# PERFECTION AND PERFECTIONISM

ANDREWS UNIVERSITY MONOGRAPHS
VOLUME III

# PERFECTION AND PERFECTIONISM

A dogmatic-ethical study of
Biblical perfection and
phenomenal perfectionism

H. K. La Rondelle, Th. D.

ANDREWS UNIVERSITY PRESS
BERRIEN SPRINGS, MICHIGAN
1971

*To Barbara, Sera and David*

# Table of Contents

CHAPTER IV

CHAPTER V

1. *Actuality of problematics of Christian perfection and perfectionism.*
The word "perfection" and its synonyms frequently occur in the Old
and New Testament in connection with *cultus* and *ethos*.[1] This makes
the notion of perfection an important idea in Biblical theology.[2] From this
it is understandable that also in dogmatic theology the word and idea
of perfection have played an important part.[3] Practically all the great
church-fathers and theologians in the course of time have interpreted
and used the term perfection.

Church-councils, including Vatican II (1963-65)[4] in their decrees and
papal encyclicals have testified to the vital meaning of perfection also
for practical theology.[5].

---

1  In the O.T. the derivatives of the stem *tmm* (to be complete, blameless)
occur 132 times, half of which (about 65) have a cultic and quantitative
meaning, while the others have a personal qualitative meaning. (The LXX
translates the first category by *anōmos*, except Ex. 12,5 [*teleios*], the second
category by the various terms *adikos, alèthinos, dikaiōs, teleios* and others).
The word *šālēm* (intact, complete, blameless) occurs 27 times, in the LXX
translated by *plèrès*, and is used in a predominantly ethical setting. In the
N.T. *teleios* occurs 17 times, *teleioun* 23 times (of which 9 times in Hebrews),
and derivatives of this root 4 times.

2  In the field of N.T. exegesis there appeared in 1959 the valuable dissertation *TELEIOS. The Idea of Perfection in the New Testament*, by Paul J. Du
Plessis. The most extensive and critical review of this book is given bij Karl
Prümm, "Das neutestamentliche Sprach- und Begriffsproblem der Vollkommenheit", in *Bib.* 44 (1963), 76-92.

3  The two dogma-historical surveys that have appeared are: H. H. Wendt,
*Die christliche Lehre von der menschlichen Vollkommenheit*, 1882, and R.
Newton Flew, *The Idea of Perfection in Christian Theology*, 1934, 1968
(reprint).

The book by Rudolf Rüetschi, *Geschichte und Kritik der kirchlichen Lehre
von der ursprünglichen Vollkommenheit und vom Sündenfall*, 1881, has a quite
restricted scope.

4  In the Decree on Eucumenism, Ch. I, no. 2 and 4: "Every Catholic must
therefore aim at Christian perfection (cf. Jas. 1:4; Rom. 12:1-2) ..."
(Quoted from: *The Documents of Vatican II*; ed. W. M. Abbott, 1966, p. 348).

5  Cf. Ecum. Council of Vienna (1311-1312), rejecting Errores Beguard-
orum et Beguinarum de statu Perfectionis. (*Denz. Schönm.*, 891 [471]).
Innocent XI condemning (1687) propositions of the quietist Michaelis de

Monasticism as well as mysticism and quietism are built on a special concept of perfection.

The Protestant Reformation of the sixteenth century and its creeds mark a revolution in the interpretation of the word perfection. It is the beginning of a new epoch of understanding.[6] Perfection, however, received its own peculiar color in the so-called Radical Reformation,[7] specifically with the revolutionary Münsterite Anabaptists, who attempted to establish a visible kingdom of God on earth. The history of later Protestantism also shows serious holiness movements, especially in times of dead orthodoxy, which followed definite methods and programs in their striving for perfection as they understood it. John Wesley and John William Fletcher may be regarded as the most conspicuous representatives in the eighteenth century.[8] In the nineteenth and twentieth centuries a great number of holiness or sanctification movements arose, like the "Higher Life Movement" in Germany, and the "Keswick Movement" and the "Victorious Life Movement" in English-speaking lands, most of which are offshoots of or influenced by the Wesleyan movement. The

Molinos on perfection (*Denz.* 2201-2255 [1221-1275]), Pius XII in Enc. *Mystici Corporis Christi*, 1943, rejecting quietism, urges all Christians "ad christianae perfectionis apicem strenue contendant" (*Denz.* 3817) and to excite others to do the same.

6  Cf. Chr. E. Luthardt, *Geschichte der christlichen Ethik*, II, 1893, p. 57 (in connection with a new evaluation of the common trades as the way of Christian perfection): "Es ist aber die unmittelbare Konsequenz der evangelischen Rechtfertigungslehre. So zeigt sich dieses Dogma [sc. of perfection] als von eminent praktischer Bedeutung." The *Conf. Augustana*, art. XVI and XXVII; *Apologia*, art. XXVII deal with the Lutheran concept of Christion perfection. For Calvin, see *Inst.* III, 3,10-15; III,6,5 III,17,15; esp. IV,13-14 (On "the erroneous claim of monastic perfection" - contra Th. Aquinas).

7  See *Spiritual and Anabaptist Writers. Documents Illustrative of the Radical Reformation*, Vol. XXV of LCC, ed. G. H. Williams, 1957, esp. pp. 19-35. For reliable information on and a positive evaluation of the three major divisions of the Radical Reformation (Anabaptism, Spiritualism, and Evangelical Rationalism), their differentiation and dramatic unity, see G. H. Williams, *The Radical Reformation*, 1962. Williams typifies the Radical Reformation as a whole as follows: "It espoused, rather, a radical rupture with the immediate past and all its institutions and was bent upon either the restoration of the primitive church or the assembling of a new church, all in an eschatological mood far more intense than anything to be found in normative Protestantism or Catholicism" (p. 857). On the tragedy of Münster, the politically supervised communism (including polygamy) of "Israel", the holy society of the "New Zion" of John Beukels, and the code of martial law for the "righteous ones", see ch. 13 (esp. pp. 371ff.). Also C. Krahn, *Dutch Anabaptism. Origin, Spread, Life and Thought* (1450-1600), 1968, esp. pp. 135-164: "Münster: The New Jerusalem". N. Cohn, *The Pursuit of the Millennium*, 1962, Ch. XII.

8  Cf. C. N. Impeta, *De Leer der Heiliging en Volmaking bij Wesley en Fletcher*, 1913.

2

dogmatic teachings on perfection of these holiness movements is generally denoted as "perfectionism".[9]

It naturally belongs to one of the major tasks of the dissertation to define theologically the constitutive elements or characteristics of "perfectionism".

This task, however, can only be fulfilled when the positive theological characteristics of Biblical perfection have first been defined, since perfectionism by definition denotes the deterioration and deformation of Biblical or Christian perfection.

The deformation, and there may be many forms of it, is always a negation of the positive, standard-setting principle and can only exist because of it.

The qualification of Biblical perfection or holiness is, for one thing, conditioned by the profound Biblical doctrine of sin. Therefore, whenever the concept of sin is deformed, or naturalized or rationalized, the idea of perfection consequently suffers under the same verdict.

It is the opinion of Biblical theologians that the problem of perfection and perfectionism is not outdated today. Since this problem is inextricably connected with the interpretation of Romans 7, the Biblical exposition of his chapter may well prove to be the decisive argument against perfectionism,[10] although the issue does not depend on this very chapter. The still continuing contest[11] about the adequate interpretation of the proper subject of Romans 7,14ff. indicates the vitality and actuality of our problem.

## 2. Non-Christian concepts of human perfection.

It is not our purpose to deal fully or adequately with the non-Christian

---

9   Cf. B. B. Warfield, *Perfectionism*, 2 vols., 1931-32 (in 1958 an abridged one volume addition, ed. by S. G. Craig, was issued). E. T. Clark, *The Small Sects in America*, 1965, ch. III:"Perfectionist or Subjectivist Sects." M. E. Gaddis, *Christian Perfectionism in America*, Unpubl. Diss. of Univ. of Chicago, 1929. K. Hutten, *Seher, Grübler, Enthusiasten*, 1968[11], pp. 443-502; and his art. in *RGG*[3] V, 220 (s.v. *Perfektionisten*). For an analysis of perfectionism, see below, Ch. V.

10   Cf. Proposition III of C. N. Impeta: „Romeinen VII weerspreekt de leer der volmaaktheid" (in dissertation, *o.c.*). The perfectionist Fletcher admitted: "If the sense which our opponents give to Rom. VII is true, the doctrine of Christian perfection is a dream" (Quoted in Impeta, *o.c.*, p. 356). Cf. H. S. Pretorius, *Bijdrage tot de Exegese en de Geschiedenis der exegese van Romeinen VII*, 1915, esp. ch. IV.

11   Cf. J. M. E. Cruvellier, *L'Exégèse de Romains 7 et le Mouvement de Keswick*, 1961, who calls the nature of interpretation of Romans 7 a touchstone (pierre de touche) for its whole religious tendency, and states: "Le problème de la sanctification, qui a toujours préoccupé les chrétiens sur le plan de la piété individuelle et a été l'occasion de controverses multiples au cours des siècles, *est devenu plus brûlant que jamais à notre époque*" (p. 5, italics supplied).

concepts of perfection or even to mention them all, since this is not our theme. Yet a short, although fragmentary, descripion of various types of non-Christian concepts will throw in relief the uniqueness of the Biblical concept and help to illuminate the distinct character of its deformations later on.

a. *Mythopoeic concepts of Mesopotamia and Egypt.*

The subject of perfection proves to be of universal value to mankind. The acceptance or projection of some sort of perfection seems to be the necessary condition for a human being to excite him to moral activity.

By nature the human being seems to possess a given religious and moral consciousness. Outside the religious sphere of Biblical revelation, man in all times has been in search of an ideal which he was painfully aware of lacking, even when this "ideal" could sometimes be spelled out only in negatives.

The old Sumero-Akkadian Hymns and Prayers[12] bear witness of complaints about suffering and misfortune because of the anger of the gods, and of the seeking of harmony with the gods by means of the religious cult, which would deliver man from his disease and misfortune.

Since the Sumerian and Babylonian man derived his sin-consciousness from the good and evil of his natural lot in life,[13] his non-moral concept of the gods[14] never could and never did lead to a doctrine or theory of sin and its deliverance.[15]

---

12 See *ANET*, pp. 383-392. Especially *Sumerische und Akkadische Hymnen und Gebete,* eingeleitet und übertragen von A. Falkenstein und W. von Soden, in "Die Bibliothek der Alten Welt", ed. K. Hoenn, 1953; esp. pp. 183ff., 235ff.

13 Cf. A. H. Edelkoort, *Het Zondebesef in de Babylonische Boetepsalmen,* 1918, p. 96: "Men leerde zijne zonden niet kennen door zich te meten aan eene goddelijke wet... Wie in lijden was, had gezondigd. De gelukkige was de vrome... de ongelukkige was stellig een zondaar." And p. 111: "Men concludeerde derhalve uit het natuurlijke tot het geestelijke. Daar was ziekte, dan waren de goden vertoornd. Daar rees weer de gezondheid, dan waren de goden weer verzoend."

14 *Ibid.,* p. 94: "Zonden en leed hingen niet organisch doch mechanisch met elkander samen."

Cf. S. H. Hooke, *Babylonian and Assyrian Religion,* 1962 (repr.), p. 95: "In the ancient myths the gods behave like men; they eat and drink, quarrel and deceive, are jealous of one another, and cannot be said to possess any moral standards." In the syncretism after Hammurabi the concept of the Babylonian high gods gradually became more moralized and the gods were supposed to reward virtue and punish sin, although the inherent contradiction of this moral concept and the intention of the magic ritualism to induce the gods to do their moral duty "was never resolved" (pp. 95-100).

15 Although some texts know about moral offences (e.g. untruthfulness, lack of clemency) especially against family ties and duties, sin usually is a cultic or ritual offence. However, in that revealing *Prayer to Every God* from the library of Ashurbanipal, 668-633 B.C., the supplicant confesses to all

The only valid recourse for the individual sufferer was to keep wailing and lamenting before his "personal" god, acknowledging his guilt, since no man is perfect, and asking that he might be shown his faults and transgressions so that he might confess them and be forgiven.[16]

Although conscious of sin, he did not have an absolute socio-ethical norm. Lacking a specifically revealed divine standard of sin and holiness, the Babylonian man received no impulse to strive for ethical perfection.[17] Yet this pessimistic judgment about the ethical situation of the Babylonian is not the full truth. When the consciousness of sinfulness is based not on moral impotency, but on ignorance of the ethical norm, when the problem is only the knowing and not the willing, then Edelkoort is correct in qualifying this Babylonian concept of man and sin basically as „an ethical optimism",[18] even when the ethical goal was wanting. If the Babylonian man had known the norm of ethical perfection, he would have believed himself quite able to perform it. The problem for him was, essentially, not himself but the gods. The object of the religious cult and the psalms was not to change man ethically, but to change the gods themselves, that these might change their will and might come to judge the acts of man differently.[19]

gods and goddesses, known or unknown, that men cannot know the will of the gods and, consequently, cannot know whether he is committing sin: "Man is dumb; he knows nothing; Mankind, everyone that exists, – what does he know? Whether he is committing sin or doing good, he does not even know ..." (*ANET*, p. 392). Cf. Edelkoort, *o.c.*, pp. 4, 72: "Het leed gaf geen inzicht in het karakter der zondige daden: het bewees alleen, dat de goden op dat ogenblik ongunstig gestemd waren ... De Babylonische goden konden dus nooit een beroep doen op het geweten." Yet there also developed in the time of syncretism a high moral eudaemonism, especially in the Šamaš-religion; cf. F. M. Th. De Liagre Böhl, *De Bab. Ass. Godsdienst*, in: *De Godsdiensten der Wereld*, 1956, pp. 105, 108. W. von Soden, "Religion und Sittlichkeit nach den Anschauungen der Babylonier", in *Deutsche Morgenländischen Gesellschaft*, 89 (1935), 143-169.

16 See the remarkable Sumerian poetic essay from the beginning of the second millennium B.C., "*Man and his God*" (A Sumerian variation on the "Job" motif), with an introduction by S. N. Kramer, in *Supplements to Vetus Testamentum*, ed. by the board of the Quarterly, Vol. III, 1955, pp. 170ff., who quotes from line 103: "Never was a sinless child born to its mother" (171). Now in *The Ancient Near East. Supplementary Texts and Pictures Rel. to the OT.*, ed. J. B. Pritchard, 1969, pp. 589-591. Cf. also Th. Jacobsen, "Ancient Mesopotamian Religion: The Central Concerns", in *Proceedings of the Am. Phil. Soc.*, Vol. 107, no. 6, 1963, 473-484, esp. 482ff.

17 See J. H. Breasted, *The Dawn of Conscience*, 1944, p. 342. Cf. Edelkoort, *o.c.*, p. 72: "Maar daarmee bestond er ook voor dien mensch geen impuls, om naar zedelijke volmaking te streven." Cf. Proposition I: "De gebondenheid van Babel's religie aan het natuurlijke heeft de ontwikkeling van een zuiver zedelijk zondebesef verhinderd."

18 *Ibid.*, p. 75; cf. also pp. 67f.

19 *Ibid.*, pp. 151, 153, 71f. "Daar was geen zedelijke wet, waarnaar zij allen

In *Egypt* the mythopoeic mind conceived the many gods of his Pantheon as being immanent in nature and therefore imperfect as individuals.[20] In the third millennium B.C. of Egyptian history there seems to be not so much resignation to the fixed plans of the gods as an indignant sense that personal worth must be rewarded.[21] In the Old Kingdom (2615-2175 B.C.) this personal worth, according to John A. Wilson, consisted of the achievements of

> an amoral people, or rather by a people whose morals were pragmatic and materialistic. They found the good life in successful activity – successful politically, socially and economically. There was little piety toward the gods – other than the pharaoh.[22]

During the Middle Kingdom (1991-1778 B.C.) man's perfection shifted to a new emphasis on good character, i.e., proper social action, social equality and fulfillment of religious cultic duties.[23] Even the (deified) king was supposed to be guided by the divine order of doing unto others what might be expected from him.[24]

---

oordeelden ... De zuiverste willekeur heerste. Op der goden oordeel was geen staat te maken. Ze konden eenzelfde daad kwaad en goed noemen, al naar het hun op dat oogenblik beliefde." Hence the prayer: "The sin which I have done, turn into goodness; The transgression which I have committed, let the wind carry away" (*ANET*, p. 392). Cf. Hooke, *o.c.*, p. 78: "Hence, on the one hand, it was thought possible, by prayers, penitence, and suitable offerings, to change the will of the gods, and in this sense the future could be controlled." De Liagre Böhl, *o.c.*, p. 109: "De tweeslachtigheid bleef bestaan. De grote massa heeft hoe langer hoe meer haar toevlucht genomen tot magische praktijken om de demonen – in hun oog de oorzaak van alle ellende – uit te drijven en een betere toekomst te voorspellen."

20  See J. A. Wilson, in *Before Philosophy. The Intellectual Adventure of Ancient Man*, ed. H. and H. A. Frankfort, J. A. Wilson, Th. Jacobsen, 1954 (Pelican), p. 76: "One element of consubstantiality [sc. with natural phenomena] lies in the fact that the Egyptian gods were very human, with human weaknesses and varying moods. They could not remain on a high and consistent plane of infallibility." See e,g. the story of the creator-god Rē, on p. 76. Cf. H. Frankfort, *Ancient Egyptian Religion*, 1949², ch. I, who excludes the Memphite Theology.

21  Wilson, *o.c.*, p. 93; cf. also p. 77.

22  Wilson, *The Culture of Ancient Egypt*, 1957⁴, p. 110.

23  See the *Instruction for King Merikare* (c. 2100 B.C.) in *ANET*, pp. 414-418. Specifically: "More acceptable is the character of a man upright ["just" (Wilson)] of heart than the ox of the evildoer" (p. 417). See also the unusual "statement of human rights" in Wilson, *Culture*, pp. 117f., because the creator-god "has made all men equal in opportunity and that, if there be any violation of this equality, the fault is man's" (p. 117).

24  Wilson, *Before Philosophy*, p. 94. Cf. H. Frankfort, *Kingship and the Gods*, 1958³, p. 51: "The king lives under the obligation to maintain *maat*, which is usually translated 'truth', but which really means the 'right order' –

The esteem of character value was conceived in direct connection with an after-life judgment[25] in which the character of the dead was judged, or rather, "counted up", in

> terms of weighing the excess or deficiency of his good against his bad and that a favourable outcome of the weighing was a prerequisite to eternal blessedness. This weighing was a calculation of $ma^cat$, justice.[26]

The perfection of man in this life already according to the *Teachings of (Vizier) Ptah-hotep* (c. 2450 B.C.) was "to strive after every excellence until there be no fault in his nature", i.e., until he attains to perfect harmony with the predestined, universal order of existence, established at the time of creation.[27] The natural order thus is identical with the moral order. Consequently, the perfect life could be taught, since man's problem was primarily his ignorance. But also man's temperament, his passionate nature was regarded as a great danger to his perfection. *Amen-em-opet* (betw. 1000-600 B.C.) describes the perfect man as the "silent" or self-disciplined man in contrast with the "heated" or "passionate" man, who was "loud of voice".[28]

The silent man is not the submissive, meek man, lowly in heart, but

the inherent structure of creation, of which justice is an integral part." See Wilson, *Culture*, pp. 116ff., how the nobles and gradually also other common people seized the deification for the hereafter, according to the Pyramid Texts and the Coffin Texts. Also *Before Phil.*, pp. 118ff. Breasted, *The Dawn of Conscience*, pp. 21f.

25  See the *Instruction for Merikare* with respect to the judgment, in *ANET*, p. 415. Cf. Wilson, *Culture*, pp. 119f.; Wilson, *Before Phil.*, p. 119. It is noteworthy that the tribunal of the gods acknowledges not only the virtues but also the faults of the dead: "Thy faults will be expelled and thy guilt will be wiped out by weighings of the scales on the day of counting up character, and (then) it will be permitted that thou join with those who are in the barque (of the sun-god)" (Quoted in *Culture*, p. 119; cf. *Before Phil.*, p. 119).

26  Wilson, *Before Phil.*, p. 119; cf. p. 120: "There was a real emphasis on this $ma^cat$ in the Middle Kingdom in the sense of social justice, righteous dealing with one's fellow-men." Also Wilson, *Culture*, p. 48: "It was the cosmic force of harmony, order, stability, and security, coming down from the first creation as the organizing quality of created phenomena and reaffirmed at the accession of each god-king of Egypt." Cf. Frankfort, *Ancient Eg. Rel.*, p. 64: "The conception of Maat expresses the Egyptian belief that the universe is changeless and that all apparent opposites must, therefore, hold each other in equilibrium." *Maat* therefore indicates at the same time "a social, an ethical and a cosmological conception" (p. 63).

27  Frankfort, *Anc. Eg. Rel.*, p. 62. A different translation in *ANET*, p. 412, line 85ff.

28  See *ANET*, pp. 422ff. Cf. Wilson, *Before Phil.*, p. 126; Frankfort, *o.c.*, pp. 65f., 69f.

according to the peculiarly Egyptian wisdom the patient, calm, successful, man, who is master of himself under all circumstances, since he is in harmony with the existing order.[29] Therefore also pride and boasting are disqualified:

> It was not a sin of the creature against his maker but a loss of the sense of proportion, a self-reliance, a self-assertion which passed the bounds of man and hence led to disaster.[30]

The perfect man is the man who is *effective* because his life is in harmonious attunement to society and nature, the universal order, i.e., with *Ma͑at*. The imperfect man is not a sinner in the sense of Biblical religion, but a fool. He does not need repentance because of his rebellion and corrupt nature, but a better understanding of *Ma͑at* and a new discipline which make him worthy of the divine mercy.[31] Since the Egyptian gods remain basically impersonal gods, being immanent in nature,[32] their powers for good or evil are also not ethical but cosmic forces which vindicate the established, divine order.

Having no specific divine commands to guide and direct man, the traditions of the sages, the accumulated human wisdom of generations, became the normative instruction for the harmonious and happy, i.e., the perfect, life in Egypt. The whole funerary literature testifies, however, of a growing preoccupation with death and eternal life, and, in the *Book of the Dead* during the New Empire in particular, of a fear for the judgment in the hereafter. In the *Instruction for Merikare* the righteous man has reckoned with the divine, cosmic order by living in

---

29   Frankfort, *o.c.*, p. 60, who concludes: "Silence is a sign not of humility, but of superiority."

30   *Ibid.*, p. 69. See his quotation from *Ptah-hotep*.

31   Cf. *ibid.*, p. 73: "The Egyptian viewed his misdeeds not as sins, but as aberrations." And on p. 77: "Man is not seen in rebellion against the command of God nor does he experience the intensity and range of feelings from contrition to grace which characterize the main personages of the Old and New Testament."

32   See Frankfort, *o.c.*, pp. 25-29, 76f. On p. 81 he states: "The gods were immanent in the phenomena and therefore remained impersonal." From this point of view H. Moderau at least gives a onesided evaluation: "Diese neue Gerechtigkeit bedeutet also einen gewaltigen Fortschritt in der Entwicklung der Moral der alten Ägypter, nämlich ihre höchste Vergeistigung und tiefste Verinnerlichung und aus diesem Grunde fand sie nun ihren Platz vor allem im Herzen des Menschen als moralische Gerechtigkeit." (In his art. "Die Moral der alten Ägypter nach Kap. 125 des Totenbuches", in *Arch. f. Orientforschung*, *XII* (1938), 258-268; quotation from 265). His statement on 266 that the worshipper entertained a personal relationship with his god is also only relatively true, since such a personal relationship was created by the worshipper, not by the deity (as in the Bible).

harmony with *Ma<sup>c</sup>at*. He therefore will reach the tribunal of the gods being perfect, "without wrongdoing",[33] thus deserving eternal life.

According to Wilson this Egyptian ethos of individual assertiveness and assurance changed so greatly around 1300 B.C. that "it ultimately reversed itself."[34] The feelings of insecurity and imperfection caused by the (second) political revolution apparently gave room to a great upsurge of the anti-ethical forces of magic and ritualism as the proper approach to the afterlife judgment.[35]

Although a sense of personal shortcoming and wrongdoing, a consciousness of "sin" (possibly more ritual than ethical), is expressed in Egypt's wisdom literature at this time,[36] the *Book of the Dead*[37] only reveals, within the framework of magical charms and spells, how the deceased one denied every sin against the gods or man by his asseverations of absolute innocence and perfection before the forty-two gods and Osiris:

> I have not lied nor sinned against anyone. I have not oppressed dependents. I have not done crookedness instead of truth. I know not sin; I have not done anything evil... I am pure... Behold, Osiris. N. is coming unto you. He is without sin, he is without

---

33 See *ANET*, p. 415: "The council which judges the deficient; thou knowest that they are not lenient on that day of judging the miserable... A man remains over after death, and his deeds are placed beside him in heaps... as for him who reaches it without wrongdoing, he shall exist yonder like a god, stepping out freely like the lords of eternity."

34 *Culture*, pp. 144ff., who states on p. 145: "Thereafter [sc. the Twentieth Dynasty] the Egyptians groped blindly for what they had lost, groped for a thousand years, groped for what they knew had been a treasure, but groped in vain: the inner spirit was dead, and the outer expression could never recapture what was lost. What was that inner spirit?... confidence, a sense of assurance and of special election..." And on p. 146: "The Egyptians relished their life. They clung to life, no with the desperation that comes from a horror of death, but with a happy assurance that they had always been victorious and so would defeat mortal change itself. There may be some sense of unreality here, but there is no morbidity and no mysticism." Cf. Wilson, *Before Phil.*, pp. 78, 121ff.

35 Cf. Wilson, *Before Phil.*, p. 127: "Thus this period came to have a strong sense of fate or external determining force." Also pp. 129f. on the power of the priesthood.

36 See Wilson, *o.c.*, p. 128, who gives this citation: "Though the servant is normally (disposed) to do evil, yet the Lord is normally (disposed) to be merciful."

37 See *The Egyptian Book of the Dead. Documents in the Oriental Institute Museum at the Univ. of Chic.*, ed. Th. G. Allen, 1960, pp. 196-202 (BD 125a-c). Cf. W. F. Albright, *From the Stone Age to Christianity, 1957* (Anchor), p. 187 who concludes: "The prevailing dynamism of the Pyramid Texts becomes [sc. in the *Book of the Dead*] magic before our eyes, and it thus diverges increasingly from the route followed by the evolution of religion." See also pp. 225-227.

guilt, he is without evil ... He lives on truth, he sips of truth. He has been joyous of heart, he has done what men request and what the gods are pleased with. He has gladdened the god with his desire. He has provided bread for the hungry, water for the thirsty, clothing for the naked. He has given (use of) a ferry boat to the boatless. He has given offerings to the gods and mortuary offerings to the blessed. May ye indeed rescue him before the lord of mummies, for his mouth is clean and his hands are clean (and he is one) to whom is said 'Welcome, welcome, in peace'.

When the declarations[38] of perfection of character in the *Book of the Dead* are considered on the basis of *Ma*ᶜ*at*, the universal order of existence, they could be regarded as sincere asseverations of perfection, without a sense of falsity. There is not the least trace of a pleading for atonement or redemption from guilt,[39] since there is no need for it in the ancient Egyptian mind.

Both Moderau[40] and Breasted[41] indicate, however, that the priestly rule of the first millennium brought about a general corruption of the conscience by selling these mortuary texts with a spell[42] as a magical

---

38   J. H. Breasted, *Development of Religion and Thought in Ancient Egypt*, 1959 (repr. of 1912), pp. 301, 304,307 is justified in replacing the phrase "Confession" by "Declaration" of moral worthiness. See other declarations of personal perfection or "excellence in character" in Breasted, *Ancient Records of Egypt. Hist. Doc.*, I, 1927³, pp. 115, 125-127. Confessions of human imperfection or sin are rare and can be found in the *Instruction of Amenemope*, ch. 18; *ANET*, p. 423 (cf. Moderau, *l.c.*, 267), and *for Merikare*, *ANET*, p. 416; esp. n. 17. For other confessions of sin, see B. Gunn, *Journal of Egyptian Archeology*, III (1916), 84, 88.

39   Cf. also Moderau, *l.c.*, 268, who refers to H. Junker; and J. Spiegel, "Die Idee vom Totengericht in der ägyptischen Religion", in *Leipziger Ägyptologische Studien*, Heft 2, 1935, 77f. Significant is W. F. Albright's remark, "Yet there is not a single intelligible declaration which could not be conscientiously repeated by a member of the Society for Ethical Culture today..." (*From the Stone Age*, pp 226f.).

40   *L.c.*, 268 (see above, n. 32).

41   *Development*, pp 307ff.

42   See *Book of the Dead*, BD 30 A-B. The function of the stone scarab, the sacred beetle, with the words "O my heart, rise not up against me as witness", possibly was to prevent the heart from betraying the character of the deceased. (Cf. Breasted, *Development*, p. 308; Frankfort, *o.c.*, p. 118). P. Barguet, *Le Livre des Morts des Anc. Eg.*, 1967, pp. 21f., however, on the basis of BD 30B ("Tell no lie against me in the presence of the great god") and BD 90 explains the spell also in a positive way. Cf. on ch. 90, J. Zandee, "Hoofdstuk 90 van het Egyptisch Dodenboek", in *NTT* 7 (1953), 193-212. Cf. also F. W. Read, *Egyptian Religion and Ethics*, 1925, p. 118 on the magic spell in the *Book of the Dead*: "But there was no sense of *falsity* in all this. To say 'I am Osiris' was not to speak falsely, because when a magical spell is properly uttered it brings to pass, according to the belief of the sincere magician, the very thing he has affirmed".

*vade mecum* for use in the hereafter. These scholars conclude that the *Book of the Dead,* in so far as it had become a magical agency for securing moral vindication *in spite of* an unworthy life, had become a positive force for evil.

b. *Graeco-Roman concepts of perfection.*

In the Greek culture of antiquity the ethical concept of perfection, although still embedded in the religious consciousness, developed into a moral system at the top of which was postulated the ideal of perfection, felicity, *eudaemonia*.[43] The Greek strived for this *summum bonum,* this perfection of the soul, with all human exertion in a more or less ascetic spirituality.[44]

At first the idea of ethical goodness was not yet distinguished from the idea of utilitarian goodness.[45]

The religious philosopher *Socrates* (469-399 B.C.) declared that the perfection of felicity to be strived for was the *homoiōsis theōi*, the being made like God, a God who is rational, wise and good.

The perfection of the soul could only be reached, however, after this life, when the soul would be completely freed from the hindrance of the physical body.[46] Self-knowledge, insight and virtue would be the way to perfection. But virtue also became primarily knowledge, intellectual insight.[47]

The whole problem, to Socrates, thus boiled down to the problem of ignorance, because whoever *knows* the good is by nature capable and willing to do the good as well.[48] The ethical norm is the city-law.[49] The

43 *SVF* I, fg. 184.

44 *SVF* III, fgs. 15ff., 59ff., 280. Cf. C. J. de Vogel, *Theoria. Studies over de Griekse Wijsbegeerte,* 1967, p. 101. L. Edelstein, *The Meaning of Stoicism,* 1966, p. 1.

45 W. Wiersma, *PERI TELOUS. Studie over de leer van het volmaakte leven in de ethiek van de oude Stoa,* 1937, p. 4. One school, the Cyrenaici, defined perfection (felicity) to be the pleasure of lust, although led by reason (Aristippus).

46 This Socrates demonstrated in the way he drank the poisoned cup, without fear of death, urging Crito to offer a cock to Asclepius as a sacrifice, which meant a thank-offering for healing (*Phaedo* 118 d e), "zonder twijfel geeft hij daarmee te kennen dat hij de dood ziet als een ontwaken tot een beter leven" (De Vogel, *o.c.*, p. 99).

47 There just could not exist any conflict between will and insight.

48 He even stated: "Nobody is acting wrong willfully" (quoted by W. J. Verdenius, in *Het Oudste Christendom en de antieke cultuur* I, 1951, p. 24); De Vogel, *o.c.*, p. 64f.: "Een probleem van het kwade echter schijnt voor Socrates niet of nauwelijks te hebben bestaan ... terwijl hij in de morele orde het kwade terugbrengt tot onwetendheid."

49 Plato had derived his city-law from the projection of his ideal state. Aristotle's principle was: man is a social being. To obey the laws is to obey God. Cf. F. Flückiger, *Geschichte des Naturrechtes* I, 1954, pp. 49f.

city-law included the religous cult, which was to be followed as a duty of law.[50] The new point is, however, that the perfection of felicity is no longer an arbitrary gift of the gods or the disposal of fate, but the achievement of man's own art of life, self-mastery, and cultivation of his soul.[51]

Only those souls who in this life have cleansed themselves perfectly, i.e., have disengaged themselves from physical lusts, will be accepted as "wholly pure" souls in the family of the gods.[52]

*Plato* (427-347 B.C.) concentrates all his exertions exclusively on the purification and salvation of his own soul, by disengaging himself from the body, its passions and all wordly ambitions. Accepting the substantial dichotomy of body and soul from the mystical Orphic-Pythagorean sects, Plato started with the pre-existence of the imortal, divine soul which had sunk down in the physical body as in a prison-house.

The way to perfection, then, was to concentrate only on the activity of the soul; that is, thinking. By thinking the soul disengages itself from the body and attains to the vision of its own, divine being, which is the remembrance, *anamnèsis*, of its pre-existent divinity.[53] As the object of thinking and acting Plato postulated a hierarchically ordered, self-existent world of ideas, the highest of which was the one Idea of the good. Envisaging that the attaining to the highest good, after a long education in the mathematical and astronomical sciences, would occur by a mystical as well as an intellectual vision,[54] Plato was bridging the gap between

50  Flückiger, *o.c.*, p. 54: "Alle Städte haben heilige Gesetze, welche die Bürgerschaft verpflichten." Also p. 57. Socrates was officially condemned to death on the ground of "impiety" against the local deities with the attempt to introduce other, new gods; in reality, however, because of his critique of his opponents' cultic superstitiousness and their religious indifference for their own soul perfection. Cf. Flückiger, *o.c.*, p. 57f. Notice Socrates' answer to his judges: "Men of Athens, I respect and love you, but I shall obey the god rather than you, and while I live and able to continue, I shall never give up philosophy or stop exhorting you and pointing out the truth to any one of you whom I may meet, saying in my accustomed way: 'Most excellent man, are you ... not ashamed to care for the acquisition of wealth and for reputation and honour, when you neither care nor take thought for wisdom and truth and the perfection of your soul?'" (In Plato's *Apologia Sokratous*, 29 d e; with ET by H. N. Fowler, in *Plato*, The Loeb Classical Library, Vol. I, 1943). On Socrates' religious motivation, see E. Fascher, *Sokrates und Christus*, 1959, pp. 36-94.

51  Cf. M. Wundt, *Geschichte der griechischen Ethik* I, 1908, p. 391: "Der Eudämonie gilt das Suchen der Zeit. Die alten Werte waren zerbrochen... Nur einem Dämon vertrauten die Menschen noch: dem Dämon in der eigenen Brust. Und da er nicht mehr als göttliches Wesen empfunden wurde, getraute man sich, ihn selbst nach eigenem Willen zu gestalten."

52  *Phaedo* 82 a-c.

53  *Phaedo* 72 e ff.; *Phaedrus* 247 c ff.

54  *Symp.* 211d-212b; *Phaedr.* 249; 250b. Cf. Wundt, *Geschichte* I, p. 464:

mysticism and philosophy. According to Plato, man's obligation is to strive after virtue or inner harmony of the soul, the perfection of his nature, and thus to perfect himself here and now[55] by making himself morally alike to "God" as much as possible: *homoiōsis theōi kata to dunaton*.[56] In this vision of "God" the trained soul attains to the level of the "gods" and becomes a perfect soul.[57] At death each immortal soul will be judged in Hades.[58] The morally perfected soul will be allowed to return to its orginal dwelling-place with the stars (gods) ; the other souls, still possessing character-weaknesses, will be reincarnated in animal bodies, according to their respective failures.[59]

„Sie erlangt ihre Erkenntnis auf einem Wege, der eine wunderliche Mitte hält zwischen wissenschaftlicher Erkenntnis und religiöser Offenbarung"; De Vogel, *Theoria*, p. 108: "Wij aarzelen niet te zeggen dat dit weten van mystisch-religieuse aard is"; Du Plessis, *o.c.*, pp. 78-81 (references). This fundamental aspect of Plato's doctrine of perfection seems to be denied by W. J. Verdenius, when he states that the soul only becomes truly free by "philosophical insight". (In: *Het Oudste Christendom*, p. 219).

55 Cf. C. J. de Vogel, *Greek Philosophy* III², 1964, 1003, n.l. (with references; ref in the vols. of *Greek Phil.* are not according to pages, but to numbers.)

56 *Theaetetus* 176 abc (the man who is most righteous is most like God); cf. De Vogel, *o.c.*, p. 134: „de ziel moet, als zij 'goddelijk' wil worden, zich *zoveel mogelijk* aan 'God' *gelijksoortig* maken." To Plato *theos* stands for the whole transcendent intelligible order of Ideas (p. 135). H. Merki, *Homoiōsis Theōi, Von der Platonischen Angleichung an Gott zur Gottähnlichkeit bei Gregor von Nyssa*, 1952, p. 6: "Durch die erkenntnismässige Betrachtung des Göttlichen und Geordneten wird der Mensch selber göttlich und geordnet."

57 *Phaedo* 82 a 10 – c 1; *Phaedrus* 246a-249e; De Vogel, *o.c.*, pp. 109, 131f., 134. C. G. Rutenber, *The Doctrine of the Imitation of God in Plato*, 1946, p. 58: "The true imitator of God is the philosopher, for the inmost nature of philosophy is the struggle to imitate God (*Phaedr.* 278 d) ... By participating in wisdom the philosopher assimilates himself to God, growing in divinity and likeness to God". And p. 62f.: "the culmination of the educative and reasoning process: the vision of the idea of the Good ... This insight in the structure of reality is the point of imitation at which man is most godlike, for he sees God as he really is and is transformed into the likeness of his image." On the difference with religious mysticism, see pp. 64ff.

58 *Laws* IX 870 d f., 872 d f.

59 *Tim.* 42 b f.; 90 e f. It was the Orphic and Pythagorean sects which in their mystery cults offered salvation from this eternal cycle of births; cf. Wundt, *Geschichte* I, pp. 136-143.

When L. Edelstein, *The Idea of Progress in Classical Antiquity*, 1967, p. 117, states concerning Plato's conception: "Perfection is denied to him, but to strive for it continually is his prerogative. Perfectability is his from his birth and dies only with his death", Edelstein is denying the possible perfection of the soul in the vision of God in this life, as well as the continued state of perfection after death. Moreover, Plato conceived that the single person, who finally will enjoy the highest contemplation, is bound to return to the earthly community in order to realize the perfect city-state for alle here. Cf. De Vogel, *Greek Phil.*, I³, 1963, 308, 4.

*Aristotle* (384-322 B.C.) in his *Nicomachean Ethics* explains the final goal (*eudaemonia*) as the perfection of the human metaphysical nature, i.e., the full unfolding of man's potentialities, the full realization of his essence.[60]

In other words, moral life depends on itself, no longer united with religion or the self-existent Idea of the *summum bonum*.[61] For Aristotle the supreme good becomes immanent in the human life. Starting with the presupposition of the absolute transcendence of God, he founded his moral philosophy on his observation of nature. From nature he derived his doctrine that *in* all things, and also *in* man, therefore, is implanted a dynamic idea or form principle.[62] This is a teleological principle, which by nature propels man to his goal of perfection, the fulfillment of the natural destination of man.

While intellectual virtue can be acquired by teaching and insight, the moral virtues, although their potentiality is given by nature, can only be acquired and perfected by the habit of doing them. By doing we become good.

> For the things we have to learn before we can do them, we learn by doing them, e.g. men become builders by building and lyre-players by playing the lyre, so too we become just by doing just acts, temperate by doing temperate acts, brave by doing brave acts.[63]

Consequently, man carries perfection in himself, to be derived from human nature itself, and from the specific human characteristic, reason (freedom of choice) in particular.[64]

The highest value and the claim of finality are to live according to

---

60 *Physica* VII 3, 246a, 13-17; *Ethica Nicomachea* X 7.

61 De Vogel, *Greek Phil.*, II³, 1967, 564.

62 The good, he defines, is "that at which all things aim." (*Eth. Nic.* I 1, 1094a). Cf. Flückiger, *o.c.*, p. 164f.: "Das Werden ist die Selbstverwirklichung der Dinge nach dem zugrunde liegenden Formprinzip. Alles drängt der Verwirklichung seiner Wesensform, d.h. seiner Vollkommenheit zu..."

63 *Eth. Nic.* II 1, 1103a, 32f., b. 1f.; cf. II 5, 1105b, 9f.: "It is well said, then, that it is by doing just acts that the just man is produced, and by doing temperate acts the temperate man, without doing these no one would have a prospect of becoming good" (ET W. D. Ross, *The Works of Arist.*, IX, 1963). Pleasure, happiness is the sign that the virtuous disposition has been acquired. (*E.N.* II 3); cf. De Vogel, *o.c.*, p. 155: „Het is objectief gezien de meest volmaakte toestand van de mens, subjectief de meest aangename."

64 Cf. M. Wundt, *Geschichte der griechischen Ethik*, II, 1911, p. 113 (in reference to the ethics of Aristotle): "Der qualitative Inhalt dieses Gutes, das wir Eudämonie nennen, muss aus der Natur des Menschen abgeleitet werden, soll es doch die Vollendung des Menschen bezeichnen, so dass die Eudämonie nichts anderes ist als der vollendete Mensch."

reason, to common sense, which, taken by itself, is a mere formal principle ethically.[65] However, reason being the source of all virtue, the driving power comes from the passions.

The virtues, i.e., the state of personal character, can only be manifested by the habitual exercise of keeping the passions and actions in balance by means of reason, the rational principle. Thus the moral capacity is being unfolded, basically unimpeded by human nature itself, in practical reality, consisting in the proper mean, the golden mean between opposed vices.[66] In his contemplative wisdom and well-ordered life man is by nature striving after God, the first form principle and ground of all being, who as the unmoved Mover is pure, perfect Thinking himself.[67]

Yet the philosopher, although participating in a super-human divine life, will not devote himself exclusively to contemplation. He participates in the political life of the city. The perfect life in a perfect city, therefore, consists in the unity of comtemplation and action. Aristotle regarded the good of the political society as being more divine and supreme than that of the individual as a person.[68]

---

65  *Eth. Nic.* X 7, 1178a, 6ff.: "for man, therefore, the life according to reason is best and pleasantest, since reason more than anything else *is* man. This life therefore is also the happiest." Cf. Flückiger, *o.c.*, 183ff.; Wundt, *Der Intellektualismus*, p. 1, 68 ("Die rechte Vernunft soll dem Handeln sein Ziel zeigen...")

66  *Eth. Nic.* I 7, 1098a: II 6-7; cf. Wundt, *Geschichte* II, p. 120f.; Flückiger, *o.c.*, p. 182f.

Cf. John H. Finley Jr., *Four Stages of Greek Thought*, 1966, p. 102: "In the *Nicomachean Ethics* nothing clouds the possible working of free will; a rational man is quite able to make the choices on which virtue and happiness depend; nature does not impede – on the contrary, it commends – the orderly conduct of life."

Since Aristotle distinguishes a double virtue, an intellectual and a moral, Wundt's statement: "In dem theoretischen Leben muss die vollendete Glückseligkeit beschlossen liegen, weil in ihr die höchste Funktion des Menschen, die Vernunft, rein zur Entfaltung kommt" (*o.c.*, p. 127), must be amplified with the conclusion that perfection of virtue consists in reasonable thinking and in reasonable acting. And with the latter Aristotle goes along with the traditional ethical virtues which were not derived from reason. Cf. Flückiger, *o.c.*, pp. 183-185.

67  Cf. Wundt, *o.c.*, p. 128: "Die Entfaltung der Persönlichkeit ist ganz im Sinne seiner Metaphysik der Grundgedanke der aristotelischen Ethik; sie vollendet sich in der Vernunft, durch die der Mensch zugleich teilnimmt an dem göttlichen Grunde der Welt, der als höchster Zweck allem Sein die Bestimmung aufprägt." Flückiger, *o.c.*, p. 165.

68  *Politics* I 1, 1252a 3-5; cf. J. Maritain, *Moral Philosophy*, ET 1964 (French, 1960) p. 44: "The notion of the person has not emerged; and there is no suggestion that the human person – who is a part of the city and must work for its common good, and if necessary give his life for it – might

He did not know of any supra-political common good, since he derived his principle of finality exclusively from the natural order of things.[69]

The highest wisdom which Aristotle could derive from nature with respect to perfection was this programmatic ideal: "We must so far as we can, make ourselves immortal, and strain every nerve to live in accordance with the best thing [sc. reason] in us."[70]

We thus agree, therefore, with Maritain's evaluation: "There is no moral system more thoroughly and authentically humanistic. And there is no moral system more disappointing for man."[71]

The Stoic philosopher *Zeno* (c. 336-264 B.C.) has further developed this idea by transforming the subjective intellect (Socrates) into the world-intellect or world-law. In this fundamental pantheism man's intellect is a part of the divine world-intellect and is, therefore, morally good by nature. Thus the ideal of living according to the state-law was changed into living according to the divine laws of nature, since this means living according to reason.[72] Following therefore Plato and Aristotle in principle,[73] Stoicism more sharply accentuated and narrowed the life according to subjective reason or nature as the virtuous life; in other words, the perfection of man is identical with the perfection of his individual rational nature.[74] Morality thus was founded on rational

nevertheless transcend the political order of the city according as he is himself directed to supratemporal goods."

69 When Maritain states, *o.c.*, p. 46: "One might say that it took the fracas of revelation and the scandal of grace coming to complete nature to make philosophy see these supreme data of the natural order, which it had been looking at all along, without realizing it", this Thomistic conception still suffers from a fundamental depreciation of the nature and effects of sin in human nature, i.e., the intellect and the will. To state that Aristotle not explicitly but "implicitly" held or even "might have known" the true knowledge of God and man's perfection by transcending the political order of the city (p. 46) is denying the fundamental difference between the concepts of the philosophical god and man on the one hand, and the Biblical-theological knowledge of God and man on the other.

70 *Eth. Nic.* X 7, 1177b, 32-35. De Vogel (*Gr. Phil.* III², 1003, n. 1) refers to Augustine, *De lib. arb.* III 13, 38; 14, 41 and to Thomas Aquinas, *S. Th.* II 1, q. 71, concluding: "Virtues, then, in a general sense, must be defined as *perfectio naturae.*"

71 *O.c.*, p. 47; Note also pp. 47-51 for his critique on the Aristotelian ethics as being empty in its concept of God and egocentric in its conception of man and therefore basically ineffective to the "real direction of human conduct" and destiny.

72 See the development of the "eudaemonistic" ideal from Zeno to Cleanthes and Chrysippus, in: P. J. du Plessis, *o.c.*, p. 54.

73 Aristotle accepted the positive function of the feelings.

74 *Diog. Laërt.* VII 94: "*To teleion kata physin logikou hōs logikou*", quoted in De Vogel, *Greek Phil.*, III, 1017b.

Virtue no longer is qualified as a habit (Arist.), but as a diathesis, a certain state of the mind.

nature, and what was morally good was natural.[75] Virtue became a matter of the intellect. Virtue and the final good now were identified. Virtue no longer is the way to perfection, but perfection itself.

Thus virtue brings: "salvation", perfect happiness and freedom, a state of blessedness here and now.[76]

This ascetic philosophical way of "salvation" for the human soul found a universal response. Now the virtue of perfect self-possession becomes the supreme end of life, the highest good. It consists in the immutable conformity of man with reason and with himself, but also with universal Reason, the royal law of nature, since "a spark of the divine fire which animates the world animates every human being."[77]

Virtue therefore requires insight in the laws of the All.[78] The first Stoic philosophers, in their passion for the ideal of perfection, fell into an extreme intellectualism by drawing a radical line of demarcation between foolishness and wisdom. The sage or perfect man ought to live in absolute harmony with himself, with his *logos*,[79] which meant to them complete equanimity and self-possession exempt from all the disturbing passions (*pathè*) and events (*adiaphora*).

In sharp contrast with this wise man, who is in possession of all perfection, was pictured the mass of fools who possess all imperfections.[80]

Later Stoicism, feeling this ideal of perfect *apatheia* to be too high-

---

75  De Vogel, *Greek Phil.* III, 1065 a-c; cf. O. Dittrich, *Gesch. der Ethik*, II, 1926, p. 20: "Die darauf ruhende *Ethik* der alten Stoa kann nur intellektualistisch sein."

76  Cf. Maritain, *o.c.*, p. 56: "At the root of the Stoic illusion is the *absolutisation*, or rather the deification of moral virtue."

77  *Ibid.*, pp. 59f.: "If a man could only take to heart this judgment, as he ought, that we are all, before anything else, children of God and that God is the Father of gods and men, I think that he will never harbour a mean or ignoble thought about himself. Why, if Caesar adopts you, your arrogance will be past all bearing; but if you realize that you are a son of Zeus, will you feel no elation?"

78  Cf. Wundt, *Der Intellektualismus*, p. 80: "War dem Mystiker die Tugend eine gottgeoffenbarte, ein Wissen vom Göttlichen und damit ein Befolger der Gebote der Götter, so ist sie der Stoa ein Wissen von der Natur des Alls, das an die Stelle der mythologischen Göttergestalten getreten ist."

79  Cf. *ibid.*, pp. 78f.: "Alle Tugenden beruhen auf einem richtigen Urteil, alle Laster auf einem falschen ..." "Nun ist aber die Vernunft ... die eigentliche Natur des Menschen; die, welche nach der Natur leben, leben also nach der Vernunft (*Diog. Laert.* VII 86)."

80  Cf. De Vogel, *Greek Phil.*, III, 1043 a-b, who concludes: "The wise man never fails, neither in judgment nor in action; consequently he never repents and never changes his opinion." Cf. Wundt, *Der Intellektualismus*, p. 82; L. Edelstein, *The Meaning of Stoicism*, 1966, p. 13, states that "the new consciousness of man's power that arose in the fourth century, the belief in the deification of the human being," was something both Stoicism and Epicureanism had in common.

pitched an ideal to be realized at all, created a legitimate status of transition with its own middle duties, the *kathèkonta*, for the "advancing" man, the *prokoptōn*.[81] Thus the *prokopè*, the progress, the advancement in virtue became the *terminus technicus* for the real tendency and characteristic of Stoicism.[82]

*Seneca* (c. A.D. 3-65), to whom the cult of virtue was the true religion, developed in a special way a systematic way of advancement, a ladder of moral progress by which the human will dominates the passions and vices.[83]

The prerequisite is always a certain natural disposition or tendency, the *euphuia*[84] and the effectiveness of the natural will of man, the *prohairesis* (choice).[85]

For Seneca there is perfect harmony between reason and nature, so that perfection of the reason at the same time means perfection of human nature. Relying solely upon his own strength,[86] man will be able to attain perfection just by striving to live according to his own nature.

> Praise the quality in him which cannot be given or snatched away, that which is the peculiar property of the man. Do you ask what this is? It is soul, and reason brought to perfection in the soul (ratio in animo perfecta). For man is a reasoning animal. Therefore, man's highest good is attained, if he has fulfilled the good for which nature designed him at birth. And what is it that this reason demands of him? The easiest thing in the world, – to live in accordance with his own nature.[87]

This perfection of peace in the body and in the soul can be attained in this life, even when life may be short. When man's whole being is founded upon reason, then his perfect state of mind will allow him to follow the perfect duties, the *katorthōmata*. Then he wil be full of human and divine virtue.[88]

---

81  Cf. Wundt, *Geschichte*, II, pp. 254ff.

82  Cf. Epictetus, *Peri Prokopès* (*Diss.* I 4; *SVF* III 543).

83  *Ep.* 75; 71, 36f.; 80, 4. Cf. R. D. Hicks, *Stoic and Epicurean*, 1962, p. 120, on the three classes of Seneca; pp. 121ff. on the three stages of Epictetus.

84  *SVF* III 266.

85  Sen., *Ep.* 71, 36. Cf. G. Stählin, "Fortschritt und Wachstum", in: *FS J. Lortz*, II, 1958, pp. 17f.

86  *Ep.* 92, 2, *nisi sibi innixus*; cf. *De Ira* II, 13, 1-2: "Since we are born to do right, nature herself helps us if we desire to be improved." Sin, evidently, comes from without, bringing the perversion of nature; cf. *Ep.* 94, 53; 115, 11-12.

87  *Ep.* 41, 8-9, quoted in J. N. Sevenster, *Paul and Seneca*, "Suppl. NT" IV, 1961, p. 141. See also pp. 142f. Also in M. Hadas, *The Stoic Philosophy of Seneca*, 1968, p. 189f.

88  Cicero (A.D. 106-143) has popularized this Stoic philosophy and its

Virtue, therefore, makes a man worthy of the company and honor of the gods. Thus everybody can make "his character the source of life" (Zeno).[89]

The transition into the final stage of wisdom and perfection occurs unconsciously.[90] The Stoic, however, no longer believing in divine punishment or reward in this life, or after this life,[91] in his moral idealism defined the moral purpose of a good conscience in itself as his reward and perfection.[92] In this philosophy of individualism the Stoic no longer is concerned with his fellowmen. He is only interested in the cultus of the virtue in his own soul.[93]

Sin to the Stoic could only mean a deviation from the path of reason because of ignorance, not a conscious transgression of a positive divine commandment.[94]

One vital characteristic of all these speculative religious philosophies should be mentioned here especially. That is their more or less outspoken religious claim to present in their systems of philosophical insight the way of *salvation* for man's existential problems.[95]

---

double morality in particular, in his *De officiis*. With respect to the notions *kathèkon* and *katorthōma*, see A. Bonhöffer, *Die Ethik des Stoikers Epiktet*, 1894, pp. 193ff. Cf. De Vogel, *Greek Phil.*, III, 1033.

89  *SVF* I, fg. 203. Cf. the ultimate anthropocentricity of Seneca's ethics, as contrasted with the Pauline concept of virtue, Sevenster, *o.c.*, pp. 146-166.

90  Cf. *Ep.* 71, 4; 75, 9; *SVF* I, fg. 2529. (Perfection cannot be expected except "late in life and at the setting of life's sun.")

91  Edelstein, *The Meaning of Stoicism*, p. 8. According to Seneca the wise man, the "advanced" man, was equal to God and had nothing to ask from Him. *Ep.* 41, 1. 4. Cf. De Vogel, *Greek Phil.*, III, 1222.

92  Cf. Sen., *De benef.* IV 12, 4; *Ep.* 66, 9. This concentration on man's grandeur and his moral progress is well grasped by Edelstein, *o.c.*, p. 11f.: "Based on the belief in the infinite perfectibility of man's character, this ethos of perfectionism is the essence of Stoicism from its very beginning to its end." Although Edelstein recognizes the striking "identity of ethical standards" between Stoicism and Christianity (p. 91), he also indicates a basic difference: "In denying transcendence even on a limitative concept Stoicism becomes flat: it makes the world appear two-dimensional instead of three-dimensional, and therefore it indulges itself in a superficial optimism, a superficial trust in reason. The Stoics unflinchingly believed that reason leads man to the good ... identifying all reasoning with moral insight" (p. 97).

93  W. Wiersma, in: *Het Oudste Christendom*, I, p. 300f.

94  A. Bonhöffer, *Epiktet und das Neue Testament*, 1964 (repr. 1911), p. 369, who observes this esp. in Epictetus: „Kein Satz kehrt wohl bei Ep. häufiger wieder, als dass jede Seele unwissentlich sündigt und nur deshalb sündigt, weil sie ihren wahren Vorteil nicht kennt und ihr Glück auf einem, falschen Wege sucht." See also p. 372 for Ep.'s philosophy that ethical perfection can be attained by the use of one's reason.

95  Cf. R. A. Markus, in *Christian Faith and Greek Philosophy*, 1960, p. 150: "Through all the various formulations of the ideal life by different philosophical schools runs the notion of deliverance or salvation as the goal." C. A. van

Philosophy throughout antiquity also meant a different way of life, usually implying discipline and asceticism, since it made totalitarian claims on man and his destination.[96]

It can be understood that the Hellenistic soul finally was not satisfied with this arid intellectualism, and in his search for new values, in reaction, began to turn to the secret doctrines of mysticism and its ecstatic way to direct knowledge of God, to deification and perfection.[97]

This tendency was greatly strengthened by the influx of Oriental religious cosmology, as well as of Egyptian-Syrian mystery cults.[98] And, remarkably, in this religious syncretistic movement Jewish elements were also absorbed.[99]

An essential feature of syncretistic religiosity was this belief: "In the world of matter here exists a remnant from the spirit-world, and the deliverance of this remnant is the aim of the soteriological process."[100]

Because of this universal hunger for the right knowledge of God, the cosmos and the soul, this worldwide religious movement has come to to be called *Gnosticism*.[101]

Peursen, *Filosofische Oriëntatie*, 1958, p. 118: "Het wijsgerige inzicht betekent verlossing, verlossing in dit geval met name ook van de schuld die aan het bestaan inhaerent is."

Rohde, *Psyche*, II, 1925, p. 279, n. 1: "Die Dialektik ... wird zum Heilswege auf dem die Seele ihre eigene Göttlichkeit und ihre göttliche Heimat wiederfindet" (quoted in Du Plessis, *o.c.*, p. 80).

96   Cf. Markus, *o.c.*, p. 149f.

97   R. Seeberg, *Textbook of the History of Doctrines*, I, 1966[7], p. 94, seems to present an adequate description of the aims of syncretism which extended to the post-Christian era: "It was by no means the aim merely to satisfy the thirst for knowledge, but it was sought to realize the upper world in personal experience through religious revelation and through the formulas and forms of the mysteries, and at the same time to secure a sure path for the soul in its ascent to the upper world at death."

In view of the fact that the way to perfection is being sought by symbolic rites and mystic ceremonies, it seems unjustified to separate Hellenistic mysticism and Gnosticism as P. J. du Plessis does (*o.c.*, pp. 81, 85, 93; especially when informations for both are drawn from one source, the *Corpus Hermeticum*).

98   See J. Doresse, *The Secret Books of the Egyptian Gnostics*, ET 1960. W. C. van Unnik, *Newly Discovered Gnostic Writings*, SBT 30, (Dutch: *Openb. uit Eg. Zand*), 1960, pp. 28-37. In the Gnostic library of Nag Hammadi the term *teleios* frequently occurs. The Valentinians and other sects regarded Seth as the first of the race of the perfect ones. See further, Du Plessis, *o.c.*, pp. 89-91. H. Ridderbos, *Paulus*, pp. 16f.

99   E.g. in the *Corpus Hermeticum*. Greek, Egyptian, Oriental and Jewish influences have been amalgamated. Cf. Ridderbos, *o.c.*, p. 21. G. van Moorsel, *The Mysteries of Hermes Trismegistus*, 1955. On the debated relationship of Judaism and Gnosticism, see ch. IV (pp. 43-79) of the valuable study by G. van Groningen, *First Century Gnosticism. Its Origin and Motifs*, 1967.

100   Seeberg, *o.c.*, p. 96; see the other nine chief features, on pp. 95-98.

101   See Van Groningen, *o.c.*, whose main thesis is that Gnosticism arose

What *gnosis* sought after was not the mere intellectual understanding of the meaning of things: [102] it looked for the ascension or return of the soul to the eternal life, its resurrection, the experience of its pre-existent divine life through the process of self-consciousness, the receiving of mystical revelations. [103] In short, it sought after the vision of "God", which delivered from the tyranny of historical reality: from the flesh, matter, time, natural and moral law. [104]

The goal is personal deification of the spirit. [105]

The cultic gnosis meant the substantial transformation into a present, instantaneous perfection. [106]

due to "scientistic" motivations. G. Quispel, *Gnosis als Weltreligion*, 1951. Van Unnik, *o.c.*, pp. 23, 35. He stresses the diversity and *inner* development of Gnosticism, since it was no finished system or dogmatics, certainly not in the first century A.D. Ridderbos, *o.c.*, p. 29. J. Zandee, "Oude en Nieuwe Vormen van Gnostiek", in *NTT* 22 (1967/68), 161-184. H. J. W. Drivers, "The Origins of Gnosticism as a Religious and Historical Problem", in *NTT* 22 (1967/68), 321-351. W. C. van Unnik, "Balans: 20 Jaar na een keerpunt in het Onderzoek van de Gnostiek", in *NTT* 23 (1968/69), 189-203, states (190) that research in Gnosticism with respect to Christianity "only stands at the beginning". On 199 he refers to the definitions which the study group on Gnosticism, convened at Messina in April 1966, proposed: *Gnosis* is"connaissance des mystères divins réservés à une élite", which would indicate "une série cohérente de characteristiques: ... la conception de la présence dans l'homme d'une étincelle divine, qui provient du monde divin, qui est tombée dans ce mond soumis au destin, à la naissance et à la mort, et qui doit être réveillée par la contrepartie divine du Soi pour être finalement réintégrée."

102 Philosophy was only the façade for Gnosticism.

103 Seeberg, *o.c.*, I, pp. 94ff. Doresse, *o.c.*, pp. 146ff., 113 n. 116. Cf. Zandee, *l.c.*, 170: "In de gnostiek is de kern, waar alles om draait, een hoger weten, waartoe de mens het vermogen in zich heeft. Hij is daartoe niet in staat door zijn verstandelijk inzicht, maar door een vonk van het goddelijke pneuma, die in hem is gezaaid. Dit is zijn ware Zelf, zijn hoger ik. De eindverlossing is, dat deze vonk weer tot het eeuwige licht terugkeert en dat de veelheid in de oorspronkelijke Eenheid wordt opgelost. Dat tussen begin en einde ligt, de zin van het leven, is een proces van zelfbewustwording."

104 Hence the rise of Neo-pythagoreanism, its asceticism, cultic revelations and soothsaying. Cf. Wundt, *Der Intellektualismus*, pp. 89-91. In Egypt: the Hermetic mystery cult. Cf. H. Jonas, *Gnosis und spätantiker Geist*, II/1, 1954, p. 49: "In der Hermetik ist das Vollendungsideal einer unmittelbaren *gnosis theou* entschieden ausgebildet, und Gnosis in diesem Sinne besagt wesensverwandelndes, selber vergöttlichendes Schauen Gottes."

Since in the ecstasy the *psuchè* is transformed into *pneuma*, the following way of life is also called gnosis (p. 52).

105 *Corp. Herm.* I, 26; XII, 9; XIII, 14. See more interesting quotations in Jonas, *o.c.*, pp. 50-53. W. D. Davies, *Paul and Rabbinic Judaism*, 1965², p. 191.

106 Cf. Jonas, *o.c.*, p. 58, note 3 on *teleiōsis*. In the Christian *Letter to Rheginos* from Nag Hammadi the eschatological resurrection is spiritualized, *De Resurrectione, epistula ad Rheginum*, ed. M. Malinine, H. Puech, G. Quispel, *et al.*, 1963; 45, 28; 49, 22; 49, 25. Zandee, *l.c.*, 168, therefore concludes: "Het

It should be remembered that the specific characteristic of Gnosticism, in spite of its mysticism, was its philosophical starting point.

How to interpret the problem of being, the origin of evil, the mixture of the spiritual and the natural?[107]

The starting point of Gnosticism is the problem of wrong. The interest of Gnosticism, therefore, is based on this ethical-philosophical motif, its metaphysics being the outcome of its ethics.[108]

Carsten Colpe has eminently summarized the idealistic metaphysics and the "gnostische Weltgefühl" of pre-Christian Gnosticism:

> Wir kennen im Hellenismus und z.T. im synkretistischen Judentum das Bewusstsein der Daseinsangst, des astrologischen Fatalismus, das Gefühl des Eingeschlossenseins und der Einsamkeit in der Welt, die Sehnsucht nach dem Himmel, die Erkenntnis eines kosmischen Dualismus, die Anschauung von der Präexistenz des Ich oder vom Ursprung der Seele im Himmel und ihrer Rückkehr dorthin.[109]

The conclusion of all Gnostics, also of the "Christian" Gnostics, was that the world and man were created by a second and imperfect God,[110] and that the soul as a spark of the divine light was imprisoned in the dark world of matter.

Hence there was the existential urge in Gnosticism to receive knowledge about the true and supreme God and the divine spark in man, and thus to attain to an instantaneous perfection of salvation right here

---

ontvangen van de gnosis is de geestelijke opstanding. Wie dit heeft doorgemaakt is reeds tijdens zijn aardse leven gestorven en opgestaan." Cf. R. M. Wilson, *Gnosis and the N.T.*, 1968, pp. 117ff. with lit.

107 Cf. Eusebius, *Hist. Eccl.*, V 37; Tert., *de Praescr. haer.*, c 7; *adv. Marc.* I, 2. See Van Groningen, *o.c.*, p. 181, n. 2, quotes a number of questions which would lead the Gnostic to salvation: "What were we? What have we become? Where is it we were? Where have we been cast? Whither are we hastening? How are we redeemed? What is generation? What is regeneration?"

108 Seeberg, *o.c.*, p. 94f., 100. Ch. Bigg, *The Christian Platonists of Alexandria*, 1968 (repr.), p. 54.

109 *Die religionsgeschichtliche Schule: Darstellung und Kritik ihres Bildes vom gnostischen Erlösermythus*, 1961, p. 200.

110 Bigg, *o.c.*, p. 110: "If Adam was created perfect, said the Gnostic, he could not have fallen. He was then created imperfect, and in that case the Creator was the cause of his imperfection, and must therefore be imperfect Himself." About the Christian Gnostics Basilides, Valentinus and Marcion, Bigg states: "They approach the problem from a non-Christian point of view, and arrive therefore at a non-Christian solution" (p. 55). Augustine, in another connection, says that the problem of evil is raised by most people because they want to excuse rather than to accuse themselves. *De lib. arb.* III 5, 12.

and now.[111] The discovery of man's essential divinity as the way of salvation was at bottom the way to himself.[112]

It becomes evident that when Gnosticism appropriated Christ as a principle of Gnostic redemption, modified according to its own presuppositions, it became a deadly menace to the authentic Christian way of salvation and perfection by faith.[113]

On the exact religious-historical relationship between Gnosticism and Christianity opinions still vary.[114]

Is seems that the thesis of G. Quispel is gaining ground, which states that "it was from Christianity that the conception of redemption and the figure of the Redeemer were taken over into Gnosticism."[115]

Colpe, however, without accepting the traditional redeemed-redeemer myth of the *religionsgeschichtliche* school, points to the redemptive function of the notions of "Self" and "Spirit" in pre-Christian Gnosticism.[116]

---

111  Cf. Van Unnik, *o.c.*, p. 76, with respect to the *Apocryphon of John*: "The solution too is typical of Gnosticism. Man is saved by becoming aware of his true nature, of the divine spark within him; for though lying ensnared in the trammels of matter and desire, yet in his deepest thoughts he harbours a portion of divinity." Cf. W. R. Rüssel, *Gestalt eines christ. Humanismus*, 1940, p. 93.

112  Du Plessis, *o.c.*, p. 88.

113  See Van Groningen, *o.c.*, pp. 181ff. Cf. Chr. E. Luthardt, *Geschichte der christlichen Ethik*, I, 1888, p. 130: "Die Gnosis hat nun Christus als das Erlösungsprinzip aus dem Christenthum sich angeeignet, aber in ihrem Sinn, und etwa nach den Voraussetzungen der orientalischen Naturreligion modifiziert". Van Unnik, *o.c.*, p. 23: "It was combated as a lethal threat to the proclamation of the Gospel: and the bishops had, I would say, every justification for pointing out how great the gulf is between Biblical Christianity and Gnosticism, even though Gnosticism made use of biblical texts." See esp. with respect to *The Gospel of Truth*, pp. 67f. Bigg, *o.c.*, p. 62: "But in the second century, while it [sc. Gnosticism] was yet living and aggressive, it constituted a danger greater than the Arian controversy, greater than any peril that ever menaced the existence of the faith." Cf. also Seeberg, *o.c.*, pp. 99ff. and R. McL. Wilson, *The Gnostic Problem*, 1958, pp. 76, 256. G. Kruger, art. "Gnosis", in *RGG*[3] VI, 737.

114  Cf. Colpe, *o.c.*, ch. I, "Überblick über den Forschungsgang."

115  *The Jung Codex*, p. 78; quoted and accepted by Wilson, *o.c.*, pp. 75, 218-228. Cf. Colpe's acknowledgment (*o.c.*, pp. 197ff.) of the fact that many Gnostic sects, in the sense of the Hermetic concept, do not know a mythological redeemer, like the Ophites, Nicolaites, and others. "Bei diesen Gruppen genügt die Gnosis, per definitionem das erlösende Wissen, zur Erlösung" (p. 198). The functioning of a "prophet" in this Gnosticism must not be confused with that of a "redeemer". Cf. Wilson, *o.c.*, pp. 218-228. He states on p. 225: "The point of all this is that it seems to indicate that the Gnostic redeemer is not pre-Christian, but simply a more radical interpretation of the Christian Jesus in terms of current belief." Cf. also p. 254, n. 317.

116  *O.c.*, p. 207.

It seems safe to conclude that in the syncretistic atmosphere at the time of the apostolic Church, there existed, besides the Greek philosophical ideologies, also undeveloped tendencies of Gnostic cults, with or without a redeemer-myth.

We can agree, therefore, with the conclusion of P. J. du Plessis: "The word *teleios* is an important term in Gnostic circles, as designation of the saviour and the saved. If the myth underlying the theology is shown to be a post-Christian phenomenon its utility to New Testament exegesis is one of antithetical comparison."[117]

It was Irenaeus, more than Tertullian, who stood out in unmasking Gnosticism as the endeavor to "change the subject-matter itself" of the Christian faith by conceiving "some other God" than the Creator of this universe, and "another Christ".[118]

c. *Humanistic ideals of humanity.*

It is remarkable that the ancient Graeco-Roman ideal of life found a new and wide response in the time of the Renaissance and in the "almost normative form" of modern secularized *Humanism*.[119] The humanistic ideal, having cut off itself from its Christian religious root, has come to incite man to become conscious of his inner powers, calling him to *unfold* his humanity in a glorious and harmonious realization by means of philosophy, art and science.[120] Rejecting all special revelation and dogmatic authority, modern Humanism presents a completely independent anthropology consisting of its own totalitarian philosophy with ultimate answers. The starting point is faith in the nobility and dignity of man, based on the natural and autonomous human spirit.[121] Recognizing also

---

117 *O.c.*, p. 32.

118 *Adv. Haer.* I 10,3 – "argumentum ipsum", "alium quendum Deum", "alium Christum". Cf. R. A. Markus, in *Christian Faith and Greek Philosophy*, p. 145, with respect to Irenaeus: "He saw gnosticism fundamentally as a human attempt to arrive at this saving knowledge by its own efforts." ... "What the gnostics had done, in his view, was to allow human thinking, speculation and imagination, to usurp the place of faith."

119 H. Kraemer, *Kerk en Humanisme*, 1957², pp. 18f., 25. Although the concept of a Christian Humanism can be traced from Justin and the Christian Platonists of Alexandria, the so-called Biblical Humanism as a movement started with Wessel Gansfort and Erasmus. The latter came in fundamental controversy with the Reformation on the issue of the free or bound will. In 1952 the International Humanistic and Ethic Union was founded in Amsterdam.

120 *Ibid.*, p. 18. Although there is a great variety in types of Humanism, especially in this century, all present forms of Humanism bear the characteristic of an ethical Humanism which has cut off man's relation with God and places man all by himself. This the great classic philosophers did not want or intend. Cf. C. J. de Vogel, *Het Humanisme en zijn historische achtergrond*, 1968, p. 229.

121 *Ibid.*, p. 22. Cf. J. P. van Praag, *Humanistisch Credo*, 1964, p. 6: "Het

the dark, the earthy, even the demonic in man, the Christian humanist H. W. Rüssel believes in the possibility of victory on the basis of the divine spark of the logos in him.[122]

In modern Humanism the transcendent factor has certainly not disappeared,[123] although it has become an outspoken anthropocentric ethical philosophy and art of life.[124] The humanist, whether religious or not, holds to the fundamental principle that man carries the principle of truth in himself.[125]

This philosophical presupposition and starting point of Humanism manifests a fundamental kinship or congeniality with the basic principle of Stoic and Gnostic anthropocentrism.[126]

---

is een levensovertuiging, waarin de mens uitgangspunt is. Omdat de humanisten geen ander deugdelijk uitgangspunt hebben. Zij ervaren de christelijke openbaring niet als werkelijkheid. Daarom moeten zij van de mens uitgaan. Om der wille van de waarheid."

Self-unfolding of man is the great ideal of this completely secularized Humanism. Cf. De Vogel, o.c., pp. 159ff., 167ff. On p. 1 she states: "Humanisme betekent dan: een geloof in de mens en zijn mogelijkheden, zonder deze terug te voeren tot of afhankelijk te zien van een metafysische Oorsprong."

Kraemer, o.c., p. 73, refers to the conviction of Kohnstamm, Psychologie van het ongeloof, p. 75, who stated that modern Humanism is the strongest, perhaps the only remaining rival of Christianity.

122 Cf. Rüssel, o.c., p. 189: "Aber er bleibt nicht an der Tragik stecken, sondern er glaubt an eine mögliche Überwindung. Und diesen Glauben schöpft er aus seiner Einsicht vom Primat des Logos in der Welt... Dieses Ja gilt dem göttlichen Funken, den er in Jedem Menschen spürt." However, how can man ever be truly human, when he still is partly divine?

123 Yet always being conceived of as being strictly immanent. The notion of transcendency with Karl Jaspers also remains an empty borderline concept which sheds no real light on the meaning of humanity. Cf. G. C. Berkouwer, De Algemene Openbaring, 1951, pp. 183-192.

124 Rüssel, o.c., p. 9, qualifies religious Humanism strikingly as: "Der Humanismus ist... ein recht merkwürdiges Geflecht von Wissenschaft, Werturteilen, Lebenshaltungen, Traditionen, Stimmungen, die aber alle um das Problem des Menschen kreisen. Und zwar des Menschen, wie er sich als einmalige gültige Norm in der griechischen-römischen Antike geoffenbart hat." (italics supplied). Also quoted by Kraemer, o.c., p. 24. Cf. Berkouwer, o.c., p. 193: "Het humanisme stelt op deze mens nog zijn vertrouwen in een greep naar zijn transcendentie ..."

125 Kraemer, o.c., p. 74. The concept of perfection with the (R.C.) Christian humanist Herbert W. Rüssel is that man, in his redeemed and glorified state, will see his embryonic divinity come to perfect development and deification (cf. his o.c., p. 194).

126 Cf. Edelstein, The Meaning of Stoicism, pp. Xf.: "European humanism from Petrarch to Erasmus and to Matthew Arnold is imbued with Stoic thought. ... And today their [sc. of the Stoics] creed is glorified by Albert Schweizer. (See P. Barth, Die Stoa⁶, Stuttg. 1946, 347)."

Kraemer, o.c., p. 74, profoundly qualifies religious Humanism as "an embryonic and mitigated edition of the heart of all Oriental religions and

Edelstein's remark is therefore to the point: "Like all Hellenistic philosophies it [sc. Stoicism] is, moreover, whether for better or for worse, nearer to the subjective tendency of modern thought than is the classical realism of Plato or of Aristotle..."[127]

### 3. *The basic issue of the starting point: philosophy or theology?*

These short indications may suffice at this moment to show that the striving for perfection is a vital theme not only in the Bible, but also in profane philosophy and religion, although the content and the way of Biblical perfection will prove to be fundamentally different.

A further element of importance which can be gathered from the examples presented is that the concept of God will exercise a specific influence on the concept of human perfection and vice versa. In other words, divine and human perfection appear to be correlative notions. Where the concept of God has no ethical traits, the human ideal does not rise higher than that, as is manifested in the Babylonian penitential psalms. When the perfection of God reveals specific ethical traits, as in the ancient Egyptian wisdom literature and in Greek philosophy, the ideal of human perfection is bound to be likewise. When God was being identified with the cosmic law or world-intellect, as in Stoicism, the ideal of human perfection became the perfect domination of human reason over all passions and affections, to live consistently with one's own nature or reason. The "revelations" about the perfection of the supreme God in the dualistic mystery cults of Gnostic syncretism led to the moral philosophy of either strict ascetic or libertinistic ideals of human perfection.[128] Du Plessis is correct in summarizing the purpose of Greek religiosity:

> To find the *to hou heneka*, the ultimate reality, the other dimen-
> sion, god, was the final and highest purpose of all religion. Only
> one who has reached this *telos* was truly *teleios*.[129]

We are struck by the fact that man in every culture never has been satisfied with himself as he was. He was always on his way, striving for, searching for a perfection which he believed would restore him to the original perfection he must have had, or which would again bring him into harmony with the deity to which he was akin.

In this mysterious inner urge for perfection which could only be found

---

religious philosophy, with the exception of Islam." In other words, the buttressing esoteric kernel of the great Oriental religions constitutes a grandiose manifestation of religious humanism. Cf. pp. 80f.

127  *O.c.*, p. ix.
128  Cf. Seeberg, *o.c.*, p. 98. Davies, *o.c.*, p. 192.
129  *O.c.*, p. 94.

in "God", we may see verified the apostolic statement made in Athens to the Greek philosophers:

> And He made from one every nation of men to live on all the face of the earth ... that they should seek God, in the hope that they might feel after Him and find Him. [130]

The crucial theological question is, however, What was the starting point of the Babylonian, the Greek and the Hellenist which led to their concept of ultimate human perfection?

It will not be contested that in all these situations, even when the basic motif may be recognized as an unconscious wrestling with God, the conscious starting point was the subjectivistic principle of man himself, his own physical and spiritual problems, wishes and questions. [131] The world of Greek philosophy in particular is characterized by a natural trust in reason. [132] Consequently, their concepts of God were fundamentally the speculative projections of the perplexed human mind of its concept of the deity. This may explain the fact that these gods could not and did not manifest themselves as gods of reconciliation and grace by which man was really saved from his mysterious but haunting problems of sin, guilt and death. [133]

130   Acts 17, 26-27.
131   Maritain's qualification of Aristotle's ethics may be taken as representative of all Greek and humanistic philosophy: "Happiness as ultimate subjective End did not lead the philosopher to discover a supreme Good which is loved more than Happiness, a Good worth more than Happiness and for the love of which our Happiness itself is loved. Thus the supreme Good was identified with Happiness. The last End relative to the human subject, the last End as *my* fulfillment or *my* supreme perfection, or as End in which *my* nature and *my* being are realized, the last End taken subjectively, blocked Aristotle's vision of the last End in and for itself, which at the same time he implicitly recognized." J. Maritain, *Moral Philosophy*, 1964, p. 50. Cf. Du Plessis, *o.c.*, p. 88: "Recognizing their true ego forms the first stage of ascent towards salvation ... Being homogenous with the divine, he is *au fond* virtuous, wise and perfect."
132   Cf. for ancient Greek philosophy, Wiersma, *o.c.*, pp. 4f.; De Vogel, *Greek Phil.*, III², p. 127: "Zeno starts from the question of 'what is the primary impulse of man'." The epitome of wisdom to the Greek mind always was "Know thyself!" Cf. Edelstein, *The Idea of Progress in Classical Antiquity*, 1967, p. 179: "Yet, on the whole, trust in reason and in the possibility of mastering one's fate by free decision of the will had not yet been questioned." Cf. Edelstein, *The Meaning of Stoicism*, p. 97.
133   Cf. Van Unnik, *o.c.*, p. 76f., e.g. on the *Apocryphon of John*: "In this the role of Jesus Christ is clearly no more than that of mediator of the true Knowledge, which is the real saving power. Jesus has no central place in the work of redemption ... The reason is that in this *Apocryphon* the fall from God is not envisaged as sin committed in defiance of his holy commandment, and there is consequently no question of an atonement."

Even when striking parallels of terms and expressions can be presented between the New Testament and the Hellenistic world, e.g., *teleios, physis, syneidèsis,* and others, this is no guarantee that the same term carries the same content in both situations. On the contrary, the completely different starting points entail inevitably a different structure and nature of the phrases, corresponding to their respective orientations.[134] The etymological structure or religious-phenomenological origin of a term is not decisive for its theological meaning, but rather the semantic use of it within the framework of its own religious or philosophical context.[135]

The meaning of Biblical perfection of man, therefore, should be derived from the Biblical starting point, as witnessed by the Hebrew prophets and Christian apostles.[136]

The peculiar nature and structure of the apostolic doctrine of human perfection discloses a concept which is strictly *sui generis*, carrying with it its own credentials. In the Scriptures the whole problem of perfection is not approached from an abstract-philosophical or metaphysical-ontological point of view or interest, but is placed in the concrete connections of life, within the framework and scope of the dynamic soteriological-Christological and eschatological-historical dimensions. From this the theological meaning of humanity, its creation, fall, sin, guilt and death

---

134  Cf. Sevenster's conclusion in his *Paul and Seneca*, p. 240: "This study has, it is hoped, shown that great care must be taken when drawing parallels ... However, in order to determine the true significance of such statements, both Paul's words and those of the writer quoted must be read in their context." "Paul may occasionally have derived terms and expressions from the Hellenistic world around him and even from the Stoic school(. . .), he may now and then use phrases which are at first sight reminiscent of Seneca, but he always makes them instrumental to the particular purpose of his own preachings."

135  See J. Barr, *The Semantics of Biblical Language*, 1961, ch 6: "Etymologies and Related Arguments." This same hermeneutical principle is also defended by J. Dupont for Paul's use of the term "gnosis", which formally is the technical term of Gnosticism, while the content of its meaning with Paul is qualified by the O.T. (*Gnosis. La connaissance religieuse dans les Épîtres de Saint Paul*, 1960², pp. 539, 542). Cf. H. Ridderbos, *Paulus*, p. 31: "Maar wel is men ervan teruggekomen de grondstructuren van Paulus' prediking en leer, alsmede het specifieke van zijn voorstellingswereld en uitdrukkingswijze, ergens anders te zoeken, dan in zijn joodse afkomst." On Bultmann's hermeneutical approach, however, see Du Plessis, *o.c.*, pp. 20-32 (*teleios* as Gnostic terminus technicus).

136  Cf. Du Plessis, *o.c.*, p. 19: "Only by taking the full N.T. kerygma into account is the danger of false analogy avoided. Here lies the shortcoming of Reitzenstein – not that he attempted to read the visions of Paul in the mirror of the mysteries, but his ineptness to do full justice to the totality of Pauline teaching, by comparing individual texts as absolute fragments of religious truth."

28

can be discovered, as well as the norm and authority of genuine human perfection, since man is revealed in his inalienable relation with his Creator and Redeemer. The deepest and fundamental problem of man, his evil, guilt and perfection, is a religious as well as a moral problem.[137]

When sin is not merely a natural attribute of man, but the way of man's relating himself to God, then even man's profoundest reasoning about humanity and metaphysics and "God" will be sinful and evil.[138]

It should be realized that causal thinking as such never can and never will lead to God, but only to a pseudo-god.[139] The metaphysical idea of God is fundamentally different from the religious God of revelation and experience. The identification, or even partial identification, of a metaphysical concept of God, derived from the reality of nature, with the Biblical-theological concept of God, inevitably must lead and has led to basically false concepts of God and man.[140]

137   Cf. A. W. Begemann, *De relatie tussen wijsbegeerte en theol. en haar bel. gestalten in de Hell. periode van het oud-Gr. denken*, 1965 (inaug. rede), p. 7, n. 4: "In de critiek van het theoretisch denken zijn alle grondmotieven uitdrukkelijk als religieus in het licht... gesteld." Cf. p. 24 (all philosophy is religious). We are touching here the crucial problem of the close relationship and yet fundamental structural difference between theology and philosophy. See esp. K. Barth, "Philosophie und Theologie", in *Philosophie und Christliche Existenz*, FS H. Barth, ed. G. Huber, 1960, pp. 93-106, with the significant statement on p. 100: "Es gibt so etwas wie ein blitzendes Schwert, das ihm [sc. der Theologe] den Weg des Philosophen abschneidet." K. Rahner, "Philosophy and Theology", in *Theological Investigations*, VI, 1969, pp. 71-81 (German: *Schriften zur Theol.*, VI, 1965/1966). J. Hessen, *Religionsphilosophie*, I, 1955², pp. 13ff. H. Kraemer, *Religion and the Christian Faith*, 1956, chs. 6 and 26 (Dutch: *Godsdienst, godsdiensten en het Christelijk geloof*, 1958). When R. A. Markus, *o.c.*, p. 154, states, "To grant philosophy its autonomy and to assert the theologian's freedom to use whatever intellectual structures seem to him to commend themselves, inevitably gave rise to a theology cast in new Aristotelian moulds," this may be true for Thomas Aquinas. This statement is unacceptable, however, when intended to state an absolute truth, since the basic structure of the apostolic kerygma is a given which not only did not rise from flesh and blood (philosophy) but even thwarts and delivers from the absolutism of all philosophical systems. More careful is G. P. Guthrie, *Kant and Ritschl. A Study in the Relation between Philosophy and Theology*, Unpubl. Diss. of Univ. of Chicago, 1962, pp. 219-222, who on the one hand recognizes that religion is seeking a metaphysics, but, on the other hand, that no metaphysics is fully adequate to the Christian reality: "The finding of an adequate metaphysics awaits the eschatological realization of the Kingdom of God" (p. 222). Cf. Van Peursen, *o.c.*, pp. 124ff., 129ff.

138   Cf. Van Peursen, *o.c.*, p. 127.

139   Hessen, *o.c.*, I, pp. 32f.

140   Cf. on Thomas' fundamental philosophical principle *analogia entis creati et increati*, Flückiger, *Gesch. des Naturrechtes*, pp. 436ff. When Thomas, *S.Th.* II-II, 4, 2, states: "Credere est actus intellectus, secundum quod movetur a voluntate ad assentiendum," he qualifies religion basically as an act of the

The rational-metaphysical knowledge of God is the product of the human mind, intended to bring *solution* to rational problems, e.g. theodicy. The God of revelation and religious experience, who, on the contrary, is Subject instead of object, lays claim on man, manifesting Himself in His living reality and holiness, and brings *salvation* for man's existential problems of the heart, culminating in eschatology.

The root-problem seems to be epistemological in nature, i.e., whether or not the religious experience is acknowledged as an independent phenomenon in its own right, with its own sphere or realm of value and reality.[141]

In other words, when religion must be explained out of its own value-reality, then a *third* way of receiving knowledge must be acknowledged, besides sensorial and rational knowledge, i.e., the religious knowledge, the experience of the HOLY ONE, in which not the I, the striving human mind, is the subject, but the HOLY GOD is the working Subject in point of fact.[142] It is not I who is seizing God, but I am seized by God, in the way of faith.[143]

The approach of *Calvin*,[144] therefore, seems to be the most adequate:

Nearly all the wisdom we posses, that is to say, true and sound

*intellect.* Cp. II, 26, 2 (the beatitude of God as well as of man consists in understanding, in the intellectual operation). Where Thomas conceives that religious truth can also be grasped by philosophy, *i.e.*, the realm of the *praeambula fidei* or natural theology, he no longer respects the proper limits of the provinces of theology and philosophy, but creates a synthesis, a system of partial identity of a philosophical god and the religious God. Cf. J. Hessen, *Thomas von Aquin und wir*, 1955, pp. 166ff. Note pp. 11f. about the real danger of absolutizing a philosophical system, e.g. of Aristotle, letting religious truth of the Gospel depend on a philosophical system. Basing the religious realm on the natural (philosophical) realm with its autonomy of the intellect inevitably led to a certain naturalizing of the religious concept (pp. 118ff.).

141 Cf. Hessen, *Rel. phil.*, I, p. 32. C. G. Rutenber, *The Doctrine of the Imitation of God in Plato*, 1946, p. 14.

142 Cf. Hessen, *Th. Aquin*, p. 117: "Der Gedanke, dass es ausser Erfahrung (Sinneswahrnehmung) und Denken noch eine dritte Erkenntnisquelle gibt: das innere Schauen, Erfahren und Erleben, das uns die tiefste Wirklichkeiterkenntnis und zugleich die höchste Werterkenntnis vermittelt, ist dem Stagiriten [sc. Aquinas] fremd." Cf. also his *Relig. phil.* II, pp. 87f., 95, about Aristotle's and Thomas' illegitimate identification of religious and rational knowledge. Since R. Otto, *Das Heilige*, 1917, the third source of knowledge has also been recognized generally. (ET: *The Idea of the Holy*, Galaxy Book, 1958).

143 Cf. Is. 6,1-8; Jer. 1,4ff.; 20,7-9; Phil. 3,12; 1 Cor. 8,3; Gal. 4,9.

144 *Inst.* I, 1, 1-2. This continues the fundamental principle of Irenaeus, who so emphatically stressed divine revelation as the starting point, faith alone being the channel to receive saving knowledge.

wisdom, consists of two parts: the knowledge of God and of ourselves.

Again, it is certain that man never achieves a clear knowledge of himself unless he has first looked upon God's face and then descends from contemplating him to scrutinize himself.

In the Bible man comes to true self-knowledge neither by striving after God nor by isolating himself from God. The surprising, unsuspected way, however, appears to be God searching for man, demanding from him an account of his being as he is before the face of God, not to condemn but to reveal to him the true knowledge of man, his "misère" and "grandeur" (Pascal), and to save him by His inscrutable love.[145]

Especially with respect to Humanism and its struggle for true humanity, the crucial question must be asked with inexorable earnestness today: "Is the source of truth and authority lying in autonomous man or in God; is the final and deepest starting point for the decisions and choices in all domains of life the self-determination of sovereign man or obedience to the sovereign God of revelation?"[146]

As far as the concept of God is concerned, the non-Christian humanist considers it most adequate to refrain from attaching to "God" any attributes, nay, even from speaking about him, since "this power withdraws from all conceptions."[147] When the humanist says, I do not experience the Christian revelation as a reality and therefore it is no truth for me,[148] he acts as if the objective possibility of divine revelation can be excluded. The question may be asked, however, has this humanist, who is claiming openness of mind, ever wrestled or confronted himself really with the mysterious fact of God *having* spoken by the prophets and in Christ Jesus?[149]

Can man ever arrive at an adequate knowledge of the objective norm of genuine and perfect humanity, when he remains orientated to the

145  Jn. 3,16.
146  Kraemer, *Hum.*, p. 91. The attitude of despising death or rebelling against it, a legitimate form of humanism (Van Praag, *o.c.*, p. 8), can not be regarded as a serious understanding or gauging of this mystery.
147  P. Schut, in *Rede en Religie in het Humanisme*, 1962, p. 141: "Elke speciale godsvoorstelling doet geweld aan de eenheid en volheid van dit besef [sc. van kleinheid van mens t.o.v. de kosmos], omdat ook wanneer de religieuze mens in de wereld zoals die voor hem verschijnt een bovenmenselijke macht vermoedt, deze macht zich onttrekt aan elke voorstelling, aan elke poging hem eigenschappen toe te dichten, zelfs over hem te spreken."
148  Cf. Van Praag, *o.c.*, p. 6.
149  Hebr. 1,1f. Cf. De Vogel, *o.c.*, p. 168: "De vraag voor ons allen, zolang wij het nog 'niet voelen' en niet begrijpen, kan alleen deze zijn: *heeft God werkelijk gesproken? is Hij werkelijk gekomen?* Want als dat zo is, dan geldt Zijn woord ook voor mij. Dan wil Hij ook mij, die het niet voelt."

subjectivistic cult of the ego? Is he justified in making totalitarian pronouncements on man, his ultimate meaning and his destiny, on the basis of *his* concept or notion of humanity within the closed circle of an absolute independent humanism?[150] It should be emphasized seriously that there begins right here a fundamental misapprehension, as if the Hebrew-Christian faith also has to do with just a *notion* or *concept* of God as the product of logical conclusions or wishful thinking.[151]

The genuine and unique characteristic of the Old and New Testament religious experience is that God, the Creator of man, has *spoken* Himself when man did not seek for Him,[152] has manifested Himself in dramatic saving acts in history,[153] while the greatest and fullest self-disclosure of God has been manifested concretely in the Man Jesus of Nazareth, the Christ of promise.[154]

According to the apostle Paul, who was a contemporary of the Stoic

150   Cf. A. A. van Ruler, *Overheid en Humanisme*, n.d., p. 23f.: "Wij stoten, dunkt mij, door tot het hart van de zaak, als ik formuleer: gezien het alles-omvattende van het moderne humanisme zullen christendom en humanisme elkaar wel uitsluiten... Dit is het grote bezwaar tegen het humanisme: dat daarin de humaniteit gevaar loopt." Kraemer, *o.c.*, p. 29: "De van de mens uit onherstelbare breuk tussen hem en God wordt door het Humanisme voor-bijgezien... Het kwellende raadsel, dat ook in de subliemste aanlopen der mensheid het zaad van corruptie en ondergang blijkt te liggen en dat alleen in het licht van de Bijbelse visie iets van zijn mysterie verraadt, vindt geen werkelijke aandacht."

151   Cf. Van Peursen, *o.c.*, p. 125: "De Bijbel handelt nimmer over God, maar spreekt vanuit God over mens en wereld... God is hier subject, geen object." E. Brunner, *The Divine – Human Encounter* (German: *Wahrheit als Begegnung*, 1963[2]), 1964[2], pp. 87ff.

152   Is. 65,1; Rom. 10,20; Hebr. 1,1f.

153   Cf. G. E. Wright, *God Who Acts*, SBT *8*, 1964[7], and *The Old Testament and Theology*, 1969, ch. 2: "Revelation and Theology", which ch. is a refutation of the critique on Wright's notion of saving acts in history by J. Barr, *Old and New in Interpretation*, 1966, chs. I-III. Wright states on p. 48: "The point is not that God speaks as well as acts in the Old Testament, but instead that the two are interrelated. A Biblical event is not simply a happening in time and space, but one in which the word of God is present (the 'speaking' of God), interpreting it and giving it special significance".

154   When De Vogel, *o.c.*, p. 169, states: "Van mijzelf uit 'voel ik het niet zo' – maar hier *zie ik het*: dat er een heilige God is, en dat er Iemand is die 'de zonden der wereld' op Zich heeft genomen om ons tot Hem terug te brengen", then the words '*hier zie ik het*' suggest too much an identification of religious knowledge with rational knowledge, disguising the truth that the saving knowledge of Christ is fundamentally a religious experience of the HOLY ONE, as in Luk. 5,8, which exceeds the nature of a rational insight. Also Justin Martyr, who combined Stoic philosophical teaching about the *logos spermatikos*, the "seminal word," with the Christian faith, maintaining that all philosophers of the past who lived "with the logos" were basically Christians (*Apol.* I 46), is compromising the unique experience and radical novelty of God's revelation in Jesus Christ. Cf. Markus, *o.c.*, p. 158.

32

philosopher Seneca, the world, i.e., the Greek philosophical world, had not come to know God by means of its wisdom.[155]

The only way to come to know the true God is by faith in Christ who is "the power of God and the wisdom of God".[156]

This kerygma means that the starting point in man, even religious man, being placed in himself, is an unrealistic abstraction from his inalienable relation with the living Creator and, consequently, is insufficient to reveal adequately the real meaning and destiny of humanity.[157]

It requires not only philosophical honesty and unconcern, by-passing all caricatures and deformations made by empirical Christianity,[158] but also an earnest decision of the heart to expose oneself to the reality of God, to real confrontation with the HOLY ONE, who comes to us as our Creator and Redeemer, to listen in receptiveness to His requirement concerning the perfection of our humanity. It seems as if the old prophet Micah,[159] in the eigth century B.C., is summing up the ideal of human perfection in these appealing words:

> He has showed you, O man, what is good; and what does the Lord require of you but to do justice, and to love kindness [ḥesed, steadfast love, loyalty], and to walk humbly with your God?

When Jesus Christ required of His disciples a righteousness which would exceed that of the self-righteous Jewish scribes and Pharisees, and designated His demand in the words, "You, therefore, must be perfect, as your heavenly father is perfect,"[160] He undoubtedly was in harmony with the words of Micah above, and unmistakably intended the very same thing.[161]

---

155  1 Cor. 1,20.
156  1 Cor. 1,24. Even the religious Greek philosophers in Athens are called to repentance (Acts 17,31). Cf. also Jn. 14,6.
157  Cf. Berkouwer, o.c., p. 187: "dat is het drama der secularisering; dat het probleem van de mens vanuit dit afvallig apriori van het begin af radicaal verkeerd wordt gesteld en daarom onoplosbaar blijft". Cf. Begemann, o.c., p. 24, summarizing Paul's kerygma: "Wie Hem kent, de enige en waarachtige God, met de enige en waarachtige kennis, uit Zijn openbaring, die kent ook Zijn schepping, mens en kosmos en historie. Nog niet wetenschappelijk maar wel in wijsheid. Die verstaat zin, oorsprong en bestemming aller dingen."
158  Cf. Begemann, o.c., p. 7: "De moderne theologieën vertonen alle de symptomen van zelfvergiftiging met filosofie: theologiae speculativae."
159  Mic. 6,8; cf. Am. 5,14-15. Cf. N. Glueck, Hesed in the Bible, 1967, p. 61, on Mic. 6,8: "Here, as in Hos. 4:1, the words seem to be arranged together in a sequence of ascending significance. Love of humanity includes within it righteous conduct and is already included in an humble attitude toward God ... Every man becomes every other man's brother, ḥesed becomes the mutual or reciprocal relationship of all men toward each other and toward God."
160  Mat. 5,20.48.
161  Compare the context, vss. 20-48.

With this statement, however, the theological meaning of the Old and New Testament perfection of man is not yet answered or elaborated in its various aspects and far-reaching dimensions.[162]

We are standing now before the inescapable dogmatic and ethical question with respect to an adequate interpretation of the Biblical testimony about the perfection of God and the corresponding human perfection as the intention of the Covenant of salvation.[163]

To this Biblical dogmatic and ethical reflection on the theocentric human perfection this study hopes to make a contribution.

162  Kraemer, *o.c.*, p. 46, stated: "Het Bijbels anthropocentrisme, dat organisch in het Bijbelse theocentrisme gegeven is, wacht nog steeds op een theologische verwerking, die duidelijk in het belijden der Kerk aan het woord komt." Noteworthy in this respect is K. Barth's suggestion to call theology "theanthropology", in *FS* H. Barth (see above, n. 137), p. 106.

163  Cf. Berkouwer, *o.c.*, p. 193: "In de worsteling om het wezen van de mens en van de naaste culmineert welhaast de relatie tussen het menselijk denken en de Openbaring Gods in onze tijd."

Chapter II            *The distinctive idea of divine perfection*
                                      *in the Old Testament*

1. *Methodical consideration.*

Is it correct to start with the Old Testament or should the New
Testament be the starting point in the search for the meaning of Christian perfection?

Two reasons present themselves for starting with the Old Testament.

First, methodologically the organizing principle of Biblical theology
requires that Biblical material be dealt with from a historical rather
than a logical point of view.[1]

Secondly, since the New Testament itself constantly stresses its
fundamental harmony and unity with the Old Testament, and, moreover,
its being rooted in the Law and the Prophets, accepting the Old Testament as its legitimate and authoritative foundation, it seems proper to
ask the Old Testament for its own witness on this vital subject.

Believing that the Old Testament can and does stand on its own feet
and is able to proclaim its own message,[2] we also maintain that the
authentic, true meaning of the Old Testament has been revealed by
Jesus Christ and the apostolic kerygma of the New Testament.[3] The real

---

1 Cf. G. Vos, *Biblical Theology*, 1963 (repr. of 1948), pp. 5, 23. He states
on p. 25: "Biblical Theology draws a *line* of development. Systematic Theology
draws a *circle*. Still it should be remembered, that on the line of historical
progress there is at several points already a beginning of correlation among
elements of truth in which the beginnings of the systematizing process can
be discerned."

2 Cf. Van Ruler, "De waarde van het O.T.", in *Religie en Politiek*, 1945,
p. 129: "Waar het om gaat, dat is dat het geheele O.T. weer in eere wordt
hersteld, en dat het geheele O.T. weer geëerbiedigd wordt als hèt oorspronkelijke Woord van God, en dat we uit het gehééle O.T. de kennis van Christus
leeren putten."

3 See W. Eichrodt, *Theology of the Old Testament*, I, 1961 (German,
1959⁶), p. 26. Cf. G. von Rad, *Old Testament Theology*, II, 1965, p. 321
(German, 1960, p. 341): "The question before us, however, is this: does not
the way in which comparative religion takes the Old Testament in abstraction,
as an object which can be adequately interpreted without reference to the
New Testament, turn out to be fictitious from a Christian point of view?"
Although he (p. 322) acknowledges the methodological right to approach the
O.T. through the N.T., he nevertheless prefers the more salvation-historical
and typological approach of the N.T. through the O.T. This last we also prefer

problem in New Testament theology has ever been, *how* to approach the ethos and the ground plan of the kerygma of Jesus Christ and the theology of Paul in particular.[4]

Several different ways of approach have been tried in the past in order to find the proper point of orientation for the fundamental structure of New Testament theology. However, most of these endeavors have labored under a dominating philosophical presupposition which introduced elements or notions which were utterly foreign to the kerygma and theology of the New Testament.[5]

Others who approached the Gospel from the angle of a personal appropriation of the salvation in Christ made either the personal religious mystic experience or personal morality the heart or motivating power of the New Testament kerygma.[6]

Although such concepts call attention to basic aspects of the Gospel of sovereign grace in Christ, they are still, in their subjectivistic one-sidedness, deformations of the ground plan of the Covenant promises as given in the Old Testament and basically fulfilled in Christ Jesus.[7]

Undoubtedly the new finds of manuscripts in Qumran and Nag Hammadi from the first centuries A.D. have led to a new consciousness of the significance of the Old Testament and the Jewish-Rabbinical background for the form and content of the New Testament kerygma.[8]

---

as our method, since we believe in the organic historical character of the Bible and, consequently, in a *historia revelationis*; cf. A. Kuyper, *Enc. der hl. Godgeleerdheid* III, 1894, pp. 149f. Cf. also C. Spicq, O.P., "The Work of Biblical Theology", in *Theology Digest*, 7 (1959), 29-34; C. Gamble, "The Literature of Biblical Theology: A Bibliographical Study", in *Interpr.* 7 (1953), 466-479; and: "Guiding Principles for the Interpretation of the Bible", Ecum. Study Conf., Oxford, 1949, in *Interpr.* 3 (1949), 457-459.

4   Cf. H. Ridderbos, *Paulus. Ontwerp van zijn theologie*, 1966, p. 5: "... waar de toegang is te zoeken tot het imposante gebouw van Paulus' theologie. Het is duidelijk, dat er allerlei deuren zijn, waardoor men kan binnengaan. Maar welke is de *hoofd*-ingang, die het gehele gebouw beheerst?"

5   H. Ridderbos, *o.c.*, pp. 7f., refers to four different basic conceptions of approach: the *Hegelian* Paul (Tüb. School), the *liberal* Paul (Holzmann, Wrede), the *mystical* Paul (rel. geschichtliche school) and the *existentialistic* Paul (Bultmann).

6   *Ibid.* Pietism, mysticism and moralism stressed the pneumatic and ethical aspects of the Pauline gospel at the cost of its salvation-historical basis.

7   Cf. *ibid.*, p. 40: "Uit de geschiedenis van het onderzoek is gebleken, hoe gemakkelijk men zich de toegang tot Paulus' prediking verspert of ook verengt, wanneer men bepaalde facetten van zijn heilsverkondiging ten koste van andere gaat centraal stellen en verabsoluteren." Ridderbos, p. 40 even qualifies the forensic-soteriological aspect (the *sola fide*) of the Reformation as too narrow a ground motif for the Pauline kerygma, especially with Luther; see p. 6.

8   *Ibid.*, pp. 30ff.: ".. een sterk herleefde bestudering van de joodse praemissen van Paulus' prediking." Notice the piercing question on p. 31: "Zal men

Ridderbos observes a growing sense of unanimity in theology to the effect that the foundation of the Pauline gospel is not to be found in any theological system or philosophical idea or religious sensation, but in the salvation-historical and eschatological action of God in Jesus Christ.[9]

> Het beheersende motief van Paulus' prediking is het heilrijk handelen Gods in de komst en het werk, in het bijzonder in de dood en de opstanding van Christus. Dit handelen is enerzijds de vervulling van het werk Gods in de geschiedenis van het volk Israel, de vervulling daarom ook van de Schriften, en het strekt zich anderzijds uit naar de totalitaire voleinding van de paroesie van Christus en de komst van het koninkrijk Gods.[10]

This broadened concept will do more justice to the manifold dimensions of the Biblical kerygma of the perfection of humanity, since the basic categories are now: creation-sin-redemption-completion (the end, *telos*; i.e., eschatological perfection).[11]

2. *The Old Testament witness to divine perfection.*

The witness of the Old Testament reveals that the Hebrew religious experience and concept differed fundamentally in structure and character from all the contemporary non-Hebrew religions and philosophies.[12] The idea of divine and human perfection is not the harmony with the natural order, an abstract postulate, or the result of mere consistent logical thinking, nor the ethical ideal of pure moral virtues, as in the (later) Greek philosophies.

---

de paulinische begrippen dan ook niet eerder moeten bezien in het licht van het Oude Testament en het rabbijnse Jodendom, dat men kent dan in dat van het hellenistische gnosticisme van de tweede eeuw of later, dat men niet of nauwelijks kent?"

9 Cf. *ibid.*, p. 34. In reference to the N.T. gospels see already E. C. Hoskyns, "Jesus der Messias", in *Mysterium Christi. Christologische Studien britischer und deutscher Theologen*, 1931, pp. 89f. (making the O.T. the only legitimate approach to the N.T.).

10 *O.c.*, p. 34.

11 Cf. also Hessen, *Rel. phil.* II, 1955[2], p. 197: "Demnach werden wir von *Schöpfung, Offenbarung, Erlösung und Vollendung* handeln müssen. Dabei werden alle wichtigeren Grundkategorien des religiösen Bewusstseins zur Sprache kommen."

12 Th. C. Vriezen, *De Godsdienst van Israël*, 1963, Ch. II, has shown this convincingly; cf. p. 59: "Ondanks vele tekenen van verwantschap met de hem omgevende religies is overduidelijk, dat Israëls godsdienst totaal daarvan verschilt. Hij heeft een eigen signatuur." Cf. G. von Rad, *o.c.*, II, ET. pp 338ff. H. van Oyen, *Ethik des Alten Testaments*, 1967, p. 19: "Das Wesentliche im Vergleich mit der Umwelt liegt darin, dass dem Jahweglauben das genuin mystische Element fehlt: die Theogonie... das *Werden* der Götter..."

Although the uniqueness of the basic Hebrew pattern can be characterized in different ways,[13] which all contain genuine aspects of its unique character, the origin and root of this uniqueness undoubtedly may be found in the self-revelation [14] of God, that is to say the concrete, dramatic historical revelation of God's will and work to Israel.[15]

Is is an extremely significant fact that the Old Testament never uses the term "perfection" (*tāmîm*, *šālēm*) as a predicate of Yahweh. The God of Israel is nowhere qualified as the *ens perfectissimum*,[16] as being perfect in Himself.

His "perfection" is only described in terms of relationship with man, and with His covenant people in particular.[17]

Van Oyen therefore even concludes:

> Der Glaube an einen personenhaft wirkenden, sich in der Geschichte offenbarenden Gott muss als ein völlig einzigartiger (bisher unbekannter und der Umwelt gegenüber völlig konträr strukturierter) angenommen werden.[18]

All knowledge or truth about Yahweh's perfection is, consequently, encounter-truth, and deals with notions of His dynamic manifestation

---

13   E.g., awesomeness for God's holiness (Bleeker); religion of the divine will and obedience (Van der Leeuw); the dynamic historical nature of Israel's religion (von Rad); the communion of the holy God with man (Vriezen); the covenant as divine reality in history (Eichrodt).

14   Cf. Vriezen, *Hoofdlijnen der Theol. v. h. O.T.*, 1966³, p. 199: "Er blijft een geheimenis Gods, dat niet ontsluierd wordt. Maar het geheimenis heft de zelfopenbaring niet op, evenmin als omgekeerd." H. Kraemer, *Religion and the Christian Faith*, 1956, p. 146 (Dutch, p. 121): "Revelation of God, if taken in the real sense, is divine selfdisclosure issuing from divine initiative."

15   Cf. von Rad, *o.c.*, II, p. 303: "For Israel, history was the place in which she experienced her election by Jahweh and from which alone she could understand her own identity." (German, p. 320). See also on p. 338 his proposition "that it is in history that God reveals the secret of his person [Zimmerli], a proposition valid for Old and New Testament ideas alike." (German, p. 359). Vriezen, *Hoofdlijnen*, pp. 205f., rightly stresses the idea that the historical events only could be understood by means of the interpretation of Israel's prophets: "Israël heeft door het openbarende Godswoord de gebeurtenissen in de geschiedenis leren ervaren als Gods daden."

16   As Thomas postulates God in his fourth proof of God's existence, "taken from the gradation to be found in things" (Arist.), *S.Th.* I-I 2, 3. Small wonder that Thomas' way of knowledge about this philosophical (impersonal) God has to be the *via negativa*, *S.Th.*, I-I, 3.

17   Cf. H. van Oyen, *o.c.*, p. 17: "Es handelt sich im A.T. nicht in erster Linie um eine Besinnung über Gott und die von ihm gestellten Lebensprobleme, es sind keine Glaubensrätsel zu übernehmen, sondern es steht der konkrete. Verkehr Gottes mit seinem Volke im Vordergrund, wobei der existentielle Gehorsam auf sein Wort hin den Leitgedanken abgibt So ist die 'ethische' Seite des Glaubens eo ipso das Wesen der Sache."

18   *O.c.*, p. 20.

38

in definite historical situations in behalf of the keeping or fulfillment of His Covenant.[19]

Because of this unique dynamic character of Israel's knowledge of God, Vriezen concludes:

> Mann kann darum kaum von alttestamentlichen Begriffen reden; Worte sind immer lebendige Kräfte, aber in der Bibel sind sie besonders schwer befrachtet und nur richtig zu verstehen von der Ganzheit aus.[20]

"Perfection" indeed never signifies a norm *an sich*, outside or above Yahweh, one that He also must answer to or fulfill.[21]

Perfection as an abstract, self-existent ethical idea or norm is a Greek philosophical concept, which stands in fundamental antithesis with the Old Testament witness of perfection as the dynamic, historical self-disclosure of God to Israel and its patriarchs.

In the Old Testament Yahweh Himself is the norm of perfection, righteousness, truth, mercy and grace. In order to grasp the meaning of Yahweh's perfection we should consider the use of this phrase in its various historical settings and dynamic connections.

As may be expected, the Hebrew poetic device, the *parallelismus membrorum*,[22] will enlighten the intentions and scope of this divine qualification by means of synonymous expressions or explanatory elucidations.

---

19 Cf. H. Wheeler Robinson, *Inspiration and Revelation in the O.T.*, 1960 (1946), p. 189: "The only way in which we can know Him is by His willing entrance into our human experience, i.e., by some form of activity or manifestation which we *can* know. This is one of the cardinal truths of revelation as asserted in the Old Testament, i.e., that the initiative is with God." Also N. H. Snaith, *The Distinctive Ideas of the O.T.*, 1950[4], p. 47: "He was never thought of by the Hebrews as apart from the world, away in splendid isolation."

20 *Die Erwählung Israels nach dem Alten Testament*, 1953, p. 116.

21 Cf. the statement from Plato's *Eutyphron*: "The good is not good therefore that it pleases God, but the other way round, because it is (an sich) good it pleases also God" (quoted in Flückiger, *o.c.*, p. 143).

Probably to Plato even God was bound to obey by necessity (*anangkè*) the eternal reality of ideas, since this postulation is required when human thinking by necessity is able to know the absolute idea or reality of truth through the insight of the mind. This is the very foundation of all intellectualistic "Naturrecht" as explained by Flückiger, p. 143: "Die von der menschlichen Vernunft ergriffenen Ideen sind ewige Seinswahrheiten, die auch Gott vorgeordnet sind, von denen wir also kraft unserer Einsicht in ihre Seinshaftigkeit wissen, dass auch Gott sie wollen muss – so dass wir demnach in unserer autonomen, vernunftsmässigen Erkenntnis des ideellen Seins zugleich auch des (notwendigen) Willens Gottes einsichtig werden können."

22 See J. Pedersen, *Israel*, I-II, 1946 (repr. of 1926), p. 123.

The Rock, His work is perfect [tāmîm]; for all His ways are justice [mišpaṭ]. A God of faithfulness ['emûnāh] and without iniquity, just [ṣaddîq] and right [yāšār] is He.[23]

This God – His way is perfect [tāmîm]: the promise of the LORD proves true; He is a shield for all those who take refuge in Him.[24]

*The law of the LORD is perfect* [temîmāh], reviving the soul: the testimony of the LORD is sure [ne'emānāh] making wise the simple.[25]

We observe that the word "perfect" is neither applied to the empirical natural world nor to the static metaphysical world, but to the dynamic world of God's actions and the concrete revelation of His will.

The divine actions are characterized as perfect, however, only because they are all intent upon the fulfillment of His covenant promises, on God's being faithful to the obligations He has taken upon Himself in the covenant with Israel. The phrases "His work is perfect", "His way is perfect", His Torah[26] is perfect, are elucidated by the paralleling explanatory expressions "A God of faithfulness", "the promise of Yahweh proves true", "the testimony of Yahweh is sure".[27]

It is the unique characteristic of the God of Israel that He has made *promises of* blessing to the forefathers, Abraham, Isaac and Jacob, and that He is going *to fulfill* them to their seed.[28] Of vital significance is Yahweh's promise to Abram[29]:

Know of a surety that your descendants will be sojourners in a land that is not theirs and will be slaves there, and they will be oppressed for four hundred years; but I will bring judgment on the nation which they serve, and afterward they shall come out with great possessions.

While Yahweh was already known to the patriarchs as the Almighty,[30]

23 Dt. 32,4; cf. Is. 45,19: "*I* the LORD speak the truth, *I* declare what is right."

24 2 Sam. 22,31 (= Ps. 18,30 [MT vs. 31]).

25 Ps. 19,7 (MT vs. 8).

26 Torah carries the broad meaning of "word of revelation", encompassing not only the legal but also the atonement aspects of God's revelation; cf. Vriezen, *An Outline of O.T. Theology*, 1966 (Dutch, 1954²), pp. 253-256 (in ch. IX, 2b: "The Law").

27 ne'emānāh, reliable, trustworthy.

28 Gen. 12,1-3; 26,24; 28,13-15. Cf. H. W. Wolff, "The Kerygma of the Yahwist", in *Interpr.* 20 (1966), 131-158 (German, in *EvTh* 24 (1964), 73-94).

29 Gen. 15,13-14.

30 Gen. 17,1; 28,3; 35,11; 48,3 ('El Šadday); cf. 14,19.22 ('El ᶜElyon) God Most High, maker of heaven and earth. For setting and background see F. M. Cross, Jr., "Yahweh and the God of the Patriarchs", in *HThR* LV (1962), 225-259.

the Creator and Judge of all the earth,[31] and the Fear,[32] to Moses and Israel God revealed Himself as the faithful Fulfiller of the patriarchal promises[33]:

> I am the God of your father, the God of Abraham, the God of Isaac, and the God of Jacob ... I have seen the affliction of My people who are in Egypt, and have heard their cry because of their taskmasters; I know their sufferings, and *I have come down to deliver them out of the hand of the Egyptians, and to bring them up out of that land to a good and broad land, a land flowing with milk and honey.*

And this is confirmed by the words: "I *promise* that I will bring you up out of the affliction of Egypt."[34] When Moses asks for the name of God in order to answer the possible question of the people of Israel about the identity of his Sender, God says: "*I AM WHO I AM.* Say this ... : I AM has sent me to you."[35]

Taken in its contexts and concrete scope, especially Ex. 6,3-8, this name

---

31 Gen. 18,25.
32 Gen. 31,53; cf. 28,17 "How awesome is this place!" (Bethel).
33 Ex. 3,6-8; cf. 2,24; 6,6f.
34 Ex. 3,17 (RSV).
35 Ex. 3,14. Cf. Th. Vriezen, *'Ehje 'ašer 'ehje*, in *FS A. Bertholet*, 1950, p. 508: "Die Antwort Gottes an Mose unterstreicht seine Aktualität, seine Existentialität." Cf. Vriezen, *Outline*, p. 236: "This does not reduce God to a lifeless abstraction, a 'Being' or 'eternal Being' in the Greek sense of the word. On the contrary, God is in Israel the One who is always really present!" (Dutch, p. 196). See p. 235 (notes), for other interpretations and lit. Also R. Mayer, "Der Gottesname Jahwe im Lichte der neuesten Forschung", in *BZ* NF 2 (1958), 26-53, esp. 44, where he stresses the idea that Yahweh is the living God of the patriarchs: "Es ist also der Begriff des Seins im Sinne tätiger Existenz, auf dem der Nachdruck an der Exodusstelle ruht." See also S. Mowinckel, "The Name of the God of Moses", in *HUCA* 32 (1961), 121-133, who indicates that not the name of Yahweh was the new revelation in Ex. 3 – see Gen. 4,26b – but the deeper meaning of being the God who "really acts". Most of all we refer to the elucidating study of J. A. Motyer, *The Revelation of the Divine Name*, Tyndale Monograph, 1959, esp. pp. 12-31, who has convincingly presented his right to translate Ex. 6,2-3 as follows: "And God spoke to Moses, and said to him: I am Yahweh. And I showed myself to Abraham, to Isaac, and to Jacob in the character of El Shaddai, but in the character expressed by my name Yahweh I did not make myself known to them." In other words, the patriarchs knew the name Yahweh but only in the character of 'El Šadday, not yet in the character or nature of Redeemer, who is going to fulfill His promises. After all, "how could an unknown name provide any legitimization?" (p. 20). Cf. also U. Cassuto, in n. 36. W. F. Albright, *Yahweh and the Gods of Canaan*, 1968, pp. 168-172, argues strongly that Yahweh is the *hifᶜil* form of the verb *hwy*, meaning He causes to be, or It is He who creates what comes into existence.

carries this theological significance: I am faithful to My promise; I am the Reliable One, on Whom you can count; I will not fail you, I will be with you. Now I am going to fulfill My covenant promise! [36]

In other words, the name Yahweh does not reveal God's mysterious essence as such, but His dynamic actuality as the *Deus praesens* who will prove that His promise and oath are reliable. He will fulfill His Words through the *Election, Deliverance* and *Covenant* of Israel.

As G. E. Wright truly observes: "The Exodus and the conquest then follow as a witness to Yahweh's faithfulness to his promises."[37]

Moses [38] teaches:

> Yahweh set his love upon you and chose you ... because Yahweh loves you, and is keeping the oath which he swore to your fathers, that Yahweh has brought you out with a mighty hand, and redeemed you from the house of bondage, from the hand of Pharaoh king of Egypt.
>
> *Know therefore that Yahweh your God is God, the faithful God who keeps covenant and steadfast love ...*

---

36   Cf. Ex. 3,12; 6,5; Dt. 31,8, Moses to Joshua: "It is the LORD who goes before you; He will be with you, He will not fail you or forsake you; do not fear or be dismayed." It may be that also Dt. 32,39 "I AM HE" intends to convey this practical meaning. Even when Vriezen, *Outline*, pp. 235f. explains: *"I Myself am there, count on Me! ...* God can only be denoted as the Real One according to the functional character of His Being, not in His Being itself", he fails to make the necessary connections with the material significance of the "I AM" as the God of patriarchal promise: "Yahweh, the God of your fathers, the God of Abraham, the God of Isaac, and the God of Jacob, has sent me to you: this is my name for ever, and thus I am to be remembered throughout all generations" (Ex. 3,15.6; cf. Luk. 20,37f.). Because of his failure to apply this theological *function* to the given *content* Vriezen finally concludes that the name Yahweh is *without quality* ("Qualitätslosigkeit", *FS Bertholet*, 510). Also Joh. Lindblom, "Noch Einmal Die Bedeutung des Jahwe-Namens in Ex. 3,14" in *ASTI*, III (1964), 4-15, does not qualify the name *YHWH* sufficiently by its theological context when he concludes: "Er ist der einzig wirklich Gott".

M. Reisel, *Observations on 'ehyeh ašer 'ehyeh*, 1957 (Diss.), p. 18 combines the static and dynamic interpretation, i.e., the absolute and eternal Existence of God together with: "His continuous Readiness to fulfil His promises."

U. Cassuto, *A Com. on the Bk of Exodus*, 1951ff. (ET 1967), p. 79, has indicated most fully the theological signification of the name *YHWH*, when he explains Ex. 6,3ff.: "In My character as expressed by this designation, I was not known to them, that is, it was not given to them to recognize Me as One that fulfils His promises, because the assurance ... I had not yet fulfilled." See also pp. 77f., 81, 38-40.

37   *The O.T. against its Environment*, 1962, p. 50. He also states: "In all our main historical sources the deliverance from Egypt is seen as the fulfillment of God's promises to the Patriarchs."

38   Dt. 7,7-9; cf. also 8,18; 9,4-5; 10,15; 29,12-13.

N. Flüglister[39] therefore is justified in concluding: "Das Pascha-Geschehen ist also, so betrachtet, nicht so sehr ein absoluter Anfang und Neubegin, sondern eher die Frucht und Folge eines schon bestehenden Bundesverhältnisses." However, the Exodus out of Egypt was not an end in itself but only the glorious means to lead Israel to the presence of Yahweh, in order to serve the Savior-King as His kingdom, as a holy nation, to be His sanctuary within the framework of a new convenant.[40] In the religious consciousness of Jeremiah the Exodus and the covenant even constitute a directly connected unity.[41]

In this way the name of Yahweh is qualified by His faithful or perfect keeping of His covenant with the patriarchs and with Israel. Therefore Yahweh's perfection means His saving and sanctifying will to remain in fellowship and communion with His covenant people and through them with the world. And since "love" is the will to communion and intercourse, God's perfection may be called His constant redeeming love, His perfect or steadfast love (ḥesed) which again is normed by His covenant. Therefore the ḥesed of Yahweh is often accompanied by the explanatory adjectives ʾemet or ʾemunah, faithfulness.[42] We might say that the term perfection with respect to God is not primarily an ethical word, but rather one of religious knowledge. Ethical knowledge of God is rooted in the religious-soteriological experience.[43] This makes the order religio-ethical of supreme importance. God's perfection primarily denotes the religious quality of salvation defined by God's nature and will, expressed in the covenant. The covenant with Israel, however, is a covenant of grace. In the covenant God's perfection is revealed,

---

39 *Die Heilsbedeutung des Pascha*, StANT VIII, 1963, p. 234. He further refers to Yahweh in His quality as *Gōʾēl* for Israel, on the basis of the patriarchal covenant, esp. pp. 176f.; notice p. 234: "Pascha-Heil und Abrahambund bilden nach dieser Geschichtsauffassung eine innige Einheit."

40 Ex. 15,17f.; Ps. 114,1-2.

41 Jer. 31,32; 34,13f. (MT *beyôm; en hèmerai*). Cf. Flüglister, *o.c.*, p. 237: "Im Pascha ist der Bund bereits eingeschlossen; Pascha und Bund sind eins".

42 See N. Glueck, *Ḥesed in the Bible*, ET 1967 (German 1961², BZAW 47), ch. III: "Hesed as Divine Conduct". Also the valuable introduction by G. A. Larue: "Recent Studies in *Ḥesed*", pp. 1-32. On p. 72 (German, p. 36) Glueck states: "Wherever *ḥesed* appears together with ʾemeth or ʾemunah, the quality of loyalty inherent in the concept *ḥesed* is emphasized." He refers to the following verses: Gen. 32,11; 47,29; Ex. 34,6; Dt. 7,9; II Sam. 2,6; 7,15-16; 15,20; Josh. 2,14; Is. 55,3; Hos. 2,21-22; 4,1; Mic. 7,20; Pss. 25,20; 26,3; 31,24; 36,6; 40,11-12; 57,4; 61,8; 69,14; 11 : 9; 85 : 11; 86,15; 88,12; 89,2.3.12.25.29. 34.50; 92,3; 98,3; 100,5; 115,1; 117,2; 119,41; 138,2; Prov. 3,3; 14,22; 16,6; 20,6; 20,28; Lam. 3,22-23. Further, A. R. Johnson, "Hesed and Hāsîd", in *FS* S. Mowinckel, 1955, 100-112; H. J. Stöbe, "Die Bedeutung des Wortes ḥäsäd im Alten Testament", *VT* II (1952), 245-254.

43 2 Sam. 22,31 (= Ps. 18,30) gave as explanation of "His way is perfect": "He is a shield for all those who take refuge in Him."

therefore, primarily as God's saving work of grace. God's perfection means His perfect or full, complete, undivided, faithful will and dedication to man, to save him, to revive him, to keep him saved in the way of sanctification in the fellowship and partnership with the loving Creator, even when man is unfaithful and turns away from his perfect Lover.[44]

Probably the most profound, unsuspected revelation of God's perfection as the stability of His steadfast love and the continuity of His unalterable compassion for His covenant people is His effusion in Hosea 11,8-9:

> How can I give you up, O Ephraim! How can I hand you over, O Israel! How can I make you like Admah! How can I treat you like Zeboiim!
> My heart recoils within me, my compassion grows warm and tender. I will not execute my fierce anger, I will not again destroy Ephraim; *for I am God and not man, the Holy One in your midst,* and I will not come to destroy.

As Yahweh has revealed Himself to Israel in redeeming faithfulness to His covenant promises, so He truly is.[45]

God's perfection, therefore, is a soul-stirring appeal to man estranged from his Creator, in order to arouse his thoughts and feelings about the wonderful works and words (torah) of his loving Redeemer-Creator.

The religious exhortation is [46]:

> Remember the wonderful works that He has done,
> His miracles, and the judgments He uttered.
> O give thanks to the LORD, call on His name,
> make known His deeds among the peoples!
> Sing to Him, sing praise to Him,
> tell of all His wonderful works!
> Glory in His holy name;
> let the hearts of those who seek the LORD rejoice!

To forget His benefits is to forget Yahweh, which is described as a sinful neglect.[47]

---

44 Cf. Hos. 11,1-7; Ez. 16. Even God's anger and judgments on Israel are intent upon the realization of His undiminished fullness of love and will to re-union.

45 In Ps. 12, God's promises, in antithesis with the double-heartedness of the ungodly, are qualified as pure (*tehōr*), as refined silver, *"purified seven times"* (vs. 6, MT 7).

46 Ps. 105,5. 1-3.

47 Ps. 103,2; 119,16.

44

The torah of Yahweh is called "perfect" because its *effect* on man is perfect[48]:

> The law of Yahweh is perfect, reviving the soul ... making wise the simple ... rejoicing the heart ... enlightening the eyes ...

Vriezen[49] suggests that the reason why *tāmîm*, which means wholeness, entirety, is never used as a predicate of Yahweh can best be explained by the feeling that *"tāmîm"* was not regarded as sublime or "elevated" enough to denote the holy God: "God is rich in (ethical) virtues, but transcends the human ethical standards."

This last statement undoubtedly is true. The question may be asked, however, whether the term *tāmîm* ever was intended to be a description of God's essence in the same "elevated" sense as holiness and righteousness. The fact that this term is not used at all as a predicate of Yahweh in the Old Testament is certainly noteworthy. The word is used of His work, His way, His covenant promise; they are said to be *tāmîm*, perfect! *Tāmîm* thus indicates a specific notion of *functionality* and *actuality* in Yahweh's relation to Israel, which is of utmost importance for the knowledge of Yahweh and His virtues. It intends to express the distinctive idea that Yahweh's act of delivering Israel is a *complete* fulfillment of His covenant promise; that His way of leading and protecting Israel is the *faithful* fulfillment of His word; that His Torah or instruction to Israel is *fully* efficacious. *Tāmîm* functions only in a specific way, to indicate the fullness and wholeness, the stability and reliability of God's will, His love and work *to redeem* His covenant people perfectly. We might say, this divine perfection is perfect in its dynamic scope of being intent upon the perfection of man and world.

As God is wholly for man, so man is redeemed in order to be wholly for God and wholly for his fellowman and the surrounding world.[50]

Yet it remains true that God's perfection is not completely characterized with the functioning of His love. The prophets spoke about the One God with more than one word! Two characterizations seem to have made the deepest impression on Israel's prophets: Yahweh's (perfect) righteousness and (moral) holiness. And it is to these qualities that God is calling His covenant people to be renewed and recreated, in order to reflect in humanity this glory of the likeness of God.

The redeemed Israel is called to the *yir'at Yhwh*, the "fear of the LORD", which is the dynamic experience of God's holiness and love,[51]

---

48  Ps. 19,7f.
49  *Hoofdlijnen*, p. 335, n. 4; ET p. 161, n. 4.
50  Cf. Dt. 6,4ff.; Lev. 19,18.
51  Cf. Vriezen, *Hoofdlijnen*, pp. 333ff.; ET pp. 159ff. On the unparalleled

and *"to walk in all His ways* and cleaving to Him"[52]; in other words, to the *imitatio Dei* in the social ethos of righteousness and mercy. "You shall be holy; for I the LORD your God am holy".[53] God's quality of holiness (*qodeš*) denotes a category completely *sui generis*, and does not belong to the realm of abstract philosophical thinking at all, even exceeding the province of ethical notions.[54]

It belongs to the realm of religious experience of the heart, to the overwhelming, almost crushing confrontation and communion with the reality of God personally, by which a new light from above enlightens the heart and conscience and all moral values in the revealing light of heaven.[55] Only in this experience of the reality of God's holiness can man fully detect and evaluate himself as he is before the HOLY ONE and sense the reality and hideousness of his sin.[56]

phenomenon of the prevalence of confident trust and love in Israel's fear of God, see W. Eichrodt, *Theology of the O.T.*, II, 1967 (German, 1964[7]), ch. XXI, pp. 268-277, 290-301.

52  Dt. 11,22; 10, 12.

53  Lev. 19,2; 11,44f. See H. van Oyen, *Ethik des A.T.*, p. 55; and E. Jacob *Theology of the O.T.*, ET 1958, pp. 173-177. See also F. J. Helfmeyer, *Die Nachfolge Gottes in Alten Testament*, BBB 29, 1968, who convincingly refutes A. Schulz, *Nachfolgen und Nachahmen*, StANT VI, 1962, p. 221, n. 70, concerning the *imitatio Dei* motif in the holiness requirement and the socio-ethical commandments of Deuteronomy. The point of Helfmeyer is: "Im Gegensatz zu der Feststellung von Schulz, dass diese Motivierungen keine Aufforderung zur Nachahmung, sondern lediglich zur Dankbarkeit enthalten, legt der Kontext von Dt. 10,18f.; 15,15 sehr wohl den Gedanken der Nachahmung bzw. der göttlichen Vorbildlichkeit nahe" (pp. 218f.). See also p. 219. With respect to the specific German dilemma of the concepts *Nachfolgen* and *Nachahmen*, it seems Th. Süss, in his article "Nachfolge Jesu", in *ThLZ* 3 (1953), 130-140, is correct when he takes the position that both concepts belong together and are only two aspects of one and the same ethics (131). *Nachfolge* in the broad sense includes and leads to *Nachahmung* which is the closer conformity with the great Example, e.g.: "Jesu Ethik ist Ethik der Nachfolge und eben damit Ethik der Verähnlichung mit Jesus; Ethik der Gleichgestaltung in der Nachfolge" (131). By our use of the term *imitatio Dei* we mean this dynamic concept of following and conforming. The richness of this *imitatio Dei* becomes more explicit in the *imitatio Christi* in the NT. See further below, n. 102.

54  Cf. Snaith, *o.c.*, pp. 21-50; p. 21: "This [sc. *qodeš*] is the most intimately divine word of all. It has to do ... with the very Nature of Deity; no word more so, nor indeed any other as much." Cf. G. Fohrer, *Geschichte der israelitischen Religion*, 1969, pp. 164f. J. Pedersen, *Israel* III-IV, ET 1940, pp. 264-295. On the twofold aspects of Yahweh's holiness, its inviolability or dreadfulness, and its blessing, see H. Ringgren, *The Prophetical Conception of Holiness*, 1948.

55  E.g. Is. 6,1-8 (the *trishagion*): "Woe is me! For I am lost; for I am a man of unclean lips, and I dwell in the midst of a people of unclean lips, for my eyes have seen the King, the LORD of hosts!" (vs. 5).

56  Cf. Job's confession in Job 42,1-6: "I had heard of Thee by the hearing

When the conviction of sin(fullness) and fear are the correlates of divine holiness, sin is qualified not as merely a transgression against some moral code, but as rebellion against the Person of God,[57] as *disobedience* to the Lawgiver, as the *forsaking* of the Covenant God,[58] as *not revering God as holy.*[60]

However, the revelations of God's holiness are never aimed at crushing man or disclosing his misery, not even to point out his (sinful) creature-feeling as such. On the contrary, they intend his atonement,[61] the repentant return to worship his holy Creator in awe and trust,[62] the reviving of his spirit and heart,[63] his being sent on divine mission,[64] his restoration into kingship over the world and his elevation unto being the full-fledged partner of God again, his walking with God in harmony and unity,[65] his being holy also, thus receiving the covenant blessings.

In others words, God's holiness is not intent upon creating distance and estrangement, but upon true communion and close fellowship and loyalty between God and man, and consequently, between man and his neighbor.[66]

Therefore it is of vital importance to notice how Yahweh's righteousness and holiness are intent upon the creation of that kind of human interrelationship, which is akin to the God-man relation, and is a reflection and fruit of it.

The anointed kings of Israel were called to establish this saving, social righteousness as representatives of the great King of the universe.[67] And when this social righteousness is being distorted into social unrighteousness, the prophets of Yahweh[68] arise with soul-stirring messages to awaken the social conscience and call the people to return to the

of the ear, but now my eye sees Thee; therefore I despise myself, and repent in dust and ashes." For this experience with regard to Christ, see Lk. 5,8; 4,34 par.

57    Dt. 28,15; Is.1.2.4; Hos. 7,13; Jer. 14,20; Ps. 51,4; Am. 1,3.6.9.11, etc.
58    Jer. 2,13; Is. 1,3; Hos. 4,7.
59    Dt. 32,18.
60    Dt. 32,51 (Moses!).
61    Is. 6,6-7; Hos. 11,9.
62    Hos. 6,1f.; 12,6; 14,1; Is. 8,13; 10,20; 17,7; 29,19.23.
63    Is. 57,15; Ps. 111,9-10.
64    Is. 6,8.
65    Am. 3,3; Mic. 6,8.
66    Is. 5,16: "But the Lord of hosts is exalted in justice, and the Holy God shows himself holy in righteousness." Cf. also 58,7-9.
67    See Ps. 72; Dt. 17,14-20.
68    Especially the four eighth-century B.C. prophets, Is., Mic., Hos. and Amos. Cf. God's complaint in Is. 5,4: "What more was there to do for My vineyard, that I have not done in it? When I looked for it to yield grapes, why did it yield wild grapes?" See also vs. 7.

covenant God in order to avoid the heralded jugdment day for the land and people of Israel.

In this connection it is important to notice that Moses uses the terms justice (*mišpāṭ*), just (*ṣaddîq*), and right (*yāšār*) as virtual synonyms of God's perfection.[69]

The redeeming acts of Yahweh on behalf of the covenant people Israel in leading them out of Egypt and into the land of promise are called by Micah the *ṣidqôt, the righteousnesses of Yahweh.*[70]

In the manifestation of God's righteousnesses two aspects of Yahweh's righteousness are revealed:

a) His *saving acts* for His faithful Israel;

b) His *destroying acts* for the enemies of Israel who threaten the covenant people and hinder the covenant from being fulfilled to Israel.[71]

God's righteousness then may be qualified as His faithfulness to establish and fulfill His covenant with Israel. Israel, therefore, in times of distress and oppression can invoke God's *righteousnesses* as the way of salvation and deliverance.[72] God assures His chastised covenant people that He will strengthen, help, and uphold them with the right hand of His righteousness.[73] Thus God is righteous when bestowing mercy. He is both not partly but fully, and in this sense, both perfectly.

The connection between *qodeš, ṣedeq, ḥesed* and *tāmîm*, therefore, appears to be very intimate. We might say, that God is *tāmîm* means that His way or the revelations of His holiness, righteousness and steadfast love are perfect. And this perfection man is called to follow, not in

---

69  Dt. 32,4.

70  Mic. 6,5; RSV translates *ṣidqôt* with: "the saving acts." Cf. Jud. 5,11; RSV translates: "the triumphs".

71  When Israel was persistently unfaithful to its obligations of the covenant (Hos. 4), the divine judgment of the Assyrian and Babylonian captivities were also qualified as God's righteousness, Yahweh being faithful to His covenant, because the intention of the captivity was the restoration of a renewed and faithful Israel. Dt. 28; 30,1-3; Dan. 9,9-19; Jer. 30-33; Neh. 1,3-11; Ps. 105-106; Hos. 11,7-11; esp. 2,19-20.

72  Ps. 31,1f.; 35,24; 71,2. In Ps. 88,11-12, God's righteousness is being used synonymously with *ᵓemûnāh*, faithfulness; and with *ḥesed*, in RSV translated with "steadfast love"; in the sense of covenant loyalty; cf. Ps. 103,17; 40,10 ("Thy righteousness" is translated in RSV by "Thy saving help"). Cf. Fohrer, *o.c.*, p. 165.

73  Is. 41,10 (*ṣidqi*); RSV translates: "my victorious right hand". In Is. 45,8 God's righteousness brings salvation for and even righteousness among Israel.

the sense of striving for an unattainable ideal, but in the sense of a gracious *imitatio Dei*, to be realized only in the communion or walk with his Creator, the Almighty covenant God.[74]

Thus the Scriptures indicate the perfection of Noah, Abraham, Job and true Israel.

Noah was a righteous man, blameless in his generation; Noah walked with God (Gen. 6,9).

The Lord appeared to Abraham, and said to him, I am God Almighty; walk before me, and be blameless (Gen. 17,1; see also Gen. 26,5).

There was a man in the land of Uz, whose name was Job and that man was blameless and upright, one who feared God, and turned away from evil (Job 1,1).

For the Lord God is a sun and shield; he bestows favor and honor. No good thing does the Lord withhold from those who walk uprightly (Ps. 84,11).

Blessed are those whose way is blameless, who walk in the law of the Lord! (Ps. 119,1).

Men of perverse mind are an abomination to the Lord, but those of blameless ways are his delight (Prov. 11,20).

The history of the patriarchs and the people of Israel shows emphatically, however, that in the individual and the collective existence of Israel sin and its consequences could not be banished in all respects. They all died in the final hope of the ultimate perfection of God's glory in all

---

74   E. Jacob, *Theology of the Old Testament*, ET 1958 (French 1955), pp. 173-177. On p. 174 he states: "ᵓ*emunah* and ᵓ*emet* denote at the same time the faithfulness and veracity of God and the faith of man. It is the same with the use of the term *chesed* ... ; the word is used at one and the same time for the attitude of God to man, of man to God, and of man to his fellow. By *chesed* man best attains to the imitation of God and the *chesed* he shows to his neighbour is always *chesed Elohim* (2 Sam. 9,3; 1 Sam. 20,14); the more complete expression ᶜ*asah chesed* we ᵓ*emet* is used of God and of men (2 Sam. 2,6; 15,20; Gen. 24,12; 2 Sam. 10,2) and every Israelite's ideal to become *chasid* is realized in a perfect way by Yahweh himself (Jer. 3,12; Ps. 145,17)." On p. 175 Jacob asks the significant question whether the frequent formula "I am Yahweh" in the Levitical laws "does not also signify that the principle of imitation lies behind all the legislation."

dimensions of life and the world; in other words, in the hope of the coming of God's kingdom.[75] The Old Testament saints knew about the protological,[76] soteriological and eschatological perfection of God's work.[77]

75    See Heb. 11. Cf. W. Eichrodt, *Man in the Old Testament*, SBT 4, 1966 (1951ff.), p. 36: "And as mankind appears at the beginning of Israel's records as a single entity, so too, in Israel's view of the future, mankind appears as the united community of nations receiving God's new world, and thus returning to their origin (Isa. 2,2-4; Zech. 9,9f.; Zeph. 3,9; Isa. 45,22-24, etc.)."

76    Cf. Job 37,16; Gen. 1,31: "And God saw everything that He had made [man also] and *behold, it was very good.*" Cf. G. von Rad, *Genesis*, 1961 (German 1956), p. 59: "It could also be correctly translated 'completely perfect' (Pr.) and rightly refers more to the wonderful properness and harmony than to the beauty of the entire cosmos."

77    See Is. 11,6-9; 35; 65,17; 66,22-23; Dan. 12,2 (man's resurrection); 2,44; 7,27; cf. Nic. H. Ridderbos, "Het O.T. in de pred.", in *GTT* 56 (1956), p. 147: "De zonde heeft in het O.T. wel degelijk een centrale plaats. En de worsteling, die het O.T. beschrijft, heeft wel degelijk tot inzet, dat er een volk zal komen, dat Jahwe dient met een ongedeeld hart." Vriezen, *De godsd. v. Israël*, pp. 63f.: "In deze visie, waarin Israëls religie haar hoogtepunt bereikt, heeft het zich wel heel duidelijk losgemaakt van de godsdienstige voorstellingen van de gehele omringende wereld." *Ibid.*, Outline, p. 369: "The eschatological vision is an Israelite phenomenon which has not really been found outside Israel." Eichrodt, *Theol. of the O.T.*, II, p. 107: "The eschatological Creator God is not the enemy but the perfector of the first creation." And now the recent, outstanding study of H. D. Preuss, *Jahweglaube und Zukunftserwartung*, BWANT 87, 1968, esp. pp. 99-102, 205-214. Preuss convincingly shows that the expectation of eschatological perfection in the O.T. was not an addition to the Yahweh-faith, or an outside influence on it, but the intrinsic idea and legitimate development of it. On pp. 9-102 he firmly establishes his thesis: "Die Zukunftserwartung mit Abschlussaspekt soll als Grundstruktur des Jahweglaubens erwiesen werden" (p. 5).

# Chapter III     *The distinctive idea of human perfection in the Old Testament*

A. HUMAN PERFECTION IN ISRAEL'S PROTOLOGY.

1. *The function of Genesis I in the Hebrew Canon.*
What is the theological significance and function of the first creation account at the beginning of the Hebrew canon?

When Israel's faith must be evaluated primarily not as creation-faith, but as redemption-faith,[1] what then is the relevancy of Israel's protology as described in Genesis 1,1–2,4a? Von Rad argues that Israel's protology in the Old Testament is continually pre-conditioned and motivated by Israel's soteriology.[2] Never does the creation-faith function as an independent, self-existent religious actuality or kerygma. All creation doxologies are only subservient to the disclosure of the central and universal functioning of Israel's soteriology.[3]

In his Commentary on Genesis von Rad states:

> Faith in creation is neither the position nor the goal of the declarations in Genesis, chs. 1 and 2. Rather, the position of both the Yahwist and the Priestly document is basically faith in salvation and election. They undergird this faith by the testimony that

---

1 Modern O.T. scholars like von Rad, Noth, Wright, Zimmerli, Westermann, Vriezen and Lohfink are united in the conclusion that Israel's religion has a "ground structure" which has its central or focal point in Ex. 1-15, i.e., the Exodus deliverance from Egypt. *E.g.*, G. von Rad, "Das theol. Problem des alttestamentlichen Schöpfungsglaubens", in *Ges. Stud. z. A.T.*, 1965, p. 136: "Der Jahweglaube des Alten Testaments ist Erwählungsglaube, d.h. primär Heilsglaube." Vriezen, *Outline*, pp. 187f.; stating on p. 189: "No wonder, then, that the idea of the Creation lies far more in the periphery than this historical experience of salvation and does not rank first in the message of the prophets." He regards this unique relationship "as one of the most striking proofs of the special origin of this religion" (*Ibid.*).
2 *O.c.*, p. 142: "Und dieses soteriologische Verständnis des Schöpfungswerkes... halten wir für die ursprünglichste Äußerung des Jahweglaubens über Jahwe, den Schöpfer der Welt."
3 Von Rad, *o.c.*, p. 139: "In ihnen [sc. creation doxologies] klingt das prophetische Wort ins Universale aus, und somit geben sie ihm eine neue Tiefendimension." Cf. C. Westermann, *The Praise of God in the Psalms*, 1965 (German 1961), p. 126, n. 78, underlining von Rad's conclusions.

this Yahweh, who made a covenant with Abraham and at Sinai, is also the creator of the world.[4]

The remarkable fact remains, however, in this valuable insight, that, while the theological structure of Israel's faith shows her soteriology to be central and fundamental (Yahweh "from the land of Egypt" Hos. 12,9), yet her protology is given the prerogative to stand at the beginning of the canon.[5] Does this procedure have only formal significance?

Vriezen[6] sees the "real meaning" of Gen. 1 "in the attempt to place the cosmogony wholly in the light of the belief in the One God", the living Savior and Redeeming God of Israel. Here Vriezen certainly indicates a vital function of the creation story in Genesis. It is the indirect polemical "de-mythologizing" (Entmythisierung) character of Gen. 1, an aspect which has been recognized more and more in the light of the various cosmogonies or theogonies of antiquity.[7]

The uniqueness of Israel's faith in antiquity proves to be its radical break with the mythopoeic approach to reality by means of elimination, transformation and historicizing of the ancient creation myths in Israel's own protology, salvation history, and even in her eschatology.[8]

---

4  *Genesis. A Commentary*, 1961 (German 1956), p. 44.

5  Cf. O. Loretz, *Schöpfung und Mythos*, 1968, p. 49: "Denn die unbestreitbare Vorrangstellung, die der Bericht, Gn. 1,1-2, 4a nun einmal besitzt, ist nicht von ungefähr."

6  *Outline*, p. 187, stating on the same page: "Gen. 1 ... cannot simply be regarded as a naive, adopted, ancient mythological conception ..." Cf. Westermann, "Das Verhältnis des Jahweglaubens zu den ausserisrael. Rel.", in *Forschung am A.T.*, 1964, p. 207: "Die eigentliche Entmythisierung besteht nicht in der Abänderung von Einzelheiten, sondern in der Verpflanzung aus dem mythischen in den geschichtlichen Zusammenhang."

7  Cf. W. H. Schmidt, *Die Schöpfungsgeschichte der Priesterschrift*, WMANT 17, 1964, pp. 21-32, 177-180; who states on p. 180: "Die Interpretation ist getrieben von der Frage: Wie ist von Gott als Schöpfer dem Glauben gemäss zu reden? ... Beide [sc. Mythos und der Glaube Israels] sind sich vielmehr fremd. Der Glaube findet das mythische Weltverständnis vor; wo er es aufnimmt, um sich auszusprechen, sucht er es zu überwinden ... So lässt das A.T. die mythische Rede nicht bestehen, sondern entfernt sie entweder völlig oder greift ihre Wörter auf, um sie neu zu verstehen." Cf. Loretz, *o.c.*, p. 48; B. W. Anderson, *Creation versus Chaos*, 1967, pp. 30ff.; N. M. Sarna, *Understanding Genesis*, 1966, pp. 7ff.; G. E. Wright, *Biblical Archeology*, 1962², p. 104; B. S. Childs, *Myth and Reality in the O.T.*, SBT 27, 1962², pp. 31-43. On the close but critical relation with Babylonian prototypes, see E. A. Speiser, *Genesis*, The Anchor Bible, 1964, pp. Lvi, 9-11.

8  G. E. Wright, *The O.T. against its Environment*, 1962 (1950ff.), p. 27: "On the one hand, the myth was historicized and used metaphorically to describe Yahweh's great victories in history, especially that over Pharaoh's army in the crossing of the Red Sea (e.g. Isa. 51,9-10). On the other hand, it was used in eschatology as a description of God's victory over his enemies in the great Day to come (cf. Isa. 27,1) (...)." H. D. Preuss, *o.c.*, p. 96ff.

This removed Israel's protology and eschatological hope from the sphere of myth into the religious assurance of an actual past and future. It gave Israel the distinctive character of a people of destiny, on the way from a historical past to a promised future which they treasured as "a historical hope."[9]

The religious reason why Gen. 1,1–2,4a wants to recount the creation story as "history"[10] may be seen in the dramatic fact that Israel knew God only as the Lord of history, who at once transcends both nature and history.[11]

Therefore the ethical character of Israel's Creator in His sovereign work of creation and history stands out in a glorious uniqueness amidst the ancient mythological creation stories.[12] And the fact, known by prophetic revelation, that the Creator of the world has used all His creative powers and virtues for the sake of delivering Israel from her over-

---

N. Füglister, *Die Heilsbedeutung des Pascha*, StANT VIII, 1963, p. 206, significantly refers to Yahweh's victory as Creator, Savior and Perfector over the dragon Rahab, as pictured in Ps. 89,10-12; Job 26,12f.; Is. 30,7; 51,9-11; Pss. 74,12-19; 87,4; and concludes: "Auf diese Weise werden Schöpfungsbeginn, Erlösung und Endheil mittels ein und derselben Bildaussage aneinandergerückt und gegenseitig verklammert. Den derselbe Jahwe ist ja zugleich Schöpfer der Welt, 'Schöpfer Israels' und Schöpfer der 'neuen Erde und des neuen Himmels' (...)." On the eschatological application, see esp. H. Gunkel, *Schöpfung und Chaos in Urzeit und Endzeit. Eine rel. gesch. Unters. über Gen. 1 und Ap. Joh. 12*, 1924[2], esp. pp. 110f., 367ff.; and H. Wallace, "Leviathan and the Beast in Revelation", in *BA* XI (1948), 61-68.

9  W. Eichrodt, *Theol. of the O.T.*, 1961 (German 1959[6]), pp. 301, 461. He urges the distinction "between the provenance of the mythological material in which the salvation-hope of Israel is clothed and the origin of the hope itself" (p. 495). Cf. J. Moltmann, *Theologie der Hoffnung*, 1965[4], pp. 274f.

10  Von Rad, *Genesis*, p. 45. W. H. Schmidt, *o.c.*, p. 30, n. 4: "Gen. 1 will Geschichte erzählen." See also pp. 183-187. He states on p. 187: "Weil die Welt aus dem Geschehen begriffen wird, hat in Gen. 1 das Verbum so starken Vorrang vor den Substantiv. Gen. 1 beschreibt nicht, sondern erzählt." He refers to *toledoth* in Gen. 2,4a to stress that Gen. 1 does not intend to be a report in the abstract ("Schöpfungsbericht") but the history or "generations" of God's work of creation ("Schöpfungsgeschichte"). K. Runia, *K. Barth's Doctrine of H. Scripture*, 1962, pp. 99f. prefers to qualify Gen. 1 as "'prophetical' historiography." See esp. B. W. Anderson, *Creation versus Chaos*, pp. 33, 35, 40f.

11  Cf. G. E. Wright, *The O.T. ag. its Environment*, pp. 22f., who states on p. 26: "That is the remarkable fact that the God of Israel has no mythology. Since history rather than nature was the *primary* sphere of his revelation, Israel's effort was to tell the story of her past in terms of God's activity." Cf. Eichrodt, *o.c.*, I, p. 496. Runia, *o.c.*, p. 98: "Exactly *in* Israel the idea of history first was discovered."

12  Cf. H. Th. Obbink, *Het Bijbelsch Paradijsverhaal en de Babylonische Bronnen*, 1917, p. 161. He concludes finally to a "purely formal conformity" between Gen. 1 and the Babylonian creation myths. H. Wheeler Robinson, *Insp. and Rev. in the O.T.*, 1960 (1946ff.), p. 222.

powering enemy, setting free His covenant people to serve Him,[13] constituted the continual appeal to wholehearted worship and thanksgiving of Yahweh as Creator and Redeemer. Thus Israel, in her situation, came to know the Creator and Redeemer who revealed to her His creation power in His redemptive acts. Does not the fact that Israel's faith placed the book of Genesis, with its creation stories at the beginning, before the book of Exodus, testify not merely that Israel's Redeemer God is the only true and living God, the almighty Creator of all men in every nation and tribe, but also that Israel's religious-ethical way of life is rooted in the will of the Creator Himself?[13a] The fact that Israel, and we, only know the Creator through His salvation does not mean that God is Creator only within the realm of redemption.

God's Redeemership presupposes his Creatorship, just as the Gospel presupposes the Law.[14] However, the starting point for true worship and obedience of God is the experience of His redemption. Hence there is a *double* aspect of Israel's worship of Yahweh, which becomes explicit in the twofold motivation of Israel's Sabbath-keeping: the Decalogue is introducing Yahweh as *Redeemer of Israel*,[15] while the Sabbath commandment is based on Yahweh's *Creatorship of the world*.[16] This describes Israel's obedience to God, and her Sabbath-keeping in particular, not as a religion of law or legalism, but as a religion of grace.[17]

We therefore agree wholeheartedly with von Rad when he states that the position of the author of Gen. 1 is the central place of the redemptive

---

13  Ex. 3,18; 19,5-6; 20,1ff.

13a Speiser, *o.c.*, p. Lvii: "The answer to this question [sc. why Gen. 1-11 were included in Israel's Primeval History] may be sought in the fact that neither J nor P was interested in national history as such. Rather, both were concerned with the story of a society and, more particularly, a society as the embodiment of an ideal, that is, a way of life. A history of that kind transcends national boundaries and may conceivably be retraced to the beginnings of the world."

14  Cf. H. Bavinck, *G.D.* III, 139; IV, 496: "Het evangelie onderstelt de wet."

15  Ex. 20,1-2; on the deuteronomic "foundation" of the Sabbath commandment (Dt. 5,14-15), see E. Jenni, *Die theol. Begründung des Sabbatgebotes im A.T.*, Th.St. 46, 1956, pp. 15-19 ("eine anerkannt deuteronomische Interpretation des vierten Gebotes").

16  On the grace-character of the Sabbath as the gift of the eternal gracious will of God, see Jenni, *o.c.*, pp. 22f.

17  Cf. Nic. H. Ridderbos, "Het O.T. in de pred." in *GTT* 56 (1956), 149: "Dat Israëls religie niet een wetsreligie, maar een genadereligie is." W. H. Velema, *Wet en Evangelie*, 1959, pp. 23ff., therefore is justified in rejecting the idea that the Old Covenant possessed traits of a "work-covenant". Referring to Lev. 19; Dt. 8,1-18; 10,12-22; 11,1-7 and Calvin, *Inst.* II, 7,1, Velema characterizes the law as a gift of the covenant of grace. Von Rad, *O.T. Theol.* I, 1962 (German 1957), pp. 229-231; and *Studies in Deut.*, 1953, pp. 71f.

Covenant with Israel.[18] However, when von Rad goes to define the function of Gen. 1 as being the dogmatic legitimization of the redemptive relationship, he seems to exhaust the significance of Gen. 1 in this function of being only a means to the end of redemption.[19] We should, however, in the joy of discovering this basic structure of Israel's faith not lose sight of the significance of the self-existent dimension of the theocentric function of Israel's faith in the Creator of heaven and earth.[20] In other words, must not God be acknowledged and praised as truly for the mysteries of creation as for the mystery of redemption? The many more or less extensive accounts of Yahweh's work in creation, as e.g., in Gen. 1; Pss. 8;33;104; Is. 40,12-28, certainly function as something *more* than a mere introduction or undergirding of redemptive faith.[21] These very passages are continually given in a doxological context, with the clear intention to excite all humanity to the praise of Israel's God for the sake of His glory, wisdom, and goodness as Creator.[22]

N. H. Ridderbos thus is justified when he states about the significance of Gen. 1:

> This enrichment of revelation also serves to enable Israel the better to sing its praises to God. The assertion of van Rad that Gen. 1, by its testimony to the effect that Jahwe is the Creator of the world, is intended to undergird Israel's faith in its salvation

---

18  *Ges. Stud.*, p. 143.

19  *O.c.*, p. 143: "So ist doch auch hier Jahwes Weltschöpfung nicht an sich und um ihrer selbst willen betrachtet, sondern ... ist von einem durchaus heilsgeschichtlichem Interesse bestimmt." Cf. von Rad's *Genesis*, p. 44, the "undergirding" function of Gen. 1.

20  Cf. J. Barr, *Old and New in Interpretation*, p. 76: "But the actual content of the creation story does not reveal any particular dependence on the Exodus theme; in fact, its absence of dependence on what is usually regarded as the 'central' theology of Israel is one of the marked things about it."

21  We may also point to Gen. 9,6; Prov. 14,31; 17,5 where insults or murder are judged by God in His attribute as Creator. This motivation is also found in Amos 4,13.

22  Von Rad, *Ges. Stud.*, p. 144, also has to acknowledge that in Pss. 19 and 104 "wirklich Zeugnisse eines reinen und selbständig in sich ruhendes Schöpfungsglaubens vorliegen; hier ist tatsächlich die Weltschöpfung Jahwes das Thema..." He qualifies these Psalms then, however, as *non*-authentic testimonies of Israel. C. Westermann, *The Praise of God in the Psalms*, p. 126 acknowledges, on Ps. 33: "Creation is here the secondary theme. It is the creation that is spoken of for the sake of the Creator, and not the Creator for the sake of the creation (...)." Westermann, *Isaiah 40-66*, p. 57 states on Is. 40,20: "In praise as found in the Psalms, the theme of the divine majesty is developed along two lines. First, God is creator and lord of history." Cf. H. Zirker, *Die Kultische Vergegenwärtigung der Vergangenheit in den Psalmen*, BBB 20, 1964, p. 137: "Lob ist Antwort auf Schöpfung und Heilsgeschichte." See also p. 136.

and election, is therefore onesided because too anthropocentric.[23]

By this Ridderbos does not imply that Gen. 1 and the other creation passages suggest that man can come to know the Creator or Yahweh by means of nature itself. On the contrary, their continual connection with the special revelation of Israel's covenant of redemption indicates that the Creator can only be truly known and praised together with Israel.[24]

Yet Loretz,[25] who acknowledges that the creation narrative, with its culmination in the Sabbath rest, wants to indicate an unbreakable relation between Israel and all creation and humanity, again subordinates the whole creation to Israel's covenant of redemption, when he concludes: "Das Geschehen der Welt ist von Anfang an auf Israel ausgerichtet".[26]

Such a construction of creation and Israel carries into Biblical theology a principle which is not derived from Scripture, but from a preconceived dogmatic concept, i.e., that of K. Barth.[27]

> Barth is no longer satisfied with the noetic interpretation of creation in the light of Israel's soteriology. He transforms this

---

23 *Is there a conflict between Gen. 1 and natural science?* 1957 (Dutch, *Beschouwingen over Gen. I*), p. 64; he states on p. 65: "In my opinion the revelation embodied in Gen. I occupies a place of central significance in the whole revelation."

24 Cf. N. H. Ridderbos, *De Psalmen*, I, 1962, pp. 206f., *ad* Ps. 19; C. Westermann, *The Genesis Accounts of Creation*, 1966² (German 1961²), p. 36; who states on p. 37: "The real goal of these creation stories cannot be lost sight of, namely the praise of the Creator." See, however, also below, n. 32. Of vital importance remains Calvin's familiar imagery that we can only read the book of nature with the help of the spectacles of God's special revelation (*Inst.* I, 6, 1; I, 14, 1), and that from the *opera Dei* in nature we know the hands and feet, but not the heart of God (*C.R.* XXIII, 11).

25 *Schöpfung und Mythos*, pp. 49f.

26 *O.c.*, p. 77, appealing to Barth, *C.D.* III, 1, § 41. More cautious is Westermann's conclusion, *Genesis*, BKAT, I 4 (1970), p. 241: "Es ist dann auch nicht möglich, Gn 1 bzw. die Erschaffung der Welt und des Menschen direkt und ohne Vorbehalt als Anfang der Heilsgeschichte oder als deren Vorbereitung zu sehen. Gn 1 steht deswegen am Anfang der Bibel, damit alles, was dann später von Gottes Handeln an den Menschen, von Gottes Geschichte mit seinem Volk, von Erwählung und Bund zu sagen sein wird, in diesem weiteren Horizont des Wirkens Gottes an der ganzen Schöpfung gesehen werde. Dieses Wirken Gottes im weiteren Horizont geht zwar auf das Wirken Gottes an seinem Volk, also das Wirken in Rettung, Erwählung, Bund zu, aber es geht nicht darin auf."

27 Even when Loretz, *o.c.*, p. 77, n. 61, seemingly criticizes Barth by stating, "Die von K. Barth gesehene Finalität der Schöpfung dürfte im Schöpfungsgericht kaum *mit dieser Schärfe* formuliert sein" (italics supplied), he does not reject the underlying Barthian concept that creation is only "the external basis of the covenant" and "the covenant as the internal basis of creation."

theological structure into an ontological precedence of salvation above creation. Thus the whole act of original creation becomes subservient to the act of salvation.

The noetic order, salvation-creation, is transformed into an ontic order.[28]

This is the result of taking the original perfection of man in Genesis [29] not fully serious as a historical reality, for the sake of letting his Christological concept of revelation bear absolute sway.[30] And whereas Barth is not starting from man's perfection in creation but from the incarnation of Christ, the inevitable result is that he bases his antropology on Christology.[31]

When the creation account in Gen. 1,1–2,4a is, however, allowed to stand on its own feet and to speak its own message in the light of Israel's covenant, the structure of its kerygma appears to be basically *theocentric* instead of Israel-centric and, with that, intent upon the praise of the Creator of His work in creation.[32] This is to say that Israel's covenant of redemption is structured with the universal scope of an intended

28  Cf. *C.D.* III, 1, p. 370 (*K.D.*, p. 423) : "What *we* consider to be the truth about the created world is one thing. Quite another is the covenant of grace, the work of Jesus Christ, for the sake and in fulfillment of which creation exists as it is."

29  To Barth the *status integritatis* (Gen. 1,31) transmitted in the form of "pure saga", belongs to the sphere of pre-history, *C.D.*, III, 1, pp. 90f. (*K.D.*, pp. 98f), and is only intended as contrasting background for "the proper history of the O.T., i.e., the history of the covenant of grace between creation and perfection" (p. 212; *K.D.*, p. 239). How much the original human perfection is overshadowed appears from the words: "But this does not mean that it intends to speak of an original excellence of the existence of the creature" (*l.c.*). It rather intends to be "a promise whose fulfillment is to be sought beyond the immediate horizon of the passage" (*l.c.*).

30  Barth's fear that the triumph of grace is denied when the *status integritatis* is accepted appears from the following statement: "It is obviously not his intention to unfold the history of the creature's original state of innocence and peace, thus moving the reader to homesickness instead of hope, and therefore to an optimistic view of human origins" (*l.c.*).

31  See the critique of G. C. Berkouwer, *Man: The Image of God*, 1968², pp. 94ff.

32  See Ps. 148. Cf. H. Bavinck, *G.D.* III, 200. Eichrodt, *Man in the O.T.*, pp. 28-35. Westermann, *Forschung am A.T.*, 1964, p. 206: "Hinter den Schöpfungserzählungen steht der Preis des Schöpfers" ... "Auch Gen. 1 ist ein, wenn auch indirekter verhaltener Preis des Schöpfers. Das ursprüngliche Reden ist das Loben des Schöpfers, nicht der Bericht vom Schöpfungsakt." It seems, however, that W. construes too much of a tension, if not an antithesis, between God's creation acts and God's praise. There is no need to minimize God's acts of creating the world and man in order to emphasize the praise of the Creator, provided we concede that the whole creation was made "very good."

appeal to all nations so that all humanity ultimately may bow the knee in praise to Yahweh as the Creator of heaven and earth.[33]

By qualifying the *original* perfection of man (*hā-ādām*, mankind!) as the *imago Dei*[34] (not the perfection of Israel as the image of Yahweh), Genesis 1 as part of the Hebrew canon proclaims the universal and totalitarian claim of Israel's religion, summoning all men and women on the earth to receive a new self-understanding and meaning of life and thereby to praise and worship the Creator exclusively in the way that Yahweh has revealed this to Israel.[35]

But does not this give room to the idea that Israel's theocentricity excludes and supplants all anthropocentricity?

When the author of Psalm 8 pondered on the meaning of *man* in Gen. 1 ("What is man?", vs. 4), his eyes were suddenly opened for the surprisingly ("yet", vs. 5) grand and glorious position of man in this world ("little less than God", vs. 5). His surprise sprang forth from a gauging of his relationship with the perfect Creator of heaven and earth. The understanding of human existence in the light of Gen. 1 meant to him something more than mere information about man's origin and the beginning of the world. It gave him the sense of identity and mission, the new dimension of being instituted as the ruling lord of all things on earth, in responsibility to a God who gave him participation in His own glory, dignity and honor (vs. 5). The overwhelming grandeur and nobility of this Creator evoked from him the worshipful Hallelujah:

O Yahweh, our Lord,
how majestic is thy name in all the earth! (vss. 1 and 9; cf. Pss. 104)

2. *Man – the Imago Dei.*

The theological qualification of man as being created in the *imago Dei*, which in the Old Testament further occurs only in Gen. 5,1f. and 9,6, has nevertheless led to a multifarious history of interpretation[36] in which

33  Cf. Gen. 12,2f.; Is. 45,22f.; 42,6; 49,6; 56,7; Ps. 113. Note especially Rev. 4,11; Eph. 3,8ff.

34  Cf. W. H. Schmidt, *o.c.*, p. 143: "Das sagt Gen. I 26f nicht nur auf Israel beschränkt, sondern vom Menschen als Geschöpf. Als Gottes Schöpfung ist der Mensch Gottes Bild, und als Bild Gottes ist er Gottes Schöpfung." On the collective meaning of Adam in Gen. 1,26f., see lit. on p. 145, n. 1.

35  See Gen. 12,3; 22,18; 26,4; 28,14. Cf. G. E. Wright, *The O.T. ag. its Env.*, p. 51: "Through the ancient conception of blessing the writers are saying that God's purpose is to use Israel for a universal blessing." Also his *The Old Testament and Theology*, ch. 3: "God the Creator". Westermann, *Forschung am A.T.*, p. 207: "*Hier* [sc. in Gen. 1] liegt der entscheidende Unterschied; er wurzelt in der Ausschliesslichkeitsforderung des Gottes Israels."

36  See the summary of lit. on the interpretation and on the history of

the *imago Dei* unfortunately has often been shriveled into an abstract theologoumenon amidst the variety of opinions and conflicting interpretations.

The traditional position, developed in the early Church since Irenaeus, remodeled and elevated into a theological key doctrine by medieval Scholasticism,[37] was to distinguish between a natural and a supernatural similarity with God, in close connection with the terms *ṣelem* and *demût* in Gen. 1,26.[38]

It took the *image* as man's rational nature and free-will, while the *likeness* was taken as man's original perfection and righteousness.[39]

This patristic and medieval tradition was basically continued in modern theology when it interpreted the *imago Dei* as man's ontic qualities like the rational or moral nature of man, or his religious-moral predisposition, the human body, or his personhood and self-consciousness,[40] or man's dominion over the other creatures.[41]

All these ontological and ethico-anthropological interpretations, however, labor under the defect of a preconceived dualism of man, in which man is considered primarily by himself, or in relationship with the ontic qualities of the other creatures of God, but never in his dynamic Biblical relationship with his Creator.[42]

---

interpretation in W. H. Schmidt, *o.c.*, p. 132, n. 1. Further especially G. C. Berkouwer, *Man: The Image of God*, ch. 3. C. Westermann, *Genesis*, BK, I 3 (1968), pp. 203-214.

37   Cf. Ir. *Haer*. 5, 6, 1; Thomas Aquinas, *S.Th*. I, q. 93, a. 4, 6; q. 95, a. 1; and Prologue to I-II.
See O. Weber, *Grundlagen der Dogmatik*, I, 1964³, pp. 619ff. O. Loretz, *Die Gottebenbildichkeit des Menschen*, 1967, pp. 23-32.

38   Easily promoted by the Septuagint translation of Gen. 1,26: *eikona kai homoiōsin*, although later Judaism uses only one expression (*eikōn*) for the *imago Dei*, J. Jervell, *Imago Dei*, 1960, pp. 21ff.

39   F. K. Schumann, *Imago Dei*, in *FS* G. Krüger, 1932, p. 168. Thomas *S.Th*. I, q. 93, a. 4, distinguishes between three stages in the *imago Dei*:
1) the natural disposition of rational knowledge and love of God
2) the imperfect knowledge and love of God as the conformity of grace
3) the perfect knowledge and love of God as the likeness of glory.

40   Walther Eichrodt states that the *imago Dei* means "personhood". Man "has a share in the personhood of God; and as a being capable of self-awareness and of self-determination he is open to the divine address and capable of responsible conduct." (*Theol. of the O.T.*, II/III 1967 (German 1964⁵), p. 126).

41   See H. Bavinck, *G.D.* II, 495; Loretz, *o.c.*, pp. 9-39. W. Schmidt, *o.c.*, p. 134, for source material on the various positions.

42   Notice the critique of K. Barth, *C.D.* III, 1, p. 184 (*K.D.*, pp. 206f.): "It is not a quality of man. Hence there is no point in asking in which of man's peculiar attributes and attitudes it consists. It does not consist in anything that man is or does." And of G. C. Berkouwer, *Man: The Image of God*, pp. 59ff., who states on p. 93: "And if we seek to define man merely in terms of

Karl Barth has tried to overcome the traditional ontological dualism of the *imago Dei* by replacing the concept of the *analogia entis* by that of an *analogia relationis:*

> Is it not palpable that we have to do with a clear and simple correspondence, an *analogia relationis*, between this mark of the divine being, namely, that it includes an I and a Thou, and the being of man, male and female?[43]

Hence Barth concludes that the *imago Dei* consists of the I–Thou relationship in the Godhead as it is "repeated in the relation of man to man."[44]

But this interpretation also cannot be the full reflection of the Biblical relationship of Creator and man, since Barth's *imago Dei* is conceived of primarily as "simply the existence of the I and the Thou in confrontation".[45] In this way, however, man's religious relationship with God is not given its Biblical priority, since man is not determined as a religious being by this social relationship.[46] Even when Barth states, "In this way He wills and creates man as a partner who is capable of entering into covenant-relationship with Himself",[47] the question remains whether this "partnership", which may be deduced from Gen. 1,28-29, is identical with the

various qualities and abilities, we are not giving a Biblical picture of man." And of von Rad, in *ThWNT* II, 388f.: "Die Gottesebenbildlichkeit liegt weder in der 'Persönlichkeit' des Menschen noch in dem 'freien Ich' noch in der 'Würde des Menschen' noch im 'freien Gebrauch der moralischen Anlage (...)." O. Weber, *o.c.*, p. 622: "Ja, wir müssen zugespitzt sagen, dass es *Sünde* ist, wenn der Mensch "in" sich, in seiner Verfügungsgewalt haben will, was er allein in seinem Verhältnis zu Gott hat." See also H. Kraemer, *Religion and the Christian Faith*, 1956, p. 249, who stresses that in Gen. 1 man's only value and dignity lies not in his "personality" but in his election and destiny to partnership with God.

43 *C.D.* III, 1, 196 (*K.D.*, p. 220). We correct the E.T. by following the original text which puts the statement in the form of a question. Barth makes an exegetical appeal to the *plural* in Gen. 1,26 ("Let us make...") as an indication of God's "plurality in the being of God" (p. 192; *K.D.*, p. 216) and to the "definitive explanation given by the text itself" (p. 195, *K.D.*, p. 219), i.e., "male and female created he them," Gen. 1,27.

44 *O.c.*, p. 185 (*K.D.*, p. 207).

45 *O.c.*, p. 185 (*K.D.*, p. 207).

46 Cf. also the critiques of Berkouwer, *o.c.*, pp. 72f., 100f. calling the alternative of an *anologia entis* or *relationis*, "a false dilemma." O. Weber, *Grundlagen der Dogmatik*, I 1964³, pp. 633f. W. Schmidt, *o.c.*, p. 135, n. 3. Some who follow Barth, but not completely on this point, interpret the *imago Dei* again, like Eichrodt, as personhood, although now as being confronted by the Word of God. J. J. Stamm, "Die Imago-lehre von K. Barth", in *Antwort*, 1956, p. 98; *Ibid., Die Gottebenbildlichkeit des Menschen im A.T.*, 1959, p. 19. Westermann, *The Genesis Accounts of Creation*, 1966², p. 21. Fr. Horst, "Der Mensch als Ebenbild Gottes", in *Gottes Recht. Ges. Stud. z. Recht im A.T.*, 1961, pp. 230.

47 *O.c.*, p. 185 (*K.D.*, p. 207).

content of *imago Dei* (vss. 26-27) or rather is the immediate consequence of it.[48]

We meet with quite a different approach to the Biblical concept of the *imago Dei* in the Old Testament theology of Th. C. Vriezen.

Starting from the soteriological understanding of Israel's creation-faith, Vriezen stresses the undeniable fact that the character of the Creator God in Gen. 1 is the same as the communion-seeking Covenant God of Israel.[49]

And although the living covenant relationship of Yahweh with Israel is expressed with the significant terms "son(s)", "children",[50] or even of "wife", the demythologizing function of Gen. 1, aiming to safeguard the specific Israelite[51] notion of the *distance* between God and mankind, purposely has avoided the designation "son" or "child of God" in its creation story.[52]

In order to express the same intimate relationship of Yahweh with Israel (father–child) for mankind, Gen. 1 uses the terms "image" and "likeness of God".

> In other words the expressions image and likeness (between which we should not make a fundamental distinction) were chosen to denote on the one hand the absolute difference between God and man, on the other their relationship.[53]

Thus Vriezen sees the *imago Dei* as a dialectical symbol, as "a 'critico-theological' idea which on the one hand indicates a direct, positive communion, but on the other hand excludes any equality of the two partners in this relation."[54] The positive intention of the expression "image of God" is, however, "to depict the same intimate relationship as between father and child."[55]

For this Vriezen also uses an exegetical argument referring to Gen. 5,3[56] where Adam's son Seth is said to be in the likeness and after the

---

48  Cf. W. Schmidt, *o.c.*, p. 136, n. 1.
49  *Theology of the O.T.*, 1960 (repr. 1958), pp. 143f.
50  He refers to Hos. 11,1; Ex. 4,22; Deut. 14,1; Is. 1,2; 30,1.9; Jer. 3,14. We might add Deut. 32,5ff., 19f.
51  Vriezen, *o.c.*, p. 144 refers to the common naturalistic pagan anthropology of the ancient Orient, which placed man in a directly physical relationship with the deity, but lacking the divine strength and immortality.
52  See Vriezen, *o.c.*, p. 146, n. 3. Thus in contrast with the pagan concept that El was "the father of men".
53  Vriezen, *o.c.*, pp. 146f.
54  *O.c.*, p. 145.
55  *Ibid.*, p. 146.
56  *Ibid.*

image of his father. Thus he substantiates his theological interpretation of the *imago Dei* in Gen. 1,26 with Gen. 5,3 as a Father-son relationship of love.[57] This interpretation of the *imago Dei* receives new depth when Vriezen summarizes[58]:

> It denoted man in his peculiar relationship to God, in his vocation to be God's vice-regent on earth but most of all to reflect in his nature the nature of God, just as the child is the image of the father.

This dynamic theological concept of man as the *imago Dei* is also held up by G. C. Berkouwer[59] when he asks:

> Does not Scripture's treatment of the image ... deal with wealth and glory, and is not the image of God in man related to the likeness of a child to his father? Does it not refer to man's activity, his response to God, his imaging of God, his serving God?

And that Berkouwer is thinking basically out of a soteriological understanding of the "inviolable humanity" of the *imago Dei*[60] appears when he notes[61]:

> That the creation of man in God's image in thus spoken of, in the midst of a world of fallen man, indicates that we may never think of man apart from the original aim of his creation. Such passages do not mean to turn our attention to some abstract thesis of the image of God as an *analogia entis:* they deal with a humaneness, a being human, in a context of God's salvation.

With this interpretation, we feel, Vriezen and Berkouwer are showing us what is the dynamic Biblical concept of man as created in the image or likeness of God.

---

57  Also O. Loretz, *Die Gottebenbildlichkeit des Menschen*, 1967, pp. 56-64, starts from the exegetical argument that Gen. 5,3 contains the key to the solution of the *imago Dei*. So already H. Gunkel, *Genesis*, 1966[7], p. 112, who, however, limits the *imago Dei* practically to "Gestalt und Aussehen."

58  *O.c.*, p. 208. It appears on the same page that Vriezen does not equate the *imago Dei* with the lordship over the world, but "because man stands in a special relationship to God he is entrusted by God with dominion over the world."

59  *O.c.*, p. 57.

60  *O.c.*, p. 59, in reference to Gen. 9,6 and James 3,9.

61  *O.c.*, p. 59. Cf. Westermann, *The Genesis Accounts*, p. 21: "This description of man means, rather, that man can maintain his humanity only in the presence of God. Man separated from God has not only lost God, but also the purpose of his humanity."

The Old Testament is never interested in explaining either the *being* or nature of God as He is in Himself or the *being* of man as such.[62]

Therefore the *imago Dei* cannot refer to the divine or human ontic qualities as such but rather to the actual functioning of the specific and living love-relation between man and his Creator.[63]

> Westermann, *Genesis*, pp. 214-218, reduces the concept of the *imago Dei* in Gen. 1 strictly to man's relationship toward God: "dass die Eigentlichkeit des Menschen in dem Gegenüber zu Gott gesehen wird" (218). The *imago Dei* is only conceived as the explication of the divine *act of creating* man for God (217), in basic analogy with the creation of man in the Sumero-Babylonian texts (men as servants of the gods, 216). It seems, however, that he is not justified in severing Gen. 1,26f. so radically from its canonical contexts, i.e., from the creation of the first 6 days, the human sphere of living, which includes also man's social relationship. No longer can the defining function of Gen. 5,3 be acknowledged. When W. in his criticism of W. H. Smidt (and H. Wildberger) asks the question, "Welchen Sinn aber soll es haben, dass die Menschheit auf Erden Gott repräsentiert oder vertritt?" he rejects the possible relationship of man toward the other creatures without an argument ("zweifellos nicht gemeint", 211). However, on p. 216 he must recognize that: "In Gen 1 werden die Menschen von Gott erschaffen, damit sie über die übrigen Kreaturen herrschen". On the basis of his conjecture that this connection "probably" was added later (216) he reduces the intention of the *imago Dei* in Gen. 1,26f. to man's relationship with God.
>
> The question arises whether the Creator of man is then still the same as the Creator of the world, especially when W. on p. 242 declares: „Ein Gott, der nur noch als der Gott der Menschen verstanden wird, ist nicht mehr der Gott der Bibel".

Just as Gen. 1 describes God in his activity and work in love on behalf of man, so the "image of God" suggests that man likewise will be motivated and directed in his activity on earth out of love for God, his Father.[64] In this way the *imago Dei* is at once gift and task, privilege

---

62 Biblical theology is not speculative, but theology of life relationships. Cf. Kraemer, *Rel. and the Christian Faith*, p. 248 ("relational theology, and not speculative").
W. H. Schmidt, *o.c.*, p. 190: "Das Hebräische denkt weithin aus der Relation, indem es die Dinge aus dem Zusammenhang, der Beziehung zu anderem, erfasst."

63 Cf. Weber, *o.c.*, p. 617 (referring to W. Zimmerli): "So wie nicht Gottes 'Wesen' ergründet, sondern sein *Handeln* erzählt wird, so ergründet der priesterliche Zeuge nicht das 'Wesen' des Menschen, sondern seine 'Aufgabe'".

64 Cf. von Rad, *Genesis*, p. 57: "One will admit that the text speaks less

and responsibility.[65] In other words, man's living relation with God must be reflected, made manifest in his relation with the world.[66] Just as God in the perfection of His character was creating the world in wisdom and loving care for man, so man is made and called to make manifest and develop that divine character as his own in earthly reality, because he is the son of this Father Creator.[67] Consequently, because he rules the earth, being thus the son and representative of the divine Ruler, man proclaims God, praises God.[68] When Seth is called the son of Adam "in his own likeness, after his image"[69] this does not merely signify similarity in outward appearance and mutual love relationship[70] but most of all representation of the religious-moral character of his father as manifested in practical behavior and visible acting.[71]

of the nature of God's image than of its purpose. There is less said about the gift than about the task."

65   Cf. Weber, *o.c.*, 619, n. 1: "Dass der Mensch das *repräsentative* Geschöpf ist". With that man's inalienable *officium* for this world is given, as stated in Gen. 1,26b: "And let them have dominion over..." Cf. Schmidt, *o.c.*, p. 142: "Während in Gen. I 28 der Auftrag dem Menschen in einem besonderen Segen ausgesprochen wird, folgt die Herrscherstellung des Menschen in I 26 aus seiner Schöpfung nach denn Bilde Gottes."

66   Cf. Schmidt, *o.c.*, p. 142f. Von Rad, *o.c.*, p. 58: "Just as powerful earthly kings, to indicate their claim to dominion, erect an image of themselves in the provinces of their empire where they do not personally appear, so man is placed upon earth in God's image as God's sovereign emblem... The decisive thing about man's similarity to God therefore, is his function on the nonhuman world."

67   Cf. H. H. Rowley, *The Unity of the Bible*, 1953, p. 79: "God made man in his own image, and his essential law for man is that he shall reflect the image of God and become like him in character."

68   Cf. Schmidt, *o.c.*, p. 144: "Entsprechend wird nach dem Alten Testament Gott proklamiert, wo der Mensch ist. Der Mensch repräsentiert, bezeugt Gott auf Erden... ; so erscheint Gott dort, wo der Mensch erscheint."

69   Gen. 5,3.

70   As Loretz, *o.c.*, p. 63, rightly states: "Menschliches Leben im Sinne des Schöpfungberichtes ist demnach ein Leben der Freundschaft mit Gott oder ein Leben, das vom Vater-Son-Verhältnis bestimmt wird."

71   That in Hebrew thought the father-son relationship meant a moral and spiritual relationship rather than a mere physical kinship, is well expressed by S. F. Lofthouse, "Fatherhood and Sonship in the Fourth Gospel", *ExpT* 43 (1931/32), 443: "With the Hebrews... the two terms [sc. father and son], and esp. "son", are used when a physical relationship is out of the question, and where the son is so called because he is the representative, the manifestation, the embodiment of him, or of that, of which he is said to be the son. We can talk of a son of peace, of worthlessness (Belial) or of consolation. And we would probably understand in this sense the phrase 'sons of God' (*B[e]ne Elohim*) if it does not carry us back to the realms of mythology." Cf. also L. Dürr, "Heilige Vaterschaft im antiken Orient. Ein Beitrag zur Geschichte der Idee des 'Abbas'," in *Heilige Überlieferung. FS* I. Herwegen, 1938, pp. 1-20, esp. 9f.

Werner H. Schmidt therefore rightly emphasizes:

> Wenn Adam einem Sohn 'nach seiner Ähnlichkeit, gemäss seinem Bilde' zeugt, so ist damit nicht nur gemeint, dass der Sohn eine dem Vater äusserlich ähnliche Gestalt hat, sondern dass der Vater im Sohn wiedererscheint. Der Sohn ist der Nachfolger, der Stellvertreter des Vaters – nicht nur in seiner Gestalt, sondern in seinem Wesen, eben als Sohn. Der Sohn 'wiederholt' sozusagen den Vater (*O.c.*, p. 144).

This Biblical destiny of man therefore exceeds that of the Babylonian creation epic *Enuma eliš*, in which man is created in order to serve and look after the gods in the cultus as a slave.[72]

In Israel's protology man's relation with God is one of honored walk or fellowship of life and moral will with God, as a son has with his father, Gen. 5,22.24.[73]

This is not conceived of as a thing to be taken for granted, which then could easily lead man to *hubris*, but as a miracle of love evoking worshipful adoration and joyful praise of the Creator.[74]

> In this light the religious meaning of the second and third commandments of the Decalogue adds a new religious-anthropological dimension. This has been indicated significantly in reference to the second commandment by Berkouwer when he deals with a "basic connection" between the prohibition of images of God[75] and the creation of man in God's image:
>
> > There lies, in any human attempt to make an image of God, an attempt to control Him, to bring Him close by... The high-handed attempt to control the image of God is *per se*

72 *ANET*, "The Creation Epic", Tablet VI, pp. 68f.: "He [sc. man] shall be charged with the service of the gods that they might be at ease!"

73 Cf. R. Borchert, *Stil und Aufbau der priesterlichen Erzählung*, Unpubl. Diss. of Univ. of Heidelberg, 1957, pp. 115-116. He concludes from his comparison of Gen. 5,22.24 in their context that the Priestly author of Gen. 5 wants to indicate that death is the result of the not walking with God: "dann besteht der 'Sündenfall' nach P in dem 'nicht-mit-Gott-Wandeln', dessen Folge (Strafe) der Tod ist" (p. 116). Eichrodt, *Theol. of the O.T.* II, p. 394, n. 2, states that the walking with God in Gen. 5,24 must be understood "in P's usual sense as perfect righteousness".

74 E.g. Ps. 8. Cf. W. Eichrodt, *Man in the O.T.*, SBT 4, 1966 (1951ff.), p. 30.

75 Especially in the light of the ancient Oriental concept of an image or statute of God as the actual revelation of the deity. Cf. J. Jervell, *Imago Dei*, p. 125: "Die orientalische Auffassung vom Bilde ist in aller Kürze die, dass im Bilde das Abgebildete realiter präsent ist... Nach sumerisch-babylonischer Auffassung ist die Gottheit in ihrem Bilde gegenwärtig". Jervell then elaborates this "religious-soteriological function" of the cultic image. See also Loretz, *Gottebenbildlichkeit*, "Exkurs I", pp. 106-109, on the vital role of the "image" in antiquity.

illegitimate, and is in its very origin an act of unmistakable alienation from God. And it is, simultaneously, an act of extreme self-alienation, since man thereby seeks to construct an 'image of God', although he himself, in communion with God, should *be* that image in all of his being.[76]

How this same principle functions in reference to the third commandment, i.e,. how the name of Yahweh in "oath", curse and sorcery was used as a means in order to control Yahweh, is indicated by J. J. Stam[77]:

> Wer der Namen hat, der hat auch die Person des Benannten. Deshalb spielen die Namen von Gottheiten in Beschwörungen eine hervorragende Rolle.

Here again the same intention becomes apparent, to safeguard the living relationship between Yahweh and His "son" Israel, since Yahweh did not reveal Himself or commune with Israel through cultic images or magic formulas, but as "Yahweh", i.e., as the faithful covenant God who not only takes the initiative to redeem his son Israel but also keeps communion with him through the event of His sovereign Word, in the way of praise and true obedience.

This Biblical notion of the *imago Dei* intended to keep Israel free from mythological concepts of God and man such as were common in the surroundings nations. In it Israel was given a new vision of God's theological transcendence, without losing His communion with men.[78]

Israel's faith that man and nature were no deified self-representations of God, but were brought into existence by a direct act of special creation,[79] not only led to a fundamental demythologization of the world

---

76   *O.c.* (see above, n. 42), pp. 81f. Instructive is the illustration taken over from Exodus 32 (pp. 82f.). Cf. Vriezen, *De Godsd. v. Israël*, p. 63: "Het beeldenverbod, dat in de oud-oosterse wereld een volkomen *novum* was."

77   *Der Dekalog im Lichte der neueren Forschung*, 1962², p. 47.

78   Von Rad, "Aspekte altt. Weltverständnisses", in *Ges. Stud. z. A.T.*, 1965, p. 316, elucidates: "Im Bilderverbot war für Israel die Grenzlinie zwischen Gott und Welt anders und doch wohl viel schärfer durchzogen, als das in den Bilderreligionen geschah. Jahwe war nicht eine der tragenden Weltkräfte, auch nicht ihre Summe, sondern ihr Schöpfer." "Jahwe war Israel viel persönlicher nahe, nämlich im anredenden Wort und in der geschichtlichen Tat."

79   Gen. 1,3ff.; Ps. 33,6-9, "For He spoke, and it came to be; He commanded, and it stood forth" (vs. 9); Ps. 148,5; cf. von Rad, *O.T. Theol.* II, p. 360: "Spricht das A.T. von Schöpfung, so sieht es die Welt als ein Gegenüber Gottes, als einen Bereich, der seine eigene Herrlichkeit hat von der Hymnus und Weisheit nicht genug reden können, aber doch als geschaffen, d.h. vollkommen mühelos vom Schöpferwort ins Dasein gerufen." To the point is C. F. Weizäcker's remark, *Geschichte der Natur*, 1948, p. 53: "Die Vorstellung der an sich seienden unendlichen Natur... ist der Mythus der neuzeitlichen Wissenschaft" (Quoted in von Rad, *o.c.*, p. 352 n. 10).

and nature,[80] but most important, created a new horizon for a genuine, full-fledged concept of *humanity*.[81]

Also the Greek concept of cosmos and man could not envision man in his genuine humanity, since man was continually an essential part of god, or enshrouded by a deified cosmic world.[82]

Only the unphilosophical Hebrew (and Christian) idea of *creation*[83] could deliver man from all deifications of himself, nature and cosmos, and open the perspective of a creative human kingship over the world.[84]

However, man came to understand himself as the (restored) partner of God, not in the sense of modern secularism, but through the knowledge and experience of Israel's covenant of grace.[85]

From these observations it seems justified to draw this conclusion

80 Cf. von Rad, *Ges. Stud.*: "Schöpfung, das hiess radikale Entgötterung, Entdämonisierung der Welt" (p. 317). "Es war Israels Glaube, der es ermächtigt hat, die Welt als Welt zu Verstehen. ... Hier und nur hier konnte jenes unglaublich realistische Bild vom Menschen wachsen. Hier nur konnte sich jene unvergleichliche Grosszügigkeit und Freiheit der Menschenschilderung entfalten" (pp. 319, 320).

81 J. B. Metz, "Die Zukunft des Glaubens in einer hominisierten Welt", in *Weltverständnis im Glauben*, 1965, pp. 46-49, 60f., states that belief in creation conquers the "divinisierte und numinisierte Welt" and is founding the "hominisierte Welt", which is not yet the "Humanisierung der Welt".

82 J. B. Metz, *Christelijke mensbetrokkenheid*, 1964 (German 1962), pp. 54f., calls the Greek form of thinking "cosmocentric".

83 Kraemer, *Rel. and the Chr. Faith*, p. 436: "'Creation' is an entirely unphilosophical concept which goes completely against the grain of the genuine philosophical mood". He refers to Heb. 11,3.

84 H. R. Schlette, *Christen als Humanisten*, 1967, p. 43 states: "Die andere Denkform ist die Biblische-christliche, derzufolge sich der Mensch erfährt als geschaffenes, endliches Wesen, das den übrigen Werken Gottes frei und souverän gegenübergestellt ist und darin befreit ist zur Freiheit selbst und damit, zur Arbeit an der Welt, zur Geschichte, zur echten Zukunft des Neuen, d.h. des Noch-nicht-Gewesenen". He seems to view the true freedom of man in the rational insight or thought of creation itself. This would deny the Biblical soteriological order redemption – freedom *from* and *to* the world (creation) and will only lead to a speculative anthropocentrism. It is the evaluation of sin and grace which basically forms the line of demarcation between Humanism and Biblical theo-anthropocentric faith. Cf. Kraemer, *Kerk en Humanisme*, p. 30: "Het theocentrisme in de Bijbel echter drukt, principieel gesproken, de mens en de wereld niet weg, maar zet ze op de juiste plaats, is theo- en anthropocentrisme in één."

85 Cf. von Rad, *Theol. des A.T.*, II, 1965⁴, p. 364: "Aber dieser rationale Weltaspekt hat sich in Israel nicht verabsolutiert, er blieb irgendwie umklammert vom Glauben, und man blieb sich seiner Grenzen Gott und seinem Walten gegenüber stets bewusst." Significant and representative for Israel's self-understanding is its wisdom, exceeding all secularized world-understanding, as worked out in the revealing chapter Job 28, culminating in this disclosure: "And He said to man, Behold, the fear of the Lord, that is wisdom; and to depart from evil is understanding."

from the creation account of Gen. 1: the theological qualification of man as the *imago Dei* contains the implied religious-moral kerygma that man is called to reflect and honor in his character and life, in his authority and dominion over the earth, the very perfection of character of his Maker. Just as the Creator, who crowned man with glory and honor, praises man as functioning "completely perfect" (von Rad[86]), so man is called to follow and imitate God and to join all creation in proclaiming the glory of God and praising the beauty and majesty of the perfection of God's character.[87]

Because of the revealed fact that man is created in an inalienable relation of praise with his Father-Creator, man can only fulfill and attain to the perfection of his humanity when he exalts God. To Israel human life without praise or exaltation of God has turned into *death*, because man will exalt, nay, must exalt or deify something else instead of God, sometimes even man himself.[88]

In others words, where man loses his hold on God, the God of Israel, man loses his *perfect* humanity, the living functioning of the *imago Dei*, his living communion and friendship with God. He still remains a son of God possessing humanity, but his *imago Dei* functions in darkness, in ultimate insecurity and fear; he has become a *lost* son, a *disobedient* creature, even an enemy of God.[89] Therefore Israel's theocentricity does not exclude but includes true anthropocentricity. God is no competitor of man's glory but *upholds* it, calling man to be His honored covenant

---

86  *Ad* Gen. 1,31. Cf. Westermann, *The Genesis Accounts*, p. 10, wo interprets the expressions "And God saw ..., and it was good", "it was very good" as "indirect praise of God", which finds its echo in the praise of Ps. 139,14: "Wonderful are thy works! Thou knowest me right well."

87  Pss. 19; 113; 148. Cf. A. M. Dubarle, "La conception de l'homme dans l'AT," in *Sacra Pagina*, Congress Vol. I (1959), 528 (quoted in Westermann, *o.c.*, p. 213): "La possession de l'image de Dieu n'est pas une propriétée statique conférée une fois pour toutes. C'est une vocation à imiter par ses actes celui, dont on porte la ressemblance. C'est un appel d'une vie religieuse: 'Soyez saints, parce que je suis saint'."

88  Cf. Ps. 73,27: "For lo, those who are far from Thee shall perish ..." Is. 38,9. Westermann, *The Praise of God in the Psalms*, p. 160: "Exalting is a part of existence. It is so much a part of it, that when one has ceased to exalt God, something else must be exalted. Then God can be displaced by a man, an institution, an idea. Exalting remains a function of existence. World history demonstrates this. Man *must* exalt something ... If the praise of God, as the Psalms express it, belongs to existence, then the directing of this praise to a man, an idea, or a institution must disturb and finally destroy life itself. The Psalms say that only where God is praised is there life."

89  Cf. Loretz, *Gottebenbildlichkeit*, p. 97. E. Brunner, *Revelation and Reason*, 1946, p. 74: "Thus sin does not mean the annihilation of the original element in man but its perversion."

partner and son.[90] It is God who has crowned man with honor and glory.[91] It is man's Maker who also provided a unique way to *keep* man in this glorious and honored position and function by means of the cultic feast of fellowship on the Sabbath of the Creator.[92]

### 3. *The function of God's rest and blessing on the seventh day.*

The profound significance of God's rest on the seventh day of the creation week in connection with man[93] has been observed by Old Testament scholars and given occasion to some systematic theologians to construct what might he called a theology of the Sabbath.[94] Here we are only concerned with the theme of God's rest within the framework of the question, What does Israel's protology teach with reference to human perfection? What is the meaning and function of the rest of God, His blessing and hallowing the seventh day[95] for man as *imago Dei?*

Even when we recognize the fact that Gen. 2 does not formulate the rest of God on the seventh day as the "institution of the Sabbath" or as an "Adamic Sabbath commandment", the question remains whether what von Rad stated is correct: "Darin liegt das Wagnis von Gen. 2,2f., dass ... das Ruhen Gottes ... ganz um seiner selbst willen bezeugt ist."[96]

Does not such a view isolate the account of God's rest in Gen. 2,2 from the explicitly expressed finality of God's rest in vs. 3, namely God's *blessing* and *sanctifying* the seventh day "because on it God rested from all his work which he had done in creation"? God's rest therefore cannot be considered "as a matter for itself", divorced from the meaning and function of God's blessing and hallowing the seventh day. Von Rad recognizes this dynamic relationship in his Genesis Commentary when he indicates a definite eschatological scope of God's rest for man:

90  Cf. Loretz, *o.c.,* p. 102: "Eine Pädagogik, die Gen. 1,26ff. ernst nimmt, wird es vermeiden, vom Menschen kleinlich zu denken."

91  Ps. 8,5.

92  See von Rad, *Genesis,* pp. 59f.: "The declarations about a Sabbath at creation contain one of the most remarkable and daring testimonies in the entire Priestly document ... it is anything but an appendix."

93  Recognized also for the post-lapsarian man by the N.T., Heb. 4,3f., 9-10.

94  In particular Karl Barth, *C.D.,* III, 1, 213-228 (*K.D.,* pp. 240-258); III, 4,47-72 (*K.D.,* pp. 51-79). Calvin, *Inst.* II, 8,28-34. Th. Aquinas, *S.Th.* II-III q 122, a 4. A. Kuyper, *Tractaat van den Sabbath. Hist. Dogm. studie,* 1890. M. L. Andreasen, *The Sabbath,* 1942. E. Jenni, *Die theologische Begründung des Sabbatgebotes im Alten Testament,* Th. St. 46, 1956. H. W. Richardson, *Toward An American Theology,* 1967, pp. 112ff.: "The Sabbath as Sacrament". For a modern Jewish treatise, see A. J. Heschel, *The Sabbath: Its Meaning for Modern Man,* 1951.

95  Gen. 2,2-3.

96  "Es ist noch eine Ruhe vorhanden dem Volke Gottes," in *Ges. Stud.* 1965, p. 108, n. 8. The article is from 1933.

Even more, that God has 'blessed', 'sanctified' ('to sanctify' means to separate exclusively for God), this rest, means that P does not consider it as something for God alone but as a concern of the world, almost as a third something that exists between God and the world ... Thus at creation God prepared what will benefit man in this life, what in fact will be necessary for him, yes, that which one day will receive him eschatologically in eternity.[97]

Here again it will be necessary to consider God's resting, blessing and hallowing in Gen. 2 in the light of the central foundation of the gracious covenant relation of Yahweh with Israel.[98] The resting, blessing and sanctifying of the Creator are all acts of the communion-seeking covenant God for the sake of man and for his fellowship as son with his Father God. It would be an unbearable disharmony with the total structure of the creation account and the Scripture canon as a whole, to consider the rest of God in Gen. 2,2f. as a "benefit" hidden from man until the covenant of grace with Israel was established, as von Rad suggests[99]: "Nothing of that is apparent to man. How could 'the' man be informed of this mystery?"

Here an isolation from the context, i.e., Gen. 1,26f. becomes apparent. When man really is taken as the *imago Dei*, as the privileged son[100] and responsible representative and partner of the Father Creator, from the very beginning living in the intimate relationship of trust and friendship, then God's acts, and the intentions of His work, cannot be conceived as a hidden and unknown mystery for the pre-lapsarian man.[101]

---

97 *Genesis. A Commentary*, p. 60. Von Rad acknowledges that the eschatological dimension of God's rest is only expressed in Hebr. 4. Cf. Jenni, *o.c.*, p. 25: "Das Werk Gottes am siebten Tage, das Segnen und Heiligen eben dieses Tages, zeigt, dass auch an diesem Tage Gott der Welt zugewandt ist."

98 Correctly so Jenni, *o.c.*, p. 27.

99 *O.c.*, p. 60.

100 Adam as son of God, made explicit in Lk. 3,38.

101 Cf. in reference to Abraham, the *friend* of God, Gen. 18,17: "Yahweh said, 'Shall I *hide* from Abraham what I am about to do ... ?'". Cf. 2 Chron. 20,7; Ps. 25,14. See further G. Ch. Aalbers, *De Goddel. Openb. in de eerste drie hoofdstukken van Genesis*, 1932, pp. 26, 30, appealing also to Ex. 20,8f., where the knowledge of creation is presupposed. Significant is also Barth, *C.D.* III, 1, p. 217. (*K.D.*, p. 245f.): "But the seventh day has also a direct meaning for the creature. The biblical witnesses are obviously not suggesting that creation, with man at its head, went to work on this day of divine rest following the last working day. The clear inference is that creation, and supremely man, rested with God on the seventh day and shared His freedom, rest and joy, even though it had not as yet any work behind it from which to cease, and its Sabbath freedom, rest and joy could only look back to God's work and not its own." And on p. 227 (*K.D.*, p. 256f.) he states: "It makes it clear that there is to be between the Creator and the creature not only an indirect but a direct connection, not only a relationship but genuine inter-

When the author of Gen. 2,2f. with God's acts of "blessing" and "sanctifying" really means that God's rest is not considered "as something for God alone but as a concern for the world" (von Rad), then it only becomes all the more compelling to let God's rest *function* in Israel's protology.

Only in this way will the perfection of God's creation be a meaningful reality. Only then can the perfectly created man actually function perfectly, with the implication that man as the *imago Dei* knows and follows the will and example of his divine Father. The reality of the *imago Dei* requires the *imitatio Dei*,[102] i.e., as son of the Creator man is bound to

course." In this connection the concept of the Midrash is noteworthy, which visualizes that Adam not merely was created in the image of God but that this fact also was revealed to him and therefore to him was given the commission of the *imitatio Dei*. See H. J. Schoeps, *Aus frühchr. Zeit*, 1950, p. 289.

102 Cf. R. Schnackenburg, *Chr. Existenz nach dem N.T.* I, 1967, p. 18: "Aus der Hinordnung zu Gott folgt das 'Wandeln vor Gott'." In this connection Helfmeyer's statement is interesting, *Die Nachfolge Gottes*, pp. 216f.: "Die Versuche, aus der Gottebenbildlichkeit des Menschen die Möglichkeit und Notwendigkeit der Nachahmung Gottes abzuleiten, setzen mehr das von der hellenistischen Philosophie geprägte rabbinische Verständnis als alttestamentliche Vorstellungen voraus. Denn Zweck der Gottebenbildlichkeit ist nach dem Zeugnis der Schrift nicht die Fähigkeit und Aufgabe, Gott nachzuahmen, sondern die Herrscherstellung des Menschen in der Welt."

In the light of our previous section (Man – the *Imago Dei*) it may be clear that Helfmeyer's last sentence is creating a false alternative, since man is called to manifest his *imago Dei* in relation to the world, i.e., his *imitatio Dei* is his sonship realized in his rulership over the world (see above, n. 66). There cannot be any *imitatio Dei* in the abstract, neither does Rabbinic Judaism intend to state this. It is true that the Jewish ethic of the *imitatio Dei* takes a central place in Judaism, and is rooted in man's creation as *imago Dei*, as appears from M. Buber "Nachahmung Gottes", in *Werke* II, 1964, pp. 1054-1065, esp. 1060ff.; H. J. Schoeps, "Von der Imitatio Dei zur Nachfolge Christi", in *Aus frühchristlicher Zeit*, 1950, pp. 286-301, esp. p. 290: "Die jüdisch verstandene Nachahmung Gottes gründet in der Geschaffenheit des Menschen zum Ebenbild, sie vollendet sich in der messianischen Zukunft; aber aufgegeben ist sie allezeit wegen der Korrelation von Gott und Mensch in der Schöpfung, zum Gesetz geworden am Sinai: 'Heilig sollt ihr sein, denn heilig bin Ich, euer Gott.'" Also I. Abrahams, "The Imitation of God", in *Studies in Pharisaism and the Gospels*, II, 1924, pp. 138-182 (Repr. in Library of Biblical Studies, ed. H. M. Orlinsky, 1967), esp. p. 146: "The whole Torah from Genesis to Deuteronomy thus bids Israel to imitate God. On this idea a whole Code of moral perfection is built up; on no other idea (except perhaps that of holiness which ... enters essentially into the ideal of imitation) is the Rabbinic scheme of the God-like life so thoroughly and consistently worked out." Cf. also S. Schechter, *Aspects of Rabbinic Theology*, 1961, pp. 199-209. M. Kadushin, *The Rabbinic Mind*, 1952, pp. 169f., 219. G. Friedlander, *The Jewish Sources on the Sermon on the Mount*, The Libr. of Bib. Stud., 1969 (1911), ch. VII: "The Ideal Life in the Gospels and the Torah." From these writings it is apparent that Rabbinic scholars do not agree with Helfmeyer's asserted antithesis between Rabbinic Judaism and the O.T. on the idea of *imitatio Dei* in the

reflect the perfect work and rest of his Father in his own way of perfect rulership and rest in communion with his Creator. Moreover, without the divine communion and fellowship on the seventh day, without man's entering into God's rest on that day, the whole creation would be cut off from its Maker and necessarily have to find its purpose and sense in itself. Then God's rest indeed would rather be the cryptic indication of God's return to the aseity (the absolute self-existence) of the inner glory of His being and existence, leaving man and the world to themselves.

The identification of the covenant God with the Creator of man opposes this speculative theology. Therefore Westermann, Barth and Jenni are quite right in rejecting this ontological speculation of God's rest in Israel's protology.[103]

God's resting should not be interpreted in the abstract, in the mere negative sense of non-activity, but rather concordant with Israel's positive understanding of her resting on the Sabbath day as being free for cultic communion with God.[104] In other words, God's rest then means His ceasing the work of creation *in order to* be free for the fellowship with man, the object of his love, for the rejoicing and celebration of His completed work together with his son on earth, the *imago Dei*, "His festive partner".[105]

---

first sentence. Our critique of Rabbinic theology would only be that it appears that in it no justice is done to the central function of the *soteriological* motif of Israel's covenant of atonement and the Sabbath in order to attain the moral perfection of the *imago Dei*. See A. Marmorstein, *The Doctrine of Merits in old Rabbinical Literature*, 1968 (repr.) esp. pp. 172-184. S. Bernfeld, *The Foundations of Jewish Ethics*, 1968 (repr.), pp. 92ff., 102ff. On the *imitatio Dei* motif in the O.T., see also below, Ch. III, B, 1; pp. 101-103, and in the N.T., see Ch. IV, 1, a; esp. n. 72.

103   See C. Westermann, *Genesis*, BK, I 3, 1968, pp. 232-237, esp. 235; I 4, 1970, pp. 241-244. K. Barth, *C.D.* III, 1, pp. 214ff., 222f. (*K.D.*, pp. 241ff., 251f.). E. Jenni, *o.c.*, pp. 25f. W. Zimmerli, *1 Mose 1-11. Die Urgeschichte*. Zürcher Bibelkommentare, 1967[3], pp. 101-106, is ambiguous. On the one hand he interprets the Sabbath of God in Gen. 2,2f. as the divine, sanctified rest which was kept "secret" by God until He called Israel as His own people (pp. 102, 105). Only then the creation Sabbath "became the Sabbath for men" (p. 102). On the other hand, he wants to recognize the creation Sabbath as originally intended for mankind: "Hier [sc. in Israel] wird offenbar dass Gott auch diese letzte, köstlichste Gabe der Schöpfung nicht für sich behalten will, sondern auch hier den Menschen in seine Gemeinschaft zieht" (p. 102); and: "Im Sabbat öffnet sich der Zugang zu einer köstlichen Gottesgabe. Am siebenten Tag hat Gott von all seinem Werk geruht und den Tag gesegnet. Wer in rechter Verfassung zu ihm herankommt, wird auch des in ihm liegenden Segens der Gottesruhe teilhaftig" (p. 105).

104   Cf. Jenni, *o.c.*, p. 28. Thomas, *S.Th.* II-II, q. 122, a. 4, *ad* 3: "And this is that man occupy himself with Divine things..."

105   Cf. Barth, *C.D.* III, 1, p. 215 (*K.D.*, p. 243): "And the reason why He

Then the divine blessing and sanctification of the seventh day can receive their rich and dynamic significance for man. Then God's rest can function as the appointed means for the benefit, even the further perfection of man, since the powers of life on this day of rejoicing, springing forth from communion with the divine Blesser, also inspire and sustain him throughout the whole week. This is basically indicated by Westermann in his *Genesis*, p. 236, when he interprets the blessing and sanctifying of the seventh day in Gen. 2:

> Hier is mehr gemeint als der Sabbat. Die mit dem Abschluss der Schöpfung einsetzende Menschheitsgeschichte wird nicht nur von der Kraft des Segens bestimmt sein, die allem Lebendigen eignet; mit der Heiligung des siebten Tages tritt ein neues, die Menschheitsgeschichte bestimmendes Moment auf: die Sonderung des Heiligen im Fluss des Geschehenden als Andeutung des Ziels des Geschöpfes, das Gott sich zu seiner Entsprechung schuf; ein Ziel, das nicht innerhalb der sechs Werktage liegt, sondern im gesonderten, geheiligten Tag.

While Westermann does not further indicate the positive aim of the sanctified day for humanity than "beneficial and succesful power will flow forth from this day" (237) because of the praise of the majesty of the Creator (238), Jenni connects the Sabbath more emphatically with the cultus, although he can only speak retrospectively from Israel:

> Durch das Segnen wird der Tag selber ein Segen. Im Ausdruck liegt etwas von der strömenden Kraft, die vom Gesegneten ausgeht. So wird der Sabbat zu einer Kraft für die ganze Woche, der Kultus zu einer Segensmacht für das ganze Leben und das Bundesvolk zu einem Heil der ganzen Welt. [106]

refrains from further activity on the seventh day is that He has found the object of His love and has no need of any further works." Also pp. 216f., 220, 223 (*K.D.*, pp. 244f., 248f., 252). Barth interprets the divine *cessation* of work also as the divine *completion* or satisfaction with creation (appealing to Gen. 2,2a and Calvin), *ibid.*, p. 220 (*K.D.*, p. 249f.); in other words, this rest of God belongs indispensably to the story of creation. Barth therefore rejects the emendation of the LXX in Gen. 2,2a changing "seventh" into "sixth". See on this Jenni, *o.c.*, p. 26. Westermann, *o.c.*, p. 233. Furthermore, Th. Jänicke, in *Gott bleibt der Erde treu. Reden über die ersten Kapitel der Bibel*, von H. Gollwitzer, *et al.*, on the connection of *imago Dei* and creation Sabbath of Gen. 2,2-3: "Das heisst an dieser Stelle: Er ist zum Mitfeiern geschaffen. Auch der Mensch geht nicht in seinem Werken auf. Er ist nicht durch die Arbeit Mensch geworden, und er ist nicht allein für die Arbeit da. Er darf er selber sein, und er *soll* es sogar sein ganz abgesehen von seinen Werken."

106  *O.c.*, p. 29. Cf. Berkouwer, *The Providence of God*, p. 62: "This seventh day – this day of God's rest – is blessed and sanctified by God and thus given in grace to the world – given for man, as Christ has taught us (Mark 2:27)".

In this light it becomes untenable to objectify the divine rest as "almost a third something" between God and man, as von Rad does, or to maintain what H. W. Richardson [107] asserts:

> Just as man is intended by God to have dominion over all other creatures, so the Sabbath Day is established so that it might have dominion over him. It is the good which man is made to serve ... For man is made for Sabbath holiness.

Here the Sabbath rest of God seems so be made an almost self-existent idea which is more in accord with Greek idealism than with Hebrew realism. This does not imply that God's Sabbath has no divinely given structure, only that it bears the character of a $b^e rit$,[108] which is upheld by the hand of God.[109]

The creation Sabbath may then be evaluated theologically as the creation covenant of the Creator with humanity and the blessing and sanctification of the seventh day as the invitation to man to manifest his *imago Dei* in the way of the *imitatio Dei* in the communion with his Creator. Thus the Sabbath prevents humanity from seeking the dignity of man in himself, or in something else but in the lifegiving blessing of God's communion and of participation in God's joyful rest.

Jenni's interpretation of Ex. 20,8-11 has a definite bearing on Gen. 2,2f.:

> Eben weil Gott am Schöpfungssabbat den Tag geheiligt hat, ist er heilig. Und weil ihn Gott geheiligt hat, muss man ergänzen, darum soll ihn auch der Mensch heilig halten. Vielleicht steht hier der Gedanke der Gottebenbildlichkeit des Menschen dahinter: Was Gott tut, soll auch der Mensch auf seine geschöpfliche Weise tun.[110]

---

Cf. also W. H. Gispen, *Schepping en Paradijs*, 1966, p. 92. Westermann, *o.c.*, pp. 232-244, rightly stresses in Gen. 2 the gift-character of the Sabbath as the blessed and sanctified seventh day for the whole humanity and creation, "die Gabe einer Daseinsordnung" (232), "eine Gabe des Schöpfers an die Menschheit..., nicht nur eine Vorausnahme des israelitischen Sabbat" (236).

107 *O.c.*, p. 116. Yet it is also possible to speak legitimately of the Sabbath rest of God as the final purpose of creation. Only, it all depends on how this is worked out. In the light of Mk. 2,27 it seems clear that Richardson creates a false dilemma. Cf. also Westermann, *The Genesis Accounts*, p. 22: "Man is not the goal of God's creation... The goal is really the solemn rest of that day." And Loretz, *Gottebenbildlichkeit*, p. 75: "Abschluss, Höhepunkt und Vollendung der Schöpfung ist jetzt nicht mehr der Mensch, sondern Gottes Sabbat."

108 Expressed as such only in Ex. 31,16f.

109 Cf. Jenni, *o.c.*, p. 23: "Gott ist es ja, der den Schöpfungssabbat und damit den Sabbat überhaupt heiligt. Der Sabbat steht innerhalb der Schöpfung. Er ist wie alle Geschöpfe unter Gottes Herrschaft... Der Sabbat ist keine Grösse, die ausserhalb des Handeln Gottes stünde. Er ist eine $b^e rit$ ..."

110 *O.c.*, p. 30. He sees this relation indicated in Ex. 20,11, but notes that

This conception of the *imitatio Dei* is attractively expressed by **Calvin** in his Commentary on Gen. 2,3[111]:

> No slight stimulans it given by God's own example, and the very precept itself is thereby rendered amiable. For God cannot either more gently allure, or more effectually incite us to obedience, than by inviting and exhorting us to the imitation of himself.

In Israel's protology the creation Sabbath functions therefore as the supreme divine assurance and promise that man is not created for himself but for the fellowship and praise of God.[112] The blessing and sanctification of the seventh day of creation week functions further as the legitimation and foundation of Israel's covenant Sabbath in remembrance of Yahweh's work as Creator, and thus of the basic unity and harmony of His plan of creation and plan of salvation. In other words, Yahweh has remained faithful to His original plan and purpose with man and His Sabbath rest.[113]

---

this verse conveys nothing more than Gen. 2,2f. Important is the conclusion of N. H. Ridderbos, *Is there a conflict?*, p. 42: "We must certainly retain the idea that the Sabbath ordinance is rooted in creation."

111 As rendered in Calvin's *Commentary on Genesis*, 1948, p. 106. Cf. also *Inst.* II, 8, 30-31. Barth, *C.D.* III, 1, 217, 226 (*K.D.*, pp. 246, 256) stresses the *imitatio Dei* motif in Gen. 2,3b. Also P. Schoonenberg, *Het Geloof van ons Doopsel*, I, 1955, p. 63 (ET: *Covenant and Creation*, 1968, p. 61: "an exemplary deed of God") who further points to Ex. 16.

N. H. Ridderbos, *o.c.*, p. 42: "His purpose was that man should follow in His footsteps, be His imitator in the matter of work and rest." J. Eadi, *Commentary on the Ep. to the Ephesians*, 1861[2], now in Classic Comm. Libr., p. 363, *ad* Eph. 5,1, makes this significant statement which applies here: "God's example has an authoritative power."

112 Cf. Jenni, *o.c.*, p. 26: "Der Sabbat ist der Ausdruck dafür, dass die Schöpfung nicht Selbstzweck ist und sich selbst überlassen wird, sondern nur in der Gemeinschaft mit Gott ihren Sinn hat. Das Ziel der Schöpfung ist der Lobpreis Gottes durch den ganzen Kosmos mit dem Menschen an seiner Spitze." In this sense we can agree with Jenni when he speaks of "der Sabbat als Ziel der Schöpfung" (p. 25).

113 Barth, *C.D.* III, 1, 218f. (*K.D.*, p. 247f.), interprets the first creative narrative of the Bible as teleology, so that Israel's protology is absorbed in her soteriology and eschatology. The creation Sabbath therefore with Barth functions exclusively as the sign of promise that man finally will enter God's rest. The creation Sabbath then is the beginning of the history of the divine covenant of grace. "Creation took place in order that man's history might commence and take place as the history of the covenant of grace ..." (p. 219, *K.D.*, p. 248). More careful is Jenni, *o.c.*, p. 27: "... den Schöpfungssabbat in seinem Zusammenhang nach vorwärts als die *Ermöglichung der Bundesgeschichte*." He substantiates this thesis by the interpretation of the divine *sanctifying* of the seventh day as the creating of a special space of time, secluded from profane life, for the religious cult and, with that, for the

With that also is given the qualification of Israel's covenant Sabbath as being founded in Yahweh's prevenient and sovereign grace and benevolence for all men.[114]

## Consideration of Barth's position

Barth's position on creation as "the external basis of the Covenant" is built upon the dogmatic *a priori* that the original perfection of man and the world has no *historical* reality. He bases his position upon the more ethical-philosophical questions of H. F. Kohlbrügge, (in his *Schriftauslegungen*, Vol. I, 1904, pp. 23f.), i.e., how precisely could God rest after creation of this world and on what grounds could He be satisfied with it and with man in particular. Since Barth thinks that this divine rest "certainly cannot be explained or justified by what we learn from Scripture about the world and particularly about man", he feels justified in interpreting the *imago Dei* and paradisiacal peace as "elements" of an eschatological *promise*.

However, only when we choose our actual starting point in the reality of sin and imperfection, with the problem of wrong, as in Gnosticism, can we arrive at the question, "Ought not creation to have proceeded to beings who would have been far more worthy of the divine completion and rest?"[115]

Barth, following Kohlbrügge, does not want to move on to the Gnostic solution of the problem, i.e., that then the creator must be imperfect himself,[116] but seeks the solution in the Christological-soteriological interpretation of God's Sabbath rest and, with that, of creation. He quotes with agreement the following statements of Kohlbrügge:

> 'Could God have rested if He had not done all these things with a view to Christ? Or did He not know that the devil would soon spoil all creation, including man? But as God created heaven and earth through Christ or in Christ, so He has created all things with a view to Christ. On the seventh

Covenant history," da für P sich der Bund im rechten Kultus verkörpert," and of the divine blessing of the seventh day as the outgoing power of life for all days of the week, for all life and by means of the covenant people for the whole world (p. 29).

114  Cf. the impressive comparison with the doctrine of predestination by Jenni, *o.c.*, p. 23: "So wie die Lehre von der ewigen Erwählung der in der Geschichte sich ereignenden Berufung den Ewigkeitswert gibt und so das Heil als unverdiente Gnadengabe vom Zugriff des Menschen ausschliesst, so wird die geschichtliche Einsetzung des Sabbats als einer Satzung des Heilsbundes am Sinai auf dem ewigen Gnadenwillen Gottes zurückgeführt und so aller Willkür und Unverbindlichkeit entnommen." See also p. 22.

115  See *C.D.* III, 1, 222 (*K.D.*, p. 251).

116  See above Ch. I, n. 110.

day God was well pleased with His Son. He saw creation perfect through Christ; and He *therefore* declared it to be finished, and rested.'

Barth then concludes himself:

There is no avoiding an eschatological explanation of this rest . . .
*God rests* when He completes . . . *because He looks forward to a completely different fulfillment and completion of its relationship to Him, and therefore of its own reality.*[117]

Barth cannot say, therefore, that the Creator was pleased with man as he functioned in his original historical reality. Consequently, the satisfaction, joy and rest of the Creator have to be interpreted teleologically and soteriologically, i.e., with the view to Christ's "restoring" work, not with the view to the actual present reality of man.[118]

Barth justifies his way of interpretation by placing us before the dilemma of (his!) alternative to interpret the creation as a *hexaemeron* (period of six days) or as a *heptaemeron* (period of seven days).[119] The *hexaemeron* point of view considers man and world "arbitrarily for its own sake", so that "the whole history of the covenant of grace is then left hanging in the air." This position of "the fathers" (e.g. Calvin) therefore only "betrayed a great obtuseness" and a narrowed horizon, since the covenant history in this way receives "no basis in creation, and therefore in the natural being and existence of the world and man."[120]

However, the other position which accepts "the necessity and fundamental importance of the institution of the Sabbath in v. 3" of Gen. 2, is able to answer legitimately all the questions of the "order" and "correspondence" of the events of Israel's covenant history with world-events "without disturbing" them.[121] Here therefore "the sphere of grace is not a foreign body; its history is in order; it is possible, without destroying the creaturely world . . ."[122]

---

117  *C.D.* III, 1, p. 222 (italics supplied; *K.D.*, p. 251). Cf. G. C. Berkouwer, *The Triumph of Grace in the Theology of K. Barth*, 1956, ch. III: "The Triumph of Grace in Creation". Berkouwer indicates here that Barth interprets the creation account not noetically merely but ontologically from Christological soteriology (p. 54). Noteworthy is Barth's interpretation of Gen. 1,2 by 2 Cor. 5,17: "It tells us that even from the standpoint of the first creation, let alone the new, chaos is really 'old things', the past and superseded essence of the world" (*C.D.*, III, 1, 110; *K.D.*, p. 121).
118  In this respect also the witness of Job 38,7 is relevant.
119  See *C.D.*, III, 1, 220, 224 (*K.D.*, pp. 249, 254).
120  *Ibid.*
121  *Ibid.*, p. 224f. (*K.D.*, p. 254).
122  *Ibid.*, p. 225.

And he concludes: [123]

> Is not this line of development obvious from the very outset? When He rested from His work, did not God from the very outset reserve this sphere for this further utterance and activity which transcends His work of creation as such?

We feel that Barth has seen a vital and fundamental relationship in Israel's protology when he emphasizes the life and perfection-giving function of God's rest as the invitation to man to participate in the divine rest on the seventh day. This concept we gladly acknowledge as true Biblical theology. Yet we feel that Barth has unconsciously mingled this grand conception with an idea which is foreign to Israel's protology and, therefore, places us before what is not a true dilemma or alternative.

We may start perhaps with this statement of Barth: [124]

> He was satisfied with what He had created and had found the object of His love. It was with man and his true humanity, as His direct and proper counterpart, that God now associated Himself in His true deity. Hence the history of the covenant was really established in the event of the seventh day. Hence it already commenced *secretly* on this day. Hence its whole range may be seen from this point.

Already the term "secretly" in the last statement indicates that not everything is so "obvious", as Barth suggests some pages farther on. It will be noticed that Barth's thesis rests on a series of logical or rational derivations. The argument starts with the inference that God wanted to associate Himself with the just-created man "in the fullest possible way". As the immediate consequence of this "the history of the covenant was really established in the event of the seventh day. Hence it already commenced secretly on this day." (See quotation above.)

The real point is, however, that Barth means with "covenant" the covenant of *grace* (!), in unbroken continuity (backwards) with the covenant of redeeming grace with Israel.[125] The section therefore concludes:

> Creatureliness, and therefore creation, is the external basis of the covenant of grace in which the love of God for man moves towards its fulfillment. It is in this teleology that it is presented in the first creation narrative of the Bible.[126]

The question thus arises, When God made a "covenant" with Adam on the seventh day, why is this covenant a covenant of

---

123  *Ibid.*, p. 225.
124  *Ibid.*, p. 217 (italics supplied; *K.D.*, p. 245).
125  Cf. also *o.c.*, p. 219 (*K.D.*, pp. 247f.).
126  *O.c.*, p. 219 (*K.D.*, p. 248).

redeeming *grace?* Is not this *grace* correlative with *sin* instead of with *nature?*

Barth starts from this affirmation as his soteriological dogmatic *a priori!* Therefore, since his primary interest here is to safeguard the correspondence and order between Israel's covenant of grace and creation, Barth finds his argument in the *rational* derivation that God's covenant with Adam on the seventh day of creation necessarily also must have been a covenant of grace.

Only then Israel's covenant will no longer stand in an unbearable discontinuity with the order of the creaturely world, since it has its basis now in creation.[127] The consequence of this rational view seems to be, however, the implication of the potentiality of sin in creation.[128] The question is not only whether this line of reasoning is Biblical, but primarily whether Barth's whole question is a legitimate one in the framework of Biblical theology. Is not the problematics whether nature, history and grace can be brought into a harmonious connection, in a logical continuity, really a *philosophical* question which belongs to the category of a *theologia speculativa* and not of Biblical theology?[129]

The proper question in Biblical theology is not whether grace and nature, covenant and creation are in perfect logical harmony

---

127  Cf. *o.c.*, pp. 224f. (*K.D.*, p. 254) : "But these questions can be answered legitimately only if we keep to what is written, namely, that the Sabbath also belongs *to creation* ... In a world created in this way, with the inclusion of the divine rest on the seventh day, the sphere of grace is not a foreign body, its history is in order ..." (Italics supplied).

128  Here a curious *tension* becomes visible in Barth's protology. K. Runia, *o.c.*, p. 102, formulates it as follows: "On the one hand, he emphatically maintains that God did not create man as a sinner. God is not the author of sin and therefore creatureliness is not automatically identical with sinfulness. On the other hand, Barth as emphatically denies the so-called state of integrity. Genesis 1 and 2 do not speak of such a golden age. They only prefigure God's grace in Christ towards man." Cf. Berkouwer, *o.c.*, p. 82. Notice Barth's interpretation of the *valde bonum* in Gen. 1,31 as a "contrasting reminder of God's original will for His creatures" as a Christological promise, but not as an original *historical* reality. *C.D.* III, 1, 212f. (*K.D.*, pp. 239f.). Here Barth's concept of the creation narrative as a *"saga"* plays its hermeneutical role. On this, see Runia, *o.c.*, pp. 91ff. It seems that Runia is correct when he interprets Barth's position as: "God created man good, but *as soon as* this created man acts as an independent, responsible being, i.e. *as soon as* this man enters into his own history, he acts against God" (referring to *C.D.* IV, 1, 508f.; *K.D.*, pp. 566f.). Cf. A. A. Hoekema, *K. Barth's Doctrine of Sanctification*, 1965, p. 19.

129  We find a striking analogy in the speculative protology and eschatology of Judaism. Cf. N. A. Dahl, "Christ, Creation and the Church", in *The Background of the N.T. and its Eschatology* (*FS* C. H. Dodd), 1964, p. 428: "This synthetic view is, in somewhat divergent forms, characteristic of the more speculative trends in Judaism. The 'new creation' is seen as the final establishment and perfection of the first one, rather than as an independent parallel act."

or analogy, but whether the God of grace is accepted by faith also as the God of creation and history, and thus as the First and the Last.[130] For *then* the unity of covenant and creation is accepted by an act of faith. This question of unity is not answered in the Scripture canon by way of inference or derivation but by direct and unequivocal proclamation in Gen. 1 and 2,[131] in Ex. 20,11 and 31,17, in the Psalms and the great prophets.[132] Yet these proclamations do not aim at the mere teaching of the doctrine that the unity of covenant and creation is grounded in the identification of Yahweh with the Creator. All these Biblical proclamations are conditioned and motivated by their soteriological connections and doxological intentions.

Their objective is not to furnish a rational insight to God's Providence, but to summon Israel and all the nations of the world to give *praise*[133] to the only living God and Creator, "a righteous God and a Savior", because He is calling "all the ends of the earth" to turn to Him "and be saved."[134]

The concern of Barth to guard the divine "triumph of grace" as a triumph already *before* the fall of man must be acknowledged as a true and vital Biblical motif, on the basis of Eph. 1,3-14 and Rom. 8,29. Only, we would rather define this "triumph of grace"

---

130  Cf. Is. 44,6; 41,4. See the incisive critique of R. Prenter on Barth, "Die Einheit von Schöpfung und Erlösung. Zur Schöpfungslehre Karl Barths", in *ThZ* 2 (1946), 161-182. He states on 174: "Hier muss in aller Schärfe erwidert werden: die Einheit von Schöpfung und Erlösung kann in dieser Welt niemals anders als im Glauben – und das heisst in dem *echten* Glauben, der *nicht sieht* und doch glaubt! –festgehalten werden. *In keiner Weise macht der Glaube an Gott den Schöpfer, der sich uns auch als Schöpfer in Jesus Christus geoffenbart hat, uns die innere Einheit von Schöpfung und Erlösung einsichtig*" (Italics in text).

131  In Gen. 2, by identifying the Creator with the institutor of the seventh-day Sabbath rest, a religious usage completely unknown in antiquity. Cf. E. Lohse, in *ThWNT* VII, 3 (s.v. *sabbaton*): "Bedeutung u. Inhalt des at. lichen Sabbats sind jedenfalls nicht von babylonischen oder anderen ausserisraelitischen Vorbildern her zu erklären, sondern ausschliesslich vom Glauben Israels an Jahwe bestimmt". Vriezen, *Outline*, p. 283; Loretz, *Gottebenb.*, p. 44, n. 3. Gispen, *Schepping*, p. 92f.

132  Is. 40,22-28; 43,1.15. Cf. Westermann, *Isaiah 40-66*, 1969, p. 49: "Praise of God's majesty is frequently developed along the two lines (e.g. Ps. 33), that he is the creator and lord of his creation, and that he is lord of history". Again on p. 17, he says: "Because *as creator he was the lord of history, and as both, the deliverer of his people*. The fusion of these three spheres of divine action – creation, control of world-history, and deliverance – excluded any other possibility than that God was one." (Italics supplied). Westermann, *The Praise of God in the Psalms*, p. 150: "There is ... no Psalm category that arose merely out of some thought concept (such as the theme, nature)..."

133  Jer. 10,10-12; Is. 43,21.1.15; Ps. 102,18; cf. Is. 38,18f.; Ps. 115,17f. On the *praising* of Yahweh as a mode of existence, see the beautiful pages in Westermann, *The Praise of God in the Psalms*, pp. 155ff.

134  Is. 45,21f.

as the *provision* of redeeming grace for any eventual *sin* and *guilt* of man as a "triumph" over Barth's speculative metaphysical power of "chaos" or "nothingness" which "confronts" and "*threatens*" God's creation.[135]

The problem only really starts when Barth projects this triumph of grace into the "history" of the *perfect* creation and Sabbath rest, thus denying the historical *status integritatis*,[136] and with that, the historicity of the fall as a transition from the *status integritatis* to a *status corruptionis*.[137]

The inevitable consequence is that Barth projects back, on the basis of Israel's salvation history,[138] the soteriological dimension of the Sabbath rest of God into the original Sabbath rest of the Creator in Gen. 2.[139] Thus he arrives at the conclusion that God's rest in Gen. 2 is a prefiguration, anticipation and inauguration of the redeeming work of Christ and the covenant of grace. This is Barth's Christological understanding of the Sabbath day and of the divine Sabbath rest. Thus, Barth feels, the logical correspondence and inner concordance and unity of creation and redemption is

---

135   Cf. Berkouwer, *The Triumph*, pp. 58, 68ff., 73f. "Jesus is the Conqueror! That is the gospel which Barth preaches when he speaks of the chaos" (p. 74). "The reality of the chaos can only be circumscribed in this way, then, that it points to the possibility which God in His creative word *rejected* and *excluded*" (p. 70). "The threat comes from that over which God has pronounced His rejecting and scorning No! Salvation is salvation from chaos, from the abyss which borders upon all creaturely reality" (p. 71). See Berkouwer's critique on pp. 244ff.

136   Cf. *C.D.* IV, 1, 508 (*K.D.*, pp. 566, 567): "The biblical saga tells us that world history began with the pride and fall of man ... There was never a golden age. There is no point in looking back to one. The first man was immediately the first sinner". Barth appeals especially to the Pauline Adam-Christ parallel, in the interpretation of which Adam no longer functions as an historical "Adam-reality" (pp. 512f.; *K.D.*, pp. 571f.). See also his *Christ and Adam, Man and Humanity in Romans 5*, 1962 (German, 1952), p. 84.

137   Cf. Berkouwer, *The Triumph*, p. 84.

138   Cf. Dt. 5,12-15. Jenni, *o.c.*, p. 5. "Die Erinnerung an die Erlösung aus der Sklaverei in Ägypten gibt nach dem Deuteronomisten den Anlass zur Feier des Sabbats überhaupt" (p. 17). Jenni describes this "historicizing" of the Sabbath as the deuteronomic "*grounding*" of the Sabbath, a view which is criticized by A. R. Hulst, "Bemerkungen zum Sabbatgebot", in *Studia Biblica et Semitica* (*FS* Th. Vriezen), 1966, pp. 152ff., who prefers to say that Dt. places the Sabbath "in den heilsgeschichtlichen Zusammenhang" (p. 156), since here not the Sabbath but man is placed at the center. Hulst clearly indicates the soteriological motif: "Das Ruhen am Sabbat, so wie Dt. es versteht, enthält einen Hinweis auf und dient als Zeichen fur die *menuḥa*, die Ruhe, die ja bekanntlich im Dt. ein Heilsgut ist" (p. 156). This is also affirmed by Jenni, *o.c.*, p. 19, who even states that in Dt. the Sabbath "selber ist ein Stück Heilsgut".

139   Barth's exegetical appeal to Heb. 4,3-11 with its reference to Gen. 2,2 plays an important substantiating role, *C.D.* III, 1, 227 (*K.D.*, p. 257) and must therefore be considered. See below.

safeguarded and maintained. It is the grand vision of Barth's theology that it has undeniably indicated the vital significance of the Biblical Sabbath as the symbol of *continuity* and *unity* between God's work in creation and redemption.[140] But the Scriptures never bring God's work of redemption into any sort of naturalistic, deterministic relationship of continuity with His work of creation, neither in Ex. 20,11 nor in Heb. 4,3.

Yet there is a definite and significant relationship, which Berkouwer also notes:

> The day of rest, then, has a rich significance for all mankind, for Israel first, but now for all. It illustrates preeminently the close relationship existing between creation and redemption.[141]

For Berkouwer, however, this "close relationship" between creation and redemption is not characterized by the quality of that axiomatic immediacy as it is for Barth. This difference, we feel, correlates with a different structure of hamartiology.[142] Where Barth's concept of creation as it were emanates from his concept of redemption,[143] Berkouwer's interpretation of Scripture is determined more by the Biblical mystery of the *unsuspected* and *surprising* character of God's redeeming grace in view of the salvation-

---

140   Cf. also Berkouwer, *The Providence of God*, pp. 63f.: "That the Scriptures do indeed indicate a bond between the sabbath of Genesis 2 and God's later work of salvation in Jesus Christ. Scripture teaches quite plainly that the fall did not force God to change His plans. He does not appear as disappointed at the failure of His experiment, and then obliged to design an entirely new plan. On the contrary, the Scriptures reveal the unbreakable unity of the work of God in creation and redemption. This unity is clear already in the fourth commandment of the decalogue, and not less in Hebrews 4, where the writer exhorts to enter into the believer's rest in the same context as he speaks of the Sabbath of creation".

141   *O.c.*, p. 62; also p. 64: "The maintenance of the sabbath after the fall is of unusual significance." "A very intimate relation between the creation sabbath and the abiding sabbath as a token of the coming salvation of the Lord (cf. Ezek. 20:12)".

142   Cf. Berkouwer, *The Triumph*, pp. 221ff., 231ff. He points especially to the Biblical dimension of the historical "reality of guilt and the alienation which it effects. If sin is ontologically impossible, a transition from wrath to grace in the historical sphere is no longer thinkable" (p. 233). Cf. also Barth's position on God's wrath as the "modus" of the divine love (p. 235f.). Cf. *C.D.*, IV, 1, 508 (*K.D.*, p. 567): "The first man was immediately the first sinner". See A. A. Hoekema, *K. Barth's Doctrine of Sanctification*, pp. 18f. "In all these ways Barth denies the ultimate seriousness of sin" (p. 20).

143   Cf. Berkouwer, *o.c.*, pp. 254f.: "Barth teaches that that which is self-evident to *God* – because of the divine self-distinction between what God *is* and what He is *not* – must in history be revealed to us. Within *this* framework of thinking the *decisiveness* of history can no longer be fully honored."

historical reality and offensiveness of *sin*, and by the dynamic function of personal faith.[144]

While Berkouwer has kept the *noetic order* of Scripture, *redemption-creation*, and thus safeguarded the ontological reality of man's perfection in creation, Barth has illegitimately and radically transformed this Biblical noetic order into an *ontic* order, thus swallowing up the reality of Biblical protology into its soteriology.

Here it becomes apparent that Barth's "triumph of grace" contains a metaphysical construction which requires a destruction of Biblical protology in order to let its soteriology have absolute sway.

Hebrews 4 also can give no basis for Barth's radicalism. When the author in his exhortation of Hebrews 4 is suddenly drawing a line from God's promise of rest to Israel back to the reality of the Creator's resting after His completion of creation, he is not trying to bring redemption and creation into an intelligible mutual relationship. On the contrary, he is rather revealing the unsuspected and surprising dimension of the *prevenient* sovereign will of the covenant God as Creator in order to deprive all unbelief and wavering of its justification and to exhort and assure the pilgrimaging Church all the more of the immutability of the divine promise of rest.[145]

This motif reappears impressively in Hebrew 6 where the author refers to God's promise and oath to Abraham, in which the *oath* of God functions "to show more convincingly to the heirs of the promise *the unchangeable character* of His purpose ... that through *two unchangeable things*, in which it is impossible that God should prove false, we might have strong encouragement to seize the hope set before us."[146] In a similar way the referring to the resting of the Creator on the seventh day of creation in Heb. 4,3 functions as an unshakable assurance "to show more convincingy to the heirs of the promise [of rest] the unchangeable character of His purpose", i.e., God's eternal purpose of the perfecting fellowship of man with God[147] just as it was, and God intended[148] it to be, in the beginning.

144  Cf. Berkouwer, *o.c.*, pp. 381-383.
145  Cf. Jenni's conclusion concerning the function of the revealed relation of *Covenant* Sabbath and *Creation* Sabbath in Ex. 31,17: "Und so den *Gnaden-charakter der Heilsgabe unumstösslich* deutlich zu machen." "...und so aller Willkür und Unverbindlichkeit entnommen" (*O.c.*, pp. 22, 23). In other words, the plan of salvation was no afterthought.
146  Heb. 6,17f.
147  Cf. C. K. Barrett, "The Eschatology of the Ep. to the Hebrews", in *The Background of the N.T. and its Esch.*, ed. W. D. Davies and D. Daube, 1964², p. 372: "[Heb. 4,11] implies, to enter into God's 'rest' is the opposite of unbelief and disobedience; it means that man shares at length in the perfection of God's ultimate purpose for mankind." Heb. 4,9-11, which interprets the Sabbath rest of God at creation as the *sabbatismos* ("Sabbath-keeping" in analogy with the verb *sabbatidzō* in LXX, Ex. 16,30; Lev. 23,32; 26,35) which *remains* for the people of God "*today*" testifies again of the deep

Thus this "word of exhortation" of Hebrews 4 at the same time proclaims the indissoluble *unity* of God's work in creation and redemption. It does not imply any suggestion that the cause of sin or the fall of Adam may be projected back into divine creation itself, i.e., in the imperfection or vulnerability of creation.

The New Testament witness does not transform or absorbently transpose the Old Testament protology into a Christological soteriology or eschatology.[149]

The Old Testament does however *correlate* or parallel Israel's redemptive events with the divine acts of creation and with the eschatological deliverance, concentrating all three in the dramatic proclamation of the one sovereign God.[150]

In this way the New Testament also throws light on the Old Testament protology by its Christological interpretations of creation, redemption and final perfection, by concentrating all three on the one Lord and Savior Jesus Christ, who is the First and the Last.[151]

When the New Testament deals with the eschatological transformation of the world it never interprets this expectation as the final perfection or realization of creation, as a repristination of protology, but as the eschatological purification and renovation or *restitution*[152] of the first things: Paradise and the tree of life and the perfect fellowship with the Creator will be restored.

This goes to show how fundamental the function of Israel's protology is in its dimension of religious historical reality. What existed in the beginning will come back, even if the eschatological

and fundamental unity of the Biblical protology, soteriology and eschatology. Is not this also implied in Heb. 13,8? Cf. C. Spicq, *L'épître aux Hébreux*, II, 1953[2], p. 83: "Par ailleurs, ce repos divin [sc. du Createur] auquel participeront les hommes est celui du Dieu redempteur et provident, à la fin du monde." F. F. Bruce, *The Ep. to the Hebrews*, 1964, p. 78, rightly points to Heb. 11,10.16 and 39.

148   With the qualification of this verb Barth would certainly agree; *C.D.* III, 1, 227 (*K.D.*, p. 257): "From creation – preceding and superseding every human decision of obedience or disobedience – there remains (*apoleipetai*) for the people of God the Sabbath rest (*sabbatismos*), the divinely willed and ordered fellowship, relationship and agreement between His own and human freedom..."

149   Cf. Dahl, *o.c.*, pp. 424f.

150   Cf. Westermann, *Isaiah 40-66*, p. 17; and on Is. 41,20; 65,17f. See Berkouwer, *The Providence of God*, p. 72, on the meaning of the verb *bārāʾ* in Isaiah. Also H. D. Preuss, *Jahweglaube und Zukunftserwartung*, BWANT 87, 1968, pp. 96-108.

151   Rev. 1,17; 2,8; 22,13; 21,5-6; Heb. 13,8.

152   Rom. 8,19ff.; Eph. 1,10; 2 Pet. 3,10-13; Rev. 20,13; 21,1; Mat. 19,28. Cf. Dahl, *o.c.*, p. 434, on the parallel of Christ as *prōtotokos pasēs ktiseōs* and *prōtotokos ek tōn nekrōn* in Col. 1,15-20: "In a very impressive way, the idea of universal restitution is here combined with the conception that the reconciliation is a parallel to the creation."

"regeneration" or recreation [153] of the world will be superior [154] to the first creation because of the history of salvation during which the pilgrimaging people of God have experienced the closest communion with their Creator. They have already entered the transforming *sabbatismos*, the Sabbath rest that remained since the creation, through the saving ministry of Jesus and His Spirit. Yet the full restoration of the *sabbatismos* in the renewed creation constitutes the expectation of the Christian hope.[155]

In the New Testament the divine atonement is not based externally in creation, nor creation internally in the atonement, but both are paralleled with and rooted in the same God and Mediator, Christ Jesus (Col. 1,15-20 and Eph. 1,3-14).[156]

Both works, creation as well as the sacrificial atonement, are presented therefore as being completed, as works perfectly finished [157] when they were accomplished. There is no automatic or self-evident connection between both, since sin and atoning love are no naturalistic attributes respectively of man, and God.

The only guarantee and perfect assurrance of the inner concordance and harmony between creation and redemption does not lie in any rationalizing harmonization between both but exclusively in the recognition by faith of the absolute identification of the sovereign will and love of the Creator and Redeemer, Christ Jesus.

153  See J. Behm, in *ThWNT* III, 451 (s.v. *kainos*).

154  Cf. Calvin on Gen. 2,7 comparing this text with 1 Cor. 15,45 which teaches us "that the state of man was not perfected in the person of Adam ... it had no firm and settled constancy" (*Com. on Genesis*, p. 112). This can be accepted in the sense of character perfection or development. Preuss, *o.c.*, p. 100: "Es ist im Alten Testament durch die Verknüpfung von Schöpfung und Geschichte daher auch nicht – wie oft und sonst im Alten Orient – von Schöpfung und Wiederkehr, sondern von Schöpfung und Neuschöpfung die Rede. Es geht nicht ... nur um eine eschatologische 'Wiederkehr' des Paradieses."

155  Cf. Berkouwer, *The Providence of God*, p. 65; C. K. Barrett, *o.c.*, p. 372.

156  Cf. Dahl, *o.c.*, p. 432: "The accord between the work of salvation and the eternal purpose of God is made especially clear in Eph. 1.3-14. To the actual 'blessing' in Christ, 1.3, corresponds the election in him before the foundation of the world, 1-4." In other words, the triumph of grace is rooted in the provision and decision of the divine predestinating love "before the foundation of the world."

157  Heb. 4,3b; Gen. 2,1-2; Jn. 19,30. When Christ at the cross said "It is finished", this can not mean that only now His work of creation was finished but that His atoning sacrifice for the sins of the world was finished, completed (Heb. 1,3; 9,26; 10,12). Cf., however, Barth, *C.D.*, III, 1, 227 (*K.D.*, p. 257), "the one man Jesus Christ, who as He was and is God's image ... also kept the commandment of the Sabbath, with the promulgation of which God completed the whole work of *creation*". (it. sup.). Here it becomes very apparent how Israel's protology with its original perfection is absorbed in Barth's soteriology. Rev. 21,5-6 indicates that when all things are made new in the final perfection, the divine word will be fulfilled: "*gegonan*", It is done.

But this is a knowledge of truth, based only on the revealing testimony and authority of the New Testament!

4. *Perfection – the aim of the "probationary command".*

Starting from the canonical unity of the story of Gen. 2,4b–3,24[158] which intends to explain why humanity is situated in its present state of disharmony with God and with itself,[159] we learn that Paradise was lost because of man's fateful answer to the divine command in reference to the so-called "tree of the knowledge of good and evil".[160]

What is the theological meaning of this narrative about the fall of man?

This "tree" has given rise to many a speculation on its purpose and function.[161] While Loretz approaches this story from the angle of the de-mythologizing[162] function of the creation accounts, which function he unobtrusively and illegitimately transforms into a decisive hermeneutical

158 Cf. von Rad, *Genesis*, p. 73: "There is no question that the narrative of chs 2f. . . . is to be understood as a whole with a consistent train of thought". "That here a factual report is meant to be given about facts, to be sure, the nature of which is very concealed and mysterious." Already H. Th. Obbink, *Het Bijbelsch Paradijsverhaal en de Babyl. bronnen*, 1917, p. 19: "Afgezien van verschillende oneffenheden . . . vormt Gen. 2,4b-3,24 één afgerond geheel." Cf. O. Loretz, *Schöpfung und Mythos*, 1968, p. 107.

159 Cf. Obbink, *o.c.*, p. 130: "Alles wat hij in Gen. 2 mededeelt krijgt het karakter van een inleiding op Gen. 3: de 'zondeval'. Niet hoe 't vroeger was, interesseert den schrijver, maar hoe 't nù is, en hoe dat zóó is geworden." Cf. S. Porúbčan, *Sin in the Old Testament. A Soteriological Study*, 1963, p. 407: "It should be clear, therefore, that the real literary *genre* of this writing is the *memory of the past transmitted by tradition*. Man fallen into sin and experiencing its consequences remembers his own state and condition before the sin and compares one with the other. I think that any serious explanation of Gen. 2-3 has to be made from this point of view." A special divine revelation for the inscripturation of the creation tradition moreover is accepted by G. Ch. Aalders, *De Goddel. Openb. in de eerste drie hfst. v. Gen.*, 1932, p. 29. Also by G. Vos, *Biblical Theology*, p. 30. P. Schoonenberg, *Het Geloof van ons Doopsel*, I, pp. 168f., 174, on the other hand rejects any historical source for the author of creation and regards the described factuality as the result of retrospective prophetical or divine interpretation of history and of the post-Paradise situation, very much akin to Barth's position. N. Lohfink, *De Actualiteit van het Oude Testament*, 1966, pp. 87f., 91, qualifies the account as the product of "human reflection", as a theology of history, as retroprojective covenant theology, as "geschichtliche Ätiologie," although with a real "historical intention".

160 Gen. 2,17. Of importance is the definite article before the substantive "knowledge", and its absence before "good and evil". See below.

161 See Aalders, *o.c.*, pp. 455ff. Loretz, *Schöpfung*, pp. 111ff.: "Dieses Wort vom Baum der Erkenntnis und dem mit dem Essen verbundenen Tod gehört zu den umstrittensten Aussagen von Gen. 2-3."

162 Especially Lohfink, *o.c.*, pp. 79f., has exposed the *de-mythologizing* function of Gen. 2-3 in an intriguing way.

key or norm,[163] we feel that neither the literary-critical analysis nor the religious-historical phenomenology can explain adequately the secret of the Biblical uniqueness and therefore cannot furnish the hermeneutical norm to interpret this *typical Israelite* Paradise story.[164]

Loretz concludes that the Genesis account of the eating of "the tree of knowledge" not only adopts the terminology of myth but thereby also automatically adopted the imagery of myth: "Im Genesisbericht wird das Verbot dieses todbringenden Geschlechtsverkehrs dem Menschen als Gehorsamsprobe aufgegeben."[165]

Yet the Hebrew re-interpretation of the myth would no longer be the first sexual act, but "the first 'No' of man to Yahweh."[166] Already H. Obbink had rightly stressed that the account does not call the forbidden tree the "tree of knowledge", but "tree of knowlegde of good and evil," concluding: „Daarmee reikt hij boven de zo evengenoemde voorstellingen uit. Die naam omvat niet alleen méér maar ook iets anders dan kennis van geslachtsverschil."[167] The whole meaning of Gen. 2 and 3 is concen-

---

163  *O.c.*, pp. 112ff.; in particular by his comparison with the mythical form of speech of the Gilgamesh epic, e.g.: "Die Formulierungen in Gn. 2,16-17 und die des Gilgameschepos zeigen zur Genüge, dass einerseits mit dem Geschlechtsverkehr ein Verlust der bisherigen Lebenskraft und zugleich ein Gewinn an Wissen verbunden war." H. Schmidt, *Die Erzählung von Paradies und Sündenfall*, 1931, p. 47, had already interpreted the de-mythologizing account of Gen. 3 as an "aetiological saga" concerning the origin of sexual love. Loretz, however, divorces Israel's protology from the rest of the Scripture canon and, with that, from its indispensable hermeneutical center, the covenant of Yahweh with Israel.

164  Cf. Obbink, *o.c.*, pp. 31ff. "Alles wijst in dezelfde richting: een israelietisch verhaal met behulp van vreemd materiaal opgebouwd" (p. 32). "Maar waar het gaat om het verstaan van de *bedoeling* van den Jahvistischen schrijver, kan het [sc. the literary critical analysis] ons niets leeren. Die bedoeling wordt niet toegelicht door de beteekenis der woorden in hun babylonisch milieu maar door de waarde die ze hebben in het bijbelverhaal. De babylonische woorden kunnen in het Genesis-verhaal geheel andere waarden hebben. En van welke waarden ze daar de dragers zijn kan alleen blijken uit het milieu, waarin de Jahvist ze plaatst" (p. 33). Lohfink, *o.c.*, p. 82. On the history of interpretation, see M. Metzger, *Die Paradieserzählung. Die Geschichte ihrer Auslegung von J. Clericus bis W. M. L. de Wette*, Abhandl. z. Phil., Psych. u Päd., Bd. 16, 1959. See also Th. Ch. Vriezen, *Onderzoek naar de Paradijsvoorstelling bij de oude Semietische volken*, 1937.

165  *Schöpfung*, p. 113; also: "Die Verbinding zwischen: Geschlechtsverkehr-Erkenntnis von Gut und Böse (d.h. Erreichung der höchsten Wissensstufe) - Sein-wie-die-Gotter tritt auch an einer Stelle des Gilgameschepos deutlich hervor." Already E. Albert, "Ein neuer Erklärungsversuch von Gen. 2 and 3", in *ZAW* 33 (1913), 166, indicated the inadequacy of the sexual interpretation. Also S. Porúbčan, *Sin in the O.T.*, 1963, p. 419, n. 24 (with lit.). And Vriezen, *Paradijsvoorstelling*, p. 146.

166  *Schöpfung*, p. 122.

167  *O.c.*, p. 138. He points to Gen. 2,23-24 as the indication that the con-

trated in and depending on the interpretation of the words, the "tree of the knowledge of good and evil."[168] Here man is placed before an existential question and task. The transgression of the prohibition to eat from this tree is presented as the transgression of the absolute and fundamental line of demarcation between man and God, as the becoming "like God, knowing good and evil",[169] which transgression deserves the most serious verdict of losing Paradise.

On the basis of the story itself, i.e., Gen. 3,5.22, "the knowledge of good and evil" might be interpreted as the inalienable absolute knowledge of God, which is due to Him alone.[170]

When man lays hands upon this divine knowledge he falls into sin, denying the place and responsibility of this humanity and *imago Dei*. By the act of disobedience man basically emancipates himself from his Creator and declares his fundamental independence from God, not merely in the unlimited realm of intellectual knowing but of the will.[171] The expression "good and evil" is interpreted to be the Hebrew idiom of the conjunction of opposites in order to signify "totality", everything".[172] A step further would be to conclude that "the" knowledge of good and evil (totality) is a signification of the sovereign will of the Creator of man as the very foundation for all ethical knowing and acting. Or, as K. Barth[173] explains:

sciousness of sexual difference was given from the very start of the creation of the woman. Especially Gen. 3,22 indicates that the intention of the account exceeds the awakening of sexual consciousness: man has become like God. "Gelijk aan God kàn hier [sc. in Israel] geen betrekking hebben op geslachtsbewustzijn, noch op 't geslachtelijk voortbrengen van leven." (*Ibid.*) Cf. also Vriezen, *Outline*, p. 209; Barth, *C.D.* III, 1, 285f. (*K.D.*, pp. 325f.).

168  Obbink, *o.c.*, p. 139.

169  Gen. 3,22.5.

170  Cf. Vriezen, *Outline*, pp. 43, 205, 209 ("the symbol of higher divine knowledge"). R. Guardini, *Der Anfang aller Dinge. Meditationen über Genesis, Kap. I-III*, 1961, p. 65: "Mahlzeichen von Gottes Hoheit, sonst nichts". M. A. Beek, *Profiel van het O.T.*, 1960, pp. 54f. refers to H. Heine's delicate intuition. Heine called the serpent "der kleinen Privatdozentin die schon 6000 Jahre vor Hegels Geburt die ganze Hegelsche Philosophie vortrug. Dieser Blaustrumpf ohne Füsse zeigte sehr scharfsinnig wie das Absolute in der Identität von Sein und Wissen besteht, wie der Mensch zum Gotte werde durch die Erkenntnis, oder was dasselbe ist, wie Gott im Menschen zum Bewusstsein seinerselbst gelange."

171  Cf. von Rad, *Genesis, ad* Gen. 3,5.

172  H. A. Brongers, "Merismus, Synekdoche und Hendiadys in der Bibel - Hebräischen Sprache", in *OTS*, XIV (1968), 105: "Es handelt sich in den Sündenfallstellen um eine totale, allesumfassende Kenntnis, die nur Gott besitzt, die aber auch vom Menschen leidenschaftlich begehrt wird." Von Rad, *ad* Gen. 3,5. Especially Barth, *C.D.* III, 1, 286f. (*K.D.*, pp. 326f.), with Biblical references.

173  *C.D.* III, 1, 257f. (*K.D.*, pp. 292f.).

To know good and evil, to be able to distinguish and therefore judge between what ought to be and ought not to be, between Yes and No, between salvation and perdition, between life and death, is to be like God, to be oneself the Creator and Lord of the creature. The one who can do this bears the supreme attribute and function of the deity.

The eating of this tree then would indicate the high-handed or presumptuous sin of seizing the divine prerogative of self-government, i.e., the human self-exaltation to the equality of God, to absolute autonomy.[174] By eating of the forbidden tree man fell into the sin of rebellion, since by this act of disobedience to the explicit command of his Creator man robbed God of his sovereign prerogative to know everything and hence to define what is good and evil for man.[175]

When it is the Creator's prerogative to define what is good and what is evil for man, i.e., that good is what God wills, evil, what God forbids, then the prohibition to eat from a certain tree implies *more* than a "probationary command".[176] Its primary function and aim, then, would be rather the appointed opportunity for man to confirm and develop his original perfection into a developed or settled perfection, i.e., into a perfection in action, by way of a *conscious* moral decision of the human will to submit to and to follow his Father and Lord in His sovereign command as an act of honoring and praising God.[177]

---

174  Cf. G. Aalders, *o.c.*, p. 473: "Het autonoom willen zijn is zonde." Also pp. 467f.: "De mensch oordeelt dat het eten van den boom niet kwaad maar goed is, en handelt dienovereenkomstig" (p. 468). Cf. von Rad, *ad* Gen. 3,6: "It begins to dawn on him that he is better off as an autocrat than in obedience to God. (E. Osterloh, Ev. Th., '37, 439)."

175  Cf. von Rad, *ad* Gen. 3,5: "That the narrative sees man's fall, his actual separation from God, occuring again and again in *this* area (and not, for example, as a plunge into moral evil, into the subhuman!), i.e., in what we call Titanism, man's *hubris* – this is truly one of its most significant affirmations." Vriezen, *Outline*, p. 43: "Man shakes off the Child-Father relation with God and is thrown into the great struggle of life because he wants to take matters into his own hands; *man's self-exaltation, his 'hybris' towards God is sin* (Gen. III; Gen. VI, 1ff.; Gen. XI), but sin against God also involves sin against one's fellow-man (Cain-Lamech)."

176  Cf. Obbink, *o.c.*, p. 142: "Als dan de Jahvist verhaalt dat Jahve den mensch verbiedt van den boom der kennis van goed en kwaad te eten, dan bedoelt hij daarmee te zeggen: wat goed en wat kwaad is, staat niet aan den mensch te beoordeelen, maar ligt in God's hand. De mensch heeft alleen te gehoorzamen, ook zonder motivatie." Cf. also Vriezen, *Paradijsvoorstelling*, p. 147: „en zoo te leeren dat dit zonde is: als God goed en kwaad willen kennen, d.i. over goed en kwaad te willen beschikken."

177  Cf. Aalders, *o.c.*, p. 471, appealing to H. Visscher, *Het Paradijsprobleem*: "Het gaat hier om het voortschrijden van automatisch tot welbewust

The command *not* to eat from this tree was a command that could never be derived from man's own moral insight, and was, consequently, based *only* on God's autonomous decision.[178] Thus the educative purpose of the prohobition may be described as to provoke in man his moral consciousness, decision and development in following his Creator by faith and trust.[179] On this ethical condition and task man's life and immortality depended.[180]

Humanity, therefore, "is to be lived in acknowledgment of the judicial office of God, in conscious gratitude, and to that extent in the form of decision and obedience."[181] The development of human perfection thus is not seen in the way of disobedience and severance from God, in other words, by *eating* of the "tree of the knowledge of good and evil,"[182] but

---

goed handelen." K. Barth, *C.D.* III, 1, 260ff., 264ff. (*K.D.*, pp. 296ff. 300ff.). W. Zimmerli, *1 Mose 1-11*, p. 136.

178  Cf. A. Kuyper, *De Gemeene Gratie*, I, 179-186. Bavinck, *G.D.* II, 532.

179  See Bavinck, *o.c.*, II, 536: "In het proefgebod werd heel de zedewet voor Adam op één worp gezet; het belichaamde voor hem het dilemma: God of de mensch, zijn gezag of eigen inzicht, onvoorwaardelijke gehoorzaamheid of zelfstandig onderzoek, geloof of twijfel." Aalders, *o.c.*, p. 473: "Het gaat ten principale om de vraag, *waar* de normen liggen: in den mensch zelf of in God ... en waarom het nog steeds gaat en gaan zal tot aan het wereldeinde: wie stelt de norm? doet God dat, of zal de mensch die aan zichzelf ontlenen?" G. Brillenburg Wurth, *Het Christelijk Leven*, 1957², p. 68: "Door de crisis echter ... ontwaakte zijn zedelijk bewustzijn in volle klaarheid. En dat was het, waar het God juist om te doen was." Barth rejects any crisis or trial here, since man was not placed "like a Hercules at the cross-roads, [with] the choice of obedience and disobedience." "It is simply the freedom to be humble; his capacity to recognize and to praise the divine judicial office; ... keeping to its own place as such, affirming and maintaining it, to hold fellowship with the Creator ... conscious, spontaneous and active assent to His divine decision" (*C.D.* III, 1, 264ff.; *K.D.*, pp. 301ff.).

180  Bavinck, *G.D.* II, 522: "Ze [sc. Adam's original immortality] was niet absoluut maar conditioneel, ze hing van een ethische voorwaarde af." Vriezen, *Outline*, p. 205: "Man would not live with God as His child, but wanted to face God as an equal, and this original sin brought death on him. But man himself, made from the dust of the earth, is already mortal; the fact that he *must* die is due to the punishment of sin inflicted by God, because that is the reason why he must leave the garden of Eden with the tree of life." Cf. Schoonenberg, *Geloof v. o. Doopsel* I, 172f., 174.

181  Barth, *C.D.* III, 1, 263 (*K.D.*, p. 299).

182  In contrast with the ethical idealism of I. Kant, *Mutmasslicher Anfang der Menschengeschichte*, in *Werke in sechs Bänden*, VI, 1964, p. 92, who evaluates the fall of man as the development "from the tutelage of nature to the state of freedom", "from moral unconsciousness to moral self-consciousness." Especially E. Albert, in *ZAW 33* (1913), 161-191, tries to "prove" that Adam and Eve are pictured as children under age who are ethically indifferent, so that "die Aufklärung, die Reife nur durch Sünde hindurch erlangt wird" (Gunkel). Consequently, the sin was only "a child's sin": "so stehen nun 'Sünde' und Strafe hier in keinem richtigen Verhältnis" (p. 183). H. Monte-

in the way of conscious obedience by faith and trust in the Father Creator.

Thus it appears that the divine commandment is not a foreign element but rather the necessary condition for the functioning of a perfect humanity, for the walk with God.[183] The most intimate relationship of man with God can never eliminate man's creatureliness and with that his subordination in his sonship. His human knowing and acting can only reflect in praise and adoration the divine wisdom and the depth of the Creator's unsearchable judgments and inscrutable ways.[184] This concept of the probationary command as intending to settle man's perfection, to develop his religious and moral maturity, is visualized by A. Kuyper[185] and G. Vos.[186]

Small wonder that this profoundly spiritual view of Genesis 2-3 has been qualified as "one of the greatest statements of the Old Testament on anthropology."[187] Von Rad, following Hempel, sees the entire narrative

fiore, *A Radical Restatement of Chr. Faith*, 1966, p. 24, even stated (quoted in Loretz, *Schöpfung*, p. 11): "If man can choose evil, he can also choose good: he can choose God. That is why, if we must speak misleadingly of a Fall, resulting in knowledge of good and evil, then for heaven's sake let us regard it as a Fall Upwards."

183  Cf. T. E. Fretheim, *Creation, Fall, and Flood*, 1969, p. 77: "Commandment was an essential ingredient of human life before sin entered the picture. Commandment was thus a manifestation of God's grace. It set the limits within which man as creature can most truly be man – acknowledgment of God as the giver and center of life." Guardini, *o.c.*, p. 66: "Von der Frucht des Baumes nicht zu essen, bedeutet keinen Verzicht auf Wesentlichkeiten deines menschlichen Seins, sondern den Gehorsam, in welchem du deine Endlichkeit anerkennst; und damit die Entscheidung für die Wahrheit [sc. dass nur Gott 'Gott' ist, du hingegen Geschöpf]."

184  See Ps. 92,5; Rom. 11,33.

185  *De Gemeene Gratie*, I, 192: "Hadden ze dit daarentegen *niet* gedaan, en staande voor de verzoeking om *zelven* de grens tusschen goed en kwaad te trekken, met helder bewustzijn dit geweigerd, dit afgeslagen en dit niet gewild en niet gedaan, dan zouden ze van dat oogenblik af tot het hooger inzicht zijn gekomen, om van nu voortaan niet alleen krachtens het instinct van hun schepping, maar nu ook willens en wetens God te eeren als *Koning, Wetgever en Rechter*, en alzoo tot de hoogste gemeenschap met het waarachtig zedelijk leven zijn ingegaan."

186  *Biblical Theology*, p. 31: "Man has been created perfectly good in a moral sense. And yet there was a sense in which he could be raised to a still higher level of perfection ... The advance was meant to be from unconfirmed to confirmed goodness and blessedness; to the confirmed state in which man could no longer sin, and hence could no longer become subject tot the consequences of sin." See also pp. 41, 43. He distinguishes between "probation" and "temptation".

187  Vriezen, *Outline*, pp. 205f. He states on p. 42: "The author of the narrative of Gen. II-XI may, no doubt, be looked upon as the most profound of the Old Testament authors." M. Noth, *Überlieferungsgeschichte des Pentateuch*, 1948, p. 256.

of Gen. 2-3 functioning as a theodicy of Yahweh as Lord of history of the world, "for it is concerned to acquit God and his creation of all the suffering and misery that has come into the world."[188] In other words, that all sorrow and death – in contrast to Babylonian mythology – do not come from the Creator, but from sin, which is a knowledge against God.

The question arises, How does Yahweh, the covenant God of Israel, reveal in Gen. 3 that He is not merely interested in a theodicy, His own justification, but also in a soteriology, His salvation of the sinner?[189]

The continuity and spiritual unity of Yahweh's work in creation and salvation appears from the divine answer to the fall of man.

### 5. *Divine answer to the fall*

N. Lohfink has pointed to a striking parallelism between the structure of the historical development of the covenant people and the story of the fall in Gen. 2 and 3.[190]

Just as Yahweh has found and chosen Israel outside the land of Canaan, i.e., in Egypt, and has led Israel graciously through the desert into the land of promise, giving it His commandments as covenant law together with the covenant blessings and curses, likewise Yahweh's dealing with man in Gen. 2 and 3 is presented in the same order. First man is formed of dust from the ground.

Then Yahweh Elohim places man in the wonderful garden, and gives him a commandment with the promise that in keeping it he will live, since the garden has the "tree of life". Disobedience would result in the curse of death, i.e., man would have to leave the garden and face hard labor and suffering until death. This vital parallelism reveals how the character of sin is qualified before God as a rupture of the covenant, with suffering and death as the consequences of sin.[191]

---

188 *Genesis*, p. 97. Also Lohfink, *o.c.*, pp. 91f.

189 Von Rad, *o.c.*, p. 98, warns not to be misled by the isolation of Israel's protology in Scripture so as to distinguish it basically from Israel's soteriology. Was not her protology "the revelation of Yahweh"? Von Rad acknowledges "manifold and important connecting lines" between both (p. 99). Lohfink, *o.c.*, pp. 92f., sees Yahweh's salvation only begin with Gen. 12 and the promised blessing for the world in the seed of Abraham. Gen. 3 only serves as the "dark background" for Gen. 12.

190 *O.c.* (see above, n. 159), pp. 83-88. Lohfink concludes that the present form of Gen. 2 and 3 would not have been possible without the covenant theology of Israel. This seems to be justified since the God of Gen. 2-3 is the God of Israel, Yahweh.

191 Cf. Lohfink, *o.c.*, p. 86: "Als Israel zijn verhouding tot God niet gedacht had in de uitgesproken juridische categorieën van een verdrag, dan zouden het moment van de vrijheid in de zonde en het verband tussen zonde en slechte afloop zeker niet zo duidelijk beseft zijn." G. Vos, *Bib. Theol.*, p. 48, gives a valuable discussion of death as a return to dust, and the curse on sin.

Sin is not seen here as an impersonal sinful impulse of human nature, but as disobedience, emancipation and autonomy,[192] as the turning of man's back to God, as a no longer walking with God,[193] as a denial of true humanity, since man, created in the image of God, owes to his Creator total obedience and implicit trust.[194]

In this respect the narrative of Gen. 2 and 3 appears to carry a kerygma which exceeds the mere historical dimension. The story at the same time teaches that all sin at all times at bottom is disobedience to the Creator and covenant God. This becomes evident, however, only where God again reveals His will for man in explicit commandments, i.e., in Israel. In *this* respect Barth's connecting Israel directly with Adam is legitimate and revealing:[195]

> The story of Adam is the history of Israel contracted into the life story of a single man. For both in the story of Adam and in the history of Israel, man's response to God's revelation is the same. In both he lets himself be enticed away by the voice of the stranger, he rebels against the God who has been revealed to him, he becomes disobedient and is made subject to the power of death.

But the theological parallel also suggests a soteriological implication. Just as the consuming wrath of God on Israel, because of their high-handed sin of making and worshipping the molten calf, was turned away through the mediation of Moses when he fell back on the sovereign promise of God to the patriarchs,[196] so it may be asked whether in Paradise the wrath of God was not also turned away from man, after his rebellious act, by mediating grace.

We realize that this suggestion does not arise from the Paradise

He takes the conjunction "until" in Gen. 3,19 not simply chronologically but as climactic in the curse.

192   Obbink, *o.c.*, p. 159.
193   Cf. also above, n. 73 (on p. 65).
194   Cf. Loretz, *Gottebenbildlichkeit*, p. 56: "Der aus Lehm geformte Mensch muss nach biblischer Lehre zu Gott im Verhältnis des Gehorsams und des Vertrauens stehen" (referring to Is. 29,16; 45,9; Jer. 18,4.6; Wisd. 15,7; Rom. 9,20f.).
195   *Christ and Adam, Man and Humanity in Romans 5*, pp. 76f. Barth bases his conclusion on the inference from the expression "in the likeness of Adam's transgression" in Rom. 5,14: "The whole history of Israel in all its stages is the revelation of man's sin... (in the likeness of Adam's transgression, vs. 14) in shameful identification with the sin committed by Adam in Gen. 3. Nowhere else does it become so plain that the history of humanity... is always and everywhere the history of the sin and condemnation of men" (p. 77). Also Lohfink, *o.c.*, pp. 90f., stresses the *universal* character of the Yahwist historic-theological horizon.
196   See Ex. 32,9-14.

story when taken by itself. But we maintain that Israel's primal story ought not to be taken as an independent, self-existent entity within Israel's canon of Scripture. We believe that the hermeneutical key lies in Israel's covenant of grace, and is fully disclosed in the Christo-centric fulfillment of Israel's covenant. This is also our guiding principle in interpreting the crux interpretum of Gen. 2,17b: "for *in the day* [$b^e y\hat{o}m$] *that you eat of it you shall die.*" Vriezen, *Paradijsvoorstelling*, pp. 161-161, concludes that the interpretation of this text (Gen. 2,17b) depends on the exegesis of Gen. 3,17-19, whether *death* must be considered as punishment or not. On the basis of the consideration that the Creator is pictured in Gen. 3 as a strictly *moral* God, who takes seriously the guilt of man, he concludes that God cannot be conceived as lying to man in Gen. 2,17. In other words, the outcome (in Gen. 3) proves that God's warning in Gen. 2,17 with reference to "in the day" ($b^e y\hat{o}m$) should not be taken literally, i.e., that death would come *immediately* as the result of the eating (see p. 190). $B^e y\hat{o}m$ therefore must be taken to mean "when", as it often does elsewhere. Porúbčan, *o.c.*, pp. 402ff., however, sees a problem here. He observes that capital punishment in the O.T. always refers to violently "putting to death" the sinner. He acquiesces, however, in that interpretation which gives the capital punishment of Gen. 2-3 the modified meaning of "*the loss of the privilege of immortality* and a sentence to the *gradual natural death* of a mortal being" (p. 422) for the sake of avoiding "disharmony" in the concept of God. Against this harmonizing interpretation von Rad, *ad* Gen. 2,19 and 3,14, rightfully remarks that the texts does not say, 'You will become mortal', but 'You shall die'. Consequently, the curse "cannot be made to agree absolutely with the threat of ch. 2,17, for men did not die after their deed." A rational harmonization of Gen. 2,17 with Gen. 3,17ff. at the cost of the sharp meaning of Gen. 2,17b is not warranted. This becomes all the more compelling after the thorough study of R. Knierim, *Die Hauptbegriffe für Sünde im Alten Testament*, 1967², p. 91, who concludes: "Sowohl zeitlich als auch grundsätzlich primär ist die dem A.T. mit der Religionsgeschichte weithin geläufige Vorstellung, dass der Sünder . . . sterben, und zwar natürlicherweise sofort sterben muss."

Barth's solution that "there is something far worse than . . . the actual moment of death, and that is an existence in the fear of death, in the hunger for life" (*C.D.* III, 1, 288; *K.D.*, p. 329), certainly is an existential truth, but gives no authority to change the content of capital punishment in Gen. 2,17, as von Rad properly observes.

It brings a step further, however, when the historical reality of the promise of grace, as given *after* the fall, is taken, into account. The argument that the phrase "in the day" ($b^e y\hat{o}m$) in Gen. 2,17 "cannot" mean the actual day of disobedience "in view of the sequel" (G. Vos), is theologically not decisive, since this would *a priori* ignore and deny not merely the reality but even the possibility of the *historical turning of divine wrath to grace* with respect to rebellious man. Vos himself acknowledges that the opportunity given to the human race to propagate itself was "the element of grace" (*Bib. Theol.*, p. 35).

Von Rad acknowledges that the author of Gen. 2-3 is concerned "to show that God did not make good his terrible threat but had allowed grace to prevail." In stead of concluding that such a theological exegesis would make God a liar (in Gen. 2,17) it seems more careful to draw from the similar situation of Israel under Moses the conclusion that the reality of divine grace has made its unsuspected impact on God's historical dealing with man as a distinct action of God after man's actual rebellion.

Therefore Bavinck's interpretation of mediating grace between Gen. 2,17 and 3,17ff. still may be regarded as adequate and most satisfactory: "Er is een element tusschen beiden getreden, dat deze straf gematigd en uitgesteld heeft... De aanvangen der geschiedenis zetten na den val, zij het ook in zeer gewijzigde vorm, zich voort. Dit alles is niet aan God's gerechtigheid, maar, gelijk later duidelijker blijken zal, aan zijne genade te danken. Deze treedt aanstonds na den val in werking. Zij krijgt de leiding der geschiedenis, niet ten koste van, maar in verbinding met het recht Gods." (*G.D.* III, 139f.)

The theological parallel suggests a Mediator. The Messianic interpretation of Gen. 3,15 therefore not only fits the religious-historical parallel,[197] but also is in harmony with the kerygmatic motif of the Yahwist as developed in Gen. 12ff. and explained Christo-centrically by Paul's kerygma in Gal. 3,8.16. Hans W. Wolff, in his important article "The Kerygma of the Yahwist",[198] has clearly indicated that the key to unlock the mening of the whole primal history of Gen. 1-11 lies in the

---

197 Speiser, *ad l.*, states that the term "seed" is "used normally in the collective sense of progeny." A. H. Edelkoort, *De Christus-verwachting in het Oude Testament*, 1941, p. 103, however, points out that the term "seed" also is applied to one single person, e.g., Gen. 4,25; 21,13; 1 Sam. 1,11; 2 Sam. 7,12. He adds: "Men bedenke ook wel, dat de overwinning wordt behaald op de slang (enkelvoud), het niet meer dan logisch is, dat ook de overwinnaar enkelvoudig gedacht moet worden [referring to Delitzsch, Genesis 107]." In the light of the religious-historical parallel of Babylonian mythology of Gen. 3,15, Edelkoort suggests that the conqueror of the serpent-dragon is a God, yet the de-mything function of Gen. 3,15 transposes the naturalistic struggle into an ethical struggle, and the mythological into an eschatological victory (pp. 104f.). Obbink, *o.c.*, p. 156, concludes that in the light of the Babylonian traditions, it is "more than probable" that Gen. 3,15 intends to be Messianic prophecy in the specific form of a world-Savior who will recapture Paradise lost by sin.

198 In *Interpr.* 20 (1966), 131-158 (German, in *Ges. Stud. z. A.T.*, Th. B. 22, 1964, pp. 345-373). Cf. also G. von Rad, *Ges. Stud.*, pp. 72ff.; M. Noth, *o.c.*, pp. 256f.; and H. D. Preuss, *Jahweglaube und Zukunftserwartung*, p. 97.

significant word of Gen. 12,3b. Abraham is elected and called by Yahweh to be a "blessing" for "all the families of the earth", who lie under specific curses (Gen. 3,17; 4,11; 9,25).

> The so-called primal history explains in advance *why* all the families of the earth need the blessing. This is disclosed in retrospect by 12:3b as its hidden, leading question (*Leitfrage*) ... "All the families of the earth" – this subject of his message in 12:3b is introduced in Chapters 2-11 (*ibid.*, 145).

From the patriarchal narratives (starting with Gen. 18,17ff.) Wolff concludes that according to the Yahwist the blessing of Abraham (and Israel) for all the peoples consists specifically in "the unflagging, *intercessory* activity of Abraham – Israel for those who are perishing".[199]

The intended result of this mediation by the elected people would be "annulment of guilt and punishment, community life without strife, effective material aid for life."[200]

The Yahwistic proclamation may recognize incidental fulfillments of the Promise here and there, but it persistently holds out the promised blessing for the world "as a kerygma",[201] as a continuum which gives the Old Testament Scripture its peculiar character of being still incomplete, because it remains the book of hope and expectation.[202]

When we ask the question whether the Yahwist has indicated this kerygma of hope and expectation for mankind already in Israel's primal history, i.e. in Gen. 3, it may be said that the Messianic interpretation of Gen. 3,15 is justified on the basis of Israel's kerygma of the indissoluble unity of Yahweh as covenant God and Creator.[203] This means that such

---

199  *Ibid.*, 148 (italics supplied); cf. also 150: "By Israel's intercession with Yahweh on the example of Abraham."

200  *Ibid.*, 150.

201  *Ibid.*, 154; cf.: "The fullness – 'all the families of the earth will gain blessing in Israel' – is first present only in the word, and it is placed before Israel as a task with numerous examples from life if Israel does, indeed, expect the future from the proclaimed word of her God" (155).

202  Cf. A. H. Edelkoort, *o.c.*, p. 5: "Het Oude Testament pretendeert niet in zichzelf af te zijn; het is verwachting, die naar verwerkelijking jaagt; belofte die om de vervulling roept. Wie het O.T. wil beschouwen als een in zichzelf afgesloten geheel, die doet daaraan onrecht en weerspreekt zijn eigen getuigenis. Het O.T. is het boek der verwachting". And p. 13: "De Oud-Test. eschatologie is zuiver aardsch, want het toneel, waarop het gehoopte messiaansche rijk zich zal openbaren, is niet de hemel maar de aarde ... De Oud-Test. prediking is in dit opzicht niet beneden-christelijk, maar in vollen zin christelijk." G. Vos, *Bib. Theol.*, p. 55. See also above, Ch. II, notes 75 and 77.

203  See above, Ch. III, A 3: "The function of God's rest and blessing on the seventh day."

a theological interpretation takes place in "faith", because the problematic verse is understood in the light of Israel's covenant of grace and the apostolic kerygma of the New Testament.[204]

That the Creator's answer to man's fall was a judgment intent upon the promise of gracious provision, as the sure foundation of a definite religious hope, we may see confirmed by two veiled indications in Gen. 3,20-21, which can best be understood in the light of their theological connection with Israel's covenant of grace and Messianic hope.

1) The significance of Adam's calling his wife, *after* the divine curse was pronounced, with the new name "Eve", Gen. 3,20. The added interpretation "because she was the mother of all living", seems to signify an expression of trust in God's promise as implied in Gen. 3,15.[205]

2) The very significant act of God's triumphant grace to fallen man in Paradise as stated in Gen. 3,21: *"And Yahweh Elohim made for Adam and for his wife garments of skins, and clothed them."*

Von Rad points out that this act of God is "in some tension with v. 7", where is stated that Adam and Eve made themselves aprons. But how is the situation when understood in the light of the *changed* situation after the gracious promise in v. 15? Just as sin has a trans-human dimension beyond the eating of a forbidden tree, so the response of the covenant God, *Yahweh*, means more than what the eye sees, e.g., to give man an "outfit for misery" (Gunkel) or to "preserve" fallen man as such (von Rad). It seems as if the *theological* dimension of Yahweh's act of making

---

204   See W. H. Gispen, *De Christus in het OT.*, Exegetica I, 1, 1952, p. 40: "Want in de afzondering van het volk Israel gaat het om de vervulling van de beloften van de Messias als in Gen. 3:15, 12:3 etc." N. H. Ridderbos refers to this conception of Gispen in "happy agreement," in *Is there a conflict*, p. 22. Aalders, *o.c.*, p. 525. Obbink, *o.c.*, pp. 162f. H. Bavinck, *G.D.* III, 201. But von Rad, *ad* Gen. 3,15, and Loretz, *Schöpfung*, p. 136, and Fretheim, *o.c.*, p. 88, reject any predicted *victory* in Gen. 3,15 on the basis of the linguistic meaning of the verb *šuph*. In the context of the Scripture canon, and in the light of the N.T., the theological significance of the verb *šuph* appears to be understood as complete and ultimate victory; cf. Ps. 91,13; Lk 10,19. Especially Paul in Rom. 16,20 (*suntripsei*; cf. *ThWNT* VII 924, also n. 34). See further E. W. Hengstenberg, *Christology of the O.T.*, I, 1956 (repr.), p. 26. Aalders, *o.c.*, pp. 517, 408-410. J. Schelhaas Hzn, *De Messiaansche Profetie in den tijd voor Israels volksbestaan*, 1932, pp. 48f. G. Vos, *Bib. Theol.*, pp. 53ff.

205   That is to say, not a profane human hope. See von Rad, *ad* Gen. 3,20. On the basis of his interpretation of Gen. 3,15, he is forced to say, however: "One must see the man's naming of the woman as an act of faith ... certainly not faith in promises that lie hidden, veiled in penalties, but rather in embracing of life ..." But faith in life as such is fundamentally different from faith in the Lifegiver, who had just pronounced His promise of the victorious *seed*. To interpret Gen. 3,15 as the verdict of an endless struggle of man with the serpent *without hope of victory* does not establish a foundation for Adam's act of faith to embrace life. Furthermore, the theological parallel of Gen. 2-3 with Israel's covenant promise is ignored and denied.

coats of skins to clothe or cover sinful man points veiled to the divine covering of human guilt and sin.[206]

Right from the start, after the fall, the human ethos appears to be embedded in and motivated by the religious cult of animal sacrifices.[207] This leads to the vital question, How does the Old Testament present Israel's relationship between cultus and ethos, religion and morality?

### B. HUMAN PERFECTION IN ISRAEL'S CULTUS AND ETHOS

#### 1. Cultus and *Imitatio Dei*.

Our inquiry occupies itself mainly which the theological significance and function of the cultus[1] in relation to the ethos of the *imitatio Dei* in Israel's covenant.[2] The reason for connecting ethos and cultus is obvious. What counts for the whole ancient Orient, counts in a very special way for Israel: the whole life and existence were inseparably

---

206 E. Peterson, "Theologie der Kleidung", in *Universitas.* (Zeitschrift f. Wiss. K. u. Lit.) III (1948), 1409-1414, esp. 1413, has tried to indicate the theological meaning of Gen. 3,21 as follows:

"Nein, in den Kleidern, die Gott für den Menschen macht, deutet sich schon das Versprechen an, dass wir das Kleid des Paradises wiederfinden werden. Gott überlässt den Menschen nicht einfach der Nacktheit, er überlässt ihn nicht seinem schlechten Gewissen, das hinter den Feigenblättern nicht die Verzweiflung heilen kann. Dieses Kleid [sc. aus Tierhäuten von der Hand Gottes gemacht] ist vielmehr eine Erinnerung an das verlorene Kleid, das der Mensch im Paradies getragen hat."

We object to the conclusion of A. van Selms, *Genesis I, ad* Gen. 3,21, that the killing of an animal in Paradise bore no sacral character, nothing being said of the eating of the flesh. Not only because in Israel the flesh of sacrifices (Job 1,5; Lev. 1,9.13.17; 7,8) was not always eaten, but primarily because the whole event, from a theological point of view, must be interpreted in the light of Israel's cultus, in the context of sin and atonement. That God "apparently" killed the first animal appears not at all. In fact, nothing is said about the killing of an animal in Gen. 3.

207 See Gen. 4,4.

1 We join N. Ridderbos, *Psalmen en Cultus*, 1950, pp. 4, 26, in understanding by the term "cultus" not merely the sacrificial cult but also the whole public religious service and ritual centered in the sanctuary or temple. Cf. S. Mowinckel's definition of cultus in *RGG*[3] IV, 120f. (s.v. *Kultus*): "K. kann definiert werden als die sichtbaren, gesellschaftlich festgesetzten und geordneten, wirkungskräftigen Formen, durch die das religiöse Erleben der Gemeinschaft zwischen Gottheit und 'Gemeinde' verwirklicht wird und Ihre Wirkungen ausübt. K. ist somit kein Sondergebiet der Religion, sondern ein Hauptaspekt derselben, in Relation zu dem alle ihre Phänomene betrachtet werden können."

2 The central significance of the cultus in the covenant is now widely accepted in O.T. theology.

embedded and rooted in the religious cultus.[3] Yet there can be observed a peculiarity in Israel's cultus characterizing it in such a conspicuous and concrete way that it may be called in a true sense unique in antiquity.

Israel's cultus is ultimately qualified by its salvation history, i.e., the unique deliverance from Egypt by the historical Exodus and the Sinaitic Covenant which constituted Israel as the peculiar, holy people of Yahweh. This perfect salvation from the enslaving power of Egypt, as well as the following constitution of Israel as a nation at Mt. Sinai, was introduced, accompanied and commemorated by cultic sacrifices, particularly by the ritual of the paschal lamb. The unanimous religious interpretation and testimony of the Law, Prophets and Psalms are to the effect that the Exodus salvation created a unique religious-cultic relationship with Yahweh, the God of Abraham, Isaac and Jacob. In fact, by these events Israel's religion was born as a new religion, its cultic life being concentrated in a central sanctuary.[4] It is of crucial significance that Israel's cultus is not qualified and motivated by the ancient Oriental idea of preserving and renewing creation, but by a salvation-historical soteriology.[5] On this basis the theological structure and function of Israel's cultus cannot be legitimately qualified by the pagan *do-ut-des* principle.[6]

On the contrary, in Israel's cultus at the yearly offering of the First Fruits the recitation of the fundamental credo was required: that Yahweh had graciously heard the voice of crying and seen the oppression of their fathers and delivered them from bondage and given them this land "flowing with milk and honey" in fulfillment of His promise to the patriarchs.[7] Thus Yahweh was regularly being confessed cultically as the gracious Fulfiller of His promises, the merciful Lord of history and the Savior of Israel.

Israel's whole ethos of holiness, obedience and social righteousness, consequently, was conditioned by and grounded on Yahweh's prevenient saving act for the people of Israel, in faithfulness to His promise. There-

---

3  Cf. H. Bavinck, *G.D.* III, 202.

4  Cf. A. S. Herbert, *Worship in Ancient Israel*, 1963[3] ("Ecum. Stud. in Worship", nr. 5) pp. 7f.: "The decisive event which determines Israel's faith and practice is the Exodus from Egypt. It is here that Israel's history and religion truly begin." M. Noth, *History of Israel*, § 7; pp. 90ff. H. J. Kraus, *Worship in Israel*, ET 1966, p. 127.

5  Cf. Vriezen, *Outline*, pp. 280f., stressing the basically different function of Israel's cultus compared with the Babylonian. H. Wheeler Robinson, *Insp. and Rev. in the O.T.*, p. 227.

6  Vriezen, *o.c.*, pp. 279f. calls this principle "absurd" for Israel's cultus. This does not deny the actual practice of this principle in Israel's experimental religion, which must be qualified theologically as an illegitimate phenomenon. Cf. H. W. Robinson, *o.c.*, p. 153.

7  Dt. 26,3.9ff.

fore, Israel's ethos was motivated legitimately only by the response of grateful love, trust and faithfulness.[8]

How central and dominating a role this motivation of love and trust plays in Israel's religious ethos can be seen in the emphatic and totalitarian claim of the credo of Dt. 6,4ff.: "and you shall love Yahweh your God with *all* your heart, and with *all* your soul, and with *all* your might."

Here the dynamic qualification of Israel's perfection is spelled out as loving obedience to Yahweh.[9] Yet this perfect love toward Yahweh is not the mere psychological response of Israel to the divine deliverance but the religious gift and creation of Yahweh in the heart.[10]

The *cultic* setting of this perfection of religious love for Yahweh appears not only from Dt. 6,14-15, where Yahweh's exclusive claim is grounded in His attribute of "jealousy" with respect to any love of Israel for "other gods", but also from Dt. 18,9-14. Here Israel is summoned: "You shall be *blameless* [*tāmîm or perfect*] before Yahweh your God" (vs. 13). The cultic context, the polemical contrast with the "abominable practices" of syncretism, indicates that this perfection is primarily qualified by the religious cultus. Moreover, Israel's perfection, i.e., her perfect love and obedience, is stressed not as the *prerequisite* of her election but as the *consequence* of Yahweh's mighty ṣidqôt, the Triumphs of King Yahweh, by which He set Israel free not merely *from* the power of bondage but also *for* the walk or life before Yahweh, the new ethos of obedience, the holy life.[11]

Here we observe a basic continuity with Abraham's call out of Chaldea and his commission, "I am *El Šaddai*; *walk* before Me, and be blameless [*tāmîm or perfect*]" (Gen. 17,1);[12] and also with Noah's acceptable life before Yahweh, "Noah was a righteous man, blameless [*tāmîm*] in his generation; *Noah walked with God*" (Gen. 6,9).[13]

---

8  Dt. 26,16-19; 27,9-10. G. von Rad in his *O.T. Theology* I, 1962, pp. 229-231, and *Studies in Deut.*, 1953, pp. 71f. stresses the priority of the salvatory indicative before the ethical imperative. Cf. Herbert, *o.c.*, p. 8: "It was this kind of God who is celebrated in ritual word and act as also in ethical conduct and in all human relationships. This is the basis of the various codes that may be distinguished in the Torah, whatever may be their date and provenance (cf. Exod. 34; 20-23; Lev. 17-26; Deut. 19-26)."

9  Again the ethos of perfect love here (Dt. 6) is immediately rooted in and conditioned by the prevenient Exodus salvation, vss. 12.20-23.

10  Cf. Dt. 30,6.14; Jer. 32,39f.

11  See also Lev. 26,12-13, where Yahweh's covenantal fellowship ("I will walk among you") is again explicitly rooted in the Exodus salvation and is directed toward the new ethos of perfection: "made you walk *erect*." Cf. Gutbrod, in *ThWNT* IV 1035, 34f. (s.v. *nomos*).

12  See 24,40. Cf. H. Bavinck, *G.D.* III, 202, who interprets Israel's covenant as the intended explanation of Gen. 17,1.

13  Noteworthy is Gen. 6,9 b in the LXX: *tōi theōi euèrestèsen Nōe*. Cf. also LXX: Gen. 5,22.24; 17,1; 24,40; 48,15; Ps. 26 (MT 25), 3 etc.

From these descriptions of human perfection it follows that perfection here is not conceived of as a divine ideal to be strived after but as the reality of wholehearted obedient walk (*hālak*) or fellowship with God.[14] Also Israel's ethos of obedience to the covenant Torah is characterized in the Old Testament by means of the dynamic *"way"*-terminology[15] and the idea of the *imitatio Dei*, the following of Yahweh and walking after Yahweh in His way.[16]

The term *imitatio Dei* is a controversial term which is defended by E. J. Tinsley and others,[17] but rejected as a term to express adequately the Old Testament concept of covenant relationship with God, by e.g. W. P. de Boer, *The Imitation of Paul*, 1962, pp. 29-41, who states on p. 41:

> We may conclude, however, that the imitation of God is neither one of the clear teachings of the Old Testament nor an integral part of the thinking of the Old Testament people.
> The raw materials for the idea are present; it seems to be hovering in the background of certain passages; occasionally it springs to the fore momentarily.

It all depends, however, how much theological quality one attaches to the term "imitation of God", which term de Boer accepts for the

---

14  Cf. M. Buber, *Zwei Glaubensweisen*, 1950, p. 60. It is significant that *tāmîm* is continually associated with *hālak* as the hermeneutical key for the understanding of the Biblical realism of perfection.

15  See F. Nötscher, *Gotteswege und Menschenwege in der Bibel und in Qumran*, BBB 15, 1958, pp. 23ff., 47ff. J. Muilenburg, *The Way of Israel. Biblical Faith and Ethics*, 1965, p. 23: "The primary image to express conduct or behavior in the O.T. is the 'way' or 'road' (*derek*) ... The way of a man was the course he followed through life, the direction of his going, and the manner of his walking." G. Östborn, *Tōrā in the O.T.*, 1945, p. 64, following Mowinckel, interprets Torah in Deuteronomy at once as law and as "showing the way". He claims, pp. 4-22, that the etymology of *hôrah* points to the idea that Yahweh is pre-eminently the one who 'shows the way'." And now H. D. Preuss, *Jahweglaube und Zukunftserwartung*, pp. 71ff.; also his recent art. "...ich will mit dir sein!", in *ZAW* 80 (1968), 139-173; esp. 157: "Die Geschichte ist Weg mit Jahwe. Dieser Weg begann mit dem Exodus und wird stets von ihm her bestimmt (Mi. 6,1-8)."

16  See F. J. Helfmeyer, *Die Nachfolge Gottes im Alten Testament*, pp. 77-130, esp. 128f., 219. Muilenburg, *o.c.*, pp. 34ff., 34: "The divine requirements or commands are the divine ways (Deut. 8,6; Ps. 119,15). This terminology of the way is clearly a covenantal way of speaking." E. J. Tinsley, *The Imitation of God in Christ*, 1960, chs. 3, and. 4. Michaelis, in *ThWNT* V 9ff. (s.v. *hodos*) indicates that the LXX does not know of any *way* for man which would lead to God or to the possession of virtues or perfection. The concept of the *way*, on the contrary, is conditioned by the command of God from the very outset. It should be added, however: conditioned primarily by the Exodus redemption.

17  See Ch. II, n. 53; and Ch. III, A, notes 67, 71,87,102 and 111.

New Testament on the basis of the explicitly attested father-son relationship (Eph. 5,1) (pp. 71-80). On p. 78 he emphasizes that only the real children of God are, and can be, real imitators of God, which immitation is exempted from all "sense of mimicking, aping, artificially and outwardly putting on the appearance of something that is not genuine, real and heartfelt" (p. 78). He concludes on p. 80:

> It is worthy of note that when the New Testament holds God before Christians as an example to learn from and imitate, it always does so in terms of the father-son relationship existing between God and his people. The example is no philosophical, ethical or even religious ideal, it is one's own Father.... It is *self-evident* that they will be like their Father in certain basic characteristics. This is the nature of the relationship between them. (*it. sup.*)

It is true that the Old Testament does not literally state that God should be imitated. The New Testament expresses this only once (Eph. 5,1), while the thought of the imitation of Christ is expressed literally only twice (1 Cor. 11,1; 1 Thess. 1,6). It is clear that a purely statistical point of view can never be the hermeneutical norm to establish the theological concept of the *imitatio Dei* and *imitatio Christi*.

When de Boer qualifies the *imitatio Dei* in the New Testament by the underlying theological concept of the redemptive father-son relationship, we are led to the question whether this covenantal father-son relationship is not also the underlying and motivating principle of following Yahweh in the Old Testament.

We refer back to the interpretation of the *imago Dei* by Vriezen and Berkouwer,[18] who rightly indicated the concept of the father-son relationship as basic for the Old Testament religious anthropology. From this it seems that de Boer does not evaluate sufficiently the theological concept and implication of the *imitatio Dei* in the Old Testament when he dismisses it with the remark: "It can only be said that the Old Testament never made this implication [sc. of the *imago Dei* as implying the *imitatio Dei*] specific" (p. 38). Also de Boer does not recognize sufficiently[19] the *imitatio Dei* motif in such a prominent and central religious commandment as the Sabbath in Ex. 20,8-11. In his critique on Michaelis (*ThWNT* IV, 674f.), who in Eph. 5,1 gives precedence to the *obedient* following of the will of the Father, as the very manifestation of the children of God in their *imitatio Dei*, de Boer creates an artificial antithesis when he reacts, on p. 79:

> In view of the father-son relationship the situation is such that the father's characteristics, attitudes, ways of life both

---

18  See above, Ch. III, A 2; esp. n. 71.
19  *O.c.*, pp. 40f. Cf. our exposition above, Ch. III, A 3.

can and may be excepted to come to expression in the son. This happens not in the child's obedience to commands but in his conforming to the very essence and structure of being a child.

Here the father-son relationship seems to be robbed from a most essential quality, the *normativity* of the will of God as Father (cf. Prov. 4,1ff) for his redeemed children, i.e., the law *within* the covenant of grace. How sharply de Boer separates the *imitatio Dei* from Israel's obedience within the covenant of grace appears from his statement on p. 38:

> The expression 'walking in God's ways' and 'following God' express not the imitating of God, but the obeying of him and the enjoying of covenantal fellowship with him.

However, since Israel is characterized as the "first-born son" of Yahweh (Ex. 4,22; cf. Hos. 11,1; Jer. 31,9; Dt. 14,1; 32,6ff. 19), all true covenant-obedience is based on and motivated by this father-son relationship, and may *therefore* be described as genuine *imitatio Dei*, just as de Boer acknowledges for the New Testament. The many redemptive *imperatives* and summons to *obedience* in the New Testament make the *imitatio Dei* less "self-evident" in the children of God than de Boer has pictured.

Representative of the repeated[20] characterization of perfect obedience as *"following Yahweh"*, *hālak ʾaḥʾrê Yhwh*, is Dt. 13,4 (MT5):

> You shall *walk after Yahweh* your God and fear Him, and keep His commandments and *obey His voice*, and you shall *serve Him* and *cleave to Him*."

In the previous verse this *walk after Yahweh* is described as motivated by wholehearted love to Yahweh:

> for Yahweh your God is testing you, to know whether you love Yahweh your God with all your heart and with all your soul (Dt. 13,3; MT4).

To the Deuteronomist this perfect obedience evidently was not an

---

20  See Helfmeyer, *o.c.*, pp. 77ff. on 1 Kgs 14,8; 18,21; 2 Kgs 23,3, 2 Chr. 34,31; Jer. 2,2; Hos. 11,10 etc. On Ps. 63,8 (MT 9) see pp. 103f. G. Kittel, in *ThWNT* I, 211f. judges: *"Die Nachfolge Jahwes* tritt als Redeform demgegenüber [sc. the following after other gods] stark zurück... Aber die deuteronomistische Hauptaussage heisst nicht, dass Israel 'hinter Jahwe her wandeln', sondern dass es 'in seinen Wegen wandeln' soll (Dt. 5,30 uo)." See Helfmeyer's critique (p. 216) on Kittel because he does not reckon with the term "Nachfolge Jahwes zur Bezeichnung des von Jahwe als Auszugs- und Kriegsgott geforderten Gehorsams."

impossible ideal only to be strived after, but the rightful expectation and obligatory reality in Israel's life on the basis of the prevenient experience of knowing Yahweh as Redeemer.[21]

Any appeal of a miracle-working prophet or dreamer to go after "other gods" on this basis is affirmed as being not merely unthankfulness but apostasy or rebellion (*sārāh*) against Yahweh (Dt. 13,5 [MT 6]). Only Yahweh has the rightful and perfect claim on Israel since only He "brought you out of the land of Egypt and remeemed you out of the house of bondage" (Dt. 13,5 [MT 6]).

For Israel all the "other gods" are false gods because these have not revealed their redeeming power to Israel. Here Israel's salvation-historical experience from Egypt functions not just as the citation of a credo but as the foundation of an obligation, of a legal relationship. Israel has become Yahweh's peculiar possession sealed in the Covenant.[23]

Israel is obliged to follow Yahweh, i.e., to walk in the way of His laws, to imitate His manifestations of redeeming love and mercy. In this Israel will confess and recognize Yahweh's claim of exclusivity[24] in the spirit of gratefulness[25] and "joyfulness and gladness of heart".[26] In short, the idea of the *imitatio* of Yahweh is rooted in the salvation-historical motif and motivated by wholehearted covenant love, trust and obedience

---

21 See also Jer. 2,2 whereon Helfmeyer, *o.c.*, p. 91, remarks: "Die Nachfolge selbst besteht zunächst darin, dass Israel auf dem Weg durch die Wüste hinter Jahwe hergeht, ist also zunächst räumlich zu verstehen. Aber der Kontext und die synonym verwendeten Begriffe *ḥsd* und *ᵓhbh* weiten das nur räumliche Verständnis aus zu einem theologischen." Cf. Tinsley, *o.c.*, p. 34; also note 1 on p. 34: "There is a similar alternation in the N.T. Gospels between *hodos* meaning first, the actual particular journey Jesus made, and second, the way of life his historical journeying has made possible."

22 Cf. Helfmeyer, *o.c.*, p. 79.

23 Dt. 27,9f.; 26,16-19. Cf. *ibid.*, p. 79: "Durch die Herausführung aus Ägypten hat sich Jahwe an Israel Eigentumsrechte erworben, so dass die daraus sich ergebende Nachfolge Jahwes nicht in das Belieben Israels gestellt ist im Sinne einer unverbindlichen, wenn auch motivierten Aufforderung, sondern im Sinne einer rechtlichen Verpflichtung."

24 Cf. the claims of exclusivity in the Hittite vassal treaties. See G. E. Mendenhall, *Law and Covenant in Israel and the Ancient Near East*, 1955, esp. pp. 33f.

25 Helfmeyer, *o.c.*, p. 129: "Das in der Nachfolge sich ausdrückende Vertrauen auf Jahwe, der seine Verheissungen erfüllt, ist durch die vorausgehenden Taten Jahwes begründet. Wenn also Israel seinen Gott nachfolgt, erfüllt es lediglich eine Dankespflicht." Cf. Tinsley, *o.c.*, p. 35: "The continuing dominance of the imagery of the 'Way', with its suggestion of movement and advance, meant that for the Hebrew mind the contemplation of God must take not the static form of thinking about the being and perfection of God, but the dynamic form of conforming one's conduct to what he had shown himself to be during the journey to the Promised Land."

26 Dt. 28,47.

to Yahweh. Israel's *perfectio* is her *imitatio Dei*, i.e., her following of Yahweh in the religious-cultic ethos.

A vital element is stressed with peculiar force in the Deuteronomic theology of history: *the prerequisite to enter and inherit the promised land is complete following of Yahweh!* In his paraenetical exhortation to Israel in Dt. 1 Moses is using Caleb as an example for all who will enter the good land. Explaining why Israel as a whole, except its children, is not allowed to enter the land – because they "rebelled against the command of Yahweh, and were presumptuous" (Dt. 1,26.43), "murmured" (1,27), and "did not believe Yahweh" (1,32), which they recognized as their sin (1,41) – he stresses the reason why Caleb will enter and inherit the land:

> "he shall see it, and to him and to his children I will give the land upon which he has trodden, because he has *wholly followed* [*millē' 'aḥªrê*] Yahweh!" (Dt. 1,36).

When the Caleb story (Joshua 14,6-15) explains why Hebron is given to Caleb for an inheritance "to this day", it points three times to Caleb's faithful following of Yahweh!

> "But my brethren who went up with me made the heart of the people melt; *yet I wholly followed Yahweh my God.* And Moses swore on that day, saying, Surely the land on which your foot has trodden shall be an inheritance for you and your children for even because you have *wholly followed Yahweh* my God." (Josh. 14,8-9). So Hebron became inheritance of Caleb ... *because he wholly followed Yahweh*, the God of Israel (vs. 14).

This passage is intended to be an exhortation to *all* Israelites to follow Yahweh fully, not as a glorification of Caleb (and Joshua, Num. 32,12) only.[27]

In Israel the priest, the prophet, and the king were called to be *ex officio* the exemplifying figures of the true following or imitation of Yahweh for all the people.[28]

---

27  Cf. Helfmeyer, *o.c.*, pp. 95-101; 100: "Die Betonung menschlicher Treue in diesem Text stellt klar, dass die Landnahme – als Geschenk Gottes – abhängig ist von dem Verhalten des Menschen Gott gegenüber und dass durch das gottwidrige Verhalten Israels der Besitz des Landes in Frage gestellt ist, ein typisch dtr Gedanke."

28  Cf. Tinsley, *o.c.*, p. 37: "Israel's vocation to walk in the 'Way' of the Lord was embodied in the three exemplifying figures of the O.T.: the king, the priest and the prophet. These three functionaries manifest activities, as E. Jacob says (*Theol. of the O.T.*, ET 1958, 233), which are performed in their perfection by God himself."

As the king was declared to be "son" of God, this implied that the king pledged to follow his Father-God in obedient submission to the priestly Torah, Dt. 18,18f.[29]

The context of the *following-of-Yahweh* passages in the Books of Kings and Chronicles further reveal their fundamental *cultic* application in polemical contrast with the surrounding syncretistic world.[30] This culminates in the dramatic manifestation of Elijah's exclusive claim of Yahweh on Mt. Carmel, 1 Kgs 18,21,[31] and in Josiah's cultus reform with the restoration of the *Passover* in particular, 2 Kgs 23,3ff.21; 2 Chr. 34,31-33; 35,1-19.[32]

The concrete result of the royal following of Yahweh is *cultus reform* centered in the Passover celebration according to the Deuteronomic covenant, Israel's festival *par excellence*.[33]

This leads us to the question, What is the theological relation between the perfect following of Yahweh and the *cultus*, the Passover in particular, within Israel's covenant?

In his stimulating study *De Heilsbedeutung des Pascha*[34] Notker Füglister has indicated that the first Passover occurrence at the Exodus materially connects two covenants, the Abrahamic and the Sinaitic covenant, into a close unity. The Passover-Exodus salvation, however, not only presupposes and leads to a divine covenant; the Passover salvation is also itself largely identical with the Covenant salvation.[35] The Sinaitic covenant may be described "nicht so sehr als Ziel des Pascha-Geschehens, sondern vielmehr als die Entfaltung und Sichtbarmachung des im Pascha-

---

29  Also Israel as a whole is called "son(s)" of God, Ex. 4,22; Hos. 11,1; Dt. 14,1; 32,6; Jer. 31,9, which therefore defines Israel's obedience to the Torah as obedience of sons. Cf. Tinsley, *o.c.*, pp. 38f.

30  Cf. Helfmeyer, *o.c.*, p. 81.

31  How much the *imitatio Dei* is identified with cultic obedience to the Torah appears from Elijah's rebuke of Ahab and the reparation of the altar of Yahweh, 1 Kgs 18,17.30.

32  See Helfmeyer, *o.c.*, pp. 83-88; 85: "Der durch die Ausschliesslichkeit der Jahweverehrung bedingte polemische Charakter der Nachfolge Jahwes kommt in diesem Zusammenhang zum Ausdruck durch die mit dem Bundesschluss verknüpfte Kultreform."

33  See W. D. Davies, *Paul and Rabbinic Judaism*, 1965², pp. 102ff.

34  StANT VIII, 1963, pp. 233f., referring to Gen. 15,13ff.; 17,7ff.; 46,3f.; Ex. 2,24f.; 6,3-8; 32,13; Dt. 7,8; Ps. 105,8-11.42-45; etc.

35  Füglister, *o.c.*, pp. 236ff. Appealing to Jer. 31,32; 34,13f. (*beyôm, en hēmerai*) and Galling's *Erwählungstraditionen*, he concludes: "Der Pascha-Exodus und der Sinaibund formen also bereits im at. lichen Denken insofern eine innige, unauflösbare Einheit, als sie im Grunde genommen ein und dasselbe Heilsgeschehen sind und den Inhalt ein und derselben Heilstat bilden. M.a.w.: im Pascha ist der Bund bereits eingeschlossen; Pascha und Bund sind eins" (237).

Ereignis und im Pascha-Heil bereits keimhaft enthaltenen Bundesgedan-kes und Bundesheiles." [36]

Passover celebration thus at the same time was also cultic covenant celebration, both having the same content and object.[37]

The day of Passover was explicitly instituted as a memorial day of the Exodus salvation and, consequently, as the ground of Israel's existence.[38] The cultic *anamnesis* of Passover intended not merely to represent the historic Exodus every year as a contemporaneous reality to be appro-priated by Israel,[39] but also the "Hineinversetzung" and basic identi-fication with the original redemption of the Exodus.[40]

The Passover ritual thus functions not merely as the subjective com-memoration of the *magnalia Dei*, but also as the objective sacramental participation in the Exodus salvation.[41]

This *double* aspect of the cultic Passover celebration [42] is implied in the

36  *Ibid.*, p. 241, on the basis of his observation that the Passover contained all the constitutive elements of a divine covenant: "die Bundesidee, das Bundes-gebot, das Bundesversprechen, das Bundeszeremoniell" (p. 240).

37  *Ibid.*, p. 246.

38  Ex. 12,14.17; 13,3.8-10.

39  Davies, *o.c.*, pp. 102ff. has tried to show this from the Haggadah and Mišnah Pesaḥim, on the basis of Ex. 13,8. He concludes on p. 104: "These questions will make it clear that the real member of the Old Israel is he who has appropriated to himself the history of his people: he has himself been in bondage in Egypt, has himself been delivered therefrom." Also Muilenburg: *o.c.*, p. 32: "It is the function of the cult to bring past events and future events into the immediacy of the present hour by the spoken words." See J. Pedersen, *Israel* III-IV, pp. 376-465. Tinsley, *o.c.*, pp. 51-56, esp. p. 53: "The cultic mime as a means whereby the past crucial events were made contem-porary would explain many of the features of the Book of Deuteronomy."

40  H. J. Kraus, *Gottesdienst in Israel* ("Beiträge z. evang. Theol." 19) 1954, pp. 125-128, has emphatically indicated that the center of Israel's religious cult was the dramatic *representation of salvation history*. However, not in the sense that the cultus is the place in which the original salvation history reappears, but as the sacrament which gives participation in the first Exodus salvation and covenant. He states on pp. 127, 128: "Vergegenwärtigung ereignet sich in Israel nicht in der Weise, dass die ursprüngliche Situation der Begegnung Gottes mit Israel der versammelten Gemeinde nahegebracht wird – vielmehr wird die Gemeinde in die Ursprungssituation hineinversetzt... So ist denn der Gottesdienst Israels vornehmlich dadurch bestimmt, dass die im Kultus sich ereignende Erneuerung die versammelte Gemeinde in das Heilgeschehen hineinversetzt."

41  Cf. J. Muilenburg, "A Liturgy on the Triumphs of Yahweh", in *Studia Biblica et Sem.*, *FS* Vriezen, 1966, pp. 233-251, with lit. He states on p. 233f.: "It is the most primitive of the affirmations of the old credos (Dt. 26:8; 6:21-23; Josh. 24 : 6-7; 1 Sam. 12:6), and from early times to late was celebrated and contemporized in song and ritual, Ps. 66 : 1-7; 74:12-17; 77:11-20; 80:1-3; 89:8-10 (Hebr. 9-11); 114; 135 : 8-9; 136:10ff. Cf. also Ps. 105:23-45; 106:8-12; Is. 63:7-14 ..."

42  Tinsley, *o.c.*, p. 55 defines this as "liturgical mysticism".

theological significance of the Biblical verb "to remember", which is basically reciprocal for the partners of the covenant.[43] As far as the subjective commemoration is concerned, it did cultivate Israel's faith, hope and love,[44] and stimulate the will to obey and follow the covenant Torah, i.e., the ethos of the *imitatio Dei*, on the basis of the Exodus salvation. This aspect is continually emphasized in the Old Testament as the motivation and legitimization of Israel's ethos of holiness[45] and love, e.g., Deut. 11,1: "You shall *therefore* [sc. the Exodus salvation] love Yahweh your God, and keep His charge, His statutes, His ordinances, and His commandments always." Also Israel's ethos of social right-eousness is thus founded and rooted in the Exodus deliverance, e.g., Lev. 19,36:[46]

> "You shall have just balances, just weights, a just ephah, and a just hin: I am Yahweh your God, who brought you out of the land of Egypt."

However, when Füglister speaks of Israel's cultic Word-commemo-ration of the Exodus deliverance as effective "on the psychological level" merely and "preponderantly subjective",[47] this limitation seems to divorce the cultic Word-commemoration from the power of the divine Word-event, which would rob the word of the Torah from its dynamic character, its creative reality.[48]

---

43 Füglister, *o.c.*, p. 230, points to Ex. 12,42 for Yahweh's remembrance of the passover night: "a night of watching by Yahweh". "Nun bedeutet aber in der at. lichen Mentalität Jahwes Gedenken nicht nur ein bloss subjektives Sich-Erinnern oder ein rein effektives Nicht-Vergessen, sondern ein objektiv-effektives, wirkmächtiges und Wirklichkeit schaffendes Eingreifen und Heils-handeln." Cf. O. Michel, in *ThWNT* IV, 678f. (s.v. *mimnèiskomai*), who indicates that esp. Deuteronomy presents "a theology of *remembrance*" (Dt. 5,15; 1,18; 8,2.18; 9,7; 15,15; 16,3.12; 24,18.20.22; 32,7). "Alle 'Erinnerung' steht im Dienst der Reinerhaltung des Glaubens" (679, 5f.).

44 See Ex. 14,31; Ps. 106,12 (faith); Dt. 7,17-19; 20,1 (hope); Dt. 6,5 (love); cf. Füglister, *o.c.*, p. 229: "Mit Recht kann deshalb gesagt werden ... : die Gegenwartsbedeutung der alttestamentlich-jüdischen Paschafeier und die den Teilnehmern daraus erwachsende konkrete Frucht bestand in der Er-weckung und Auferbauung des Glaubens, der Hoffnung und der Liebe."

45 See Lev. 17-26. Cf. Füglister, *o.c.*, p. 228: "Ist es doch sehr aufschluss-reich, feststellen zu können, wie tief die mannigfaltigsten at. lichen Gebote und Vorschriften im einmalig-vergangenen Pascha-Exodus-Geschehen ver-ankert sind und aus ihm heraus motiviert und legitimiert werden." See p. 229, referring to Num. 3,12f.; 8,17f. (conc. Yahweh's claim on the first-born and the substituting Levites); Dt. 28,1-8 (conc. Yahweh's right on the first fruits); 5,15 (conc. the rest of the Sabbath).

46 Cf. also Lev. 25,39ff.55; Dt. 15,15 conc. the impoverished brother; Lev. 19,33f.; Ex. 22,21; 23,9; Dt. 10,19; 24,17f. conc. the stranger.

47 *O.c.*, p. 229.

48 Cf. Dt. 30,14: "But the word is very near you, it is in your mouth and

The human commemoration of Yahweh's acts and words can never be conceived as an autonomous psychological event, being an independent constitutive factor in the efficacy of the cultic remembrance.

The act of Israel's Word-commemoration is already rooted in and called forth by Yahweh's prevenient command and, therefore, inseparably connected with the creative promise of blessing.

Consequently, to reduce the commemorative aspect of Israel's Passover cult to the activation of the "psychological-subjective" faith, hope and love would mean to break the given correlation between faith and promise.

As far as the *objective, sacramental* aspect of Israel's sacrificial Passover cult is concerned, with its ministration of the blood of the paschal lamb, we stand directly *vis-à-vis* Yahweh's remembrance of His promise of atonement and protecting forgiveness, the renewal of His saving fellowship. Füglister[49] rightly states:

> Bei jeder Opferdarbringung wird zudem Jahwe segnend gegenwärtig (vgl. Ex. 20,24), und beim Opfermahl – also auch beim Pachamahl – tritt man in heilsmächtige Gemeinschaft mit ihm.

In other words, the cultic remembrance of Passover signified theologically the dynamic renewal of Yahweh's forgiving and protecting fellowship together with a renewed incitement to the covenantal *imitatio Dei*.[50]

## 2. Does the Old Testament define perfection as sinlessness?

Did Israel's faith equate the walk of blamelessness or perfection with ethical sinlessness? It seems appropriate to investigate specifically those categories of Scripture which contain the terms *tāmîm* and *šālēm: the Book of Psalms, the Wisdom Literature,* and the *Book of Chronicles.*[51] The Psalms may be regarded as the "official"[52] and legitimate answer

---

in your heart, so that you can do it." Also Pedersen, *Israel* I-II, pp. 167f.: "Behind the word stands the whole of the soul which created it ... He who utters a word to another lays that which he has created in his own soul into that of the other, and here then must it act with the whole of the reality it contains."

49 *O.c.*, p. 231.

50 Cf. Tinsley, *o.c.*, p. 59: "Israel's love of God, for example, was to be an imitation of God's love of Israel. Not only in liturgy but in ordinary life there was to be a mimetic tribute to the kind of love shown by God during the basic period of the Journey from the Red Sea to Zion, [quoted Dt. 10,15ff.]". See also p. 60.

51 The books of *Chronicles* represent the priestly-prophetic historiography.

52 Cf. N. H. Ridderbos, *De Psalmen* I, 1962, p. 45: "De Psalmisten moeten eerder gezien worden als vertolkers van wat in de harten van een gemeenschap leeft, dan als mensen, die hun strikt persoonlijke geloofservaringen onder

of Israel to the Torah, the foundation of Israel's religion.[53]

The Psalms reproduce and conserve, as it were, the Torah in Israel's cultus,[54] in her liturgy, her songs and prayers, in short, in her religious life and ethos. Even the (possibly) original non-cultic psalms, as 1,34,37 and others, obviously have for their object exhortative religious and moral instruction.[55]

Derivatives of the stem *t m m* occur 21 times in the Psalms.[56]

The wisdom literature reflecting Israel's ethos in its practical wisdom[57] contains 33 such references.[58] As far as the books of Chronicles

---

woorden brengen. In de psalmen beluisteren we dus de uitingen van Israëls 'officiële' geijkte vroomheid." S. Mowinckel, "Psalms and Wisdom", in *Wisdom in Israel and in the Ancient N. East, FS* H. H. Rowley, 1955, pp. 205, 222. H. J. Kraus, *o.c.,* p. Lxxlv: "'Private Frömmigkeit' gibt es im Psalter nicht. Die Sänger der Klage- und Dankpsalmen kommen immer schon vom Gottesdienst der Israelgemeinde her" (referring to Ps. 22,5f.26).

53 Cf. W. H. Gispen, *De Christus in het O.T.* ("Exegetica"), 1952, p. 39: "Er bestaat nl. een zeer nauw verband tussen het boek der Psalmen en de Pentateuch ... Met recht kan men het boek der Psalmen beschouwen als een echo der gemeente, haar antwoord op de Tora." Cf. *ibid., Indirekte gegevens voor het bestaan van den Pentateuch in de Psalmen?* 1928. B. Jacob, *ZAW* 17 (1897), 279: "Die Psalmen sind ... das Echo des gläubigen und willigen Herzens auf das Gesetz der Thora."

54 S. Mowinckel, *Psalmenstudien* VI, pp. 8-65. Gispen, *De Chr. in O.T.,* pp. 39f., refers to the fact that all the great historical facts recorded in the Pentateuch meet with a wide response in the poetical songs, e.g. Pss. 11; 18; 29; 78; 95; 105; 106; esp. 19 and 119. Cf. H. J. Kraus, *Psalmen* I[2], BK 1961, pp. Llv ff.; Lxxlv (on the "individual songs of Lament and Thanksgiving") "Die Formeln und Formulierungen sind der Welt des Kultus erwachsen." On the relation of the Psalms with the cultus see the critical evaluation of N. H. Ridderbos, *Psalmen en Cultus,* who stresses the phenomenon that Israel's poetry occurred in a definite style, i.e. the cultic style. Of great significance is his remark: "Daarbij werkt goddelijke opzet. De bewoordingen van de Psalmen zijn opzettelijk algemeen gehouden, opdat deze liederen voor later gebruik geschikt zouden zijn, opdat de kerk van alle eeuwen met de woorden van deze liederen haar nood zou kunnen klagen, haar uitreddingen bezingen" (p. 29).

Cf. also A. R. Johnson, "The Psalms", in *The O.T. and Modern Study* (ed. H. H. Rowley, 1951), pp. 198f.

55 See Mowinckel, "Psalms and Wisdom", in *o.c.,* pp. 213f., 217.

56 According to G. Lisowsky, *Konkordanz z. Hebr. A.T.,* 1958[2]: Pss. 7,9 (ET 8); 26,1.11; 41,13 (ET 12); 78,72; 101,2; 25,21; *tām* (complete, perfect) 37,37; 64,5 (ET 4); *tom* (perfection, integrity) *tāmim* (complete, perfect, blameless): 15,2; 18,24 (ET 23).26 (ET 25).31 (ET 30).30 (ET 32); 19,8 (ET 7); 37,18; 84,12 (ET 11); 101,2.6; 119,1.80. No reference to *šālēm.*

57 Both Job 28,28 and Prov. 15,35 associate wisdom with "the fear of Yahweh". Mowinckel, *o.c.,* pp. 206ff. defends the thesis that in the circles of the 'wise man' a psalmography also originated: "The psalmists have learnt from the learned men, and the learned men have learnt from the psalmists: when they are speaking of the greatness and wisdom and justice of God, they often do so in the form of a hymn, just as their instruction about the 'two

are concerned, not one reference to *t m m* is found; they contain, however, the term *šālēm* 9 times, of which 8 are directly related to *lēb(ab)*.[59]

### a. The religious-moral ground plan of the Psalms and Wisdom literature.

Basic to the Psalms as well as the Wisdom literature is their common ground plan of dividing all men into only two contrasting categories or classes: the righteous (*ṣaddîqîm*) and the wicked (*rešāᶜîm*).[60]

The *ṣaddîqîm* are those who love and fear Yahweh, and do "what is right" to their fellow Israelites when these also are suppressed and persecuted, i.e., they live in loving obedience to the whole Torah.[61] The *rešāᶜîm*, and these are also found within Israel, are those who basically have a different way and basis of existence, since they lack this principle of love for Yahweh and His Torah as the motivation of their actions.

roads', the road of virtue and the road of vice, not infrequently has the form of the blessing or the cursing word" (p. 208).

W. Baumgartner, "The Wisdom Literature", in *The O.T. and Mod. Study*, p. 215, rightly opposes the suggestion which makes "wisdom an offshoot of the cultus", but also denies any connection with the psalms. Although Israel's Wisdom relates itself explicitly only incidentally with the cultus (Prov. 15,8; 21,3) as this did not constitute her theme, the protestations of one's righteousness (e.g. Job 31) and the contrast of the wise (as the righteous) with the foolish (as the wicked) are originally rooted in the cultus.

Cf. also H. J. Hermisson, *Sprache und Ritus im altisr. Kult*, 1965, p. 146: "Auch die Entstehung über 'Tod' und 'Leben', die ursprünglich im Kultus auf dem Spiel stand, das Lebensangebot des Kultus, ist zuletzt von der Weisheit usurpiert worden (Prov. 8,35f.)."

He also points to Ps. 74: "hier spricht ein 'Weiser' im Kult" (*ibid.*). According to H. J. Kraus, Pss. 1; 37; 49 and (partly) 119 belong to the class of Wisdom literature.

58  *Tōm*: Job 4,6; 21,23; Prov. 2,7; 10,9; 10,29; 19,1; 20,7; 28,6; 13,6; *tām*: Job 1,8; 2,3; 8,20; 9,20.21.22; Ct 5,2; 6,9; Prov. 29,10; *tûmmāh* (perfection, integrity): Job 2,3.9; 27,5; 31,6; Prov. 11,3; *tāmîm*: Job 37,16; 12,4; 36,4; Prov. 11,5; 28,18; 11,12; 2,21; 11,20; 28,10. No reference to *šālēm*.

59  1 Chr. 12,39; 28,9; 29,9.19; 2 Chr. 8,16 (connected with: house); 15,17; 16,9; 19,9; 25,2.

60  Prov. 2,20-22; 10,6f. 11. 16. 20f. 24f. 28-32. Especially Pss. 1 and 37 emphatically project this alternative Cf. N. H. Riddebos, *De Psalmen* I, p. 69, on Ps. 1: "Deze psalm spreekt van de twee wegen, zie vs. 6. Getekend wordt de tweeërlei bestaanswijze en het tweeërlei lot van rechtvaardigen en goddelozen." Also p. 70: "Voor het besef van de dichter zijn er slechts twee soorten van mensen: 'rechtvaardigen' en 'goddelozen'..." See further p. 47. A. Cohen, *The Psalms*, Soncino, 1945, pp. xlll and 1. Cf. however already Ex. 23,7.

61  Ps. 15,4; cf. 1,2; 18,1f. (MT 2f.); 19,17ff. (MT 8ff.); 119,14-16,35. N. Ridderbos, *o.c.*, p. 73 (on Ps. 1) rightly stresses the vital point that this obedience to the covenant law is no legalistic Pharisaic piety, but one motivated and legitimated by true love and delight in the Torah of Yahweh: "de wet is voor hem geen drukkende last..." And p. 211 (on Ps. 19): "In de wet ontmoet de dichter de levende God."

They are inimical to Israel's covenant and Davidic King.

The two different relations to Yahweh and His Torah manifest themselves necessarily in two fundamentally different ways of life or behavior, i.e., of religious and social ethos.[62]

The deepest motive of Israel's morality in cultus and *ḥokmāh* is, however, the *yir'at Yhwh*.

The wicked one or fool in Israel is therefore ultimately characterized not by his immorality but by his irreligiosity; he says in his heart: "There is no god", i.e., he does not reckon with God.[63]

What the Psalms and Proverbs continually stress and evaluate is therefore not simply the difference in ethos as such, important as this may be, but the ethos in connection with its source and fate.[64] Basic to the Psalms and Wisdom Literature is the experience of the fear of Yahweh, i.e., the spiritual knowledge of God through the Torah and the cultic covenant experience of Yahweh's atoning grace.[65]

This characterized the *ṣaddîq* basically not as the mere virtuous or ethically perfect one but as the *homo religiosus* who, motivated by Yahweh's redemptive love, wholeheartedly loves, trusts and obeys Yahweh according to the cultic and socio-ethical commandments of the divine covenant.[66]

This means that also Israel's ethics of social righteousness is conditioned and qualified by cultic redemption and blessing.[67]

G. von Rad has indicated that the ultimate norm for the determination

---

62  Ps. 1,1 successively points to sins of thoughts, acts, and words. Cf. N. Ridderbos, *ad* Ps. 1,1; also p. 47.

63  Cf. N. Ridderbos, *ad* Ps. 14,1: "Andere dingen zullen meer in het oog gevallen zijn: zedelijke verdorvenheid, verdrukking van de rechtvaardigen; maar de dichter laat zich niet op een dwaalspoor brengen: *hij ziet de wortel*" (it. suppl.). G. Ziener, *Die Theol. Begriffssprache im Buche der Weisheit*, BBB 11, 1956, p. 26: "Wenn Ps. 14,1 (vgl. Ps. 10,4) der Tor spricht: 'Es gibt keinen Gott', so will er nicht die Existenz Gottes bestreiten, sondern nur seiner Überzeugung Ausdruck geben, dass er ungestraft das Gesetz Gottes übertreten könne."

64  Pss. 1; 16; 37; 73; Prov. 10.

65  See Pss. 25,14; 102,15; 111,10.5; 119,38; 130,4; Job 28,28. Prov. 1,7; 3,7; 9,10. Eccl. 5,7; 12,13. Torah is understood as the gracious revelation of Yahweh's will, not merely the Decalogue but also the cultic ordinances of atonement for forgineness. Cf. W. Eichrodt, *Theol. of the O.T.*, II, pp. 268-277, 309-310. Vriezen, *Outline*, pp. 253-256.

66  Cf. N. H. Ridderbos, *De Psalmen* I, p. 60: "De mens is 'rechtvaardig', als hij in zijn verkeer met God en mensen beantwoordt aan de verplichtingen van het verbond; 'rechtvaardigheid' mag dan ook niet op één lijn gesteld worden met zondeloosheid." And p. 47: "'Rechtvaardigen' zijn echter niet mensen die de zedelijke volkomenheid nagenoeg bereikt hebben; het zijn geen zondeloze mensen, maar mensen, die, wanneer ze in zonde vallen, hun zonden belijden, en bij de Here vergeving zoeken." H. J. Kraus, *Psalmen* I, p. lxxv: "Der *ṣaddîq* aber ist der gemeinschaftstreue, im bundesgemässen Wandel lebende Mensch."

67  Cf. e.g. Deut. 25,13-16; Lev. 19,36; Prov. 11,1; Job 31,6.

of the righteous and the wicked one, for life and death, was the *cultic* decision!

> Wo ist denn der Ort, von dem aus Israel das Wort vom Leben, von Jahwe als dem Geber oder Verweigerer des Lebens gehört hat? ... es wurde Israel vom Kultus aus zugesprochen.[68]

The conclusion of his investigation is:

> Die letzte Entscheidung über Leben und Tod fiel also für Israel im Kultus; da erst wurde der Einzelne seines Lebens gewiss.[69]

Even when we acknowledge the indissoluble interrelationship and unity of Israel's cultus and ethos, we observe that the *ṣaddîq* is ultimately determind by his relationship to the cultus and not by his morality as such, let alone ethical perfection or sinlessness, since the cultus judges the quality of his ethos and decides his fate, life or death.[70]

The Psalms and the Wisdom Literature associate *perfection* with *righteousness* so closely that righteousness and perfection or blamelessness are used as virtual synonyms.[71] This means that the terms perfection, blamelessness, integrity and righteousness are all ethical terms defined by Israel's religious-cultic covenant with Yahweh.

b.  *Perfection in cultus and ethos: sinlessness?*

Neither the Torah nor the Psalms base themselves on the dogmatic *a priori* that the sincere Israelite can live in obedience to Yahweh's Law *without* atonement, *without* the need of forgiveness, i.e. *sinless*.[72]

On the contrary, the Psalms reveal the need and necessity for Yahweh's

---

68  *Ges. Stud.*, p. 235, referring to Dt. 30,15.19; Ez. 18,5-9; Lev. 18,5 as functioning within the liturgical-cultic setting of life.

69  *Ibid.*, p. 236. How this principle developed into a cultus mysticism which spiritualized the cultic institutions into a living spiritual reality, von Rad has impressively set forth on the basis of Pss. 16,5-11; 23; 27,4; 36,8-10; 63,3-6; 73,23-28; 142,6 (pp. 238-244).

70  Pss. 15; 24; 5,4-7 (MT 6-8). Cf. Ridderbos, *De Psalmen* I, p. 47: "De cultus maakt scheiding. Zij, die op een wettige wijze deelnemen aan de cultus, zijn rechtvaardig, de anderen zijn goddeloos".

71  Cf. already Gen. 6,9 with respect to Noah; Job 12,4 (Job); Pss. 7,9 (ET 8); 15,2; 18,22-23; 37,17-18; Prov. 11,5 (the righteousness of the blameless (ones) *tāmîm*); 13,6 ("Righteousness guards him whose way is upright, perfect, *tōm*); 20,7 ("a righteous man who walks in his integrity, perfection, *bᵉtûmmô*). Also *yāšār* (uprightness) is used synonymously with perfect(ion) and righteous(ness): Job 1,1.8; 2,3; Pss. 25,21; 37,37; Prov. 2,21; 11,3.

72  Gen. 8,21; Lev. 4f.; Pss. 14,1-3; 40,7ff.; 143,2; 130,3f., cf. Job 14,4; 1 Kgs 8,46 (= 2 Chr. 6,36); on the prophet's view of sin, see N. H. Snaith, *The Dist. Ideas*, 1957[7], pp. 65-68.

continual *forgiving* and *keeping* redeeming grace,[73] e.g., Pss. 19,12-14; 139,23-24. Generally speaking, the Psalms reveal as their leading emotion an aroused[74] consciousness of sin and contrition, not only because of some sinful act, but because of one's sinful being.[75] To the psalmists deliverance or redemption therefore means primarily salvation from *sin*, and secondarily also from distress.[76]

This is the situation because the psalmists are deeply convinced of their standing in guilt before Yahweh and, consequently, live in genuine contrition of heart, i.e., the conviction of personal sinfulness in relation to Yahweh. This deep idea of sin of the individual psalmist exceeds the ceremonial ideas of uncleanliness and purification.[77]

### aa) *Psalm 19*

Psalm 19 intensifies the priestly distinction of sins done *bišegāgā* (by error, inadvertently) and sins done *beyād rāmā* (with a high hand, presumptuously) as taught in Num. 15,27-31,[78] since David in the Psalm prays

> But who can discern his errors [*šegî᾽ôt*] ?
> Clear Thou me from hidden faults [*nistārôt*].
> Keep back thy servant also from presumptuous sins; let them not have dominion over me!

---

73 Yahweh's *ḥesed*, although rooted in the divine essence, and motivated by the general human weakness and sinfulness, is determined by the historic Covenant of grace, Pss. 25,10; 103,8.17f.; 89,1f.14 (MT 2f.15). Cf. J. J. Stamm, *Erlösen und Vergeben im A.T.*, 1940, pp. 140f., with lit. on *ḥesed*, p. 93, n. 1.

74 This repentance is not the product of an autonomous insight in evil, but the covenant gift of Yahweh who reveals the awful dimension of sin in the eyes of God by means of distress and the death of the sin offerings.

75 Pss. 51,5; 58,3; cf. G. van der Leeuw, *Religion in Essence and Manifestation* II, 1963 (German 1933), p. 522 (§ 78,2): "it is the *Book of Psalms* that exhibits the true nature of sin and guilt more clearly than perhaps any other literature...." H. J. Kraus, *Psalmen* I, p. 387 (contra H. Gunkel): "Das A.T. betont die totale Verderbnis, die wurzelhafte Schuldverfallenheit der menchlichen Existenz in einer ganz anderen Wucht als die kirchliche Erbsündenlehre."

76 J. J. Stamm, *o.c.*, p. 132f., referring to Pss. 32,5; 51,3ff. 9f.; 130,1-4; 25,7.11; 41,4.

77 Stamm, *o.c.*, p. 134: "Die Sünde ist als gegen Jahwe gerichtete Handlung verstanden (vgl. bes. Ps. 41,5), demgemäss kann sie nur durch ein Vergebungswort Jahwes annuliert werden."

78 W. Eichrodt, *Theol. of the O.T.* I, p. 161, suggests that both types of sins originally were practically distinguished by penitence, confession and reparation on the one hand, and impenitent contempt for the Law and open apostasy on the other hand. The Priestly Code later would have limited the applicability of the sin offerings simply to the inadvertent transgression of some commandment, see Lev. 4,13f. 22f.; 5,1-10.

Then I shall be blameless and innocent of great transgression.[79]

He prays for forgiveness (,,Clear Thou me") of his errors or hidden sins, i.e. sins of which he is still unconsious,[80] and for Yahweh's restraining grace to keep him from any conscious or presumptuous sin,[81] which could not be atoned for in the sanctuary.[82]

The conclusion of faith is: "Then I shall be blameless [ʾêtām, Qal. impf. of tāmam] and innocent of great transgression."

Here perfection is undeniably indicated to be *not* inherent sinlessness but *the persistent walk of life in dependence on Yahweh's forgiving and restraining grace.*[83] This perfection is felt to be at once *requirement* (as in Gen. 17,1) and *gift.*[84]

N. Ridderbos' observation is therefore to the point:

> Deze dichter beseft ten volle de rijkdom van de wet, maar weet dat hij aan die wet, op zichzelf gesteld, niet genoeg heeft, dat hij leven moet van de vergeving, vs. 13, en bewaring, vs. 14, van de HERE.[85]

In others words, the psalmist realizes that the law as such cannot make perfect. His basic need is expressed in the entreaty for forgiveness. *Forgiveness* here is indicated primarily as judicial salvation from the guilt of sin: "Clear Thou me" [naqqēnî].[86] But it points beyond mere judicial acquittal or innocence.

Ps. 19 points to the living source of a perfect socio-ethical relationship, the personal covenant fellowship with Yahweh.[87] Sin, causing separation and alienation from Yahweh,[88] is basically characterized by *enmity* to

79  Ps. 19,12-13 (MT 13-14).
80  Unconscious sins which became conscious could be forgiven by sacrificial atonement, Lev. 4,27-31; 5,2-6. Cf. Cohen, *ad* Ps. 19,13: "He therefore prays for purification from *hidden faults*, those undiscovered to himself."
81  The Hebrew can also be translated by "presumptuous men"; see, however, J. Ridderbos, *De Psalmen* I, 1955, pp. 169f. H. Bout, *Het zondebesef in het boek der Psalmen*, 1952, pp. 18f.
82  Cf. 1 Sam. 3,14; 15,24ff.
83  Cf. N. Ridderbos, *ad* Ps. 19,14: "Hier blijkt duidelijk, wat dit woord inhoudt, nl. niet zondeloosheid, maar op het gebed vergeving ontvangen voor de verborgene zonden, en zich in Gods kracht wachten voor afval" (pp. 214f.). J. Ridderbos, *ad l.*, significantly points to the addition "innocent of great transgression" (p. 169).
84  J. Ridderbos, *o.c.*, p. 169.
85  *O.c.*, p. 214.
86  Cf. Ps. 32,5 ("Thou didst forgive [nāsāʾtā, take away] the guilt [ʾawôn] of my sin [ḥaṭṭāʾtî]"). The guilt is weighing "like a burden too heavy", Ps. 38,4. Cf. Quell, in *ThWNT* I, 281, 36ff. (s.v. *hamartanō*).
87  Cf. Ps. 25,14; 42,1f.
88  Ps. 44,23ff.; 88,14; 89,46; 143,7; cf. also Is. 59,2.

Yahweh.[89] When sin is taken away[90] by forgiveness, Israel is therefore restored in the blessed knowledge of friendship and perfecting communion with Yahweh[91] and delivered from physical oppression.[92] The Hebrew understanding of forgiveness is realistic in that it does not separate guilt from the act or life of sin.[93]

Consequently, forgiveness also has a definite bearing upon the ethical life. It implies the taking away of all ruling power of sin,[94] i.e., the subduing of the sinful passions of the natural heart by the restraining power of Yahweh, the gracious $Gō^{\jmath}ēl$.[95] In Ps. 51 forgiveness is equated with a creative act of God in the heart of the contrite sinner.[96] His sin is not only remitted but he is also cleansed from his sin so that his heart is transformed into a clean heart, a clear conscience and a new obedient spirit. His guilt is taken away from him, the power of sin is conquered, broken and subdued in him. Israel's cultus therefore confesses in Ps. 19 that a perfect heart is not an attribute of human nature or the product of law and morality, but the gracious gift of redemption. Its reality does not consist of an inherent sinlessness but of forgiveness of inherent sinfulness and the continual reception of the keeping power of Yahweh, the Redeemer. This dynamic existential reality the Psalmist experiences

---

89   Cf. Van der Leeuw, *o.c.*, (§ 78,1), p. 518: "Conscience cries out to man that he hates God. The will that is hostile to God arises from man's deepest being."

90   Cf. J. J. Stamm, *o.c.*, p. 131: "Auch in den Psalmen, wie in den übrigen Teilen der alttest. Literatur, meint Vergebung die Aufhebung der zwischen Jahwe und dem Volk oder Jahwe und dem Einzelnen stehenden Sünde."

91   Ps. 25,14. Cf. Jer. 31,31-34, where forgiveness results in a new $da^{c}at$ $Yhwh$, a new $b^{e}rît$.

92   E.g. illness or persecution, Ps. 107,20; 103,3; cf. Ps. 41,4; 25,18; 79,9. Cf. Stamm, *o.c.*, pp. 131f.: "In Befreiung von Not hat das Volk schon in der Vergangenheit die Vergebung seines Gottes erfahren (Ps. 78,38; 99,8). In des Volkes Zukunft wird die Vergebung sichtbar im Nachlassen von Jahwes Zorn und in der Wiederherstellung des Landes und seiner Bewohner (Ps. 85,2f.)." See also pp. 144-147.

93   Significant is the fact that the Hebrew uses the same word for guilt and sin; e.g. Ps. 32,4-5. Cf. Quell, in *ThWNT* I, 280: "Die Promiskuität des Sprachgebrauchs in dieser Hinsicht lehrt, dass an einer scharfen begrifflichen Unterscheidung von Sünde und Schuld dem Hebräer nicht viel gelegen war, da der kausale Zusammenhang zwischen normwidriger Handlung und normwidrigen Zustand nicht dem mindesten Zweifel ausgesetzt war." Only the term *āšām* (and deriv.) in priestly law specifically indicates the objective character of sacral guilt, and is identical with uncleanliness. See also p. 281.

94   J. Ridderbos, *o.c.*, p. 169: "Wie in de zonde valt, wordt... door haar overheerst." N. Ridderbos, *o.c.*, p. 214: "Hij weet er van, dat hij alleen in Gods kracht tegen de zonde kan strijden."

95   Ps. 19,14 (MT 15).

96   Ps. 51,10. Cf. Stamm, *o.c.*, p. 132: "Was der Beter nach der Vergebung erhofft, ist zunächst nichts Aeusseres, sondern ein reines Herz und ein neuer Geist."

through the Torah in which he, consequently, meets the holiness and joy of Yahweh Himself. How far he is removed from abstract legalism his praise of Yahweh's Torah shows, in that it both makes him wise unto the fear of Yahweh and revives and rejoices his soul "sweeter also than honey", vss 7-11 (MT 8-12).

This Psalm reveals that Israel's perfection constitutes the dynamic movement of the soul between the two poles of the *fear of Yahweh* and the *joy in Yahweh*[97], on the basis of a living, personal communion with Yahweh in the way of the Torah.

Personal perfection is not described in terms of a sinless nature, but of gracious fellowship with the holy and merciful covenant God.

The Psalmist, therefore, offers this Psalm to Yahweh with the prayer that the meditation of his heart might be *acceptable* ($l^e r\bar{a}\bar{s}\hat{o}n$)[98] to God as a true offering! This reveals a very personal relationship[99] in which the deep consciousness of sin is correlated with the intense joy of salvation.[100]

bb) *Psalm 15 in cultus and ethos.*

In Ps. 15 we encounter *tāmîm*, perfection, as cultic requirement for entering the sanctuary and enjoying Yahweh's protection and blessing:

> O Yahweh, who shall sojourn in Thy tent? Who shall dwell on Thy holy hill? He who walks blamelessly [*tāmîm*], and does what is right [*ṣedeq*], and speaks truth [*ʾemet*] from his heart.[101]

After these three more general positive indications, the psalm consists of elucidating these by seven more specific negative Torah require-

---

97  Cf. Mowinckel, *Psalmenstudien* II, 130, who rightly refers to Ps. 130,4 interpreting the fear of Yahweh as: "die Angst vor der Sünde, die Dankbarkeit, die Liebe, das Vertrauen zu Gott, die Ehrfurcht vor ihm, den Heiligen, der sich auch in der Verzeihung und der Gnade als Heilig betätigt, weil Verzeihung eben Entfernung der Sünde und der Unreinheit ist."

98  Cf. Kraus, *ad l.* Mowinckel, *Ps.St.* VI, 53: "So spricht nicht ein Mensch, der sich von der Kultreligion emanzipiert hat, möge er über das blutige Tieropfer denken wie er wolle." Weiser, *o.c.*, p. 204, regards this "dedicatory formula" of Lev. 1,3f. as "proof" that this prayer is offered as a *substitute* for the sacrifice. This is uncertain, however. The same holds good for Ps. 141,2; cf. Thompson, *o.c.*, p. 156.

99  See also Ps. 19,14b (MT 15): "O Yahweh, my Rock and my *Gōʾēl*."

100  Ps. 19,8 (MT 9); cf. 4,7 (MT 8); 63,5-7 (MT 6-8). On the central and fundamental position of joy in the O.T., see W. Eichrodt, *Man in the O.T.*, 34f. H. van Oyen, *Ethik des Alten Testaments*, 1967, p. 18: "Denn das Leben nach dem Gesetz ist ein Leben in der Freude. Wer dem Ungehorsam verfällt, in dessen Leben hat die Freude ein Ende (vgl. Kl. 5,15)."

101  Ps. 15,1-2.

ments,[102] all dealing with the socio-ethical conduct within the covenant setting.[103] The psalm ends with the (priestly[104]) assurance of eternal unshakableness, returning to vs. 1. This psalm is recognized as belonging to the class or type of established "entrance or Torah-liturgies" which mention the general characteristics of the *ṣaddîq* as legitimation for participation in the cultus.[105]

This procedure of cultic requirements and professions of loyalty and innocence seems strange in the light of Israel's historical Exodus deliverance, since Israel is already legitimated to participate in the cultus on the basis of this historic covenant relation with Yahweh.

This redemptive-historical soteriology indeed emphatically remains the foundation for Israel's cultus and ethos.[106] The fact that also the *Priestly Code* has framed its cultus in a redemptive-historical setting implies the comprehensive claim that Israel's cultus is legitimated and

---

102   Ps. 15,3-5. See *ad l.* H. Gunkel, *Die Psalmen*, 1968[5], and N. H. Ridderbos, *De Psalmen* I, 1962.

103   The appeal to Yahweh, vs. 1, presupposes the Covenant. It is most remarkable that no cultic, ceremonial or nationalistic requirements but only moral ones are mentioned. Vs. 4 stresses, however, that the social ethos must be rooted in and qualified by the religio-cultic connection with Yahweh. This fundamental interrelationship of religious experience and ethos, developed emphatically in Ps. 1, underlies the whole book of Psalms. Cf. K. Koch, "Tempeleinlassliturgien und Dekaloge", in *Stud. z. Theol. der at. lichen Überlieferungen*, ed. R. Rendtorff und K. Koch, 1961, p. 59: "Es wird überall [sc. in Pss. 15; Is. 33] gegen ein unrechtmässiges Gewinnstreben und damit gegen wirtschaftliches und soziales Unrecht Stellung genommen."

104   Cf. Gunkel, *o.c.*, p. 49.

105   K. Koch, *o.c.*, pp. 45ff., esp. p. 50. H. J. Kraus, *Psalmen* I, pp. 111f., referring to similar confessions of obedience and innocence in Dt. 26,13ff.; Job 31; Ez. 18,5-7; Ps. 24. Gunkel (und J. Begrich) calls Is. 33,14-16 and Mi. 6,6-8 "prophetische Nachahmungen" (*Einleitung in die Psalmen*, 1966[2], p. 408, n. 4). See esp. G. von Rad, "'Gerechtigkeit' und 'Leben' in der Kultsprache der Psalmen", in *Ges. Stud.*, p. 227: "Wer sich diesen Forderungen unterwirft, der ist Gott wohlgefällig und ist ein Glied der grossen Kult- und Lebensgemeinschaft mit Jahwe." J. L. Koole, "Psalm XV – Eine Königliche Einzugsliturgie?" in *OTS* XIII (1963), 98-111 ably defends the possibility, if not probability, that Ps. XV primarily is dealing with the royal liturgy of enthronement, esp. pp. 104ff., referring to Ps. 21,7 and Ps. 101. Significant is his conclusion: "Andererseits wird hier deutlich, dass der König vor Gott auf genau gleicher Ebene steht mit seinen Beamten und mit dem ganzen Volke" (109). See also p. 110.

106   This is well worked out by W. Gutbrod, in *ThWNT* IV, 1029-1037 (s.v. *nomos*). Concerning the predominantly negative formulation of Israel's religious-ethical laws and Torah-liturgy (besides Ps. 15, cf. Ex. 20; Lev. 19,11ff.; Ez. 18,5-9), Gutbrod's theological qualification is significant: "Dadurch [sc. der negative Char.] wird nochmals deutlich bestätigt, dass der theologische Ort dieses Gesetzes der Bund der Erwählung ist, es wird nicht *geboten*, was die Zugehörigkeit zu Jahwe verschafft, sondern *verboten* was sie aufhebt" (1030,22ff.). Esp. 1031, 3ff.

rooted in Yahweh's historical saving acts and revelation.[107]

But more than that, Israel's festival cult as a sacred drama "remembers" the historical facts of salvation, thereby turning them "into new effectual reality by Yahweh's presence at the festival. All he formerly did, gave, and secured, he does and gives and secures again when he 'appears' at his festival."[108]

From the theological point of view, however, the soteriological character of the cultus requires Israel to *abide* and *stay*[109] in the gracious covenant communion with Yahweh by faithfully seeking counsel, refuge and joy in Yahweh's cleansing presence in the sanctuary.[110]

"Guestship" with Yahweh to many a Psalmist meant a mystical experience of eating and drinking, which probably began in the literal eating and drinking of the sacrificial meal. (Ps. 36:9, 23:5-6, 27:4, 63:6). The frequent thank offerings on the fulfillment of a vow speak of real joy in sacrificial worship.[111]

Morality *as such*[112] did not permit Israel to participate in the life-giving blessing[113] of the cultus, but Yahweh's "rich grace":

But I through the abundance of Thy steadfast love [$b^e r \bar{o} b$

---

107   Cf. Gutbrod, *o.c.*, 1035, 22ff.; also: "Er unterstreicht damit, dass der überweltliche, heilige Gott nicht unpersönliche *Kraft*, sondern persönlicher Wille ist." "So äussert sich in [priesterlichen] Gesetz die Souveränität des schaffenden u erwählenden Gottes, u es bestimmt, wie das Leben der Menschheit – u des Israels – diesem heiligen Gott gemäss sein kann. Von diesem Gesetzesverständnis aus ist das positive Gesetz bei P zu verstehen" (1035, 26f., 34ff.).

108   S. Mowinckel, *The Psalms in Israel's Worship* I, 1962, p. 19.

109   Cf. Gutbrod, *o.c.*, 1030, 46ff. about the objective of the Torah: "Es will die Bindung des Volkes und des Einzelnen an Jahwe allein gewährleisten".

110   See Pss. 16; 27; 36; 63 and 73 which testify of a living cultus mysticism which finds deep spiritual satisfaction, divine guidance and assurance in an intimate communion of life with Yahweh. Cf. G. von Rad, in *Ges. Stud.*, pp. 239ff., who speaks about a *visio Dei*. E. Würthwein, *ThLZ* 72 (1947), 145 is fully justified in concluding: "Viele Worte des Alten Testaments, vor allem des Psalters, sind Zeugnis dessen, dass man das Heil im Kultus nicht nur suchte sondern auch fand."

111   R. J. Thompson, *Penitence and Sacrifice in early Israel outside the Levitical Law*, 1963, p. 139.

112   Cf. G. von Rad, *Theol. des A.T.* I, p. 375; ET 1962, p. 378.

113   Cf. Mowinckel, *o.c.*, p. 17: "What the congregation wants to achieve through the cult, and what the 'power' from God is to create, is *life* – in the most comprehensive sense of the word... The Israelites expressed the same idea by the word 'blessing'. Blessing is to be created, increased, and secured through the cult..." Cf. J. Pedersen, *Israel* I-II, pp. 182ff.; 211: "We see that the blessing comprises everything in life."

*ḥasdᵉkā*] will enter Thy house, I will worship toward Thy holy temple in the fear of Thee.[114]

How precious is thy steadfast love, O God!
The children of men take refuge in the shadow of thy wings. They feast on the abundance of thy house, and thou givest them drink from the river of thy delights. For with thee is the fountain of life.[115]

This does not mean that morality was irrelevant, but at least that it was not the ultimate basis for participation in the cultus. Yet the ethos of righteousness and perfection, i.e., the wholehearted moral obedience to the spiritual covenant law ,the Decalogue, is upheld as the requirement for dwelling with Yahweh and for the reception of the cultic blessing.[116] The *rᵉšāᶜîm*, all who delight in wickedness and evil, the boastful, deceitful men who speak lies, are explicitly excluded from the cultus. This seems to indicate that the legitimate cultic [117] relation with Yahweh not merely *bestowed* the blessing of a new or recreated heart, as confessed in Pss. 19,13; 24,5; 51,10, but that the cultic blessing could be *renewed* and *maintained* only when the soul had not rebelled in presumptuous sin by choosing to walk in his own crooked way in apostasy from the covenant community.[118]

114   Ps. 5,7 (MT 8); cf. 69,13.
115   Ps. 36,7-9 (MT 8-10); cf. also Pss. 16,1-5; 23; 63,3-6; 73,23-28; 142,5.
116   See also Ps. 24,3-5; 118,19-20; Is. 26,2. Here a striking contrast with the heathen cultus becomes apparent, as observed by F. C. N. Hicks, *The Fullness of Sacrifice*, 1946³, p. 94: "To be a guest of Baal meant sensual indulgence and gross immorality: to be a guest of Yahweh meant the character described in Psalms XV, XXIV 1-6." Cf. A. Weiser, *The Psalms. A commentary*, 1962 (German 1959⁵), p. 169: "The spiritual grandeur of the psalm [15] rests on the high level of its ethics." Also Gunkel.
117   Ps. 5,4-6 (MT 5-7). Cf. Prov. 15,8, Ps. 1,5. N. Ridderbos, *De Psalmen* I, p. 74, n. 8. Von Rad, *Ges. Stud.*, p. 231 has rightly stressed that there were only two possibilities. The Israelite was either righteous or wicked: "Alle Zwischenstufen, alle die mittleren Färbungen, die einer menschlichen Bewertung so geläufig sind, fehlen durchaus." K. Koch, "Tempeleinlassliturgien", in *o.c.*, p. 51: "Steht zwischen den Kultgenossen eine ungeklärte Verleumdung, eine nicht gesühnte Gewalttat, ein Eidbruch oder ein Verhältnis von Gläubiger und Schuldner auf der Basis einer Zinsforderung, so ist für die bevorstehende Feier die erforderliche Einheit der Gemeinde gestört."
118   This Biblical cultic-ethical dialectic is also indicated by Mowinckel, *Psalmenstudien* I-II, p. 334: "Bezeichnend für die irrationale Art der lebendigen Religion ist es, dass die Reinigung der Gemeinde, die Wegschaffung aller Sünden und die Ausrottung aller Frevler, die Ps. 15 und 24 als Forderung, als Bedinging des Heils stellen, an anderen stellen als eine Gabe Gottes, als ein Teil des Heils dargestellt wird." Cf. his stimulating treatises on pp. 146ff. (Die Gaben) and pp. 178ff. (Die Forderungen). When A. Weiser, *o.c.*, p. 171, ends his interpretation of Ps. 15 by stating that this psalm "lacks the truth of the Gospel that man is incapable of being perfectly obedient by virtue

O continue thy steadfast love to those who know thee, and thy salvation to the upright of heart! Let not the foot of arrogance come upon me, nor the hand of the wicked drive me away.[119]

In order to stay within the covenant the Israelite had to know his God, i.e,, walk with Him, sensing *Yahweh's holiness* and his own sinful weakness, longing for Yahweh's continuing grace of forgiveness and cleansing, since Yahweh's burning holiness and kingly honor could not bear with an unholy and unclean people which was enslaved to or divided by sin.[120]

> Klaus Koch, however, supposes that the entrance liturgy (Pss. 15; 24; Mi. 6; Is. 33) had lost its *use* and *sense* in *post*-exilic time since Israel then no longer possessed "indisputable rectitude":

> > Eine Einlassliturgie ist aber nur so lange sinnvoll wie man bei den Pilgern eine unfragliche Rechtschaffenheit voraussetzen kann. Geschehen jedoch die kultischen Handlungen hauptsächlich zu dem Zweck, aus Sündern wieder rechtschaffene Menschen zu machen, so wird eine solche Tora sinnlos, weil sie beim Laien vor Betreten des Heiligtums voraussetzt, was er erst im Heiligtum gewinnen kann.[121]

> This evaluation is based on more than one curious *a priori;* first, on the presupposition that Israel in pre-exilic time was "unfraglich" perfect; secondly, on the presupposition that in post-exilic time the function of the cultus became primarily that of atonement, which would mean the changing of sinners into pious and righteous men; and that in view of *such* a function the entrance liturgy then became meaningless ("sinnlos"!), since this liturgy pre-

of his own strength..., but can reach that goal only by the grace of God, who, forgiving man his moral weakness and sins, grants him that commission by his own free will," he affirms a moralistic viewpoint which is based on an illegitimate, isolated consideration of the Torah liturgy by itself, cut off from its inalienable setting within the transforming grace of cultic atonement and from its living root in the prevenient salvation-historical grace. See our consideration of Ps. 19,12f., and Ps. 15.

119   Ps. 36,10-11 (MT 11-12).

120   Cf. Mowinckel, *o.c.,* p. 166: "Welche einzelnen Güter bilden nun den wichtigsten Inhalt des 'Segens', des 'Frieden', des 'Heils'? Zunächst braucht das Volk *Reinigung* und *Sündenvergebung.* Denn der kommende König ist der heilige, furchtbare, verzehrende Jahwä, der nichts Unreines und 'Abscheuliches' duldet. Er kann nur in der Mitte eines reinen und heiligen Volkes wohnen. Unreinheit und Sünde sind aber auch an sich böse Mächte, die die Seele und die Kraft des Volkes vergiften." P. 167: "Das heisst nicht nur, dass er ihre Sünden vergibt, ihre Unreinheit entfernt, sondern auch, dass er ihr vereiteltes Glück, ihr Heil, ihren 'Frieden', die zerbrochene 'Ganzheit' wieder herstellt." See further pp. 168f.

121   "Tempeleinlassliturgien", in *o.c.,* p. 60.

supposed in the worshipper what the sanctuary would now bring him. These presuppositions are accepted by Koch as a dogmatic *a priori*. We feel, however, that in this way no justice is done either to the fundamental theological significance of Israel's cultus to renew the refreshing fellowship with Yahweh, or to the qualification of Israel's cultic ethos. In the first place, Koch's statement that the proper function of the entrance liturgy presupposes *"unfragliche* Rechtschaffenheit"* implies for Koch that such "perfect" people do not primarily need atonement. With respect to atonement, G. Buchanan Gray[122] has already indicated that not merely sin – and guilt – offerings but also burnt offerings, Lev. 1,4, and even "the sacrificial system as a whole is expiatory", on the basis of Lev. 17,11.[123] His balanced conclusion is to the effect that the expiatory character of sacrifice was "in the earlier periods of the history of Israel anything but unknown or even exceptional."

This should prevent such a sharp contrast between pre- and post-exilic times with reference to cultic atonement as Koch maintains. Furthermore, Israel's self-understanding of socio-ethical perfection did not exclude but included the consciousness of sinfulness and the need for atonement, e.g., 1 Kgs. 8,46; Ps. 143,2. To willful sinners, the *rešā<sup>c</sup>îm*, the cultus categorically denied any legitimate participation in its blessing of atonement. But to repentant sinners the entrance liturgy was definitely not senseless, because they walked in the way of cultic perfection. It is, however, a fateful fundamental misconception of Israel's cultus to suggest that the entrance liturgy is "senseless" for those who are thereby legitimated to draw near to the presence of Yahweh, as if the beholding of Yahweh's power, glory and beauty[124] brought no new element to the worshipper's perfection!

The prerequisite of approaching Yahweh's presence in the Sanctuary at the cultic festival was not a record or sense of sinlessness, but the confession[125] of sin and guilt with the conviction of personal shortcoming and national failure, of unconscious deviations and sinfulness, in short, the spirit of true *repentance* which longs for re-establishment in God's

---

122 *Sacrifice in the Old Testament*, 1925, pp. 67ff, 82ff., esp. p. 76. The quotation is from p. 95.

123 See his references to the expiatory character of sacrifices in pre-exilic times, together with the eucharistic nature of he cultic festivals, pp. 82ff. Cf. also Füglister, *Die Heilsbedeutung des Pascha*, pp. 77ff., 250ff.

124 Pss. 63,2; 27,4.

125 Cf. H. Brongers, "Schuldbelijdenis en Genadeverkondiging in het O.T.", in *Kerk en Eredient*, IX (Sept. 1954), 135-144, who differentiates between collective and individual confessions of guilt. See also P. A. H. de Boer, "De Voorbede in het O.T.", *OTS*, III, 1943, 144ff. N. Johansson, *Parakletoi. Vorstellungen von Fürsprechern für die Menschen vor Gott in der alt.lichen Religion, im Spätjudentum u. Urchristentum*, 1940.

covenant and revitalization of the soul and unification of the people as a whole.[126] An Israelite whose eye was thus directed upon Yahweh and whose heart thus waited for this God, stood in the right covenant relation with Yahweh. Such a soul was considered cultically as righteous and perfect, and was permitted to participate legitimately in the cultus and to receive its blessing.[127] This reveals the profound spirituality of the cultic Torah liturgy, which is akin to the depth of the Sermon on the Mount, in that it is not satisfied with the mere external compliance with the moral commandments, but relates the socio-ethical "perfection" and righteousness to the inward truthfulness of the human heart, Ps. 15,2.[128] This immediate root-relation of the *walk* (ethos) with the condition and motivation of the *heart* is the characteristic structure of the Torah (esp. Dt.), the books of Kings (I-II) and Chronicles (I-II), the book of Psalms and the Proverbs.

The conspicuous theological quality of this spiritual structure is the incessant and emphatic requirement of a *whole* or perfect heart before Yahweh. When King Solomon consecrated the Temple to the religious cultus, he acknowledged before the altar of Yahweh the reality of sin in each man,[129] but then pronounced the blessing:

> *that he may incline our hearts to him, to walk in all his command-ments,* his statutes, and his ordinances, which he commanded our fathers ... *Let your heart therefore be wholly true* ["wholly true", in MT: *šālēm*] *to Yahweh our God, walking in his statutes and keeping his commandments, as at this day.*[130]

Here Solomon in the cultic service acknowledges that the *perfect* heart, which manifests itself in the ethos of a *walk* in wholehearted, moral obedience to the covenant laws, is first of all the covenant *gift* of Yahweh. The perfect walk is rooted in the perfect heart, which is possessed and motivated by Yahweh's "inclining" power of grace.

The answer to Solomon's prayer is Yahweh's assuring promise:

---

126   Pss. 25,6f., 11; 51,17.19 (ET); 34,18; also Is. 55,7; 57,15; 66,1. Cf. Mowinckel, *o.c.*, p. 167: "Nun ist aber immer die Voraussetzung des Festes, dass der Bund im Laufe des soeben vergangenen Jahres zerrüttet worden ist; Israel – oder gewisse Israeliten – haben immer Sünden begangen, die als Bruch der Bundesverpflichtungen gelten (Ps. 81; 95; 50). So sind damit alle gewisser-massen 'ungerecht' geworden und bedürfen der Rechtfertigung."
127   Pss. 123; 130; 131; 48,9ff.; 65,1ff.; also Is. 26,2-4 righteousness and "perfect peace" (*šālôm šālôm*) are conditioned and qualified by keeping faithfulness, trust in Yahweh, a mind stayed on Yahweh. Cf. von Rad, *Ges. Stud.*, pp. 230f.
128   Cf. Weiser, *o.c.*, p. 169.
129   1 Kings 8,46.
139   1 Kings 8,58.61.

My eyes and My heart will be there for all time. And as for you, *if you will walk before Me*, as David, your father walked, with integrity of heart [b<sup>e</sup>tom-lēbāb] and uprightness [b<sup>e</sup>yōšer], doing according to all that I have commanded you, and keeping My statutes and My ordinances, then I will establish your royal throne over Israel forever ... But if you turn aside from *following Me*, you and your children ... then I will cut off Israel from the land which I have given them; and the house which I have consecrated for my name [the Temple!] I will cast out of my sight.[131]

From this it appears, first that *šālēm* (1 Kgs 8,61) functions as a complete synonym of *tōm* (1 Kgs 9,4); secondly, that *šālēm* and *tōm* describe the religious-moral condition of the perfect heart as manifesting itself in the ethos or walk of obedience, which is acceptable to Yahweh; thirdly, that the perfection or integrity of heart together with the (wholehearted) obedient walk are considered as an indissoluble unity, defined as *following* Yahweh[132]; and finally that the Temple and its whole religious cultus do not function legitimately when they are divorced from the ethos of the concrete covenant walk and life.

When the correlation between cultus and ethos is broken, Yahweh will reject and destroy the cultus, i.e., bestow the covenant curse (Lev. 26) upon the cultus and Israel. It is within this framework of Yahweh's covenant that all the Psalms, and Ps. 15 in particular, and the Proverbs are placed and to be understood. The almost exclusive concentration on the social ethos in the Torah-liturgy as prerequisite for the cultic participation reveals, however, a realistic sense of the titanic tensions between cultic salvation and factual ethos in Israel.

The solution to these covenant-disturbing tensions is never sought in the separation or the substitution of the one (e.g. ethos) for the other (e.g. cultus).[133] On the contrary, the cultus here emphatically upholds the ethos of social righteousness as the rightful manifestation and

---

131  1 Kings 9,3bf. 6f.; cf. Ps. 78,72, where David's royal leadership is described as tending the sheep of Israel "with upright heart" (RSV), or, more literally, "according to the integrity of his heart [k<sup>e</sup>tōm l<sup>e</sup>bābô]".

132  In this light all the texts with *šālēm* in Kings and Chronicles are to be interpreted: 1 Kgs 11,4; 15,3.14; 2 Kgs 20,3 (= Is. 38,3; as confession of Hezekiah, which is accepted by Yahweh!); 1 Chr. 28,9; 29,19; 2 Chr. 15,17; 16,9 (here the seer Hanani equates the *šālēm* heart with trust and reliance on Yahweh, vs. 7); 19,9 (Jehoshaphat charges Levites and priests to be true and wholehearted judges); 25,2 (denying Amaziah a *šālēm* heart because of idolatry, vss. 14f.).

133  See H. J. Hermisson, *Sprache und Ritus im altisr. Kult. Zur "Spiritualisierung" der Kultbegriffe im A.T.*, 1965, pp. 118f. who discusses the validity of the three theses: 1) Gerechtigkeit statt Opfer. 2) Gerechtigkeit als Opfer. 3) Das Opfer eines Gerechten... (ist wohlgefällig), and rightly rejects the first two. Also p. 140.

necessary realization of cultic salvation.[134] And this may well be affirmed. When the cultic encounter with Yahweh's presence and power of salvation transformed the *heart*, the center of human existence and motivations, then moral conduct in all its actions will be determined thereby.[135]

The cultus therefore was justified in claiming the ethos of social righteousness or perfection as its legitimate *fruits*[136] and in this sense as its legitimation. Whence then did the tension and discrepancy between cultus and ethos arise?

From at least two causes: 1) from the participants in the cultus; 2) from the priesthood.

Ad 1) *The subjective condition of the cultic participant.*

As the gift of salvation in the cultus was no magic or automatic working power,[137] but personal encounter with Yahweh, on each participant was resting the responsibility of faith to appropriate fully this gift with all his heart in all his conduct; i.e., not to withhold any segment of his heart, will or life from service to Yahweh, his Lord. Yahweh is not satisfied with less than 100% of the heart and life, was the penetrating message of the entrance or Torah liturgy.[138]

Yet, according to Ps. 50, the tension between cultus and ethos did develop into an untenable disharmony and judgment-evoking contrast:

But to the wicked [in Israel!] God says: 'What right have you to cite My statutes, or take My covenant on your lips? For you hate discipline . . ."[139]

---

134   Cf. N. Ridderbos, *o.c.*, p. 164: "Het gaat er juist om de cultus tegen ... verval en denaturering te beschermen ..."

135   Pss. 15,2; 24,4; 51,10.12; 143,10; Prov. 4,23ff. See H. J. Kraus, *o.c.*, pp. 113f. on the legitimate authenticity of the ethos in the cultus, not as mere prophetic influx.

136   Cf. also Is. 5,1-7.

137   Kraus, *o.c.*, pp. 115, 116: "Die Heilsgabe im altt. Kult ist kein magisches Kraftzentrum, sie wird nicht bei jedem Fest in unpersönlicher Fülle ausgeschüttet." "Sein Kult ist keine naturhafte, magische Kraftzufuhr ..." Mowinckel, *Psalmenstudien* I-II, p. 167: "Der Segen ist nicht etwas, was voraussetzungslos von aussen her in den Mensch hineingelegt werden kann."

138   Cf. N. Ridderbos, *o.c.*, p. 164: "Zo klinkt ons hier tegen de boodschap, die Israël zo dikwijls is ingescherpt, dat de Here niet tevreden is met een uitwendig eerbetoon, maar dat Hij het hele leven voor zich opeist, vgl. 40:7 vv.; 50; 51:8 v.; 1 Sam. 15:22; Hos. 6:6; Am. 5:21 vv.; Jes. 1:11 vv.; Mi. 6:6 vv., enz." Kraus, *o.c.*, pp. 115f. points to Josh. 24,15.21.23f., where Joshua appeals to Israel on the basis of its responsibility in the covenant with Yahweh: "Then put away the foreign gods which are among you, and *incline your heart to Yahweh*, the God of Israel." Also Gutbrod, in *ThWNT* IV, 1030, 35 (s.v. *nomos*): "Der Herrschaftsanspruch dieses Gottes lässt keine neutrale Zone übrig."

139   Ps. 50,16f. Reference is made to the *systematic* transgression of three commandments of the Decalogue, stealing, adultery, and false witnessing, vss. 18ff.

Here the profession of righteousness with the lips no longer reflected the condition of the heart and life, since the heart here was fully bent on evil, cherished sin, and openly rejected *mûsār*, discipline.[140] Such religious-ritual formalism is declared by the "prophetic judgment-liturgy" (Kraus) to be *wickedness*, godless "religiosity", or at bottom *forgetting God*.[141] From such Yahweh witholds His salvation,[142] showing it only to the "perfect of way".[143]

Consequently, not the unconscious errors or sinfulness as such were the cause of the tension and the falling apart of cultus and ethos, but the conscious persistence and cultivation of sinful desires and practices of the natural heart against the fellow-Israelite.

Where selfishness thus reigned unbroken as the way of life, and sin had become the cherished system, there the deepest sin was unrepentance, the guilty neglect or forgetting of the *reality* of God's daily proffered cultic salvation. To those the Torah-liturgy forbade the hypocritical, formalistic participation in the cultus. Those could never truly affirm the ethos of the entrance liturgy of Ps. 15 as their heart desire[144] and way or direction of life, since they had already turned away from the cultus with their heart.

Ad 2) *The priestly failure.*

Psalm 50 already may suggest that not merely the common people of Israel formalized the cultus ritual. Israel's systematic departure from the true cultic experience could well indicate a tendency among the priesthood to misunderstand the function of the sacrificial cult, especially under the influence of post-Davidic syncretism, see vss. 8-15.[145] After Mowinckel's epoch-making study on the "cultic prophets",[146] G. von Rad,[147] E. Würth-

---

140 Kraus, *o.c.*, p. 379: "*Mûsār* bezeichnet die 'existentielle' Bindung des Gehorsams und der Zucht, in die Jahwes Bund und Bundesordnung den Menschen hineinstellen (vgl. Jer. 2,20; 5,3; 7:28; Prov. 15,10)".

141 Ps. 50,22; cf. Is. 29,13ff.

142 Ps. 50,23; cf. 91,16.

143 We follow the text correction *tam derek* in vs. 23; see Kittel *ad l.*; J. Ridderbos, *ad l.*; Kraus, *o.c.*, p. 371.

144 E.g. 15,2: "and speaks truth from the heart"; cf. Kraus *ad l.*: "Sind die innersten Denkbewegungen und Willensrichtungen 'treu' und 'zuverlässig'?"

145 Cf. Kraus, *o.c.*, p. 377: "Jahwe klagt sein Volk nicht an, *weil* diese Opfer vor ihn gebracht werden, sondern er weist streng die Wirkungen zurück, die man sich auf seiten der Opfernden verspricht... In die bestehende und in Israel rezipierte und regulierte Opferinstitution hat sich offensichtlich eine heidnisch-magische und das ganze kultische Leben beherrschende Vorstellung eingeschlichen." See further p. 378.

146 *Ps. St.* III (1922): "Kultprophetie und Prophetische Psalmen"; cf. p. 3: "Die *These*, die im Folgenden zum Beweis gestellt werden soll, ist nun diese: der prophetische Form gewisser Psalmen entspricht eine kultische Wirklichkeit." Followed by H. Junker and A. R. Johnson. For a critical evaluation on the official status of temple-prophets, see H. W. Robinson, *Insp. and Rev.*,

wein,[148] R. Rendtorff,[149] and H. J. Hermisson[150] greatly contributed to the understanding of the Old Testament relationship of prophetism and cultus on the basis of the form-critical method.

It has become clear now that, according to the Priestly Code and the Law of Holiness, it was priestly responsibility and commission to pronounce officially whether the sacrifices, presented to them, were acceptable and accepted by Yahweh as pleasing to Him, or not. This official pronouncement of approval (or refusal) took the form of a special "declaratory formula"[151] in which the judgment on the cultic sacrifice always was identified with that on the offerer himself.[152]

The sacrificial animal had to be perfect in every respect, $tāmîm$, in order to be acceptable for priestly atonement before Yahweh[153]: "to be accepted [$l^e rāṣôn$] it must be perfect [$tāmîm$]; there shall be no blemish [$mûm$] in it."[154] Also the cultic requirement of eating the sacrificial meat within *two* days was the condition on which the offering and the offerer were to be accepted and atoned.[155] It was the priestly formula which declared Yahweh's acceptance ($rāṣôn$) in the cultic offering,[156]

pp. 222-225; N. W. Porteous, "Prophet and Priest in Israel", in *ExpT* 62 (1950/51), 4-9.

147 "Die Anrechnung des Glaubens zur Gerechtigkeit", in *Ges. Stud.*, pp. 130ff.; *O.T. Theology* I, 1962 (German 1957²), pp. 259ff.

148 *ThLZ* 72 (1947), 143-152: Amos 5,21-27; and "Amos-Studien", in *ZAW* 62 (1950), 10-52.

149 *Die Gesetze in der Priesterschrift*, 1954; *ThLZ* 81 (1956), 339-342.

150 *Sprache und Ritus im altisr. Kult*, 1965, 131-145: "Propheten und Kultus."

151 *ôlāh hû* (Lev. 1,13.17); *minḥāh hî'* (Lev. 2,6.15), etc.; *tāmē' hû* (Lev. 13,15). Cf. Rendtorff, *Die Gesetze der Priesterschrift*, 1963², pp. 74ff. (Deklaratorische Formeln). Von Rad, *O.T. Theol.* I, 261: "This special aspect of the ritual act has hitherto been overlooked, but it was without doubt the most important part of the whole procedure."

152 Cf. Lev. 19,5; the peace offering was accepted together with the offerer himself ("so that *you* may be accepted"). See already Gen. 4,4f., where the offerer is taken in account even before the offering. 2 Sam. 24,23; Ez. 20,20.21; 43,27. Cf. Th. Lescow, *Micha 6,6-8*, 1966, p. 52, n. 24.

153 Lev. 1,3f.; an obvious programmatic sentence at the beginning of Leviticus; cf. Rendtorff, *Die Gesetze in der Priesterschrift*, pp. 12,77.

154 Lev. 22,21b; the specifications of the blemishes or mutilations, because of which "they will not be accepted for you", are given in vss. 23-25.

155 Lev. 19,5-8; cf. 7,18: when the flesh of the peace offering is eaten, however, on the *third* day "he who offers it shall not be accepted [$lô yērāṣeh$], neither shall it be credited to him [$lô yēḥāšēb$]; it shall be an abomination [$piggûl yihyeh$] ..."; cf. 19,7.

156 In Lev. 7,18 *rāṣāh* and *ḥāšab* are used as virtual synonyms (see previous note). Cf. Rendtorff, *ThLZ* 81 (1956), 341: "Der Ausdruck *rāṣāh* gehört also in den Bereich der priesterlichen Anrechnungstheologie hinein" (referring to von Rad, *ThLZ* 76 (1951), 129ff.).

which was identical with the declaration that Yahweh credited (ḥāšab) the perfection of purity to him.[157]

Where the sacrifices were imperfect, i.e. with blemishes or mutilations, in defiance of the cultic regulations, the sacrifice together with the offerer were to be rejected as not pleasing, as unacceptable to Yahweh for atonement.

The profanation of the cultus by imperfect sacrifices is evaluated by the prophet Malachi as a reflection of the prevailing religious-moral condition, i.e. the conscious desecration of Yahweh's Name, not merely by the common people of Israel but by the *priests* in the first place.[158] When the sacrifices, however, were perfect according to the law, and therefore were accepted by the priesthood as pleasing to Yahweh, this situation implied that the offerer complied in his obedience not merely to the cultic but also to the fundamental socio-ethical requirements of the covenant of Yahweh.

Both Israel's cultic service and wisdom required a perfect or undivided heart and life (Pss. 15,2; 119,80; 2 Chr. 16,9; Prov. 28,9.13.18). No realm of life was to be divorced from the cultus and Torah of the covenant. Yahweh's claim on the whole heart and complete life made all the secular sacred. All of life is religious.

And it was the sacred trust of the priest not merely to consider the perfection of the sacrificial animal but also the religious-moral way of life of the cultic participant: whether or not also his heart was perfect as reflected in his social ethos.[159]

The judicial authority and declaration of the priest, however, constituted only the initial part of his cultic function. Of equal importance was his sacred commission and reponsibility to administer the cultic reality of atonement by means of the sacrificial blood.

This sacred action may be described as a *sacrament*,[160] since it re-

---

157 Cf. Eichrodt, *Theol. of O.T.* I, p. 160, who states that the expiatory sacrifices of Israel had two effects: 1) atonement of the wrath of God; 2) "that the sinner is transferred from a state of defilement to one of purity." H. W. Robinson, *Insp. and Rev.*, p. 228: "The ancient symbol is an *effective* part of that which it represents. Sacrifice is an efficient act."

158 Cf. Mal. 1,6ff. 10-14. Maleachi presents a most impressive example for the intimate relationship of cultus and ethos, in which the profanation of the one reflects the deterioration of the other; cf. 2,13ff.

159 The priests also had to exercise the office of judge, Ex. 22,7.; Num. 5,11ff.; Dt. 17,8ff.; 21,5. See K. Koch, "Einlassliturgien", in *o.c.*, p. 59; von Rad, *OT Theol.* I, p. 373.

160 Eichrodt, *o.c.*, I, pp. 99f.; "The cultus is, however, not only the inwardly necessary expression of spiritual realities by means of the physical, but also *the medium by which divine power is presented* to men for their participation" (99). Von Rad, *O.T. Theol.* I, p. 262: "Thus, only the addition of the divine word [sc. the priestly *placet*] made the material observance what

presented the spiritual activity of the Holy One within the heart and conscience of the participant, causing the reality of the joy of salvation (Ps. 4,7; 63,5). In the Priestly texts the priestly act of declaration, however, is basic to the transforming act of atonement or imputation.[161]

The greatest danger which continually threatened the priesthood was to consider its own judicial declaration as the decisive principle for atonement independent from the required ethos of the Torah in the life of the participant; i.e., as the objective or automatic guarantee of Yahweh's acceptance and imputation or accrediting. In other words, the abstract judicial appeal to the priestly law in Leviticus, divorced from the religious-moral dynamism of the Psalms, could easily lead to the misconception that the mere cultic obedience of the participant together with the mere judicial approval and accrediting of the priest already guaranteed the pleasure and atonement of Yahweh.[162]

How the threat of a formalistic unity of cultus and ethos was already realized in pre-exilic times can be inferred from some cultic references in Israel's Wisdom, the Proverbs in particular:

> The sacrifice of the wicked is an abomination to the Lord, but the prayer of the upright is his delight. Prov. 15,8.

> To do righteousness and justice is more acceptable to the Lord than sacrifice. Prov. 21,3.

it was meant to be, a real saving event between Yahweh and his people." Mowinckel, *Ps.St.* III, 6. H. W. Robinson, *Insp. and Rev.*, pp. 225-228; appealing to Ps. 50,5: "It is in miniature the actual renewal of a relation"; "sacrifice establishes or renews the covenant" (p. 227). Notice the vital remark after having stated "sacrifice is an efficient act": "This opens up the right (exegetical) line of approach to the N.T. sacraments, and to the conception of the death of Christ as a sacrifice" (p. 228, n. 2).

161  Von Rad, *O.T. Theol.* I, p. 262: "Only in virtue of the declaratory word of the priest did the sacral event become a gracious act of God." Rendtorff, *ThLZ* 81 (1956), 341: "Der Priester vollzieht den deklaratorischen Akt, der Voraussetzung der Anrechnung ist, indem er die vorgeschriebene Formel spricht:..." Rendtorff, *Die Gesetze*, p. 75: "Das Urteil des Priesters macht das rite vollzogene Opfer erst zu dem, was es sein soll, verleiht ihm seine Wirkung, so dass es den Opfernden vor Jahwe wohlgefällig macht und ihm Sühne verschafft (Lev. 1,3f.)."

162  Cf. Hermisson, *o.c.*, p. 140: "Doch mag diese Art zu reden [sc. in Lev.] zu dem Missverständnis Anlass gegeben haben, ein rite vollzogenes Opfer garantiere zusammen mit der priesterlichen Anrechnung bereits Jahwes Wohlgefallen." H. W. Robinson has appropriately stated that "the Book of Psalms ... should always be associated with the Book of Leviticus, as though they were written in parallel columns" (in *A Companion to the Bible*, ed. T. W. Manson, 1947, p. 304).

The sacrifice of the wicked is an abomination; how much more when he brings it with evil intent. Prov. 21,27.[163]

In these statements of Israel's wisdom the emphasis is not on the cultic perfection of the offering but on the socio-ethical perfection of the offerer, which is declared to be acceptable to Yahweh in cultic categories.

The wicked ($r^e\check{s}\bar{a}^c\hat{i}m$) are described in Prov. 28,9 as those who turn their ear or heart from hearing the Torah; even their *prayer*, like their sacrifice, is an abomination. These few references in Proverbs indicate how the fierce tension and discrepancy between ethos and cultus was realized already in ancient times. Hermisson puts his finger on the weak spot, on the imperfection of the Old Testament priesthood, when he says:

> Die hier auftretende Diskrepanz ist zwar von vornherein eine Möglichkeit und eine Gefahr des Kultus, der bei den ihm gegebenen Mitteln darauf verzichten muss, dem Menschen "ins Herz" zu schauen.[164]

The ethos of Israel's wisdom, while never renouncing its religious cultic foundation in the fear of Yahweh, continually stresses the root relation of all social conduct with the moral condition of the heart. The heart in turn is immediately related to the evaluation of Yahweh who "weighs" the heart and the spirit.[165] This living correlation of the searching of the soul before Yahweh has kept Israel's wisdom from the claim of perfectionism, to attain to a sinless heart. Before Yahweh it realized:

> Surely there is not a righteous man on earth who does good and never sins.[166]
> Who can say: "I have made my heart clean; I am pure from my sin"?[167]

This *theonomic* ethical self-qualification lay at the foundation of the social ethos of righteousness and perfection of Israel's wisdom. However, when the heart stays in the fear of Yahweh and the conduct follows the perfect way of the Torah, then man's way or walk, and consequently he himself, is qualified as perfect, acceptable, blameless and upright, even by Yahweh!

---

163  Cf. the statement of the Egyptian Instruction for King Merikare, *ANET*, p. 417, quoted in Ch. I, n. 23. As this word dates from before 1300 B.C., the quoted statements of Proverbs may also well be pre-exilic. Cf., moreover, Is. 1,10ff.; Am. 5,21f.

164  *O.c.*, p. 122.

165  Prov. 16,3; 21,2; 24,12.

166  Eccl. 7,20; cf. 1 Kings 8,46.

167  Prov. 20,9; cf. 15,3.11.

And the Lord said to Satan, "Have you considered my servant Job, that there is none like him on the earth, a blameless [*tām*] and upright man, who fears God and turns away from evil?[168]

The Psalmist's criticism of the sacrificial cult seems to be more congenial to this cultically rooted ethos of the Wisdom Literature, than to the passionate prophetic criticism.[169] In the so-called anti-cultic Psalms, Pss. 40,6f. (MT 7f.); 50,14; 51,16-19 (MT 18-21), the cultic sacrifices were not rejected basically,[170] but even the perfect sacrificial animals were not acceptable to Yahweh *as such*.[171] Only when they were accompanied by the ethos of a dedicated and consecrated heart, i.e., by repentance, confession, reparation, forsaking of sins and praise of Yahweh were they acceptable.[172] In other words, only sacrifices which were pre-

---

168   Job 1,8; cf. 1,1; 2,3. Cf. Prov. 2,7.21; 10,9.29; 11,5.20; 19,1; 20,7; 28.6.10.18.

169   R. J. Thompson, *o.c.*, p. 139. Cf. C. H. Toy, "On some Conceptions of the Old Testament Psalter", in *Old Test. and Sem. Studies*, I, 5-7. On a survey of lit. dealing with the attitude of the Psalmists to sacrifice, see J. J. Stamm, "Ein Vierteljahrhundert Psalmenforschung," in *ThR* N.F. 23 (1955), 61-63.

170   Cf. Mowinckel, *Ps. St.* VI, p. 51, who rightly concludes that it would be "ganz falsch, die Begriffe Kultreligion und Opferreligion schlechthin zu identifizieren." The disdain of sacrifices is not necessarily identical with the rejection of the religious cultus. In Pss. 40; 50; 51, M. interprets the problematic verses as "*eine Verschiebung in der Wertschätzung* der einzelnen Momente des Tempelkultes." Further, pp. 53f., the references in Pss. 40,7f.; 51,18f. do sound absolutely, but are meant relatively, with respect to the sacrificial cultus, in the sense of Mat. 23,23. These Pss. present a "spiritual re-interpretation of the sacrifice, not a condemnation of it." Cf. Mowinckel, *The Psalms in Israel's Worship*, II, ET 1962, p. 23.

171   Cf. Mowinckel, *o.c.*, p. 54: "Man trifft sicher den Sinn des Dichters des 40. Psalms, wenn man seine Worte so erklärt: nicht an dem Opfer *an sich* hat Gott Gefallen, sondern an der aus der 'Weisheit' des Herzens entspringenden poetischen Lobpreisung in der Gemeinde. Und ähnlich auch Ps. 51,18f...." 'Opfer an sich' kann man im Hebräischen nicht sagen. Statt zur Abstraktion müssen die Hebräer zur Hyperbel greifen." Referring to Jacob, "Beitrage zu einer Einleitung in die Psalmen III", *ZAW* 17 (1897), 273-279, who sticks to the MT in Ps. 40,7b (*ʿôlāh waḥaṭāʾā*) "burnt offering and sin (!) thou hast not required." See also Ps. 69,30f. (MT 31f.) with its significant comparative. Cf. Hermisson, *o.c.*, pp. 43ff., indicating that in Ps. 40 the alternative is not cultus and ethos, since the last is already the prerequisite for participation in the cultus. "Spiritualisierung ist jedenfalls hier nicht dasselbe wie 'Ethisierung', und wenn die Propheten 'Gehorsam statt Opfer' fordern, so ist das sehr genau von der These dieser Psalmisten: Loblied als (oder: statt) Opfer zu unterscheiden." Cf. Westermann, *The Praise of God in the Psalms*, p. 77.

172   Cf. Eichrodt, *o.c.*, I, p. 160: "The sacrifice is normally accompanied by prayer and confessing of sin x) and exerts no kind of compulsive effect. Reconciliation remains the gift of God's independent majesty (Ex. 32.33f.; 33.19), which explains why there are offences which cannot be expiated by sacrifice (1 Sam. 3.14; 15.24ff.)." In note x he refers to 1 Sam.7,5f.; Lev.

sented by the participant in the spirit of Pss. 4,5; 19,12f; 50,5; 66 and of the most profound Psalm 51,17, were acceptable and, consequently, effective before Yahweh. E.g.:

> The sacrifice acceptable to God is a broken spirit; a broken and contrite heart, O God, thou wilt not despise. ... then wilt thou delight in right sacrifices ... (51,17.19a, RSV).[173]
>
> If I had cherished iniquity in my heart, the LORD would not have listened (66,18).[174]
>
> I will praise the name of God with a song; I will magnify him with thanksgiving.
>
> This will please the LORD more than an ox or a bull with horns and hoofs (Ps. 69,30-31; MT 31f.).

When the cultic participant sinned and then did not repent of his sin, but rather *cherished* his sin and, thus, chose to cultivate sin as his pattern of life, Yahweh did not accept his sacrifices. It was the sacred commission of the priesthood to deny to such the divine acceptance and accrediting of the sacrament. While the prophets in their cultus criticism do not reject the cultus and the priestly office as such, they frequently accuse the priesthood of negligence of their priestly duty and commission.[175] *Hosea* announces Yahweh's verdict against the northern kingdom:

> My people are destroyed for lack of knowledge; because you have rejected knowledge, I reject you from being a priest to Me ... you have forgotten the law of your God (4,6).

5,5; 16,21; Num. 5,7; Jer. 3,24 (cf. 2,35); Job 42,8; cf. Josh. 7,19f. and then states: "The fact that the prayers accompanying the atonement sacrifice are not very frequently mentioned can hardly mean that repentance, sorrow and confession of sin were not generally taken for granted as the subjective conditions of forgiveness: cf. II Sam. 12.13; I Kings 21.27ff.; Joel 2.12-14; Pss. 25.7; 32.5; 38.19; 41.5; 51.6ff.; 65.4; 130.3f.; Lam. 3.40ff. etc." In Ps. 50,14.23 the emphasis is on a deeper form of praise rather than on a deeper sense of sin; cf. Thompson, *o.c.*, p. 149. This is situated in its judgment against a false conception of God. On Ps. 51 see H. H. Rowley, *The Meaning of Sacrifice*, pp. 98ff.

173  Cf. Kraus *ad l.*: "Das Herz des zerknirschten Büssers und flehenden Beters trägt der Psalmsänger vor Gott in der Gewissheit, dass dieses Opfer nicht einem deklarativen Verwerfungsurteil verfällt, sondern Jahwe angenehm ist: vgl, Ps. 34,19; Jes. 57,15; 61,1 [referring to Luther, E 17, 255f.]." See also Jacob, in ZAW 17 (1897), 278.

174  Cf. Kraus, *ad l.*: "Jahwe hätte den Beter nicht erhört, wenn er nicht unschuldig gewesen wäre (zu den Gebeten unschuldig Angeklagter vgl. vor allem zu Ps. 7)."

175  See Hermisson, *o.c.*, pp. 131ff., esp. 137. Gutbrod, in *ThWNT* IV, 1033, 22f. (s.v. *nomos*): "Der Kultus, wie ihn die Propheten vorfinden, dient dazu den Ungehorsam zu decken, Gott in die Hand zu bekommen ..."

*Micah* accuses the priesthood of Jerusalem of teaching "for hire" (3,11). *Isaiah* indicates the failure of Judah's priests and prophets: "they are confused with wine ... they err in vision, they stumble in giving judgment" (28,7).

In the time of the kings of Judah the disharmony between cultus and ethos reached its sad climax in that the cultus had almost completely lost sight of the Torah and even had come to neglect the Torah or entrance liturgy of the Temple as given in Pss. 15 and 24. It is the prophet *Jeremiah* who now, in the gate of the Temple(!), addresses all "who enter these gates to worship Yahweh" with the demands of the Torah requirements in the name of Yahweh.[176] This presupposes that in his time the Torah liturgy was ignored and had been left out of the cultus ritual.[177]

Jeremiah rebukes Judah's spiritual and political leadership for its negligence to remember Yahweh's redemptive acts in Israel's salvation history, pointing also to a fundamental failure of the cultus:

> "The priests did not say, 'Where is Yahweh?' Those who handle the law did not know Me ..."[178]

No wonder that the result of this inner *breach* between cultus and ethos was the prevalence of great abuses in the social life of Israel together with the absence, even the refusal, of repentance,[179] while the ritual of cultic sacrifices flourished.[180]

In this situation of apostasy from Yahweh alle intercession, cultic and prophetic,[181] had become meaningless. Because the covenant fellowship and walk with Yahweh were systematically rejected in disobedience, and the prophetic calls to repentance were spurned, the covenant blessing was no longer pronounced; instead the covenant curse was invoked upon Israel, i.e., Yahweh's rejection of *this* Israel and of *this* cultus.

> And if by this discipline you are not turned to me, but walk contrary to me, then I also will walk contrary to you, and I myself will smite you sevenfold for your sins. And I will bring a sword

---

176   Jer. 7,1ff.
177   Thus also Kraus, *o.c.*, p. 114; Hermisson, *o.c.*, p. 121.
178   Jer. 2,4f. 8.
179   Jer. 5,3.
180   See Jer. 7,4ff., who even qualifies the Temple in this setting of life as "a den of robbers" (vs. 11). Vs. 18 shows how Canaanite cultic elements also had crept illegitimately into Israel's cultus.
181   Even Jeremiah's prayers in behalf of Judah are rejected by Yahweh with an appeal to the factual ethos in the cities, Jer. 7,16ff.; 11,14; 14,12f.; 15,1ff.

upon you, that shall execute vengeance for the covenant (Lev. 26,23-25a).

And I will lay your cities waste, and will make your sanctuaries desolate, and I will not smell your pleasing odors (vs. 31).

This curse on the cultus and Israel, the prophets Amos, Micah, Isaiah, and Jeremiah announced in their problematic anti-cultus passages. These messages did not constitute the timeless ethicizing alternative of ethos or cultus, but the special oracle of Yahweh's curse in Israel's situation of persistent apostasy from the covenant law.[182] From now on, these messages intend to say, Yahweh no longer accepts the cultus of Israel as pleasing to Him.[183] The time of forgiveness has gone, therefore the whole cultus, in all its manifestations, has now become meaningless.[184] The cultus has meaning and efficacy only so long as Yahweh says Yes to it.[185] And when the priests continue to say Yes in their declaratory formulas while Yahweh says No, the prophets take over the negative cultic declaratory formulas in the name and authority of Yahweh.[186]

The intention of the prophets, therefore, was not to separate Israel's cultus and ethos but rather to deny the legitimacy of the *cleavage* and *disharmony* between them.[187]

---

182   E. Würthwein, *ThLZ* 72 (1947), 149: "Der Prophet [i.e. Amos 5,21ff.] gibt ein Orakel, keine Tora"; 150: "[Verse] 21-23 spricht von der Nichtannahme der Opfer in einer bestimmten Situation."

183   Hos. 8,13. Cf. Würthwein, *l.c.*, 147: "*Jetzt* gedenkt er ihrer Sünden und sucht heim ihre Vergehen. Das heisst: In diesem bestimmten Zeitpunkt wird die Annahme der Opfer und die mit ihr erstrebte Sündenvergebung verweigert, weil jetzt die Zeit der Heimsuchung gekommen ist. Vgl. noch Ez. 20,40.41; 43,27."

184   Würthwein, *l.c.*, 148: "Der kultische Weg versagt, weil Jahwe sich nicht finden lässt... Dass er sich dem menschlichen Anruf versagt, das ist der schärfste Ausdruck für die Geschiedenheit des Volkes von seinem Gott. Es ist Gott-los, durch seine Sünde von Gott geschieden und darum Heil-los. Diese von Gott verhängte Heillosigkeit ist es im letzten Grunde, die den Kult sinnlos macht."

185   Cf. H. Brongers, *l.c.*, (see above, n. 125), p. 140: "Zo is het ook geen wet, dat Jahwe elke zonde, ook al wordt zij beleden, automatisch vergeeft... [referring to 2 Kgs. 24,4; Jer. 5,7; Lam. 3,42; Ps. 109,14 a.o.]. *Pardonner n'est pas son métier*! Het is niet Zijn *métier*, maar Zijn souverein recht. Dat betekent, dat Hij van dat recht ook wel eens *niet* gebruik wil maken."

186   Crucial is the phenomenon that the prophets use the cultic verb *rāṣāh* or noun *rāṣôn* in a *negative* formula: Am. 5,22; Hos. 8,13; Mi. 6,7; Jer. 6,20; 14,12. Cf. Hermisson, *o.c.*, p. 140: "Es geht schliesslich um die Vollmacht des Priesters, die Anrechnung Jahwes zuzusprechen. Diese Vollmacht nimmt nun der Prophet als Jahwes Bote für sich in Anspruch."

187   Cf. Hermisson, *o.c.*, p. 139: "Sie haben jedenfalls, als erste mit allem Nachdruck und aller Schärfe gesagt, dass so – in dieser Gespaltenheit – der Mensch Gottes Wohlgefallen nicht erlangen kann." Cf. Th. Lescow, *Micha 6,6-8, Studien zu Sprache, Form u. Auslegung*, 1966, p. 59: "Worauf die

They rejected an isolated[188] cultus which feels justified in abandoning the old Torah liturgy and ethos, and fulminated against the self-centered ethos which was radically cut off[189] from its living cultic root in salvation-historical soteriology.

The prophets therefore summon Israel to remember Yahweh's ṣidqôt, i.e., His saving acts in salvation history, denying any virtue in the sacrificial cult in order to re-establish the cultic or Torah-ethos, i.e., the *personal* covenant relationship of faithfulness and love with Yahweh and with the fellow Israelite. Thus Micah, in the setting of Yahweh's lawsuit, recounts Israel's salvation-historical deliverance from Egypt and her redemption from bondage and the following ṣidqôt of Yahweh (6,1-5). He then proceeds to expose the impotency of all cultic sacrifices, even the costliest, of the firstborn child, as causing atonement for sins, and with that the futility of trusting[190] in the cultus as such (6,6-7).

Finally he reaches the climax in that historic statement, which basically is identical with the Torah liturgy of Ps. 15[191] and therefore does not pretend to be any new ethos:

> He has showed you, O man, what is good; and what does the LORD require of you but to do justice [*mišpāṭ*] and love kindness [*ḥesed*] and to walk humbly with your God? (6,8)[192]

Here the reality of the Torah-ethos and the experience of personal religious communion with the God of salvation are restored.

prophetische Kultpolemik *eigentlich* zielte, dürfte in Jes. 58,1-2 ausgesprochen sein: Es geht um das Auseinanderbrechen von 'Kultus' und 'Ethos' um jenes falsche Verständnis der priesterlichen Anrechnungstheologie ..."

188  Cf. Hermisson, *o.c.*, p. 139: "Wo er [sc. Kultus] als ein Mittel zur Rechtfertigung der bösen Taten angesehen wird wie Jeremia es beschreibt, oder wo man auch nur meint, das Wohlgefallen Gottes würde im Kultus, unabhängig vom übrigen Leben des Menschen beschafft, da ist der Kult in der Tat sinnlos. Dieser Kultus mussten die Propheten radikal verwerfen. Dieser Kult entspricht aber ... auch nicht dem eigenen israelitischen Verständnis." See further p. 143. H. W. Robinson, *o.c.*, pp. 226, 228, who appeals to Moore, *Judaism*, I, 503f., for being justified in stating: "In theory at least, the better type of priest in the later systems would have fully agreed [sc. with the prophetic condemnation], as did the rabbis still later."

189  Cf. G. von Rad, *O.T. Theology*, I, p. 260 (contra E. Sellin): "It is arbitrary to reconstruct a spiritual 'prophetic' faith in Jahweh, and devalue the 'priestly cult religion' as an unpleasant by-product."

190  The isolated trusting in the Temple is exposed in Jer. 7,4.8-11. Cf Hermisson, *o.c.*, p. 141: "Ihre [sc. prophets] Antithesen sind als Umkehrung eines der Naiven Heilsgewissheit des Volkes entspringenden Satzes zu verstehen".

191  H. Gunkel, *ad* Ps. 15, refers to Mi 6,6-8 as a "prophetische Nachahmung, aus *Frage* und *Antwort* bestehend."

192  More detailed in Is. 1,17-18.

According to Pss. 15; 19; 50; 51 this was also the exalted purpose and divinely appointed function of the cultus itself. It provided the blessing of a new and whole heart and a new spirit, opening the way for a new religious and socio-ethical fellowship. Only when the cultus failed to uphold its legitimate and authentic spiritualizing,[193] the prophets of judgment stepped in to reject the formalized and degenerated cultus. They did this to save and revive the spiritual ethos of the personal encounter and walk with Yahweh, Israel's covenant God.

## CONCLUSION

Pss. 15 and 19 reveal how vital the function of the cultus is in upholding the social ethos of the Torah with Israel's covenant.[194] The standard to be met is a *perfect* ethos: a perfect walk or behavior or social relationship, doing what is right and speaking truth from the heart, with special attention to the socially poor in Israel.[195] This ethos is not grounded in itself, in its own perfection or utility, but in the will of Yahweh,[196] the covenant God, i.e., in His historic act of liberation, represented and applied in the cultic atonement.

Consequently, when the ethos of Israel's faith is *not* manifested in concrete reality Yahweh's will is denied and His cultus formalized and made void. The heart which is completely or perfectly possessed by the love of Yahweh and thus by love for Yahweh and His Torah, is the heart that is in harmony, in right covenant relation, with Him and with the fellow Israelite. It follows Yahweh in all ways in loving moral obedience.

Such a heart or soul is *ṣaddîq*, completely [197] righteous, since it enjoys

---

193    Cf. Hermisson, *o.c.*, p. 144, who rightly concludes: "Dann ist der Vorgang nicht so aufzufassen, als hätten die Psalmisten die Kritik der Propheten vernommen und daraus ihre eigene Konsequenzen gezogen; vielmehr sind Propheten und Psalmisten von *verschiedenen* Positionen aus zu einer Kritik am Opferkultus gelangt" [referring to Pss. 40,7; 51,18]. Kraus, *Psalmen* I, p. 114: "Die Propheten tragen das Ethos nicht als etwas Neues, Revolutionierendes in den Kultus ein – sie sind vielmehr Erneuerer, Reformatoren eines Festkultus, der sich im Verlaufe der Zeit vom Gottesrecht gelöst hat. In Ps. 15 gehört das Gottesrecht noch wesensmässig zum Kultus hinzu."

194    Cf. Eichrodt, *Theol. of the O.T.* I, p. 86: "The content of such formulas, with their echoes of the Decalogue and the major religious prescriptions related to it, bear witness to the significance of divine worship for the sacred law and its inculcation."

195    Ps. 15,2.5.

196    Cf. Gutbrod, in *ThWNT* IV, 1030, 51-1031, 2: "Aber dabei ist festzuhalten, dass die Gültigkeit des Gebotes nicht in dieser sozialen Zweckmässigkeit ruht, sondern in dem dahinterstehenden Willen des Bundesgottes."

197    Cf. von Rad, *Ges. Stud.*, p. 231: "War man *ṣaddîq*, so war man es nicht incohativ und approximativ, sondern man war es ganz."

a living covenant relationship in cultus and ethos.[198] That soul is *tāmîm*, perfect, or innocent, since he is undivided[199] and in his social conduct intent upon the will of Yahweh only. When sin overrules him, he repents of his sin and follows the way of atonement and cleansing in the recreation of his heart, its motives and objectives. The cultus of Israel calls such a man righteous and perfect. From this we conclude that in Israel's ethos the ideas of righteousness and perfection are not oriented to an ideal norm or a highest virtue, but are significations of the cultic communion relationship in Israel's covenant.[200]

Perfection is not the individualistic achievement of a human ideal or virtue, but the religious-cultic walk with the covenant God, manifested in the socio-ethical walk with the fellowman, in wholehearted moral obedience to the covenant of Yahweh.

Consequently, perfection in Ps. 15 does not stand for the state of sinlessness or ethical blamelessness, but for the right cultic relationship, i.e., the living religious covenant relationship with Yahweh and the fellow Israelite.

Of special importance is the underlying spiritual unity of the prophetic ethos of Micah 6,8 with the priestly cultic ethos of perfection of Psalm 15: the soteriological root in salvation-history, i.e., in the Exodus salvation, as their common motivation and legitimation. The impressive dominating fact that Yahweh offered His blessing of a perfect heart only in correlationship with the socio-ethical requirement of perfection not only reveals the majesty and wisdom of Israel's covenant God but also appeals to all nations to worship Him in the praise and exaltation of His name and perfect character.

c. *The Individual Confessions of Innocence and Perfection.*

Gunkel has classified the "Psalms of Innocence"[201] together with the "Penitential Psalms" and those of Confidence as the three principal types of „*Individual Laments*".[202] This already indicates that the setting in life

198   See Ez. 18,5-9 for the detailed qualification of the *ṣaddîq*.

199   Cf. J. Pedersen, *Israel* I-II, p. 336: "Innocence is a fairly accurate translation of this word [sc. *tāmîm*], when by that it is understood that no secondary wills have their seat in the soul so as to counteract the main will in which its contents centre." The wicked speak with "a double heart", Ps. 12,2 (MT 3: *beleb wāleb*).

200   Cf. Mowinckel, *The Psalms in Israel's Worship* I, 209.

201   E.g. Pss. 5; 7; 17; 26.

202   H. Gunkel, *The Psalms. A Form-Critical Introduction*, 1967, p. 35. Cf. his *Einleitung in die Psalmen*, pp. 251ff. On p. 173 he says: "Die Klagelieder des Einzelnen bilden den *eigentlichen Grundstock des Psalters*." O. Eissfeldt, *Einleitung in das Alte Testament*, 1964³ (ET 1965, p. 115), mentions about 40 Pss. in this category, see § 15, no. 9, with lit. It is, however, S. Mowinckel, *Psalmenstudien* I (1919), pp. 134ff., who expounded the Songs of Lament as official cult songs, indicating a presumed priestly oracle.

(*Sitz im Leben*) of the protestations of perfection is not the common, normal situation in life, but a special situation of deep distress in which the worshipper is usually bewailing the enemy(ies) by whom he is persecuted or slandered.

Characteristic for the Psalms of Innocence is the emphatic assurance of innocence and righteousness which they present before God, to whom they appeal as the righteous Judge and at the same time the Redeemer who has sovereign power over all distress:

> The LORD judges the peoples; judge me [*šopṭēnî*], O LORD, according to my righteousness and according to the integrity [*kᵉtummî*] that is in me (Ps. 7,8; MT 9).

> Vindicate me [*šopṭēnî,*] O LORD, for I have walked in my integrity [*bᵉtummî,*] and I have trusted in the LORD without wavering. . . . I do not sit with false men, nor do I consort with dissemblers; I hate the company of evildoers, and I will not sit with the wicked. I wash my hands in innocence, and go about thy altar, O LORD, singing aloud a song of thanksgiving, and telling all thy wondrous deeds . . . .
> But as for me, I walk in my integrity [*bᵉtummî*]; redeem me, and be gracious to me (Ps. 26,1-11).

> I was blameless [*tāmîm*] before him, and I kept myself from guilt. Therefore the LORD has recompensed me according to my righteousness, according to the cleanness of my hands in his sight.
> With the loyal [*ḥāsîd*] thou dost show thyself loyal; with the blameless [*tāmîm*] man thou dost show thyself blameless (Ps. 18, 23-25; MT 24-26; corresponds to 2 Sam. 22,24ff.).

The questions of R. J. Thompson and Chr. F. Barth are to the point: „How could true worshippers, of apparently deeply spiritual insight, nevertheless make such claims to self-righteousness?"[203] "How can these expressions be reconciled with the admittedly less frequent but no less clearly formulated confessions of personal guilt?"[204] It is obvious that these supposed contradictions did not exist in the minds of the psalmists. To them the two statements in this juxtaposition of guilt and innocence functioned rather in a harmonious, dynamic interrelationship.

H. Schmidt[205] has offered the ingenious explanation that many psalms of innocence really belong to the category of cultic prayers of persons falsely accused of some breach of law, who, for want of evidence, were required to vindicate their innocence at the sanctuary by an oath of

---

203  Thompson, *o.c.*, p. 140 (see above, n. 111).
204  Barth, *Introduction to the Psalms*, 1966, p. 40.
205  *Das Gebet der Angeklagten im Alten Testament*, BZAW 49, 1928.

purgation.[206] Yahweh Himself then would, possibly by means of some form of divination, or some form of trial by ordeal, vindicate the innocent one as the righteous one. In some cases the accused one was at the same time suffering from some form of sickness, which then was explained by the enemy as being the result of some secret sin or crime. Here again Schmidt regards the "enemies", of whom the psalmist complains, as personal persecutors of a pious Israelite who in his distress turns to Yahweh, the righteous Judge, for help.[207]

In spite of the criticism of Schmidt's interpretation of the "enemies"[208] and especially of his insistence on the detention under remand,[209] a limited number of Psalms indeed is explained best by the premise of the false accusation and the vindication of the innocent one by divine oracle at the sanctuary. Eissfeldt agrees that Pss. 7; 35; 57 and 69 may indeed be understood from the situation "eines kultischen Untersuchungsver-fahrens."[210] Thus also Eissfeldt, following Mowinckel, defines the Individual Psalms of Lament as cult songs which were recited on the occasion of ceremonies of innocence and purgation, and consequently are not to be regarded as "private Ergüsse frommer Menschen."[211] To him the assurance of hearing at the close of the Individual Songs of Lament

206 On the basis of Dt. 17,8ff.; 1 Kings 8,31f.; Ex. 22,7ff.; Num. 5,11ff. and Dt. 21,1ff. In Ps. 7 such an oath of purgation or innocence is indicated in vss. 3-5, while vss. 6-9 present the prayer for divine vindication of the accused worshipper. Before the following thanksgiving prayer in vss. 12ff. the ordeal must have taken place in which the accused one has triumphed over his accuser who now receives the curse of the oath on his own head. Thus Schmidt, *o.c.*, pp. 17f.

207 Schmidt discusses here Pss. 31,10-25; 35; 38; 41 and 69 and further refers to Pss. 25; 28; 86 and 102. On Ps. 41 he concludes, p. 32: "Es ist kein Wunder, dass die Klagegebete der Angeklagten und die der Kranken einander so ähnlich sind. *Mancher war in der furchtbaren Lage, beides in einer Person zu sein.*"

208 H. Birkeland, *Die Feinde des Individuums in der Isr. Psalmenlit.*, 1933, pp. 312ff.

209 Gunkel-Begrich, *Einleitung*, pp. 252ff. Cf. also L. Delekat, *Asylie und Schutzorakel am Zionheiligtum. Eine Untersuchung zu den privaten Feind-psalmen*, 1967, pp. 6ff. And recently W. Beyerlin, *Die Rettung der Bedrängten in den Feindpsalmen der Einzelnen auf institutionelle Zusammenhänge unter-sucht*, FRLANT 99, 1970. He criticizes both Schmidt and Delekat, pp. 43-53, but considers Pss. 7 and 26 to have a place in the cultic-sacral judgment of Yahweh on behalf of the helpless and innocent Israelite.

210 *O.c.*, p. 160. Eissfeldt also considers the possibility of calling these Pss. spiritual songs made in imitation of this category of prayers of a falsely accused one. Birkeland, *o.c.*, pp. 314f., also includes Pss. 119 and 59.

211 *Ibid.*, p. 158. Eissfeldt maintains, on the other hand, that Pss. 25; 39; 51, 130, and others, because of their strictly private and deeply religious content, were originally composed without connection with the cultus (pp. 160f.).

"most probably" goes back ultimately to the divine answer in the cultic oracle.[212] In this respect Eissfeldt's appeal to Is. 38,1-6[213] is significant and revealing.

King Hezekiah became sick "at the point of death" and received the prophetic message that he would die. In this situation he prays to Yahweh in the form of an individual song of lament:[214]

> Remember now, O LORD, I beseech thee, how *I have walked before thee in faithfulness* [*beᵉᵉmet*] and with a whole heart [*bᵉlēbāb šālēm*], and have done what is good in thy sight.

This prayer, which consists of a protestation or, better, a confession of innocence and perfection, is not remarkable so much for its content as for the fact that Yahweh, the God of Israel, *accepts* this prayer and confession, by means of a divine oracle, a special sign and Hezekiah's complete recovery.[215]

In the following *Song of Thanksgiving*, Is. 38,10-20, the king praises Yahweh for His salvation and His faithfulness.

The questions of Thompson and Barth arise here with peculiar force. How can one ever confess his personal perfection before God? And how can the holy God of Israel ever accept a confession of personal innocence and faithfulness?

To enter upon the Biblical concept and feeling of life we must first remember what we found to be the meaning of perfection in Pss. 15 and 19. Perfection in these Pss. was established to be definitely not sinlessness, but the right or perfect covenant relationship which is accompanied by an ethos of obedience, rooted in the cultic experience of deliverance from the defiling power of sin, the judicial acquittal from guilt and the transforming, existential communion with Yahweh's Holiness and Love.

This sense of Yahweh's holiness and forgiving mercy is such a fundamental reality in Israel's religion that all the official prayers and Songs of Innocence are offered, explicitly or implicitly, on the basis of this presupposed cultic-ethical fellowship with Yahweh.[216] That also Hezekiah

---

212  *Ibid.*, p. 157.
213  *Ibid.*
214  Is 38,3 = 2 Kings 20,3.
215  Is. 38,4ff.
216  Cf. Mowinckel, *Ps. St.* I, 158: "Gewiss, wenn der Betende sich auf seine 'Gerechtigkeit' beruft, so ist alles oben Erwähnte [sc. the cultus] darin mit eingeschlossen; zur Gerechtigkeit gehört auch die genaue Beobachtung der kultischen Pflichten. Es gehört aber auch dazu viel mehr. Die ganze Ethik des Lebens und die ganze Zucht der heiligen Observanz gehört dazu. Das

realized his own shortcomings before Yahweh appears from his prayer of thanksgiving: [217]

> Lo, it was for my welfare
> that I had great bitterness;
> but thou hast held back my life
> from the pit of destruction,
> *for thou hast cast all my sins*
> behind thy back.

Hezekiah, then, definitely did not intend to assert "sinlessness" when he confessed the perfection of his heart and faithfulness of his life.[218] The king's prayer, on the contrary, was directed to his complete dependence and submission to Yahweh's wise and gracious will. He confessed that he had remained in the covenant cultus and ethos faithfully with his whole heart. In all aspects of his life and rule as king of Judah he had reckoned with the will of Yahweh.[219] His ethos ("walk") had been *all the time* acceptable to Yahweh ("Before Thee", "in Thy sight"), not because of his "sinlessness" but because *"He trusted in Yahweh the God of Israel; he did not depart from following Him, but kept the commandments which Yahweh commanded Moses. And Yahweh was with him; wherever he went forth, he prospered."* [220]

Hezekiah knew his God because he walked with Him continually – "Yahweh was with him" – and received the visible and concrete signs of Yahweh's blessing in his rulership.[221] In other words, Hezekiah dwelt as guest with Yahweh in Zion because he complied fully with the cultic requirements. How the honor and glory of Yahweh was uppermost in his heart can be seen in his close cultic relationship with his God.[222]

---

tritt eben in Kultpsalmen wie 15 und 24, 81 und 132 genügend hervor, bleibt aber auch in den individuellen Klagepsalmen nicht unberücksichtigt."

217   Is. 38,17.

218   Nor does he appeal to "his own dignity and merits" as K. Frör unfortunately concludes in his "Das Gebet des Königs Hiskia", in *Humanitas-Christianitas, FS* W. v. Loewenich, 1968, p. 381.

219   Cf. 2 Kings 18,3: "And he did what was right in the eyes of Yahweh, according to all that David his father had done." He reformed and purified the cultus, vs. 4.

220   2 Kings 18,5-7a; cf. Is. 26,2-4.

221   See 2 Kings 18-19.

222   2 Kings 19,14ff. It is just as important to note that after his recovery Hezekiah on one important occasion did *not* glorify Yahweh, i.e., to the envoys of Babylon, so that the prophetic oracle announced the doom of Jerusalem, 2 Kgs 20,12ff. (Is. 39). This proves that Hezekiah's perfection was not a natural or inherent quality of his heart, but rather that the perfect relationship with Yahweh, even of a lifetime, always remains threatened by the secret, unconscious tendency to self-exaltation.

What further must be taken into account, to understand Hezekiah's confession of perfection, is his position as king of Judah, who now was in the situation of utmost distress and bitterness. His prayer actually is an appeal to Yahweh as covenant God to deliver him out of deep trouble. The confession of his perfection is not a claim on the basis of merit, but an appeal to his attitude of covenant-faithfulness in order that Yahweh, unhindered by an obstacle of wickedness or rebellion on Hezekiah's side, may now graciously fulfill His own covenant promise to help and deliver His child and servant in the time of trouble.[223] The fact that Hezekiah is the king, the anointed one of Yahweh, and therefore God's son and servant in a special sense, only adds power to his confession of innocence.[224]

N. Ridderbos[225] justly stresses:

> Wie zich tegen de koning keert, keert zich tegen de gezalfde van de HERE, tegen de stamvader van Israëls grote Koning, de Messias, vgl. 2 Sam. 76; hij brengt het heil van Israël, ja het heil van de wereld in gevaar; zie op Ps. 18:21 vv.

This observation has a vital and profound significance. Between the king of Israel and Yahweh the Davidic covenant had provided a special son-Father relationship of love and protection (2 Sam. 7,14) for the benefit of the covenant people as a whole and the needy and poor in particular (Ps. 72). In a unique way the king was the appointed mediator between Israel and Yahweh, being the representative of both.[226] What he received from Yahweh belonged to Israel, even the rulership over the nations (Ps. 2,7), the heritage of the world! How fundamental the Davidic covenant of 2 Sam. 7 was to the faith of Israel is attested by Ps. 89,26-33:

> He shall cry to me. "Thou art my Father, my God, and the Rock of my salvation." And I will make him the firstborn, the highest of the kings of the earth. My steadfast love I will keep for him for ever, and my covenant will stand firm for him. I will establish his line for ever and his throne as the days of the heavens. If his children forsake my law and do not walk according to my ordinances, if they violate my statutes and do not keep my commandments, then I will punish their transgression with the rod and their

223 Cf. Ps. 50,14-15; 91,14-15.
224 Cf. 1 Sam. 2,10; Ps. 18,6ff.
225 *De Psalmen* I, 48f.
226 In Ps. 110 the king is even named "Priest forever after the order of Melchizedek." See now G. Fohrer, *Geschichte der israelitischen Religion*, 1969, pp. 134-142: "Die Eigenart des israelitischen Königtums." Also Fohrer, in *ThWNT* VIII, 349-353 (s.v. *huios* ktl B 5b-c).

iniquity with scourges; but I will not remove from him my steadfast love or be false to my faithfulness.

When the king of Israel was in danger or trouble, by sickness or persecution or false accusation and conspiracies, he could in trust and faith cling to Yahweh's faithfulness to His Davidic covenant. This kingly appeal to Yahweh's faithfulness did not exclude but included his own faithfulness to the covenant, i.e., as the adopted son of God he was to love and obey God, and to seek refuge in Yahweh in a representative way for the whole covenant people.

This ideal reality is pictured in the so-called Royal Psalms: 18 and 101.[227]

### aa) *Psalms 18 and 101.*

#### *Psalm 18*

In this cultic individual Thanksgiving Psalm the theme is the mutual covenantal relationship of trust and love between the theocratic king and his covenant God and the victory given over all overruling enemies, closing with a hymn of praise. David is described as "the servant of Yahweh" who in times of great persecution and distress is seeking his refuge in Yahweh, his Rock and Fortress. Calling upon Yahweh in praise, he testifies in the Song: "I am saved from my enemies," vs. 3 (MT 4).

In vss. 20-30 (ET) *Yahweh's covenant faithfulness* is placed in a central position, which indicates that "this awe-inspiring God is no arbitrary God; one can rely on Him."[228] Yet, in these vss. Yahweh's covenant faithfulness is especially emphasized in its correlationship with the royal covenant faithfulness.[229] Here an adequate interpretation depends completely on the Biblical theological evaluation of Israel's covenantal relationship with Yahweh in the setting of the cultus, the heart of the Torah, as presented in the Torah liturgy of Pss. 15 and 24.

H. J. Kraus[230] has explicitly indicated that not "the legalistic spirit in Deuteronomic form" (Gunkel), but the underlying Torah liturgy of

227  N. Ridderbos, *o.c.*, I, p. 443, who accepts the Davidic authorship of Ps. 18. Cf. also Weiser, *The Psalms*, p. 186 (on Ps. 18), and p. 648 (on Ps. 101).
228  N. Ridderbos, *o.c.*, I, p. 191.
229  N. Ridderbos, *o.c.*, I, p. 191: "Door heel de psalm heen weerklinkt het: God geeft aan zijn gezalfde, die zich houdt aan zijn wegen, bevrijding en heil, en voor hen, die zich verheffen tegen zijn gezalfde en daarin tegen Hemzelf, is Hij geducht." On vss. 20-24 he refers to the fact that four times Yahweh's attitude is typified as the reflected image ("spiegelbeeld") of man's attitude.
230  *Psalmen* I, 146.

Ps. 15 constitutes the legitimate hermeneutical key to interpret Ps. 18,20ff. In other words, even the Davidic king is subordinated to the entrance liturgy like every other Israelite in order to be the guest of Yahweh and to plead and receive the divine promises of help and salvation. The same cultic-ethical declaration of loyalty is required from the theocratic king as from the common Isralite, i.e., to be righteous and walk perfectly in the covenant.

A comparison of Ps. 18,20-25 with Ps. 15,2 reveals that both Psalms use the terms *şedeq* and *tāmîm* as the requisite qualifications for Yahweh's companionship and blessing. The royal confession of righteousness and perfection, therefore, has to be interpreted on the same basis and defined with the same theological dignity as the confession of righteousness and perfection of the common participant in the religious cultus.[231] That means that also in Ps. 18,20ff. the choice and following of the good way instead of the wicked way is not an autonomous decision of the human will as a constitutive element in the covenant righteousness, but, as in Ps. 15, the cultic-ethical dynamics of the covenant,[232] which summons the recreated will to *stay* within the salvation-historical deliverance and freedom given by divine grace, i.e., to continue in the fellowship or walk with Yahweh in ultimate dependence upon His grace.

Yet there is a difference here with Ps. 15 in two respects. First, in Ps. 18 it is nevertheless the theocratic king who is standing in the need of Yahweh's blessing, help, and instruction. Secondly, directly related to the previous, instead of the priest requiring perfection, now the king himself emphatically appeals to his "own" righteousness or keeping of the ways of Yahweh, which culminates in the extraordinarily strong confession of perfection:

> I was perfect [*tāmîm*] before Him, and I kept myself from guilt [*caŵônî*]. Vs. 23 (MT 24).

To this covenant faithfulness he ascribes[233] the divine rescue at the moment of his utter helplessness, already being in the grip of death:

---

231   Cf. Kraus, *l.c.*: "So wird also in 21ff. (sc. of Ps. 18!) das Bild des bundesgemässen, zum Heiligtume zugelassenen *şaddiq* gezeichnet."

232   Cf. N. Ridderbos, *o.c.*, I, 199: "Het doen van de HERE is een spiegel-beeld van het doen van de mensen, maar hierbij is te bedenken, dat dit zo is krachtens het door de HERE gestichte verbond."

233   N. Ridderbos, *o.c.*, I, p. 198, may well conclude of the king: "Hij doet dat in een van de sterkste 'onschuldsbetuigingen', die we in de Psalmen vinden." See also his important article, "De betuigingen van 'onschuld, recht-vaardigheid' in de Psalmen", in *GTT* 50 (1950), 86-104; esp. 100f. on the three elements which exercised their influence on Ps. 18,21ff. See also Weiser, *The Psalms*, pp. 192f. (on Ps. 18,20-24).

Therefore Yahweh has recompensed me according to my righteousness, according to the cleanness of my hands in His right. Vs.
24 (MT 25).

The following should be considered:
1) With the appeal to his perfection or righteousness the king is not
confessing, let alone claiming, merits or sinlessness. He is placing these
terms in opposition to the way of wickedness (cf. vs. 21f.), which, in
connection with the mention of Saul in vs. 1, can best be explained by
1 Sam. 15,23:

> For rebellion is as the sin of divination, and stubbornness is as
> iniquity and idolatry. Because you have rejected the word of the
> LORD, he has also rejected you from being king.[234]

Consequently, contrariwise, the way of following Yahweh in obedience
to His word in cultus and ethos is the way of righteousness and perfection. Everyone who thus participates in Israel's cultus is officially
declared righteous in the priestly act of judicial salvation in the name of
Yahweh.[235]
2) In the special situation of the king of Israel – i.e. his humiliation
and suffering – not merely his personal well-being, but that of the whole
nation, even the honor and covenant faithfulness of Yahweh, were at
stake. This situation of extreme danger, then, seems identical with that of
Hezekiah's position and confession of innocence. It is therefore of theological importance to notice the peculiar evaluation of David and Hezekiah
in the post-Davidic prophetic historiography of the Books of Kings:[236]

> David "walked with integrity of heart [$b^etom$-$l\bar{e}b\bar{a}b$, in perfection
> of heart] and uprightness [$b^ey\bar{o}\check{s}er$]" (1 K. 9,4).
> David's heart was "wholly true to the LORD" [$\check{s}\bar{a}l\bar{e}m$ $^cim$] (1 K.
> 11,4). David "followed the LORD wholly" [$mill\bar{e}^{\circ}$ $^{\circ}ah^ar\hat{e}$] (1 K. 11,6).
> David has walked in the LORD's ways and done "what is right in My
> sight" (1 K. 11,33; also vs. 38). David kept the LORD command-
> ments and "followed Me with all his heart, doing only that which
> was right in my eyes" [$h\bar{a}lak$ $^{\circ}ah^aray$ $b^ekol$ $l^eb\bar{a}b\hat{o}$ $la^casot$ $raq$
> $hayy\bar{a}\check{s}\bar{a}r$] (1 K. 14,8). David's heart was "wholly true" [$\check{s}\bar{a}l\bar{e}m$]
> to the LORD (1 K. 15,3). David did what was right [$hayy\bar{a}\check{s}\bar{a}r$] in
> the eyes of the LORD "and did not turn aside from anything that
> He commanded him all the days of his life, except in the matter of
> Uriah the Hittite" (1 K. 15,5).

234   N. Ridderbos, o.c., I, 198, points to the occurrence of the same pattern,
"spiegelbeeld", of God's action toward man as found here in Ps. 18,26.
235   See on Ps. 15.
236   Cf. G. von Rad, "Die deuteronomistische Geschichtstheologie in den
Königsbüchern," in Ges. Stud., pp. 200f.

"And Asa did what was right in the eyes of the LORD, as David his father had done" (1 K. 15,11).

Amaziah did "what was right in the eyes of the LORD, yet not like David his father" (2 K. 14,3).

Ahaz "did not do what was right in the eyes of the LORD, his God, as his father David had done" (2 K. 16,2).

Hezekiah "did what was right in the eyes of the LORD, according to all that David his father had done" (2 K. 18,3).

Josiah "did what was right in the eyes of the LORD, and walked in all the way of David his father, and he did not turn aside to the right hand or to the left" (2 K. 22,2).

It is obvious that David was the only ideal king of Judah in the theological judgment of the author of the Books of Kings.[237] All the other kings, even Solomon, Hezekiah and Josiah, are measured by the perfection of David's Messianic kingship.[238] In this respect the cultic priestly judgment of Pss. 18 and 101 on the theocratic reign and covenant faithfulness of David is in complete harmony with the Deuteronomistic prophetic historiography.

Only in the prophetic evaluation is David elevated above all the other Judean kings as the one supreme example, the ideal king.

Here a new element is presented which exceeds the purely cultic qualification of perfection. It is the divine legitimization of David's throne in the prophetic Messianic promises of 2 Sam. 7, Is. 9 and 11[239] by which Judah received the exalted privilege and responsibility of sacral kingship with universal rulership in perfect righteousness and peace.[240]

---

237 In spite of David's sin against Uriah, a deep fall of which he repented intensely, and which sin is not concealed here.

238 Von Rad, *Ges. Stud.*, p. 201: "Er ist das Urbild des vollkommen gehorsamen Gesalbten und deshalb das Vorbild für alle folgenden Könige in Jerusalem."

239 See von Rad, *O.T. Theology* I, 1962, pp. 40f., who draws a comparison with the Egyptian "model": "In Israel too these and other courtly ceremonial forms were the bearers of a whole store of equally traditional ideas. The king is God's son – though in Israel certainly not in the physical mythological sense, but *per adoptionem*: he is commissioned to rule by God himself, he governs with perfect justice and wisdom, he is the great benefactor and shepherd of his people, which flourishes under his rule... Abroad, he is the dread victor who triumphs over all his foes" (p. 41). Cf. also his "The Royal Ritual in Judah", in *The Problem of the Hexateuch* (ET of. *Ges. Stud.*), 1966, pp. 221-231. Fohrer, in *ThWNT* VIII, 351, 11ff., sharply distinguishes between judicial legitimization and adoption.

240 See Fohrer, *Gesch. der isr. Rel.*, pp. 138ff., who recognizes three aspects in Israel's kingship: a) the Davidic king is described as the Son of God and the Anointed one of Yahweh; b) the king is qualified as world-ruler; c) the king is social ruler, embodying the divine righteousness. On pp. 142-143

Although Judah did not accept the ancient Oriental ideology of a divine kingship, the poet of Pss. 2 and 89 uses the divine legitimization of the Davidic king in 2 Sam. 7 as basis for asking Yahweh's special help for its king.[241] In this Messianic-eschatological light not only the prophetic-historiographical evaluation of David,[242] but also the cultic picture of the Judean kingship in the "Royal Psalms"[243] add a new dimension in depth. With this Messianic background we now return to Pss. 18 and 101 which both portray the Davidic king in the cultic confession of the ideal, we might almost say, sinless ( ! ) king.[244]

As a theocratic[245] king David, as well as any of his royal descendants, could therefore legitimately identify himself with the sacral prerogative and protection of the Davidic covenant, *provided* he stood within the cultic perfection of Israel's covenant. Here we must disagree with von

Fohrer refers to the unique phenomenon of Israel's critical attitude toward, limitation of, and even rejection of its kingship. For arguments that Israel knew no divine kingship, see p. 136. Cf. also H. J. Boecker, *Die Beurteilung der Anfänge des Königtums in den deuteronomistischen Abschnitten des I. Samuelbuches*, WMANT 31, 1969, pp. 20ff. W. H. Schmidt, *Alttestamentlicher Glaube und seine Umwelt*, Neukirchener Studienbücher Bd. 6, 1968, pp. 174ff., 193-200.

241 Fohrer, in *ThWNT* VIII, 350,30ff.-352. Cf. also W. H. Schmidt, *o.c.*, p. 200: "Dem Alten Testament hat es nicht genügt, die altorientalische Königs-ideologie in die Zukunft zu verlegen; es hat sie so umgeprägt, dass sie ihr Wesen verlor."

242 *Ges. Stud.*, pp. 201f., therefore presumes behind the evaluation of David and his descendants in 1 and 2 Kings the Messianic idea and hope: "Dieses ganz menschliche Bild [sc. of the real David in his weaknesses] ist nunmehr von einem höchst eigenständigen Vorstellungskreis überlagert, näm-lich dem von dem urbildlichen, theokratischen und dem vorbildlich gehorsamen David. Damit bezeugt Dtr. zunächst einen messianischen Vorstellungskreis, der in seiner Zeit lebendig gewesen sein muss" [referring also to Ps. 132 and Is. 1,21].

243 Cf. von Rad, *O.T. Theology* I, pp. 318-324: "The Empire and Office of the Anointed in the Royal Psalms." N. Ridderbos, *o.c.*, I, pp. 156f.

244 Cf. N. Ridderbos, *o.c.*, I, p. 57: "De koning is zoon, en daarom ook stedehouder van de HERE, van de God des hemels en der aarde, vgl. ook Ps. 2:7 vv., 18:44, 89:27 v.... De dichters... richten hun blik op wat de koning van Israël naar recht toekomt, ze hebben voor ogen wat Israëls koning kan zijn, wat hij behoort te zijn: bijna zouden we zeggen: wat hij zou zijn, als hij zonder zonde was."

245 By "theocratic" we mean that the Davidic king by his adoption as "son of God" in the Enthronement Ritual did not become a god but remained in every respect dependent upon the only God, Yahweh. It is its *theonomic* character which distinguishes Jerusalem's kingship from the kingship of the surrounding ancient Near East. See K. H. Rengstorf, "Old and New Testament traces of a formula of the Judaean Royal Ritual", in *Nov. Test.* V (1962), 229-244, esp. 238, who points to Ps. 2,8 ("Ask of Me, and I shall give thee...") as the explicit manifestation of the theocratic character of Judah's Royal Ritual.

Rad when he evaluates the promise of Nathan concerning the Davidic covenant as functioning completely *independently* of Israel's covenant, so that he even describes Israel's covenant as a law that judges and destroys, and the Davidic promise as a Gospel which forgives and saves.[246] Here N. Lohfink[247] has indicated the indissoluble connection between David's kingship and Israel's cultus and ethos in a better way:

> Davids volmaakte gehoorzaamheid en de zegen die daardoor op hem en zijn huis neerdaalt, staan integendeel volstrekt binnen de ruimte van het verbond, en ook in hem werkt de wil van God zoals die in de wet werd opgetekend.

In this way we see the theocratic king in the religious cultus appeal to Yahweh with a "Psalm of David":[248]

> I will sing of loyalty [ḥesed] and of justice [mišpāṭ];
> to thee, O LORD, I will sing.
> I will give heed to the way that is blameless [derek tāmîm]
> Oh when wilt thou come to me?
> I will walk with integrity of heart [betom-lebābî] within my house;
> I will not set before my eyes anything that is base ...
> I will look with favor on the faithful in the land, that they may dwell with me; he who walks in the way that is blameless [bederek tāmîm] shall minister to me.
> No man who practices deceit shall dwell in my house;
> no man who utters lies shall continue in my presence.
> Morning by morning I will destroy all the wicked in the land,
> cutting off all the evildoers from the city of the LORD.

B. D. Eerdmans may be correct when he remarks that the subject of this Psalm, benevolence and justice, is presented "not as ideals but as real elements of speaker's manner of life",[249] but definitely goes too far when he adds: "To the psalmist a perfect life was not beyond the capacity of human nature."[250] Here the cautious exegesis of N. Ridderbos[251] is more realistic:

246  *Ges. Stud.*, p. 202.
247  *De Aktualiteit van het O.T.*, p. 151. Cf. also J. L. Koole, in *OTS* XIII, 111: "Der Davidsbund ist in den Sinaibund eingegliedert und der Davidide spielt die Rolle Moses am Sinai und Josuas in der Amphiktyonie." Cf. also Weiser, *The Psalms*, p. 192, n. 1 (on Ps. 18,20-24).
248  Ps. 101,1-3a, 6-8. See also Koole on the intimate relationship between Pss. 101 and 15, in: *OTS* XIII, 107ff.
249  *The Hebrew Book of Psalms*, 1947, *OTS* IV, 455. Also Weiser, but Kraus applies these virtues to Yahweh.
250  *L.c.*
251  *O.c.*, I, p. 57. Cf. J. Ridderbos, *ad* Ps. 101: "In het uitspreken van zijn

Wat Israëls' koningschap kon zijn, moest zijn, werd niet gerea-
liseerd door de koningen uit Davids huis, zelfs niet door de besten
van hen. Zo moest wel het gebruik van deze psalmen het verlangen
oproepen naar de koning, in wie al deze heerlijke uitspraken van de
psalmen werden vervuld.

It should be clear, however, that the Royal Psalms must not be
regarded as pious wishes, but, as von Rad[252] explains, as "prophetic
exegeses of the Nathan prophecy", i.e.,

> the royal psalms tell us much more about the prophetic prototype
> of Yahweh's anointed and his empire than about the actual figure
> he made in history – they address to the monarchy a *doxa*, which
> in their eyes Jahweh had attached to it once for all.

Especially the history of the last kings of Judah reveals how small
the divine *doxa* became in Judah's kingship, until by order of Yahweh
only a "ruin" (Ez. 21,25ff.), or a "stump" (Is. 11,1) of it was left
over. As the priesthood failed ultimately, so did the kingship.

The priestly declarations of cultic perfection together with the royal
protestations of righteousness and perfection were no longer accepted
by Yahweh, having become objectionable to the covenant God. Both
theocratic institutions fell under the wrath of Yahweh, and were swept
away by the divine judgment. Why? Obviously for the very same reason:
because the cultic claim of perfection was radically and systematically
being divorced from the ethos or walk of perfection. Here we are standing
*vis-à-vis* an undeniable historic testimony with respect to "the capacity
of human nature": in the most blessed situation of divine favor and
wisdom, of priestly grace and prophetic guidance, humanity failed and
lost its *doxa*. Paradise lost again!

How then can it be meaningful that the prophetic kerygma announces
a *new* covenant in the face of the frustration of the old covenant?[253]
Or, as Zimmerli puts it: "Wie aber soll die Unkraft der Rechtsverwirk-
lichung in Israel, die sich vor der Katastrophe zeigte, dann überwunden

---

voornemen aangaande de vervulling van zijn ambt ontwerpt de auteur een
beeld van de ideale koning, dat in geen aardse koning ooit volle werkelijkheid
is geworden, maar dat, evenals dat van Ps. 72, naar de bedoeling van de H.
Geest heenwijst naar de grote Koning der toekomst Jezus Christus." Also
Kraus, *o.c.*, II, p. 691: "So ist der König Wächter über die Einzugsthora ...
An dieser Stelle überschreitet der Regent seine eigenen Möglichkeiten und
Fähigkeiten." "Er vergegenwärtigt in einer letzten Vollkommenheit die
richterliche Autorität Jahwes in Israel."
    252  Von Rad, *O.T. Theol.* I, p. 321.
    253  Hos. 2,16ff.; Jer. 31,31ff.; Ez. 36,26f.

werden?"[254] By the prophetic promise of the coming of a perfect Priest-King who would reign and bring šālōm, welfare, by the Spirit of Yahweh![255]

In this coming King, this second David, the hope of Israel was ultimately concentrated.[256] The most mysterious revelation of the coming Savior-King is, however, the new element predicted by Isaiah in his pictures of the ᶜEbed Yahweh who will suffer and atone for the sins of Israel, which Vriezen justly calls a culmination-point of Old Testament preaching.[257]

But here we stand at the door of Israel's eschatology, with all its universal expectations and cosmic implications of the perfection of the Messianic age, when Yahweh shall reign again in Jerusalem and shall be glorified in the presence of all and unto Him every knee shall bow.[258]

### bb) Psalms 7 and 26

It was von Rad who pointed to the remarkable fact – from the viewpoint of Christian ethics – that in the Psalms the cultic participant does not start with and focus on the disturbing moral question "Am I ṣaddîq?", but "How can it be – since we are ṣaddîqîm, that God is acting this way?"[259] This is a question which applies not only to Hezekiah's prayer and confession, Is. 38, but also to all the cultic confessions of innocence.

Righteousness and innocence were regarded as the judicial cultic blessing of Yahweh's covenant (Pss. 4,1 [MT2]; 17,2; 35,23 [MT24]; 37,6). The appeal to one's innocence and righteousness then cannot be intended to exalt ethical perfection[260] but the unassailable reality of divine forgiveness and acquittal in Yahweh's covenant. The indication is that one's standing of righteousness presupposed the cultic confession of one's guilt and unrighteousness in true penitence. Thus we can find in the same Psalm confessions of sin and the rejoicing in righteousness,[261] e.g.:

Psalm 32
    I acknowledged *my sin* to thee,

254  In *Gottes Offenbarung. Ges. Aufs.*, 1969², p. 272.
255  Is. 11,1ff.; Ez. 21,27. Cf. Zimmerli, *o.c.*, p. 272f.
256  Ez. 34,24; 37,24-27.
257  *Outline*, p. 206; cf. pp. 352ff.
258  See Vriezen, *o.c.*, pp. 360ff.
259  In *Ges. Stud.*, p. 234.
260  Von Rad, *Ges. Stud.*, p. 232: "Das ist nicht eine unbegreiflich verstockte Selbstgerechtigkeit, sondern der Kultus hat sie angewiesen, in dieser Weise das Israel angebotene Wohlgefallen Gottes zu ergreifen."
261  Cf. N. Ridderbos, *o.c.*, p. 48; and, "De betuigingen van 'onschuld, rechtvaardigheid' in de Psalmen," in *GTT* 50 (1950), 86-104 esp. 94ff.

and I did not hide my iniquity;
I said, 'I will confess my transgressions to the LORD;
then thou didst forgive *the guilt of my sin* (vs. 5).
Be glad in the LORD, and rejoice, *O righteous* [*ṣaddîqîm*],
and shout for joy, *all you upright in heart!* (vs. 11).

## Psalm 40

Do not thou, O LORD, withold thy mercy from me,
let thy steadfast love and thy faithfulness ever preserve me!
For evils have encompassed me without number; *my iniquities* have
overtaken me, till I cannot see; they are more than the hairs
of my head; my heart fails me (vss. 11f.; MT12f.). Then I said,
"Lo, I come; in the roll of the book it is written of me; *I delight
to do thy will, O my God; thy law is within my heart* (vs. 7f.;
MT8f.).

## Psalm 41

As for me, I said, "O LORD, be gracious to me; heal me, for
*I have sinned against thee!*" (vs. 4; MT5).
But thou hast upheld me because of *my integrity*, and set me in
thy presence for ever (vs. 12; MT13).

These examples already disclose that the psalmists conceived both
statements not as contradictory but as necessary corollaries. It is only
on this religious-cultic basis of identification with Yahweh's righteousness that the Songs of Innocence can have their legitimate interpretation.[262]

### Psalm 7

The situation of this Individual Lament, or, better, Prayer of Supplication[263] is clearly one of a cultic-sacral lawsuit, in which the accused
one appeals to the heavenly Judge-King by taking upon himself an oath
of purification or innocence. The oath of innocence is also the dominating
structure of Job 31, esp. vss. 5-6.

262   Cf. Ch. Barth, *Introd. to the Psalms*, p. 41: "This completely unassailable righteousness in the sight of God, and not their 'good conscience' in the
face of every reproach and accusation from men, is the essence of their
attitude." Also p. 42, where Barth rejects the phrase „*assertions of innocence*",
for „*confessions of innocence*". Von Rad's describing it as "bragging"
(„pochen") therefore seems beside the point (*Ges. Stud.* 232). See, however,
his modified statements in *O.T.Theol.* I, p. 381.
263   See the treatment of W. Beyerlin, *o.c.*, pp. 95-101 (see above, n. 209).
He classifies Ps. 7 as "Bittgebet." He states: "Dass er [sc. der Gerichtsaufruf]
vom Begehren des Psalmisten bewegt und bestimmt ist, seiner Unschuld und
unverletzten Gemeinschaftstreue entsprechend Recht zu erlangen und eine
Beendigung der bösartigen, wuterfüllten Anfeindung zu erwirken, ist ganz
offensichtlich" (p. 99).

When we give full weight to the superscription of the Psalm the accused one is David, the anointed (Messiah) of Yahweh, who is falsely accused while he is convinced of his righteousness, i.e., that he is living in the right cultic relationship with Yahweh and his fellow Israelite; in short, in harmony with the covenant and not following the ethos or walk of wickedness. David confesses that he has not harmed his fellow-covenanter, vs. 4.[264] Now he appeals to the covenant God to judge him according to the (recreated) motives of his heart and the righteousness of his cause[265] according to the covenant. Yahweh's own righteousness is at stake, since the accused one is in harmony with Yahweh's covenant.

Therefore the term "righteous(ness)" is the key-word of this Psalm.[266] It is by order of Yahweh, the righteous Judge, vs. 11, that the curse of the oath shall fall upon the evil-doer, i.e., the false accuser and persecutor, because his whole being is intent upon the breaking of the covenant. "His mischief returns upon his own head, and on his own pate his violence descends" (vs. 16).[267]

*Psalm 26*

In this Psalm the poet again confesses his innocence and integrity (vss. 1.11) in the particular situation of a false accusation. N. Ridderbos, however, is careful not to emphasize this particular aspect too much (contra H. Schmidt, Kraus), since this confession of innocence is also intended to be a very personal one. Yet this Psalm is not the prayer of a self-righteous

---

264   E.g. in his relation to Saul:
"The Lord rewards every man for his righteousness and his faith-fullness; for the Lord gave you into my hand today, and I would not put forth my hand against the Lord's anointed." 1 Sam. 26:23.
Cf. 1 Sam. 24,6.10.12; 26,9; 2 Sam. 1,14.16. This connection becomes very real when King David would have been accused by a former follower of Saul, e.g. Cush a Benjaminite, that David had robbed Saul, cf. 2 Sam. 16,5-8; 20,1. Cf. N. Ridderbos, *o.c.*, p. 110, n. 1. This concrete relationship of forgiveness and sanctification is ignored and denied by J. Köberle, *Sünde und Gnade im Rel. Leben des Volkes Israel bis auf Christum*, 1905, pp. 351f., who describes the O.T. confessions of innocence as an "imperfection" since righteousness is not sought exclusively in forgiveness. He is followed in this respect by J. J. van As, *Skuldbelydenis en Genadeverkondiging in die O.T.* (Confession and Pardon of Sin in the OT), 1961, p. 59.

265   N. Ridderbos, *o.c.*, p. 108, speaks of "zaaksgerechtigheid" here. Cf. J. Ridderbos, *De Psalmen* I, p. 64: "dat de psalmisten in dergelijke uitspraken niet pleiten op zondeloosheid, maar hierop, dat ze aan het door God met Israël gesloten genadeverbond vasthouden in geloof en werken, die niet te scheiden zijn, vgl. Jac. 2:24."

266   Cf. N. Ridderbos, *o.c.*, p. 107.

267   Cf. Ps. 34,21; also Gal. 6,7. Beyerlin, *o.c.*, p. 101, concludes: "So hat Ps. 7 im ganzen die Funktion, Jahwe auf allerlei Weise zum rettenden Handeln im Gericht zu bewegen."

Pharisee, as N. Ridderbos, Kraus and Weiser justly elucidate.[268]

In his emergency the poet confesses that his walk (ethos) has been within the covenant, and his trust in Yahweh "without wavering", and now submits his inner motives to the judgment of his God, vss 1f. Expressing his hate or aversion against companionship with the wicked and their evil devices – an aspect which is similar to Ps. 1 – the poet professes his love for the sanctuary, the place of atonement and communion with Yahweh, vss. 4-8.

Gunkel emphasizes several times its corresponding "geistige Form der Gottesverehrung" with Psalm 15.[269] In this light the confession of personal perfection in Ps. 26 is not an assertion of sinlessness[270] but a confession of his covenant ethos in order to praise Yahweh's covenant *ḥesed* and to plead in his extremity for Yahweh's renewed faithfulness according to His gracious covenant promise. Walter Beyerlin, in his recent study on the cultic Psalms of Lament, has pointed out, however, that Ps. 26 is not situated in the so-called Temple-entrance liturgy but in the cultic-sacral supplication or appeal for divine acquittal from the false accusation of religious-cultic apostasy.[271]

The function of this Psalm would be not merely to receive the judicial

268 See also Barth, *C.D.* IV, 1, 570-573 (*K.D.*, pp. 636-639), who stresses with reference to the Psalms of Innocence: "We must hear them together with the other voices which sound in the Psalms. And if we do we shall see that for all their strangeness they did not really say anything other than what Paul said [sc. in Rom. 8,30f.]" (571). G. C. Berkouwer, *Faith and Sanctification*, p. 126 (Dutch, p. 127), states in this connection: "Whoever gives an abstract moral interpretation to these Old Testament expressions of righteousness is bound to distort the Scriptures. He would make of Israel's religion and the Covenant of Grace a purely nomistic salvation. The holiness of the righteous could then be only an ethical ideal and the mercy of God becomes irrelevant."

269 *Die Psalmen*, p. 111.

270 Cf. N. Ridderbos, *o.c.*, I, p. 272; J. Ridderbos, *o.c.*, I, pp. 224f. Weiser *o.c.*, p. 243; Kraus, *o.c.*, I, p. 218: "In diesem Psalm handelt es sich nicht um sittliche Selbstqualifikation oder hybrides Unschuldsbewusstsein eines sich selbst Rechtfertigenden..." L. A. Snijders, "Psaume XXVI et L'Innocence", *OTS* XIII (1963), 112-130, reduces the idea of *tom* in vss. 1 and 11 – as in Pss. 7,9; 25,21; 41,13; 101,2 – to merely ethical guilelessness: 'ingénuité', sans arrière-pensées (mauvaises)." "L'homme sincère n'a pas d'intentions secrètes" (115). It seem that full justice is not done to the underlying *redemptive* cultic qualification and experience here. Significant is his objection against the name "Psalms of innocence" (115).

271 *O.c.*, pp. 117-122. He again classifies this Psalm as a Prayer of Supplication: "Im ganzen ist die Struktur des so gegliederten Textes am besten wieder als Bittgebet, genauer als Gerichtsappellation zu charakterisieren, die entsprechende Loyalitäts- und Unschuldsbekundungen in sich schliesst und in einem Lobpreis-Versprechen ausmündet" (p. 122). "In Ps. 26 geht es, fasst man zusammen, um eine gerichtliche Untersuchung und Entscheidung des Verwurfs der Apostasie durch Gott" (p. 119).

acquittal as such but Yahweh's cultic theophany (His *kābôd*, vs. 8), for the vindication of the accused covenant worshipper. The psalm closes with the confession of personal integrity as far as his covenant ethos is concerned, and the supplication for Yahweh's gracious redemption together with the promise of praising His name in the cultus community:

> But as for me, I walk in my integrity [*bᵉtummî*]; redeem me, and be gracious to me. My foot stands on level ground; in the great congregation I will bless the Lord (vss. 11-12).

A graphic picture of this combined motif of false accusation and perfection is found also with the post-exilic prophet Zechariah.

In ch. 3 we find Satan accusing Joshua the high priest, standing before the angel of Yahweh (3,1). In a unique way Israel's perfection before Yahweh is portrayed not as being any inherent ethical perfection but the judicially imputed righteousness and purity according to the cult covenant. By order of Yahweh the filthy garment, i.e., Israel's iniquity, is removed from Joshua and exchanged for *clean* or perfect apparel. What is, however, of no less crucial importance is the following commission and promise to Joshua:

> *If you will walk in my ways and keep my charge,* then you shall rule my house and have charge of my courts, and I will give you the right of access among those who are standing here.[272]

With unmistakable clarity the prophet reveals the twofold message that Yahweh is faithful to His covenant to forgive and to impute perfection to His covenant people, but, at the same time, that justification implies no quietism. Ethos and cultus still stand in an indissoluble, dynamic relationship, in which the ethos of living obedience or sanctification is founded and rooted in the cultic dynamism of divine justification. But most of all, that sins of weakness brought in repentance to Yahweh (the filthy garments!) can never be the cause for condemnation or rejection of Israel by Yahweh, even when the accuser is Satan.

### cc) *Psalms 37 and 119 – legalistic?*

#### Psalm 37

In this "Psalm of David",[273] which shows more affinity to the Wisdom Literature than to the cultus,[274] the "blameless" ones, *tᵉmîmim*, are

272  Zech. 3,7.
273  N. Ridderbos and Weiser defend the appropriateness of a pre-exilic Sitz im Leben.
274  Cf. however, N. Ridderbos, *o.c.*, I, p. 397, who yet recognizes the possibility of cultic use.

154

placed over against the wicked (in Israel). These last "plot against the righteous" in order "to slay those who walk uprightly" (vss. 12.14.18.32. 37). In this situation of mortal danger the old, wise man, vs. 25, offers comforting assurance[275] to the young who are tempted to doubt whether Yahweh will vindicate His own. Yahweh knows the days of the $t^e m \hat{\imath} m \hat{\imath} m$ and will soon intervene; the $\d{s}add\hat{\imath}q\hat{\imath} m$ will see it! "Their heritage will abide for ever" (vs. 18). Hence the counsel:

> Refrain from anger, and forsake wrath! Fret not yourself; it tends only to evil. For the wicked shall be cut off; but those who wait for the LORD shall possess the land (vss. 8f.).

How far this Psalm is removed from the spirit of legalism appears from the reality of the *transformed* heart of the perfect or righteous one:

> The law of his God is in his heart; his steps do not slip (or waver) (vs. 31).[276]

The Psalm closes with special emphasis on the real ground of the hope of vindication:

> The salvation of the righteous is from the LORD; he is their refuge in the time of trouble. The LORD helps them and delivers them because they take refuge in him (vss. 39-40).

*Psalm 119*

This literary "alphabetical Psalm" is well described by Kraus as "eine Sammlung von Äusserungen der individuellen Thora-Frömmigkeit der nachexilischen Zeit, die aus Elementen des Schriftstudiums, der deutero- nomischen Theologie, der kultischen Thora-Unterweisung des Einzelnen und Impulsen der Weisheitslehre entstanden ist."[277]

However, in Ps. 119 also the religious confessions of the psalmist's own righteousness and perfection (vss. 1.11.98ff.111.121.162ff.) are framed within the situation of oppression and persecution (vss. 61.78. 84ff.110, etc.). Weiser[278] rightly stresses that these last statements must be taken quite seriously:

---

275 Thus Kraus, *o.c.*, I, p. 292, contra Gunkel's idealistic interpretation of "requital" (Vergeltung). Cf. Weiser, *o.c.*, *p.* 314: "Trust in God and in his providential rule is indeed the fundamental theme of the psalm..." See also p. 315.

276 Cf. Pss. 18,36; 26,1.

277 *O.c.*, II, p. 823.

278 *O.c.*, p. 740. Cf. Mowinckel, *Ps. St.* I, 122, who even calls Ps. 119 "ein individuelles Klagelied mit Unschulds- und hymnischen Motiven", in which the praise of the Torah is not the main purpose; see also *Ps. St.* VI, 28 n. 1

It is only if we understand them as being at the root of the poet's utterances that we can apprehend the strength and the comfort which God's word and his law impart to the life of the poet.

The prayers of vss. 8, 107, 153ff. are clearly laments and supplications. Therefore the protestations of innocence and perfection are again confessions of wholehearted surrender and submission to the Torah, not merely with respect to a particular situation he is now falsely accused of, but in reference to his whole life and existence.[279] His whole *derek* or ethos is placed in the center as a walk *b*e*tôrat Yhwh* (vs. 1).

How intimately this Torah was experienced in living relationship with Yahweh as Creator can be seen in vss. 72f.:

> The law of Thy mouth is better to me than thousands of gold and silver pieces. Thy hands made and fashioned me; give me understanding that I may learn Thy commandments.

The afflicted poet, who lives in close and dynamic communion with his divine Master, does not make his perfection, righteousness or covenant obedience the autonomous ground of his supplication. On the contrary, falling back on Yahweh's *ḥesed* and *promise* (vs. 76), he prays: "Let Thy mercy [*raḥ*a*mêkā*] come to me, that I may live; for Thy law is my delight" (vs. 77). He is not boasting in self-righteousness,[280] nor uttering any moral self-evaluation, but is praying for the right attitude toward his God according to His revealed will:

> Give me understanding, that I may keep Thy law and observe it with my whole heart... graciously teach me Thy law! (vss. 34.29b).

In all this Ps. 119 is akin to Pss. 1; 19B; 37 and 40.

Von Rad threatens to create too wide a distance between the poet's

---

("sondern Vertrauens- und Gerechtigkeitsmotiv"). In the framework of his so-called "demons"-interpretation he classifies Ps. 119 in the category of cultic "individuelle Sündopferpsalmen" (*Ps. St.* VI, 28).

279 Cf. Kraus, *o.c.*, II, pp. 822f., nr. 5. Cohen, *ad* Ps. 119,1 connects the *t*e*mîmê-derek* ("whose way is blameless") with Abraham's way in Gen. 17,1: "Those to whom the epithet applies are undivided in their allegiance and completely guided by the Torah." He even translates Ps. 119,80 as "Let my heart be *undivided* (*tāmîm*) in Thy statutes..."

280 Weiser, *o.c.*, pp. 740f. acknowledges this only partly, since he describes the piety of Ps. 119 as implying a more or less deification of the law which therefore "was bound to end in the self-righteousness of the Pharisees and scribes." Kraus, *o.c.*, II, p. 829, however, judges: "Von Nomismus und von strenger 'Gesetzesfrömmigkeit' ist keine Spur zu finden. Doch selbstverständlich ist der in der Thora Lebende immer der Gehorsame, der in Gottes Wort mit seiner ganzen Existenz Verwurzelte."

literary testimony and his actual religious experience when he states concerning Ps. 119,143 (implying practically all the confessions of delight in Yahweh's Torah) that these assertions exceed "the boundaries of psychological possibilities."[281]

Is it really adequate to deny the reality of the testimony even to the original Psalmists? Von Rad[282] asserts:

> Although their utterances are couched in the form of most intimate confessions, they are not to be taken in the modern sense of a soul's testimony about itself...; they... definitely transcend human, psychological, and moral possibilities.

No doubt this evaluation is correct when judged from the viewpoint of the capacity of the human natural heart as such. However, does such psychological-moral evaluation sufficiently take into account the reality of the transforming, recreating encounter of the poet's heart with his divine *Gōʾēl* in the mystical and sacramental experience in the Sanctuary of Yahweh? Should we not leave room here for the reality of the soul experience of the poet who indeed experiences the reality of a new heart and who now testifies of the *miracle* of his new heart in which is now written Yahweh's Torah, i.e., a heart that truly and wholeheartedly loves the revelation of Yahweh? Yet, we feel, von Rad has indicated a very vital principle of the Psalms in their function as cult Songs, a principle which we also encountered in the Royal Psalms. These confessions of perfection as a *delectari* in the revelation of Yahweh together with the professions of continuous faithfulness to these revelations are functioning in the cultus as "type expressions" for the ideal *ṣaddîq* who is pictured in Ps. 119 with the qualifications of religious and psychological perfection.[283]

"What happens is that the speakers put themselves into the picture of the *ṣaddîq par excellence*, and claim it as their own."[284] This claim, however, does not legitimately occur in the spirit of a moral self-qualification but as an identification of faith, in which the soteriological foundation is maintained.[285] Von Rad sees this cultic style of perfection

---

281   *Ges. Stud.*, p. 22, n. 11.

282   *O.T. Theol.* I, p. 382.

283   See von Rad, *O.T. Theol.* I, pp. 381f. Gunkel, *Die Psalmen*, p. 514, remarks in this respect: "Ja, darüber hinaus [sc. the avowal of obedience] kann er es sich selber bezeugen, dass er das Gesetz schon jetzt hält und auch bereits gehalten hat 95.100.102.109.110.112.157 usw. Dem entspricht, dass sich im Psalm eine Bitte um Sündenvergebung nicht findet."

284   Von Rad, *o.c.*, I, p. 382. Cf. N. Ridderbos, *o.c.*, I, pp. 47,51, who indicates the similar creedal style.

285   Cf. von Rad, *Ges. Stud.*, p. 234 and *O.T. Theol* I, pp. 381f., referring to Ps. 143,2; Job 4,17.

intensified in post-exilic times in the theological circles of the wisdom tradition.[286] Here a cultic mysticism of passionate delight in Yahweh together with a deepened recognition of the inadequacy of one's own obedience was kept alive (Pss. 73,28; 37,4; Job 22,26; 27,10; Is. 58,14; 64,6).

The sharpest contrast between human righteousness and Yahweh's mercy is found in the prayer of Dan. 9,18 which further indicates "the very small extent to which legal ideas entered into the thought of later Israel on the process of declaring a man or men righteous."[287]

D. Rössler[288] has shown more precisely how this Torah-faith in late Judaism diverges in *two* ways. Besides the legalistic and casuistic Rabbinical law interpretation there was developed the Torah concept of apocalyptic theology. In this last concept the Torah was not understood as as codex or volume of statutes, but as the banner of divine election calling and uniting the true Israel. In other words, here the Torah was still acknowledged in its living covenant relationship.[289]

286  *O.T. Theol.* I, pp. 382f.

287  *Ibid.*, p. 383.

288  *Gesetz und Geschichte in der spätjüdischen Apokalyptik*, WMANT 3, 1962², esp. pp. 70ff., 100ff.

289  Cf. W. Zimmerli, in *Ges. Aufsätze*, pp. 274f.: "Das [sc. late Judaistic apocalyptic theology] zeigt, wie falsch es wäre, das Gesetz auf der ganzen Linie einfach mit Verdienstgedanken und einer rechnenden Gerechtigkeit zu verbinden."

## 1. *Christ and perfection*

When we consider the teaching of Jesus Christ on the theme of perfection according to the New Testament, we cannot limit our reflections to the two places where the term *teleios* is used, Mt. 5,48; 19,21.

We also have to inquire where the *matter* of perfection is being referred to in the four Gospels, in the form of the *"imitatio Christi"* in particular.

a. Mt. 5,48: *Esesthe oun hymeis teleioi hōs ho patèr hymōn ho ouranios teleios estin.*

This logion of Christ, spoken to His disciples in the framework of the Sermon on the Mount, constitutes the climax of a series of logia, vss. 43-47,[1] if not of the whole series of antitheses of chapter V,[2] which is colored by a conscious contrast with the legalistic piety of the scribes and Pharisees who do not enter the kingdom of heaven themselves and hinder those who were entering.[3]

1  This is implied in the term *oun* following the imperative *esesthe*. Cf. P. J. Du Plessis, *TELEIOS. The Idea of Perfection in the New Testament*, 1959, p. 168.

2  Cf. Du Plessis, *o.c.*, p. 168. J. Schmid, *Das Ev. nach Mat.*, RNT I, 1965⁵, p. 113: "V. 48 fasst den Grundgedanken der sechs Antithesen, die sittliche Forderung Jesu, mit einer sonst nirgends mehr wiederkehrenden Schärfe zusammen." W. D. Davies, *The Setting of the Sermon on the Mount*, 1964, p. 14 even stresses: "Any attempt to understand the *SM* [sc. Sermon on the Mount] in stark separation from the rest of the Gospel (and many treatments of it have been such) must therefore be deemed inadequate: it must be approached in the light of its setting in Matthew." Cf. also his *The Sermon on the Mount*, 1966, pp. 1-6, defending the essential unity of Mt. 5-7 against source, form and liturgical criticism. Also the polemical G. Friedlander, *The Jewish Sources of the Sermon on the Mount*, The Libr. of Bibl. Stud., ed. H. M. Orlinsky, 1969 (1911), p. 84, acknowledges concerning Mt. 5,48: "This statement is clearly intended to be a summary of all that Jesus has said in the Sermon up to this point. From the artistic standpoint, it must be granted that no finer culminating passage could possibly have been selected [referring to Dt. 18,13; Lev. 19,2]".

3  Cf. R. Schnackenburg, *Christliche Existenz nach dem N.T.*, I, 1967, pp. 140f., 146, referring to Mt. 23,13. J. Schmid, *o.c.*, pp. 113f.: "Was aber 5,20 in negativer Form ausspricht, sagt 5,48 in schärfster positiver Formulierung." Also U. Luck, *Die Vollkommenheitsforderung der Bergpredigt*,

Already from this contextual relationship the word in Mt. 5,48 cannot be considered as an isolated moral imperative which would imply the teaching of ethical sinlessness or perfectionism.[4]

The character of the perfection-imperative,[5] however, will be colored by one's interpretation of the *basileia tōn ouranōn*[6] – the nature of which determines its entrance-requirements – and of its relation to Jesus as the Messianic King.[7] Although it is now generally acknowledged that "the sayings in the Sermon on the Mount are set in an eschatological framework",[8] i.e., are directed to the ultimate establishment of the Kingdom of glory,[9] yet it is true that the eschatological Kingdom-motif is not the exclusive point of view. Jesus' radical religious intensifying and concretizing of the ethos of love of grace remains basic.[10]

ThEx 150, 1968, p. 17: "'Bessere Gerechtigkeit' und 'Vollkommenheit' sind für Matthäus identisch. Was diese bessere Gerechtigkeit oder Vollkommenheit enthält, wird in dem Abschnitt 5,21-48 gezeigt."

4   See e.g. H. Windisch, *The Meaning of the Sermon on the Mount*, ET 1950 (German, 1937), pp. 119f., 121f. On p. 185 he limits his perfectionism, however, by a recognition of Mt. 7,11. On perfectionism, see below, Ch. V.

5   Cf. *hagioi esesthe*, 1 Pet. 1,16; Lev. 19,2 LXX; also Deut. 18,13 LXX: *teleios esèi*. See also F. Blass-A. Debrunner, *A Greek Grammar of the N.T.*, ET from the ninth-tenth German ed.; 1961, § 362.

6   Mt. 5,3.10.19.20; 7,21. Cf. R. Schnackenburg, *Gottes Herrschaft und Reich*, 1959, p. 72: "Die neue *sittliche Haltung*, die Jesus verlangt, die 'grössere Gerechtigkeit' (Mt. 5,20), die 'Vollkommenheit' nach dem Vorbild des himmlischen Vaters (Mt. 5,48), lässt sich nur im Zusammenhang seiner Basileia-Botschaft begreifen." J. Schniewind, *Das Ev. nach Mat.*, NTD 2, 1960[9], pp. 73f., refers to the interpretations of the Sermon on the Mt as 1) Kultur-programm, 2) Gesinnungsethik, 3) Interimsmoral, 4) Todesurteil, 5) Messias-Geheimnis Jesu, 6) Gottes Gegenwart als Einzelforderungen. See H. N. Ridderbos, *De Komst van het Koninkrijk*, 1950, pp. 5-23, 217f. with lit., for a historical survey of the various concepts. H. Preisker, *Das Ethos des Urchristentums*, 1949, pp. 130-134, interprets *teleios* from the strictly eschatological understanding of *telos*, i.e., *teleios* is qualified by the degree of participating in the *telos*, the final establishment of the kingdom of God: "Der Begriff *teleios* ist aber nicht irgendwie ethisch zu fassen, sondern gibt die Endzeitbestimmtheit des Seins an" (p. 50).

7   Cf. Ridderbos, *o.c.*, p. 18: "Rijk Gods en Messias zijn correlate begrippen."

8   R. N. Flew, *The Idea of Perfection in Christian Theology*, p. 4, justly refers to H. Windisch, *Der Sinn der Bergpredigt*, 1929, pp. 9-20.

9   Cf. Windisch, *The Meaning of the Sermon on the Mount*, pp. 27ff. E. Brunner, *The Mediator*, 1947 (German 1927), p. 419 (in ch. XVI). W. Lüthi and R. Brunner, *The Sermon on the Mount*, ET 1963, p. 165: "The beginning too, and the middle, indeed its whole content is influenced by this last day and is aimed at this one final goal." Ridderbos, *o.c.*, pp. 218-220.

10   Cf. Ridderbos, *o.c.*, pp. 279f.; 285f. referring to Lk. 16,19-31, esp. vss. 29f.: "Niet slechts en niet in de eerste plaats het inzicht, dat het einde nabij is, maar het geloof in hetgeen God van den beginne geopenbaard en bevolen heeft, bepaald de rechte verhouding tot God en is het geheim van het leven naar zijn geboden."

160

The remarkable *egō* statements in Mt. 5, however, far exceeding the prophetic consciousness, testify of Jesus' consciousness of Messianic authority, i.e., that in Him God has come to the world "with His grace and justice, with His salvation and curse."[11] Matthew presupposes the redeeming and healing reality of "the gospel of the kingdom" for this perfection-imperative.[12]

The presumption of the Sermon on the Mount is that the kingdom of God in Jesus as the Messianic King has begun its operation; that the divine dominion or rulership in Christ has broken through as a present reality; that the *eschaton* is already effective in the person of Jesus,[13] without denying its final eschatological fulfillment (7,13f. 21-23). The ethos of the Sermon on the Mount is not addressed to the Gentiles or self-righteous Jews, but to the praying children of the heavenly Father[14] (Mt. 6,9ff.; 7,7-11; Lk. 11,13). These are addressed with the ethical redemptive indicative:[15] "You are the salt of the earth", and "You are the light of the world", which light does not merely become concrete in their "goods works" but is characterized by the praise and exaltation of their "Father who is in heaven" (Mt. 5,13-16). They do not boast in their

11 See Ridderbos, *o.c.*, pp. 98f. Cf. E. Käsemann, *Exegetische Versuche und Besinnungen*, I, 1964⁴, p. 206: "Denn der Jude, der tut, was hier geschieht, hat sich aus dem Verband des Judentums gelöst oder – er bringt die messianische Thora und ist der Messias." Also *Str-B* IV, 1, 1ff. E. Thurneysen, *Die Bergpredigt*, ThEx 46, 1936, p. 8: "Wichtig ist nicht das Mehr oder Weniger der Distanz die hier sichtbar wird zwischen der Lehre der Schriftgelehrten und der Lehre Jesu, sondern wichtig ist allein der christologische Sinn und Bezug, der in den Aussagen Jesu über das Gesetz liegt." Thurneysen's Christological-pneumatic interpretation – because of its Messianic joy – overlooks, however, the Messianic demands. We cannot enter on the complicated and much debated problem of the Messianic self-consciousness of Jesus. See on this the contributions in *Der historische Jesus und der kerygmatische Christus*, ed. H. Ristow and K. Matthiae, 1962; esp. of O. Cullmann, pp. 266-280. Cf. E. Fuchs, "Jesu Selbstzeugnis nach Matthäus 5", in *ZThK* 51 (1954), 14-34.

12 See Mt. 4,23f. Cf. J. Schniewind, *o.c.*, p. 207: "Alles, was Jesus bei seinen Jüngern an neuer 'Gerechtigkeit' erwartet, stammt aus der Macht und dem Wunder Gottes."

13 Cf. Mt. 11,2-6; 12,28f.; 13,16f. W. G. Kümmel, *Promise and Fulfillment. The Eschat. Message of Jesus*, SBT 23, ET 1961², pp. 105ff., 109. Schnackenburg, *o.c.* I, p. 119, referring to Lk. 4,19. Ridderbos, *o.c.*, pp. 102ff. Preisker, *o.c.*, p. 49.

14 Cf. Kittel, in *ThWNT* I, 5f. (s.v. *abba*). Especially Schrenk in *ThWNT* V, 984-987 (s.v. *patèr*); esp. 985: "Neu in diesem Sprachgebrauch ist, dass der unfeierliche Kindeslaut aus dem Alltag ohne Bedenken auf Gott übertragen wird ... Das Recht zu solcher Kindlichkeit steht in den Schranken der *basileia*." R. Schnackenburg, *Chr. Existenz* I, p. 146: "So ist wenigstens angedeutet, dass alle Kraft des Wirkens, auch des sittlichen Strebens, dem Jünger Jesu vom Vater zufliesst." Preisker, *o.c.*, pp. 49, 56f., pointing to Mk. 10,27.

15 Ridderbos, *o.c.*, p. 222.

righteousness but "hunger and thirst for righteousness", seeking first their Father's kingdom and His righteousness (Mt. 5,6; 6,33). They love and serve God with an undivided, i.e., a whole heart (Mt. 6,24).

Jesus describes them in Mt. 5,5 as the meek (*praeis*) who will inherit the earth (*klèronomèsousin tèn gèn*). With this description Jesus identifies them with the meek or righteous (*ṣaddîqîm*) or blameless (*temîmim*, perfect!) ones of Ps. 37, who bear the law of God in their heart (Ps. 37,31).[16] And when He calls them "the pure in heart" (*katharoi tèi kardiai*), Mt. 5,8, He identifies them with the Old Testament worshippers in the sanctuary, who have received "clean hands and a pure heart" (Ps. 24,4 LXX: *katharos tèi kardiai*; 51,10 [MT 12] LXX: *kardian katharan*) and who walk perfectly (*tāmîm*, Ps. 15,2) according to the covenant cultus. H. Windisch[17] even evaluates the commandments of Mt. 5,21-48 as *"thoroth-d'entrée"*, "prescriptions for admittance" when he draws this parallel:

> Just as access to the altar and participation in the cultus in the Temple at Jerusalem were hedged about by definite cultic and ethical conditions (the most familiar catalogues are in Ps. 15 and 24; cf. also Ps. 118:19f. and Isa., ch. 33), so also the Kingdom of Heaven opens its doors only to those who meet the prescriptions for admittance as revealed by Jesus.

He may intend this in a legalistic way,[18] but nevertheless scores a bull's eye from the viewpoint of Old Testament theology, since the Psalms presuppose the redemptive experience in Israel's covenant of grace.[19]

This intimate relationship of the Sermon on the Mount with the living Old Testament sanctuary worship precludes fundamentally the notion of theological perfectionism in Christ's perfection-imperative of Mt. 5,48. In other words, Jesus' perfection-imperative also presupposses the redemptive indicative,[20] i.e., the perfect forgiveness of sins. Just as in

16  The LXX of Ps. 36(37), 11 reads: *hoi de praeis kleronomèsousin gèn*. - Cf. also Mt. 5,3 (*ptōchoi tōi pneumati*) with Ps. 33(34),19 LXX; Is. 57,15; 61,1; and Mt. 5,4 (*penthountes paraklèthèsontai*) with Is. 61,2f. See above, Ch. III, B, 2 (cc).

17  *O.c.*, p. 27. Cf. also *ZNW* 27 (1928), 163-189: "Die Sprüche vom Eingehen ins Reich Gottes". Esp. p. 182: "Das Zusammenstehen der beiden Begriffe *dikaiosynè* und *eiserchesthai* [sc. in Mat. 5,20] ist der deutlichste Beweis für die Beeinflussung der synoptischen Sprüche durch die ATlichen entrée-Liturgien. Jesus hat die Tempeltorot auf die *basileia* übertragen."

18  That is to say, to place the imperative as a prerequisite *before* the salvation-indicative. This justifies Ridderbos in criticizing Windisch here as being "at least onesided" (*o.c.*, p. 223).

19  See above, Ch. III, B, 2b.

20  Cf. Ridderbos, *o.c.*, p. 221. Significant is the conclusion of Windisch, *l.c.*: "Für die *basileia* Jesu gelten ganz ähnliche Bedingungen und Bestimmungen wie für die *ekklèsia* (qhl) der Thora" (185).

the Psalms the religious-moral requirement of perfection as the covenantal *imitatio Dei*[21] is conditioned and motivated by the historic salvation of the divine Exodus deliverance, so we find Christ's call to perfection conditioned and motivated by His own redeeming acts of healing, exorcism and forgiving of sins.[22] On the basis of this Messianic authority and redemption Jesus identifies the call to perfection with the call to follow Him as the Christ in the new life of true and wholehearted obedience.[23]

Especially Matthew and John intend to reveal why the Old Testament *imitatio Dei* is now to be made manifest as the *imitatio Christi*, or, as John describes it, as the following of the good Shepherd, the Son of God.[24]

---

21  See above, Ch. III, B, 1. The threefold distinction of J. S. Banks, in *A Dictionary of the Bible*, ed. J. Hastings, III, 1900, p. 745 (s.v. *perfection*), therefore labors under a forced theological tension between the Old and New Covenants: "It [sc. OT] is negative rather than positive, refers to outward act rather than to inner disposition and spirit, and may be summed up in righteousness rather than in love." G. Friedlander, *o.c.*, p. 87, rightly criticizes Hasting's *Dictionary* with the reply: "The fact that God's holiness is man's ideal according to the Torah, should effectively disprove this unwarranted statement." (See, however, our critique on the Rabbinic *imitatio Dei*, in Ch. III, A, n. 102).

22  Mt. 4,23f.; 8,16f. 28ff.; 9,5f. Cf. Flew, *o.c.*, pp. 21f. See the instructive treatise of J. Jeremias, *The Sermon on the Mount*, 1961, esp. pp. 25-33; stating on p. 32: "The result to which we have come is that the Sermon on the Mount is not Law, but Gospel." Jeremias evaluates the sayings of Mt. 5-7 as "an early Christian catechism", in which "the Gospel preceded the demand" (p. 29). This basic Gospel structure of Mt. 5-7 is denied by E. Brunner, *The Mediator*, pp. 419f., who stresses only the "impossibility" of obedience. "It gives isolated examples of the one Good, the absolute Good, the Impossible" (p. 420).

23  Mt. 4,19-22 (*deute opisō mou-èkolouthèsan autōi*); Mt. 9,9; Mk. 2,14 *akolouthei moi-èkolouthèsen autōi*). See also Mt. 28,19-20. Cf. E. Larsson, *Christus als Vorbild*, ASNU XXIII, 1962, p. 32: "Die neutestamentliche Nachfolge wurzelt somit [referring to Lev. 11,44f.; 19,2; 20,8] in alttestamentlich-jüdischer Tradition. Ihre eigene Prägung und spezielle Bedeutung erhält sie aber dadurch, dass es sich um eine Nachfolge Jesu handelt."

R. Schnackenburg, *o.c.* I, p. 146, indicates the difference of Christ's perfection-imperative with the Greek idea of perfection: "Sie ist kein 'Ideal' dem wir uns schrittweise nähern sollen, ohne es je zu erreichen, vielmehr ist sie eine Ganzhingabe an Gott, die wir einmal als Jünger Christi vollziehen müssen und aus der heraus wir unser Leben in dieser Welt, jeder nach seiner Berufung, gestalten sollen."

24  E.g. Mt. 10,25 (and Lk 6,40); 20,25-28 (and Lk 22,24-27). Jn. 10,11.27-30; 1 Jn. 2,6 (and Rev. 14,4). See the revealing chapter (8) "Jesus the Imitator of the Father in St. John", in E. J. Tinsley, *The Imitation of God in Christ*, 1960, in which he clearly shows the parallelism between the Father-Son relationship and the Jesus-disciple relationship of love. Further G. Kittel, in *ThWNT* I, 213, 32ff. [s.v. *akoloutheō*], who concludes that *akolouthein* in the N.T. is no longer connected with God, as in the O.T., but with Christ Jesus.

We use the controversial term *imitatio Christi* not in the moralistic medieval sense of copying or reproducing the life of Christ, as, e.g., with Francis of Assisi (cf. *RGG²* IV, 398, s.v. *Nachfolge Christi*) or even with Thomas à Kempis (see Berkouwer's evaluation in *Faith and Sanctification*, pp. 136f. (Dutch, pp. 137f.)). It can only mean to us the obedient, religious-moral following of Christ – His words and deeds – rooted in the redeeming cultic communion with Him.

The New Testament concept of *imitatio* is worked out by W. P. de Boer in his valuable dissertation *The Imitation of Paul. An Exegetical Study*, 1962.

Indicating that the problem of imitation is primarily one of semantics (pp. 68-70), he concludes (p. 69):

> For the sake of clarity it is undoubtedly preferable to use the term imitation only in the way the New Testament uses it, namely, where the believer is active in learning Christ's ways and as a Christian is conforming his life to the example of Christ.

As far as the German distinction between *Nachfolge* and *Nachahmung* is concerned, see above, Ch. II, n. 53; and Ch. III, A, n. 102; and below, esp. notes 71, 72, 75, 80. In the matter of the *imitatio Christi* or following of Christ in the way of conformity, we share completely the concern for the right evangelical relationship of redemptive indicative and redemptive imperative – over against each moralistic distortion – as is expressed by Berkouwer, *Faith and Sanctification*, Ch. VII: "The Imitation of Christ" (Dutch: "De Navolging van Christus"), and by N. H. Søe, *Christliche Ethik*, 1957², § 14: "Die Nachfolge Christi und seine Vorbildlichkeit", who indicates this threefold danger (p. 71): to accomodate Jesus' life and disposition to our own ideal of life; to focus on Jesus' example in the way of a "personality-cult"; to forget the "unbridgeable gulf" between sinful man and the sinless Christ.

Helmut Thielicke, *Theological Ethics*, I, 1966 (abridged from German, vols. I and II, 1958-59), rejects the concept and piety of "imitation", not only because of its historical legalistic aspect, esp. with Pelagius (p. 185), but also because of its inherent wrong principle of confusing Law and Gospel (pp. 185f.):

> On the basis of this *imitatio* piety, the participation of the Christian in Christ can be thought of only if man stands on the same level as Christ, with only a quantitative distance but not an infinite qualitative difference between them. For after

---

Cf. also H. C. Waetjen, "Is the 'Imitation of Christ' Biblical?", in *Dialog*, 2 (Spring 1963), 124: "Matthew, in fact, more than any of the other Gospels develops a theology of discipleship which is expressed both explicitly (...) and implicitly. In both cases it is always a discipleship involving *imitatio*."

all I can imitate the example only of someone to whom I am basically akin. Hence the piety of imitation has a tendency either to reduce Christ to the human level or to exalt man in his capacity for Christlikeness.

E. Schweizer, *Lordship and Discipleship*, SBT 28, ET 1960 (rev. ed. of *Erniedrigung und Erhöhung bei Jesus und seinen Nachfolgern*, 1955), however, believes that it "would not be wrong" to speak of an *imitatio Christi* in connection with Jesus as Example although "it occurs only on the fringe of the N.T." (p. 77). But he warns against the misconception of imitation as a "method of attaining salvation, an ascetic road to salvation" (p. 20), or to imitate some isolated aspect like Jesus' unmarried state (p. 94). To follow Christ means to be borne by the atoning Jesus (the Christ *"for us"*) on the way *"with Him"*, which is already grace, a gift (p. 20), since it merely means a sharing *His* way (p. 53).

He further explains (p. 115):

> It is quite clear that there are dangers on both lines. Where the 'for us' was the sole centre there was also the possibility of misunderstanding a purely academic acceptance of truth. Where the 'with him' was the sole centre, overenthusiastic anticipation was the danger. Therefore the two assertions have been kept close together in the N.T. For eventually they are one.

Berkouwer also, *o.c.*, p. 159 (Dutch, pp. 167f.) discusses this duality of Christ as Mediator and Christ as Example. He indicates the intrinsic unity as follows in the English (summarizing) "translation":

> In the message of Atonement lies the blueprint for the future. The Atonement and the imitation of Christ are related as a spring to a well and this true imitation of Christ may and must be a leitmotif in the preaching of the church: preaching based on the premise that God was in Christ reconciling the world unto himself (II Cor. 5:14).

Illuminating is Schweizer's illustration (on p. 11) of a father who leads his son through the snow in a blizzard. The father goes in front, the son treads in the footsteps of his father, behind him. Here the father is more than an example! Otherwise the son should have fought his own way a few yards beside his father, looking to his father to see how he did it in order to do the same thing himself by imitation.

It is therefore significant that Luther described Christ not as the Example but as *"the Exemplar"*, the original prototype (*Urbild*) or representation of divine righteousness and peace. Luther explains it thus (*WA* 2,518; as in the American Ed. of *Luther's Works*, vol. 27, p. 263):

> It is not the imitation that makes sons; it is sonship that makes imitators.

This theology of *imitatio Christi* is worked out as follows by Thielicke (*o.c.*, p. 193):

> I must first be in a right relation to Christ in his quality as exemplar before I can follow him as example. I must first be set in the sun before I can become warm. I must first know that I am loved before I can love in return.... To adopt the terminology of Luther, it is not that we imitate Christ in order to be as he is, i.e. to participate in his divine likeness. It is rather that his qualities count as ours, his *alienum* becomes our *proprium*, his fate becomes our fate (Matt. 10:25) because in the state of faith we *are* as he is.

Calvin, more than Luther, has systematically worked out an outline of Christian ethics from the standpoint of the call to the *imitatio Christi*. From Mt. 16,24 ("If any man would come after Me, let him deny himself and take up his cross and follow Me") he derives two principles of discipleship, i.e, the imitation of Christ in self-denial and bearing the cross, which he extensively explains and continually relates to the fellowship with Christ. See *Inst.* III, 7,2; 8,1-2. Esp. in *CR* XLV, 481:

> Porro brevem imitationis regulam praescribit, ut sciamus, qua praecipue in re velit sibi nos esse similes: ea vero duobus modis constat, abnegatione nostri, et voluntaria crucis tolerantia.

Since fellowship with Christ means the imitation of Christ in His suffering, a sharing of His Cross, the *imitatio Christi* also implies the eschatological aspiration towards sharing in Christ's glorification, the looking forward to the consummation in eternal blessedness: "when we think of our crown, we are to raise our eyes to heaven" (*Inst.* III, 9,1). On Calvin's concept of hope and progressive sanctification, see H. Quistorp, *Calvin's Doctrine of the Last Things*, 1955, pp. 15-54.

That the imitation of Christ also implies true communication with the brethren, Calvin stresses in the Christian's self-examination before the Lord's Supper, *Inst.* IV, 17, 40.

W. Niesel, *The Theology of Calvin*, 1956 (German 1938), pp. 142-151, discussing Calvin's doctrine of the Imitation of Christ, is definitely correct when he concludes (p. 151):

> Calvin preaches neither pessimism nor optimism but calls us inexorably to the imitation of Jesus Christ. ... The ethics of Calvin are not negativist. In the strictest sense they stem from the principle of the imitation of Christ.

It is this dynamic evangelical concept of the transforming *imitatio Christi* through the Spirit, which is brought out impressively also by E. J. Tinsley, *The Imitation of God in Christ* 1960, Chs. 8-10.

On pp. 130f. he states:

The life of the Christian disciple as *imitator Christi* is not any kind of yoga or self-endeavour. It is not a process which is initiated and sustained by the Christian believer, as if the *imitatio Christi* were some kind of literal mimicry. It is a process initiated and sustained by the Spirit as Paraclete, and in it he conforms the pattern of life of believers to that of the Lord so that men may become aware that they are his disciples.

See also H. Bavinck, "De navolging van Christus en het moderne Leven", in *Kennis en Leven*, 1922, pp. 115-144, esp. pp. 123, 127, 133, who stresses that Jesus gave his whole conduct as the transforming example to be followed. The extensive scholarly study of Edvin Larsson, *Christus als Vorbild. Eine Untersuchung zu den paulinischen Tauf- und Eikontexten*, 1962, focuses the *imitatio Christi* on the organic relationship of sacrament and ethic with Paul (p. 18). To Larsson *imitatio* is not an ethical ideal as such, but "a part of the following" of Christ; not a competitive part but the "conscious, willful and active" part of it (p. 17), springing forth from the redemptive sacramental act of following Christ in baptism. Larsson' basic idea is that the Pauline baptismal theology (esp. in Rom. 6,1-11; Col. 2,11-3,4) means a sacramental-ethical following of Christ in His proto-typical crucifixion, death, and resurrection as a "new creature" (pp. 74-80, 94-104). Therefore *imitatio Christi* is only for him who has died and risen with Christ. His norm is the law of Christ, His words and acts (p. 102). The invaluable gain of this theology of *imitatio Christi* is that it precludes the ethical moralistic understanding or humanistic idealism, because of its "sacramentalizing" of the imitatio idea. (p. 75). By this Larsson does not mean that the sacrament of baptism works *ex opere operato*, since it presupposes faith in and surrender to the Gospel message, but mystical-ethical fellowship with Christ, His cross and resurrection and, ultimately His glorification, Rom. 8,29.

The following of Christ from the viewpoint of Matthew's Gospel is worked out by E. Schweizer in his instructive article "Observance of the Law and Charismatic Activity in Matthew", in *NTS* XVI (1970), 213-230. He summarizes (p. 229):

> The Church by which the first Gospel is shaped is the body of 'these little ones" who are ready to follow Jesus; to remain obedient to the law of God as interpreted by Jesus' deeds and words; to re-interpret his instructions ever anew in answer to practical problems; to proclaim his word in this way, letting it speak to present situations and to revive his miraculous power in healings. There is one authority only in this Church, *Jesus' own words and deeds, interpreting the Law of God* (italics supplied).

This theology of the following of Christ or *imitatio Christi*, however, cannot be found in the widely distributed book of the American congregationalist Charles M. Scheldon, *In His Steps. "What Would*

167

*Jesus Do?"* (A Spire Book), 1970[11] (1897ff., transl. in 14 languages). To Sheldon the consistent following of the motto "What would Jesus do in my place?" would lead to "the millennium of the Christian history" (See also the critique of Søe, *Christl. Ethik*, pp. 427-428).

How *Nachfolge* and *Nachahmung* both may be understood and experienced from the redemptive presence and power of Christ, from the sphere of the *regnum Jesu Christi*, is indicated by K. Barth, *C.D.* II, 2, 569-571, 613-630 (*K.D.*, pp. 632-634, 681-701), esp. pp. 570ff. (*K.D.*, pp. 632ff):

> In every case "following" means simply to be there, to be with Jesus, in His proximity... To want to be where Jesus is, is to abandon oneself to this total claim: to one's cross, to deny oneself, to leave all, to love one's enemies... It is good to be with Jesus and not elsewhere. This is good because it is there that God Himself is good for us. We can certainly try to be elsewhere and to be good for God of ourselves. But how far astray we shall go on such independent ways! How ineluctably we shall fail, even when we imagine we are doing well, if we deviate from the sure way which God Himself trod for us and still treads! We do not possess the teleological power to adjust our action to that goal of our determination.

A summarizing statement can be found in *C.D.* III, 4, 649 (K.D., p. 747).

Jesus' exclusive claim of *imitatio* is rooted in His conviction to fulfill the whole salvation-history of Israel with its typological significance, as is well pointed out by Leonhard Goppelt[25]:

> Es war daher ein schlechthinniges Novum in der Welt des Judentums, *als Jesus seine Person und sein Wirken typologisch auf die alttestamentliche Gottesgeschichte bezog:* 'Siehe, hier ist mehr als Jona', d.h. ein Bussruf der gewichtiger ist als der der Propheten (Mt. 12,41 par. Lk.). 'Siehe, hier ist mehr als Salomo', d.h. eine Weisheitsrede, bedeutender als die Salomos (Mt. 12,42 par Lk.). Hier ist Grösseres als David (Mk. 2,25f. par), Grösseres als der Tempel (Mt. 12,6)! Hier ist der Gerechte schlechthin!

Especially Matthew, on the one hand, identifies Jesus as the perfect

---

25 In his article "Apokalyptik und Typologie bei Paulus", in *ThLZ* 89 (1964), 321-444 (quot. from 336); now also in his book *Christologie und Ethik. Aufsätze zum Neuen Testament*, 1968, pp. 234-267 (quot. on pp. 256f) Italics are in the text. To the point is also G. Bornkamm, "Enderwartung und Kirche im Matthäusevangelium", in *FS* Dodd, who remarks on p. 244: "Das Verhältnis Jesu zu Moses ist dabei nicht in dem Sinne der Antithese gemeint..., sondern im Sinne der Entsprechung." See also p. 245.

*son* of David, with the faithful remnant of Israel, who conquered where Israel of old failed in history.[26] Even when Jesus is crucified, He suffers as the faithful *ᶜEbed Yahweh* of Is. 53 to save Israel.[27] On the other hand, Matthew identifies Jesus with the perfect *Lord* of David, the covenant God Yahweh, who remains faithful to His covenant.

In Mt. 19,16-21 the question how to participate in eternal life (*zoèn aiōnion*), is answered by the call to the concrete *imitatio Christi* (*deuro akolouthei moi*, vs. 21) as fulfillment of the Torah (see next section).

This appeal to unreserved religious commitment to His Person is characteristic of the new message and the unique claim of Jesus which far exceeds those of the Rabbis.[28] Jesus does not call His disciples merely to teach them His interpretation of the Torah as the Rabbis did, nor does He bind His followers to some captivating idea as the Greek philosophers did, but He calls them to an ultimate decision and absolute religious surrender to His Person as Messiah, as the One who speaks and acts in God's stead.[29] The disciple of Jesus therefore realizes that he will – and

---

26 See R. Bijlsma, *Schriftgezag en Schriftgebruik*, 1964, pp. 48f. Cf. Waetjen, *o.c.*, p. 124, who calls it Matthew's "'new Israel' christology." Also Davies, *The Sermon on the Mount*, p. 74, who draws attention to the relation of Matthew's temptation narrative (ch. 4) with Dt. 8. He concludes: "Jesus himself relives the history of his own people and thus becomes in himself the people of God, and the inaugurator of a new covenant." Tinsley, *o.c.*, pp. 67-72: "Jesus' Mission to be Himself the 'Way'."

27 Cf. Bijlsma, *o.c.*, p. 49. Also Waetjen, *o.c.*, p. 124, who stresses the Christological dialectics of *saved* and *saving* remnant: "And this Jesus, who calls to discipleship, simultaneously summons his followers to emulate him both as the saved remnant and as the saving remnant: [quoted Mt. 5,13-14]." On p. 125 Waetjen refers to the imitation of Christ's suffering by the church in Acts: "The Acts of the Apostles might well be called the *imitatio Christi* of the church under the 'Servant of the Lord' christology."

28 See Lk. 14,26; Mt. 8,21-22. Cf. Schnackenburg, *Gottes Herrschaft*, pp. 73f. Rengstorf, in *ThWNT* IV, 447ff. (s.v. *mathètès*), esp. 447,21f.: "Die Art und Weise, wie es zum Anschluss von Jüngern an Jesus kommt, ist demnach [sc. die Initiative Jesu] grundverschieden von der im Rabbinat üblichen Art." Also pp. 450f. A. Schulz, *Nachfolgen und Nachahmen*, StANT VI, 1962, p. 63: "Durch seine Person als Messias ist die Gemeinsamkeit im äusseren zugleich immer auch geprägt von der inhaltlichen Andersartigkeit der Strukturen." See also pp. 68, 79, 81f. Davies, *o.c.*, pp. 133f. See now the important study by Martin Hengel, *Nachfolge und Charisma. Eine exegetisch-religionsgeschichtliche Studie zu Mt. 8,21f. und Jesu Ruf in die Nachfolge*, BZNW 34, 1968; esp. pp. 55-63. (For an extensive critique on Hengel's book, see G. F. Hasel in *Bibliotheca Orientalis*, XXVI (1969), 262-264).

29 Lk. 9,57-62; 12,8f.; Mk. 8,38. Cf. *Str-B* IV, 1, 20, *ad* Mt. 7,24f.: "Die Entscheidung lautet: für Jesus oder gegen Jesus!" Also E. Fuchs, "Zur Frage nach dem historischen Jesus", *Ges. Aufs.* II, 1960, p. 156: "Dieses Verhalten [sc. Jesu] ist aber weder das eines Propheten noch das eines Weisheitslehrers, sondern das Verhalten eines Menschen, der es wagt, an Gottes Stelle zu handeln." Rengstorf in *ThWNT* IV, 450, 42f.: "Der Rabbi und der griechische

can – never grow up to take the place of Jesus, but that it is his calling and fulfillment of life to remain a disciple of Jesus Christ until the very end (Jn. 8,31f.).[30]

By so identifying the *imitatio Dei* with the *imitatio Christi*[31] (Lk. 9,32; 14,25-35; Jn. 8,12; 10,4.27f.), Jesus manifested His Messianic consciousness and claim.[32]

As the Messianic King of the kingdom of God, "the good Shepherd", He came to reveal and to fulfill the perfect "way" of the *imitatio Dei* as Son of God, thus fulfilling the Old Testament kingly and priestly perfection in the redeeming reality of His own Person.[33]

Therefore the *imitatio Christi* does not really begin with the ethical requirement, but with election, just as in the Old Testament salvation-history and law the commandments are *preceded* by the redeeming reality of divine election: "I am Yahweh your God, who brought you out of the land of Egypt, out of the house of bondage."[34] The true following

Philosoph sind dadurch zusammengeschlossen, dass sie beide Vertreter einer bestimmten *Sache* sind. Jesus aber bringt sich selbst. Das gibt selbstverständlich dem ganzen Jüngerverhältnis da und dort seine volle Besonderheit." Schnackenburg, *Chr. Existenz* I, 93ff.

30 Rengstorf, *ThWNT* IV, 452. Remarkable is the fact that the Gospel of John applies *akolouthein* of Christ even with respect to the resurrected Christ, Jn. 21,18-22. Larsson, *o.c.*, p. 42, n. 3, connects these vss. with Jn. 1,37-51 as an intended suggestion for the continuity of the *imitatio Christi*. See further E. Lohse, in *RGG*[3] IV, 1286-87 (s.v. *Nachfolge Christi*).

31 At first *akolouthein* is still being used in a general way, e.g. Mk. 5,24, but in most cases the verb possesses a qualified religious content: a total communion of life and destiny, Mk. 3,14f. Cf. G. Kittel, in *ThWNT* I, 214. A. Schulz, *o.c.*, p. 68. See on the salvation-historical function of the "holy remnant", Larsson, *o.c.*, p. 35.

32 Cf. Kittel, *l.c.* H. J. Schoeps, "Von der Imitatio Dei zur Nachfolge Christi", in *Aus Frühchr. Zeit*, p. 291: "Es ist kaum eine andere Möglichkeit offen als von seinem Messiasbewusstsein auszugehen, dass er die Forderung der imitatio Dei mit der Nachfolge seiner eigenen Person verknüpfen kann." Larsson, *o.c.*, pp. 33f.: "Mit messianischer Souveränität wählt er Menschen aus und beruft sie ihm nachzufolgen." H. Conzelmann, in *RGG*[3] III, 629 (s.v. *Jesus Christus*), also stresses the basic difference with the Rabbis. Hempel, *o.c.*, p. 76, therefore typifies Jesus as the „eschatological Charismatic", "die freilich zugleich weit über das hinausreicht, was an prophetischen Vorbildern oder Parallelen aus dem Bereich des AT und der neutestamentlichen Zeit herangezogen werden kann." See also C. H. Dodd, *According to the Scriptures. The Substructure of NT Theology*, 1952, p. 110.

33 Jn. 14,6; 10,11ff. Mt. 5,17f. Cf. Ridderbos, *De Komst van het Koninkrijk*, pp. 221ff. Du Plessis, *o.c.*, p. 169. Larsson, *o.c.*, p. 38: "Das einzigartige Selbstbewusstsein Jesu bringt es mit sich, dass seine eigene Person und seine Sendung einen zentralen Platz in seinem Unterricht einnehmen."

34 See Wingren, "Was bedeutet die Forderung der Nachfolge Christi in evangelischer Ethik?", in *ThLZ* 75 (1950), 385-392. Cf. Berkouwer, *Faith and Sanctification*, p. 186 (Dutch, p. 202).

of Jesus or *imitatio Christi*, accordingly, is conditioned by participation in the Messianic election and salvation.[35]

On the basic of this Messianic election, Christ's perfection-imperative then can only be understood adequately in the light of Israel's and the Davidic covenant of grace.

Exceeding the righteousness and love of the scribes and the Pharisees, Christ requires perfection, i.e., the undivided holy[36] love from the sons of the heavenly Father, not in order to *become* sons of God, but to be or manifest themselves as sons of God.[37] In Mt. 5,48 Christ orients this perfect manifestation of sonship not to the legal ethos but to the holy love of the Father, to the *imitatio Dei*,[38] i.e., the actual reflection of the character of the forgiving, holy love of the Father in the character of His sons and daughters.[39]

The perfect or wholehearted love of the Father in His acts[40] is to be reflected and concretely manifested in the wholehearted, or perfect, love or service of His earthly sons in their inter-human relationship.[41]

---

35  Cf. Kittel, in *ThWNT* I, 214, 24f.: "Weil sie [sc. to follow Jesus] bedeutet: dem Messias nachfolgen, ist diese Jüngerschaft ihrem Wesen nach *religiöse Gabe*; das *akolouthein* ist: Teilhaben an dem in Jesus sich darbietenden Heil." Also Berkouwer, *o.c.*, p. 140f. (Dutch, p. 143): "The voice that spoke from heaven on the mount of Transfiguration can, as well as the appeals of Deuteronomy, be taken as a call to follow the Christ: 'This is my beloved Son: fear ye him' (Mark 9:7). To 'hear' the Christ is to follow him in intimate fellowship." Wingren, *ThLZ* 75 (1950), 387. Tinsley, *o.c.*, pp. 130f.

36  Cf. Thurneysen, *o.c.*, pp. 5f.: "Die Bergpredigt handelt... von der Heiligkeit des Lebens (5,21-26), von der Heiligkeit der Ehe (5,27-32), von der Heiligkeit der Wahrheit (5,33-37), von der Heiligkeit des Rechtes (5,38-42), von der Heiligkeit der Gemeinschaft (5,43-48), also von fünf wichtigen Grundvoraussetzungen des menschlichen Lebens."

37  Mt. 5,43ff.; Lk. 6,35; cf. Mt. 22,39; Lev. 19,18.34. The designation of Israel as children or sons of God (Dt. 14,1) was recognized in Judaism, and obliged Israel to imitate the example of God's character, see *Str-B* I, 371-373. Cf. W. Lüthi and R. Brunner, *The Sermon on the Mount*, p. 78: "Everything that is demanded of us here, and not only here but throughout the whole of the Sermon on the Mount, depends on the presupposition that we are children of God." Ridderbos, *o.c.*, p. 225. E. L. Smelik, *De Ethiek in de Verkondiging*, 1967, p. 27.

38  Mt. 5,48 is structurally akin to Lev. 19,2 LXX. Cf. A. Schulz, *o.c.*, p. 234. R. Schnackenburg, *Die sittl. Botschaft des N.T.*, p. 70.

39  Cf. Schnackenburg, *Chr. Existenz* I, 140: "Die an Gottes Heiligkeit selbst orientierte Haltung fasst Matthäus am Ende und Höhepunkt der Antithesen in den Begriff 'Vollkommenheit' zusammen."

40  Mt. 5,45f. Du Plessis, *o.c.*, p. 171: "By pointing to God as the supreme Example for imitation, Jesus is referring to the way in which He reveals Himself... The correlative is therefore not ontological but modal."

41  See Jn. 13,12-16; Mt. 20,25ff.; Lk. 22,27. See Preisker, *o.c.*, p. 67: "Wo Gott gibt, erwartet er des Menschen Gehorsam aus diesem neuen Sein. Neues Sein von Gott her muss umsetzen in neues Tun des Menschen, weil Gott nicht

This means that to *respond* to love is not enough, a principle which was already indicated in the Mosiac Law, Ex. 23,4-5; see also Prov. 25,21f.

Although H. Montefiore, "Thou shalt love the neighbour as thyself", in *Donum Gratulatorium. FS* E. Stauffer, 1962, pp. 157-170, acknowledges Jesus' application of Lev. 19,18 "to anyone in need" (p. 166), "the unloved and the loveless" (p. 160), he nevertheless states:

> "Yet concerning 'the central and governing idea of Christianity' [sc. taken from Nygren] the Fourth Evangelist gives a distorted account of Jesus' teaching" (p. 167)

His point is that "the early church narrowed the concept of neighbour until it was equivalent to church member" (p. 166); and he concludes:

> "Concerning 'the central and governing idea of Christianity' there is a sea-change in outlook between the synoptic gospels and the rest of the New Testament" (p. 167).

The basic failure of this evaluation seems to be the denial of the *universal* aim and thrust of Christ's mission and redemptive love, as testified in Jn. 3,16; 10,16; 17,20; 20,30-31; 1 Jn. 2,2. Although it is true that the Johannine corpus is concerned with neighborly love in the sense of love of the Christian to his fellow believer, this is definitely not the ultimate purport or complete picture of "neighborly" love in John, just as the election of Israel was not a goal in itself (the distortion!), but implied a *world mission* (Gen. 12,3; Is. 42,6f.; 49,6; 56,6-8). Christ regarded the unity of His disciples in holy love as of primordial significance and as necessary prerequisite for the ultimate purpose of His mission and that of the Church: the salvation of all in the world who hear the testimony of His believers.

> I do not pray for these only, but also for those who believe in me through their word, that they may all be one.... *so that the world may believe* that thou hast sent me.... I in them and thou in me, that they may become perfectly one, *so that the world may know that thou hast sent me and hast loved them even as thou hast loved me* (Jn. 17,20f.23).

It is therefore certainly not fair to quote only Jn. 17,9 without mentioning vss. 20-23 as the necessary correlation, in order to prove that the author of the Fourth Gospel "limited his ideal of perfection to the disciples", as G. Friedlander does (*o.c.*, p. 89). Furthermore, Montefiore's judgment does not take into account the

Gott der Toten... Mk. 12,27; Lk. 9,60." Cf. Ridderbos, *Koninkrijk*, p. 276: "In de dienst van God komt alles aan op de integriteit, de volkomenheid, het zonder enige weerhouding bereid zijn tot de dienst."

dynamic universal scope of the Pauline kerygma, as developed in Rom. 1,5; 5,8-10; 9-11; esp. 11,32ff. It is highly significant that Montefiore in spite of his conclusion admits that neighborly love in the apostolic church in a very vital way was extended to the non-Christian:

> The real work of neighbourly love (to his Jewish or pagan neighbour) consisted in saving him from the inevitable destruction which awaited him in 'the world' (*o.c.*, p. 168).

D. Bonhoeffer[42] aptly expressed the tenor of holy love:

> In the New Testament our enemies are those who harbour hostility against us, not those against whom we cherish hostility, for Jesus refuses to reckon with such a possibility.

This means that the Christian love manifests itself – in true imitation of God's love – in *forgiving* love, for Christ's sake.[43] This merciful love,[44] however, can only be exercised by one who has experienced this forgiving love himself from God.[45]

In the Gospel according to Luke Christ does not use the term *teleios* but *oiktirmōn*, merciful[46] (6,36), "for He is *kind* (*chrèstos*) to the ungrateful and the selfish" (6,35).[47] This Lucan parallel passage agrees with Matthew's interpretation of God's perfection as the active and wholehearted manifestation of forgiving love to all people, the ungrateful or unjust in particular.[48] To Matthew the word *teleios*, however, is of

42   *The Cost of Discipleship*, 1960², p. 132.

43   Cf. Bultmann, *Jesus*, 1951, pp. 95-103.

44   Here the basic difference between the Biblical selfgiving *agapè* and the Greek self-demanding *eros* appears most conspicuously. Cf. A. Nygren, *Agape and Eros*, ET 1953. G. Bornkamm, *o.c.*, p. 115.

45   See Lk. 7,36-50. Cf. Ridderbos, *Koninkrijk*, p. 224: "De strekking... is, dat slechts bij diegenen de waarachtige liefde is, door wie ook het heil van de *vergeving* gekend wordt." See also the parable of Mt. 18,23-35, esp. vs. 33, where the prevenient merciful love of God is illustrated. Here again Jesus presents the divine mercy as the motive and norm for the interhuman relationship. Cf. A. Schulz, *o.c.*, p. 237. Bultmann, *o.c.*, p. 174.

46   The opinions differ as to which term is primary, *teleios* or *oiktirmōn*. See J. Dupont, *Les Béatitudes*, 1954, p. 60, n. 1 (with critical bibliography); also Schnackenburg, *o.c.*, I, 139. At any rate, Matthew uses with *teleios* a special O.T. terminology *tāmîm* in order to signify Jesus' command of righteousness and perfection as superior to that of the Pharisees, 5,20, and that of the Gentiles, 5,47. Cf. G. Barth, in *Überlieferung und Auslegung im Matthäus-Evangelium*, WMANT I, 1960, p. 91: "[*Teleios*]... es ist das Merkmal der Gemeinde."

47   Cf. P. Bonnard, *l'Évangile selon Saint Matthieu*, CNT I, 1963, p. 76: "Luc a bien compris que la seule perfection que l'Évangile connaisse est celle de la miséricorde (...); mais cela ne signifie pas que son texte soit plus archaïque que celui de Matthieu."

48   Cf. Mt. 6,12; 18,21-22; also Acts 14,17.

vital significance, since he thereby wants to indicate specifically that true righteousness and love are not a break with but the fulfillment of the Torah, i.e., the perfect righteousness which the Law always intended to command.[49] Accordingly, Matthew's concept of *teleios* is not oriented to the feeling of ethical sinlessness, but rather to the religious-cultic consecration to Israel's God of love and the universal scope of His mercy.[50] Such a perfection can be characterized dynamically as holy or merciful love.[51] From this it becomes clear that Christ's perfection-imperative to His disciples is meant to be no less concrete as a *present* reality than it is meant in the Torah and the Psalms.[52]

In this light the deep analogy between the Mosaic covenant of grace and the "Torah of the Messiah"[53] becomes evident: the indissoluble interrelationship and unity of religious cultus and ethos.[54] Also in Christ's "Torah" on the Mount, the blessings are followed by and inter-

---

49   Cf. U. Luck, *Vollkommenheitsforderung*, pp. 19, 21, 25, 29. He rightly concludes that to Matthew the understanding of the idea of perfection "von fundamentaler Bedeutung ist" (p. 29). In order to interpret Matthew's concept of perfection he takes his norm too exclusively from the Wisdom Literature (including the apocrypha), thus neglecting its fundamental cultic use in the Torah.

50   Cf. Bonnard, *o.c.*, ad Mt. 5,48: "Le thème de la perfection (*tāmîm*), dans les écrits bibliques, n'exprime pas tant l'idée de pureté morale que celle d'engagement total, d'appartenance sans réserve à Dieu, au sein même du péché (cf. Dt. 18.13; Lev. 19.2; 1 Pi. 1:16; Mat. 19.21). Dans leurs actes d'amour, de réconciliation, de fidélité intrépide à la loi de Christ, ses disciples feront apparaître dans ce monde quelque chose de la perfection du Royaume de Dieu (cf. 25.31-46)." Noteworthy is Flew's remark: "Christian Perfection is greater even than sinlessness" (*o.c.*, p. 93).

51   See also Lk. 15,20-24; Rom. 11,30-33. Cf. Flew, *o.c.*, p. 15: "A love that was not holy would not be perfect love."

52   It would therefore testify of an unhistorical exegesis to identify *teleios* in Mt. 5,48, or *dikaiosunè* in Mt. 5,20, with the Pauline imputative or forensic righteousness. The illegitimay of such exegesis has been clearly indicated by H. Windisch, *The Meaning of the Sermon on the Mount*. On the problematics of the ethical application of the Sermon on the Mount, see the valuable treatise of Schnackenburg, *o.c.* I, 109-130 (Ch. V), with lit.

53   As such the new interpretation on the Torah by the expected Messiah was defined in Judaism, see *Str-B* IV, 1,2d. Cf. Davies, *The Sermon on the Mount*, pp. 27,31-32.

54   See Ch. III, B; see esp. on Ps. 15. Further, V. Hasler, "Das Herzstück der Bergpredigt. Zum Verständnis der Antithesen in Matth. 5,21-48", in *ThZ* 15 (1959), 90-106. Hasler states that the matter at issue is not the legalistic problem: "Ihre Antithetik ist nicht gegen das Gesetz gerichtet, sondern gegen die Verkenning der eingebrochenen heilsgeschichtlichen Stunde, des im Rabbi Jesus angebrochenen messianischen Reiches (94f.)." Cf. E. Haenchen, "Matthäus 23", in *ZThK* 48 (1951), 38-63, who states that Mt. does not fight against human self-justification by works, "sondern gegen eine Theologie und Frömmigkeit, welche die wesentlichen Forderungen Gottes nicht beachtet (vgl. z. B. Mt. 5,20 und 23,23)" (46).

174

related with ethical demands which function as prerequisites[55] to enter the Temple and the eschatological Kingdom of God (Mt. 5,23f.20; 7,21ff.). Christ's ethos of perfection and obedience exceeds the Rabbinical wage-ethics of His days in that He restores[56] the covenant ethos of *wholeness* and *totality* of heart and personality in the service of God.[57] That *love* can be required or *commanded* (Dt. 6,5; Lev. 19,18; Mt. 22,37-40) indicates that this love appeals to the will more than to emotions or affections, since feelings cannot be commanded.[58] The love of the covenant people has to be of the same nature as the love of the covenant God, i.e., a love which expresses itself in concrete acts based on the will of God (1 Jn. 3,16; 4,10.14). That means that *love* can only be *perfect love* when man obeys God in the concrete reality of human relations: "But whoever keeps His word, in him truly love for God is perfected [*teteleiōtai*]", 1 Jn. 2,5; cf. 4,12. How the God-pleasing, perfect life of love and service is acknowledged as a concrete historical reality in this world appears strikingly from Jesus' description of the final judgment in Mt. 25,31-46 (also called the "Parable of the Great Surprise").

The blessed ones who then will inherit the Kingdom show themselves surprised that their lives and acts of love and mercy to their fellowmen are described by the King as "righteous" (vs. 37) or perfect. They

---

55   This soteriological-ethical correlation is strikingly expressed by W. Lüthi and R. Brunner, *o.c.*, p. 82: "If it is true to say that Christ demands and expects this fruit only of a child of the Father in Heaven, it is equally true that we are children of the Father in Heaven only as long as this fruit of absolute love and selflessness grows on us. If it does not grow on us, then we are not children of God: however piously we may act, it will not ring true. 'You will know them by their fruits'." Cf. also H. Ridderbos, *Koninkrijk*, p. 280. See further above, notes 17 and 20.

56   Cf. J. Schniewind, *o.c.*, p. 56: "Jesus stellt hier also keine neue Forderung auf, er sagt nicht: Eure Gerechtigkeit muss sich von der der Pharisäer sachlich unterscheiden; sondern er behaftet seine Hörer auf den ihnen in ihrer ganzen Schärfe bekannten Forderungen."

57   Cf. J. Schmidt, *o.c.*, p. 116: "Der Wille Gottes erstreckt und beschränkt sich nicht auf gewisse einzelne Handlungen, diejenigen nämlich, die im Gesetz eigens genannt werden. Er muss das ganze Leben des Menschen beherrschen." P. 117: "Sittliches Handeln ist nun nicht mehr 'Verdienste anhäufen', ein Rechnen mit Gott, sondern freie Herzenshingabe in Liebe und Vertrauen an den Herrn und Vater, dem gegenüber es keine Rechtsforderung für treue Dienste gibt." Also Schnackenburg, *Gottes Herrschaft*, p. 73: "Nur die *Halbheit* hat er gerichtet; man kann nicht Gott dienen und dem Mammon (Mt. 6,24), das Herz nicht an himmlische und irdische Schätze zugleich hängen (Mt. 6.19-21)."

58   Cf. Bultmann, *o.c.*, p. 102: "Nur wenn Liebe als Gefühl gedacht ist, ist es sinnlos, Liebe zu gebieten; das Gebot der Liebe zeigt, dass Liebe als Haltung des Willens gemeint ist." See also p. 101. Dodd, *Gospel and Law*, 1951, p. 42: "It [sc. *agapè*] is primarily an active determination of the will. That is why it can be commanded, as feelings can not."

certainly did not feel that way in their self-esteem[59] before God; hence their astonishment. The required perfection thus includes justification in its fullest sense, i.e., also sanctification. The only alternative will then be the curse of condemnation (vs. 41), since all covenantal piety which is not rooted in real fellowship with God or Christ is called hypocrisy.[60]

The new fulfillment in the Gospel is that the cultic foundation and motivation is now found and experienced not in the old Temple service, but in the decisive saving relationship with Christ Jesus (Mt. 12,6), in whom the divine Šekinah[61] is present.

As Jesus' Messiahship also implies His being the authoritative *Teacher* in Israel, Christ is presented not only as Redemeer but also as *Example* to be followed in total life-fellowship.[62] This principle of *imitatio* in the disciple-teacher relationship is well developed by Jos. M. Nielen[63]:

Nicht nur möchte der Schüler jedes Wort des Lehrers in sich aufnehmen, sondern es auch, ihm nachstrebend, befolgen, das heisst,

59 Ulrich Luck, *Vollkommenheitsforderung*, pp. 41ff., indicates that Matthew shows in 6,1-18 *how* perfection, or the "better righteousness" of 5,20, is lived. This implies that perfection is to be exercised "in secret" (6,4.6.18), but will be brought "in the open" (*en tōi phanerōi*; according to the Koine text, θ*alitsy*s) by God: "Die vollkommene Gerechtigkeit kann nur so getan werden, dass das eigene Wirken Gott zur Vollendung überlassen wird" (p. 44). "Im Tun der Gerechtigkeit ist der Mensch nicht nur von der Öffentlichkeit vor der Welt verborgen, sondern er ist vor sich selbst verborgen... Der Mensch wird aufgerufen zur Tat, zur vollkommenen Gerechtigkeit, doch diese Tat ist ihm entzogen, weil sie nur durch Gott in Kraft gesetzt werden kann" (p. 45).

60 Mt. 23,28. See Ridderbos, *o.c.*, p. 278: "Het [sc. hypocrisy] is enerzijds wel een pijnlijk nauwkeurig nakomen van allerlei voorschriften en instellingen, aan de andere kant een ontbreken van de zelfovergave aan God. Het gaat hier om een *religieuze* karaktertrek..." (referring to Mt. 15,8).

61 Davies, *The Sermon on the Mount*, pp. 23, 34, indicates how Matthew points to Jesus as symbolizing the Šekinah, the very presence of God itself, in Mt. 17,5 and 18,20. Cf. also H. Odeberg, *The Fourth Gospel*, 1968 (repr. of 1929), on Jn. 10,30 (p. 332).

62 See Mt. 5,11; 10,25.38; 16,24; 11,29. Cf. Larsson, *o.c.*, p. 38: "Wenn man konstatieren kann, dass der Empfang des Unterrichts des Meisters ein wesentliches Element der Nachfolge ist, so ist es daher selbstverständlich, dass auch die Nachahmung, die Imitation von ihm eine zentrale Rolle spielt. Ein jüdischer Lehrer unterrichtete nicht nur mit Worten. Seine Handlungsweise, ja seine Lebensführung hatte pädagogische, vorbildliche Bedeutung." See also pp. 40f., 44. Kittel, in *ThWNT* I, 214, 31: "Dasselbe *akolouthein* bedeutet aber gleichzeitig ein Teilhaben an dem Geschick Jesu" (referring to Mt. 8,19f., Mk. 8,34; Jn. 12,25-26).

63 In his article "Die Kultsprache der Nachfolge und Nachahmung Gottes und verwandter Bezeichnungen im neutestamentlichen Schrifttum", in *Heilige Überlieferung. FS* I. Herwegen, 1938, pp. 59-85; quotation is from pp. 65f. See also the challenging art. of E. Fascher, "Jesus der Lehrer", in *ThLZ* 79 (1954), 325-342; and his *Sokrates und Christus*, 1959, pp. 134-174.

durch Nachahmung des gegebenen Beispiels in die Tat umsetzen. Dass somit gerade im Judentum der Ausdruck "hinter jemandem hergehen" soviel wie "sein Schüler sein" bedeutete, hängt damit zusammen, dass viel mehr als aus den Worten des Lehrers, aus dessen praktischer Übung das "Gesetz", die Norm der jüdischen Ethik zugleich und des jüdischen Kultus, erlernt wurde. Diese Nachfolge durch das Bekanntmachen mit der Tora in Lehre und Beispiel kann man sich nicht eng genug vorstellen. Der Lehrer wird zum Meister, der Schüler zum Jünger. Das Verhältnis der beiden wird zu einer geistigen Vaterschaft und Sohnschaft.

Teaching and life constitute a unity in the person of the teacher.[64]

64  Cf. Larsson, o.c., p. 39: "Eine wesentliche Seite dieser selbstverständlichen Imitation stellt der Gehorsam gegenüber den Geboten Jesu dar." He tries to show that this traditional concept of unity between teaching and life of the teacher is not sufficiently recognized by W. Michaelis in *ThWNT* IV, 672ff. (s.v. *mimeomai*), with the result that obedience to the authority of the commandment (as Nachfolge) is placed too much in contrast with the *imitatio Christi* (Nachahmung). Cf. also Berkouwer's critique on Michaelis, in *Geloof en Heiliging*, pp. 147f. in ET only in principle, pp. 144f.: "One is bound to impoverish the N.T. revelation if he speaks so emphatically about obedience as to neglect the idea of imitation." Also W. de Boer, *The Imitation of Paul*, pp. 209f.
The same contrast between *Nachfolge* and *Nachahmung* is made by A. Schulz, o.c., p. 238, and H. Kosmala, "Nachfolge und Nachahmung Gottes", in *ASTI* II (1963), 38-85; III (1964), 65-110. Kosmala concludes in II, 68: "Es ist unverkennbar, dass der Nachahmung Gottes und verwandten Gedanken im N.T. das populär-griechische Ideal der Nachfolge zugrundeliegt. Durch dessen Aufnahme in die christliche Verkündigung wird es mit einem neuen Inhalt erfüllt." This means to K. that Eph. 5,1 presents "das zeitgenössische heidnische Lebensideal in christlicher Deutung" (66).
Michaelis even objects to the translation of the Pauline *mimeisthai* by "Nachahmen", with the argument: "Dem entspricht auch *unser Sprachgebrauch*, indem wir unter Nachahmung auch in ihren ernsthaften Formen stets ein Unselbständigwerden verstehen, bei dem der Nachahmer seiner eigentlichen Bestimmung sich entfremdet" (*ThWNT* IV, 675, n. 28; italics supplied). In this sense, of course, we agree with his conclusion: "Die Forderung einer imitatio Christi hat in den paulinischen Aussagen keine stütze" (676, 8f.). It remains, however, that the apostle Paul chooses to use *mimeisthai* instead of *akolouthein*. This fact definitely suggests that God in Christ is also our *Example* in morality and activity; cf. Berkouwer, *Geloof en Heiliging*, p. 148, n. 65 (omitted in ET; see however, pp. 144f.): "Men zal kunnen zeggen, dat alleen de navolging die in de verzoening is gefundeerd, elke verdienste uitsluit, maar dán ook *als* navolging moet worden gehandhaafd." On Gal. 6,17 and the idea of stigmatization, see pp. 158ff. (ET pp. 152ff.). H. Schlier, *Der Brief an die Epheser*, 1965[5], pp. 230-232, ad Eph. 5,1f., makes the helpful distinction between *Nachahmen* as "Imitieren", and *Nachahmen* as "Entsprechen" (p. 230). This is also the idea of A. Schulz, *Unter dem Anspruch Gottes*, 1964, p. 106, who even proposes to replace the term *Nachahmen* by "entsprechen". It is Schlier's merit that he stresses the call to imitation (Nachahmung) in

Obedience to Christ's moral teaching of repentance therefore is implied in the call to the *imitatio Christi*, which at the same time means that the moral *imitatio Christi* is not simply a matter of moral conduct, of following a set of moral habits, as suggested in Aristotle's ethics (*Eth. Nic.* II 6).[65] In the old and in the new covenant the religious experience of salvation is never divorced from its ethical obligation and moral implications of the *imitatio Dei* or *Christi*.

Love is not – and cannot be – a law to itself, but rather the condition and root of its fulfillment.[66] As law is not absorbed or annihilated in love but fulfilled in the Biblical ethos of obedience and perfection, so the theological *imitatio Christi* may not be emptied of its ethical content, reducing the following (Nachfolge) of Christ to the mere religious occurrence of redemption without any real following in His footsteps (Nachahmung).[67] This *imitatio Christi* implies that the same merciful moti-

Eph. 5,1f. as directed to *tekna agapèta*: "Die 'Nachahmung' Gottes ist seinen 'geliebten Kindren' möglich und wird von ihnen erwartet. Offenbar besteht ein Zusammenhang zwischen dem Kind-sein und der Nachahmung. Er kommt bei Paulus auch 1 Kor. 4,14.16 zum Ausdruck. Auch nach Mt. 5,44f. besteht das Sohn-sein darin, dass man so wie der Vater handelt" (p. 230). It is significant that even H. D. Betz, *Nachfolge und Nachahmung Jesu Christi im N.T.*, BHT 37, 1967, who sharply distinguishes between the kerygma of Jesus, the synoptic strata and the theology of the gospel-writers, and who also stresses the discontinuity of *akolouthein* and *mimeisthai* between the gospels and Paul, still acknowledges (p. 43): "Der Struktur nach sind aber auf beiden Seiten gleichlaufende Intentionen festzustellen. In der theologischen Interpretation nimmt die Nachfolge de facto die Struktur der Mimesisvorstellung an."

65   See Mk. 1,15; Mt. 7,24f.; Jn. 12,48f. Cf. Davies, *o.c.*, p. 137: "Jesus of Nazareth appears in a twofold form, at least – as an eschatological figure and as a rabbi, a teacher of morality." He indicates that Jewish eschatology was never divorced from ethics: "the Messianic King was to be also a teacher or interpreter of the Law." He then points to Mk. 1,15, saying: "The proclamation of the eschatological event calls for repentance: the act of God in the Gospel constitutes an appeal to man for a better life: the gift and the demand are inseparable" (137). Also W. F. Lofthouse, "Imitatio Christi", in *ExpT* 65 (1953/54), 338-342; esp. 338: "Conduct always suggests rather the memory of the great Exemplar, even in 1 and 2 Thessalonians. Nor is the importance of conduct ever pushed aside by the thought of mystical union with Christ, either 'faith-mystik' or 'love-mystik'." He concludes: "In short, in the Gospels the conventional distinction between morals and religion as the two poles, as it were, of the good life, disappears" (340). How completely the evangelical *imitatio Christi* is deprived of human autonomy, he expresses thus: "But this is not a human imitation of a Divine copy, it is God's reproduction of Himself within the heart of man" (342).

66   Cf. Ridderbos, *o.c.*, p. 287.

67   Larsson, *o.c.*, pp. 40, 44. Wingren, *o.c.*, p. 386, points to the illegitimacy of mere "being-ethic": "Zweitens aber hört die Nachfolge eben damit, so will es scheinen, auf, etwas 'Ethisches' zu sein, etwas das mit Lebensführung und Moral zu tun hat. Die Imitation, das Nachahmen der Handlungen Jesu fällt dahin. Das Reden von Tod und Auferstehung lässt uns vom Gesichtspunkt

vation with respect to the neighbor – to serve and to save him – is awakened in the saved Christian as was and still is the concern of His Master.[68] Consequently the true and acceptable praise and exaltation of Christ as Lord does not exclude, but is manifested as, the outgoing love to the neighbor, i.e., to every one who needs my help.[69]

b. Mt. 19,21: *ei theleis teleios einai, hypage pōlèson sou ta hyparchonta kai dos ptōchois, kai hexeis thèsauron en ouranois, kai deuro akolouthei moi.*

This reply of Christ to the rich young ruler can only be understood adequately from the particular siutation and context of the story. To the sincere question addressed to Jesus regarding what good deed must be done in order to have eternal life, Christ refers to the way of the Torah: "If you would enter life, keep the commandments." [70]

The question itself, however, revealed no experimental knowledge of

---

der Ethik aus anscheinend mit ganz leeren Händen dastehen." See also Berkouwer's critique on Barth's interpretation of the ethics of Mat. 5ff. as being rather the created *room* to live in (Ortsangabe) for the holy people than the concrete *content* of the requirements. (*C.D.* II, 2, pp. 687f., 690; *K.D.*, pp. 766f., 770); in *Geloof en Heiliging*, pp. 203-207. Joh. Kraus, "Imitation and being in the ethics of the N.T.", *Theology Digest*, XVII, 1969, 139-143, is also working with separate concepts of *being-ethic* and *model-ethic*. His conclusion is that we choose Christ as our model not because He gives us moral values, but because Christ answers to our presupposed knowledge of holiness and sinlessness "according to which we do evaluate Christ" (143). Small wonder that he must describe 1 Pet. 2,21 as a "consciously hellenizing interpretation" by Christians who had no Biblical concepts (139). See esp. T. Süss, "Nachfolge Jesu", in *ThLZ* 78 (1953), 129-140, who emphasizes that both following and imitation must be taken seriously. He concludes on p. 135: "Christenleben ist Leben in der Nachfolge Jesu, mit dem Ziel, ihm ähnlich zu werden und ihn wirklich und in echter Weise nachzuahmen." Also his critique on Bonhoeffer's *Nachfolge*, in 135, n. 11. See also Kierkegaard's significant distinction between *Imitators* (followers) and *admirers* of Christ, *Training in Christianity*, ET 1944, pp. 231f.

68  See Mt. 20,25-28; 25,31ff.; cf. 1 Cor. 10,33.

69  See Flew, *o.c.*, p. 92. C. H. Dodd, *The Johannine Epistles*, Moffatt NT Com., 1953, *ad* 1 Jn. 3,16, p. 85: "The practice of love, or charity, therefore, can be broadly described in terms of the imitation of Christ ... it is probable that the idea of the *imitatio Christi* had more to say than is commonly recognized by critics ..." On the apostolic ethos of *imitatio Christi*, see Wingren, *ThLZ* 75 (1950), 390-391. W. de Boer, *The Imitation of Paul*, esp. pp. 92-205. How basically this apostolic ethos of *imitatio* does safeguard the absolute priority and sovereignty of atoning grace, also in 1 Pet. 2,18-21, is impressively set forth in Berkouwer, *o.c.*, ch. VII; pp. 141ff. (Dutch pp. 143ff.). D. M. Stanley, "Become Imitators of Me': The Pauline Conception of Apostolic Tradition", in *Bib.* 40 (1959), 859-877, stresses the imitation of Paul as a mediated '*imitatio Christi*', springing forth from Paul's apostolic authority and the necessary transmission of apostolic tradition.

70  Mt. 19,17; cf. Mk. 10,19; Lk. 10,26-28; 18,20.

the covenant of grace as the way of salvation.[71] Where the redemptive experience of Yahweh's love is lacking, the required responsive motivation of love toward Yahweh and the neighbor is impossible.[72] Yet the young man asserted: "All these I have observed; what do I still lack?"[73]

This last question not only reveals the inner dissatisfaction about the first claim, but also the prevailing Pharisaic misconception of Israel's Torah, i.e., the basic lack of the redemptive cultic perfection or transforming experience of wholehearted, undivided fellowship with the holy covenant God. On this basis our conclusion must be that the ruler had *not* observed the Torah in reality, since he was lacking the very essence of the *imitatio Dei:* the motivation of perfect love.[74]

When Jesus showed him the way of perfection as the sale of all his possessions, in order to give to the poor and then to come and follow Jesus, "he went away sorrowful; for he had great possessions."[75] This

71 See Lev. 26 and Dt. 26-28, where obedience is explicitly conditioned and motivated by the great Exodus-salvation experience. It is therefore incorrect to explain Christ's answer as imposing the way of legalism, which Christ clearly rejected in Mt. 5,20; cf. 5,17-19; 23,23.

72 Significant is therefore Jesus' elucidation in Mt. 19,26: "With men this is impossible, but with God all things are possible," which statement according to Ridderbos, *o.c.,* p. 201, is a "keyword for the understanding of all his preaching and of all his commandments." Also p. 221. Cf. Schniewind, *o.c.,* on Mk. 10,23-27; p. 131f.

73 Mt. 19,20. Cf. *Str-B* I, 814-816, which indicates that the young ruler believed that he had kept the *whole* Torah, in harmony with the concept of Rabbinic Judaism that man had the ability to fulfill the commandments of God "restlos." See p. 816: "Gut Raschi: 'Was ist noch zu tun, was ich nicht getan hätte?'"

74 This conclusion is confirmed by the readings of Mk. 10,21 and Lk. 18,22. Cf. *D. Martin Luther's Evangelien-Auslegung*, II, 1954², p. 667: "Darum spricht Christus an dem Pharisaer: du liebst Gott nicht über alle Dinge, darum bist du nicht vollkommen, du sollst nichts über alle Dinge lieb haben als alleine Gott; das tust du nicht vollkommen, du offerst mir wohl im Tempel Ochsen und Kälber und gibst den Zehnten, aber damit bist du nicht vollkommen...." Calvin, *Inst.* IV, 13, 13 (rightly referring to 1 Cor. 13,3 and Col. 3,14). See further Thielicke, *Theol. Ethics*, I, 258-261. Barth, *C.D.* II, 2, 613-630 (*K.D.*, pp. 681-701), esp. p. 617 (*K.D.*, p. 686): "The commandments which he knows – he does not really know. Observing them, he has not really observed them. And coming to Jesus, he has really passed Him by.... That he should *be* something – the covenant-partner of God – is what all the commandments demand.... That he should *love* his neigbor is what God wills.... That he should *belong* to Jesus – as King of the kingdom in which he lives – is the necessary meaning and truth of the obedience.... That he is very far from this being, loving and belonging will emerge later."

75 Mt. 19,22 par. See G. Barth, in *Überlieferung und Auslegung im Matthäusevangelium, WMANT* I, 1960, p. 90: "Da Matth. keinerlei asketische Tendenz gegenüber Besitz und Reichtum zeigt, ist in 19,21 das *akolouthei* das entscheidende Ziel des Gebotes, das auf keinen Fall übersehen werden darf." And p. 92: "Die *teleiotès* besteht ja nach 19,21 in der Nachfolge." Cf. already

reaction reveals that the great possessions took the first place above Christ in the heart of the ruler, i.e., functioned as an idol. This hidden condition was brought to light only by this special test of the *imitatio Christi*[76] as the salvation-historical concretizing of the *imitatio Dei*.

The Messianic call to be *teleios*, therefore, is not a higher or a different way to the kingdom of God than obedience to the commandments (19,17), but the intensifying or radicalizing of them in following Christ.[77] Consequently, the real decision which Christ required from the rich young ruler was not primarily of an *ethical* nature, but of a radical *religious* nature: the complete self-surrender to God.[78]

The traditional Roman Catholic exegesis, which finds here the teaching of two different stages or standards of morality,[79] can only be main-

---

Melanchthon, *Apology of the Augsburg Confession* (1531), Art. XXVII, 48: "Perfection consists in that which Christ adds, 'Follow me.'" Calvin, *Inst.* IV, 13, 13.

76 This special call was identical with those of the twelve disciples, who all had to leave home, family and daily profession, Mk. 10,28ff.; Mt. 19,27ff. These passages also reveal, however, that the principle of this call also is applied to the whole church. Cf. Schnackenburg, *o.c.* I, 151f.: "Es kann kein Zweifel sein, dass Jesus die Ansprüche, die sich aus einer Reich-Gottes-Botschaft ergaben, an *alle* richtete, ebenso aber auch, dass er in die besondere Jüngernachfolge mit Aufgabe von Heim, Familie und bisherigem Beruf nur eine *begrenzte* Schar rief." Larsson, *o.c.*, pp. 45f., 46: "Eine gewisse Verwandlung des Nachfolgegedankens kann man somit schon im Rahmen der Evangelientradition beobachten."

77 Cf. G. Barth, *o.c.*, pp. 93, 96, who rightly indicates that *teleios* in Mt. 5,48 and 19,21 both are directed against a superficial moralizing of the commandments, and of the love-commandment in particular, 5,43 and 19,19. Preisker, *o.c.*, p. 133, concerning Mt. 19,21: "Gedacht ist dabei an die uneingeschränkte Hingabe an Gott und das Gesetz – und Bestimmtsein des Menschen vom *telos*, vom Ziel, vom Reich her; es geht nicht um die Erfüllung einzelner Gebote sondern um die Ganzheit im Gottgehorsam aus Gottes Gnade (Mt. 19,26)." See the valuable discussion of Ridderbos, *Komst van het Kon.*, pp. 280-287: "De toepassing van de eis der liefde." Von Campenhausen, *o.c.*, pp. 8f. Schniewind, *o.c.*, pp. 206f.

78 Cf. Ridderbos, *o.c.*, pp. 277f.; stating on p. 280: "De in Christus geopenbaarde genade Gods brengt ook de eis der liefde tot zijn hoogste spankracht." Also p. 287.

79 Preisker, *o.c.*, pp. 208, 219f., 234ff., traces the beginning of the *moralizing* in the Church back to the first letter of Clement and the so-called apostolic fathers for whom the Kingdom of God became the *object*. The commandments of the Decalogue are regarded to require a universal morality, while the "evangelical counsel" of poverty (beside those of charity and obedience) is a higher, safer and more sure way to acquire perfection, left to the free choice of the individual. This dogmatic exegesis was established by Th. Aquinas, *S Th* I-II, q. 107, a. 2; q. 108, a. 4, and is still defended basically by B. Rigaux, "Révélation des Mystères et Perfection à Qumran et dans le N.T.," *NTS* IV (1957/58), 248. J. Keulers, *Het Ev. volgens Mattheüs*, 1950, p. 241.
It is fundamentally rejected, however, by J. Herkenrath, *Die Ethik Jesu in*

tained on the premise that the rich young ruler indeed had kept all the ethical commandments of the Torah. This is the crucial point in the story.[80] Here not only Mark (10,21) and Luke (18,22) reveal the intention of Matthew,[81] but also the Sermon on the Mount, Mt. 5,48 in particular,[82] leaves no room for doubt as to the significance of perfection in Mt. 19,21. Moreover, Mt. 19,23-24 testify unmistakably that "the issue is not the determination of higher and lower moral grades, or how to attain to a higher rank among His followers, but the question of gaining admission to the Kingdom of heaven. This is a matter with which every one of His followers is concerned."[83]

We might conclude that, while *teleios* in Mt. 5,48 denotes perfect or undivided love *toward enemies* – as intensified love toward the neighbor – rooted in the Father's love, *teleios* in Mt. 19,21 signifies perfect or undivided love *toward Christ Jesus*, as the manifestation of the supreme love toward God.

This reveals the richness and depth of the content of *teleios* in the gospel of Matthew, which shows its basic continuity with the Old Testament salvation-historical and cultic tradition. This perfection is achieved not by the sum total of all human emotions, affections or moral sentiments but by the full or living son-Father relationship, i.e., covenant fellowship with the Creator and Redeemer God, as in Israel's salvation-historical and cultic relationship with Yahweh.[84]

By faith in and submission to Christ Jesus this perfection or perfect love is purified and intensified Christologically. Perfection is realized not at the end of the way of trying to follow or imitate Christ but in the relation with and in the belonging to Christ, in His redeeming fellowship all the way through. For Matthew the Christian ethics of obedience and *imitatio Christi* are founded on his Christology.[85] The *imitatio Christi* therefore is not attained by an autonomous copying of Christ, but only by the fellowship with Christ which is rooted in His redeeming call.[86]

---

*ihren Grundzügen*, 1926, pp. 164ff. Schnackenburg, *o.c.* I, 147ff., 151ff. Schmid, *o.c.*, p. 282.

80   Cf. *D. Martin Luther's Evangelien-Auslegung*, II, pp. 666ff.

81   Von Campenhausen, *o.c.*, p. 7, asserts that Matthew does accept the fact that the ruler had kept the commandments, in contrast with the *Gospel to the Hebrews* (Preuschen, *Antilegomena* III, 5, p. 6) which points to the shortcoming of the ruler towards his poor fellowmen.

82   See G. Barth, *o.c.*, p. 90: "Die Forderung, *teleios* zu sein, gilt aber 5,48 der ganzen Gemeinde. Scheitert somit die Deutung nach einer zweistufigen Ethik...." Also pp. 92f.

83   Du Plessis, *o.c.*, p. 172.

84   H. W. Robinson, *Inspiration and Revelation in the O.T.*, pp. 214ff.

85   Cf. G. Barth, *o.c.*, p. 98.

86   Mt. 11,28. Cf. Kittel, in *ThWNT* I, 214, 35f. Schnackenburg, *o.c.* I, 107:

## 2. The cultic qualification of the apostolic ethos of perfection and holiness.

### a. The Pauline Writings

When we consider the use of the terms *teleios* and *hagios* in the writings of the apostle Paul, we observe one overall and supreme characteristic: the Christo-centric soteriological and cultic motif.[87] The apostolic ethos of perfection and sanctity never constitutes an autonomous ethical quality which is reserved only for a selected *elite* class.[88] The apostolic ethos is rooted in and founded on the Christocentric historical and cultic redemption.

This cultic-ethical relationship is most explicitly expressed in *2 Cor. 6,16–7,1*,[89] where the Church is described by the significant term Temple (*naos*) in relation to her ethos of holiness. Appealing to Lev. 26,11f. and Ez. 37,27, where the cultic presence of Yahweh is rooted in the historical redemption of the covenant God, Paul applies this cultic salvation reality of the old covenant to the indwelling of the Spirit of Christ in the Christian church of the new covenant: *hèmeis gar naos theou esmen zōntos.*[90]

---

"Christusnachfolge ist die herrlichste Verheissung und darum schon in der Mühsal des Weges tiefinnere Freude." Von Campenhausen, *o.c.*, pp. 11f.: "Der Glaube in diesem Sinne [sc. die unbedingte, persönliche Bindung an den geglaubten Herrn] und kein wie immer geartetes allgemeines Gesetz bildet den lebendigen Ausgangspunkt der christlichen Lebensführung und Sittlichkeit."

87  See Du Plessis, *o.c.*, pp. 176-205; discussing Rom. 12,2; 1 Cor. 2,6; 13,10; 14,20; Eph. 4,13; Phil. 3,12.15; Col. 1,28; 3,14; 4,12; cf. 205: "If we reflect for a moment on Paul's use of the word *teleios* it is clear that the particular and most distinct aspect of perfection as he envisaged it, was the fullness of the redemptive state or the supreme soteriological bounty of belief in Jesus Christ."

88  Cf. Du Plessis, *o.c.*, p. 205: "What was attainable according to alien conviction only by the specially endowed individuals, is granted here [sc. 1 Cor. 2,6; Phil. 3,15; Col. 1,28; 4,12] to the humble and the lowly who are thus elevated beyond all standards of contemporary measures of wisdom and excellence. They are perfect because they receive the full donation of the redemptive work of Jesus Christ."

89  Cf. R. Schippers, "Cultus en ethos in het N.T.," in *Arcana Revelata*, *FS* F. W. Grosheide, 1951, pp. 105-117; he states on p. 106: "Wie haar ethos wil wekken, moet haar cultisch duiden." And on p. 114: "Aldus blijven de verhoudingen fundamenteel gelijk aan wat in het O.T. gesteld was. Het ethos krijgt geen eigenmachtigheid. Het is in de greep van de cultus en het wordt van daaruit verstaan en in practijk gebracht." We are not dealing here with the norms of the apostolic ethos as such. See for the concrete normativeness of the apostolic ethos the very instructive dissertation by W. Schrage, *Die konkreten Einzelgebote in der paulinischen Paränese. Ein Beitrag zur neutestamentlichen Ethik*, 1961. Esp. ch. VIII.

90  2 Cor. 6,16b; cf. 2 Cor. 3,18; 13,5; 1 Cor. 3,16-17; Also Gal. 2,20; Eph. 3,16-18; 5,18; 2,19-22.

On the basis of the Christological fulfillment of Israel's liturgy of atonement,[91] Paul emphasizes the daily redeeming fellowship (*koinōnia*) and moral unity of the Christian believer with his loving Lord.[92] The new relationship of the believers with God as *sons* of God[93] is analogous to the restored covenant relationship of Israel with God, only determined Christologically by the "now" of the day of salvation,[94] i.e., the salvation-historical death and resurrection of Jesus Christ:

> ... and He died for all, that those who live might live no longer for themselves but for Him who for their sake died and was raised.[95]

On this Christological redemptive indicative Paul bases his religious-ethical imperative:

> Since we have these promises, beloved, let us cleanse ourselves [*katharisōmen*] from every defilement [*molysmos*] of body and spirit, and make holiness perfect [*epitelountes hagiōsynèn*] in the fear of God.[96]

In this respect 2 Cor. 7,1 manifests a basic and clear continuity with the Old Testament cultic-ethical dynamism of Lev. 19,2 and Pss. 15 and 24.[97] Sanctity is presented again at once as a gift – the state of holiness – and a commission to the believers in Christ, the saints, to cleanse themselves from every defilement of body and spirit.[98] But, like the cultus of

---

91 2 Cor. 5,18-21. 14-15.

92 2 Cor. 6,14-15; 5,17; 4,16. Cf. Hauck, in *ThWNT* III, 804, 22ff. (s.v. *koinōnos*): "Die Teilnahme der Frommen am Heiligen hat exklusiven Charakter (2 K 6,14: *tís koinōnia phōti pros skotos*;). Sie zwingt zur Scheidung. Als Kinder des Lichtes dürfen die Christen unmöglich teilhaben an der Sünde (Eph. 5,11 ...)." Schippers, *o.c.*, p. 116, indicates how, e.g., the sexual ethos is built up from the religious cultus in Eph. 5,25-27; 4,19f.; 1 Thes. 4,3-5; etc.

93 2 Cor. 6,18. E. Nestle, *Novum Testamentum*, refers to Jer. 31,9; Is. 43,6; Hos. 2,1 (1,10).

94 2 Cor. 6,2; cf. Acts 17,30f.

95 2 Cor. 5,15; cf. vs. 21; 1 Cor. 1,30.

96 2 Cor. 7,1. Cf. Du Plessis, *o.c.*, p. 131, who points to the cultic origin of the concepts *katharizein, molysmos*, and *hagiōsynè*.

97 Cf. 1 Pet. 1,15-16. Schippers, *o.c.*, p. 115: "De heiligheid van de gemeente van het nieuwe Verbond wordt telkens analoog aan die van het O.T. getekend." Procksch, in *ThWNT* I, 116 (s.v. *hagiōsynè*), observes the ethical character of *hagiōsynè* in 2 Cor. 7,1 and 1 Thes. 3,13: "Gottes Ziel gilt der Festigung der Herzen in Heiligkeit. Auch hier erweist sich die Heiligkeit in der Herzensreinheit; es ist die in der sittlichen Aneignung vollendete *hagiōsynè*, deren Ursprung in der Versöhnung gegeben ist, worin ihr kultisches Element liegt" (116,31ff.).

98 Du Plessis, *o.c.*, p. 131, therefore is correct in concluding: "It means

the old covenant, the ethos of holiness remains conditioned and motivated by the cultic Christological redemption.

Consequently, the apostolic kerygma proclaims that the cultic fellowship with the covenant God in the Old Testament now is being surpassed by God's redeeming presence in Jesus Christ.[99]

When K. Prümm[100] critizes Du Plessis by stating:

> Wohl aber ist es im Widerspruch, der apostlischen Mahnung einen 'göttlichen Akt in Christus' als Ziel zuzuweisen. Solches 'der Vollendung zuzuführen', ist dem Können des Menschen entzogen,

he not only ignores the interpretation of Du Plessis who explained: "that they should *put into operation* what they already have [sc. the divine promises]"[101], but Prümm also denies the cultic correlation[102] of redemption and ethical imperative of the old covenant (Psalm 15!) and its basic Christological continuity in the new covenant. The real conflict, however, concentrates itself on the nature of Biblical sanctification and divine grace. When grace is qualified by the medieval Scholastic concept of a depersonalized metaphysical substance and not by the Spirit or *Christus praesens*, then theological *synergism* cannot be avoided, in which the human will is conceived as an independent autonomous factor which has to co-operate with and to use grace as the other constitutive element in sanctification.[103] In the framework of this semi-Pelagian concept, holiness can be defined as "eine bleibende Vereigenschaftung des Inneren."[104] In fundamental contrast to this idea of an inherent quality, the apostolic kerygma proclaims the cultic ethos of the indwelling Lord in the soul

that *hagiōsynè* is not an achieved quality, but a gracious act of God in Christ. Ignoring these motives is tantamount to making sanctity an autonomous ethical quality." *Contra* K. Prümm, "Das neutestam. Sprach- und Begriffsproblem der Vollkommenheit," *Bib.* 44 (1963), 84f., who describes this as an "exegetisches Fehlerteil," since Du Plessis does not acknowledge the (Roman Catholic) *synergistic* problematics here.

99   Cf. Schippers, *o.c.*, pp. 114f.: "Waar gaat het in de cultus anders om dan om de tegenwoordigheid Gods?" Schlatter: "In Jesus ist Gottes Gegenwart in höhere Weise vorhanden als im Tempel" (quoted by Schippers, p. 114).

100   *L.c.*, 84.

101   *O.c.*, p. 132.

102   This term is also to be preferred for designating Paul's ethics above such terms as "paradoxale" or even "antinomie" which J. Héring, *La Seconde Ep. de St. Paul aux Cor.*, CNT VIII, 1958, p. 61, uses.

103   Cf. Prümm, *l.c.*, 84: "Wohl aber ist es ihm gegeben etwas, was Gott (wenn auch anfanghaft schon nicht ganz ohne seine menschliche Mitwirkung[!]) gnadenhaft in seinem Inneren angefangen hat, unter Benützung der ihm stets zur Verfügung gestellten Gnade zu Ende zu führen. Darin eben besteht die Aufgabe des christlichen Leben...."

104   Prümm, *l.c.*

temple,[105] which calls for a concrete walk with God or *imitatio Christi*, i.e., constant and progressive sanctification, or increasing reflection of the glorious character of Christ.[106] Like the old covenant, this apostolic ethos of perfection rejects both quietism and moralism,[107] since its scope is not virtues as such but the incessant fellowship and communion of love with God through Christ Jesus. This must also be the meaning of the significant Old Testament term, "in the fear of God"[108] (2 Cor. 7,1). It denotes the deep religious motivation and characterization of the Christian moral ethos of perfection, since it constitutes "the basis of respect for the divine norms."[109]

The Christological-moral application of the old-covenant cultus appears most directly in *1 Cor. 5,7-8*. Here the ethical imperative to "cleanse out [*ekkatharate*][110] the old leaven" of sin is based on the cultic celebration of Passover as fulfilled in the atoning death of Jesus Christ:

> For Christ, our paschal lamb, has been sacrificed. Let us, *therefore*, celebrate the festival, not with the old leaven, the leaven of malice and evil, but with the unleavened bread of sincerity and truth.

Just as the cultic command to eat only unleavened bread seven days, from the day of Passover, and to remove all leaven from "all your territory," is grounded in the remembrance of the historic deliverance from Egypt (Dt. 16,3ff.), so the apostolic ethos of sincerity and truth is

---

105   2 Cor. 6,16ff.; 1 Cor. 3,16; Gal. 2,20.
106   2 Cor. 3,18; 4,15; Eph. 3,17; 4,20-32; 5,1-2.18; Col. 3,1-10. Cf. Du Plessis, *o.c.*, p. 132: "Sanctity calls for constant sanctification, by steadfast devotion and acts of self-sacrifice. In terms corresponding with the O.T. idiom, it is 'a way to be walked' and to be consolidated.... Putting this religious quality into operation entails both spiritual and moral endeavor."
107   Cf. Du Plessis, *o.c.*, p. 132.
108   See W. Eichrodt, *Theol. of the O.T.* II, ET 1967, pp. 268-277. H. A. Brongers, "La Crainte du Seigneur," *OTS* V (1948), 151ff. Cf. Th. C. Vriezen, *Hoofdlijnen der Theol. van het O.T.*, 1954², p. 247: "Deze vreze des Heren is zelfs de staande uitdrukking geworden voor wat wij religie, godsdienst noemen." Lit. on p. 145.
109   Eichrodt, *o.c.*, II, p. 273, who further states: "There is a very close, almost stereotyped connection, in admonitions to observe the law, between the fear of God and walking in his ways (Deut. 10.12,20; Josh. 24.14; cf. Ps. 86.11). Indeed, the word by which God reveals his will is seen as the best guidance to a right fear of God (Deut. 4.10; 17.19; 31.13). The wisdom teachers, too, group together the fear of God and the avoidance of evil (Prov. 3.7; 8.13; 14.2; 16.6; Job 1.8)." The specific application in 2 Cor. 7 has to do with the abstaining from the heathen cultus and the immoral practices of syncretism, cf. 2 Cor.6,14ff.; cf. 1 Cor. 5,1ff.; 6,13ff.; 8; 1 Thes. 3,11-13; 4,3-8; 5,23.
110   Cf. *Str-B* III, 359, referring to Ex. 12,15.19; 13,7.

rooted explicitly in the redemptive-historical fact of deliverance from the defiling power of sin by the death of Christ as the perfect paschal Lamb of the new covenant.

The apostolic ethos of perfection appears explicitly in *Romans 12,1-2*. Conspicuous again is the cultic designation and motivation, reminiscent of the old-covenant Temple cultus:

> ... to present [*parastèsai*][111] your bodies as a living sacrifice [*thysian*], holy [*hagian*] and acceptable [*euareston*] to God, which is your spiritual worship [*logikèn latreian*][112] (Rom. 12,1).

Significant is Paul's specific emphasis on the religious-cultic service of the *body*, in clear continuity with 6,13, betraying an anti-Gnostic polemic.[113]

The cultic structure of Romans 12,1-2 is clearly prepared by the structure of Romans 6, where the ethical imperative of vss. 12ff., 16-19[114] is founded on the Christological salvation history[115] and the transforming cultic redemption of baptism.[116] The cultic death of the old self in baptism

---

111 The verb *parhistèmi* functions as the technical term to present sacrifices and offerings in the Levitical cultus, cf. Lk. 2,22. O. Michel, *Der Brief an die Römer*, 1955, p. 260, indicates that the LXX uses for this the technical term *prosagein* or *prospherein*; *parhistanai* being the customary Hellenistic cultic term. All the more emphatic then is Paul's description of the Christian ethos: "Das neue Leben des Christen steht unter dem Zeichen des Opfers, das sich leiblich und geistig auswirkt" (260).

112 1 Pet. 2,5 uses *pneumatikos* instead of *logikos*. Michel, *o.c.*, p. 260, concludes: "Wir haben offenbar in Röm. 12,1 und 1 Petr. 2,5 d e n g l e i c h e n liturgisch-hymnischen S t i l vor uns. Zugrunde liegt die Vorstellung von einem rechten Priesterdienst und einem offenbarungsgemässen Opfer, das in der eschatologischen Gemeinde dargebracht wird."

113 Cf. Michel, *o.c.*, *ad* 12, 1, p. 261: "Die paul. Vorstellung ist eigenartig und setzt sich von der Hermetik ab. Dort ist Gott unausdrückbar, und man darf ihm nur die ebenso unaussprechliche Verehrung der Gedanken und Gefühle darbringen (*logikè thusia*). Pls dagegen geht es um konkreten und völligen Gehorsam gegen den Anspruch des Evangeliums in der ganz unmystischen Sphäre des 'Leiblichen'."

114 The passage Rom. 6,13.16.19 uses five times the verb *parhistanein*, as in 12,1, to present the cultic consecration and service to God.

115 Especially worked out in Rom. 5,12-21. Cf. G. C. Berkouwer, *De Zonde* II, 1969, pp. 273-298; he states on p. 297: "Als Paulus in Rom. 5 Christus ziet als de grote initiator der nieuwe mensheid tegenover de Adamitische mensheid, dan gaat hij in Rom. 6 in dezelfde denkwijze voort en handelt hij over het (corporatieve) begrepen-zijn van de velen in Christus." See E. Larsson, *Christus als Vorbild*, pp. 48f.; he states on p. 50: "Paulus will mit seiner Darstellung der Taufe zeigen, wie die Folgen von der Tat Christi den Christen zugute kommen. Er tut dies, indem er das Taufgeschehen mit der Heilsgeschichte in Verbindung bringt."

116 Larsson, on pp. 63f., n. 2, rightly rejects the various theories of

is not pictured as being man's own activity but God's, "hid with Christ in God" (Col. 3,3) yet no less real, just as the salvation-historical act of atonement at the cross of Christ was God's hidden but real act. Into Christ's substitutionary death at the cross the baptismal act by faith transfers, connects, and gives legal participation.[117] This implies not only the death of the "old man" or nature, but just as truly the resurrection of the "new man"[118] by an act of God (Eph. 2,4ff.; Col. 2,12f.). Paul summons the Christian Church to manifest this cultic hidden reality of death to sin and resurrection to righteousness in empirical reality by the new ethos of sanctification, the new obedience of "slaves" or servants of God.[119]

This new walk therefore cannot be described as a pure ethical life but rather the empirical aspect of the cultic-sacramental transformation of fellowship with Christ's death and resurrection: "so that as Christ was raised from the dead by the glory of the Father, we too might walk in newness of life," Rom. 6,4b.[120]

The new ethos is the life with Christ (Rom. 6,8), the life "to God in Christ Jesus" (Rom. 6,11b). In this sense the apostolic ethos of holiness is the life of total communion of life and destiny with Christ who now lives "to God" (Rom. 6,10).[121]

The apostle Paul seems to qualify his ethos as a cultic *imitatio Christi*:

*simultaneousness*, which are inspired either by existentialistic philosophy or by Christ-mysticism or by O. Casel's and V. Warnach's cultic-mystery representation. On the debated question concerning the revelation of salvation history and baptismal event see V. Warnach, *Archiv f. Liturgiewiss.*, V/2 (1958), 275-332: "Die Tauflehre des Römerbriefs in der neueren Theologischen Diskussion," esp. 324ff. For a fundamental critique on Warnach see H. Ridderbos, *Paulus*, pp. 454-458. Also Grundmann, in *ThWNT* VII, 790-792 with resp. notes and much lit. (s.v. *synmeta ktl*).

117   See the valuable section on baptism in Ridderbos, *Paulus*, pp. 442-462. Cf. also Grundmann, in *ThWNT* VII, 790, 3ff.

118   J. A. T. Robinson, *The Body*. SBT 5, 1961, pp. 79, 57, unjustly identifies the "new man" in Christ, and the church, with the resurrection body of Christ. Cf. Ridderbos, *o.c.*, pp. 409, 417.

119   Rom. 6,12-14.22.19. Cf. Larsson, *o.c.*, pp. 68f.: "Dieser Todesprozess muss aber auf ethischem Gebiet vollendet werden, da der 'Leib' und das 'Fleisch' des Menschen immer noch empfänglich sind für die Impulse der Sünde." P. 84: "Das Auferstehungsleben ist schon wirklich, aber doch verborgen."

120   Cf. Rom. 7,6b: "... in the new life of the Spirit." Rom. 6,5.10-11; Col. 3,3; 2 Cor. 5,17 (*kainè ktisis*); Gal. 6,15. Larsson, *o.c.*, p. 69, who rightly stresses the reality of the cultic creation of the resurrection life, although the final eschatological resurrection of the body is not excluded.

121   *tōi theōi*; cf. Larsson, *o.c.*, p. 72: "Der Dativ gibt hier an, dass er in Gemeinschaft mit Gott lebt und von ihm abhängig ist, Blass-Debr. § 188, 2 Anh. Diese seine Stellung ist für die Christen als Vorbild von Bedeutung. Auch sie sollen bedenken, dass sie in einem totalen Gemeinschafts - und Abhängigkeitsverhältnis zu Gott stehen."

"So you also [*houtōs kai hymeis*] must consider [*logizesthe*][122] your-
selves dead to sin and alive to God in Christ Jesus" (Rom. 6,11).

In the following passage (vss. 12-23) the ethos of sanctification or
perfection is motivated by this cultic *imitatio Christi* which is rooted in
the baptismal identification with the substitutional death and resurrection of Jesus Christ. When death no longer has dominion over the
risen Christ, the followers of Christ who are risen with Him in baptism
no longer stand under the dominion of sin, but under the gracious, holy,
royal power of Christ as their new ancestor, king and master.[123]

In Rom. 12,1-2 the apostle returns to the ethical implication of his
cultic-baptismal theology with the renewed appeal, "by the mercies of
God," to consecrate the whole bodily existence as a cultic sacrifice
acceptable to the covenant God.

By the "body" Paul indicates the total man, including his mind (*nous*),
Rom. 12,2.

Paul summons the baptized "brethren" that first of all their thinking
and willing (*nous*) should be constantly engaged in a new "cultic thinking,"[124]
even to "*prove*" the perfect will of God in order to serve God in society
according to the divine pleasure. In Rom. 12,1 tot 15,13 Paul develops
more systematically than elsewhere his Christian ethics out of his Christian
theology, out of his baptismal theology in particular.[125]

To Paul the philosophical ethos of serving man, church and world by
a perfect dedication to an ethical ideal or virtue is not sufficient, and

122  This verb – to be taken in the imperative form – functions in this context as *to believe*; cf. Col. 2,12. Michel, *Com. ad loc.* Larsson, *o.c.*, pp. 72, n. 1;
83. Cf. Ridderbos, *o.c.*, p. 295.

123  Cf. Berkouwer, *De Zonde* II, p. 297: "Het heil. [sc. in Rom. 6] wordt
corporatief omschreven als het medegekruisigd-zijn van de oude mens met
Christus (Rom. 6:6) en vanuit deze realiteit roept Paulus op tot onderwerping
aan Christus' koninklijke heerschappij, Rom. 6:8, 9." In this light it becomes
clear why the apostle Paul never builds his ethos on the dignity of humanity
in its original creation for God; cf. Robinson, *o.c.*, pp. 32, 35f.

124  Cf. Michel, *o.c.*, p. 261, n. 1: "Die urchristliche Gemeinde ist als Tauf-
gemeinschaft in ein neues kultisches Denken hineingestellt." And on p. 262:
"Der Getaufte und Geistbegabte wird aufgerufen in seinem Denken (*nous*)
sich erneuern zu lassen." Schrage, *o.c.*, p. 164, rightly emphasizes: "Die
Neuwerdung ist freilich kein Akt des Nous selbst und also kein 'Akt der
Selbstbesinnung' und kein 'Zur Vernunft – Kommen' wie in der Stoa, sondern
eine an ihm geschehene Umformung."

125  This is not merely "Vergegenwärtigung" of salvation history, but
participation in it. This has been recognized especially by C. H. Dodd, *The
Epistle of Paul to the Romans*, who places Rom. 12,1-15, 13 under the heading:
"The Righteousness of God in Christian Living." Cf. also Michel, *o.c.*, p. 258,
n. 1. Schrage, *o.c.*, p. 165: "Die Begründung allen sittlichen Handels bei Paulus
ist gewiss keine rationale, sondern eine pneumatisch-sakramentale, aber das
schliesst den Gebrauch der ratio in der *Erkenntnis* des Guten für den Christen
nicht aus."

not what he is aiming at. No more is he satisfied with the Rabbinical concept of striving after righteousness on the basis of a moral code and casuistry.[126]

Paul's Christian ethos seeks to manifest in concrete social life what he has received in the cultic redemption: Christ, and the life with Him.[127] The holy law of God is fulfilled and magnified in Christ.[128] As His life cannot be copied but is given to be followed in union with Him, each Christian is called to prove "what is the good and acceptable and perfect will of God," Rom. 12,2.[129] The apostle uses the significant concept of *dokimazein* here in order to indicate the two-fold responsibility of the Christians who stand between the received redemption in baptism and the future apocalyptic judgment.[130] This does not mean that the Christian ethos is determined by fear of the final judgment, but by the ethical responsibility to *abide* in moral union with Christ. This Christian responsibility is exercised by way of self-examination as preparation for participation in the sacrament of the Lord's Supper.[131] This self-examination can only be exercised *coram Deo* on the basis of knowing or *dokimazein* the divine will, not as a fixed moral code as such,[132] but in intimate union

---

126  1 Pet. 1,18. See the excellent statement of Dodd, *o.c.*, p. 189: "He does not attempt to define the ethical end, or *summum bonum*, and to deduce from this a scheme of virtues ... such as Aristotle and the Stoics attempted, would be just as foreign to his conception of morality as the Pharisaic *Halakha*, or Rule of Conduct, derived from a fixed code of commandments accepted as divine and unalterable. He does not think of right conduct either as conformity with a code or as the adding of virtue to virtue in a discipline of self-culture."

127  Cf. Michel, *o.c.*, p. 258, n. 1: "Das menschliche Tun ist nicht mehr der Weg zur Selbstvollendung in Verdienst und Tugend, sondern ein Zeugnis für die Gnade, die der Mensch empfangen hat."

128  C. Michel, *o.c.*, p. 258, n. 1: "Entscheidend ist, dass Pls auch in seiner Ethik das Gesetz des Moses nach der Auslegung Jesu aufrichtet (Röm. 3,31)." It is significant, therefore, that Paul qualifies his ethos of life not by the law but by Christ, Phil. 1,21.

129  The grammatical construction allows this translation. But the RSV also does not change the text materially. The "good and acceptable and perfect" remains normed by the preceding *to thelèma tou theou*. Cf. Du Plessis, *o.c.*, p. 177. Also Michel, *o.c.*, p. 262. *Contra* Dodd, *o.c.*, pp. 200f., who rather defines the will of God by what is good, acceptable, perfect in itself. Schrage, *o.c.*, p. 168, indicates that the will of God not merely denotes His moral will, but also implies His whole salvatory will as Creator and Redeemer, e.g. Rom. 1,10; 15,32; 1 Cor. 12,18; 1,1; Gal. 1,4.

130  See Grundmann, in *ThWNT* II, 259, 46ff. (s.v. *dokimos*). Also below, Ch. IV, 3a: "The meaning of apocalyptic in Pauline soteriology."

131  1 Cor. 11,28 before the Lord's Supper: *dokimazetō heauton*; cf. 2 Cor. 13,5; Gal. 6,4. See the section on the Lord's Supper, in Ridderbos, *Paulus*, pp. 463-478; esp. pp. 474ff.

132  As such Paul describes the Jew, Rom. 2,18: *dokimazeis ta diapheronta katèchoumenos ek tou nomou.*

with Christ, under all circumstances.[133] As children of light their walk must be determined by the *dokimazein* what is pleasing to the Lord.[134] Thus the twofold commission of the Christian to *prove* himself in the religious cultus and to *prove* the perfect will of God are placed in an unbreakable correlation. This cultic-ethical self-proving in the light of Christ's self-revelation[135] receives its seriousness and urgency, however, from the emphatically attested fact that Christ in the cultus of the Lord's Supper is not exclusively present as Redeemer but also as judging Lord.[136] The Christian is called to periodic self-critique in the light of the holy self-sacrifice of Christ's body and blood, in order to partake "worthily" of the table of the Lord.[137] Here it becomes most conclusively clear how the Christian ethos of righteousness and holiness is *constantly* motivated by the religious cultus, *until* the day of Christ's second parousia.[138]

Since the Lord's Supper represents at once the *already* fulfilled sacrifice of the new covenant, and the *not yet* fulfilled communion with the Lord in glory, this cultic celebration of the accomplished redemption also awakens and summons one to a divinely approved moral behavior[139] which

133   Phil. 1,10: "*ta diapheronta* ist das, worauf es in der jeweiligen Situation ankommt" (Grundmann, *ThWNT* II, 263, 13f.).

134   Eph. 5,8.10. Cf. K. Barth, *Der Römerbrief*, 1929, *ad* Rom. 12,2, p. 422: "Die primäre ethische Handlung ist ein ganz bestimmtes *Denken*. Busse heisst *Um*denken. Die Schlüsselstellung des ethischen Problems, der Ort, wo die Drehung geschieht die auf ein neues Tun hinweist, ist dieses Umdenken." That Paul's renewed *nous* and its *dokimazein* are intent upon a concrete act and ethos, appears from Eph. 5,8; Phil. 4,8-9 (*tauta logizesthe – tauta prassete*); Col. 1,9-10. Cf. also Schage, *o.c.*, pp. 165f. Of vital significance is Schrage's treatise on the similarity and the difference between the Christian and the non-Christian morality, the Stoic morality in particular, pp. 197-210.

135   1 Cor. 11,27-29.

136   1 Cor. 11,29-32. Hence the warning example of Israel's religious-moral failure while enjoying their sacraments, 1 Cor. 10,1-11. Cf. Ridderbos, *o.c.*, p. 476, who rightly rejects all notions of magical or intrinsic power of the cultic elements.

137   See Ridderbos, *o.c.*, pp. 477f.: "Het lichaam van Christus onderscheiden, d.w.z. het in zijn heilige en heilrijke betekenis erkennen, betekent ook: zichzelf onderscheiden, d.w.z. zichzelf onder het oordeel en de kritiek doen doorgaan, welke met de heiligheid van Christus' lichaam in overeenstemming is." Cf. C. F. D. Moule, "The Judgment Theme in the Sacraments," in *FS* C. H. Dodd, 1964, pp. 464-481; esp. p. 472: "Emphatically, therefore, the Eucharist is an occasion of judgment – either of voluntary self-judgment, in acceptance of God's verdict on fallen man, or else of unwilling liability to God's judgment as it falls upon those who, in the blindness of selfish secularism, side against the Lord Jesus. (It is *ptōsis kai anastasis*, cf. Luke II.34)."

138   1 Cor. 11,26, "until He comes."

139   1 Thes. 2,4, God testing, *dokimazōn*, the hearts of the Christians continually. Cf. Ridderbos, *o.c.*, p. 474, who states that the Lord's Supper is celebrated "in nimmer aflatende zorg voor het blijven in de gemeenschap van Christus, voor de heiligheid van Gods volk en het vlieden van de afgoden, 1 Kor. 10.14."

will stand the final test of God's apocalyptic *dokimazein*.[140]

It is the special characteristic of Paul's theonomic self-understanding – which he also emphatically applies to the Christian Church – that Christ not only begins, continues and completes His work of grace in the believers, but also will finally judge and justify them according to their fruits of righteousness by faith, their ethos of faith in concrete reality.[141]

The distinctly expressed *condition* for ultimate justification is continuation or *perseverance, epimenein*, in "the faith, stable and steadfast, not shifting from the hope of the gospel which you heard" (Col. 1,23).[142] It means being kept and established in living *fellowship* with Christ through His spiritual gifts, waiting for His glorious revealing, sustained by His faithfulness "to the end" (*heōs telous*, 1 Cor. 1,7-9; cf. 1 Thess. 3,13; 5,23). The apostle therefore feels prompted to write to the Christians at Philippi:

> And it is my prayer that your love may abound more and more, with knowledge and all discernment, so that you may approve what is excellent [*eis to dokimazein ta diapheronta*], and may be pure and blameless for the day of Christ, filled with the fruits of righteousness which come through Jesus Christ, to the glory and praise of God (Phil. 1,9-11).

The Letter to the Ephesians which visualizes the building up of the body of Christ until it attains to a "perfect man" (*andra teleion*; 4,13) as the ultimate goal of all charismatic gifts in the Church, at the same time proclaims:

> For we are his workmanship, created in Christ Jesus for good works, which God prepared beforehand, that we should walk in them (Eph. 2,10).

The good works of the "perfect man" remarkably are described as "prepared beforehand by God" (*prohetoimazein*), forever excluding glory to human righteousness.[143]

---

140  Cf. 1 Cor. 3,13; 9,27. Grundmann, *ThWNT* II, 260, 44ff.: "Die bevorstehende Prüfung im Gericht und das dauernde Stehen unter Gottes Augen bedingen eine Lebensführung, die auf Bewährung gerichtet ist, und zwar auf Bewährung des anvertrauten Heiles in der konkreten Situation des jeweiligen Lebens."

141  1 Cor. 1,8; Col. 1,22; both: *anegklètos*, irreproachable, guiltless, blameless. Cf. Grundmann, in *ThWNT* I, 358, 25ff. (s.v.), rightly referring to Rom. 8,33f. Cf. also 2 Tim. 4,7-8; Phil. 1,6.9-11.

142  On the Biblical correlation of faith and perseverance, see Berkouwer, *Faith and Perseverance*, ET 1958. On the theological concept of perseverance in Calvin, see J. Moltmann, *Prädestination und Perseveranz*, "Beitr. z. Gesch. u. Lehre der Ref. K.," XII, 1961; ch. II.

143  Cf. F. W. Grosheide, *De Brief van Paulus aan de Efeziërs*, 1960, *ad 2*,

This dimension of the priority of sovereign grace in the sanctification of the Church is proclaimed in Eph. 5,26-27:

> ...that he might sanctify [*hagiasèi*] her, having cleansed [*katharisas*] her by the washing of water with the word, that he might present the church to himself in splendor, without spot or wrinkle or any such thing, that she might be holy and without blemish.

Here baptism is signified as the divine cleansing which intends to sanctify the Church completely and to restore it into the full glory of the *imago Dei*, in conformity to the Son of God: "holy and without blemish."[144] Yet, this designation of holiness and perfection will not be the moral self-understanding of the Christian Church, since all the redeemed will glory exclusively in their Creator and Redeemer, joining the never-ceasing cultic hymn of the heavenly beings:[145]

> Holy, holy, holy, is the Lord God Almighty,
> who was and is and is to come!
> Worthy are Thou, our Lord and God, to receive glory
> and honor and power, for Thou didst create all
> things, and by Thy will they existed and were created.
>
> Worthy art Thou . . . for Thou wast slain and by Thy
> blood didst ransom men for God from every tribe and
> tongue and people and nation, and hast made them a
> kingdom and priests to our God, and they shall
> reign on earth.
>
> For Thou alone art holy!

b. *The Letter to the Hebrews*

In this "word of exhortation" (*logos tès paraklèseōs*, Heb. 13,22), the author presents his appeal to go on to perfection (6,1),[146] within the

10, p. 41: "De apostel denkt hier aan den heiligen wandel, die na het verlost zijn door het één zijn met Christus, den Ambtsdrager (*Christos* staat voorop), mogelijk, doch ook geëist is." Cf. Berkouwer, *Faith and Sanctification*, pp. 191f. (Dutch, pp. 213ff.).

144  Calvin, *Inst.* III, 3, 11, interpreted not only *katharisas* but also *hagiasèi* as imputed holiness. Eph. 5,27, however, can also be seen as a parallel of Rom. 8,29, i.e., in its eschatological-apocalyptic dimension and fulfillment of God's eternal purpose. See the instructive section on Rom. 8,28-30 in Larsson, *o.c.*, pp. 293-307.

145  Rev. 4,8.11; 5,9; 15,4.

146  *epi tèn teleiotèta pherōmetha*. Du Plessis, *o.c.*, p. 209, defends on good linguistic and contextual grounds the interpretation that the author is appealing to his readers to leave the elementary subject matter of Christ behind them and to go on now to consider the teaching of perfection, i.e., what

framework of a Christologically determined salvation history and eschatology.

The concepts of *teleios*, and especially *teleioun* (to make complete or perfect) and derivatives[147] occur so many times and function in such a specific Christological soteriology that Christian perfection constitutes the central, unifying idea of the whole letter.

Of all the writings of the New Testament the Letter to the Hebrews most explicitly and thematically relates the apostolic ethos of perfection to the Christological cultus, Christ being the exclusive High Priest.

Hebrews focuses ultimately on the heart and conscience (*syneidèsis*) of the Christian believer as the very essence and being of humanity, but never in an abstract or isolated way. Incessantly the indissoluble correlation between conscience and cultic atonement with its sanctifying power is indicated. Its seriousness and reality is stressed within the framework of the progression from the old to the new covenant, the continuity and yet the superiority of the new covenant cultus. The atoning daily and yearly sanctuary services of the old or first covenant as such could not perfect the conscience of the worshipper (*mè dynamenai kata syneidèsin teleiōsai ton latreuonta*, 9,9; cf. 7,18f.). The author does not intend to state that the first covenant did not know the reality of this transforming soul experience, but only that animal sacrifices as such[148] could not take away sins (10,1.4).

The context reveals as its specific intention to indicate the Christological fulfillment of the sanctuary cultus once for all, both with respect to the blood of the many sacrificial animals and to the (high-) priestly ministration of this blood within the sanctuary.[149] The Old Testament cultic sacrifices and priests as such could never cleanse or perfect the heart or conscience from the pressing guilt of sin.[150] But Christ by His single[151] offering has brought about the purification of sins and the

---

perfection is. This interpretation thus rejects the translation of the RSV: "let us ... go on to maturity."

147   See O. Michel, "Die Lehre von der christlichen Vollkommenheit nach der Anschauung des Hebräerbriefes," in *Th St Kr* 106 (1935), 348-355, who also presents these statistics: *teleios* (2x): 5,14; 9,11. *teleioun* (9x): 2,10; 5,9; 7,19; 7,28; 9,9; 10,1; 10,14; 11,40; 12,23. *teleiotès*: 6,1. *teleiōsis*: 7,11. *teleiōtès*: 12,2. *telos* (5x): 3,6; 3,14; 6,8; 6,11; 7,3. Cf. Du Plessis, *o.c.*, pp. 118-122; 206-233.

148   In other words, the author places his Christological soteriology over against the Jewish "religious externalism induced by cult emphasis," cf. Du Plessis, *o.c.*, p. 229.

149   Cf. Du Plessis, *o.c.*, p. 230: "Thus perfection of the saints in Hebrews is, by virtue of its O.T. roots and the consummation in Christ, a soteriological and redemptive historical concept. ... Perfection on this analogy is described as the expiation for sin, of which the cultic propitiatory services of the O.T. high priests are mere shadows."

150   Heb. 7,11.19; 10,1-4. On 10,2, see below: Ch. IV, 3c (cc).

151   The meaning of *ephapax* is not merely the numeral once-ness of

cleansing of the conscience of the worshipper.[152] The forgiveness of sins through Christ brings the reality of a cleansed or perfect conscience,[153] i.e., a conscience free from divine condemnation and the defiling power of sin.

This supreme work of Christ's perfecting ministry is summed up in the declaration that the new covenant is fulfilled in the forgiveness of sins (10,15-18).

The reality of perfection therefore can only be received in the cultic way of "drawing near," *proserchomai*,[154] to the Mediator Jesus Christ in the heavenly sanctuary, the "new and living way" (10,20):

> Let us draw near with a true heart in full assurance of faith, with our hearts *sprinkled* clean from an evil conscience and our bodies *washed* with pure water (Heb. 10,22).

This verse indicates that this cultic *proserchesthai* to the heavenly sanctuary is conditioned by the cultic qualification of complete cleansing of heart and body, a recognized allusion to *baptism*.[155] The ultimate perfection of the glorious *visio Dei* again is conditioned by the continual or persevering *abiding* in the way of sanctification, 12,14 (*diōkete ... ton hagiasmon*).[156]

There is, however, in Hebrews a specific color in the qualification of the term *teleios*. Rooted in the Christological soteriology, the author

Christ's atoning sacrifice, but also the decisive term for the all-sufficient expiation once for all. Cf. Du Plessis, *o.c.*, pp. 231f.; "qualitatively and quantitatively wholly efficacious. Perfection is thus conditioned and constituted from beginning to end by the 'one for all' and 'once for all' of His unique sacrifice."

152 Heb. 1,3; 10,10-14.

153 Heb. 10,1-2. 15-18. Cf. Du Plessis, *o.c.*, p. 231. Cf. J. Schneider, *The Letter to the Hebrews*, ET 1957, p. 89: "The difference between the Old and New Covenant, consequently, does not lie in the cultic principle, but in the *means* which are at hand for carrying it through."

154 This verb has a specific cultic technical meaning, cf. 10,1.22; 4,16; 7,19.25; 12,18.22. Cf. Schneider, in *ThWNT* II, 682, 3-8 (s.v. *proserchomai*). Du Plessis, *o.c.*, p. 231: "Using the framework of cultic O.T. tradition to provide basic motifs he arrives at a provocative image of the perfection of the saints. It is drawing near to God, and they who do so become beneficiaries of salvation and are called the people of God."

155 Cf. Michel, *o.c.*, *ad* Heb. 10,22, pp. 346f.: "Die beiden Partizipien stammen aus der Kultsprache, meinen aber jetzt mehr: die Taufe besprengt das Herz und wäscht den Leib; weil das Wasser der Taufe reinigt, heisst es selbst 'rein' (*katharon*).... Die Taufe reinigt nicht nur äusserlich, sondern auch innerlich, übertrifft also die verschiedenen Waschungen des Alten Bundes, die nur der *sarx* gelten (9,10)."

156 Cf. Procksch, in *ThWNT* I, 115, 22-27 (s.v. *hagiasmos*). Oepke, in *ThWNT* II, 233, 32ff. (s.v. *diōkō*).

emphasizes a double characteristic in the life of the *teleios*. On the one hand, the *teleioi* are not "dull of hearing" (cf. 5,11 *nōthroi tais akoais*), which indicates that the *teleioi* will remain receptive, teachable, growing in Christian theological knowledge.[157] On the other hand, the *teleioi* are not "sluggish" (*nōthroi*) in faith, patience and assurance of hope, but showing "the same earnestness in realizing the full assurrance of hope *until the end*" as the saints showed who lived and died in the full assurance that they would inherit the promises (cf. 6,11-12).[158] These *teleioi*, consequently, were perfect or mature in faith and hope, but were not perfected in the final eschatological sense (see 11,39-40).

The specific quality of *teleiotès* (6,1) in the section 5,11-6,20 is the indispensable progress for the whole church in intellectual-theological discernment of good and evil (5,14: *pros diakrisin kalou te kai kakou*), which has to do not with ethical properties as such but with "heilsam-forderlicher Lehre und schadlicher Irrlehre."[159]

c. *The First Letter of Peter*

This letter, which shows a remarkable correspondence to Pauline theology, is characterized by a dominating Christo-centric *imitatio Dei*.[160] Of decisive significance is Peter's transference or better, continuation, of the divine election of Israel in the chosen believers in Jesus Christ, who therefore are now addressed as "a chosen race, a royal priesthood, a holy

157  Preisker, in *ThWNT* IV, 1120 (s.v. *nōthros*), compares this aspect with "das Einatmen (= verstehendes Aufhorchen und Aufnehmen)."

158  Preisker, *l.c.*, compares this aspect with: "das Ausatmen (= gläubige Zukunftsgewissheit)."

159  Grundmann, "Die *nèpioi* in der Urchristlichen Paränese," in *NTS* V (1959), 193. Cf. Du Plessis, *o.c.*, p. 208: "This extremely grave peril [sc. of Heb. 6,4ff.] attached to apostasy as intellectual, moral and spiritual deterioration forms the framework of the image of maturity exhibited here.... These ... do not, however, obscure the primary property of *teleios* here as the *maturity of apperception* in pedagogical or tutorial respect." See in particular the contrast in Heb. 5,13-14 between *nèpios* and *teleiōn*, which is used almost identically with *didaskalos*, 5,12. H. P. Owen, "The 'Stages of Ascent' in Hebrews v.ii-vi.3," in *NTS* III (1956-57), 243-252, projects three stages in Hebrews, which "normally" would be (1) catechetical instruction; (2) moral perfection or maturity; (3) religious vision of Christ. Because of the moral inertia of the Hebrews, and the eschatological urgency of the time, the author would have modified the first two stages eschatologically by implying them into his appeal to proceed at once to the third stage: "a fresh vision of Christ." Owen concludes: "In vi.1 the author plainly implies that the *sterea trophè* will confer the moral maturity (*teleiotès*) that normally precedes it" (249). It seems to us that Owen takes his guiding principle too much from Philo and therefore supposes too readily that to the author of Hebrews moral training and growth are *not "normally"* rooted in the transforming religious cultus or the *Christus praesens*.

160  Cf. A. Schulz, *Nachfolgen und Nachahmen*, pp. 240f.

nation, God's own people," in order to testify of the new "wonderful deeds" of the covenant God in salvation history.[161]

Remarkable is the implied anti-typical thrust of 1 Petr. 1,18-19, where the redemption from the bondage of heathen morality by "the precious blood of Christ, like that of a lamb without blemish or spot" receives salvation-historical significance by its suggested anti-typical comparison with Israel's deliverance from bondage by the cultic Passover lamb.[162] The holy covenant God, who called Israel to be holy, now calls the Christian Church to fundamentally the same holiness:

> But as he who called you is holy, be holy yourselves in all your conduct [*anastrophè*],[163] since it is written, "You shall be holy, for I am holy" (1 Pet. 1,15.16).

This qualification of the Christian ethos by the cultic ethos of Israel's covenant evidently does not pertain to the cultic ritual of the old covenant, but to the cultic ethos of holiness. Since Israel's cultic ethos of perfection was correlated and motivated by forgiving and keeping grace (Pss. 15; 19, etc.), it seems definitely insufficient to contrast Israel's *cultic holiness* with "sittlicher Reinheit" (Schneider[164]) or with "die *ethische* Vollkommenheit des göttlichen Wesens und seine Nachahmung" (A. Schulz[165]).

1 Peter immediately connects the moral obedience with the continuous mediatorial efficacy of the blood of Jesus Christ (1 Pet. 1,2).[166]

In 1 Peter baptism is characterized specifically as the redemptive cultus (*sōizei baptisma*, 3,21), which points beyond an external, symbolic ritual of washing, the cleansing of the *conscience* (*syneidèseōs agathès*).[167]

---

161   See 1 Pet. 2,9-10; cf. 1,2.

162   See also 1 Cor. 5,7. Cf. J. Schneider, *Die Kirchenbriefe*, NTD 10, 1961[9], *ad* 1 Pet. 1,19: "Er wird in erster Linie an das Passahlamm denken, dessen geopfertes Blut und Fleisch die Erlösung aus der ägyptischen Knechtschaft einleitete (vgl. 1 Kor. 5,7)." See also 1 Pet. 1,10ff.

163   This term also in 1,18; 2,12; 3,1.2.16; cf. Eph. 4,22.

164   NTD 10, p. 51; on p. 55 he only seemingly modifies his previous anti-thesis by the qualifications "Bereicherung und Vertiefung."

165   *O.c.*, p. 243.

166   Cf. Schneider, *ad loc.* (NTD 10): "Wie das durch das Opfer des Versöhnungstages im Alten Bunde gewonnene Blut über dem Volke Israel ausgesprengt wurde, so soll das Blut des Sühnopfers Christi die ständig reinigende Kraft für die Sünden der Gottesgemeinde des Neuen Bundes sein (vgl. 1 Joh. 1,7). Die sühnende Kraft des Blutes Christi ist eine immer wirksame Realität" (p. 44). See also Hauck, NTD 10[8], pp. 39f.

167   See Schneider, NTD 10, p. 85. Cf. Hauck, *ad* 1 Pet. 3,21: "Sie [sc. baptism] wird zum Rettungsmittel indem menschliches Rufen und göttliches Antworten und Retten sich hier begegnen.... Solche rettende Kraft eignet der Taufe nur 'durch die Auferstehung Jesu Christi'" (p. 71). See also Acts 2,38; 3,19.26.

This means that the baptismal rite, through the saving power of the resurrected Christ, places the whole existence and ethos of man on a new foundation.[168] The whole ethos of the baptized Christian becomes the *imitatio Christi* as total communion with Christ and therefore as the following in His footsteps, as sheep following their Shepherd.[169] This means concretely that in all social relationships they are to manifest "good behavior [*anastrophè*] in Christ,"[170] and with a "clear conscience" are to render service "by the strength which God supplies; in order that in everything God may be glorified through Jesus Christ."[171]

### d. *The Letter of James*

In the Letter of James[172] a cultic qualification of his ethos of perfection[173] does not appear explicitly. Yet his whole ethos is motivated by the presupposed covenant of grace with Israel.[174] Christian perfection, for James, stands in basic continuity with the cultic social ethos of perfection of the old covenant and of the wisdom literature in particular, i.e., the loving respect for and care of the neighbor or fellow-covenanter.[175]

The "perfect law" (1,25) is seen not in its isolated, legalistic function as a yoke of servitude, but in its legitimate function as the gracious covenant Torah in which faith and morality form a dynamic unity. As the royal covenant law (2,8), it liberates and blesses[176] those who sincerely obey the *whole* covenant law, which includes the cultic way of atonement.

As John in his first epistle (4,12) does not recognize as perfect love a "love" which is not manifesting itself in actual brotherly love, so James does not recognize as perfect faith a "faith" which remains barren, or dead, is not manifesting itself in works of faith (2,4ff.20).[177]

168  Schneider, *o.c.*, p. 50, acknowledges the supposition that 1 Pet. 1,13-2,10 even may be regarded as "ein Stück Taufparänese."

169  1 Pet. 2,19-25.

170  1 Pet. 3,16.

171  1 Pet. 4, 11; see his appeal to servants, 2,18ff.; to wives of unbelieving husbands, 3,1ff.; to husbands, 3,7.

172  Schneider, *o.c.*, p. 3, describes this letter as "paränetische Lehrschrift (Didache)."

173  *Teleios* is his favorite word: 1,4 (2x). 17.25; 3,2. Cf. Du Plessis, *o.c.*, pp. 233ff.

174  See 1,1.12; 2,8 (quoting Lev. 19,18). The "twelve tribes" are the Jewish Christians outside Palestine (Schneider). Cf. Du Plessis, *o.c.*, p. 240.

175  See 1,26f.; 2,5f. 15f. His emphasis on the fateful function of the tongue is especially akin to the ethos of the Psalms and the Proverbs, cf. Js. 3,5 with Ps. 12,3; Prov. 12,18; Js. 3,8 with Ps. 140,3; Prov. 18,21; Js. 3,6 with Prov. 16,27. Noteworthy also is the fact that James refers to the abiding dignity of the *imago Dei* of creation (3,9).

176  1,22-25; 2,8-12; cf. Ps. 119,44-45 (on the concept of liberty); Ps. 19,7f. (on the perfect function of the law). Cf. Du Plessis, *o.c.*, p. 237.

177  Cf. also Gal. 5,6.22; 1 Cor. 7,19; 13,2-3; Rom. 5,5; 6,2; 1 Thes. 2,13. On 1 Jn., see below, section 3c (aa).

James therefore is not contrasting faith and works,[178] but only acknowledging as true religion that religious cultus which is conditioned and motivated by the wholehearted surrender to God – as in Abraham[179] – and by wholehearted service to the neighbor,[180] in an indissoluble unity.

### 3. Christian perfection and sinlessness.

As we have done with our inquiry of the Old Testament soteriology[181] so we now face the question directly whether Christian perfection is identical with ethical sinlessness in the New Testament.

A fundamental answer – in the negative – has already been given when it was established that the meaning of *teleios* in the Torah of Jesus Christ (Mt. 5,48; 19,21), although exceeding the Rabbinical righteousness, does not set up a different standard or ethos than was required in the Torah and cultus of the old covenant.[182] Christ Jesus came not to abolish but to fulfill te Torah and its Covenant.

When He as the Messiah established a new covenant – with a new cultus – on the merits of His own blood, He thereby brought the imperfect old covenant cultus to an end, but at the same time *renewed* Israel's covenant into a "better covenant" with a "much more excellent ministry."[183] This indicates that the new covenant, through Christ's sacrifice and priestly ministry, functions more powerfully to bring about the covenant-fellowship between God and "Israel."[184]

178   This is the case in the concept which James combats and rejects, 2,18. Those who construe a conflict between James and Paul do this on the illegitimate basis of identifying James' works (of faith) with Paul's works of the law. Cf. Berkouwer, *Faith and Justification*, ET 1954, pp. 134ff. (Dutch, pp. 137ff.).

179   2,21ff. Cf. Berkouwer, *o.c.*, p. 136 (Dutch, p. 138): "This faith was not something isolated, an abstract acceptance of something as true, but a truly experienced reality that dominated his entire existence.... The statement of Genesis 15:6 is seen as fulfilled, completed, incarnated in the concrete reality of Abraham's obedience of Genesis 22."

180   See 1,8 (*dipsychos*) 2,1; cf. Ps. 12,2 (*beléb wāléb*) where the double-hearted men are described as the wicked, who have "a heart that thinks one thing and a heart that devises another thing"; Du Plessis, *o.c.*, pp. 235f., 99.

181   See above, Ch. III, B, 2.

182   See above, Ch. IV, 1.

183   Heb. 7,22. 25-28; 8,6.

184   See Calvin, *Inst.* II, 10, 2. And specifically J. de Vuyst, *"Oud en Nieuw Verbond" in de Brief aan de Hebreeën*, 1964; esp. on Heb. 8,6-8; pp. 96-125. Noteworthy is his illustration on the continuity and discontinuity of the old and new covenant: "gelijk de sluiting van het huwelijks-'verbond' niét de verbreking van het verlovings-'verbond' in ontrouw maar wel de opheffing van het verlovings-'verbond' in trouw betekent, zo betekent de sluiting van het nieuwe verbond niét de verbreking van het oude verbond in ontrouw maar wél de opheffing van het oude verbond in trouw; gelijk juist de genoemde opheffing van het verlovings-'verbond' uitdrukking geeft aan de bestendiging en de

The questions arise, Does not the perfect new covenant-fellowship through Christ with the holy God require and provide for absolute ethical sinlessness? Does not the transforming, recreating power of God change sinful man into such a victorious holy Christian that he has no more selfishness, no more sinful passions and impulses? In other words, Does not the new covenant, more than the old covenant, hold out the promise of essential holiness or perfection? Do not some specific verses at least, taken by themselves, suggest, if not teach, such a doctrine of perfection(ism)? Does not 2 Pet. 1,4 explain that the "precious and very great promises" make our escape from the corruptive passions a reality by making us "partakers" of the *"divine nature"*? And does not 1 Jn. 3,9 unequivocally state: "No one born of God commits sin; for *God's nature* [as *sperma* is translated in RSV] *abides in him, and he cannot sin* because he is born of God"?

Furthermore, does not Heb. 10,2 indicate that the new-covenant worshippers who have been cleansed "would *no longer have any consciousness [syneidèsis] of sin"*?

While these texts require a special investigation in this connection, the answer to our questions is not dependent on some isolated verses or statements. The real problem concentrates itself on the meaning of Gal 5 and Rom. 7-8 within the framework of the apostolic message as a whole.

a.  *The meaning of apocalyptic in Pauline soteriology.*

In order to be able to understand better the meaning of the struggle and inner discord in the Christian life as described in the letters to the Romans and Galatians, we must recognize the determining function of Paul's apocalyptic theology for his soteriology and ethics.[185] Paul never takes man as an entity by himself, but relates him ultimately to the spiritual power or dominion which rules over him and which he serves. This salvation-historical point of view is most explicitly worked out in Rom. 5,12-21. Paul usually indicates this with the terms "in Christ," or "in the spirit" on the one hand; and "in Adam," or "in the flesh" on the other hand.[186]

ontvouwing der normen en de vervulling van het vroegere verlovings-'verbond' in het hierop volgende huwelijks-'verbond', zo geeft de ópheffing van het oude verbond uitdrukking aan de bestendiging en de ontvouwing der normen en de vervulling van het oude verbond in het nieuwe verbond" (pp. 113f.).

185   Cf. Ridderbos, *Paulus*, p. 297, referring to the "not-yet" in Rom. 13,12a; 16,20: "Dit heilshistorische gezichtspunt heeft dus ook zijn zedelijke implicaties.... Onder hetzelfde heilshistorische gezichtspunt zullen wij de uitspraken hebben te beschouwen, die van de *voortgaande begeerte van het vlees* in het leven der gelovigen spreken [quoting Gal. 5,17]." E. Käsemann, "Zum Thema der urchristl. Apokalyptik," in *Exeg. Versuche u. Besinnungen*, II, 1965², p. 129: "Apokalyptik begründet sogar die besondere Gestalt der paulinischen Anthropologie."

186   See Ridderbos, *Paulus*, pp. 58-60, 242f.; he states on p. 60: "Wij hebben

The apostle relates the whole Christian existence and moral struggle to the eschatological antithesis between the powers of darkness and the kingship of Christ, Col. 1,13. That Christ Jesus has risen victoriously from the dead and is exalted as Priest-King of the world above all anti-godly power and dominion[187] must now be made manifest in the lives and acts of the Christians, i.e., in their social ethos. Since they are now, after baptism in Christ, living under the triumphant resurrection power of Jesus Christ, their King, they may show their freedom in Christ by their *nova oboedientia*[188] to the holy will and law of God.

Thus Paul's ethics is basically determined by his Christology. *Christ must reign* over and in His people. The point at issue with the Gnostic perfectionists was – and is – however, *whether* the Christians – because all cosmic powers and principalities are disarmed and put under the feet of Christ – now, in baptism, have received total transformation and final salvation, so that they may live here and now already essentially sinless and perfect.

It appears conclusively from Paul's apocalyptic theology that he clearly and firmly opposes such perfectionism in his soteriology and hamartiology. He discloses in 1 Cor. 15,25-26 that Christ's present kingly rule *still* meets opposition from enemies and powers which – although subjected to Christ – have not been finally destroyed as yet.

> For he must reign until he has put all his enemies under his feet. The last enemy to be destroyed is death. For God has put all things in subjection under his feet (1 Cor. 15,25-27a).

He closes his apocalyptic exposition with the emphatic statement that only "at the last trumpet" (vs. 52) will *sin*, as the sting of death, be swallowed up in victory (vss. 54-56), when this *sōma psychikon* will be changed or transformed into a *sōma pneumatikon* (vs. 44).[189]

---

hier met een van de grondmotieven van Paulus' heilsprediking te doen...."
And on p. 242: "Er [sc. 'in de Geest zijn'] wordt niet een subjectieve bewust-zijns-toestand, maar een 'objective' zijns-wijze mee aangeduid. De gedachte is, dat de gelovigen, zoals zij vroeger 'in het vlees' waren en door het vlees als zondige macht in hun bestaan bepaald waren, thans 'in de Geest', d.w.z. onder het regime, de bevrijdende heerschappij van de Geest gebracht zijn en daarom niet meer dienstplichtig zijn aan het vlees, noch onderworpen aan de gezind-heid van het vlees, Rom. 8,5-12."

187  Eph. 1,21; Col. 2,15.
188  Rom. 6,4ff.; 1 Cor. 7,19. Cf. Käsemann, *o.c.*, II, pp. 120, 126.
189  See Büchsel, in *ThWNT* IV, 355, 19ff. (s.v. *apolytrōsis*): "Aller Geist-besitz in der Gegenwart ist nur Anzahlung auf das Erbe, das darin bestehen wird, dass das gesamte Dasein des Menschen geistgegeben, geistgemäss, *sōma pneumatikon* 1 K. 15,44 sein wird." Also E. Schweizer, in *ThWNT* VI, 419, 1ff. (s.v. *pneuma*). J. Schneider, in *ThWNT* VII, 602, 7f. (s.v. *stenazō*). Cf. H. Clavier, "Brèves remarques sur la notion de *sōma pneumatikon*," in *The Back-*

What does it mean that the Christian or reborn man still has a *psychikon* body, "flesh and blood" which cannot inherit the kingdom of God (1 Cor. 15,50)? Does it have *ethical* significance that the perishable, dishonorable weakness "must" be changed into the imperishable, the glory and power (vss. 42f.); that the mortal "must put on" immortality (vs. 51) *before* he will bear "the image of the man of heaven (*tou epouraniou*)" (vs. 49)? The point of the apostle is directed against the Hellenistic enthusiasm or Gnostic perfectionism which conceived that having the Holy Spirit meant the reception of *heavenly substance!*

The intention of Paul becomes apparent when he culminates his apocalyptic revelation with the disclosure of the *mystèrion* that only at that final future "moment, in the twinkling of an eye" not merely "death" but also the cause or "sting" of death will be "swallowed up in victory."

He leaves no room for doubt concerning the meaning of his apocalyptic imagery. "The sting (*kentron*) of death is *sin*, and the power of sin is *the law*" (vs. 56). In other words, *until* the day of final[190] triumph and glorification the reborn believers must recognize the law of God and, through its disclosing spiritual efficacy,[191] the *powerful* reality of *sin* in their bodies, in their flesh and blood, i.e., in themselves.[192]

The apostle, therefore, first indicates the redemptive necessity of the futural-eschatological resurrection of the dead against those who denied this Christian hope (vs. 12) – either by their Gnostic sacramental realism[193] or by their idea of a primordial inherent "spiritual body."[194] Paul addresses the Christian church as a whole with the consoling assurance of the Gospel, based on the decisive[195] reality of Christ's kingship

*ground of the N.T. and its Eschatology. FS* Dodd; pp. 342-362; esp. 361: "On peut assurer que la caractéristique essentielle du *sōma pneumatikon* selon Paul, n'est pas d'être ou non un corps en esprit, mais un organe de l'esprit, commandé par l'Esprit, par le Saint-Esprit."

190  L. Schmid, in *ThWNT* III, 667, 28ff. (s.v. *kentron*) denies the apocalyptic framework and perspective ("*then* shall come to pass," vss. 54f.) when he applies vs 55 ("O death, where is thy victory – thy sting?") already to the *present* thanksgiving of vs. 57, also bypassing vs. 56. Also G. Th. Rothuizen, *Primus Usus Legis. Studie over het burgerlijk gebruik van de wet*, 1962, p. 181, n. 255, has lost sight of the determining apocalyptic cadre of 1 Cor. 15, when he contrasts vs. 54 (de "*overwonnen*" dood) with vs. 26 (de nog *te overwinnen dood*). It seems symptomatic for Rothuizen's interpretation of Rom. 7,14ff. that he describes the "conquered" death by "the sting of sin"(?). It is written, however, the other way round: sin is "the sting of death"! (vs. 56; cf. Rom. 5,12). And sin as the stimulating power of death will not be swallowed up in victory *before* the *psychikon* body is changed into a *pneumatikon*, immortal body.

191  Cf. Rom. 7,14, see below.

192  In vs. 51 Paul states: "*we*" shall be changed.

193  Cf. 2 Tim. 2,18. Käsemann, *o.c.*, II, p. 120f.

194  Schweizer, *ThWNT* VI, 418, 8ff.

195  Cf. also Schweizer, *ThWNT* VI, 414, 15: "Die Entscheidung fällt bei

as *Pneuma zōiopoioun*:[196] sin no longer has dominion in the lives, i.e. in the ethos,[197] of the Christian believers.

> But thanks be to God, who gives us the victory through our Lord Jesus Christ (vs. 57).

The fact that the reborn Christian, in spite of his *psychikon* body, *already now* may be in his walk or ethos a conqueror over the innate sinful weakness, does not mean therefore the possession of any inherent holy quality or perfection. To be a conqueror in Christ is only realized by way of the covenant fellowship with the exalted Lord and Savior, and manifested in the concrete ethos of being "steadfast, immovable, always abounding in the word of the Lord," with the eye of faith seeing the day of ultimate reward (vs. 58; vf. also Heb. 11,13.26). Until *that* day the Christian believer will still have to fight in the victorious power of the resurrected Christ who overcame sin and death, against the intrinsic tendencies to sin, brought to light by the spiritual law of God. In other words, the reborn Christian is awakened to a religious-moral battle with himself, since his body or whole being is *not yet* inclined to the Spirit of Christ. Even therefore the holy law of God still has a hold on the Christian![198] It might even be said that the Christian knows of a fiercer battle, nay even a battle on a different level than the moral struggle of an unregenerate man, since the Christian's carnal nature is *stirred up* and *stung into* sinful action through the exposing and convicting activity of the holy law as instrument of the Spirit of Christ.[199]

This same apocalyptic structure and perspective of 1 Cor. 15, which limits every ethical enthusiasm, apparently also underlies Paul's theological exposition of Rom. 5,12–8,24. In Rom. 8,18-23 the apostle Paul recognizes not only that the creation with eager longing and groaning waits "for the revealing of the sons of God," but also that

> We ourselves, who have the first fruits of the *Spirit*, groan inwardly as we wait for adoption as sons [*huiothesian*], *the re-*

---

Pls in der Eschatologie. Entschiedener als alle vor ihm hat er Kreuz u. Auferstehung als die grosse Wende verstanden, nicht nur als Ouvertüre zur Parusie. Er musste darum also das Leben im Geist als das Leben der neuen *ktisis* selbst verstehen!"

196   Not just as "living Spirit," but life-giving Spirit, i.e., with creative power.

197   Cf. 1 Cor. 15,33-34; 5,7-8.

198   Cf. W. Sanday-A. C. Headlam, *The Epistle to the Romans*, ICC, 1915, p. 172: "The Law had its hold upon him only through sin."

199   This Christological-pneumatical reality is overlooked by Rothuizen when he states that he cannot see why the inner discord of Rom. 7,14ff. might be "typical" of the Christian faith (*o.c.*, p. 181).

*demption of our*[200] *bodies* [tèn apolytrōsin tou sōmatos hèmōn] (vs. 23).

In other words, the Christians, individually and as a Church-body, are still in need of final eschatological salvation and ultimate perfection since they still remain in their *"unredeemed"*[201] *bodies* until the day of final glorification.[202]

Since the "redemption of our bodies" (Rom. 8,23) constitutes the culmination point of this apocalyptic passage, this is not without significance for the interpretation of Paul's soteriology, his pneumatology and hamartiology specifically.

On the one hand, Paul from his apocalyptic relativizes the absolutism of the *Holy Spirit's* ruling "already now," in that he calls the Spirit in the Christian *the first fruits* (aparchè) of the future "spiritual" body (Rom. 8,23) or as guarantee (arrabōn) of the futural "dwelling" (2 Cor. 5,5).[203]

On the other hand, Paul qualifies the absolutism of *sin-deliverance* "already now," in that he calls the Christian's ethos of sanctification the continual presentation of his body as a living and holy sacrifice to God (Rom. 12,1);[204] as the constant battle against his own fleshly or selfish impulses, *although* they are already crucified in the body of Christ; cf. Col. 3, vs. 5 with vs. 9f.; Rom. 8, vs. 10 with vss. 12-13.

---

200   See Büchsel, *ThWNT* IV, 355, 2f.: "Die *apolytrōsis tou sōmatos* ist R. 8,23 nicht die Erlösung vom Leibe, sondern die Erlösung des Leibes. Das beweist der Vergleich mit v. 21 unweigerlich." Also E. Schweizer, *ThWNT* VII, 1059, 4ff. (s.v. *sōma*). Contra Rothuizen, *o.c.*, p. 180, n. 257.

201   We may say that the body is already redeemed (cf. Rom. 6,6; 8,13) and still maintain with Rom. 8,23 that it is not yet redeemed; considering also the analogous dual application of the *huiothesia* in Rom. 8,15f. (soteriological: *already*; cf. Gal. 4,5f.; Eph. 1,5) and Rom. 8,23 (apocalyptic: *not yet*); cf. also 1 Jn. 3,2. The same with *apolytrōsis* in Eph. 1,7; Col. 1,14 (now), and Eph. 1,14, 4,30 (future). This dual application of redemption, in which the one is qualified and limited by the other is rooted in the salvation-historical reality of two separate Advents of Christ Jesus.

202   Cf. Käsemann, *o.c.*, II, p. 130: "Präsentische Eschatologie allein und nicht von der futurischen umfangen, – das wäre auch beim Christen nichts anderes als die Hybris des Fleisches, wie sie der Enthusiasmus ja genugsam zu allen Zeiten bezeugt. Das wäre Illusion und nicht Realität. Gerade die Apokalyptik des Apostels gibt der Wirklichkeit, was ihr gebührt, und widersteht der frommen Illusion. Christliche Gemeinde hat die Realität der Kindschaft nur in der Freiheit der Angefochtenen, welche auf die Auferstehung der Toten als die Wahrheit und Vollendung des regnum Christi vorausweist."

203   See Schweizer, *ThWNT* VI, 420f.: "*Pneuma* als Zeichen des Kommenden."

204   Cf. Schweizer, *ThWNT* VII, 1059, 6-14 (s.v. *sōma*): "So wird wohl sichtbar, dass der irdische Leib für Paulus unter Sünde und Tod steht und dadurch belastet ist."

It is on the basis of the atonement of Christ's own body that Paul summons the Christian believers, in whom the Spirit dwells, now to cultically present their bodies and their members (manifestations) in the service of righteousness in order to live in the moral ethos of sanctification as its fruit (*ton karpon hymōn eis hagiasmon*, Rom. 6,22b).[205]

To be transferred by faith into the dominion or status of holiness, therefore, means to obey the commission to "*cleanse ourselves* from every defilement of body and spirit, and make holiness *perfect* [*epitelein*, to complete] in the fear of God" (2 Cor. 7,1). And it is this very moral appropriation[206] or bodily manifestation by the Christians of Christ's perfection which is emphatically placed under the apocalyptic "*judgment seat of Christ*, so that each one may receive good or evil, according to *what he has done in the body*" (2 Cor. 5,10,[207] cf. also 1 Cor. 3,12-15; Rom. 14,10; Eph. 6,8). Here lies the critical, anti-perfectionistic instance which brings into right focus the whole thrust of Paul's ethos of sanctification or perfection, which is rooted in and motivated by Christ's atoning death and resurrection:

> And He died for all, that those who live might live (*zōsin*) no longer *for themselves* but for Him who for their sake died and was raised (2 Cor. 5,15).

It is true that already the continual apostolic redemptive imperatives and admonitions, like Gal. 5,13-25 and Rom. 6,12ff.; 8,12-13.23; Col. 3,5ff.; Eph. 4,22ff., which disclose the unabated conflict with self after rebirth *until the day of glorification*, substantiate[208] the doctrine that the Chris-

---

205  See Procksch, in *ThWNT* I, 115, 11ff. 25f. (s.v. *hagiasmos*).

206  Cf. Procksch, *o.c.*, 116, 21ff. (s.v. *hagiōsynè*): "In 2 K. 7,1 ... erscheint die *hagiōsynè* als *menschliche Eigenschaft*. Ihre Grundlage besteht in der Versöhnung kraft deren das *ethnos hagion* besteht. Doch dieser von Gott geschaffene Zustand fordert seine Vollendung (*epitelein*) in der sittlichen Aneignung, die nur auf Grund der Gottesfurcht (*en phobōi theou*) möglich ist."

207  Cf. Schweizer, in *ThWNT* VII, 1059, 28f. (s.v. *sōma*). Grundmann, in *ThWNT* II, 259, 50f.; 260 (s.v. *dokimos*) rightly describes the Christian existence between baptism and final judgment as follows: "Das Verhalten, das sich daraus ergibt, ist das Ringen um die Bewährung, nämlich um die Bewährung des empfangenen Heiles, um in der Prüfung des Gerichtes als bewährt zu erscheinen."

208  Cf. H. Bavinck, *G.D.* IV, 249: "De vermaningen, die door heel de Schrift heen en inzonderheid bij de apostelen in hunnen brieven aan de gemeenten voorkomen, zijn het sterkste bewijs, dat zij aan eene zondeloosheid der geloovigen niet denken, maar overal en altijd hun gebrek en tekortkoming onderstellen. Zoolang zij in dit leven zijn hebben zij strijd te voeren tegen den satan, wereld en eigen vleesch; dat vleesch begeert steeds tegen den Geest en de Geest tegen het vleesch, en deze staan tegenover elkander, alzoo dat zij niet doen hetgeen zij willen, Gal. 5:17."

tian does not have holy flesh and can never claim ethical sinlessness or inherent holiness.

This indicates that the question of absolute ethical sinlessness therefore does not stand or fall with the way of interpreting Rom. 7,14ff.

It becomes, however, especially apparent from Paul's apocalyptic hamartiology in 1 Cor. 15, that not only the redemptive *imperatives* to the redeemed Christians but also the typification of those who are baptized in Christ according to the redemptive *indicative* in Rom. 6,4-11; 8,1-11 may *not* be interpreted in an ethical-perfectionistic sense. The reason is that, although Christ's righteousness is *imputed* fully to the believer by faith, the *impartation* of Christ's perfection in his heart and bodily manifestations has only been realized in *principle*. Or, in Pauline terminology, while the forgiven believer is under no condemnation of the law, since his old man or nature, *palaios anthrōpos*, is legally crucified through his justification by faith, in *empirical reality* this enemy of God is not dead as yet and therefore still has to be brought under the reign of Christ!

This implies that the reborn Christian, while having only one nature, the *neos* or *kainos anthrōpos*, before the law, at the same time in empirical reality, until he receives the apocalyptic *pneumatikon sōma*, possesses *two* natures, the old *and* the new man, although not on equal terms. It is his calling, in continual covenant fellowship with Christ's justifying and sanctifying grace, continually to put off the old man, to put away, even to put to death, all "the members" (*melè*) or sinful motions or deeds (*praxeis*) of his body[209] (Rom. 8,12-13; Eph. 4,22.25-31; Col. 3,5-9) and *continually* to put on the new man or nature which, in the way of the *imitatio Dei* (Eph. 4,32; 5,1; Col. 3,13), is manifested in the ethos of righteousness, holiness and knowledge of the recreated *imago Dei* (Eph. 4,24.32; Col. 3,10-17).

While Eph. 1,7.13f. stresses the present reality of redemption (*apolytrōsis*) as forgiving grace together with the sealing of the Holy Spirit as the guarantee of our *future* redemption (*apolytrōsis*, vs. 14,4,30), Eph. 4,29-30 still admonishes the Christian Church not to grieve the Holy Spirit by the manifestation of their old man or nature in their social ethos *within* the Church.[210]

---

209  Chr. Maurer, in *ThWNT* VI, 644, 9ff., states that Paul uses *praxis* in Rom. 8,13 and Col. 3,9 in the sense of the evil propensity or natural inclination of the body: "So ist R 8,13 nicht an die Taten zu denken, die der Leib vollbringt, sondern an die böse Art und Weise, die ihm innewohnt, wenn er *kata sarka* lebt. Es gibt, nicht nach dem Fleische in der durch die Sünde beherrschten Existenz zu leben, die zum Tode führt, sondern *im Geiste die bösen Handlungsweisen des Leibes zu ertöten*, um dadurch zu leben. Der Leib als solcher soll nicht getötet, sondern dem neuen Herrn verpflichtet werden. Ähnlich liegt es Kol. 3,9" (644, 13-19).

210  Büchsel, in *ThWNT* IV, 356, 4-11 (s.v. *apolytrōsis*), is basically correct,

It is therefore *illegitimate* to treat Rom. 8,2-11 as if it intends to describe the empirical life and reality of the justified believers and on this basis to place it in glaring contrast with the picture of the self-condemning and inner divided believer of Rom. 7,14-25.

The passage of Rom. 8,2-11 does not intend to picture the actual reality of the Christian's life and self-consciousness, but holds before the baptized believers the objective[211] reality of faith of the redemptive indicative in which those who are in Christ ought to live according to the legal indicative of having died to the law "through the body of Christ" (cf. 6,6; 7,4). It points out that those who have *died* with the body of Christ at the cross in their old man (*palaios anthrōpos*, 6,6), can only *be alive* for God when their bodies *remain dead* (8,10) and their new life reveals that the indwelling *Christ* or Spirit – not *their* new spirit or self – *fulfills the law in them* (8,4).

The theme of Rom. 8,1-11 seems to be the emphatic presentation of the only two ways of existence *coram Deo* – in continuity with the old-covenant cultus and liturgy[212] – which are described as the ways (*peripatein*) of "life" and "death" within the new covenant (vss. 2,6-11).

Vss. 2-10 fix the attention on the only two determining ways of standing before God. The way of life belongs to him whose *mind* is governed by the Spirit of Christ, i.e., the one who concentrates his thinking (*phronein*) and willing on *ta tou pneumatos*, which includes the spiritual law of God. His mind (*phronèma*) constantly seeks to be controlled by God and is therefore in harmony with God, submitting wholeheartedly to God's law; cf. vss. 5-7. Such a way of thinking and living is pleasing to God. The way of life *outside* of Christ is characterized by absolutely opposite qualities. It is the life *kata sarka* because the *mind* or heart takes its ideal, norm and delight in *ta tès sarkos*, which basically means self[213] in all its manifestations from Pharisaic self-righteousness

---

only he passes over in silence the real struggle of the repentant Christian when he concludes from Col. 1,14; Eph. 1,7; Rom. 8,24: "Wir haben sie [sc. Sündenvergebung] nur als die uns geschenkte Zusage, die zwar jetzt schon Auswirkungen in unserem Leben zeitigt, aber im Vollsinne des Wortes greifbare, unser Dasein auch äusserlich erneuernde Wirklichkeit erst im Endgerichte wird. Im Worte Gottes ist die Sündenvergebung schon vorhanden, und dies Wort ist zugleich wirksame Kraft R 1,16, aber Gottes Gaben auf sein Wort und was es enthält zu beschränken, ist ganz unpaulinisch. So sind die Gläubigen also Erlöste, aber nur so, dass sie zugleich auf die (Vollendung der) Erlösung warten."

211 See Ridderbos, *Paulus*, p. 242, concerning the phrase "you are in the Spirit" in Rom. 8,5-12: "Er wordt niet een subjectieve bewustzijns-toestand, maar een 'objectieve' zijns-wijze mee aangeduid."

212 See Ch. III, B, 2a.

213 Cf. 2 Cor. 5,15. Schweizer, in *ThWNT* VII, 133, 16 (s.v. *sarx*): "Ein Leben, das sich auf die *sarx* ausrichtet, ist zugleich ein Leben, das der *sarx* dient (R 8,12) und ihr Denken durchführt (R 8,6)." And 132, 33f.: "Das Ver-

to open transgressions of law (8,5-8; cf. Phil. 3,19; 2 Cor. 3,14 [*noèmata*] 15 [*kardia*]). Therefore this mind (*phronèma*) is hostile to God, vs. 7, in that it does *not* submit to or take delight in the law of God.[214] Consequently, this mind and this existence are still under the condemnation of death.

Between these two ways of existence, typified as fundamental opposites which stand in irreconcilable antithesis, no room is left for a middle way. The one existence in Christ is life, the other in the flesh is death. *Tertium non datur!* Each variation within both existences, either in the Christian life with its weaknesses and failures,[215] or in the non-Christian life with its shining virtues, is left out of consideration, in basic continuity with the ground plan of the Psalms and Proverbs.[216]

The Christian – being in Christ – is no longer under condemnation of the law of God since he has died to the law through the body of Christ; 8,1; 7,4. This same redemptive indicative is qualified in its dynamic aspect in 8,2:[217]

> For the law of the Spirit of life in Christ Jesus has set me free from the law of sin and death.

As this verse serves as the terminological bridge between Rom. 7,14-25 and 8,1ff., we are now confronted with the crucial question: With which of the two ways of existence in Rom. 8, is the struggling, self-condemning subject of Rom. 7 to be identified? Before we enter upon this question, however, we still have to ask first the question whether Paul's apocalyptic has any bearing on Rom. 7. It seems to be no coincidence that both Rom. 7 and 8 find their culmination in the longing for deliverance from the body, 7,24 and of the body, 8,11.23.

This ultimate concern for and concentration on the redemption of the "body" in Rom 8 also corresponds with Paul's apocalyptic revelation with respect to the *psychikon* body of the believers (still with the sting of death!) in 1 Cor. 15.

The question urges itself, whether Paul refers to the same body in

---

fallensein an die *sarx* prägt sich also in der Gesetzlichkeit des Pharisäers ebenso aus wie in der Unmoral des Heiden."

214  Paul even adds significantly in vs. 7: *oude gar dynatai*, which indicates that the whole matter of the two ways of existence in 8,1-11 is not a question of moral man with his autonomous mind, but the mind or heart in its relation to the covenant God.

215  Only from vss. 12f. begins the exhortation to the Christians to realize now the concrete ethos in the life without condemnation of the law, by continually putting the body to death, i.e., to conquer the sinful motions through acts of righteousness.

216  See Ch. III, B, 2a.

217  Cf. also 6,18.

Rom. 7,24 as in Rom. 8 and 1 Cor. 15; and, with that, whether the longing for deliverance (*rhusetai*)[218] from the "body of death" in Rom. 7,24 is not likewise determined by the cry for ultimate redemption of the body of death as in Rom. 8,11.23 and 1 Cor. 15. Anyway, when Rothuizen[219] concludes that Rom. 8,2 describes the deliverance of the "death-body" in Rom. 7,24 as "deliverance from sin" (for the non-Christian), and the deliverance of the body in Rom. 8,23 as "deliverance from suffering" (for the Christian), he does not seem to reckon with two vital factors which forbid a separation of sin and suffering. First, the modifying function of Paul's apocalyptic in 1 Cor. 15, which reveals that neither law nor *sin* (the sting of death) will be empirically dead in the body of the Christians until they receive the apocalyptic *pneumatikon* body.[220] Secondly, Rom. 8,13 summons the same Christians to put to death the active, sinful motions of their body, which might well be an indication that the cry of deliverance in Rom. 7,24 is not merely a past experience, but rather an ever recurring and deepening experience for the Christians. They not only acknowledge their *psychikon* body[221] but feel the abiding need of forgiveness under the working of the holy law, even when they are conquerors over sin in their social ethos.

It therefore seems inadequate to interpret the cry for deliverance and the answer of faith and thankfulness in Rom. 7 as pertaining exclusively

218  See W. Kasch, in *ThWNT* VI, 1003f. (s.v. *rhuomai*), who indicates the twofold application of this O.T. oriented verb, e.g. in Mt. 6,13. While 1 Thes. 1,10; Col. 1,13 use the verb in a strictly soteriological sense, Rom. 5,9 uses the verb in a strictly eschatological sense.

219  *O.c.*, p. 181, n. 257.

220  Also the "groaning" (*stenazein*) of the Christians with respect to their body in 2 Cor. 5,2-5 is not merely related to the burden of physical sufferings in persecutions, but also, if not primarily, to a soteriological interest (cf. Rom. 8,13.23). Cf. J. Schneider, in *ThWNT* VII, 601, 23f. (s.v. *stenazō*) on 2 Cor. 5,2: "Das Sein in der Behausung des irdischen Leibes wird von den Christen als schwere Belastung empfunden. Es ist ein Zeichen dafür, dass sie noch nicht im Stande der vollkommenen Erlösung sind." With A. Oepke, in *ThWNT* I, 774, 21f. (s.v. *gymnos*), we understand the phrase "so that... we may not be found naked" to mean: not to be condemned to "das endgültige Schicksal der Ungläubigen, für welche kein Himmelsleib bereit ist." Noteworthy is the basic difference from the groaning of the souls in the bodies in the hermetic literature, see Schneider, *o.c.*, 602, 23ff.

221  Cf. Ridderbos, *Aan de Rom.*, p. 161, who interprets *sōma*, *melè* and *sarx* as "de mens in zijn concrete, zondige lichamelijke bestaanswijze." Sanday-Headlam, *o.c.*, p. 184: "Sin and death are inseparable: as the body involves me in sin it also involves me in mortality." J. Murray, *The Ep. to the Romans*, I, 1959, pp. 266ff., rightly warns against identifying Paul's ethical conception of "flesh" with the body as contrasted with the mind or spirit of man, as if (the law of) sin has its seat in the physical as such. "Here is a cry for deliverance from the body of this death because the body is the instrument and sphere of operation of the law of sin..." (269).

to present deliverance from guilt and the power of sin. It would rather be in harmony with the revealed dimensions of sin and grace as death and eternal life (5,21; 6,23; 8,23) to understand Rom. 7,24-25a in their fullest sense, i.e., also in their apocalyptic eschatological dimensions.[222]

It is highly significant that the apocalyptic redemption of man is described explicitly as *to teleion* by the apostle Paul in 1 Cor. 13,10. By this he does not mean to suggest the notion of gradual development from to *ek merous* to *teleion*, but the essential replacement or transformation of the body with its partial proficiencies by "the constitutive perfection of the eschatological age."[223]

The focus of Paul's apocalyptic-eschatological perfection is the future *visio Dei*, the face-to-face vision of God (*tote de prosōpon pros prosōpon*, vs. 12) in contrast with the dim vision of divine knowledge to which the believers now attain.[224] In others words, even the divine *gnōsis* and *prophèteia* of the *pneumatikoi* or *teleoi* in the church at Corinth (1 Cor. 2,6; 3,1; 12,8) are not yet *teleiai*.[225] In his letter to the Philippians, apparently again arguing from an anti-perfectionistic view,[226] he addresses himself specifically to those who would regard themselves already as *teleioi* in a more Gnostic sense than in the true Christological-soteriol-

222   For this eschatological interpretation, see also Murray, *o.c.* I, p. 269. O. Michel, *Der Brief an die Römer*, Meyers Kommentar, 1955, p. 155. Barth, *C.D.* IV, 1, 591 (*K.D.*, p. 659).

223   Du Plessis, *o.c.*, pp. 205, 185, rightly concludes: "And therefore, there is not only room, but necessity for a future dimension to the present state of affairs" (185).

224   Flew, *o.c.*, p. 52. He uses the terms "relative perfection" and „absolute perfection" to denote resp. the states of present redemptive perfection and apocalyptic perfection. This terminology is inadequate since these adjectives suggest the notion of quantity; moreover, "relative" perfection implies perfect forgiveness. Cf. Du Plessis' qualification of *teleios* in Col. 1,28: "What is bestowed in Christ is quite perfect and needs no supplementation whatsoever. Perfection is the absolute *redemption which is in Christ*" (p. 199; see also p. 184 on 1 Cor. 2,6).

225   Cf. Delling, in *ThWNT* VIII, 76, n. 45 (s.v. *teleios*).

226   We do not mean exclusively, but *beside* the anti-judaistic point of view. Cf. Käsemann, *o.c.* II, 126: "Die reformatorische Paulusdeutung bringt es zwangsläufig mit sich, dass wir den Apostel vornehmlich in jener Auseinandersetzung sehen, welche antijudaistisch in seiner Gesetzes- und Rechtfertigungslehre tatsächlich statt findet. Die religionsgeschichtliche Forschung hat das Verdienst, dem die antienthusiastische Front an die Seite gerückt zu haben." On Phil. 3,12.15 see the excellent treatise in W. P. de Boer, *The Imitation of Paul*, 1962, pp. 171-175, with critical bibliography. He concludes: "It seems quite likely that Paul's reactions against Judaistic tendencies, against perfectionist tendencies, and against libertinistic tendencies were all called forth from the same source. There were teachers propagating Jewish-Gnostic interpretations of the Christian gospel in Philippi" (173). Cf. also H. Köster, "Häretiker im Urchristentum," in *RGG³*, III, 19f.; G. Bornkamm, "Paulus," in *RGG³*, V, 177.

ogical sense (3,15).[227] His appeal is directed against the false feeling of
security of having arrived already at ultimate perfection.[228] He therefore
urges those who are apprehended by Christ to share His sufferings and
to press on (*diōkein*, vss. 12,14) in the power of His resurrection. What
lies ahead, the final goal, is nothing less than the glorious "resurrection
from the dead" (vss. 10-11, also 21). Here Käsemann's[229] thesis proves
itself correct:

> Der antienthusiastische Kampf des Apostels wird jedoch letztlich
> und zutiefst im Zeichen der Apokalyptik ausgefochten.

b. *Militia Christiana in Romans 7?*

The tenor of Rom. 7,14ff. has been interpreted mainly[230] as applying

227   See W. Schmithals, *Paulus und die Gnostiker*, 1965, pp. 59-86: "Die
Irrlehrer des Philipperbriefes." S. defends the position that the heretical
teachers are to be identified as Gnostic Jewish-Christians: "Die einzige uns
aus urchristlicher Zeit bekanntgewordene libertinistische Bewegung innerhalb
der christlichen Gemeinden ist aber die Gnostische" (p. 62). And, appealing
also to T. Zahn: "Je älter die Gnosis ist, desto mehr ist sie jüdisch" (p. 63).
On pp. 67ff. S. presents five strong indications that Phil. 3,8-21 can be understood best – if not exclusively – as an anti-Gnostic polemic, in which Paul
takes over the keyword *teleios* from Gnostic common parlance and therefore
intentionally denies that he is a *teleios* himself in this sense, Phil. 3,12. Yet
he addresses himself "in paradoxer Rücksicht" to the *teleioi* (vs. 15) with the
intention: "Lasst uns die Vollkommenheit in dem demütigen Bekenntnis
unserer Unvollkommenheit suchen." See p. 72 on *hosoi oun teleioi* in vs. 15.
Also De Boer, *o.c.*, p. 174, who takes this phrase, following J. B. Lightfoot,
as a term of "reproachful irony," as in 1 Cor. 8,1; Rom. 15,1. In other words,
vs. 15 should be interpreted by vss. 12-14. This interpretation seems to us more
likely than the idea of "maturity of judgment" (Ridderbos, *Paulus*, p. 300),
or "(unity) in the faith in Christ" (Du Plessis, *o.c.*, p. 146), in Phil. 3,15.
228   See his emphatic "Not that I have *already* obtained this or am *already*
perfect [*èdè teleleiōmai*]," (better: or have already been made perfect) vs. 12.
(Noteworthy is the contrast with e.g. 1 Cor. 4,8). Du Plessis correctly concludes
that here the *eschatological* significance is foremost as "the climax of all
devotion," since "*teteleiōmai* thus distinguished from *teleios* constitutes a
further stage" (p. 196). Yet, when he stresses that the resurrection must
be preceded by fellowship with Christ in sufferings with the argument,
"Obviously Paul cannot be resurrected while he is still alive" (p. 194), he
apparently overlooks the fundamental Gnostic heresy of 2 Tim. 2,18 (*èdè
gegonenai*!) against which this *èdè* in vs. 12 is directed. The same holds good
for J. J. Muller, *The Epistles of Paul to the Philippians and to Philemon*,
NICNT, 1961², p. 121. His distinction on p. 125 between "principal perfection"
(the state of perfect justification) and "ethical perfection" ("toward which all
must constantly strive..."), as applied to resp. Phil. 3,15 and 12, denies the
anti-Gnostic *teleios*-polemic here. Cf. also Preisker, *Das Ethos des Urchristentums*, p. 130.
229   *Ibid.* II, 126.
230   For a detailed historical survey, see Pretorius, *o.c.*, Hst. I. Michel, *o.c.*,
pp. 156f., with ref.

either to the *unreborn* but morally conscious man, who wants and strives
to be good until he despairs of himself *or* to the Christian who, through
the effective spiritual power of the law, still observes an inner discord
in himself between his reborn heart or mind and his flesh, i.e. its
defiling passions. It is obvious that in the latter situation – when Rom.
7,14-25 is applied to the Christian believer – every kind of perfectionism
which proclaims a transformation into inherent holiness or the possibility
of realizing ethical sinlessness *before* the glorious advent of Christ is
judged and exposed as a dream.[231] It does not mean, on the other
hand, that all interpreters who choose the first view – that Rom. 7,14ff.
pictures the struggle of "the natural man"[232] – therefore defend some
kind of perfectionism.

It is commonly stated, on the basis of vss. 7 and 13, that the proper
objective or theme of Rom. 7,7-25 is the function of the law with respect
to sin[233] or justification.[234] However, to consider the theme of vss. 7-25
as the function of the law on man as such seems to objectify the law and
to abstract its function from its living relation with the crucified Christ
and the Christian believer, within the baptismal theology of the apostle
Paul. The proper function of the law of God on man in general – the
primus usus legis – cannot be conceived as a theme by itself,[235] since the

231  See note 10 of Ch. I. Cf. also Berkouwer, *Faith and Sanctification*,
pp. 55-67 (Dutch, pp. 52-66), esp. p. 57 (Dutch, p. 58): "Suppose we assume
at this point that what Paul has sketched for us in Romans 7 is the profile
of the battling believer. We have then an excellent basis for reflection on the
Perfectionist view of man." Bavinck, *G.D.* III, 59.

232  This interpretation by Ridderbos, *Aan de Rom.*, pp. 160, 167, seems
inadequate from the very fact that the man of Rom. 7,14ff. *has* the holy law
of God, in contrast with "the natural man" who does *not* have the covenant
law, Rom. 2,14.

233  Bultmann, "Römer 7 und die Anthropologie des Paulus," in *Imago
Dei*, FS Krüger, 1932, p. 59 (repr. in: *Der alte und der neue Mensch in der
Theologie des Paulus*, Bd. XCVIII Wiss. Buchges., 1964, p. 35) strikingly
indicates concerning the sense of Rom. 7,7-25: "Und zwar ist das Motiv dieser
Apologie wohl nicht eigentlich die Pietät oder der Gedanke an erschreckte
Leser, sondern die klare Einsicht, dass der Schuldcharakter der Sünde preis-
gegeben wird, wenn die Anerkennung des Gesetzes als der Forderung Gottes
hinfällt, an der der Mensch schuldig wird." Also Pretorius, *o.c.*, p. 163.

234  Cf. Cruvellier, *o.c.*, p. 61: "Le tableau du conflict dramatique des
versets 14 à 24 n'a pas d'autre but que de nous prouver que personne ne peut
être justifié devant Dieu par la loie." Ridderbos, *Paulus*, p. 135: "de onge-
noegzaamheid van de wet en haar krachteloosheid vanwege het vlees."

235  Cf. D. Bonhoeffer, *Ethik*, 1936[6], p. 326, rightly emphasizes all three
elements or "uses" of the law, if the unity of the law of God is not to be
sacrificed. He states: "Es gibt keine Verkündigung *nur* für die Ungläubigen,
sondern nur eine solche, die *auch* den Ungläubigen gilt. Eine Klare Aufteilung
in zwei Menschengruppen ist theologisch unsachgemäss" (332). "Die Bibel
kennt keine vom Evangelium gelöste Verkündigung des primus usus...

holy law is only given in correlation with the covenant of atoning grace. To consider the function of the law in Rom. 7 without the covenant setting, without the Christological-soteriological framework, is a presumption not only out of order in Paul's *theologia crucis* as developed in the previous chapters of Romans, but also in the Biblical covenant theology as a whole.[236]

Even when H. Ridderbos[237] writes:

> Vanuit Christus gezien – dit is de grote veronderstelling – onthult de wet pas recht wie de mens is buiten de openbaring van Gods gerechtigheid zonder de wet en buiten het in Christus geschonken regime van de Geest.

he still considers the intended subject in Rom. 7 to be *not* the Christian man, but man in general outside Christ about whom is given the judgment and evaluation of the Christian, from the viewpoint of his experience with the law as revealed in Christ. And then specifically about that moral man outside Christ who is fascinated and captivated by the law.[238] It is, however, remarkable that Ridderbos also cannot fully maintain his view in logical consistency to the very end, since he must acknowledge that the language of self-knowledge and wretchedness in vss. 14 and 24 can only be understood and gauged "in depth" "from the knowledge of redemption."[239] But *how* or *when* did this moral man ever come to the

keinen prinzipiellen Unterschied zwischen der Predigt an Ungläubige und Gläubige" (338f.). See his critique on the confusion in the Lutheran creeds with respect to the usus-doctrine, pp. 339f.

236 See the valuable treatise of the divine correlation between the law of God and the covenant of grace in Berkouwer, *De Zonde*, I; ch. VI; esp. pp. 160-179 concerning an isolated function of the *usus elenchticus legis*: "Hebben we, om tot kennis der zonde te komen, alleen met de *wet* te maken?" (p. 160). He concludes: "Maar dan is het ook duidelijk, dat het niet mogelijk is aan deze 'kenbron' (de wet) een aan het evangelie *voorafgaande* kennis der zonde te ontlenen, een kennis, die zou opkomen uit het kennisnemen van een op zichzelf staande legale relatie. Het is de wet der liefde, waarover we bij de usus elenchticus spreken en daarom is de weg naar de kennis alleen vanuit en in verband met het Evangelie mogelijk en werkelijk" (p. 176). Cf. also Bonhoeffer, *Ethik*, pp.379f.: "Was immer das Wort der Kirche an die Welt sei, es kann nur Gesetz u n d Evangelium sein."

237 *Paulus*, p. 159.

238 *Ibid.*, p. 138: "Het is speciaal de door de wet *geboeide* zedelijke mens, met wie Paulus zich daarom zo gemakkelijk kan vereenzelvigen, omdat hij zelf ook eenmaal zo was. Die mens wordt hier beschreven in zijn strijd en nederlaag, met de wet als bondgenoot en de zonde en het vlees als tegenstanders, in zijn hoge aspiraties en zijn volkomen falen."

239 *Ibid.*: "Ongetwijfeld moet men zeggen, dat met name in de dramatische erkenning van het volkomen bankroet, als in vs. 14 e.v., en vs. 24, de natuurlijke mens de taal der ellende spreekt, zoals die pas vanuit de kennis

point of crying out (to whom?) or confessing his own "wretchedness," and, moreover, *at the same time* exclaiming his thankfulness for redemption by Jesus Christ? When Ridderbos explains this last exclamation of thankfulness by the passing remark that "therefore at a certain moment as it were a spark is discharged from 'the other side'"[240] this curious phrase obscures the matter at issue rather than clarifying it. The real problem of Rom. 7 does not seem to be how the law is driving "the natural man" to a conviction of his moral wretchedness which then would make him already an anonymous Christian, so that "at a certain moment" (?) the "spark" of Christ's all-sufficiency fittingly can be discharged.

The very problem is how, in what way the man of Rom. 7 *ever came* to his conviction of ultimate self-condemnation and simultaneously, of existential redemption in Christ!

Is not the simultaneousness of both religious experiences in vss. 24-25 already an indication that the holy law and Christ are correlated and thus indissolubly connected in an existential experience of faith? How futile in Paul's estimation is the efficacy of the law by itself, i.e., divorced from Christ's atonement, even with the unbelieving Jews who have the law and read it fervently, becomes strikingly apparent from his explanation in 2 Cor. 3-4. The reading of Moses or "the old covenant" without the life-giving Spirit through faith in Christ is only a killing letter, not because the law as such kills, but because a *kalymma* lies over the hardened minds (*noèmata*) or hearts (*kardia*) of those who want to be justified by the law. The law can only condemn to death those who are not in Christ, because of *sin*, i.e., their unbelieving, sinful heart, mind, self.

It is Paul's outspoken conviction that only the glorious light of the Cross of Christ reveals the law in its proper work of condemning all law-righteousness as sin before God:

> I bear them witness that they have a zeal for God, but it is not enlightened. For, being ignorant of the righteousness that comes from God, and seeking to establish their own, they did not submit to God's righteousness. For Christ is the end of the law, that every one who has faith may be justified (Rom. 10,2-4).

In the kerygma of Paul's baptismal theology, baptism into Christ means baptism into Christ's death or the identification of the believer's "old man" with the crucified body of Christ, in order to participate in what happens to Christ before the law, *coram Deo*. The death of Christ then

---

der verlossing in haar diepte gepeild en verstaan kan worden. Daarom springt *op een gegeven moment* a.h.w. ook de vonk over van 'de andere zijde': 'Goddank, door Jezus Christus, onze Heer!'" (it. sup.).

240  See previous note.

becomes also the believer's death before the law.[241]

It is of crucial significance, however, that Paul describes this crucified "old man" in 6,6 as *"sinful body"* (*to sōma tès hamartias*), in Gal. 5,24 as "the flesh with its passions and desires" (*sarx syn tois pathèmasin kai tais epithymiais*), in Col. 2,11 as "the body of flesh" (*to sōma tès sarkos*). Ridderbos classifies with these terms also "this body of death" (*to sōma tou thanatou*) of Rom. 7,24, stating that all these terms do not signify the human body as such, but its "sinful way of existence."[242]

Paul is cautious not to suggest that the Christian has already now received in baptism the sinless resurrection-body of Christ, so that he would no longer have his sinful death-body.

> For if we have been united with him in a death like his, we shall certainly be united with him in a resurrection like his. We know that our old self was crucified with him so that the sinful body might be destroyed, and we might no longer be enslaved to sin. For he who has died is freed from sin. But if we have died with Christ, we believe that we shall also live with him (Rom. 6,5-8).

In this baptismal theology Paul seems to have built in the anti-perfectionist reservation[243] that the Christians cannot as yet claim the quality of the resurrection-body of Christ. While expressing the union of the Christian with Christ's *death* in the *perfect* tense, he avoids this tense for their union with Christ's resurrection, using here only the *future* tense.[244] If we want to define whether the subject of Rom. 7,14ff. in its inner struggle is the natural or the Christian man, whether this struggle fits the existence *kata sarka* or *kata pneuma* before the holy

---

241 See Ridderbos, *Paulus*, pp. 447-456, who states on p. 456: "Het specifieke van het gedoopt worden in Christus' dood is niet, dat de tijd wegvalt of dat de dopeling met Christus in zijn dood gelijktijdig gemaakt wordt, maar dat de gelovige door de doop deelgenoot wordt van hetgeen met Christus is geschied. De doop doet ons niet nog eens opnieuw sterven met Christus, maar rust veeleer daarop, dat Hij voor ons en wij met Hem gestorven zijn, omdat Hij de tweede mens, de laatste Adam is, die plaatsbekledend en representatief de velen in Zich omsloot en verenigde toen Hij stierf en opstond."

242 *Ibid.*, p. 251: "Al deze uitdrukkingen zijn kennelijk niet van het lichaam zelf, maar van de zondige bestaanswijze van de mens bedoeld. Dit praegnante gebruik van lichaam is echter uitzondering." In note 57 on p. 251 Ridderbos quotes Dreijdanus on Rom. 7,24 who interprets the longing for deliverance from this *"death-body"* to mean that the body "must be cleansed, renewed, sanctified." Ridderbos accepts this statement with the *"reservation"* of the eschatological redemption of Rom. 8,23. It occurs to us that Greijdanus' interpretation could lead to the wrong notion that the body or old man can be sanctified or cleansed. The new man is not the corrected or cleansed old man!

243 Käsemann, *o.c.* II, 126f.

244 Not so in Col. 2,12, but here the resurrection is immediately related to faith in God.

law in Rom. 8, the struggle with the flesh as such cannot be the decisive criterion, since they "have died to the law through the body of Christ" (7,4), but rather the commitment of the heart or mind to the flesh or the holy law *coram Deo*. In order to establish the theological meaning of the confession "Wretched man that I am! Who will deliver me from this body of death?" (vs. 24), we first have to ascertain the meaning of the "body of death" in its relation to the law of God and man's social ethos.[245]

The theme of Rom. 7 seems to be not the unassailable dignity of the law as such, but of the law in its dominating and condemning efficacy on a person as long and as far as he lives in the "old man" or sinful death-body, i.e., as long as the law of sin operates in man, vss. 1-4. This general principle receives its significant application, however, with reference to the two seemingly rhetorical questions of Paul, whether the being *discharged from the law* through faith in the crucified body of Christ (vss. 6,4) finds its cause in the nature of the law itself. Is the law sinful, vs. 7, and does the law bring death to me, vs. 13? Ridderbos[246] states that vss. 14-25 intend to reveal how the law *fails* in the man outside Christ. Otherwise, if the theme concerning the law is no longer the condemnation of the law, as in vss. 1-6, but the *goodness* of the law, this would disturb the whole tenor of Rom. 5-8, and stand in contrast with 7,1-6.

But could not the apostle speak in a different way about the law of God in order to cut off false conclusions? Hence the specific intercalation of 7,7-25 on the basis of two false conclusions which identify completely the condemnatory function of the law with the law itself. Paul therefore is stressing intentionally the inalienable goodness and holiness of the law of God (vss. 10,12), at the same time disclosing the *real* cause of the condemnatory efficacy of the holy law. The law of God only condemns the "law of sin and death" which reigns in the flesh (vss. 13,18).

Consequently, man should not cry for deliverance from the law of God, but for deliverance from his own body of death with its inherent law of sin (vs. 24).

The real matter at issue seems to be concentrated on the question whether vss. 14-25 intend to indicate the *death* of the sinful body, in spite of man's moral militancy, or the militant *resistance* of the crucified death-body to the spiritual law or reign of Christ in the baptized man.

---

245  Cf. Schweizer, in *ThWNT* VII, 135, 26ff. (s.v. *sarx*): "Der Mensch ist nicht wesentlich bestimmt von seiner Natur her, weder von seiner körperlichen Beschaffenheit von der ihn umgebenen materiellen Welt her. Er ist letztlich qualifiziert durch seine Relation zu Gott und damit auch zum Mitmenschen." How this concept is in basic continuity with the religious anthropology of the O.T., may be seen from 123, 1-12.

246  *Aan de Rom.*, p. 164.

*The death of the subject of Romans 7.*

In order to come to grips with this problem it is of vital importance to ascertain the meaning of vss. 9-11, i.e. the theological meaning of the phrase:

> *I was once alive apart from the law [chōris nomou], but when the commandment came, sin revived and I died* (vs. 9).

Could this be Paul's theological description of his own Rabbinical experience before and when he was apprehended by Christ?[247] Or is he describing "a happy childhood – happier and freer in retrospect, no doubt than it ever really was – before the troublesome conscience awoke"?[248]

Writing Rom. 7 from the standpoint of an apostle of Jesus Christ, his evaluation may well be compared with the retrospective descriptions of his religious experience in Phil. 3,6-10 and Gal. 2,19-20. Just as the rich young ruler himself asserted that he had kept all the divine commandments (Mt. 19,20), while from the Christian standpoint he had not attained to the law at all (cf. for "Israel" Rom. 9,31), so Paul now counts his legalistic life as a Pharisee – which

---

247 Cf. A. J. Bandstra, *The Law and the Elements of the World*, 1964, p. 142. "In the light of Gal. 2:15-20, we conclude that it is most probable that in Rom. 7:14-25 Paul is describing his own experience and that of his fellow Jewish Christians at the point at which the message of grace in Christ 'had hit its mark' in them, or, if you will, their conversion experience." This is basically the traditional Augustinian-Reformation interpretation which distinguishes here between *status securitas, legalis* and *regenerationis*.
Ridderbos, *o.c.*, p. 151, following here Pretorius, *o.c.*, p. 105, calls it "improbable" that Paul would describe his pre-Christian life as a life "without law". Pret. refers to 1 Cor. 9,20; Rom. 9,31f. to corroborate this „improbability." In 1 Cor. 9 Paul is indicating the style of his missionary work as an apostle of Christ that he might "win those under the law." In Rom. 9,31f. he is recognizing Israel's zeal for God which nevertheless fails to fulfill the law *coram Deo*. If we ought to take Rom. 7,9 *not* as a description of Paul's Rabbinical self-consciousness before his conversion, but as his Christian-theological evaluation *coram Deo* concerning his Rabbinical zeal for the law which knew no radical condemnation but rather self-justification, it seems not only probable but a *theological* necessity to characterize *such* a life with the law as a life *without* the law. Is not this also the intention of Rom. 9,31, that Israel in all their zeal for the law *eis nomon ouk ephthasen*? It all depends, therefore, whether the law is taken and interpreted *within* its divinely ordained Gospel setting, or divorced from it.
248 Dodd, *o.c.*, p. 128 *(ad* Rom. 7,9). Cf. Ridderbos, *Aan de rom.*, pp. 150, 151. Pretorius, *o.c.*, pp. 106f. 155f. Also Sanday-Headlam (in ICC), *ad* Rom. 7,9. Murray, *o.c.*, I, p. 251, disagrees with this position by stating: "But there is no need or warrant to restrict what he describes as being 'alive from the law' to the years of unreflecting childhood (cf. Phil. 3:4-6)." P. Althaus, *Der Brief an die Römer*, NTD 6, 1959⁹, pp. 66f. takes it as the sad history of sin in man in general, the Jew in particular: "Das Selbstbekenntnis ist nichts anderes als das Selbstverständnis des Christen Paulus in Bezug auf sein vorchristliches Sein."

he previously regarded as the perfect life: "as to the righteousness under law blameless," Phil. 3,6 – "loss" and "refuse" (Phil. 3,8), because he had felt no *condemnation* by the law!

Although the revelation of Jesus Christ brought to Paul the realization that Christ is the end of all law-righteousness, Christ to him did not abolish the just requirement of the law.[249] On the contrary, only through being apprehended by Christ was the holiness of the law brought home to his conscience with its infinite divine claim and condemning power, revealing his transgression of the law, crushing all self-righteousness in him before God. "For I through the law *died* to the law, that I might live to God" (Gal. 2,19). In the following verse he explains this *death* of self to be his crucifixion *with Christ* so that he was no longer living in his old self, but Christ in him (vs. 20). In others words, in Gal. 2,19f. Paul is identifying the coming of the law in its condemning power with the coming of Christ to him.[250]

The question thus must be asked, whether Paul is indicating the same religious experience of faith (of Gal. 2,19) in Rom. 7,9. Certainly Gal. 2,19 testifies in favor of it, since in both cases the law of God is the instrument to cause the death of the self-righteousness "I".[251]

---

249   See e.g. Rom. 3,31; 7,10.12; 8,4; 9,31.

250   Cf. P. A. van Stempvoort, *Oud en Nieuw. De brief aan de Galatiërs,* 1951, p. 58: "Paulus zelf is gestorven: door de wet. Dit laatste kan hier niet betekenen dat de wet kennis der zonde geeft. Alsof Paulus als farizaeër reeds vertwijfeld zou zijn geweest. Verre van dat." Calvin on Rom. 7,9. Even Rothuizen, *o.c.,* p. 185, n. 285, must acknowledge about the man with the law in Rom. 7: "Hoe positief ook: moeilijk kunnen we, op deze wijze geschilderd de farizeeër plaatsen." See also his other references. Definitely inadequate, because of its autonomous self-understanding, is Sanday-Headlam, *ad* Rom. 7,24: "But St. Paul was not an ordinary Pharisee. He dealt too honestly with himself, so that sooner or later the self-satisfaction natural to the Pharisee, must give way..." p. 183). And: "only because of his intense sincerity and honesty in facing facts" (p. 187).

Also in H. Ridderbos, *The Epistle of Paul to the Churches in Galatia,* NICNT, 1956, *ad* Gal. 2,19, p. 104, the *Christological* definition of this death to the law is lacking. W. Hendriksen, *Galatians,* NTC, 1968, *ad* Gal. 2,19, p. 102, tries to relate the law to Christ.

251   Cf. Bavinck, *G.D.* III, 57-58. Bandstra, *o.c.,* pp. 141ff. Ridderbos, *Aan de Rom.,* p. 152, interprets Rom. 7,9 ("sin revived and I died") as the general objective situation of man under the law, as the *coming* under the wrath of God, 4,15, just as the life in sin is defined as "death" in Col. 2,13; Eph. 2,1.5. Also Pretorius, *o.c.,* p. 105, interprets Rom. 7,9 as the death which is characterized by a sinning stirred up by the law. This interpretation can only be maintained on the basis of the law working in isolation from the covenant of grace, which we feel is theologically unjustified. Furthermore, if this death of "I" in Rom. 7,9 is to be characterized as the coming under the wrath of God by consciously sinning against the law, while still remaining outside Christ, it follows that this death of the *I* worked by sin through the law has to be

Without denying that Paul as a Pharisee may have felt the convicting power of the holy law of God, it cannot be doubted that only when he came face to face with the divinity of the resurrected Lord Jesus did the full weight of the far-reaching claims of God's law and – by contrast – the true hideousness of his own self-righteousness pierce his conscience, leading him to the conviction of his own sinfulness *coram Deo* and of his condemnation to death.[252]

Ridderbos[253] has stated that the power of Christ and of the Spirit (Rom. 7,25; 8,2ff.) cannot in any way be integrated in the death situation of Rom. 7,14-25. We would like to submit that the "death" which is the result of the sin-reviving, *pneumatikos* law of God (7,9ff., 13-14) cannot be the work of the law as a moral code aside from the convincing power of the Holy Spirit[254] or the Spirit of Christ.[255]

Does not Rom. 7,4, just as Gal. 2,19-20, define the spiritual death of the "brethren" *Christologically?* They have "died to the law through the body of Christ."[256] We therefore take the position that the power of Christ or the Spirit *underlies* the dynamic and fruitful activity of the *pneumatikos* law *coram Deo,* in Rom. 7,9-25.

The sin-reviving efficacy of the holy law is Christologically determined from the beginning to the end.

---

basically distinguished from *another* death of the *I* when the law is revealed in Christ, as stated in Gal. 2,19-20. Consequently, Paul would speak of two basically different *kinds* of *dying* of the *I*, both through the same law.

Murray's interpretation of "I died" in Rom. 7,9 as "the death of the complacent self-assurance" as still basically different from "death to sin" is based on his *separation* of the proper function of the law from the gospel of Christ. It seems unwarranted, however, to distinguish between *these* two kinds of death.

252 Cf. Lk. 5,8; Is. 6,5; Job 42,5f. Cf. K. Barth, *C.D.* IV, 1, 584 *(K.D.,* p. 654), on Rom. 7,9: "It is not the heathen, secular, godless man who lives in this self-knowledge and is constantly forced back to it, but the man who is elected and called: Paul the Christian and the apostle interpreting the experience of Israel."

253 *Paulus,* p. 135.

254 Cf. Luther on Rom. 7,9-10: "But through the knowledge of the Law, or rather through the Spirit's revelation I recognized that the commandment worked death in me." (*Com. on the Ep. to the Romans,* abr. tr. by J. Th. Mueller, 1965[4], p. 95).

Cf. Murray, *o.c.*, I, p. 254: "Paul's usage will show that the word 'Spiritual' is derived from the Holy Spirit." (referring to 1 Cor. 2,13.15; Eph. 5,19; Col. 3,16; 1,19 etc. O. Michel, *Der Brief an die Römer,* p. 150. J. Wesley, in *Forty-Four Sermons,* repr. 1964, p. 391, rightly applies Heb. 4,12 also to the law of Rom. 7. *Contra* Ridderbos, *Aan de Rom.,* p. 148: "zó werkt de wet zich uit bij de zondige mens."

255 Calvin justly refers to 2 Cor. 3,14 for the interpretation of Rom. 7,9. See also above, note 236.

256 See also Rom. 6,6; Gal. 5,24. Cf. Bavinck, *G.D.* III, 58.

Through the spiritual law in the light of the Cross the eyes are opened to the exceeding sinfulness of one's own carnal or selfish nature, which leads to the conviction that "nothing good" dwells in one's flesh, being a "captive" to the death-body until the apocalyptic day of 8,23; 1 Cor. 15,50-56.[257]

It is this battle of the new man in Christ against his empirical old man which causes his utmost repentance because he recognizes that his carnal nature is "sold under sin," i.e., the old man or death-body remains under the power of sin against the will of the mind or heart of the new man.[258] From his hamartiological point of view Paul identifies the "law of sin" in the body with the empirical reality of the body.[259]

The mind, *nous*,[260] or inner man, *esō anthrōpos*,[261] is clearly

---

257   The designation in Rom. 7,18 of the sin-conscious man: "I cannot do" the good, because "sin dwells within me" (vs. 20), need not be interpreted to mean the absence of actual works of obedience of faith, but the religious confession that the fleshly *"I"* cannot do them; cf. 1 Cor. 15,10; Gal. 2,20.

258   Vss. 21ff. 25b. See also 2 Cor. 10,3-5, where Paul in a different context explicitly states that the Christians are not carrying on a war *kata sarka* although walking *en sarki*. The weapons of the Christians are not *sarkika*; they *"take every thought [noèma] captive to obey Christ."* He uses again the same verb *aichmalōtizein* as in Rom. 7,23. We therefore feel that Berkouwer is justified in concluding: "Paulus is dan ook *in* z'n verkocht-zijn, in de ervaring van de overmacht niet een slaaf van de zonde." (*o.c.*, p. 58) Rom. 6,16 defined a *doulos* as a servant who obeys *willingly* and *wholeheartedly*.

259   See Murray, *o.c.*, I, pp. 268f. on the significance of the translation "the body of this death" or "this body of death," opting for the last one: "It is in this way that the body can be regarded as the body of this death – the bodily members are the spheres in which the law of sin is operative unto that death which is the wages of sin" (269). Michel, *o.c.*, p. 154: "Der Hinweis auf die Leiblichkeit des Menschen darf auf keinen Fall übersehen werden; die Begriffe: Begierde, Fleisch, Sünde, Tod haben alle eine enge Beziehung zur gegenwärtigen Leiblichkeit des Menschen: in der Leiblichkeit und an der Leiblichkeit setzt der Kampf an. 'Der Kampfplatz ist der menschliche Körper' (ZnR 362)."

260   See the elucidation of *nous* in Cruvellier, *o.c.*, pp. 87-93, who rightly asks those who take *nous* as the *natural* capability of man: *"Nous serait-il plus près de Dieu que sarx? Y a-t-il un conflit dualiste dans l'homme que Paul ne dépeint nulle part ailleurs?"* (91). He concludes: "Les exégètes qui voient dans Rom. 7 le tableau du chrétien n'ont pas les mêmes difficultés pour expliquer la nature de *nous* de Rom. 7 que les exégètes fidèles à l'interprétation de *ego* comme designant le non chrétien; le *nous* du chrétien ayant été renouvelé il n'est pas étonnant qu'il prenne plaisir à la loi de Dieu et qu'il s'oppose à la loi du péché qui est dans les membres comme c'est le cas dans Rom. 7" (93).

261   See 7,22; cf. 12,2; Phil. 2,13. It is not without significance that the qualification *esō anthrōpos* in Rom. 7,22 is further only used for the *reborn* man: 2 Cor. 4,16; Eph. 3,16. Moreover, that man has "delight in the law of God" is a description given only to the children of the covenant, e.g. Ps. 1,2; 119,35.47. See Cruvellier, *o.c.*, p. 86.

determined by the new-covenant experience of delight in, and willing obedience[262] to (douleuō) the law of God, vss. 22,25.

We now come to the crucial question, With which of the two contrasted objective ways of existence in Rom. 8,1-13 is the battle of Rom. 7 to be identified? The subject of Rom. 7,9-24 can *never* be identified with the existence in which the mind or heart is set on the things of the flesh,[263] and therefore *has* to be identified legally with the existence in which the mind or heart is set on the things of the Spirit, while the body is dead because of sin, 8,10-13. We might summarize this identification with three considerations.

First, the subject of Rom. 7 must be identical with the perfect Christian of Rom. 8 because there is a corresponding recognition of and delight in the holy law of God *coram Deo*, cf. 7,16.21-22.25 with 8,5b.7.

Secondly, the inner man or mind of Rom. 7 hates and opposes self, the old man (vss. 14-15)[264] and repents of his own wretchedness (vs. 24), which corresponds to the battle of the Christian with his (legally) "dead body" in Rom. 8,10.13.[265]

Thirdly, the battle with the indwelling power of sin in Rom. 7 (which seems to know no victory and only defeat) is still basically different from the sinful walk or ethos *kata sarka* in Rom. 8. The non-Christian in Rom. 8 still has the heart and mind (*phronèma*) of the old man or body, which is emphatically egocentric, his mind being set on himself, hostile to God and His law (vs. 5a.7) in contrast to the man in Rom. 7 (vss. 22.25).

It can be observed moreover, that the spiritual man in Rom. 8 is not described in his actual, empirical battle with self! In other words, the passages, Rom. 7,9-25 and Rom. 8,1-13, should not be contrasted with each other on the presupposition that Rom. 7 knows no Spirit or victory, and the Christian in Rom. 8 knows no flesh (vs. 13!) or defeat.[266] While

262  Vs. 21. This *ho nomos* may not be robbed of its religious *pneumatikos* character by changing it basically into the concept of *lex naturae* like "constraining principle" (Sanday-Headlam, in ICC, *ad loc.*) or "norm, gezondheid" (Ridderbos, *ad loc.*).
263  Cf. Schweizer, in *ThWNT* VII, 132, 4ff. (s.v. *sarx*): "Die für Paulus charakteristische Verbindung von Fleisch und Sünde ist die alttestamentlich vorgegebene: sündig ist das Bauen des Menschen auf Fleisch." Also 135, 34f.; 136, 1-10. Ridderbos, *Paulus*, p. 108: "Terwijl 'vlees' bij Paulus de zonde aanduidt in héél haar van God afgekeerde en afkerige strekking."
264  In sharp contrast with the "mind of the flesh," *nous tès sarkos*, in Col. 2,18.
265  Pertinent to the Christian struggle is also that the apostle Paul repeatedly has to *summon* the Christians to fix their *phronein* on Christ, Phil. 2,5; Col. 3,2. Cf. Bertram, *ThWNT* IX, 228, 10-23 (s.v. *phrèn ktl*).
266  Also Ridderbos, *ad Rom.* 8,13 (*Com.*, p. 179), acknowledges here the empirical existence of the Christians who are forensically *en pneumati*: "'Lichaam' betekent ook hier weer de door de zonde beheerste menselijke

Rom. 7 describes, in terms of personal exemplary experience, the actual Christian battle and self-consciousness before God, Rom. 8 (1-10) seems to present more the two antagonistic objective ways of being in God's sight, either the being *kata pneuma, en pneumati,* or the being *kata sarka, en sarki.*[267]

In this concept it can never be adequate to interpret Rom. 8 and 7 as mutually exclusive experiences for the Christian. The theme of the apostle Paul in Rom. 7,13ff. seems to be the continuing[268] death of self, caused by the abiding efficacy of the *pneumatikos* law of God. This does not mean that the moral struggle of "the natural man" between his reason and sensuality, conscience and lust, mind and heart, is denied.[269] The real question is only whether it is the intention of Rom. 7 to unfold this pre-Christian moral dualism, *or* the religious-moral dualism of the reborn I and the old man before God.[270] It is attractive to interpret Rom.

bestaanswijze, vgl. bij 6:12." It is noteworthy that he does not refer to this sinful body in his interpretation of the apocalyptic redemption of the body in 8,23 (p. 188).

267  Paul identifies both ways of existence with *life* and *death*; cf. Foerster, in *ThWNT* II, 412, 20ff. (s.v. *eirènè*). Ridderbos acknowledges in his *Com.*, pp. 174ff. these two contrasting ways of existence with their resp. *phronein* in Rom. 8. He emphatically identifies the existence *en sarki* with Rom. 7,7-25, and the existence *en pneumati* with Rom. 8,1ff. (pp. 143, 146) ; see also *Paulus*, p. 242), because he does not consider here the distinction between the objective forensic states of Rom. 8,1-11 on the one hand, and the *subjective, empirical standing within the state of justification* (in Rom. 7,14-25) on the other hand. A comparative exposition between Rom. 7,14-25 and the existence *en sarki, kata sarka* in Rom. 8 would be helpful. On Rom. 7,7-25 (as the religious self-understanding of the Christian in the state of justification) see K. Barth, *C.D.* IV, 1, 581-591; esp. 588 (*K.D.,* pp. 649-659; esp. 656), where Barth refers to vss. 17 and 20 with the remark: "Here we have a direct proof that in this whole chapter Paul is speaking of himself as a Christian and an apostle and not placing himself in the situation either of an unbelieving Jew – perhaps his own before his conversion – or of an unbelieving Gentile." See also p. 589 (*K.D.,* p. 657) on Rom. 7,24-25.

268  Also Ridderbos, *o.c.,* p. 158, acknowledges that Rom. 7,14ff. intends to say "dat de mens uit kracht van de wet niet leven kan, maar gestorven is *en nog steeds sterft*" (it. sup.). See also his *Aan de Romeinen,* p. 154. Cf. Barth, *C.D.* IV, 1, 583 (*K.D.,* p. 650).

269  This is recognized in Rom. 2,14f. See Schrage, *o.c.,* pp. 191ff., with lit. Cf. Ridderbos, *Paulus,* p. 137, who also points to the struggle of man against sin, in the Qumran literature. Significant is, however, the question of Berkouwer to H. Ridderbos in *GW* 14 (1959), 345: "Is Rom. 2 ook maar in de verte een illustratie voor het probleem, dat ons in Rom. 7 voor de aandacht wordt geplaatst? ... Het gaat natuurlijk niet om een tegenstelling tussen Rom. 2 en 7, *maar wel om een ander probleem*" (it. sup.). Or, stated concretely, can the *doing* of the law by the Gentiles in their autonomous morality (Rom. 2) be taken as a legitimate illustration for the *not-doing* of the law by those who *have* the law of God? Cf. also Bavinck, *G.D.* III, 58.

270  Cf. Pretorius, *o.c.,* pp. 166f.

222

7,14-21 as the outworking of Rom. 7,5, i.e., the moral struggle between the mind and sensuality, and Rom. 7,25a; 8,1-17 as the outworking of Rom. 7,6, i.e., the "new life of the Spirit." In other words, to interpet Rom. 7,7-24 and 7,25a; 8 in a chronological-redemptive order, so that the true Christian is described as *no longer* experiencing the feeling of impotency, sinfulness and wretchedness of Rom. 7. Or as Dodd[271] states of Paul's describing "his individual case as typical":

> It would stultify his whole argument if he now confessed that, at the moment of writing, he was a miserable wretch, a prisoner to sin's law (verses 24,23). He would have thought it quite abnormal that any Christian should feel so . . .

Yet, Paul's description of the Christian's self-consciousness in Rom. 8,23 – i.e. simultaneously (!) to rejoice in the Spirit and to groan inwardly because of the body – does not seem to justify Dodd's suggestion. After all, Biblical sanctification definitely does not mean the feeling of holiness and righteousness but rather the very opposite!

The closer one approaches and walks with the holy God, the deeper the holy requirement of the law is written in the heart or conscience, the more the believer is impressed with his own inherent sinfulness and unworthiness, leading him to ever deepening repentance, humility and praise of the only holy One[272] and His holy law.[273]

The fact that the efficacy of the law always *remains*, exposing the abiding carnal nature, the indwelling selfishness which is truly hated[274] by the Christian himself, constantly keeps him aware of his own imperfection, his daily need of deliverance by Christ. Then the confessions "Wretched man that I am!" and "Thanks be to God through Jesus Christ our Lord!" can both fully be taken as true exclamations of the apostle's own condition while writing his letter to the Romans.[275] In this concept the last statement of Rom. 7 (vs. 25b) only confirms the contemporaneity of the *two* realities of the *one* Christian person. In other words, Rom. 7,14-25 can just as well be applied to the Christian's self-consciousness before the holy God.[276]

It seems not irrelevant in this respect to refer to the context in which "wretched," *talaipōros*, is used in the only other instance that it occurs in the New Testament, in Rev. 3,17. Here it is the reproof of the glorified Christ, which He addresses to the *church* in Laodicea in order to break

---

271   *O.c.*, p. 126.
272   Cf. Rev. 15,4 (in the song of the conquerors!). See also note 252.
273   Rom. 7,13-14.16.22.
274   Rom. 7,15.
275   Also Pretorius, *o.c.*, p. 166. Barth, *C.D.* IV, 1, 583f. (*K.D.*, pp. 657f.).
276   Cf. Pretorius, *o.c.*, pp. 164f. Barth, *C.D.* IV, 1, 589 (*K.D.*, p. 657).

through the false self-esteem which this Christian church has in her own self-consciousness (vs. 17: "For *you say* . . . ; not knowing that *you are*"). From the divine call to repentance (vs. 19) it appears that the "lukewarmness" of that church was not the *fact* of her being wretched in herself, but that she did not recognize and acknowledge herself as such *before God*. The summons to repentance from her divine Lord intends to awaken her again to the only true self-evaluation which is acceptable to God, the confession of her sinfulness in radical terms: "*wretched, pitiable*, poor, blind, and naked" (vs. 17b.).[277]

Also in Rom. 7 we do not get the impression that Paul is dealing with the non-Christian man in general but rather with the "brethren," "those who know the law," vs. 1. And vs. 14 may well be understood in direct continuity with vs. 1:

> We know that the law is *pneumatikos*; but I am *sarkinos, pre-pramenos hypo tèn hamartian*.

This is not an objective theological analysis, but the confession of his dramatic new-covenant experience (vss. 9-12), which he presents as a continuing reality.[278]

As long as the holy law of God is exercising its dynamic *spiritual* (*pneumatikos*) activity of exposing the exceeding sinfulness of self, the hateful carnal nature, he remains convicted that his (reborn) will and religious-moral self-manifestation are defiled before God because of the carnal,[279] selfish contamination. In other words, Paul confesses his total[280] wretchedness in the sight of God, not as Ahab who sold himself[281]

---

277    Cf. also Lk. 18,9-14 concerning the confession which was rejected, and the one which led to justification.

278    Significant are the emphatic *present* tenses in vss. 14-25. Cf. Bavinck, *G.D.* IV, 248; III, 57. Barth, *C.D.* IV, 1, 583 (*K.D.*, p. 650).

279    As *sarkinos* is being used as a synonym of *sarkikos* in 1 Cor. 3,1-3, Cruvellier unnecessarily weakens the confession of Rom. 7,14 when he states on p. 75: "Le chrètien, qui n'est plus charnel dans le sens de: 'celui qui a une mentalité charnelle,' reste charnel dans le sens qu'il vit encore dans la chair et participe à ses conditions; c'est ce que Paul exprime par *sarkinos*." Cf. Rothuizen, *o.c.*, p. 180, n. 253 with other references. Calvin's term *vestigia* (*ad* Rom. 7,18; *Inst.* II, 2, 27; IV, 15, 12) is not merely "too light a word for the climate of 7:14" (Rothuizen, *o.c.*, p. 187), but wholly inadequate since it uses a quantitative category, beside the fact that Calvin applies 7,14 to the *un*regenerate man.

280    Cf. Michel, *o.c.*, *ad* Rom. 7,14: "Das grosse Recht der augustinisch-reformatorischen Auslegung besteht in der Erkenntnis, dass letztlich nur der Christ zu einer derartig radikalen Aussage über den Menschen kommen kann; jeder nichtchristliche Standpunkt muss notwendig abschwächen" (p. 150, n. 3).

281    1 Kgs. 21,20.25. Cf. Berkouwer, *o.c.*, pp. 58f. (Dutch, pp. 57f.). Pretorius, *o.c.*, p. 165. Murray, *o.c.* I, 261: "It is one thing to sell oneself to do iniquity; it is another to be sold under the power of sin. In the former

willingly in presumptuous sin, but as a captive who is sold against his will.[282] It is not the social-moral dimension (*coram hominibus*) but the religious one (*coram Deo*) in Rom. 7,18 which has led the Church of the Reformation[283] to apply to herself the testimony of the apostle, in full harmony with Christ's teaching in Jn. 15,5 ("apart from me you can do nothing"):

> For I know that nothing good dwells within me, that is, in my flesh. I can will what is right, but I cannot do it.

Such a radical self-condemnation *coram Deo*, without ultimate despair, can only be given to him who is conscious of the radicality[284] of divine forgiveness. Only to the man who is redeemed from his law-righteousness through the revelation of Christ's atoning death, is it given to confess that all his good works are effected by the defiling power of his carnal nature or indwelling sin.[285]

So much so that he even acknowledges that his prayers and most elevated thoughts continually need the forgiving mediation of Christ Jesus, 8,34 and the intercession of the Holy Spirit, 8,26-27.[286]

Only he who is confronted with the reality of the divine holiness in Christ, and in his heart is convicted by the law of God, is fully awakened to the religious dimension and *power* of sin in himself.

Only he is drawn into the existential experience of God's *holiness* and, *by contrast*, his own *sinfulness*, even with all his religiosity and morality.

---

case the person is the active agent, in the latter he is subjected to a power that is alien to his own will."

282  In Rom. 7,15.20 Paul obviously distinguishes between the *sarkinos* man (7,14) who in his *mind* or heart delights in God's law and yet does the very thing he "hates" in the light of the judgment of the holy law with which he identifies himself (vss. 22, 25) and thus condemns himself (vs. 24); and the man who lives *en sarki*, walking *kata sarka*, setting his *mind* deliberately on the things of the flesh (8,5) and thus justifies himself. Cf. Bavinck, *G.D.* III, 58.

283  E.g. *De Heidelbergse Catechismus*, Zondag 44, on the significance of the continuing preaching of the Ten Commandments. *Ned. Geloofsbelijdenis*, art. 24. Cf. also *Canones* V, art. IV. It is this dimension *coram Deo* which is ignored by Dodd and therefore proves his quoted citation inadequate.

284  Cf. Bultmann, *Jesus*, p. 169: "Indem der Mensch die Vergebung annimmt, verurteilt er sich selbst am tiefsten, beugt er sich wahrhaft unter Gottes Gericht." See Ez. 36,31; Is. 57,15; Ps. 51,17 (RSV); Gal. 6,14.

285  Cf. Cruvellier, *o.c.*, p. 88: "L'homme étant un tout, *nous* n'est pas independant de *sarx*; l'homme est *sarx* et *nous* en même temps." Barth, *C.D.* IV, 1, 582 (*K.D.*, p. 649): "The justified man speaks of his sin as in Rom. 7." The German text goes on with: "Keiner sonst könnte es, täte es in dieser Unerbittlichkeit" (omitted in ET). See further above, n. 280.

286  Thus not merely a part of man, the "periphery," or the "center" of his being (A. Kuyper, Bavinck) needs redemption and is redeemed, but the *whole* man is continually to be redeemed in the forgiveness of sin (Berkouwer).

It is the essence of godly repentance that it experiences and testifies simultaneously complete sinfulness and complete redemption in divine forgiveness. As Rom. 7 culminates in the doxological professions, we need not wonder that all endeavors in theology to interpret this deeply religious testimony of Paul in terms of rational understanding and to construct them into a system of unity have failed one way or another.[287] The dynamic correlation of law and grace belongs to the category of miracles. The consolation of Rom. 7 lies in the continuing actuality, the abiding promise of perfect redemption where the law of God is proclaimed and brought home most fully, i.e., in Jesus Christ. It was especially John Wesley[288] (following J. A. Bengel)[289] who energetically proclaimed the abiding correlation of the holy law and Christ:

> But when it has brought us to Him, it has yet a further office, namely, to keep us with Him ... How clearly does this agree with the experience of every true believer! While he cries out, 'O what love have I unto Thy law! all the day long is my study in it'; he sees daily, in that divine mirror, more and more of his own sinfulness. He sees more and more clearly, that he is still a sinner in all things – that neither his heart nor his ways are right before God; and that every moment sends him to Christ ...
>
> Therefore I cannot spare the law one moment, no more than I can spare Christ; seeing I now want it as much to keep me to Christ, as I ever wanted it to bring me to Him. Otherwise, this 'evil heart of unbelief' would immediately 'depart from the living God.' Indeed each is continually sending me to the other – the law to Christ, and Christ to the law.

As applied to the Christian religious experience, we are led to identify the testimony of Rom. 7,14-25 with the expression of Luther's theological

---

287  See the excellent article of E. Ellwein, "Das Rätsel von Römer VII," in *KuD* I (1955), 247-268; esp. 266ff.; He concludes: "Das heisst also: Was im logischen Raum auseinanderfällt, der status hier und der status dort, der Stand des Verzweifelnden und der Stand der Gotteskindschaft, gehört im existentiellen Vollzug des Glaubens, in der lebendigen Bewegung des Glaubens zusammen. Dann ist Röm. 7 die ständige erinnerung daran, dass wir nur aus der Vergebung, nur von der fremden Gerechtigkeit Christi her, nur aus seiner 'süssen Wundertat,' aus dem Wunder das Heiligen Geistes, vor Gott leben können und dürfen. Dass wir, immer wieder am Gesetz Gottes zuschanden werdend, nur an und in der Gabe Christi Ruhe finden für unsere Seele" (267). Cf. Berkouwer, *o.c.*, pp. 60, 61 (Dutch, pp. 58, 59): "There is no transparency here, only grief over sin, meekness, confession of guilt, and a glorying in salvation (Rom. 7:25)." "Every attempt to make this heterogeneity transparent to the eye by some division of human functions is doomed to failure."

288  We quote from his *Forty-Four Sermons*, repr. 1964, pp. 392, 393. Sermon XXIX, on Rom. 7,12.

289  See Ellwein, *KuD* I, 260-262.

statement that the Christian is *simul iustus et peccator*;[290] not in the sense of *partly* righteous *partly* a sinner, but at once *fully* righteous and *fully* sinful, thus exceeding all logical and psychological-anthropological considerations.

### c. Problematic texts

aa) 1 Jn. 3,9: *Pas ho gegennèmenos ek tou theou hamartian ou poiei, hoti sperma autou en autōi menei· kai ou dynatai hamartanein, hoti ek tou theou gegennètai.*

The only legitimate way of interpretation is to consider this statement in relation to its immediate context and in the light of the wider context of the whole letter and the specific religious-historical situation.

The intention of this letter is, by means of this reassuring testimony (1,2) to warm and protect the threatened churches because of the serious errors and heresies which would lead the churches away from the simplicity of the Gospel and into apostasy from their Lord,[291] in order that they might be ready to meet Christ Jesus with confidence at His coming, i.e., the day of jugdment (2,28; 4,17).

The heretical doctrine which led to separation,[292] is characterized by a docetic Christology,[293] and a Gnostic conception of sin and morality,[294] although it is not possible to deduce from the epistle a polemic against a particular Gnostic system.[295]

John acknowledges a direct connection between moral conduct and

290 See Luther on Rom. 7,25 (in *o.c.*, p. 98f.). Since Luther here still explains this formula to mean *peccator in re, iustus in spe* (see his explanation of *imputation* by the illustration of a gradually recovering patient) we accept Luther's formula only in his later interpretation (after 1531) of forensic imputation. Cf. W. Joest, "Paulus und das Luthersche Simul Iustus et Peccator," in *KuD* 1, (1955), 269-320. A. Nygren, *Commentary on Romans*, ET 1949, pp. 309f. D. Demmer. *Lutherus Interpres. Der theologische Neuansatz in seiner Römerbriefexegese*, 1968. On the ecclesiological application, see M. Schwintek, *Die Kirche der Sünder*, Th. Arb. XXVIII, 1969, pp. 114-119.

291 Cf. e.g. the three sentences beginning with "If we say" in 1,6.8.10; and "he who says" in 2,4.6.9. See M. de Jonge, *De Brieven van Johannes*, 1968, pp. 11-24; also his article "Geliefden, laten wij elkander liefhebben, want de liefde is uit God" (1 Joh. 4:7), in *NTT* 22 (1967/68), 352-367; esp. 356f.

292 2,19. According to A. E. Brooke, *A Crit. and Exeg. Com. on the Joh. Ep.*, ICC, 1948, p. L, the recent withdrawal of a particular party from the Church "was most probably the occasion of the First Epistle."

293 8,22-24; 4,1-3; 5,1ff. 20.

294 1,6-10; 3,3-10.

295 Cf. Du Plessis, *o.c.*, p. 174. De Jonge, *o.c.*, p. 15: "Hoe zij dit zelf christologisch en soteriologisch formuleerden, is niet helemaal duidelijk." And p. 17: "In de hier bestreden dwaalleer ontmoeten we kennelijk een vroeg stadium van het docetisme..."

Christology, and is basing his individual and social ethics on his Christology and salvation history, i.e., on the concrete, authentic, empirical life and death of Jesus Christ which was "from the beginning", 1,1-4; 2,4-6.14.[296]

In this way he contrasts the Christological-ethical dualism[297] of darkness and light – as one of sin and righteousness – with the Gnostic metaphysical dualism of divine spirit and evil matter.[298]

John interprets the specific Gnostic phrases that "God is light", and "we are in the light", "we are born of God", "we have fellowship with Him", "we have no sin", etc.[299], by his Christological soteriology. The consequence for Christian ethics therefore is clear: to *know* God is to *love* Him (4,8) to abide in Him (3,6)[300] by the *imitatio Christi* in true obedience to His commandments (2,3-6).[301]

Thus, by opposing not the Gnostic phrases as such but their ideology to divorce morality from the religious experience, John exposes the incongruity of their claims and their ethos,[302] which remainded a walk "in

296  Cf. De Jonge, *o.c.*, pp. 23f., 53. F. Hauck, *Die Kirchenbriefe*, NTD 10, 1957, p. 8.

297  De Jonge, *o.c.*, pp. 19, 49, 50ff., stresses John's Jewish-apocalyptic background in this respect, together with the typical N.T. redemptive-historical realization of salvation in Jesus Christ. Cf. O. Cullmann, *Christ and Time*, 1962 (rev. ed.), pp. 81-93 (ch. 5). Especially S. Kubo, "1 John 3:9: Absolute or Habitual?", in *AUSS* VII (1969), 47-56, esp. 48f., argues the *inadequacy* of the comparison of Jewish apocalyptic "parallels" of sinlessness with the eschatology of John: "The eschatological background of the late Jewish writings does not fully explain the situation in 1 Jn since no absolute perfection is envisaged as in those writings" (49).

298  Cf. also 1 Tim. 4,3. Hauck, *o.c.*, p. 114.

299  See C. H. Dodd, *The Johannine Epistles*, 1953³, p. XIX: "He is prepared to use such expressions, properly defined, in a fully Christian sense. It is their false and unworthy use that he reprobates." Cf. R. Bultmann, in *RGG*³ III, 838 (s.v. *Johannesbriefe*).

300  See Flew, *o.c.*, p. 102: "The knowledge of God is the Johannine term for fellowship with God. . . . By our knowledge of God we are actually in the heart of God, [quoted 1 Jn 5,20]. To know God is not a momentary experience. It is an 'abiding in God.'" It therefore seems unwarranted to interpret 3,6 ("No one who abides in him sins; no one who sins has either seen him or known him") as "Entsündigung durch Christusschau". "So wird die Entsündigung aus dem 'Eindruck der Persönlichkeit' des sündlosen Erlösers abgeleitet" (H. Windisch, *Die Katholischen Briefen*, HNT 15, 1930², p. 121).

301  See M. de Jonge, *o.c.*, p. 53.

302  De Jonge in his article, *o.c.*, 359, states that it does not appear that the „spiritual antinomianism" expressed itself in excesses, the only sin mentioned being lovelessness toward their brethren. This judgment, shared by Brooke, *o.c.*, p. L, although formally correct, certainly does not hold good for "some of the heretics (who) believed themselves to be so far above good and evil that their conduct scandalized even the easy-going censors of Roman society" (Dodd, p. XX).

Cf. also De Jonge, *o.c.*, 358: "Maar het is niet te gewaagd om te veronder-

darkness": "If we say we have fellowship with Him *while we walk in darkness, we lie and do not live according to the truth*" (1,6).

That the "Christian" Gnostics not only claimed to be reborn Christians but probably also asserted to have received an inherent sinlessness together with the new nature, seems to appear from the claims: "We have no sin", and "we have not sinned".[303] In other words, they made the claim to know God, to have fellowship with Christ, to be born of God (3,9) as children of light, and, consequently, to be righteous or perfect, in the sense of sinless. *Sin* they interpreted as ignorance, not as lawlessness or a moral relationship.[304]

In their moral indifferentism they denied the ethical imperative of the *imitatio Christi* as being superfluous, unnecessary and irrelevant for the pneumatics. Where the *psychè* had been transformed into *pneuma*, perfection was reached already in the here and now in the substance of the new nature as such.[305]

stellen dat het hier gaat om pneumatici, die zichzelf nu reeds deelgenoot achten van het rijk van de Geest, deswege neerkeken op en zich afscheidden van minder begaafden, mensen die meenden dat de geboden Gods voor hen hadden afgedaan en dat zij uit de Geest levend, *ad hoc* hun beslissingen konden nemen." It is certainly remarkable that the term *hè teleia agapè* of 1 Jn. 4,18 is used later by the Gnostics for their sexual debauchery, Ir. I, 13,6; Hipp. VI, 19,5; cf. W. Schmithals, *Paulus und die Gnostiker*, 1965, pp. 80f.

303  Cf. 1,8.10. We follow R. Schnackenburg and S. Kubo (contra Brooke and Westcott) who see no reason to depart from the meaning of sin as guiltiness, as found in the Fourth Gospel (9,41; 15,22.24; 19,11) so that the two expressions in 1,8 and 10 virtually become identical. Cf. Kubo, *o.c.*, 53: "The heretics are not saying that they are *not* guilty although they sinned, but that they are not guilty because they have *not* sinned (verse 10)."
This implies that 1 Jn 1,8 and 10 are directed not "to the situation of a genuine Christian and his occasional failings but to the claim of the heretic..." (p. 54). See also Flew, *o.c.*, p. 109. Cf. E. Gaugler, *Die Johannesbriefe*, 1964, p. 85, with respect to the Christian believer: "So sagt er nicht: Die Finsternis ist bedeutungslos. Man soll sie gar nicht ernst nehmen. So beschwindelt sich der gnostische Perfektionist" (quoted in De Jonge, *Brieven*, p. 158).
304  Dodd, *o.c.*, p. 72, referring to Rom. 6,1, overlooks the underlying Gnostic doctrine of inherent holiness; cf. his assertion: "But we need not look for any particular heretical doctrine here" (p. 72). More correct therefore is F. Büchsel, *Die Johannesbriefe*, ThHNT XVII 1933, p. 49: "Vermutlich verstanden sie die Gerechtigkeit als Wesenseigenschaft, die ihnen vermöge einer besonderen 'Natur' eigne und ihnen demgemäss auch dann verbleibe, wenn sie sündigten. Vgl. Irenäus adv haer I 6,2..."
305  This conclusion is drawn by inference from later Gnostic sources like *Corpus Hermeticum* on the presupposition that the Gnostic religiosity against which John and Paul write is basically the same. See W. Schmithals, *Paulus und die Gnostiker*, pp. 33, n. 101; 38. H. Jonas, *Gnosis und Spätantiker Geist*, II/1, 1954, pp. 49, 52. Cf. Kubo, *o.c.*, 54: "the possession of gnosis by

Moral behavior could have no influence on the *pneuma*, and deliberate[306] immoral conduct to some even testified of the certitude of their perfection and the very proof of their superiority as *pneumatikoi*.[307]

They could not sin anymore! Hence their exalted profession: "We have no sin; we have not sinned!" while they were walking in darkness, as far as the *imitatio Christi* was concerned. Thus their orthodoxy in confessing to be born of God showed itself incompatible with the apostolic orthopraxy (2,6).

In this crisis of the Church John does not introduce any new principle, but falls back with renewed emphasis on the victorious ethos of love and righteousness already manifested in Jesus Christ (2,7-17),[308] which stands in fundamental antithesis with "love for the world".[309]

The reborn child of God participates in the moral character of God, since he is anointed by the Holy One with His Spirit (2,20.27).[310] On this

means of a mystical communion with God brought them to a state of perfection." Schnackenburg, *Christliche Existenz* II, 1968, p. 101: "Sie sündigen nach ihrer Meinung nicht, weil sie eine vollkommene Gottesgemeinschaft besitzen (1,6), Gott 'erkannt' haben (2,4) und in ihm 'bleiben' (2,6)."

306   Cf. E. Schweizer, in *ThWNT* VI, 392, n. 381: "Immoralität wird darum Programm, weil sie die Unverlierbarkeit der pneumatischen Substanz am besten demonstriert (Iren Haer I 6,2)".

307   Cf. Käsemann, "Zum Thema der urchristlichen Apokalyptik", in *Exeg. Vers. und Bes.* II, pp. 105-131. He concludes: "Es darf heute ja als ausgemacht gelten, dass die dominierende Gruppe in Korinth das Erlösungsziel bereits mit der Taufe erreicht zu haben wähnte und christliches Dasein auf Erden für sie einzig noch bedeutete, himmlisches Wesen zeitlich zu repräsentieren" (p. 120). Referring to 2 Tim. 2,18 and 1 Cor. 15: "Hier leugnet ja nicht hellenistische Aufklärung die zukünftige leibliche Auferweckung, sondern ein Sakramentsrealismus, der vollkommene Erlösung schon darin erfolgt sieht, dass mit der Taufe ein himmlischer Geistleib vermittelt und der irdische Leib zur wesenlosen, vergänglichen Hülle degradiert wurde. Darin wurzeln alle Misstände in Korinth: die Verachtung der Zucht und Sitte, die mangelnde Rücksicht auf den schwächeren Bruder bei der Herrenmahlsfeier und im Alltag, die Auflehnung der ekstatisch begabten Frauen, die Überschätzung der Glossolalie und sexuellen Askese, die als Bekundungen des engelgleichen Seins betrachtet werden. Die Pneumatiker sind den Gesetzen der Psychiker, ja der Macht des Schicksals entnommen und repräsentieren nunmehr in der Welt himmlische Freiheit. Was so anthropologisch sichtbar wird, hat seinen Grund jedoch in der Christologie" (p. 121).

308   The "old" commandment is also the "new" commandment in Christ and in the Christian, 2,7-8.

309   2,15-17. Noteworthy is the sharp anti-Gnostic thesis: "If any one loves the world, love for the Father is not in him."

310   So that also the Christian's *joy* of salvation may be complete [*peplèrōmenè*] 1,4; cf. Jn. 3,29; 15,11 ("that My joy may be in you, and that your joy may be full [*plèrōthèi*]"; 16,24 ("that your joy may be full [*peplèrōmenè*]"; 17,13 (that they may have My joy fulfilled in themselves

eschatological reality (as indicative),[311] John bases his imperative:

> And now, little children, *abide in Him* ... If you know that He is righteous, you may be sure *that every one who does right is born of Him* (2,28-29).

All emphasis is concentrated on the ethico-soteriological function of the incarnation:

> You know that He appeared to take away [*arèi*] sins, and in Him there is no sin ... The reason the Son of God appeared was to destroy [*lysèi*] the works of the devil (3,5.8).[312]

And based on this Christology there then follows the soteriological indicative, in fundamental and irreconcilable antithesis with the Gnostic hamartiology:

> No one born of God commits sin, for His Seed [*sperma*][313] abides in him, and he cannot sin because he is born of God (3,9).

This expression needs to be understood in the light of the intentional sharp antithesis of the whole letter between light and darkness, sin and righteousness, life and death apart from any qualification within the Christian existence.[314]

---

[peplèrōmenèn]"). Here the Christian faith exceeds the Rabbinical expectation of "completed joy" in the future age, see *Str-B* II, 429, 566.

311  Cf. G. Delling, in *ThWNT* VI, 296, 20ff. (s.v. *plèroō*).

312  See J. Heise, *Bleiben. Menein in den Johanneischen Schriften*, 1967, p. 146: "Das Tun der Sünde ist verstanden nicht als etwas Beliebiges, was frei gewollt oder auch unterlassen werden kann, sondern als etwas dem Menschen Aufgezwungenes. Deshalb kann es sich in der Sendung des Sohnes auch nicht nur um die Reinigung und Erlassung von Sünden, sondern es muss sich um die absolute Beseitigung und Auflösung der Macht der Sünde handeln... Die Sendung des Sohnes ist das eschatologische Ereignis, in dem die Sünde ihre alle umfassende Macht verlor, denn vom Sohn gilt: *hamartia en autōi ouk estin* (Vs 5b), er ist *der Gerechte*".

313  The RSV translates *sperma* here with "nature", by which the sense is given a static metaphysical purport.

314  Cf. Preisker, *o.c.*, p. 207, concerning 1 Jn. 3,9: "Himmlische Lebensgewalt und Sündigen kann und darf er nicht in einem Atemzug und nicht nebeneinander denken und aussprechen." F. Hauck, *o.c.*, p. 135: "Gotteskinder und Teufelskinder sind als reine Gegensätze bezeichnet. All Zwischenstufen, dass auch in der Seele des Frommen ein Ringen, in der Seele des Unfrommen ein Sehnen statt hat, sind ausser Betracht gelassen (Röm. 7,24f.). Denn nicht den Kampf, der in der Brust des Menschen stattfindet, will er schildern, sondern die tiefe, entgegengesetzte Wesensbestimmtheit, die in der einen und anderen Seele statt hat, will er aufweisen."

Sakae Kubo [315] elucidates this point very well:

> Sin is what the heretic does; righteousness is what the Christian does. The verse needs to be understood in this sharp contrast. There are only two sides, and for the moment there are no gradations or intermediate stages between or within them. Either you sin and are a heretic, a member of the forces of darkness and of the devil, or you do not sin and are a Christian and member of the forces of right and of God. To say in this context that the author means only that the Christian does not habitually sin is appreciably to weaken his point. He cannot and he does not sin because he is a child of God.

What does John mean by the qualification *"one born* of God"? Using this designation in 2,29; 3,9; 4,7; 5,1.4.18 (all in the perf. pass.) as a present reality, he describes this redemptive reality in religious-moral and ultimately in Christological terms: he does right (2,29); he commits no sin, (3,9; 5,18); he loves (4,7); he believes in Jesus as the Christ (5,1); he overcomes the world (5,4).

It is significant that John in 3,4-10 stresses the dynamic religious-ethical correlation between the believer who abides in Christ (vs. 6), and God's Seed (or Spirit of Christ) who abides in the child of God (vs. 9b); in other words, the moral communion of God and the believer in Christ.[316] But what is more, John bases the impossibility of the believers' sinning not in the Christian as such, but in the transforming and keeping [317] presence of God's Seed,[318] i.e., in the *Christus praesens* who is "greater than he who is in the world" (4,4). In other words, the decisive qualification of the one born of God is his personal fellowship with God in

---

315  *O.c.*, p. 50 (see above, n. 297).

316  Also Bultmann, *Die drei Johannesbriefe*, 1967, pp. 57f., indicates that freedom from sin is conditioned in vs. 6 by the *menein* of the believer in God, while in vs. 9 by the *menein* of God's seed (Spirit) in the believer. Concerning this redemptive correlation he states: "Geschenk und Forderung gehören in der Weise zusammen, dass es das eine nicht ohne das andere gibt, jedoch so, dass das Geschenk das erste ist, das die christliche Existenz begründet" (p. 58).

317  Cf. 5,18.

318  Cf. Hauck, *o.c.*, p. 135. R. Schnackenburg, *Die Johannesbriefe*, pp. 190f., 176f., suggests too sharp a contrast between Spirit and Word in the Johannine concept of *sperma*: "Die Joh. Texte halten sich ausschliesslich an die Analogie der Zeugung und sehen als Zeugenden Gott bzw. das Pneuma an. Die Wort-Gottes-Theologie verbindet sich in Joh. und 1 Joh. nicht mit dem Zeugungsgedanken" (p. 177). Dodd, *The Joh. Ep.*, pp. 77f., however, supposes that the author associates (e.g. 1 Jn 2,24) "seed" with the Word of God, or the Gospel, in the light of the "fairly well established association of the ideas 'seed' and 'word'". Most satisfactory is S. Schultz in *ThWNT* VII, 545,31 (s.v. *sperma*): "als Same Gottes jetzt den *Geist* meint, der sich in seinem Wort offenbart".

232

Christ.[319] John is emphatically upholding the incompatability of the Spirit of Christ in the Christian with sin and immorality, the walk in darkness.

The incompatability and impossibility of co-existence of light and darkness is stressed again in 1 Jn. 4,20:

> In any one *says*, "I love God", and hates his brother, he is *a liar*; for he who does not love his brother whom he has seen, *cannot* [*ou dynatai*] love God whom he has not seen.

To John this fundamental antithesis is to be identified with the contrast of *life and death* (3,14). To have real fellowship (*koinōnia*) with God, to John means much more than a formal confession of faith or a profession in the abstract of philosophical enlightenment or mystical ecstacy or even ethical idealism.

Fellowship or communion with God and fellowmen means to him the transforming and continuing *imitatio Dei in Christo* as manifested in the cultic ethos of holiness and love:

> but if we walk [*peripatein*[320]] in the light, *as He is in the light*, we have fellowship with one another, and the blood of Jesus his Son *cleanses* us from all sin (1,7).

To John the life of holiness is to be lived on the level of miracle.[321]

The impossibility of sinning therefore to John does not spring forth from any inherent metaphysical quality but from the reality of the victorious[322] and cleansing union of faith with the Crucified and Risen One who is essentially holy and righteous.[323] In this sense the "impossibility"

---

319  See Büchsel, *Joh. briefe*, p. 52: "Für die ganze Beweisführung in 4-6 und 7-8 ist bezeichnend, dass die Unmöglichkeit des Sündetuns der Christen von Christus, nicht von den Christen aus bewiesen wird. Ein Umgewandeltsein des Wesens der Christen als solches wird nicht behauptet, aber ihre Sündlosigkeit wird aus der Beziehung, die Christus zu ihnen hat, geschlossen. Das salus nostra posita extra nos bleibt gerade hier, wo salus im vollsten Sinne als bei den Christen vorhanden behauptet wird, aufrecht erhalten. Die Sündlosigkeit der Christen ist nur im Urteil des Glaubens an Christus behauptet und nur als Glaubensbesitz vorhanden." Cf. also Büchsel in *ThWNT* I, 669f. (s.v. *gennaō*).

320  While *peripatein* in extra-Biblical Greek has no moral connotation, this verb in the N.T., and in John's letter in particular, carries a religious-moral character, and denotes the general ethos of the covenant (*hālak* in LXX); Büchsel, *Joh. briefe*, p. 18. See Seesemann, in *ThWNT* V, 944, 14ff. (s.v. *(peri) pateō*).

321  Cf. Flew, *o.c.*, p. 116.

322  See 5,4.

323  5,6. Cf. Flew, *o.c.*, pp. 110f.: "It is of the essence of that experience that they should walk with a Person Who is perfectly righteous and they must be like Him (I. 111. 7; cf. I. 11.29)". Heise, *o.c.*, p. 123: "In Jesus bleiben ist

is qualified cultically by the forgiving and cleansing power of the mediating *Paraclètos* with the Father and our faith in the Son which *overcomes* the world.[324] We are struck here by the underlying unity and continuity with the religious-cultic ethos of the Psalms, specifically of the entrance liturgy as expressed in Psalm 15,1-2.[325]

As in Psalm 15, participation in the cultic cleansing from sin by the blood of the Lamb is not based on the Torah ethos but placed in an unbreakable, living correlation with the social ethos of righteousness and love as established by the new-covenant cultus: the walk in the light as He is in the light.

This Christological cultic relationship recognizes that the reborn child of God *continues* to confess his sins and receive forgiveness and cleansing (1,9),[326] even *while* walking in the light (1,7).[327]

Since this walk in the light is basically the same as the *perfect* walk with and before God in the old-covenant cultus, the moral ethos of John ("No one born of God commits sin, for His Seed abides in him, and he cannot sin because he is born of God") can and may be compared with the ethical description of the perfect ones in Ps. 37,31: "The law of his God is in his heart; his steps do not slip";[328] and Ps. 40,8: "I delight to do Thy will, O my God; Thy law is within my heart".[329]

And just as the old-covenant perfection did not consist of an inherent sinless nature but the living, sanctifying fellowship and walk with God

---

nicht Bewegungslosigkeit, sondern peripatein kathōs ekeinos periepatèsen." Büchsel, in *ThWNT* I, 670, 16ff., makes the enlightening remark: "Als parallele Vorstellung muss man die von der Teufelskindschaft der Juden J 8,34-47 vergleichen. Auch diese ist wesentlich etwas Sittliches, sie beweist sich in Lüge und Mord. Auch sie ist ein persönliches Gemeinschafts- bzw Abhängigkeits-verhältnis."

324  See 1 Jn. 2,1; 1,9; 5,4f. On the meaning of *kosmos*, cf. De Jonge, *o.c.*, pp. 91-95, referring to 1 Jn. 2,16. Schnackenburg, *o.c.* I, 160-171; II, 103f.

325  See above, Ch. III, B, 2b.

326  Noteworthy is the present tense *katharisèi*, cf. De Jonge, *o.c.*, p. 58.

327  Cf. De Jonge, *o.c.*, p. 58: "De dwaalleraren zeggen in het licht te zijn en dus niet te zondigen. Echter ook juist in het licht zijn we aangewezen op zondevergeving, daardoor kunnen we telkens weer in het licht en uit het licht leven." Bultmann, *o.c.*, p. 28: "Ist das Sein des Gnostikers ein statisches, so ist das christliche Sein ein dynamisches. Dem Gnostiker ist durch seine Gnosis seine Zugehörigkeit zum Licht der Gottheit ... ein für allemal zum Besitz geworden. Der Christ hat durch seinem Glauben das Licht nie als dauernden Besitz erworben. Er hat seinen Glauben im *peripatein* zu bewähren, ist immer unterwegs und steht nie als ein Fertiger vor Gott sondern ist auf Vergebung angewiesen".

328  See above, Ch. III, B, 2c; cf. Ps. 18,36.

329  Cf. also Rom. 8,7-8; cf. De Jonge, *o.c.*, p. 157: "Zoals de 'vleselijke mens' de wet niet kan vervullen, zo kan de geestelijke mens ook niet zondigen hij is 'dood voor de zonde' (Rom. 6:2)."

in wholehearted obedience to His will as revealed in the Torah, i.e., of the experience of forgiving and restraining grace,[330] so John does not intend to say that the *walk in the light* is the result of a sinless nature which cannot sin as such.[331] This appears clear from his consolation in 2,1:

> My little children, I am writing this to you so that you may not sin, *but if any one does sin*, we have an advocate with the Father, Jesus Christ the righteous.[332]

This comforting message is not intended to be an excuse for sinning or for a walk in darkness, but reveals the consciousness that also in the reborn children of God the sinful nature still is at work always trying to regain the supremacy.[333]

John distinguishes between two categories of sin in basically the same way as in the hamartiology of the old-covenant cultus, e.g. Num. 15,27-31, and of the Psalms.[334]

There is a basic difference for John between sin within the walk in darkness, and sin within the walk in the light. These sins might be designated cultically as deliberate, presumptuous sin[335] and unintentional sin, i.e., all sin which is repented of. John himself designates them in 5,16f. as "a mortal sin" which is hopeless because man himself has radically broken with God[336] and "sin which is not mortal" which can be forgiven.

---

330  Ps. 19,13f.; see above, Ch. III, B, 2b.

331  Cf. De Jonge, *ad* 1 Jn. 3,9; p. 154: "Gave en opgave blijven onafscheidelijk verbonden; 'niet-kunnen-zondigen' betekent niet automatische zondeloosheid." R. Schnackenburg, *Die Johannesbriefe*, 1963², p. 191: "Das 'Bleiben' des Gottessamens im Menschen (V 9a) fordert zu seiner Ergänzung den Imperativ, in Gottes Art zu bleiben (4,16)."

332  See also 1 Jn. 5,16. Cf. S. Kubo, *o.c.* ,p. 50: "In the idealistic context of 1 Jn 3:9, the Christian cannot sin, but in the realistic context of 2:1, he may. It is possible for a Christian to sin; but this possibility must not qualify 3:9, and thus weaken and even destroy the author's argument." F. Hauck, *o.c.*, p. 136, compares 1 Jn. 3,9 with 1 Jn. 1,8-10 in the first passage of which John calls attention to "das Grundsätzliche", in the second to "das Tatsätzliche", in polemical contrast with the heretical claims.

333  This also appears from 3,19-20, where John deals with the accusing and condemning heart. Cf. Flew, *o.c.*, p. 114: "Perhaps our author has in mind some whose tortured consciences condemn them because of their own failures." Schnackenburg, *o.c.* II, 103, with respect to 1 Jn. 2,16: "Bei aller Formelhaftigkeit liegt darin ein Wissen um destruktive Neigungen des menschlichen Herzens."

334  See above, Ch. III, B, 2b Schnackenburg, *o.c.* II, 116-122 ("Sünde zum Tod und Sünde nicht zum Tod") neglects this O.T. connection.

335  Cf. also Heb. 10,26.

336  See F. Hauck, *o.c.*, p. 152: "Da unserm Verfasser 'das Leben' in der Gottesgemeinschaft besteht, ist 'Sundigen zum Tode' ein solches, das in der

And immediately after this distinction of sin in two categories John repeats as it were 3,9 when he states:

> We know that any one born of God *does not sin*, but He who was born of God [Christ [337]] *keeps* him, and the evil one does not touch him (5,18).

Here the cause of not sinning in the life of the Christian is explicitly indicated: not the power of the human will or any inherent holiness, but the gracious keeping power of Christ, the Son of God, who is "the true God and eternal life" (5,20).[338]

In the light of the previous hamartiological distinction it becomes transparent what John has meant all the way through by the impossibility of sinning. The Christian cannot sin in mortal sin, i.e., presumptuous sin, because the child of God is being *kept* from this way of sinning by the forgiving and restraining grace, the indwelling Spirit of Christ. The child of God is no longer under the overruling power of the evil one, as the world still is (5,18-19); he is now living in Christ (5,20).

The crucial point in 1 Jn. 3,9 for us is that John is not teaching the doctrine of an inherent holiness or sinlessness, but continues the soteriology and hamartiology of the old-covenant cultus. Only, in the new salvation-historical epoch of Messianic fulfillment the walk with God is now realized exclusively in the walk with Christ, the Son of God, who as the Word of life or the Spirit is also living and reigning within the heart of the believer through the apostolic kerygma. This ultimate purpose is stated not only at the end of the letter (5,20), but already at the beginning:

> so that you may have fellowship with us, and our fellowship is with the Father and with His Son Jesus Christ ... that our joy may be complete (1,3f.).

bb) 2 Peter 1,4: *and become partakers [koinōnoi] of the divine nature [theias physeōs].*

This phrase, containing the hapax legomenon *theia physis* which can only be explained by its context,[339] forms part of a greater passage in

---

völligen bewussten und entschlossenen Verneinung der Gottes- und Christus-Gemeinschaft besteht (vgl. Hebr. 6,4-6)... Wo der Mensch selbst mit Gott gebrochen hat, da will der Verfasser nicht, dass Fromme für ihn eintreten soll (vgl. 1 Sam. 2,25; Jer. 7,16; 11,14; 14,11f.)".

337   Cf. De Jonge, *o.c.*, pp. 228f.

338   Cf. Hauck, *o.c.*, pp. 153f.

339   Bo Reicke, *The Epistles of James, Peter and Jude*, "The Anchor Bible", 1964, understands *theia physis* as "an accommodation to popular Greek philosophy, esp. Stoicism... in order to emphasize the same point that Paul

which the motivating subject is God's "divine power" (*theia dynamis*, 1,2) concentrated in "His precious and very great promises" (1,4) given for the specific purpose

> that through these you may escape from the corruption that is in the world because of passion, and become partakers of the divine nature (1,4).

This shows that the phrase "partakers of the divine nature" is placed in contrast with "escaping [*apophygontes*] the corruption that is in the world because of passion [*tès en tōi kosmōi en epithymiai phtoras*]".

The wider context of the letter reveals that the *epithymiai*, in harmony with the rest of the New Testament,[340] stand for the fleshly lusts or defiling passions (cf. 2,10.8; 3,3), which are placed, however, in the framework of the false religious teaching of libertinism (2,1ff.19[341]; 3,3ff.), to be compared with the philosophy of the antediluvian world and of Sodom and Gomorrah (2,5ff.).

The author stresses the necessity of *fruitfulness* in the righteousness of God and the knowledge of the Savior Jesus Christ, in order to find "an entrance into the eternal kingdom of our Lord and Savior Jesus Christ" (1,1-11).

He unfolds this required fruitfulness in the knowledge of the Lord Jesus by way of a systematic unfolding of character perfection (1,5-8).

The appeal to this activity in virtue, self-control, steadfastness, godliness and brotherly love is not based on any ethical autonomy but explicitly in God's powerful "precious and very great promises" and in the *cleansing* from the "old sins" by Christ Jesus (1,3f.9). Moreover, thus human co-operation in sanctification is described as a *confirmation* of the prevenient call and election of God, "for if you do this you will never fall" (1,10).

Here we are reminded of the imagery of walking in the way of the perfect ones in Israel's cultus (cf. Pss. 15,5b; 37,31).

Just as the entrance liturgy in its cultus offered and required the perfect heart and walk (Ps. 15,1-2) for the dwelling of the believer with God on His holy hill, so in 2 Peter 1 the same covenant promises are

---

expresses by relating how a convert is freed from the world through baptism, is clothed in Christ, and *becomes* a new man (Rom. VI 5; Eph. IV 22ff.)" (p. 153; cf. also p. XXXVI).

On the basic difference between Philo's soteriology and that of the gospels with respect to *physis*, see J. N. Sevenster, *Het verlossingsbegrip bij Philo*, 1936, pp. 149f.

340   Cf. also 1 Pet. 1,14; 2,11; 4,2f.; Jud. 16.18; 1 Jn. 2,16f.; Gal. 5,16.24; Eph. 2,3; 4,22.

341   These false teachers promise freedom "but they themselves are slaves of corruption [*tès phthoras*]", 2,19; cf. 2,12.

continued and acknowledged to lead to the divine *doxa* and *aretè*, i.e., the *theia physis*.

In the light of the Old Testament covenant this participation in the *theia physis* may be regarded as identical with the cultic *imitatio Dei*.

This phrase therefore does not indicate a deification of human nature by an inherent sinlessness or a supernatural or divine substance,[342] but the *promised* transformation of the sin-dominated heart into the divine character of holy love and righteousness. Materially the phrase is identical with the cultic imperative of the old covenant, which is applied to the Christian Church in 1 Pet. 1,15f.: "You shall be holy, for I am holy".

An enlightening similarity between 1 and 2 Peter is the objective of the covenant God with His new-covenant people.

1 Peter applies the purpose of Israel's election to that of the Christians: "that you may declare [*exaggeilète*] the virtues [*tas aretas*][343] of Him who called you out of darkness into His marvelous light" (2,9).

2 Peter 1,3-7 may be regarded as a more extensive repetition of 1 Peter 2,9. Again God is introduced as calling us, but now "to His own glory [*idiai doxèi*] and virtue [*aretèi*][344] (2 Pet. 1,3). This specific call is summarized in vs. 4 as to become "partakers of the divine nature" through the covenant promises.

The whole scope of both 1 and 2 Peter reveals the practical nature of the knowledge of God and Christ in the way of sanctification. The actual behavior or moral conduct[345] is motivated by gracious fellowship with God in Christ. Both letters, moreover, are especially concerned with the nature of *progressive* sanctification: "that by it [sc. the pure spiritual milk] you may *grow up to salvation* [*auxèthète eis sōtèrian*]" (1 Pet.

---

342   Cf. G. C. Berkouwer, *Conflict met Rome*, 1949², pp. 228f. Even in the RC exegesis it is acknowledged that humanity is not deified in the speculative ontological way of Greek idealism.

See A. Hulsbosch, "De Genade in het N.T.", in *Genade en Kerk*, 1953, pp. 97f. Hauck, *ad loc*, still interprets the term *theia physis* as implying the Greek concept of liberation from the "earthly-corporeal" body.

*Schneider, ad loc.*, identifies participation in the *theia physis* with freedom from "die fleischliche, der Sinnenlust unterworfene sündige Art des natür-lichen Menschen" (p. 104), which the Christian will receive in the eschatological *visio Dei*. However, this interpretation denies the soteriological truth and reality of the present freedom from the dominion of sinful passions through the knowledge of the Savior; see 2 Pet. 1,4; 2,19-20; 3,11.14.

343   RSV: the wonderful deeds. See Bauernfeind, in *ThWNT* I, 460f., who rightly refers to Is. 42,8.12; 43,21; 63,7 LXX to interpret *aretè* here by *doxa*.

344   RSV: excellence.

345   Notable is the conspicuous function of te term *anastrophè* in 1 Pet. 1,15.18; 2,12; 3,1f.16; 2 Pet. 2,7; 3,11. In Heb. 13,7 the outcome of the life (*anastrophè*) of the Christian leaders is made the *criterion* by which to imitate their faith, *mimeisthe tèn pistin*. Cf. also 1 Tim. 4,12; Js. 3,13.

2,2); "But *grow* [*auxanete*] in the grace and knowledge of our Lord and Savior Jesus Christ" (2 Pet. 3,18).[346]

In this contextual relationship the partaking of the divine nature or character of glorious virtue is described in 2 Petr. 1,5ff. as the way of progressive sanctification which leads assuredly through the entrance into the eternal kingdom (vs. 11).

The following series of virtues, starting with faith and ending with love, is not intended to suggest a synthesis of disconnected virtues which one after another must be attained. The repeated grammatical construction of the new virtue with the previous one by means of the preposition *en* indicates that each virtue is rooted in, and in germ contained[347] in, the previous one, that is, ultimately all virtues are contained in *pistis*.

The tenor of the enumeration of *aretè, gnōsis, egkrateia, hypomonè, eusebeia, philadelphia* and *agapè* then can be no other than to emphasize the call to cultivate and unfold fully the grace and knowledge of Christ as Savior into efficaciousness and variegated fruitfulness.[348]

In other words, only when all these divine virtues are manifested in the concrete reality of the individual and social ethos do the Christians partake of the divine nature in reality. If these virtues of faith are lacking, the old sins are not really cleansed or subdued:

> For whoever lacks these things is blind and shortsighted and has forgotten that he was cleansed[349] from his old sins (2 Pet. 1,9).

This leads us to the conclusion that 2 Pet. 1 identifies the partaking of the divine nature with the cultic cleansing through the blood of Christ.[350]

This implies the dynamic *imitatio Dei in Christo*, i.e., the life or ethos of holiness and godliness (2 Pet. 3,11).

---

346   Cf. also Col. 1,10 as the life worthy (*axiōs*) of the Lord, fully pleasing to Him (*eis pasan areskeian*); 2,19 in the corporative sense, as rooted in the Head, Christ; also Eph. 2,21; 4,15; 2 Cor. 10.15. Noteworthy is the remark of W. H. Velema, *De Geestelijke Groei van de Gemeente*, p. 30: "Groei drukt vooruit uit, dat de voortgang bij het leven behoort, niet te organiseren is door mensen, en daarom Gods zaak is." See 1 Cor. 3,7. Cf. B. Reicke, *o.c.*, p. 154.

347   Cf. H. von Soden, *Briefe des Petrus*, ThHNT 1899[3], p. 216.

348   See 2 Pet. 1,8; cf. Gal. 5,6.22f. (as the fruit of the Spirit!); 1 Cor. 9,25-27. B. Reicke, *o.c.*, pp. 154f., therefore is justified in stating: "A detailed list of such ethical relationships is presented. Some of these constituted wellknown Hellenistic ideals and were esp. prominent in the propaganda of the Stoic philosophers; the author seems to have borrowed them from his contemporaries. However, they have been transplanted into the structure of Christian faith."

349   A reference to baptism (B. Reicke).

350   Cf. also 1 Pet. 1,2.

Here the apostolic ethos of perfection reveals again its basic continuity and spiritual unity with the cultic perfection of the old covenant.

cc) Hebrews 10,2: Otherwise, would they not have ceased to be offered? If the worshipers had once been cleansed [*hapax kekatharismenous*], they would no longer have any consciousness of sin [*syneidèsin hamartiōn*].

Does this verse substantiate the idea that the superior glory of the new-covenant mediation of the Lord Jesus Christ – in contrast with the Levitical sanctuary service – provides for such a cleansing from sin that the Christian believer may experience the total absence of the consciousness of sin, i.e., the assurance of ethical perfection or sinlessness?

With such a preconceived idea one may try to find support for it in the apparent meaning of the words isolated from their context. The context, however, should determine the specific content of each phrase.

All commentaries bring out the salvation-historical theme of Hebrews which stresses the shadow character of the Levitical sanctuary service, with its many repeated animal sacrifices. These could only function as a temporary indicator and prophecy of the coming, all-sufficient atoning sacrifice of the incarnate Son of God, 10,1.5-9. On the basis of this salvation-historical fulfillment of the typological cultic ritual, the Son of God has appeared "once for all" [*hapax*], "to put away sin by the sacrifice of himself" (9,26), "having made purification for sins" [*katharismon tōn hamartiōn poièsamenos*] (1,3).

The emphatically presented antithesis between the impotency and inefficacy[351] of the whole Mosaic system of mediation by means of the blood of the many repeated sacrificial animals, on the one hand, and the abiding perfect efficacy of Christ's offering of His body once for all,[352]

---

351 Already recognized in the O.T.: 1 Sam. 15,22; Ps. 50,8ff.; 51,16ff.; Hos. 6,6; Is. 1,10ff.; Jer. 7,21f.
Cf. H. Montefiore, *A Commentary on the Ep. to the Hebrews*, 1964, p. 164: "In fact the levitical sacrifices can only cleanse ritual sins (IX. 13), and they can never, even for a moment, effect a perfectly clear conscience (IX. 9)".

352 Cf. B. F. Westcott, *The Epistle to the Hebrews*, 1955 (1889), *ad* 10,2; pp. 305f.: "The inefficacy of the sacrifices is proved by their repetition. If it be said that the repeated sacrifice dealt only with the later sins; the answer is that we have to deal with sin and not with sins only: to be assured that our true relation with God has been re-established. A sacrifice which effects this for humanity, and we need no less, cannot be repeated."

H. van Oyen, *De Brief aan de Hebreeën*, 1962³, p. 158: "De opmerking, dat ten gevolge van de hernieuwde zonden hernieuwde offers noodzakelijk waren, kan op de schrijver geen indruk maken, daar de zonde niet door hem incidenteel, geatomiseerd gedacht wordt, maar als een schuldig zijn van de ganse mens voor God, een prijsgegeven zijn aan de overmacht der zonde, waarvan men als een doem moet worden bevrijd."

on the other hand, is applied to the subjective redemptive experience of the worshipper with respect to his *consciousness of sin*. It is the conscience [*syneidèsis*][353] which the blood of the old-covenant sacrifices could never *cleanse* [*katharizein*] (9,14) or *perfect* [*teleioun*] (9,9; 10,1). The author evidently identifies the theological meaning of a *cleansed* (purified) conscience and a *perfect* conscience.[354]

Such a conscience he simply calls a good or "clear" conscience [*kalè syneidèsis*][355] (3,18), in contrast with an "evil" conscience [*ponèra syneidèsis*] (10,22). This evil conscience could never be perfected or cleansed from its "dead works" (9,14), i.e., sinful works (6,1), or from the condemning and accusing self-infliction, by the repetition of animal sacrifices. On the contrary, these could only serve as "a reminder of sin year after year" [*anamnésis hamartiōn kat'eniauton*] (10,3).

This cultic reminder of sin has to be taken not in the sense of mere intellectual or moral reflection but in the Hebrew sense[356] of a burdened, smiting heart[357] or haunting guilt-consciousness, which became most pronounced on the Day of Atonement.[358] This sin-remembering function of the whole Mosaic ritual all year round is further enhanced by the self-evident *impossibility* of animal blood to "take away sins", [*aphairein hamartias*] (vs. 4).[359]

---

353  Cf. Westcott, *o.c.*, p. 293, on the N.T. idea of *syneidèsis*. On the reason why the O.T. has no word explicitly for conscience, see Maurer, in *ThWNT* VII, 906f. (s.v. *synoida*).

354  Cf. also O. Michel, *Der Brief an die Hebräer*, Meyers Kommentar, 1966[12], p. 333, in note 4, comparing Heb. 9,14 and 9,9: "Reinigung ist also identisch mit Vollendung."

355  Maurer, *ThWNT* VII, 907, 25-35, rightly indicates that the idea of personal purity of heart is rooted in the atoning cultus; and that the O.T. concept of a "clean" or "pure heart" (Pss. 51,10; 24,4; 73,1; Prov. 22,11) lies at the foundation of the N.T. concept of a "clear conscience."

356  Cf. Michel, *o.c.*, pp. 332f., n. 4; stating on p. 334: "*anamnèsis* (im N.T. hier und 1 Kor. 11,24; Lk. 22,19) ist nicht nur Erinnerung, sondern auch Erwähnung (vulg. commemoratio). Kündendes Wort und sich vollziehendes Handeln können im kultischen Ereignis zur 'Erinnerung' werden."

357  Cf. 2 Sam. 24,10: "But David's heart smote him..."; cf. 1 Sam. 24,5.

358  See Lev. 23,27-32. Cf. F. F. Bruce, *The Epistle to the Hebrews*, NICNT, 1967[2], pp. 227f.: "If the old sacrificial order had possessed true cleansing efficacy – that is to say, if it had been able to cleanse the conscience – then the worshippers would have enjoyed unrestricted communion with God. It is the presence of sin in the conscience that hinders such communion; 'if I regard iniquity in my heart', said the psalmist, 'the Lord will not hear' (Ps. 66:18)". Cf. Westcott, *o.c.*, p. 305, on *kat'eniauton*.

359  Michel, *o.c.*, p. 334, interprets this *apharein* as forgiveness, since this verb "ist im A.T. ein gebräuchlicher Ausdruck für die Vergebung (Ex. 34,7.9) und Tilgung der Sünden (Lev. 10,17), weist daher an dieser Stellen auf die Verwendung der Opfersprache im Hebr. hin." Although these O.T. references, together with many from the Psalms (e.g. Ps. 32), indicate the reality of

The religious need of the repentant worshipper can only be met in the perfect sacrifice of Jesus Christ whose blood alone can fulfill the reality of the covenant promises [360] of Jer. 31,33-34; Ez. 36,25f., which culminate in the divine blessing: "I will remember their sins and their misdeeds no more".[361]

Again this promise implies not the intellectual oblivion of sins in God but the gracious freedom from condemnation, because He no longer counts or reckons the sins against the covenant believers (cf. Ez. 33,16), owing to the all-sufficient sacrifice of Jesus Christ.

The final conclusion of the author is, therefore, that this freedom from condemnation in the conscience is now proffered and experienced in the redemptive reality of forgiveness of sins because of the single sacrifice of Christ's body.[362] This glorious present reality necessarily makes any other offering, and with that the whole Mosaic ritual, superfluous:

> Where there is forgiveness of these [see v. 17], there is no longer any offering for sin (vs. 18).

When the sacrificial blood of Jesus Christ is continually efficacious to bring the worshippers, through the cleansing of forgiveness, into the right relationship with God and to serve Him, their conscience can no longer trust in sacrificial animals and Levitical priests. If the Levitical sacrifices had had intrinsic, i.e. "once for all", efficacy to cleanse the conscience, the same sacrifice could *not* have been repeated continually.[363]

---

forgiving grace in the old covenant, which the author of Hebrews basically does not deny (4,1f.; 11,1), the scope of his intention is to reveal the *obsolete* character of the Mosaic offerings in the light of the efficacious reality of the perfect offering of Christ Himself (8,13). In the light of their glorious fulfillment, he exposes the radical powerlessness of animal sacrifices to cleanse the conscience from guilt.

Cf. H. Strahtmann, *Der Brief an die Hebr.*, NTD 9, 1954[7], *ad* 10,2; p. 127.

360　See Bruce, *o.c.*, pp. 172ff., on the three aspects of the new-covenant relationship with God: a) the implanting of God's law in their hearts; b) the knowledge of God as a matter of personal experience; c) the blotting out of their sins.

361　On the Hebrew sense of "remembering", see Bruce, *o.c.*, p. 175.

362　Cf. also Eph. 1,17.

363　J. Héring, *L'Épitre aux Hébreux*, CNT XII, 1954, *ad* 10,2, p. 94, who concludes that the reiteration of the Jewish sacrifices was necessary "non pas seulement parce que l'homme continue à pécher, mais aussi parce qu'il n'est jamais sûr d'avoir obtenu le pardon," misses the point since the proper Levitical declarative cleansing from sin was the unquestionable assurance of forgiveness, Lev. 4,26.35. The decisive argument of Heb. 10 is not the *subjective* feeling of the worshipper as such, although it may seem so in vs. 2, but the *objective* validity and efficacy *coram Deo* of the animal offerings which, because of their endless repetition, proclaim their own complete insufficiency as a foundation for *divine* cleansing or forgiveness.

*One* sacrifice then would have been continually all-sufficient to cleanse the troubled conscience from condemnation. If the worshippers had been cleansed or forgiven on the basis of the efficacy of an animal sacrifice itself, then "they would no longer have any conscience of sin" (10,2), and would have found rest from the accusings of their troubled conscience by trust in the sacrifices themselves. Now that Jesus Christ has appeared, and His sacrifice and priesthood are the appointed reality and fulfillment of the whole Mosaic ritual, the futility and inadequacy of trust in the shadowy sacrifices in order to obtain a perfect conscience, i.e., a pure and holy heart, are all the more exposed.[364] Only trust in Christ's sacrificial blood as "the blood of the covenant" (10,29; cf. Mt. 26,28) can lead to the continual experience of a perfect conscience, i.e., a conscience which has a perfect relationship with God, because it is cleansed from the guilt and defiling power of unforgiven[365] sin (9,14).[366] This establishes the superiority, the more powerful efficacy of the new covenant. The fact that Hebrews is emphasizing so much the perfection of the heart or *conscience* implies that the cultic perfection of the new covenant does not provide for perfection of the *flesh* or body in the Christian believer. This *ever-abiding* efficacy of Christ's all-sufficient offering of His body is stressed repeatedly by the *perfect tenses* in Heb. 10,10 and 14.

The three perfects: cleansed[367] (vs. 2), sanctified (vs. 10) and perfected (vs. 14) do not primarily indicate the way of progressive sanctifi-

---

364 Cf. J. Schneider, *The Letter to the Hebrews*, p. 96: 'Here [sc. in Hebrews] for the first time in the history of Christianity the cult of the Old Covenant is illuminated in such a way as to make its true character understandable. The Old Covenant can only be judged and understood in the light of Christ. That is the important insight which the author of the letter of Hebrews conveys to us. He places the Old Covenant into the whole chain of the history of salvation."

365 That Hebrews considers cleansing and forgiveness as synonymous terms follows from 9,22.

Cf. Michel, *o.c.*, *ad* 10,2; p. 332: "das Bewusstsein um die Sünden als unvergebener Schuld". H. Strathmann, *o.c.*, *ad* 10,2; p. 127: "the unrest of the evil conscience". O. Kuss, *Der Brief an die Hebr.*, RNT 8/1, 1966, *ad* 10,2; p. 139: "dem lastenden Druck der Sünde." A. W. Pink, *An Exposition of Hebrews*, II, 1954, *ad* Heb. 10,22; p. 96: "An 'evil conscience' is one that accuses of guilt and oppresses because of unpardoned sin."

366 Cf. Hauck, in *ThWNT* III, 430, 2ff. (s.v. *katharos*): "Der Opfertod Christi wirkt so eine Reinigung von Sünden (1,3) und Befreiung von den sündigen Trieben (9,14: *nekra erga*, beflekkende im Gegensatz zu den im Dienst Gottes geschehenden)". Also Michel, *o.c.*, p. 333.

367 Cf. also 2 Pet. 1,9. Michel, *o.c.*, *ad* Heb. 10,2, p. 333: "Gemeint ist das innere Wissen um das Urteil Gottes über den Menschen. *Hapax kekatharismenous* weist darauf hin, dass eine einmalige und totale Reinigung erfolgen muss, die nicht nur von der vergangenen Schuld befreit, sondern auch einen neuen *Anfang* im Leben des Menschen setzt."

cation but point to the reality of the completed sacrifice of Jesus Christ. His offering alone can effect perfect cleansing, i.e., perfect forgiveness, and perfect sanctification, and imparts this perfection *now* as the divine redemptive rest to all who draw near to God through Christ.[368]

This actuality is confirmed by the two participial phrases *rherantismenoi* and *lelousmenoi* in 10,22, which are veiled allusions to the one-time act of baptism[369] by which the believer has been washed and therefore is "clean all over".[370]

The worshippers are established in a perfect relationship of peace with God or not at all; they are cleansed from sins or not at all. Hebrews 10,10.14 is therefore not indicating – although not excluding[371] – what Christ will ever do for the worshippers in the future, but emphatically concentrates on that perfection which Christ's single sacrifice now *has* accomplished and in which all the believers, through baptism, may participate for all time.[372] It is this very *completion* of Christ's priestly

---

368 Heb. 4,16; 7,25; 10,12-13 (the sitting down at the right hand of God, waiting for the final triumph, stresses the victorious reign of Christ as Priest-King on the basis of His completed reconciliation at the Cross). Cf. H. van Oyen, *o.c.*, p. 163: "Reiniging, heiliging en volmaking, ze zijn alle het werk van Christus aan ons. Reeds in dit leven wordt de gelovige door Christus volkomen; vervolmaakt echter is hij pas wanneer hij deel krijgt aan de eeuwige sabbatsrust (verschil tussen *teleios* en *teteleioomenos*)".

G. Vos, *The Teaching of the Ep. to the Hebrews*, 1956, pp. 121-124, tries to show that the ritual verbs *katharizein, hagiazein* and *teleioun* do not signify ethical operation or moral perfection, but the atonement "*exclusively*" in its forensic effect, in order to fit the worshipper for the service of God.

Also W. Neil, *The Epistle to the Hebrews*, 1955, p. 107, *ad* Heb. 10,10.14, who interprets *hagiazein* in the Pauline sense of justification, to "put into a right relationship with God." Probably Spicq, *L'Épitre aux Hébreux*, II, 1953², p. 312, comes closest to vss. 10,14: "La distinction que fait Hébr. entre le participe parfait *hègiasmenoi esmen* (x, 10) et le participe présent *tous hagiazomenous* (v. 14) atteste que si l'oeuvre du Christ est parfaite, achevée du côté de Dieu, elle est progressive dans ses effets appliqués aux hommes."

Also F. Delitzsch, *Com. on the Ep. to the Hebr.* II, ET 1870, *ad* 10,14, pp. 162f., indicates that *teteleiōken* comprises perfection which "is not as to its effect a past work, but one perpetually realized in those who accept it".

369 Also Michel, *o.c.*, *ad* 10,22, pp. 346f. Maurer, *ThWNT* VIII, 917, 33f.: "Der Hebraerbrief spricht von der Reinigung des Gewissens, welche in der Taufe geschieht."

370 Cf. Jn. 13,10; 15,3; Acts 15,9; 1 Cor. 6,11. Notable are the aorists: *apelousasthe, hegiasthēte, edikaiōthēte*); Eph. 5,26 (*katharisas*).

371 See the *apocalyptic* fulfillment of the promised perfection in the glorious *visio Dei* and kingdom of God, 11,39-40. 13ff. 35; 12,14; 13,14.

372 Cf. Westcott, *o.c.*, p. 66: "The first passage (X 14) gives the one sufficient and abiding ground of man's attainment to perfection in the fact of Christ's work. Man has simply to take to himself what Christ has already done for him (*teteleiōken eis to diènekes*)." And *ad* 10,14: "The virtue of Christ's work remains ever available as long as the need of man exists" (p. 315).

sacrifice of Himself on earth (9,26) which vss. 10,11-14 stress again: Christ does not need to stand daily, like the Levitical priests, in order to secure redemption; He can *"sit down"* at the right hand of God and then *"wait* until His enemies should be made a stool for His feet".

Having completed the atonement at the cross by a single offering, Christ thereby *"has perfected* for all time *those who are sanctified [tous hagiozomenous]"* (10,14). This cannot mean that perfection would be a stage *after* sanctification, since Christ's perfecting act is indicated as a one-time act in the past ("has perfected"). On the contrary, Christ's act of perfection or cleansing at the cross is the foundation and source for the process of progressive sanctification.[373]

This Christological cultic redemption fulfills the foreshadowing, typological cultus of the old covenant. As *cleansed* worshippers, who possess a *perfect* heart, or clear conscience by baptism, they may and should now draw near to the presence of God in His sanctuary (10,19.22; 13,18).[374]

The fact that these worshippers "no longer have any consciousness of sin" (10,2) thus indicates that their conscience is cleansed from the "apprehensive or terrifying sense of what they deserved".[375]

373 Westcott, *o.c.*, *ad* 10,14, places the *hègiasmenoi esmen* (vs. 10) and *hagiazomenous* (vs. 14), in analogy with *sesōsmenoi* in Eph. 2,5 and *hoi sōzomenoi* in Acts 2,47; 1 Cor. 1,18; 2 Cor. 2,15. To him the process of sanctification means the progressive realization of the validity of that "which has been potentially obtained for them" (p. 315).

374 Cf. Michel, *o.c.*, p. 333 (in note), indicates that Heb. 10,22 is inspired by the O.T. motif of the perfect or whole heart (1 Chron. 29,19), which is rooted in the cleansed heart. This is indicated by the divine gift of a circumcised heart in Dt. 30,6 LXX; which heart is presented as a requirement in Dt. 10,16. Maurer, *ThWNT* VII, 918, 5f., goes too far when he suggests that the "good conscience" in Heb. 13,18 is a "formula" to describe a Christian, since the *service* to the living God is the goal of this purified conscience (9,14).

375 Pink, *o.c.* II, 37, referring to Rom. 8,1: "If we really believe that the wages of sin were paid to our sinless Substitute, how can we be fearful that they will yet be paid to us!"

# Chapter V

## An analysis and an evaluation of phenomenal perfectionism

We use the term perfectionism te denote any form of theological falsification or religious distortion of the Biblical concept of perfection. The perfectionist concept, however, claims to present the only true way of perfection and salvation.

In order to define perfectionism it is therefore necessary first to define our Biblical norm and theological religious standard, with reference to both the Old and the New Testament.[1]

It must be admitted, however, that the above stated negative definition of perfectionism is quite a theoretical, abstract concept. Can a man or community of men who try to serve God perfectly, who strive after holiness with all intensity, be defined adequately by a purely negative term? Can the living reality of the many variegated forms of perfectionism be truly evaluated by a simplistic black-white scheme? Is this true to reality itself? Our inquiry into perfectionism thus must occupy itself with the various concrete phenomena of perfectionism, each in its own historical setting, and then try to evaluate them in the light of the Biblical concept and religion.

It is good to remember that the Biblical ideal of the perfect life with God and men cannot be seen embodied completely in Israel and its kingship and priesthood. Such an ideal is found only in liturgical hymns of the book of Psalms.[2] The message and fate of the many prophets of Israel constitute a telling proof in this respect.[3] This leads us to consider whether the phenomeon of religious perfectionism has not arisen by way of reaction and protest against the prevailing laxity or apostasy of the established religious institution.

Any dogmatic evaluation of heresy or deviation from the perfect ideal which does not truly consider its concrete historical setting of life is unable to do justice to its real motivations and intentions. Just as divine revelation bears an indissoluble historical character and may not

---

1   See above, Chs. II-IV.
2   In 2 Cor. 3,7 the apostle Paul defines the whole Mosaic dispensation as "the dispensation of death," just because of the impressive failure of the way of perfection in the concrete reality of Israel's existence as a whole.
3   See 2 Kgs. 17,7-20 and 2 Chr. 36,15f.; cf. also Mt. 21,33-43; 23,37.

be divorced from its historical setting, so it seems that also our analysis of perfectionism can be meaningful only when the concrete historical situation of its origin and development is taken into consideration. Accordingly it is proper to ask whether there have been individuals or communities in history which *claimed* to follow perfectly the way of Biblical revelation, yet deviated from it fundamentally in one way or another. What are their theological and religious motivations and objectives?

Why did they separate – separation appears to be the typical characistic of perfectionism[4] – from the established main body, its theology and discipline? Since our study is not focusing on the New Testament exclusively, but on the whole complex of Biblical revelation, the method that commends itself is to study the historical phenomenon of perfectionism in the old as well as the new covenant era.

This invites us to consider those specific communities or movements which separated themselves more or less from the main body of Israel and, later on, from the Christian Church, with the explicit claim to have been called to a higher or more strict standard of religious holiness, purity and perfection, than was considered sufficient or neccessary in the established body.

In order to stay within prescribed limits we can select only some major types of religious perfectionism.[5] The most conspicuous religious perfectionist community during the old-covenant period appears to be the Qumran sect. It is evident that we can assess this particular pre-Christian concept adequately only if we refer to the specific Old Testament norm of religious-cultic perfection.

For the Christian era we will deal with the specific claims of Christian perfection as held by the Encratites, Montanists, Novatians, Pelagius, the Alexandrian Christian Platonists, the medieval monks, and finally with Wesley's concept of perfection. After our analysis, we will try to classify these major types of religious perfectionism.

1. *The Qumran Community.*

It is now generally[6] recognized that the Qmran community or Dead

---

4   This does not imply that *each* separation or segregation or secession necessarily is caused by the specific motivation of theological perfectionism. The theme of our investigation, however, is not the legitimate but rather the illegitimate separation, which is commonly designated as separatism.

5   For a survey of all the known sects in all times, see the still useful J. H. Blunt, *Dictionary of Sects, Heresies, Ecclesiastical Parties, and Schools of Religious Thought*, 1874. For literature on modern perfectionism, see above, Ch. I, n. 9.

6   See M. Hengel, *Judentum und Hellenismus*, WUNT 10, 1969, p. 394, n. 626. W. H. Brownlee, *The Meaning of the Qumran Scrolls for the Bible*,

Sea Sect belonged to the Essenes which are described by Josephus[7] as a brotherhood of segregated Jews, totaling about four thousand men, who practised community of goods and submitted themselves to a severe discipline, asceticism, and Levitical purity. This secluded and strictly hierarchically ordered cloister community on the northwestern shore of the Dead Sea was founded about 150 B.C. by a persecuted Priest who claimed to have the specific prophetic charisma. The Qumran texts call him the Teacher of Righteousness.[8] The community flourished until the Roman invasion in 63 B.C., but continued to exist until A.D. 68.

Martin Hengel[9] indicates that the character of this separatist Jewish community must be understood from the background of the great religious-cultic crisis within Judaism under the impact of Hellenism since 175 B.C.[10]

This historical setting helps to explain the apocalyptic interpretation of history, the intensified eschatological sense that they were living in the last days of the cosmic conflict between truth and falsehood, light and darkness. But it also casts light on their radicalized religious-ethical dualism which saw holiness and wickedness being crystallized in two distinguishable communities or camps.[11]

As Hengel states:

Die in den Augen des Lehrers und seiner Anhänger unheilvolle

1964, pp. 111, 134. F. M. Cross, Jr., *The Ancient Library of Qumran and Modern Biblical Studies*, 1958, pp. 37ff. There are still a few scholars, however, who argue that the Covenanters of Qumran were not Essenes, e.g. Leah Bronner, *Sects and Separatism during the Second Jewish Commonwealth*, 1967, pp. 86-149. C. Roth, *The Dead Sea Scrolls. A New Historical Approach*, 1965, pp. 22f., 81f. G. R. Driver, *The Judaean Scrolls. The Problem and a Solution*, 1965, pp. 109ff.

7  *Wars* II, 8; *Antiquities* XVIII, 1.

8  See Hengel, *o.c.*, pp. 407ff. H. Ringgren, *The Faith of QUMRAN. Theology of the Dead Sea Scrolls*, ET 1963 (Swedish, 1961), pp. 23-43. Bronner, *o.c.*, pp. 118-149. Driver, *o.c.*, pp. 51-76. On the role of the Teacher, and the basic contrast between him and Jesus, see the outstanding study of Gert Jeremias, *Der Lehrer der Gerechtigkeit*, SUNT 2, 1963, esp. ch. 9. Further Brownlee, *o.c.*, pp. 126-151. J. Daniélou, *The Dead Sea Scrolls and Primitive Christianity*, ET 1958, Ch. II. An extensive critical bibliography is given by H. Braun, *Qumran und das N.T.*, II, 1966, §§ 3-5.

9  *O.c.*, pp. 409ff.

10  See 1 Macc. 1,11 for the beginning of the crisis.

11  According to 1 QH (*Hodayot* or *The Thanksgiving Hymns*) 7,12, the Teacher of Righteousness is called to "make distinction between the righteous and the wicked" The ET is from M. Mansoor, *The Thanksgiving Hymns.* "Studies on the Texts of the Desert of Judah," III, ed. J. van der Ploeg, 1961. The sigla used to denote the Qumran writings follow the standard system, adopted by D. Barthélemy, O.P., J. T. Milik, *et al.*, *Qumran Cave I. Discoveries in the Judaean Desert* I, 1955, pp. 46-48.

Entwickelung des jüdischen Volkes liess ihnen nur noch die Möglichkeit der Absonderung einer kleinen Minderheit, des heiligen Restes und wahren Israels, als Ausweg offen. Aus dieser Situation ist auch das minutiöse Festhalten des Lehrers und der Gemeinde an der *Tora* zu verstehen.[12]

The specific mission of the Righteous Teacher, in his self-understanding, was to establish the pure Remnant of Israel, the perfect "new covenant" community which alone would be fitted for fellowship with Yahweh and His angels. Through him exclusively they would receive the secret knowledge[13] necessary for victory in the final conflict.

*The Manual of Discipline*[14] states:

> All those who devote themselves to do the ordinances of God, shall be brought / into the covenant of mercy for the community, into the council of God. He shall walk perfectly before Him ⟨according to⟩ all the things / which have been revealed at the times fixed for their revelations. He shall love each one of the sons of light / according to this lot in the council of God, and hate each one of the sons of darkness according to his guilt / at the time of God's vengeance.

Gripped by a deep passion to walk perfectly[15] in all the ways of the Torah and by the conviction that they practised ritual and moral perfection, they did not hesitate to call themselves "the perfect ones,"[16] "the men of holiness,"[17] "the men of holy integrity"[18] and "the council of holiness."[19]

---

12  *O.c.*, pp. 413f. The judgment of M. Black, *The Scrolls and Christian Origins*, 1961, p. 118, that the origin of the Qumran community must be sought in the priestly legalistic attempt "to reform the Law," does no justice to the religious motivation of the sect and its priestly interpretations. Protest against cultic apostasy rather was the motif, cf. p. 32. At Qumran any criticism of the Torah was inconceivable. In all their intensified Torah obedience and literalism the Qumran sectaries only intended to fulfill the Mosaic Law.

13  See Hengel, *o.c.*, pp. 415ff. on the "Intellektualisierung der Frömmigkeit," which he traces back to the ḥasidic-apocalyptic Wisdom tradition.

14  1 QS 1, 7-10. The ET is from P. Wernberg-Møller, *The Manual of Discipline*. "Stud. on the texts of the Desert of Judah," I, ed. J. v. d. Ploeg, 1957.

15  Cf. the repeated designation of a perfect walk, 1 QS 1,8; 2,2; 3,9; 8,18.21; 9,6.8.9.19. B. Rigaux, "Révélation des Mystères et Perfection à Qumran et dans le N.T.," in *NTS* IV (1957-8), 237-262, concludes that Qumran has borrowed its terminology of perfection from the O.T. (238). Cf. also Burrows, *More Light on the Dead Sea Scrolls*, 1958, p. 100.

16  1 QS 3,3 (*temîmîm*) ; 4,22; 8,1.

17  1 QS 5,13.18; 8,17.23; 9.8.

18  1 QS 8, 20.

19  1 QS 8,21.

Over against any partly or fragmentary obedience they emphatically demanded complete and radical obedience to all the commandments.[20]

True repentance or conversion, therefore, implied to them entrance into the monastic Qumran community, i.e., the taking upon oneself the oath "to return to the Torah of Moses, according to everything which He has commanded, with all heart and soul, according to everything which has been revealed from it to the sons of Zadok, the priests who keep the covenant and seek His pleasure."[21]

These separatist covenanters thus believed that, guided by revelation, they had separated themselves "from all the men of deceit who walk in the way of ungodliness," by which were meant, without restriction, all those outside their own community, whether they be Gentiles or Israelites, because all these could not "be reckoned as being in His covenant."[22]

In others words, they rejected Israel as a whole as being the covenant people, accepting only their own communal fellowship as the valid new-covenant people, the elect out of the "official" Israel. Small wonder that to the covenanters of Qumran there was no salvation outside their own new-Israel community.[23]

The almost military discipline within the community was intended to be a perfect following of the Mosaic Law:

> Who transgresses a word of the Torah of Moses with a lifted hand or a slack hand, he (or: they) shall banish him from the council of the community / and he shall never come back again.[24]

Bertil Gärtner has clearly shown that the Qumran community intended to follow the priestly ideal of sanctification and Levitical purity because of its dominating priestly leadership:

> This concentration on sanctification, expressed in a multitude of regulations for ceremonial purity and an intense exclusiveness, was not merely an expression of personal piety, but is to be seen against the background of the priestly office ... There is a striking

---

20 H. Braun, *Spätjüdisch-häretischer und frühchristlicher Radikalismus*, I, BHTh 24, 1957, p. 28, n. 2, counts 192 times where the term *kôl* occurs in the Manual, 64 of which are applied to the totalitarian character of the requirements. He states on p. 29: "Der Gehorsam soll nun auf der *ganzen* Linie erfolgen. Der Mensch gilt als verloren bereits dann, wenn er nicht *alles* tut; das blosse Überwiegen der Gebotserfüllungen genügt nicht."

21 1 QS 5,8-9. Cf. Rigaux, *o.c.*, 238: "La perfection de la voie, c'est avant tout l'obéissance aux préceptes divins, tels qu'ils sont pratiqués à Qumrân; c'est l'acceptation de toute la vie monastique, conçue comme l'expression d'une volonté divine."

22 1 QS 5,10-11.

23 Cf. Braun, *o.c.*, I, p. 25. Hengel, *o.c.*, p. 407.

24 1 QS 8,22; cf. 7,2.17.24; 9,1; 8,17.

correspondence between the rules binding the priests in their holy office and the methods used by the Qumran community in order to build up their organization and preserve their holiness. [25]

The demanded holiness, therefore, was determined by the cultic requirements. Just as the Temple priests had to be "perfect" in the presence of Yahweh, so "the members of the Qumran community were commanded to be 'perfect' in the exercise of their cultic functions." [26]

It is of vital significance to recognize that the Qumran community, on the basis of its Temple symbolism and self-application, regarded itself as actually having entered upon present-eschatological salvation, i.e., cultic-spiritual salvation.[27] Yet, we certainly fail to do justice to the soteriology and ecclesiology of the Qumran sect, if we should overlook its fundamental eschatological motivation, its sense of apocalyptic mission to prepare itself for the final war in the last days.[28] The separation from "men of deceit" by going out into the desert had as its positive objective to fulfill prophecy:

> ...in order to clear His way; / as it is written: "In the wilderness make clear the way of ..., level in the desert a highway for our God." [29]

This eschatological-apocalyptic motif is recognized by Helmer Ringgren when he states:

> In this way the congregation is to become a pure and holy com-

---

25  *The Temple and the Community in Qumran and the New Testament. A Comparative Study in the Temple Symbolism of the Qumran texts and the N.T.*, "Soc. for N.T. Studies Monographs" I, 1965, p. 4, and further. None of those who were disabled or afflicted by any bodily imperfection were allowed to enter the Community. This was only for those of physical perfection.

26  *Ibid.*, p. 7.

27  See esp. H. W. Kuhn, *Enderwartung und gegenwärtiges Heil. Unters. z. d. Gemeindeliedern von Qumran*, SUNT 4, 1966, pp. 167ff., 178ff. He indicates the interrelationship between Qumran's soteriology and apocalyptic, even the intertwining of each other.

28  See K. Elliger, *Studien zum Habakuk-Kommentar von Toten Meer*, BHT 15, 1953, pp. 275ff. He states: "Das schwergewicht liegt ganz entschieden nicht im Ethischen, sondern im Dogmatischen, genauer in der *eschatologischen Verkündigung*" (p. 278). Cf. E. Osswald, "Zur Hermeneutik des Habakuk-Kommentars," in *ZAW* 68 (1956), 243-256. He concludes: „Die Beachtung des hermeneutischen Prinzips, von dem sich der Verfasser des Kom. Leiten lässt, führt jedoch zu der Erkenntnis, dass die Aktualisierung der Habakuk-Botschaft nicht das Wesentliche ist. Das alles Beherrschende ist vielmehr das Bewusstsein in der Endzeit zu leben, in der die Geheimnisse den Auserwählten bereits enthüllt sind."

29  1 QS 8,13-14; cf. 9,19.

munity, which through their obedience to the Law becomes a holy temple and atones for the sins of the people, thus preparing the way for the fulfillment of the promises and God's final victory.[30]

On this basis Cross is fully justified in characterizing the Qumran community as "an apocalyptic community, a *Heilsgemeinschaft*, imitating the ancient desert sojourn of Mosaic times in anticipation of the dawning Kingdom of God. They are priestly apocalyptists, not true ascetics."[31] On the basis of the *War Scroll* (1 QM) Y. Yadin[32] has unravelled the complicated organizational structure of the Qumran community in its military aspect as an attempt to model the Remnant community according to that of Israel of old in the desert. They believed themselves to be the chosen ones who would wage the final war – together with the angels – against the wicked ones, the servants of Belial.[33] This eschatological war, which would last forty years and bring the eternal extermination of all the wicked,[34] would usher in the Messianic era.[35]

In this particular apocalyptic setting also the command of the *Manual of Discipline* to hate the sons of darkness must be considered.[36]

A most vital statement on this point is made in 1 QS 10, 17-19:

> For I know that in His hand is the judgment / of every living being, and that all His actions are truth. When affliction starts I will praise Him, and also at His salvation I will cry out in exultation. I will not return evil to anybody, / with good I will pursue mankind. For with God rests the judgment of every living being, He being

---

30  *O.c.*, p. 137. Cf. also Braun, *o.c.*, I, pp. 31f.: "Dieser Eifer, diese Vollkommenheit sind nun aber erst dort recht verstanden, wo man für sie die Nähe des Eschatons einkalkuliert: der Wandel ist qualifiziert durch die Einsicht in die dem eschatologischen Ende zustrebenden Zeitperioden." Daniélou, *o.c.*, p. 57.

31  *O.c.*, p. 56; cf. also pp. 73-74 ("apocalyptic asceticism").

32  *The Scroll of the war of THE SONS OF LIGHT ag. THE SONS OF DARKNESS*, 1962. L. Rost, in *ThLZ* 80 (1955), 206, concludes that the War Scroll is *older* than all the other Scrolls, and pictures a more militant group than the quietists of later Qumran. But G. Jeremias, *Der Lehrer der Gerechtigkeit*, p. 176, defends the *Hodayot* as the oldest.

33  Cf. K. Schubert, *The Dead Sea Community. Its Origin and Teachings*, ET 1959 (German, 1958), pp. 88ff. He states: "In this last battle the angels of God join with the sons of Light as a decisive factor" (p. 92).

34  1 QS 4,12-14; 1 QH 3,28-36.

35  *Ibid.*, pp. 91f. M. Black, *The Dead Sea Scrolls and Christian Doctrine*, 1966, p. 4, agrees with the École Biblique in Jerusalem that the Qumran or Essene group in its final phase had ceased to be "the pacific ascetics, idealized by Josephus and Philo, they had by then thrown in their lot with Zealot and Pharisaic groups." C. Roth, *o.c.*, pp. 22ff., defends the position that the Qumran covenanters were always Zealots; on this identification, however, see Burrows, *More Light*, pp. 271-273.

36  1 QS 1,10; cf. also 1 QS 9,21f. 15f.

252

the one who repays man ... A man of perdition I will not prosecute
until the day of vengeance.

Braun[37] and V. Hasler[38] have suggested that Jesus' polemic against
the tradition "You have heard that it was said, 'You shall love your
neighbor and hate your enemy' " (Mt. 5,43) was specifically directed
against the Qumran ethics. This seems to be a welcome solution to a
long standing problem in regard to Mt. 5,43.[39] K. Schubert[40] even states
definitely: "The Qumran texts give us the answer."

E. F. Sutcliffe, however, in his challenging article "Hatred at Qumran"[41]
concludes with regard to the presumed command to hate the enemy:

> But neither is this teaching to be found at Qumran. The hatred
> preached there is exclusively of wicked men, as has been seen above.
> Hatred and rancour against fellow members of the Community
> or Congregation are strictly forbidden. And as regards external
> enemies, instigators of persecution, they are not to be repaid with
> evil but on the contrary with good, 1 QS X, 17f. It seems clear
> that Christ's words do not refer to Qumran.[42]

This would mean that the sect was to hate all the sons of darkness
only because they were God's enemies, not because they were their own
personal enemies just as in the Biblical Psalms. This consideration leads
A. R. C. Leaney[43] to the conclusion: "It is therefore wrong to claim that
the tradition referred to in Matt. 5,43 is here identified." Also Ringgren[44]
admits that "hatred of those outside the community is limited to the time
appointed by God for his vengeance", referring to 1 QS 1,10f.[45] R. E.
Brown[46] explains that the formulae of hate occur in the initiation rites

37  O.c., II, p. 58.
38  "Das Herzstück der Bergpredigt," in *ThZ* 15 (1959), 102f.
39  The injunction to hate one's enemy cannot be found in the O.T. nor in
Rabbinic sources.
40  O.c., p. 143. He recognizes the setting of an eschatological war of vengeance; cf. p. 92: "A general, eschatologically-determined hatred of enemies
was therefore propagated among the Qumran Essenes."
41  In *RQ* 2 (1960), 345-355.
42  O.c., 355; cf. also 352: "Thus the doctrine held at Qumran on the
subject of hate was the same as that they found in the pages of the Old
Testament. There was to be no private hatred or revenge. On the contrary,
enemies were to be repaid with good."
43  *The Rule of Qumran and its Meaning. Introd., transl. and comm.,* "The
N.T. Library," 1966, *ad* 1 QS 1,9; p. 121.
44  O.c., p. 138, n. 57.
45  Sutcliffe, o.c., 350f., observes: "Before that time [sc. "the time appointed
for vengance"] is manifested by God, it would be wrong to harm even the
Sons of Darkness."
46  "The Qumran Scrolls and the Johannine Gospel and Epistles", in
Stendahl, *The Scrolls and the N.T.,* 1957, pp. 183-207, esp. p. 198.

of the *Manual of Discipline* and that "they may be ancient, stylized re-
nunciations of evil as personified in the sons of Belial." *The Thanksgiving Hymns* would better represent the ideal of personal piety at
Qumran. To him the most striking characteristic in this respect is the
prevalence of the theme of brotherly love in both the Qumran and the
Johannine literature. Here Qumran rises far above the literature of late
Judaism.[47] Yet, in relation to this aspect of fraternal affection Brown
recognizes a "puzzling" trend in the ritual curses on all outsiders (1 QS
2,7-8) and the complete separatism (1 QS 5,11; 9,17-18).

The origin of these diverging trends must be sought, however, it seems
to us, in Qumran's peculiar *apocalypticism*, which is inspired by the
authoritarian exclusive claims of revelation by its Teacher of Righteousness.[48] Qumran's ethics of concealed "eternal hatred" with respect to the
outsiders can probably best be described as non-retaliation.[49]

As far as *soteriology* is concerned, a most remarkable *new* characteristic in late Judaism has been recognized in the Qumran writings.

In conspicuous contrast with the piety of Pharisaic Judaism, moral
perfection is conceived as a work of grace at Qumran. It is the sovereign
predestinating God who elects a man and motivates him to perfect
obedience by His Spirit.

> For as for me, the judgment concerning me belongs to God. In
> His hand is my perfection of way and also my rectitude of heart. /
> By His righteousness my sin is wiped out (1 QS 11,2-3). For he
> [sc. man] is steeped in sin. From the womb and unto old age, (he
> is) amid treacherous guilt. For, verily I know, that righteousness
> belongs not to a mortal, nor is integrity of W a y to a son of man.
> Unto God Most High are all the works of righteousness and way of
> a mortal is not established save through the spirit (which) God
> fashioneth for him (1 QH 4,29-31).

> And I know through Thy understanding that it is not by the
> hand of flesh... And that man's W a y [is not his own], and
> neither can mortal direct his own steps. And I know that in Thy
> hand is the purpose of all spirit... [and] his [work] (1 QH 15,
> 12-13).

As has been generally recognized, the Dead Sea Scrolls, more than the

47  *Ibid.*, p. 199.
48  See below.
49  See 1 QS 9,21. Cf. K. Stendahl, "Hate, Non-Retaliation, and Love",
*HThR* 55 (1962), 343-355. Brownlee, *The Meaning of the Qumran Scrolls*,
p. 198: "The Essenes [B. means the Qumran community] went part way in
forbidding vengeance, but they allowed the vengeful spirit to remain. Only
Jesus forbids and removes the vindictive spirit itself."

Old Testament, emphasize man's impurity, weakness, nothingness, depravity.[50] This deep religious consciousness of man's inherent sinfulness is especially characteristic of *The Thankgiving Hymns* or Psalms,[51] but is also an essential part of the liturgical confession of sin at the yearly festival of covenant renewal.[52]

As J. van der Ploeg[53] aptly formulates: "Many expressions and utterances in the Hymns seem to be no more than a broad development of the saying of Genesis: 'The thoughts of the heart of man are evil from his youth' (Genesis 8:21)".

Human sinfulness is not explicitly traced back to Adam's fall, nor merely conceived as "original sin,"[54] but experienced religiously as an abiding corollary of God's absolute righteousness and holiness. This religious relationship reveals that the Qumran worshipper does not concentrate on his sinful wretchedness by itself. Ringgren observes: "Not a single psalm deals exclusively with nothingness, sin and guilt, but as a complement there is always a reference to God's grace and compassion."[55] The implication seems to be that only the redeemed Qumran saint by heavenly enlightenment really knows about man's sinfulness.[56] Only he has the esoteric knowledge of God's plan for this world, and of the beginning and end of the existence of good and evil. God has created both the spirit or angel of truth (light) and the spirit or angel of iniquity (darkness). They struggle for the supremacy in man on equal terms.[57] The predominant view of the Society Manual (3,15-4,26) is that every

---

50   See Ringgren, *o.c.*, pp. 94ff. Burrows, *More Light*, pp. 290ff. Also J. Ph. Hyatt, "The View of Man in the Qumran 'Hodayot'," in *NTS* II (1955/56), 276-284. And esp. H. Braun, "Römer 7,7-25 und das Selbstverständnis des Qumran-Frommen", in *ZThK* 56 (1959), 1-18. After an extensive survey of the moral self-qualifications in 1 QS and 1 QH, he concludes: "Diese terminologische Übersicht ergibt: Der Mensch gilt den Qumran-Frommen als Sünder in seinem Tun und in seinem Sein" (7).

51   See Mansoor, *o.c.*, pp. 58-62. S. Holm-Nielsen, *Hodayot. Psalms from Qumran*, "Acta Theol. Danica," II, 1960, pp. 274ff.

52   See 1 QS 1,24-2,1. Braun, *o.c.*, 11, calls attention to the fact that this yearly confession of sin clearly intends also to confess the abiding, inherent sinfulness of all the saints. He further refers to 1 QS 4,30; 7,27-29; 9,14.15; 12,30-32; 13,15.16; 16,11; 18,12.13.25.26; 10,11 (sin as an engraved law!), 11,9.10.12.14.15.

53   *The Excavations at Qumran*, ET 1958 (Dutch, 1957), p. 118.

54   Cf. Hyatt, *o.c.*, 283: "He comes close to a doctrine of original sin or inherited sin. At any rate he stands in the line of those who emphasize the origin of sin in some inherited defect of man's nature or the influence of Satan, fallen angels or the like (cf. for example, I Enoch X. 7-8; IV Ezra IV. 30-2), rather than in man's misuse of his freedom of will (as, for example, in II Baruch 54.15,19)."

55   *Ibid.*, p. 104; cf. Braun, *o.c.*, 8,11.

56   Cf. Braun, *o.c.*, 8.

57   1 QS 4,17.25. Cf. Brown, in *o.c.*, pp. 188f.

man has to be enrolled in one of the two armies in the struggle between good and evil, but each according to his predetermined destiny.[58]

The doctrine of predestination in its curious form of a double predestination – the history of both the righteous and the wicked is ordained beforehand – appears to determine the structure of the whole Qumran theology, its eschatology and soteriology in particular.[59]

This absolute predestination, which usually is traced back to Persian influence (Zoroastrianism), of the whole order of history and of the individual destiny, is a *novum*[60] in Judaism. It causes the curious problem of two conflicting trends in the Qumran soteriology and ethics, especially between determinism on the one hand, and the responsibility and possibility of reformation on the other hand, between the election of grace and an austere law observance.[61] What God has willed and ordained for

58   Cf. Hengel, *o.c.*, p. 399: "Das apokalyptische Drama konzentriert sich auf die Anthropologie, ohne dass der kosmische Aspekt verloren geht."

59   See esp. 1 QS 3,15-4,26; 1 QH 1,7; 4,38. Cf. Hengel, *o.c.*, p. 397: "Alles ist von Uranfang an prädestiniert, einschliesslich der einzelnen Menschenleben mit ihren Gedanken und Taten." See the discussion in Holm-Nielsen, *o.c.*, pp. 281f., on the problem of predestination and responsibility. Van der Ploeg, *o.c.*, p. 117, concludes that this predestination is based on God's *foreknowledge* of all the free actions of men, "and He had used this prescience to lay down His unalterable plan for the world." From 1 QS 3,17ff., concerning the two spirits, he concludes "that man chooses freely between the good and the evil spirit; once he has made his choice, the spirit he has chosen makes him behave well or ill" (p. 119). But how, in this concept, can election ever be the source of assurance of salvation and ultimate religious praise, as the Qumran documents testify? Undoubtedly Herbert Braun is more correct, when he concludes: "Gottes prädestinierendes Heilshandeln weckt die wählende Entscheidung und das Ja des Menschen. So kommt es durch Gott beim Menschen zu rechten Taten, zu rechtem, unsträflichem Wandel und zu einem festen Stand in der Anfechtung [referring to resp. 1 QH 16,10; 1 QS 10,12; 1 QS 10,13; 1 QH 6,9; 1 QS 11,16; 1 QH 4,32; 6,67; 18,12; 1 QS 11,11.13; 1 QH 4,36; 6,10; 7,31; 9,12]" (*o.c.*, 10). See also his *o.c.*, I, p. 42: "... seine Bekehrung ist ein ausgesprochener Freiwilligkeitsakt." For a full discussion, see H. W. Huppenbauer, *Der Mensch zwischen zwei Welten*, ATANT 34, 1959, esp. pp. 95ff. His conclusion is: "Der Dualismus der Qumrangemeinde, ist also ein *relativer, ethisch-kosmischer* Dualismus" (p. 113).

60   Hengel, *o.c.*, p. 397. Cf. S. Schulz, "Zur Rechtfertigung aus Gnaden in Qumran und bei Paulus", in *ZThK* 56 (1959), 155-185, esp. 157f.

61   As is well-known, the doctrine of predestination in Christian theology since Augustine has always tended to prevent or neutralize the idea of human meritoriousness and law-righteousness. The curious fact presents itself, however, that even within Christianity, in late medieval Scholasticism specifically, the doctrine of predestinating grace (*solo gratia*) could be combined at the same time with the doctrine of justification by works alone (*solis operibus*), manifested in the piety of observances. See H. Oberman, *The Harvest of Medieval Theology. Gabriel Biel and Late Medieval Nominalism*, 1963, pp. 175ff., 185ff. F. Nötscher, *Gotteswege und Menschenwege in der Bibel und in Qumran*, BBB 15, 1958, pp. 84-87, however, recognizes in Qumran "no sharp boundary"

His chosen ones is interpreted as a manifestation of God's grace by the covenanters.[62] Because of the accelerated eschatological intensity, the Qumran covenanters felt themselves utterly dependent upon God. The *Thanksgiving Hymns* express the heartfelt thanks for the divine election by grace and for membership in the congregation of the elect.[63] To them life within the Remnant community was like being already in Paradise.[64] Hengel,[65] taking into account the whole corpus of extent Qumran texts, does not hesitate to conclude with respect to its soteriology and ecclesiology:

> Dabei ist jedoch nichts, was am und durch den Menschen zu seinem Heil geschieht, in seiner eigenen Leistung begründet. Da er von Anfang an entweder zur Gerechtigkeit oder zum Gericht bestimmt ist, gründet die "Erlösung" durch die Aufnahme in die Gemeinschaft ausschliesslich in Gottes freier Erwählung.

Also G. Vermes[66] observes an outspoken doctrine of *sola gratia:*

> No note of self-righteousness sounds in the Qumran writings; on the contrary, the sectary is amazed by the blessings showered on him and expresses himself in the Hymns in tones of self-abasement.

In sharp contrast to this interpretation stands the unqualified judgment of W. H. Brownlee:

> Unlike Jesus, the Teacher of Righteousness founded a community enmeshed in legalism. The strict rules of the Essenes' Manual of Discipline indicate their stern legalism.[67]

between divine grace and moral efforts. "Man hatte über ihr gegenseitiges Verhältnis wohl keine klaren Vorstellungen..." (p. 86).

62   See Braun, *o.c.*, 9.
63   See Mansoor, *o.c.*, pp. 62-65, on "Salvation Through Election."
64   See 1 QH 8,4ff. Cf. Holm-Nielsen, *o.c.*, pp. 297f.
65   *O.c.*, p. 406.
66   *The Dead Sea Scrolls in English*, 1962, p. 35.
67   *The Meaning of the Scrolls*, p. 150. Cf. also Burrows, *More Light*, p. 89. Black, *o.c.*, p. 122, speaks of a "legalistic perfection" or "perfectionism." It is very curious to see how Black on p. 126 acknowledges that "the Qumran saints had discovered the secret of 'evangelical' religion, trust in the everlasting mercy of God alone, and in His spirit to guide and direct daily life and conduct." On p. 128 he affirms that the Qumran religion forms "a continuation of *Psalmenfrömmigkeit*, the spirit of profound trust in God's mercy in the Psalms, and in the prophets." To "solve" his discrepancy, Black seeks the way out of a remarkable presumption: "Perhaps we ought to allow more for different 'philosophies' within Qumran itself" (p. 125). This "solution" is already unacceptable because Black himself must admit with regard to the evangelical piety of the *Hodayot*: "It certainly gave the theological foundation for the religion of these sectarian saints" (p. 126).

Braun, although more careful than Brownlee, also finds a *synergistic* soteriology in the *Manual of Discipline:*

> Neben dem Grenzfall des gnädigen, souveränen und prädestinie-renden Gottes, steht der radikal seine Gehorsamsleistung vollbrin-gende Mensch, der in ängstlicher Abhängigkeit die Totalleistung des Gehorsams erstrebt.[68]

It must be said that Braun gives a considerably more moderate judg-ment in his article "Römer 7,7-25 und das Selbstverständnis des Qumran-Frommen",[69] where he states:

> Beide, Paulus wie Qumran, lehren den Heilsstand als betonten Gegensatz zu der vergangenen heillosen Situation (15).
> Die Terminologie für Sünde und Heil ist in Qumran reicher und mannigfaltiger als bei Paulus (16).

He acknowledges that the Qumran piety rejects boasting in ones own righteousness. Yet he still doubts whether its way of *sanctification* can stand the test of the Pauline *sola fide*. For what reason should Qumran maintain its casuistry and intensified law obedience?

He sums up his argument as follows:

> Paulus würde auf die Unvereinbarkeit von wirklicher Gnade und Tora-Weg, von wirklicher Gnade und einer ungebrochenen, un-dialektischen Kraftemfang, von wirklicher Gnade und kasuisti-scher Ausrichtung des Wandels hinweisen (18).

The basic failure of Braun's assessment seems to us to be his illegiti-mate identification of Torah obedience and law-righteousness or legalism. This antimonian bias, however, never can do justice to the Old Testament Torah imperative as found e.g., in Pss. 1; 19 and 119, let alone to the problematic Torah intensifying of a Judaism at "boiling point."[70]

Braun's proposed incompatibility would also be difficult to maintain in the light of the Sermon on the Mount, esp. Mt. 5,17-19, and e.g., the Epistle of James. But Paul also has more to say about the law than that "Christ is the end of the law", Rom. 10,4,[71] and that Christians are

---

68  *Radikalismus* I, 47. To the point is the critique of Hengel, *o.c.,* p. 406, n. 673: "Braun ... kommt zu einer falschen Beurteilung, weil er die Hodajot nicht heranzog". With an appeal to Josephus, Hengel rejects synergism in the early Essene writings.

69  *ZThK* 56 (1959), 1-18, esp. 15-18. His concept remains hampered, however, by his antinomian, negativistic evaluation of each Torah imperative.

70  The expression is from W. D. Davies, in Stendahl, *The Scrolls and the N.T.,* p. 282, n. 86.

71  The rest of this verse indicates, as has generally been recognized, that

"discharged from the law, dead to that which held us captive, so that we serve not under the old written code but in the new life of the Spirit" (Rom. 7,6).[72]

Our concern here, however, is the Qumran soteriology, whether its theology and piety bear a legalistic, synergistic structure. The adequate criterion to test the Qumran theology, however, is not the Christological soteriology – Braun basically confuses the issue by his redemptive-historical anachronism – but only the Old Testament way of religious-cultic perfection.[73]

The more adequate question would be, Is the Qumran way of justi-fication and sanctification in harmony with the Old Testament way of salvation? And, in the framework of this question, particularly, Has the law of God in the radicalized Torah obedience kept its rightful place and function within the sola gratia?[74]

Although the Qumran piety and observance may seem to be a legal-istic perfectionism in the light of the Christological soteriology of the New Testament, some scholars suggest that this outward appearance may be deceptive.[75]

Davies[76] recognizes the following two aspects in the Qumran religion:

The obedience to the Law demanded in the sectarian sources is

---

Christ is the end of *law-righteousness*. See on this H. Ridderbos, *Paulus*, pp. 167ff., 311ff.

72   See also 2 Cor. 3. Ridderbos, *o.c.*, pp. 238ff., points to the twofold regimen and sphere of efficacy. An antinomian bias also underlies the final conclusion of G. Jeremias, *o.c.*, pp. 352f., when he contrasts the Teacher of Righteousness with Jesus by the radical analogy of Law *against* Gospel.

73   Although a comparison between the Teacher of Righteousness of Qumran and Jesus of Nazareth stands in its own right, it just is *unhistorical* to measure a pre-Christian Jewish sect – even when it *continues* in the post-Christian era – solely by a N.T. Gospel norm. No more is Rabbinic Judaism the adequate norm, against which the apostle Paul is directing his theological formulations. The only adequate norm is the O.T. revelation. This principle is also ignored by G. Jeremias, *o.c.*, pp. 352f.

74   A number of scholars have acknowledged that Jesus' intensifying and radicalizing of the Torah went even further than the ethics of Qumran. Even Braun states, *Qumran und das N.T.* II, 86: "Ja, man wird sagen müssen: Jesus sei noch kompromissloser als Qumran (Howlett); seine Gesetzesstrenge übertreffe die Qumrans (Burrows, Klarheit)". Cf. also his *Qumran und das N.T.* I, 15, *ad* Mt. 5,20. Here again this particular issue with respect to the O.T. soteriology is mystified by the *exclusive* dilemma of Qumran and N.T. Christological soteriology.

75   Cf. Hengel, *o.c.*, p. 403, who refers to others when he states: "Im Blick auf die 'perfektionistisch' anmutende vollkommene Toraerfüllung könnte man von einer 'eschatologisch radikalisierten... Heiligungsbewegung' sprechen. Aber dies ist nur *eine* Seite der Gemeinschaft."

76   In Stendahl, *The Scrolls and the N.T.*, p. 180.

even sharper than in Rabbinic Judaism. But at the same time there is found, especially in the Hymns, an awareness of the need of God's justifying help which surpasses anything known to us in pre-Christian Judaism.

To Davies the coincidence of a "legalistic" and a "charismatic" piety, i.e., the fact that there seems to be no essential tension, "no sense of an essential incompatibility", between Law and Spirit, is one of the most striking aspects of the Scrolls.[77]

This observation already suggests that the Qumran theology did not *onesidedly* radicalize or intensify Law obedience. It likewise radicalized hamartiology, i.e., the knowledge that the Qumran saint has *no* righteousness of his own!

This has been developed more fully by A. Dietzel[78] and S. Schulz[79] from the Qumran texts themselves. Dietzel shows how the worshippers of this "new Israel "community thanked God for forgiveness and cleansing from their sins, on the basis of God's redemptive judgment (*mšpṭ*), both present and future.[80] The most remarkable disclosure from the *Manual of Discipline* and specifically from the *Thanksgiving Hymns* is the religious-theological doctrine of justification in the sense of unmerited favor of God.

> [I] lean On Thy lovingkindness and the overflowing of Thy compassion. For Thou atonest a sin, and cl[eanest ma]n from guilt through righteousness (1 QH 4, 36-37).[81]

> For as for me, the judgment concerning me belongs to God. In His hand is my perfection of way and also my rectitude of heart. By His righteousness my sin is wiped out (1 QS 11, 2f.).
> Certainly I belong to wicked mankind. My sins, my iniquities, my transgression, as well as the perverseness of my mind / certainly belong to the assembly of worms and of them that walk in the darkness. For the way of man is ⟨not⟩ his (own affair).
> It is not man who makes firm his step, but to God belongs the judgment and ⟨in⟩ His hand is / the perfection of way ...

---

77  *O.c.*, p. 181. Cf. Schulz, *o.c.*, p. 175.

78  "Beten im Geist. Eine rel. gesch. Parallele aus den Hodajot zum paulinischen Gebet im Geist," *ThZ* 13 (1957), 12-32.

79  *L.c.* (see above, n. 60).

80  On the function and meaning of *mšpṭ*, which occurs 45 times in QH alone, see Dietzel, *o.c.*, 20f.; cf. also Braun, *Radikalismus* I, 45, n. 4 (with regard to 1 QS only).

81  Cf. 1 QH 17,12.15; 3,21; 11,10. Mansoor, in a note on 4,37, explains that *to atone*, as referred to God, is synonymous with *to forgive, to pardon a sin*. Holm-Nielsen, *o.c.*, p. 282, n. 18, clarifies 4,37 by the verb "remove" and "cleanse," and continues: "it signifies a forensic act on the part of God."

As for me, when / I totter, the mercy of God is my salvation for ever. When I stumble over fleshly sin, the judgment concerning me (is passed) by the righteousness of God which stands for ever. / When my affliction starts He rescues my soul from perdition. He makes firm my steps on the way. In His compassion He draws me near, and in His mercy He brings / my judgment. In the righteousness of His truth He judges me. In His great goodness He condones all my sins.

In His righteousness He pronounces me clean of impurity / of man and (of) sin of mankind, in order that I should praise God for His righteousness, and the Most High for His glory (in the following way): Praised be Thou, my God, who openest the mind of Thy servant unto knowledge. / Direct in righteousness all his actions (1 QS 11,9-10.11b-16).

Small wonder that Mansoor,[82] who observes "a striking similarity, on the surface at least" between the Qumran and the Pauline doctrine of salvation through election, concludes:

> Salvation, for the Sect as for Paul, means not only forgiveness and cleansing from sin but also participation in a divine fellowship.[83]

And Dietzel is led to the conclusion:

> In den Hod. ist die Hoffnung auf Gottes Erbarmen radikalisiert. Für einen Verdienstgedanken bleibt kein Raum mehr (15).[84]

And Schulz acknowledges: "Die Ordensregel wimmelt bekanntlich von Geboten und Verboten, während der Schlusspsalm von dem Thema der Rechtfertigung sola gratia getragen wird" (175). Possibly the Qumran community understood itself as a complete parallel or renewal of the Mosaic covenant people, so that its Thanksgiving Psalm functioned basically for Qumran as the Biblical Psalms did for the old covenant people.[85]

So gesehen, sind die Hymnen und der Schlusspsalm in der Ordens-

---

82  *O.c.*, pp. 63f. He compares 1 QH 15,12-22; 4,30-31; 7,29-31; 11,9-14, with Eph. 2,8; 2 Tim. 1,9-10; Rom. 3,21-24; Gal. 2,15-16.

83  *Ibid.*, p. 64. Cf. also D. Flusser, "The Dead Sea Sect and Pre-Pauline Christianity", in *Scripta Hierosolymitana*, Publ. Hebrew Univ., Vol. IV, ed. Ch. Rabin and Y. Yadin, 1965², pp. 215-266.

84  Cf. also Hengel, *o.c.*, p. 406, n. 673: "Bezeichnenderweise fehlen Begriffe für den Lohn im Blick auf Gott nahezu völlig." Cf. also A. Metzinger O.S.B., "Die Handschriftenfunde am Toten Meer und das N.T.", in *Bib.* 36 (1955), 467.

85  "Der qumranische hat wie der sinaitische Bund seinen historischen Ort im Auszug in die Wüste, seinen von Gott erwählten Bundesmittler, seine festumrissene (Kult-)Gemeinde, seine Tora, Prophetie und Psalmen!" (176).

regel letzlich nicht anderes als Ausdruck und Antwort auf die Rechtfertigung aus Gnaden, auf das Sola gratia, das dem Lehrer der Einung als Bundesmittler geoffenbart, den Seinen gelehrt und von diesen selbst erfahren und gepriesen wurde (177).

Schulz goes so far as to conclude that even in comparison with the Pauline justification and sanctification the new Israel of Qumran possesses no righteousness of its own: "Auch dem frommen Menschen eignet keine Gerechtigkeit" (181).[86]

Both Dietzel[87] and Schulz[88] recognize that the Qumran saint knows present salvation through God's redemptive act of justification, though its terminological formulation is not as explicit as the Pauline doctrine of imputative or declaratory righteousness. Accordingly, many scholars[89] translate *mšpṭ* by "justification", instead of by "judgment". By applying the form-historical method to the Qumran literature, Schulz arrives at the conclusion that the doctrine of *justificatio sola gratia* is constitutive of its didache.[90]

Braun, in his above mentioned article, even acknowledges in the Qumran soteriology an emphatic *simul iustus et peccator!* [91]

But he certainly does not maintain this position when he states that the *justificatio sola gratia* functions only *before* redemption.[92] His point is that the Qumran justification only delivers for the purpose of a stricter

---

86 Schulz therefore proposes the significant conclusion: "Damit dürfte die Paulinische Anschauung von der Rechtfertigung des Sünders sola gratia in ihrer theologischen *Grundstruktur* als vorchristlich erwiesen sein" (182). See n. 1 on p. 182, for similar conclusions by other scholars. And, on the basis of Paul's presumed acquaintance with the Qumran theology: "Paulus hat mit Hilfe legitimer Erkenntnisse und Offenbarungen eines sektiererischen, antipharisäischen Judentums seine Rechtfertigung aus Gnaden in polemischer Antithese zur rabbinische *zᵉkut*-Lehre, wie sie im offiziellen Judentum seiner Zeit gelehrt und von ihm selbst einmal praktiziert worden war, entwickelt!" (184).

87 *O.c.*, 22, n. 37.

88 *O.c.*, 166f. He states: "Die Sache aber, um die es hier geht, der mitgeteilte Urteilsspruch Gottes als Rechtfertigung und rechtskräftige Reinigung, auf Grund dessen das Vollmitglied des Qumran-Jaḥad als vollkommen erachtet wird, wird sowohl in den Hodajot als im Schlusspsalm der Ordensregel ausgesprochen" (167).

89 Schulz mentions Brownlee, Burrows, Dinkler, Allegro. Dietzel also Bardtke and Molin.

90 *O.c.*, 168ff. He observes that this theme of *sola gratia* is only taught in the older stratum of literature, like 1 QS and 1 QH; not in CD and 1 QpHab.

91 *O.c.*, 12.

92 *Ibid.*: "Dass der Mensch keine Rechttaten hat, die ihn vor Gott retten können (1 QH 7,17), gilt also für die Situation des Menschen *vor* dem Heil, besagt aber nichts gegen die Tora als Heilsweg für den Begnadeten" (12).

observance of the Torah than in Pharisaic Judaism.[93] Sin is not conceived as existing in the actual will to obey the Torah, only as a negative influence beside and against this positive will. Confession of sin is only incited by *outward* causes, not by the need of an inner cleavage. It does not realize that sin enters into the very will to obey the Torah.[94]

Here a number of questions arise. First of all, does this point of view do justice to the emphatic declaration of the Society Manual that "the spirits of truth and deceit struggle *within the heart of man*",[95] even until the very apocalyptic end of time?[96]

Is not this struggle within the heart unmistakable evidence of an inner cleavage?

Secondly, does the apostle Paul really indicate that the inner cleavage is one *within* the good will? He himself is confounded by an inner ethical dualism (Rom. 7,15f.). He confesses that the root cause is sin within him, indwelling sin (Rom. 7,17). But he never seems to trace this indwelling sin back specifically to his good will, only to his "flesh":

> For I know that nothing good dwells within me, that is, in my flesh. I can will what is right, but I cannot do it.[97]

Paul delights in the law of God in his inmost self, in his mind or heart, but realizes before God his impotency to fulfill the law, because of the power of sin in his members or flesh.[98]

In other words, the battle in Rom. 7 is between the flesh and the

---

93  *Ibid.*:"Die Gnade dagegen schärft die Tora ein und leitet dazu an, mit der Tora ernst zu machen. Die Gnade verleiht Kraft und Willen zur Tora" (12).

94  *Ibid.*, 14: "Oft sind es Bedrängnisse und Anfechtungen von aussen und Gottes Hilfe darin, welche zum Bekennen der früheren Sünden und der jetzigen Sündlichkeit und Hinfälligkeit treiben, 1 QH 3,26-36; 4,3f.; 6,9; 9,8-10."

95  1 QS 4,23f. Braun, in the quotation of the previous note, does not completely want to restrict the causes of confession of sin to outward incitements ("oft"), yet he neglects to evaluate the *inward* causes. He even continues: "Nie aber ist es die Not der Gespaltenheit, die als *solche* sich ausspricht und das Sündenbekenntnis hervorbrechen lässt." P. von der Osten-Sacken, *Gott und Belial*, SUNT 6, 1969, pp. 24f., makes a different separation between vss. 23 and 24, which does not alter the reading materially, however; cf. p. 25, n. 1.

96  1 QS 4,19-20. The exact time of the end has not been revealed to the Community, 1 QpHab 7,7ff., only that it is imminent, the sect itself being "the last generation", 1 QpHab 2,7; CD 1,12. Cf. also Schulz, *o.c.*, 162.

97  Rom. 7,18. In vs. 20 he describes his "flesh" as indwelling sin: "sin which dwells within me", in vs. 24 as "this body of death".

98  7,22ff.

renewed will or mind, just as in Gal. 5,17ff.[99] Consequently, Braun's critique seems to fail on both sides.

Karl G. Kuhn,[100] who sees the same opposition depicted in Mk. 14,38 par. ("the spirit indeed is willing, but the flesh is weak"), stresses that Paul's use of the concept "flesh" shows "great similarity" to that of the Qumran texts. Most interesting is his comparison of Rom. 7,14: "But I am carnal, sold under sin", with 1 QS 11,9-10:

> *But I* belong to the mankind of perversion and to the *company of the flesh of evil*. My transgressions, my wickedness, my sin together with the rottenness of my heart (mark me as belonging) to the company of worms and to those who walk in darkness" (transl. in Kuhn's art., p. 102).

Kuhn observes here a formal (the "I"-style) as well as a material identity.[101] Even when Paul's Christological and existential interpretations of his anthropology in Rom. 7 and 8 are taken into account, Kuhn affirms a structural analogy with the Qumran anthropology.[102] This means that both Paul and Qumran use the term "flesh" not only in a "neutral" or amoral sense of bodiliness,[103] but also in the specific theological sense of "the sphere, the realm where ungodliness and sin have effective power."[104]

He then points to the "completely new accent and meaning" which the "I"-sayings have in the Qumran texts, in comparison with those of the Biblical Psalms, due to the metaphysical dualistic framework of Qumran. Yet, the new accent of ethical dualism in the Qumran anthropology presents "the true immediate parallel to the 'I'-sayings of Rom. 7."[105]

Schulz therefore believes that new light is cast on the problem of Rom. 7. He suggests that Rom. 7,14ff. may be a reworked and Christianized Qumran thought pattern.[106]

Would this mean that Paul's cry in Rom. 7,24 is merely an echo of the

99  See above, Ch. IV, 3b.

100  In his art. "New Light on Temptation, Sin, and Flesh in the New Testament" in *The Scrolls and the N.T.*, ed. K. Stendahl, 1957, pp. 94-113, esp. 104. This art. is a revised translation from *ZThK* 49 (1952), 200-222.

101  *O.c.*, p. 105; cf. also pp. 102f. He refers also to 1 QH 3,23-25.

102  *O.c.*, p. 106: "we find nevertheless that the over-all anthropological pattern inside which Paul affirms what is new with Jesus Christ is that of the Qumran texts. This analogy is found in both terms and concepts, as was particularly clear in the concept 'flesh'."

103  *Ibid.*, p. 107. In this sense "the body of flesh" is a *terminus technicus* in Judaism.

104  *Ibid.* The Gnostic sense would be to identify the flesh as such with evil.

105  *Ibid.*, p. 103.

106  *O.c.*, 181, n. 4: "Auch hier dürfte eine Qumranvorlage überarbeitet und verchristlicht worden sein!"

Qumran religious experience? W. D. Davies suggests that Paul's own struggles under the Law in his pre-Christian days must now be considered anew for the interpretation of Rom. 7.[107] With that he does not suggest a projecting of the religious experience of Qumran in Paul's pre-Christian days. This cannot be done, since Paul was a Pharisee, and Pharisaic Judaism meant a theology and religious experience basically different from those of Qumran. Davies rather thinks of a polemical use of the term "flesh" (in its moral connotation) by the apostle Paul, as directed against the metaphysical dualism of the Qumran ideology.[108]

The valuable observation in this respect, made by Braun, is that both Paul and Qumran see the sinfulness and imperfection of the redeemed believer *continue* in the state of grace.[109] Unfortunately Braun describes the function of the law at Qumran within the state of grace as "way of salvation" (Heilsweg), i.e., as the specific alternative to the Pauline deliverance *from* the Torah. Here the concept of the *joy in the Tora* of the Book of Psalms, e.g. 1; 19; 119, as the only legitimate way of piety and sanctification, has completely been lost sight of and ignored.[110]

It will not do suddenly to identify the Qumran pietistic ethics with that of Pharisaic Judaism, as Braun basically does.[111]

Otzen seems to honor the motives of the Qumran piety far better when he evaluates them as an intentional return to the true piety of the prophets, i.e., to a spiritualizing of the Torah in its claims on the human heart as depicted in Micah 6,8.[112] The Qumran community, after its

---

107   "Paul and the Dead Sea Scrolls: Flesh and Spirit", in Stendahl, *The Scrolls and the N.T.*, pp. 157-182; see n. 86, on p. 282.

108   *O.c.*, p. 164: "Paul shares its terminology at certain points but not its doctrinal formulations." He sees the basic difference in the Pauline antithesis of flesh and spirit on the one hand, and the Qumran antithesis of the two spirits, on the other hand, p. 171.

109   *O.c.*, pp. 15f. Braun, who agrees with W. G. Kümmel's conclusion with regard to Rom. 7, refers specifically to Gal. 5,16f. for this statement, since Rom. 7 is not applied by Kümmel to the Christian existence.

110   Here Calvin's *third* use of the Law appears to be of crucial significance (*Inst.* II, 7, 12), i.e., that the Spirit-filled believers long to obey God and still profit by the law in two ways: "to learn more thoroughly each day the nature of the Lord's will to which they aspire, and to confirm them in the understanding of it."

111   See e.g. the argument of B. Otzen, *l.c.*, 126: "Den beiden Schriftgruppen [sc. Test. XII and Qumran writings] ist gemeinsam, dass sie fern von der pharisäisch-rabbinischen *Gesetzlichkeit* stehen und beide eine *Frömmigkeits- und Nächstenethik* aufstellen". Otzen specifically refers to the *Manual of Discipline* for a pietistic ethics, as quite different from late Judaism.

112   *O.c.*, p. 129: "Das Gesetz ist nicht aufgehoben, wird aber durch die Innerlichkeit der prophetischen Frömmigkeit vergeistigt." Also 155, 157. He refers esp. to 1 QS 2,11-18; 4,9.

wandering to Damascus, stood under a definite anti-Pharisaic influence, if the *Manual of Discipline* is compared with the *Damascus Document*. The new influence is clearly opposed to the contemporaneous Pharisaic externalism of the Torah obedience.[113]

The *Hodayot* picture the way of sanctification as the new consecration for God in total obedience *after* the cleansing from sin, *after* justification by grace.

> And for the sake of Thy glory, Thou hast cleansed man from transgression so that he may consecrate himself For Thee (1 QH 11,10).

> And Thou sheddest (Thy) favor upon me through Thy compassionate spirit and Thy [glo]rious splendor. To Thee, alone, is righteousness, for Thou hast wrought al[l these].
> For, indeed, I know that Thou inscribedst (every) righteous spirit. And (therefore) I have chosen to purify myself, according to Thy wi[ll], for the soul of Thy servant [abhorreth] all deeds of injustice. And I know that no man beside Thee can be just. And I, therefore, entreat Thee, through the spirit which Thou didst put [in me] to bring unto fulfillment Thy [lovingkind]ness (Thou hast shown) unto [Thy] ser[vant]... to cleanse me with Thy holy spirit and draw me near (to Thee) in Thy good pleasure, according to Thy great lovingkindness ... (1 QH 16,9-12).

A highlight in the religious self-consciousness of the Qumran believer, to us, is the following praise of Israel's God as the source of holiness together with the acknowledgment of his own "perverseness":

> But God I will call my righteousness, / the Most High (I will call) base of my happiness, fountain of knowledge, well of holiness, height of splendour, the power of everything with eternal glory.

---

113  *Ibid.*, 155: "Der Einfluss stammt aus Kreisen, die wohl das Gesetz als Grundlage haben, aber nicht wie die Pharisäer kramphaft an den Gesetzesregeln festhalten und die Petitessen der Thora pflegen; die Äusserlichkeit der pharisäischen Frömmigkeit ist ihnen fremd." Otzen thinks of the anonymous group of the ᶜ*Am-Haᵓareṣ* (156).
On the matter of casuistic laws of Sabbath observance, see the interesting comparison of the *Damascus Document* with Rabbinical literature, in S. T. Kimbrough, Jr., "The Concept of Sabbath at Qumran", in *RQ* 5 (1966), 483-502. His conclusion is that Qumran's concept of Sabbath "does not seem out of step with Judaism, nor so apparently more strict than the Pharisees and the resulting Rabbinical tradition" (502). He states: "The Sabbath Halakah of *Dam. Doc.* is very rigid." That it was more rigid, however, than that of Pharisaism appears from CD 11,13-14, where is codified that a beast, when fallen into a cistern or pit, "let it not be lifted out on the Sabbath"; cf. Mat. 12,11. Cf. Moore, *Judaism* II, pp. 26-27.

⟨I⟩ will choose what / He points out for me, and I will accept the way in which He governs me (1 QS 10,12-13).

When the Qumranians call themselves "men of holiness" and "the perfect ones", therefore, it seems not to express a feeling of self-sufficiency. All their perfection was ascribed completely to God's work.[114]

The new obedience is stressed as the result of the graciously given Spirit of God:

> Unto God Most High are all the works or righteousness and way of a mortal is not established save through the Spirit (which) God fashioned for him. To make perfect a way for the sons of man, so that they may know all His works through the might of His power and the abundance of His mercies upon all the sons of His pleasure. (1 QH 4,31-32). And with (Thy) established truth Thou dost uphold me and in Thy holy spirit Thou dost delight me and even unto this day ... (1 QH 9,32).[115]

Since the Qumran community, in contrast with Rabbinic Judaism, believed that the time of the end *had* come, and with that, the eschatological promise of the Spirit *was* being fulfilled, the *Hodayot*, like the apostle Paul, know of a praying of the Spirit in man as well as a praying of man in the Spirit.[116]

It cannot be denied that the Qumran piety placed more emphasis on the ideal of a perfect heart and wholehearted religious-moral rectitude than on cultic purity and asceticism.[117] The ideal of moral perfection is perhaps nowhere expressed so clearly as in the following words of the *Manual of Discipline*:

> Belial (worthlessness) I will not keep in my heart. Neither shall lewdness and iniquitous deceits be heard in my mouth, nor shall craftiness and lies be found on my lips. The fruit of holiness shall be on my tongue, and detested words shall not be found on it (1 QS 10,21-22).[118]

114 Cf. van der Ploeg, *o.c.*, p. 119: "Thus the consciousness of their own sinfulness suppressed the thought of their own perfection." Vermes, *o.c.*, p. 41. Mansoor, *o.c.*, p. 60.

115 See further 1 QH 7,6f.; 16,7. Cf. Dietzel, *l.c.*, 23f., who concludes: „der Geist ist das von Gott geschenkte Mittel zum Vollzuge des neuen Wandels" (24).

116 See Dietzel, *o.c.*, pp. 24-32.

117 Cf. Ringgren, *o.c.*, p. 140: "In any case, asceticism is not a means of disciplining the body in its capacity as sinful flesh." See further in Ringgren on the ideal of poverty.

118 For the same ideal of moral perfection in the *Testaments of the Twelve patriarchs*, esp. *Test. Iss.* 7,4, see B. Otzen, "Die neugefundenen hebräischen Sektenschriften und die Testamente der zwölf Patriarchen", in *StTh* 7 (1954), 125-157, esp. 133.

And that this ideal was intended to become a gracious, living reality in the society and the character of the individual Qumran believers, appears from the following:

> And (verily) I know that there is hope for them that turn from transgression and for them that abandon sin ... to walk about In the way of Thy heart, with no injustice (1 QH 6,6-7).[119]

Since the Qumran soteriology is so deeply influenced and embedded in the Old Testament way of salvation, it is likely that the sharp religious-ethical dualism of Qumran was intended to be the cultic dualism of the Biblical Psalms. Accordingly, the self-designation *ᵓebyôn* ("poor") and *ᶜānî* ("oppressed") may well be intended to be the fulfillment of prophecy as depicted in the Psalms.[120]

What then was the attitude of the priestly apocalyptists of Qumran toward the cultic way of salvation of the Old Testament, and the sacrificial cult in the Temple in particular?

As appears from *The War Scroll* (1 QM), *The Damascus Document* (CD) and the *Habakkuk Commentary* (1 QpHab.), the Qumran community did not reject the sacrificial cult in the Temple in principle, only in its contemporary ritual manifestation because of its desecration by an unfaithful priesthood.[121]

Baumgarten[122] observes with respect to the Qumran covenanters and the Essenes:

> Both continued to honor the Temple and the priesthood as holy institutions, although they ceased to offer sacrifices. Both had sacred rituals which were at first modelled after and ultimately came to replace the Temple worship.

119  Cf. also 16,11; 1 QS 4,2-7.
120  Cf. Ringgren, *o.c.*, p. 141. He refers to scholars who even identify the Qumran community with the Ebionites, i.e., Jewish-Christians. J. Daniélou, *Qumran und der Ursprung des Christentums*, 1959² (French, 1957), pp. 164-167, ET. pp. 122-124, takes the position that the Ebionites stand between the Qumran Zadokites and Christianity.
121  See Cross, *o.c.*, pp. 75f. J. M. Baumgarten, "Sacrifice and Worship among the Jewish Sectarians of the Dead Sea (Qumran) Scrolls", in *HThR* 46 (1953), 141-159, shows that the sectarians "turned to Prophetic denunciations of sinful offerings" (154); e.g. Amos 5,22-27 (in CD 7,14f.). Concerning the differences in the resp. writings as being no real contrasts, see Hengel, *o.c.*, p. 406, n. 674.
122  *O.c.*, p. 157. On the basis of the archeological discovery of meticulous burials of animal bones at Qumran, Cross (*o.c.*, p. 76, also n. 122) is inclined to believe now that the Qumran sect actually maintained its own independent sacrificial cult. But this remains very doubtful.

Gärtner especially has discovered that the Qumran community was organized as a parallel to the Jerusalem priesthood, continuing some definite forms of Temple liturgy, as appears e.g. in the Levitical proclamations, blessings and curses, in 1 QS 1,18-2,25.[123] He indicates how the community's concentration on the Law did not obscure the predominant cultic liturgy taken from the Temple service. And because "they transfered the whole complex of ideas from the Jerusalem temple to the community", they also transferred the holiness and the atoning function of the Temple to their Qumran community. The conclusion therefore seems to be justified that the "sacrifices" of thanksgiving and the godly life of perfect obedience to the Law of Moses were regarded at Qumran as atoning for sin.[124] In other words, the "spiritualization" of the Temple service and worship at Qumran meant a realistic *replacement* of the blood sacrifices of the Jerusalem Temple, but only temporarily, i.e., for the time of present defilement of the Temple. They looked forward to the future purification of the Temple in the final war, when the Temple cultus would be restored again.[125] But for the time being the Qumran community regarded itself as the Temple in which spiritual sacrifices were offered, a unique phenomenon in Judaism.[126]

As Gärtner summarizes:

> These are not merely images and symbols; they express a reality. Since the community has taken over the holiness and the functions of the temple it is now in point of fact the only means of maintaining the holiness of Israel and making atonement for sin. It is necessary that atonement should be made for the sins of the people; the desecration of the official temple has rendered it useless for these ends; there must be a substitute, and that substitute is the life of the community, lived in perfect obedience to all the precepts of the Law; all its commandments, purifications and prayers.[127]

---

123  *The Temple and the Com. in Qumran*, pp. 9f., referring esp. to 1 QM 2,1ff. See also Leaney, *The Rule of Qumran and its Meaning*, pp. 91-95: "The Temple and the Priesthood."

124  *Ibid.*, pp. 18f., 44-46, 87. He refers, among others, to 1 QS 8,9; 9,3ff.

125  *Ibid.*, p. 19: "This vision of the restoration of the temple and the reestablishment of the cultus represents one side of the demand for perfection in the life of Israel made by the Messianic epoch. The other was made up of the consummate power of the Law among a righteous people. The Law and the temple thus belong to the same complex of ideas." Cf. Driver, *o.c.*, p. 119.

126  Gärtner, *o.c.*, p. 47: "No direct parallel to this temple symbolism has been traced in Judaism." Leaney, *o.c.*, p. 95: "If the whole sect represents the Temple, the laity represents the sanctuary and the priests of the sect the holy of holies."

127  *O.c.*, p. 44.

We owe much to Gärtner's scholarly work, since we are now able to evaluate better the intensified Torah obedience of the Qumran community. The specific cultic setting and concentration casts light on the strict observance of Levitical purity. The concept of atoning *mediation* in place of the Jerusalem cultus was part of Qumran's self-understanding. The line of demarcation between Israel as a whole and its Remnant was not yet absolute and final.[128]

The apocalyptic end and judgment was conceived as being imminent, but not yet present.

An assessment of the Qumran theology and piety, in spite of the revealing documents which have been published so far, still must be tentative, since many manuscripts have not yet been published.

Were the Qumran saints perfectionists? Does their religion or ethics bear the mark of perfectionism? It would be inadequate to say that they were just separatists or ascetics or legalists, striving for religious-moral perfection. Their motivation was to maintain specifically the cultic purity of the Jerusalem Temple and its atoning, mediating efficacy, in obedience to the Pentateuchal Law, within an apocalyptic setting and urgency. When the official cult was desecrated by an illegal priesthood in Jerusalem according to Levitical law,[129] the priestly Teacher of Righteousness set up his own cultus within his own community. His ritual puritanism led him to construct (or accept) a different cultic (solar) calendar, according to which the Qumran Zadokites began to regulate their liturgy and their celebration of Levitical festivals.[130] Thus Qumran strove for a perfect keeping of the covenant of Israel in assumed apocalyptic times.

As far as its soteriology is concerned, the deep religious *Hymns* confess the conviction of an *abiding*, inherent sinful nature together with the joyful trust in God's justification *sola gratia*. In view of this testimony it does not seem fitting to make an unqualified judgment that Qumran's theology taught a religious synergism or legalistic perfectionism. However, the severe moral and ritual rules and the concentrated urge for perfection according to the Law tend to legalistic perfectionism.[131]

---

128  Cf. Holm-Nielsen, *o.c.*, p. 284, who indicates that even "a falling away can occur from within the community, from amongst the elect."

129  Cf. Leaney, *o.c.*, pp. 165, 94f. Yadin, *o.c.*, pp. 198-201.

130  See Leaney, *o.c.*, pp. 92ff., who points out that Qumran followed the calendar of I *Enoch* 72-82 and *Jubilees*. He associates the claimed connection of the Qumran Zadokites and the angels with their similar service in the presence of God: both serve "before God"; cf. also Lk. 1,8.19. Cf. K. G. Kuhn, "Zum Essenischen Kalender", in *ZNW* 52 (1961), 65-73.

131  Cf. also Hengel, *o.c.*, p. 403: "die 'perfektionistisch' anmutende vollkommene Toraerfüllung". Bronner, *o.c.*, pp. 148f., 157, 162, places the Qumran

In other words, the *sola gratia* is seriously overshadowed by the extreme ritual and ascetic injunctions. The legal structure of Qumran's concept of sanctification becomes evident when we consider the yearly investigation of the progress in perfection (ritual and moral) of each individual member, as appears from 1 QS 5,24; 9,2; 10,21. Qumran even seemed to have defined degrees of perfection. Perfection apparently was conceived in judicial terms, measured by the sons of Zadok, while the *sola gratia* still was affirmed.[132] This combination of works according to the Law, and the praise of the *sola gratia*, is the peculiar characteristic of Qumran's piety. As Davies acknowledges: "The attainment of 'perfection' envisaged in these passages is clearly a matter of works and yet it is a gift of God. (DSD [sc. 1 QS] XI:2)."[133]

He touches the crucial issue when he observes that "perfection" in the *Manual of Discipline* "is not directly thought of in terms of the *imitatio Dei*: It is rather complete obedience to the Law as understood by the community." In other words, the Law tends to become an almost self-existent entity beside God, which, consequently, must be punctiliously observed for its fulfillment. Yet, the Law is rooted in the living God, although a distance between Law and God seems to be experienced.

There are, however, some definite aspects of the Qumran piety which qualify it incontestably as religious perfectionism, basically because of its extreme and decisive principle of apocalyptic ritual puritanism. Ritual-ethical purity proved to be its guiding principle since it led to separation from the official sacrificial cult and to the establishment of a counter priestly cultus in Qumran, rejecting the Jerusalem priesthood merely on the basis of Levitical purity and ethics.[134] Ritual puritanism even drove the Qumran community so far as to discontinue the Mosaic way of cultic redemption through blood sacrifices, and to regard its own ritual-moral observance as atoning for sins.[135] Furthermore, the sectarian character of

---

rituals *between* the stern rules of the Essenes, and the moderate regulations of Pharisaic Judaism. In the judgment of Rabbinic Judaism "The Qumran community was styled as 'heterodox' while the Essenes were considered 'heretical'" (p. 162).

132 Cf. Nötscher, *Gotteswege*, p. 84: "Wie Sündenvergebung und Recht-fertigung betrachtet man auch den 'vollkommenen Weg' im Sinne der rechten Lebensführung als ein Gnadengeschenk aus der Hand Gottes."

133 In *HThR* 46 (1953), 115.

134 Cf. G. Molin, *Die Söhne des Lichts*, 1954, p. 143: "Es sind einfach die viel weitergehenden Reinheitsvorschriften für Priester auf die ganze Gemeinde übertragen, weil sie priesterlichen Dienst übt und in ihrem Leben dem ver-weltlichten, unreinen Jerusalemer Priestertum ein anderes, besseres gegen-übergestellt." He interprets their wearing of white garments, according to Josephus, also from this priestly motivation and imitation. Further K. Elliger, *Stud. z. Hab.-Komm.*, p. 277.

135 J. Ph. Hyatt, "On the meaning and origin of Micah 6:8", in *AThR* 34 (1952), 232-239, recognizes in the *Man. of Disc.* an attitude "toward sacrifice...

their observances becomes specifically evident from their exclusive, self-imposed entrance rules; only the *physically* [136] perfect ones were allowed membership. The sect of Qumran came to regard the sons of Zadok, and then also the whole community, as the only legitimate priests, and their own Torah interpretations as the exclusively perfect insight, through special revelation. It is this last point, the Gnostic principle that Israel's God would have revealed His final secrets exclusively to the Qumran community – and its Teacher of Righteousness in particular – which gave them their sense of apocalyptic mission, i.e. the conviction of being the elected, faithful Remnant of all Israel, which alone will be saved in the final war. These final secrets, or "marvelous mysteries", of Yahweh were conceived as hidden in the words of Scripture, but disclosed solely to the Righteous Teacher as saving gnosis [137] by means of a special charisma. The Teacher of Righteousness claimed to be not merely the teacher and leader of the Qumran community but also its bringer of salvation. [138]

The prophetic words in Hab. 2,4b: "But the righteous shall live by his faith(fulness)", are interpreted to mean that only those "law keepers" in the house of Judah will be saved from condemnation in the final judgment, who in the time of persecution have been "faithful to the Teacher of Righteousness" (1 QpHab 7,18-8,3).

---

similar to that expressed in Micah 6:6-8" (239), referring to 1 QS 9,3-5. The Damascus Covenanters, however, did offer sacrifices. Cf. also S. E. Johnson, in *ZAW* 66 (1954), 115, who states concerning the Dam. Cov. that to them "the true keeping of Torah was a valid equivalent to animal sacrifice, but sacrifice was not excluded."

136 Illuminating is Jeremias' comparison of the Qumran Teacher and Jesus Christ in this respect, *o.c.*, pp. 339f.: "Die Kluft zwischen dem Lehrer und Jesus trennt zwei Welten. Auf der einen Seite steht der Lehrer mit radikalsten Versuch, die ethisch einwandfreie, reine Gemeinde Gottes zu verwirklichen, –auf der anderen Seite Jesus, der nicht zu den Gerechten geht, sondern zu Sündern (Mk. 2,17), der die Verworfenen und Verachteten zu sich ruft und mit den Sündern Tischgemeinschaft hält. Die Krüppel, Lahmen und Blinden, die in der Q.-Gemeinde keinen Platz haben, schildert Jesus im Gleichnis als Gäste beim Freudenmahl (Lk. 14,21 ...)." This comparison becomes specifically relevant for our assessment of Qumran's piety when we consider that Jesus' attitude towards sinners is the true reflection of Yahweh's mercy, the very revelation of Israel's covenant God and His perfect love (cf. *ibid.*, p. 343). Cf. also A. Vögtle, *Das öffentliche Wirken Jesu auf dem Hintergrund der Qumranbewegung*, "Freib. Univ. Reden" NF 27, 1958.

137 Cf. 1 QH 1,21; 7,26; 9,24; 15,12; *et al.* Cf. Hengel, *o.c.*, p. 417, who correctly observes: "Die apokalyptisch-essenische Erkenntnisvorstellung nimmt im Grunde wesentliche Züge der gnostischen vorweg: [referring to Bultmann, in *ThWNT* I, 693]." Cf. Mansoor, *o.c.*, pp. 68ff. Holm-Nielsen, *o.c.*, pp. 286. Elliger, *o.c.*, p. 286.

138 See G. Jeremias, *Der Lehrer der Gerechtigkeit*, pp. 175f. ("der Heilbringer"), 266f. This does not mean the Messiah, however, as A. Dupont-Sommer concluded. See pp. 268ff., 319ff.

He alone possesses the decisive "banner" of divine knowledge, the key to unlock all the mysteries of the prophecies, by special inspiration of God (1 QpHab 2,7ff.; 7,4), and therefore is the sole appointed messenger of this saving knowledge (1 QH 2,13).

Qumran's specific apocalyptic eschatology and ethics thus is grounded and motivated by the inspiration or revelation of its Righteous Teacher. Not in the sense that the Old Testament prophets are officially set aside or placed in a secondary position, but that the Righteous Teacher claims to have the inspired divine interpretation of these prophetic messages with regard to the present crisis situation.

His interpretation, however, is an independent criterion and authority. Elliger is correct when he observes that here the authority and inspiration of the "interpreter" is elevated above that of Scripture itself.[139]

Israel's acceptance or rejection of his Scripture interpretation determines its salvation or condemnation. Yet, strangely enough, this esoteric or hidden knowledge of "the wondrous secrets" had to be kept concealed from the sons of destruction.[140] Here Qumran's exclusivism comes most painfully to the front.

As Otto Betz[141] summarizes well:

> Israel lebt im Irrtum, weil ihm die verborgenen Dinge in der Schrift unbekannt sind (1 QS 8,11). Es hat diesen Zustand selbst verschuldet; denn es unterlässt das Suchen und Forschen in Gottes Gebot (1 QS 5,11), versäumt so, den Gottesweg zu bereiten, und verfällt deshalb dem Gericht (1 QS 5,12f).

P. Wernberg-Møller[142] has shown that the author of the *Manual of*

---

139 Elliger, *o.c.*, p. 278: "Damit wird faktisch die Inspiration des Lehrers der Gerechtigkeit der der heiligen Schriften übergeordnet, auch wenn sie sich nur als 'Auslegung' (II 8) gibt...." Cf. G. Jeremias, *o.c.*, p. 324: "Er ist Prophet. Seine Kenntnis stammt direkt von Gott, der ihm die Geheimnisse offenbart. Er fasst die Propheten zusammen, er weiss um die Geheimnisse die in ihren Worten verborgen sind. Schon dieses prophetische Bewusstsein stellt den Lehrer unmittelbar neben Jesus."
140 1 QH 5,24f.; 1 QS 9,17-20. Cf. Flusser, in *o.c.*, pp. 250f. Holm-Nielsen, *o.c.*, p. 284.
141 *Offenbarung und Schriftforschung in der Qumransekte*, WUNT 6, 1960, p. 158.
142 "Some reflections on the Biblical Material in the Manual of Discipline", in *StTh* 9 (1955), 40-60. On pp. 64f. e.g. he refers to the spiritualizing of the implied fasting of Lev. 16,31 in 1 QS 3,8; and to the esoteric application of the "strong city", protected by "walls and bulwarks" in Is. 26,1-3 to the secrets of the society in 1 QS 10,24f. On pp. 53ff. he discusses "cases of words taken in meanings other than those intended in the biblical context"; on pp. 57ff. cases of words that are given different meanings by rearranging the letters or the vowels.

*Discipline* manifests an arbitrary spiritualistic-allegorical way of interpreting the Old Testament Scriptures, with the tendency toward an increasing liberty from the letter of the Torah. Betz,[143] especially, has pointed to the crucial significance of the eschatological Scripture interpretation, in which the esoteric-allegorical application constitutes the motivating principle of Qumran's apocalyptic self-consciousness. This underlying principle of esoteric or secret light on the Torah reveals that the Qumran sect completely identified the Scripture interpretations of the Teacher of Righteousness with divine revelation and took his specific revelations as the superior norm of interpretation.[144] This uncritical apocalyptic-allegorical principle of Torah interpretation and self-understanding by the Qumran community constitutes its most essential form of religious-theological perfectionism.

We might describe this form of charismatic apocalyptic interpretation of the Torah, together with its outward manifestations of ritualism, asceticism, and exclusiveness, as *apocalyptic perfectionism*.[145]

This term tries to avoid the illegitimate idea that at Qumran the extreme ascetic-ethical, ritual and separatist principles would have arisen and existed *beside* or independently from its peculiar apocalyptic con-

---

143  *O.c.*, pp. 155-182. He concludes: "Dabei steht nicht etwa der Heilbringer, sondern das Heilsvolk im Vordergrund. Das hohe Selbstbewusstsein der Sekte, die als die Gemeinde der Erwählten und Heiligen allen Stürmen der Endzeit trotzen und mit den Engeln zu einer ewigwährenden Gemeinschaft zusammengeschlossen werden soll, wird durch das geistlich verstandene Wort der Schrift bestärkt" (pp. 181f.).

144  Cf. 1 QH 2,13; 4,24; 7,1-5, 20-21. His interpretation is accepted by the covenanters as "sucklings" drink the milk from the breasts of their mother. Also Rigaux, *o.c.*, p. 247, interprets the *Pešarim* of the Teacher of Righteousness as a *new* revelation in connection with the Scripture text. "Le parfait était celui qui acceptant cette doctrine la vivait intégralement" (248). "En somme, nous nous trouvons devant une réinterprétation apocalyptique des écrits sacrés basée sur l'autorité des fondateurs et des maîtres de Qumrân" (261). See also above, n. 139.

145  When Burrows, *More Light*, p. 92, states: "In four of its most distinctive characteristics – asceticism, legalism, ritualism, and exclusiveness – the Qumran community thus represents the opposite extremes from the religion of Jesus", we have a reservation only about his too unqualified assessment of "legalism". Even Braun acknowledged in Qumran's soteriology the religious experience and doctrine of *simul iustus et peccator* (see above). The issue at stake is only whether Qumran taught a synergistic way of sanctification. When Leaney, *o.c.*, p. 125, states, *ad* 1 QS 1,17: "This ideal of legal perfection [sc. complete obedience to all that God has commanded] must not be confused with the inner qualitative perfection which is the ideal of the Christian ethic", it seems more fitting to ask, Does this ideal of legal perfection come in conflict with the religious-cultic perfection of Israel's covenant? Only when law by itself is substituted for the living presence of Yahweh does the conflict arise. On this point there is no clear *communis opinio*.

viction. Apocalypticism rather constituted the underlying, motivating principle of Qumran's perfectionism.[146]

George Molin[147] has called the Qumran community the "Latter-day saints" of late Judaism, who in holy earnestness followed the way of the Law to its utmost consequences. He states:

> Dass sie den Weg des Judentums konsequent zu Ende gingen, wer will es ihnen verübeln? Kannten sie einen anderen doch nicht. Sie gingen ihn mit einem heiligen Ernst, der beschämend wirkt. Aber hie und da dämmert es auf ihren Schriften, besonders in den Hymnen, dass der Mensch von sich aus mit aller Mühe nicht gerecht sein könne, dass er ganz auf die Gnade Gottes angewiesen sei.[148]

From our analysis of human perfection in the Old Testament,[149] it follows, however, that legalism or synergism is a falsification of the cultic-ethical way of covenant perfection. Not the law or moral code by itself is the ideal of covenant perfection, but the personal fellowship with the Redeemer-Creator God, i.e., the walk with the covenant God in the way of His Torah. In the Qumran community there is a distance kept between the Pentateuchal Law and God, and that vacuum is filled with the autority of the Scripture interpretation of its Teacher of Righteousness. History has shown that his apocalyptic perfectionism with respect to his asceticism, ritualism and exclusivism carries in it the germ of catastrophic disappointment and disillusionment, in spite of its religious passion and enthusiasm.

## 2. *The Encratites.*

Harnack observes that the first Christian perfectionists, starting perhaps already in the time of the apostle Paul (as indicated in his Letter to the Romans), were those "circles of ascetics in the Christian communities who required of all, as an inviolable law, under the name of Christian perfection, complete abstinence from marriage, renunciation of possessions, and a vegetarian diet."[150]

---

146  Cf. Elliger, *o.c.*, p. 277: "Und das Drängen auf das Halten des Gesetzes ist nur die praktische Konsequenz seiner Überzeugung von der Nähe des Endes...." Also Betz, *o.c.*, p. 142. On the relationship of apocalypticism and Gnosticism, see Schubert, *o.c.*, pp. 71ff.

147  *O.c.*, p. 146.

148  Cf. Betz, *o.c.*, p. 182: "Vergegenwärtigt man sich die Kraft des Glaubens und Gottvertrauens und die Glut der Hoffnung, die diese Männer in Qumran beseelten, so kann man ihr katastrophales Ende nicht bedenken, ohne tief erschüttert zu sein."

149  See above, Ch. III, B.

150  *Hist. of Dogma*, I, Dover ed. 1961 (German, 3d ed.) § 3; pp. 238f. He refers specifically to Clement of Alexandria's *Stromateis* III, 6,49. For all the

They tried to imitate the poor life of Jesus through this rigorous asceticism. To them the bearing of "the whole yoke of the Lord" actually meant the perfect fulfilling of the law of Christ.[151] Those Christians – at first without being organized or holding to a specific creed – who tried to imitate Christ by making abstinence from flesh, wine, marriage, and possessions their rule of life were called the *Encratites* or "continent people", and, later, the Severians.[152] J. Strahan[153] gives the following setting of life of the Encratites in the Christian Church:

> They rejected the prevalent distinction between a higher and a lower, though sufficient, morality. The Church, which applauded their counsel of perfection in the few, resolutely declared war against their principle when they sought to make it an inflexible law for all. Therefore they refused to follow the Church, scorning the weak compromise she offered. They insisted that, if *enkrateia* was right at all, it was right universally. To be a Christian was to be an Encratite.

Following their excommunication, after A.D. 170, Encratism gradually lost its identity by being swallowed up by Gnosticism, on the one hand, and by being replaced by Montanism, on the other hand.[154]

The most important representative of Encratism is the Mesopotamian Apologist Tatian, a disciple of Justin Martyr.[155] Of his writings only one

sources, see A. Hilgenfeld, *Die Ketzergeschichte des Urchristentums. Urkundlich dargestellt*, 1966 (repr. of 1884), pp. 543-546.

151 Harnack, *H.D.*, I, 238.

152 Eusebius, *Hist. eccl.* IV, 29. Cf. J. Strahan, in *ERE* V, 301 (s.v. *Encratites*) who states: "Their spirit was widely diffused.... The life of celibacy and the renunciation of all worldly goods, after His pattern, was the essential mark of Christian perfection." The Severians even rejected the Epistles of Paul since the Pauline ethics obviously was not perfectionistic enough, see esp. 1 Tim. 4,3. Cf. Harnack, *H.D.* I, 239. On the basic difference between *enkrateia* in Greek and Hellenistic philosophy on the one hand, and in Biblical religion on the other hand, see Grundmann, in *ThWNT* II, 338-340 (s.v. *enkrateia*).

153 In *ERE* V, 301.

154 Harnack, *H.D.* I, 239. He states that Tertullian's "only reason for not being an Encratite is that this mode of life had already been adopted by heretics, and become associated with dualism" (II, 103).

155 For Tatian's later fragments and the judgment of early Church fathers on Encratism, see *Corpus Apologetarum Christianorum*, ed. J. C. Th. Otto, Vol. VI, 1969 (repr. of 1851), pp. 164-175. And Hilgenfeld, *o.c.*, pp. 384-397. Irenaeus, *Adv. Haer.* I, 28, 1, condemns three errors of Tatian's teaching: 1) the invention of "aeons" between God and men; 2) the denouncing of marriage as "corruption and fornication"; 3) the denial of salvation to Adam. Eusebius, *H.E.* IV, 29, reports that Tatian even was regarded by many as the author of Encratism. Cf. Heussi, *K.K.* §§ 12d; 13S. It should be remembered, however, that not all Encratites stood behind Tatian. Hippolytus, *Phil.* VIII,

has been transmitted as a whole, his *Oration to the Greeks* (c. A.D. 176). His popular *Diatesseron*, the standard Church lectionary of the Four Gospels in novel form in Syria until the fourth century, is only extant in diverging manuscripts.[156] For our purpose especially important is a transmitted fragment of an early Christian tract in an Armenian manuscript, first published in 1836, which J. Rendel Harris[157] identified as Tatian's missing *Peri tou kata ton Sōtèra katartismou* (Perfection according to the Savior) mentioned by Clement Alexandrinus, *Strom.* III,12. This ancient Christian tract presents a most interesting concept of Christian Perfection or Perfect Discipleship. In the translation of Rendel Harris the following idea is developed:

> Wherefore, even as our Saviour Himself and the Prophets and His Apostles separated themselves from this present world through their piety and their dwelling and their eating and drinking and their glorious words, so also should we be imitators of our Teacher and of our Comrades his first disciples. For we ourselves will part from this present world, by our piety and our sobriety, and our habitation of the world, and by our eating and drinking and our spiritual course of life; nor should ye mingle with the affairs and the discourse of the world. For if we by our mode of life and our dwelling and our eating and our drinking and our words are not separate and disjoined from the men who are here, our Lord might just as well have come to the winds and the stones and discoursed to them His noble commands from His father, and He should not have been sent to us in person.[158]

The conspicuous characteristic of this presentation is its negative, separatistic trend. Further, its repeated ascetic stress, e.g., on eating and drinking. Of major importance is, however, its dogmatic theological tendency of a legalistic piety and *imitatio Christi*, which is only confirmed by the rest of the extant writing. The copying of Jesus', the prophets' and the apostles' style of life is never motivated by the redeeming walk with

---

7, 20, knows Encratites who have an ortdodox Christology and theology, and differ from the Church only in their vegetarian manner of life, and their abstinence from wine and sexual life.

156   F. F. Bruce, *The Spreading Flame*, 1964[3], p. 286, reports that John the Baptist is presented as a vegetarian in the *Diatesseron*, using milk instead of locusts. This, however, seems not to be the case in all manuscripts. On the problem of the Diatesseron, see M. Elze, *Tatian und seine Theologie*, "Forsch. z. Kirch, u. Dogm. gesch." 9, 1960, pp. 124-126.

157   See the *Reprint of Bull. of the John Rylands Library* 8, 1924, 17-24. Elze, on p. 7, calls Harris' arguments "schwache Argumente," but does not indicate why. Elze bases his investigation of Tatian's theology solely on Tatian's *Oration to the Greeks*.

158   *O.c.*, pp. 17f.

or the gracious presence of Jesus Christ, nor incited by the sense of gratitude for the received deliverance. Rather the continuous impression is given that the "perfect discipleship" of Christ consists in the autonomous decision and militant effort to fight for the Heavenly King in order to "attain to glory through the conflict of our strivings, and the war of our heroism, and through our obedience, and we come to stand before the Heavenly King, and to receive from His great presents, renown and honour and glory . . ."[159]

The Christological soteriology of the New Testament seems to be forthrightly denied, however, when it is stated:

> For by the observation of His commandments we shall be set free from Satan, who fights against us in varied forms: and tenderly doth the Holy Spirit care for us as He did for the Prophets.[160]

Tatian's Encratite perfectionism is supported by the heroic consciousness of attaining to the same perfection as Christ by the Encratite way of life and struggle, i.e., of having become perfect in true knowledge and conduct and of having destroyed the human "nature of wickedness."[161] That Tatian's concept of perfection seems to point to the idea of inherent perfection appears from his application of the merchantman in the parable, who sold all his possessions in order to buy the one costly and precious pearl:[162]

> When we gain the pearl of our Lord, that is, His commandments, gay and glad is our Soul and Spirit and our Heart is delighted within us, and fair we are and beauteous we become in ourselves through the pearl that is within us.

Although one should not draw definite conclusions with reference to Tatian's theology on the basis of a small tract, the tentative conclusion must nevertheless be that this treatise on Perfect Discipleship presents the literal imitation of Christ as the exclusive way of true piety. This conclusion from Tatian's tract on Perfection appears to be in complete agreement with the conclusions of Martin Elze's study of the theology of Tatian's *Oration to the Greeks*. In this study Elze establishes the fact

---

159  In Harris, *o.c.*, p. 21.
160  *Ibid.*, p. 18.
161  *Ibid.*, p. 20: "and when we became perfect and strong in it . . ." Cf. also Tatian's *Oration*, ch. 30.
162  In Harris, *o.c.*, p. 22. In the application of the parable of the man who found a treasure in a field, Tatian again applies the treasure ultimately not to Christ but to "the gladsome treasure of His mouth" (p. 23).

that Tatian's starting point and leading principle is not the orthodox Christological soteriology but the philosophical idea of truth as an indivisible and exclusive principle of unity.[163] This philosophical *a priori* is found to determine basically Tatian's theology, its monotheism and docetic Christology in which Christ is portrayed as the heavenly moral Instructor and Example.

In Tatian's anthropolgy and dualistic ethics Christ comes only to enflame the inherent spark of the Spirit in man so that man himself may overcome his inner disunity by denying his natural body, natural generation, marriage and all wordly life.[164]

Because of Tatian's intellectualistic idea of sin and presumed inherent spark of the Spirit in man, there is no deed for a specific Redeemer.[165]

In the light of this philosophical presupposition it becomes more understandable why Tatian in his Perfect Discipleship develops such a rigoristic, ascetic doctrine of moralistic perfection and imitation of Christ. A significant consequence – or presupposition! – of Tatian's austere asceticism is his moralistic understanding and devaluation of the Old Testament as being useful only for an immature man:

> For first we did drink like milk the instruction of the teaching [sc. of the O.T.]: and when we became perfect and strong in it, then, led onward, we approach the prescriptions of the Gospel; and this is the Perfection of Age, a Perfect and Strong Meat.[166]

---

163  See Elze, *o.c.*, pp. 127-129. For an explanation of the origin of the *Diatesseron* from this fundamental idea, see p. 126. Interesting is Elze's remark that Tatian remains basically a philosopher, p. 129; cf. *ERE* V, 301.

164  On Tatian's anthropology and ethics, see Elze, *o.c.*, pp. 88-100. Cf. also R. M. Grant, "The Heresy of Tatian" in *JThS*, NS 5 (1954), 62-68, who substantiates the critique of Irenaeus, *A.H.* I, 28, 1.

165  See *Oration*, chs. 29-30. Elze, *o.c.*, p. 99, concludes: "An all dem fällt auf, dass Tatian keine Soteriologie im Sinne einer Lehre von einem Erlöser vorträgt.... Für einen Erlöser ist in seinem theologischen System kein Raum.... Seine Lehre behandelt Gott, Welt und Mensch, wie wenn es eine philosophische Abhandlung wäre. Darüber hinaus kann ihn auch sein Ansatz nicht führen, der ja gleichfalls ein philosophischer ist."

166  *Tatian: Perfection acc. to the Saviour*, in R. Harris, *o.c.*, p. 20. Cf. also Harnack, *H.D.* I, 239, who states that the Encratite Tatian, because of his severe asceticism, "could no longer maintain the identity of the supreme God and the creator of the world". How close Tatian comes to the Gnostic ethos and theology, appears also from Harnack's remark: "The Gnostics were the first critics of the Old Testament in Christendom" (*ibid.*, 258; cf. 227ff.). Cf. Harris, *o.c.*, p. 31.

Hilgenfeld, *o.c.*, pp. 391f., concludes from fragments of Tatian in Clemens Alex. that Tatian *differentiated* between the imperfect God of the O.T. and the perfect God of the N.T., but that Tatian did not go so far as Marcion, who constructed a direct contrast between them.

The question now to be asked is, If Tatian's doctrine of Christian perfection is not in harmony with the Biblical way of perfection and, therefore, may be characterized as *perfectionism*, what then are the specific constitutive elements which define Tatian's Encratite concept of Perfect Discipleship as perfectionism?

Is it Tatian's vegetarianism and teetotalism as such? This is difficult to maintain since this way of life is condemned neither by Christ and the apostles, nor by the Church. Is it Tatian's celibacy as such? Christ and the apostle Paul both explicitly made room for this way of life within the Christian Church.[167]

Consequently, it is not the personal style of Tatian's ascetic-ethical imitation of Christ which is the definite perfectionistic element. Is it, then, Tatian's undeniable moralism or legalism, since his ascetic imitation of Christ is presented as an autonomous act of self-denial with the aim of following the example of Christ? Moralism, in the sense of the idea that morality earns salvation, does not yet necessarily mean perfectionism.[168]

Tatian's perfectionism rather pertains to his particular conviction that Christ's example not only *can* but *is* perfectly followed and manifested in the Encratite way of *imitatio Christi*, i.e., in the conduct of austere asceticism.

The conviction of perfect fulfillment leads inevitably to the exaltation of one's own fulfillment as the *only and exclusive way of salvation*, and consequently, as the required way for *all* the Christian fellowbelievers in the Church.

Here the intolerant, schismatic character of early Christian perfectionism appears, since it required of all the other Churchmembers the same strict asceticism as an inviolable, inflexible law, in the way of Church policy and discipline.[169] Thus all consciences were put on one level and the Gospel was turned into law, in the passionate endeavor to manifest the life of perfection in a truly heroic anticipation.

### 3.  *The Montanists*

In the fertile valley of Phrygia in Asia Minor around A.D. 160 the Montanist movement arose within the Christian Church. It was called "the

---

167   See Mt. 19,12; 1 Cor. 7,7-9. On monasticism, see below.
168   Cf. Bavinck, *G.D.* IV, 246. Berkouwer, *Faith and Sanctif.*, p. 49 (Dutch, p. 45).
169   Cf. Harnack, *H.D.* I, 239. *ERE* V, 301. Harris, *o.c.*, p. 13, therefore seems to be more correct in the second than in the first half of his statement: "Tatian himself is among the heretics on the ground of his Encratism, being condemned as a Vegetarian, and Teetotaller and Celibate, or quasi Celibate, and for making his peculiar views into matters of discipline, for the perfect at least."

New Prophecy" before, and "the Phrygian heresy" after its excommunication.[170] Unfortunately no original works of the founders of Montanism
have been transmitted, except a few isolated oracles in the Church
fathers.[171] From these oracles it appears that Montanus, as well as Prisca
and Maximilla, claimed to have the particular prophetic charisma, receiving visions of Christ and apocalyptic dreams, a phenomenon not
unknown in the early Church.[172] The unique significance of Montanism,
however, is expressed by Maximilla when she declared, according to
Epiphanius: "After me there will be no longer a prophetess but the
end."[173]

The new revelation concerned not merely the imminent end of the
age but also the exact place where the new Jerusalem of John's Apocalypse (ch. 20) would descend from heaven on earth, specifically in
Pepuza.[174]

To this place Montanus called all the Christian believers to be gathered
and to become the restored, pure, spiritual Church, the perfect bride of
the coming Lord. The schismatic character of this apocalyptic movement
sprang forth from its peculiar doctrine of prophetic inspiration, according
to which the fullness of the prophetic charisma had not yet come with

170   See the art. of H. Kraft, "Die altkirchliche Prophetie und die Entstehung des Montanismus", in *ThZ* 11 (1955), 249-271.
171   See the survey in Hilgenfeld, *o.c.*, pp. 591-595, who presents the few
extant statements from Montanus, Prisca, and Maximilla. As regards the
judgment of the early Church concerning the "new prophecy", see *ibid.*, pp.
560-579. For a treatment of Montanism against its own background, see the
helpful study of W. G. Murdoch, "A Study of Early Montanism and its
relation to the Christian Church," Unpubl. Diss. of Univ. of Birmingham,
Engl., 1946. For a critical examination of the oracles of Montanism see chs.
IV-V. See also the critical treatment by K. Aland, "Bemerkungen zum Montanismus und zur frühchristlichen Eschatologie", in his *Kirchengeschichtliche
Entwürfe*, 1960, pp. 105-148.
172   Cf. Ignatius, *Ad Rom.*, VII. *Ad Philad.*, VII. *Pastor Hermae*, I. *Didache*,
XI.
173   *Panarion* XLIII, 2: *met'eme prophètis ouketi estai, alla sunteleia.* In
Hilgenfeld, *o.c.*, p. 593. In *MPG* 41, 857.
174   Epiph., *Pan.* XLIX, 1. Cf. Harnack, *H.D.* II, ch. III; pp. 94ff. Seeberg,
*H.D.*, Bk I, § 12. It should be noted that Tertullian never mentions this
particular place, Pepuza, in his extant writings. In *Adv. Marc.* III, 24, 4, he
even explicitly states that the New Jerusalem will descend in Judea in
Palestine. Aland, *Kirch. Entwürfe*, p. 123, justly remarks: "Hier zeigt sich
deutlich der Abstand Tertullians vom ursprünglichen Montanismus". R. R.
Williams, *A Guide to the Teachings of the Early Church Fathers*, 1960, p. 66,
states: "These could very well be described as the Latter Day Saints of the
early Church". This analogy with the Mormons of today must be restricted,
however, to this particular element of a local return of Christ, since the
Montanists, in contrast with the Mormons, formally accepted the Christological
soteriology of the N.T. Cf. also A. A. Hoekema, *The Four Major Cults*, 1965²,
pp. 53-62. The doctrine of inspiration also seems to be similar.

Christ or His apostles but only with Montanus and his prophetesses.[175].

It was not so much its rigid asceticism and church discipline but the fundamental claim that the inspiration of Montanus by the Paraclete was of an authority superior to that of the apostles, that was the deepest cause of its religious-ethical deviation from Biblical perfection. Montanism visualized basically three successive stages of revelation: Law, Gospel, and New Prophecy. Tertullian, who became a Montanist himself, tried to present this idea in the concept of a progressive but organic development of discipline. The Law and the Prophets constitute the time of infancy, the Gospel the time of youth, the Paraclete (Montanism), however, the time of manhood and maturity.[176]

Tertullian did not conceal the fact that this concept implied a basic *replacement* of the one by the other, not merely a further development from the one into the other. The New Prophecy abrogates what Paul or even Christ had still allowed, e.g., the second marriage.[177] With an appeal to Jn. 16,12, Tertullian taught that the superior moral teaching of the Paraclete, in relation to that of Christ and His apostles, was similar to the law of Moses in relation to the promise of Abraham. In both cases Grace was followed by the Law. But only, through the Paraclete having come in His fullness in Montanism, the Church attained to perfection.[178]

175  Cf. Hilgenfeld, *o.c.*, p. 596: "Neu war die Behauptung, dass die Fülle des h. Geistes noch nicht durch die Apostel, nicht einmal durch Christus selbst, sondern erst durch Montanus und Genossinnen gekommen sei, oder dass erst seit dem die Zeit der eigentlichen Charismen begonnen habe." Cf. K. Aland, in *RGG*³ IV, 1117f. (s.v. *Montanismus*).

176  *De Virgin.*, I. The concrete following of the Paraclete now meant that "virgins be wholly covered". And according to *De Exhortatione Castitatis X*, Prisca is quoted as having said that chastity, sexual continence and purity are prerequisites for the spiritual communion and the reception of revelations.

177  *De Monogamia*, XIV: "Si enim Christus abstulit quod Moyses praecepit, quia *ab initio non fuit sic*, ... cur non et Paracletus abstulerit, quod Paulus indulsit?" Eusebius, *H.E.* V, 8, 2f., quotes Apollonius (c. 212 A.D.) who accuses Montanus among other things of teaching "the dissolution of marriages". Although the attitude of Montanism towards marriage was considered extreme, there seems to be, however, no verification for Apollonius' statement. This rather applied to the Marcionites who denied a married person baptism unless he consented to a divorce; cf. Tert., *Adv. Marc.* I, 19; V, 7. Tertullian's own position became more strict in this respect. Rejecting a second marriage, he defended marriage as honorable and holy, in *Adv. Marc.* I, 29. In his *De Monog.*, III, he praised the unmarried state as one of higher sanctity. In his *De Exhort. Cast.*, IX, he came to impugn marriage as tolerated adultery. At the same time Tert., arguing from 1 Cor. 7, claimed, however, that the Paraclete was introducing "nothing of novelty"; *De Monog.*, III.

178  Of special importance in this respect is *The Acts of the Martyrdom of Perpetua and Felicitas*, ed. J. Rendel Harris and S. K. Gifford, London, 1890, who believe that this document was written by Tertullian. Referring to its Preface, Murdoch summarizes: "He [sc. Tertullian] believed that now, through the Paraclete, the Church had arrived at perfection and that all

The oracles of Montanus and his prophetesses, therefore, were regarded by Tertullian as possessing an authority superior to the apostolic writings. As Hilgenfeld points out:

> Nicht als Prophetie an sich zerfiel die montanistische Bewegung mit der Grosskirche, sondern als eine neue, über das Evangelium und die apostolische Kirchenordnung hinausgehende Prophetie, welche die Souveränetät des Parakleten dem Amte und Herkommen der Kirche gegenüberstellte.[179]

Tertullian, as Montanist, considered the Old and the New Testament merely as primitive writings, (*pristinae Scripturae*[180]), to the Canon of which he added the Montanistic prophetic writings (*Prophetia nova cum documentis martyrum*). As Murdoch states:

> In Tertullian's opinion, this *instrumentum novissimum* transcended the New Testament and contained the final revelation for the Christian life (given by the Paraclete), and also contained records that testified to the actual existence of the perfect life.[181]

The Montanists considered their own prophetic revelations as the third Testament, endowed with the final and superior authority to legislate the perfect preparation for the Kingdom of God.[182] This belief led them to inflict a stricter discipline than that presented in the New Testament. The expectation of the impending Kingdom so fully determined Montanus' ethos that he urged his Christian followers not merely to evade or to endure martyrdom but to seek after it, to long for it as an end to be desired, i.e., the promotion of the glory of God.[183]

---

prophetic utterances should be set forth to the Church in public lection and received into her *instrumentum*" (*o.c.*, pp. 125f.).

179  *O.c.*, p. 597. Since Montanistic eschatology nowhere spoke of the coming of Jesus Christ, and located a specific territory for the New Jerusalem, etc., Aland, *Kirch. Entwürfe*, p. 133, concludes: "Er [sc. the Paraclete] repräsentiert die höchste Offenbarungsstufe, höher als die Evangelien und die Apostel, hat also auch die Vollmacht, die überkommenen eschatologischen Vorstellungen zu verändern, ja von Grund aus umzugestalten".

180  *De Monog.*, IV. *De Resurrectione*, LXIII.

181  *O.c.*, p. 127.

182  W. Nigg, *Das ewige Reich. Geschichte einer Hoffnung*, 1954, pp. 78-89. He states on p. 81: "Die Montanisten erstrebten das überaus kühne Ziel einer Geistkirche, indem sie ihre Offenbarungen sammelten und als ein drittes Testament aufstellten." They appealed specifically to Rev. 19,10.

183  In Tert., *De Fuga In Persecutione*, IX 7: "Nolite in lectulis, nec in ardoribus et febribus mollibus optare exire sed in martyriis, uti glorificetur qui est passus pro vobis". It must be said that later Montanists, however, lost this zeal for martyrdom which possessed the early Montanists; cf. Eus. *H.E.* V, 18, 5.

This burning apocalyptic expectation of the Kingdom – on the authority of their new prophetic revelations – was also the motivating power of their asceticism[184] and their distinction between two exclusive classes of the Christian Church: the Physics (*psychikoi*; animales) and the Spiritualists (*pneumatikoi*; spirituales).[185] Only those who followed the New Prophecy of Montanism were the Spiritualists; the others were following the flesh.[186]

While Montanism may be regarded as a reaction of a form of primitive Christianity against an institutionalizing, secularized Church, we must agree with Hilgenfeld when he states that not only Romanism but also Montanism went to extremes with respect to primitive Christianity.[187] Montanism urged and imposed a moral perfection through a burdensome asceticism and a schismatic exclusiveness. Since this ethos of perfection was determined and motivated by its peculiar apocalyptic enthusiasm, we could characterize Montanism basically as apocalyptic perfectionism.[188]

### 4. *The Novatians.*

The schismatic Novatian Church, which existed from the middle of

184  Montanism was charged with heresy and novelty also with respect to its strict rules of fasting, see Tert., *De Ieiunio* I. Murdoch, *o.c.*, p. 97, states: "To Tertullian, fasting became an end in itself, rather than a means to an end. He attributed a God-propitiating significance to fasting, celibacy and martyrdom, and called them merita." Cf. also Harnack, *H.D.* II, 132.

J. Schwital, *Grosskirche und Sekte*, 1962, pp. 48ff., observes that Montanism maintained the orthodox Christological soteriology. He concludes: "Beide Momente, die Naherwartung und das Geisteswirken, gaben den Impuls zu einem Leben der Busse und der Heiligung. Es ist nicht verwunderlich, dass in einer solchen Zeit der eschatologischen Spannung strenge sittliche Forderungen erhoben wurden. Sie verlangten die Einmaligkeit der Ehe, die Beachtung einer strengen Fastenordnung und einer strengen Sittenzucht" (p. 48). Harnack, *H.D.* II, 102, evaluates the Montanist asceticism as steering between the Marcionite and the Encratite mode of life.

185  See Clement, *Strom.* IV, 13 (*MPG* VIII, 1300). Tert., *De Iei.*, I, Cf. Hilgenfeld, *o.c.*, p. 598.

186  Cf. Tert., *De Iei.*, I; Epiph., *Pan.* XLVIII, 1.

187  *O.c.*, p. 599: "Aber mit seiner Monarchie der Propheten in der Kirche und mit seiner entsprechend gestalteten Kirchenverfassung ist auch der Montanismus über das Urchristenthum hinausgegangen."

188  Compare also our evaluation of the Qumran community, at the close of section 1, above. Tert. is basing his asceticism explicitly on the apocalyptic urgency, *Adv. Marc.* I, 29. Aland, *Kirch. Entwürfe*, p. 127, summarizes early Montanism as "Seine Enderwartung ist ausserordentlich intensiv, das Ende wird in unmittelbare Nähe gerückt ... Im Hinblick auf das nahe Ende werden die ethischen Forderungen ausserordentlich verschärft." The apocalyptic perfectionism of Montanism implies an exclusivistic asceticism (the two classes) and possibly a fundamental legalism, where Christ no longer is in the focus of the kerygma and the saints are raised from the dead earlier or later during the earthly millennium *according to their merits*, *Adv. Marc.*, III, 24 (if these concepts actually have been held in early Montanism).

the third until the seventh century A.D., constitutes a unique phenomenon in the history of western Christianity. Not theological but ecclessiastical, disciplinary, and legislative reasons actually led to this widespread schism in the early Church.[189]

The problematic ordination of Novatian as counterbishop of Rome in A.D. 251 coincided with the claim of Cornelius, the newly elected bishop of Rome, of having the power of the keys to extend forgiveness to all the repentant lapsed members (*lapsi*) of the time of the Decian persecution. Novatian, a distinguished orthodox theologian and presbyter at Rome, wanted to retain, however, the ancient praxis of the Church of excommunicating once for all the so-called mortal sinners, i.e., all those who after baptism had sacrificed to idols.[190] Only God could forgive those sins. The Church could only forgive transgressions of the commandments of the Church, i.e., venial sins. To Novatian the Church had no right to anticipate the judgment of God, and this the Church was *doing* when it readmitted the repentant *lapsi*.

The decisive, guiding principle of Novatian was to maintain and establish a pure Church, which would consist only of actually holy man. The Novatians styled themselves the *Katharoi*, Catharists, i.e., the moral Purists.[191] According to Cyprian[192] the Catharists believed that they would become contaminated if they worshipped together with unholy members:

> They say that one is polluted by another's sin, and ... contend, by their own asseveration, that the idolatry of the delinquent passes over to one who is not guilty according to their own word.

After his excommunication by the synod at Rome in A.D. 251, Novatian

---

189   See A. Harnack, in *RE*[3] XIV, 223-242 (s.v. *Novatian*), which may be regarded as the most thorough treatment of Novatianism. On the source material, see pp. 225-229. He states: "Wir haben es hier mit einem Schisma zu thun auf dem Boden des Katholicismus, einem Schisma, welches lediglich aus der Kontroverse über die Berechtigung, den Umfang und den Erfolg der kirchlichen Schlüsselgewalt entstanden ist" (225). Cf. also his *H.D.* II, 118-122.

P. Löffler, in *RGG*[3] IV, 1539 (s.v. *Novatian*), traces the schism back to the personal disappointment of Novatian of not having been elected as the Roman bishop: "Dabei ging es offenbar zunächst um einen persönlichen Gegensatz zwischen N. und Cornelius, der sich jedoch bald zu einem sachlichen vertiefte." Also E. W. Watson, in *ERE* IX, 399-401 (s.v. *Novatianists*). J. Quasten, in *LThK* VII[2], 1062-64 (s.v. *Novatianismus*).

190   Harnack (*RE* XIV, 237; *H.D.* II, 118) and Seeberg (*H.D.* I, 180) conclude that while Novatian applied mortal sin only to the *lapsi*, the later Novatian Churches extended mortal sin to all unabashed transgressions of the moral law.

191   Eus., *H.E.*, VI, 43. Cf. also Seeberg, *H.D.*, Bk I, 179.

192   *Ep.* LI, 27; ET from *ANF* V, 334.

began to organize his holy counter-Church, with its own hierarchy, and to rebaptize all the converts from the Catholic Church.[193] To him "the Church must be a real communion of salvation and of saints; hence she cannot endure unholy persons in her midst without losing her essence. Each gross sinner that is tolerated within her calls her legitimacy in question."[194]

No wonder that many Montanists in the East and the West joined the Novatian Church.[195]

Undoubtedly Novatianism, with its emphasis on the *communio sanctorum* and the sanctified life of the baptized believers, preserved a valuable element of primitive Christianity. Yet it failed to manifest this ideal of ecclesiological perfection in empirical reality, because it reduced the discipline of penance basically to the sins of idolatry and adultery.[196] Thus it cultivated a sharp distinction between repentance acceptable to the Church, and repentance not acceptable to the Church but acceptable to God only.[197]

Harnack notes that "the Novatian Churches speedily ceased to be any stricter than the Catholic in their renunciation of the world."[198] Both churches soon represented the same religious ethos, so that the Council of Nicea[199] in A.D. 325 decided to readmit the clergy of the Novatians to the clergy of the Catholic Church, acknowledging also the baptism of the Catharists.

Basically, the constitutive element of Novatianism comes down to moral purity on the ecclesiological-disciplinary level. Since it made outward moral characteristics the ultimate norm for ecclesiastical unity and discipline, while falling short in brotherly love[200] in view of the severe

---

193  Eus., *H.E.*, VI, 43.

194  Harnack, *H.D.* II, 119. Watson, in *ERE* IX, 400, states: "With the claim to purity we come to what grew into the *raison d'être* of Novatianism, though, in fact, so far as Novatian was concerned, it was an afterthought, and not the occasion of his action."

195  See Harnack in *RE* IX, 240.

196  Cf. Schwital, *Grosskirche und Sekte*, p. 51: "Da die Novatianer in der Lehre und in der Verfassung von der katholischen Kirche nicht abwichen, erschien ihre Bussdisziplin zweifelhaft und ihre Praxis der Wiedertaufe nicht gerechtfertigt. Die Unterscheidung von lässlichen Sünden und Todsünden, die sie mit der Kirche gemeinsam hatten, führte zur Abstumpfung des Gewissens (A. v. Harnack, DG, I, 451ff.). Damit verlor aber die novatianische Kirche ihr Selbstverständnis." Also Harnack, *H.D.* II, 122.

197  Harnack, *RE* IX, 239, evaluates this Novatian purism with respect to the *lapsi* to be both "unjust and unmerciful", since many of the lapsed members were punished heavier than other gross sinners.

198  *H.D.* II, 121.

199  In canon 8. The Council considered the Novatians as schismatics but not as heretics; cf. Hefele, *Conciliengeschichte*, I², pp. 407f.

200  Cf. A. C. Coxe, in *ANF* V, 608, regarding Novatian: "His heresy,

tests of the Decian persecution, we could perhaps indicate the schismatic purism of Novatianism best by calling it ecclesiological perfectionism.

### 5. *Pelagius*.

In Pelagius we face the consistent outcome of a long-standing moralistic theology which was strongly influenced by the prevailing popular Aristotelian-Stoic philosophy and ethics.

Pelagius and Caelestius, two earnest ascetics, together with bishop Julian of Eclanum, formed the league which tried to incite a morally listless Christendom to exert its will to obey God's commandments, and to lead Christianity to moral, which meant monachist-ascetic perfection.[201] Pelagius' deep concern for moral rectitude and sinless perfection appears most strikingly in his letter to the noble virgin Demetrias,[202] who had resolved to take the vow of virginity. He encourages her to be blameless and innocent, a true child of God, shining as a beacon amidst a crooked and perverse generation, appealing to Phil. 2,15. Ferguson believes that "the moral laxity of the time shocked him [sc. Pelagius] into calling his contemporaries to a stricter asceticism and a deeper loyalty to the Gospel."[203]

Pelagianism only became problematic and even heretical when Augustinianism became its forceful counterpart which ultimately triumphed at the general Church Council at Carthage in A.D. 418.[204]

Focusing our inquiry on Pelagius' doctrine of perfection, two specific

such as it was, turned upon unrelenting discipline, and was a sin against charity, which is greater than faith itself. It violated the 'seventy times seven' maxim of our Lord, and the comprehensive precept, 'Forgive and ye shall be forgiven'. It wounded Christian unity at a perilous period, and when every breach in the wall of the fold was sure to let in the wolves." On the accusation of mercilessness, in the literary polemics of the East, see Harnack, in *RE* IX, 340.

201  See Harnack, *H.D.* V, 170ff. Seeberg, *H.D.* I, 331-338. J. Ferguson, *Pelagius*, 1956, pp. 18-22: "The Corruption of the Church". Pelagius was known as a *vir sanctus*: "His asceticism was widely famed and admired" (p. 46). On Caelestius, see pp. 48ff.

202  Transmitted in the corpus of Jerome's works; see *MPL* 33 (Aug. II), 1099-1120.

203  *O.c.*, p. 47.

204  F. Loofs, *Leitfaden zum Studien der Dogmengeschichte*, I-II, 1959[6], § 53, p. 336, shows that the condemnation of Pelagianism did not imply the acceptance of all of Augustine's anti-Pelagian ideas. See § 54. Loofs' characterization of Augustinianism and Pelagianism is illuminating: "Unabhängig voneinander, haben beide unter dem Einfluss differenter philosophischer Einwirkungen den Vulgärkatholizismus ihrer Zeit in verschiedener Weise modifiziert. Während Augustin von der m y s t i s c h e n Philosophie der Zeit, dem Neuplatonismus, die entscheidenden Impulse bekommen hat, ist Pelagius von der älteren, moralistisch-r a t i o n a l i s t i s c h e n Popularphilosophie, insonderheit von der der Stoa, abhängig gewesen" (p. 339).

aspects of his theology must be recognized. With reference to his doctrine of the Christian's call to sinless perfection, to live *anamartètōs*, after baptism, Pelagius is no innovator. He only accentuates and capitalizes on an agelong Christian tradition, already found in Justin[205] and Athanasius.[206] Even when Pelagius acknowledges that sinless moral perfection is only rarely manisfested, his doctrine of the *possibility* of sinlessness – directly related to his rejection of the idea of inherited original sin – was not an innovation of Pelagius. As Loofs points out, in this respect there was a "Pelagianism before Pelagius".[207]

The other aspect of Pelagianism is its onesided emphasis on the doctrine of *justificatio sola fide*.[208] Even Augustine fails to recognize this remarkable aspect of Pelagianism, when he accuses Pelagius of teaching *gratia, qua justificamur, non gratis, sed secundum merita*.[209] Since the original copies of Pelagius' *Expositions of Thirteen Epistles of St. Paul*,[210] which are referred to by Augustine,[211] have been recovered only in this century, we are now able to establish with certainty what Pelagius really taught, and also that Augustine's unqualified accusation does no justice to Pelagius.[212]

Pelagius is even more explicit than Paul when he adds *"sola"* to *fide* in his comment on Eph. 2,8, *Non meritis prioris vitae, sed sola fide, sed tamen non sine fide; iustificat deus, non per opera bona quae non habuit....Quo proposuit gratis per solam fidem peccato dimittere*. Pelagius relates this *sola fide* only to baptism, however.[213] Loof's conclusion is

---

205 *Dial.*, XXXXIV, 4.

206 *Contra Gentes*, II. *Or. c. Ar.*, III, 33. Cf. Loofs, *Leitfaden*, pp. 268, 339.

207 See *RE* XV, 755, 48-50: "Dennoch ist auch hier, bei der Annahme möglicher Sündlosigkeit ebenso, wie bei der Verwerfung der Fortpflanzung der Adamssünde, offenbar, dass es einen 'Pelagianismus ante Pelagium' gab."

208 Loofs, *Leitfaden*, pp. 309f., indicates how the *sola fide* in the popular concept was applied only to the forgiveness of past sins, in baptism.

209 Aug., *Contra Duas Epp.*, VIII. *De Dono Persev.*, II, 4. Cf. Loofs, in *RE* XV, 755, 54f. (s.v. *Pelagius und der pelagianische Streit*). Augustin referred to "the three main errors" of Pelagianism as being 1) the denial of original sin, 2) the meritorious character of grace, 3) the possibility of sinless perfection after baptism.

210 Under this title the Scottish scholar A. Souter published the exegetical works of Pelagius, together with an introduction, in *Texts and Studies* IX, ed. J. Armitage Robinson, 3 vols 1922-1931 (Repr. 1967). The following quotations from *Exp*. are taken from this edition (vol. 2).

211 *De Peccatorum Meritis et Remissione*, III, 1, 1 (CSEL). Souter, *o.c.*, I, pp. 4, 34, presumes that part of Pelagius' expositions at least was written not earlier than about 406, and that Augustine came to know Pelagius' Commentary as early as 412, some three years after its completion.

212 For a list of all the undisputed works of Pelagius, see R. F. Evans, *Four Letters of Pelagius*, 1968, pp. 34f.; or R. F. Evans, *Pelagius. Inquiries and Reappraisals*, 1968, p. xiv.

213 See *Exp*. ad Eph. 2,5.8-9; *ad* Rom. 5,17. Cf. Loofs, *Leitfaden*, p. 336.

striking: "Das 'sola fide' hat vor Luther keinen so energischen Vertreter gehabt als Pelagius."[214]

Yet Pelagius' emphasis is not, as Luther's, exclusively on the *sola fide*. An exclusive emphasis on forensic justification would only stiffen the lax Church all the more in quietism and moral apathy, in Pelagius' opinion.[215]

The specific thrust of Pelagius appears more fully in his warning to the baptized Christians that they must now also manifest a moral sanctification, a practical Christianity. A *sola fide* which does not conquer sin and lead to holiness of spirit and body, does not save us for the kingdom of glory: *Nolite errare, putantes vobis solam fidem sufficere ad salutem, cum omne peccatum permanens excludat a regno, sicut [et] ad Galatias ait:* [Quoted Gal. 5,19-21].[216]

Warning even against sins of thought, he summons a wordly Christendom to rise to moral perfection, "depriving it of the pretext that it was impossible to fulfill the divine commandments".[217] Ascetic perfection, however, to Pelagius is not an end in itself, only the means to the actual development of moral character in spiritual virtues, and the victory over all vices.[218]

Pelagius was deeply concerned about the sin problem among the baptized Christians, which is a very real problem indeed. All his Pauline expositions served to exhort his readers to live better lives, to give their whole person to God, body and soul, so that they would actually strive for and also attain to sinless perfection. Pelagius uses the verb *perficere* very widely in his writings, referring to the "accomplishment" of good works and actual virtues in the lives of Christians.[219]

---

214 *RE* XV, 753, 41f. This judgment, although formally true, still is inadequate materially because of Luther's basically different Christological soteriology and pneumatology. Luther himself called Pelagianism one of the three main heresies, specifically as the type of work-righteousness, *WA* 50, 269.

215 Cf. the opinion of Loofs on Pelagius' opposition to the religious phrase of Augustine "da, quod iubes et iube quod vis (*Conf.*, X, 40), in A.D. 405: "Der moralistische Ernst des Pelagius sah in dem "da, quod jubes" vermutlich nur eine Phrase fauler Frömmigkeit (vgl. ad Demetr. 20 . . .)" (*RE* XV, 758, 26f.). Also Ferguson, *o.c.*, p. 47: "It seemed to Pelagius to turn the individual into a mere marionette, impotent before the leading-strings of God, and to destroy the very foundation of that moral effort he had set himself to inculcate in himself and others".

216 *Exp. ad* 1 Cor. 6,9.

217 Harnack, *H.D.* V, 189.

218 *Ibid.* V, 190; cf. also Harnack's evaluation in this respect: "The Pelagians deserve respect for their purity of motive, their horror of the Manichaean leaven and the *opus operatum* . . ." (203).

219 For (incomplete) listings of the use of *perficere* by Pelagius, see Evans, *Four Letters*, p. 81; and Souter, *Texts and Studies* IX, vol. 1, 107 (*perfectus, perfectior, perfecte,* and *perfectio*).

Christians must already now by their actions strive to manifest that perfection which they will enjoy in the kingdom of God.[220] The Thessalonians, e.g., had achieved perfection and by their word and example also incited others to become perfect.[221]

Moral or sinless perfection is the aim of true humanity. Created in the image of God, man ought and, therefore, can be just as righteous, holy, and true as God is.[222]

Pelagius believes that many patriarchs, prophets and saints of the Old Testament attained to sinless perfection, e.g., Abel, Enoch, Melchizedek, Abraham, Isaac, Jacob, and many more.[223]

He specially mentions also some women, like Deborah, Anna the mother of Samuel, Judith, Esther, Elizabeth, and Mary the mother of Jesus.

Perfect faith does not merely mean to believe Christ but also to believe in Christ.[224]

To abide in Christ means, according to John, to walk as He walked, i.e., to imitate the fullness of His virtue.[225]

If faith is not manifested in works of faith – which are not works of the law [226] – it is dead, according to James.[227]

Intellectual belief is not enough. Faith without love and peace is just as incomplete as love without faith for the perfect Christian.[228] From all these simple interpretations and direct applications [229] we can observe how Pelagius, by his exclusive focus on the ethical implications of the Christian faith, tried to counterbalance the contemporary neglect in Christianity.[230] Sinless perfection after baptism was not merely possible

---

220  *Exp. ad* 2 Cor. 5,9: *Iam modo tales esse* [*actu*] *conamur quales futuri sumus in regno, natura incorruptibiles sine dubio et perfecti.*

221  *Exp. ad* 1 Thess., *argumentum:* [*Thessalonicenses*] *non solum ipsi in omnibus perfecti erant, sed etiam alii eorum verbo profecerent et exemplo.*

222  *Exp. ad* Eph. 4,24: *Exposuit quid sit hominem ad imaginem dei esse creatum, ut scilicet iustus* [*sit*] *et sanctus* [*sit*] *et verax* [*sit*], [*sic*]*ut deus.*

223  See his *Ep. ad Dem.*; cf. Aug. *De Nat. et Grat.,* XXXVI, 42. Aug. replies by asking the question, what would these holy men and women testify about their own sinlessness? Would it not be in the words of 1 John 1,8?

224  *Exp. ad* Gal. 3,11: *Perfecta fides est non solum Christum, sed et Christo credere.*

225  *Exp. ad* Eph. 4,13: ... *virtutem plenitudinis imitari.*

226  Pel. explains "works of the law" only as works of the *ceremonial* law like circumcision, etc., see *Exp. ad* Rom. 3,28. This aspect was criticized fundamentally by Augustine, *De Spiritu et Littera,* XIV.

227  Cf. *Exp. ad* Gal. 3,10.

228  *Exp. ad* Eph. 6,23: *Pax et caritas et fides perfectum faciunt Christianum: tam enim sine fide infructuosa est caritas, quam fides sine caritate vel pace.*

229  Cf. Evans, *Four Letters,* p. 64: "Simplicity and directness characterize the prose of Pelagius".

230  Cf. Ferguson, *o.c.,* pp. 165.

but a duty to achieve.[231] In other words, Pelagius was primarily a moral reformer, concerned with moral perfection, and only secondarily with religious salvation and theological soteriology.[232] From his moralistic point of view, Pelagius therefore concludes that God can never command the impossible from man, when he requires him to attain to the standard of ethical perfection or moral holiness.[233]

Basic to Pelagius' doctrine of perfection, however, is the intellectualism of the ethics, i.e., the idea that human nature is indestructibly good. In other words, Pelagius' ethics is not rooted ultimately in the religious-cultic redemption from sin, but in man's being a creature created in the image of God. Being a fundamental creationist, instead of a traducianist, with reference to the individual soul of each man, Pelagius believes that each new-born man begins with a "tabula rasa", i.e., without original sin.[234]

He therefore views grace as man's "condition of willing", i.e., his possession of free will. He contrasts this grace of human nature with the "condition of necessity" of irrational creatures.[235]

"Nature was created so good that it needs no help."[236]

Guided by reason, man's will is free to choose the good, according to Pelagius. As Harnack explains: "The possibility of good as a natural faculty is from God, willing and action are our business".[237] All emphasis lies on the possibility of doing good or evil by nature.[238] It was Torgny Bohlin who first observed how Pelagius' theology is basically governed by his anti-Manichaean polemic.[239]

The fundamental concern of Pelagius was the Manichaean doctrine of

---

231   Loofs, *Leitfaden*, p. 338.

232   Cf. Ferguson, *o.c.*, pp. 48, 159. He sees the contribution of Pelagius "in his denial of original sin, and his assertion of individual responsibility and the possibility of sinlessness" (p. 159).

233   Cf. Jerome, *Dial. adv. Pel.*, I, 16, 21. And Pel., *Ep. ad Dem.* It would be incorrect, however, to conclude that Pelagius boasted or claimed to have sinless perfection himself, as Jerome derives in *Dial.*, II, 23-24. In fact, Pel. saw pride as his constant temptation; cf. *De Poss. non pecc.*, II, 1. See Ferguson, *o.c.*, pp. 166f.

234   Ferguson, *o.c.*, p. 164, refers to *De Cast.*, III, 5: *Nemo enim corruptus nascitur, nec ante legitime temporis spatium quispiam corruptione violatur.*

235   Harnack, *H.D.* V, 193-194; 200f.

236   *Ep. ad Demetriadem*, quoted in Harnack, *H.D.* V, 194.

237   *H.D.* V, 194.

238   The *liberum arbitrium* in the sense of the *possibilitas utriusque partis* is indestructible; cf. Loofs, *Leifaden*, p. 342.

239   *Die Theologie des Pelagius und ihre Genesis*, Uppsala and Wiesbaden, 1957. Even when Bohlin goes too far in making the anti-Manichaean polemic the exclusive center of Pelagius' theology, what Evans states in his *Pelagius*, p. 22, remains true: "One of the chief theological interests of Pelagius was and remained the combatting of Manichaean fatalism."

creation which he saw affected Augustine's and Jerome's doctrine of the *necessity* of sinning. If sin is not a "substance", however, then the flesh cannot impose upon man a natural necessity of sinning.[240] The rational will remains indestructibly free over against any external necessity.

The human will and nature are so completely divided by Pelagius that sin and virtue can never pass into nature. Sin, therefore, can never become an evil nature; otherwise, God would be its author. Human nature is always the momentary self-determination of the will and therefore not corrupt. Decisive is the voluntary imitation of an example or instruction, the good one (Jesus) or the bad one (Adam).[241] The forgiveness of sins *sola fide* only applies to the past. The present life is formed only by the good choice and action.

Consequently, the obedience to the divine will, after baptism, is meritorious![242]

By conceiving the Pauline doctrine of *sola fide* in an *exclusively* judicial sense, Pelagius divorced the *sola fide* from the way of sanctification. This marked his moral ethos as an ascetic moralism, a humanistic concept closer to Seneca than to Paul.[243] Harnack even goes so far as to say "that in its deepest roots it is godless," because it abandons "the pole of the mystical doctrine of redemption, which the Church had steadfastly maintained side by side with the doctrine of freedom."[244]

The redemptive significance of the Cross is no longer central or vital to Pelagius' ethics and theology.[245] Here lies the innovation of Pelagianism.[246] Grace to the Pelagians meant fellowship with the Holy Spirit or

---

240 See Evans, *Pelagius*, pp. 100-106. He concludes: "Pelagius' insistence than men can be without sin is an emphatic assertion of the doctrine of creation by a just God; it is nothing more, and is nothing less".

241 See Harnack's critique on the equal impossibility of cultivating a virtuous character, *H.D.* V, 196.

242 *Ep. ad Demetr.*, XXV. In this respect Augustine's criticism was thus correct. Cf. Harnack, *H.D.* V, 200, that "Julian's main object was to show that the human constitution bore merit and salvation in its own lap." Julian "held the opinion that there was no difference between a good Christian and a good heathen" (201).

243 Cf. Loofs, *RE* XV, 758, 17ff. See also Harnack's fundamental criticism in *H.D.* V, 199, n. 3: "Here, as in Stoicism, there is a gap in the system. Why is rational man irrational and bad? How can he possess *ratio* and an evil will at the same time? And how is the sinful habit explained?"

244 *H.D.* V, 203. Ferguson, *o.c.*, p. 183, rejects the evaluation "godless" but takes it out of its context in Harnack.

245 See Ferguson, *o.c.*, pp. 164, 183. He explains: "It is in fact to the teaching not to the Cross that we are to look for our salvation. To follow his example is all that we need for life. Even the preaching of the Cross brings the same message – that Jesus conquered on the Cross to give us an example of how to conquer" (pp. 130f.).

246 Harnack, *H.D.* V, 203.

infused supernatural inspiration (*gratia inspirationis*) which changed the *concupiscentia mala* into the *concupiscentia bona* (*dilectio*), as it meant to Augstine. Grace only meant the freedom of choice, i.e., grace of nature; or the illumination of the divine law or instruction or example.[247] In other words, law and gospel are basically identical and both are ethical helps, only needed because of the clouds of ignorance and the power of the habit of sinning. With these illuminating helps, the state of sinless perfection can be attained by the power of the human will. The Christian has in the example of Christ, in baptism, and the Christian dogma's means which really are unnecessary but, in the actual situation of universal sinning, are given by the Creator to make sinless perfection more easily available.[248] As Ferguson[249] points out:

> He [sc. Pel.] was of that temperament which sees in Jesus the example of human perfection, rather than God confronting Sin. It is the moral teaching of Jesus, and the pattern of humility and love which He presented, that show us the way of life.

Since Pelagius wanted to be orthodox, he came to define grace as the capacity for sinlessness implanted in man by the Creator.

This definition he gave in his book *De Natura*. When Augustine read the book of Pelagius in A.D. 415, it shocked him into the firm conviction that Pelagius' teaching on grace was a "poisonous perversion of the truth, hostile to salvation by Christ".[250]

Evans has demonstrated that the cause for Augustine's shock was not so much the error of Pelagius' teaching in *De Natura* as the new claim of Pelagius that his doctrine of grace, freedom and sinless perfection, was essentially Catholic orthodoxy.[251]

Pelagius supported his own position by quoting from Lactantius, Hilary of Poitiers, Ambrose, John Chrysostom, Xystus the Martyr bishop of Rome, Jerome, and even from Augustine's early anti-Manichaean book *De Libero Arbitrio*.[252]

---

247 Harnack, *H.D.* V, 200f. Seeberg, *H.D.* I, 336f.

248 *Ibid.*, V, 202f. Cf. Evans, *Pelagius*, p. 25: "The issues are rather the relation of man as a creature of God to sin, and the meaning of the idea of sinlessness." See also p. 105.

249 *O.c.*, pp. 164f. Cf. Loofs, *Leitfaden*, p. 337.

250 Aug., *De Gestis Pelagii*, XXIII (ET from NPNF, Vol. V, p. 203). On this, see Evans, *Pelagius*, pp. 79-89.

251 Evans, *o.c.*, p. 85: "Pelagius becomes a serious threat at that moment when Augustine sees him marshalling the forces of Catholic orthodoxy behind him." Augustine answers with his *De Natura et Gratia*.

252 Evans, *o.c.*, p. 89, formulates the issue between Pelagianism and Augustinianism as follows: "Which theological synthesis, which attempt to bring clarity, which novelty will prevail?" It is interesting to see how

It cannot be doubted that Pelagianism is the most outspoken form of moral perfectionism within Christianity. Although its objectives no doubt were pure and, in a time of moral laxity, rightly emphasized moral sanctity, its ethics was based on a fundamental theological moralism and legalism, in spite of its forensic justification *sola fide* in baptism.[253]

H. H. Esser well summarizes the basic difference between Pelagius and Paul by pointing to Pelagius' fundamental anthropocentric starting point and anthropological-moral restriction of his ethics.

> Pelagius versucht, mit einem in sich geschlossenen anthropologischen System die Möglichkeit des menschlichen ethischen, d.h. letztlich Gott entsprechenden Handelns ontologisch zu sichern, und geht dazu vom Schöpfungsstande des Menschen aus und folgt dem Menschen durch seine Geschichte, während Paulus keinen andern Ausgangspunkt seiner Erkenntnis kennt als die einzige Möglichkeit und Wirklichkeit des neuen Menschen in Jesus Christus; und dieser Erkenntnisgrund bestimmt ausschliesslich die ganze Sicht aller vergangenen und noch ausstehenden menschlichen Geschichte. Die ontische Befindlichkeit beschlagnahmt bei Paulus souverän alle ontologischen Aspekte.[254]

Pelagianism constitutes an unmistakable proof, especially to Protestantism, that a static concept of justification *sola fide* can do no justice to the dynamic concept of Biblical justification in which the ethos of moral holiness remains rooted in and determined by the living faith-obedience relationship, i.e., the transforming religious-moral union and progressive walk with God in Jesus Christ.

A formal acceptance of forensic justification and an emphasis on moral sanctification does not yet necessarily mean an adequate Biblical soteriology.

The criterion whether the ethos of perfection has the right focus of

---

Augustine, while denying the empirical reality, acknowledged the possibility of sinless perfection or "perfection of character" if aided by the grace of God (*ope adjuvante divina*), *De Spir. et Lit.*, I; *De Pecc. Mer.*, II, 6. 7ff. 21. For Augustine the *possibility* of sinless perfection or "perfection of purity" is not the great error, but the idea that men without the divine assistance may either attain or progress toward perfection through the exercise of natural free will in obedience to the divine commandments, *De Spir. et Lit.*, II. Evans, *Pelagius*, pp. 74ff., ably defends the thesis that Augustine in *De Spir. et Lit.* reacts, at least in part, to teachings which he had read in Pelagius' Pauline Commentary.

253 For an adequate analysis and critique of Pelagius' understanding of law and Gospel in Paul's Letters, see H. H. Esser, "Thesen und Anmerkungen zum exegetischen Paulusverständnis des Pelagius", in *Studia Patristica*, Vol. VII, "Texte und Unters.", Bd 92, 1966, pp. 443-461.

254 *O.c.*, pp. 458f. (see previous note).

the Biblical kerygma may be found in its Christological soteriology[255] which implies the Christological pneumatology.

Since Biblical perfection in the Old and the New Testament remains embedded within the religious covenant cultus, excluding the notion and experience of inherent sinless perfection,[256] the decision of the Council at Carthage in A.D. 418 is justified in rejecting the moral perfectionism of Pelagianism.[257]

### 6. The Christian Platonists of Alexandria.

Alexandria has been called the brain of Christendom, because the powerful Christian Catechetical School at Alexandria produced a succession of doctors in the third century who ably defended the Christian faith against Gnostic Hellenism. Clement and his disciple Origen are the two most influential Alexandrian apologists, who presented their Christian message in a Hellenistic philosophical guise.[258] Although Clement wrote a special book, *The Exhortation to the Heathen* (*Protreptikos*), to win pagans to the Christian faith, he, and Origen, wrote for the educated

---

255 See Schwital, *Grosskirche und Sekte*, pp. 18, 44. F. Schleiermacher, *Der christliche Glaube*, §§ 11; 22. K. M. Beckmann, *Der Begriff der Häresie bei Schleiermacher*, 1959. Schwital succesfully applies this criterion to define the four basic heresies in Christianity: Gnosticism, Marcionism, Manichaeism, and Pelagianism. He arrives at the conclusion: "Das christologisch-soteriologische Prinzip ist heute zum Kriterium für eine eindeutige Bestimmung des Häretischen geworden" (p. 122).

256 See above, Chs. III, B; IV, 3.

257 In this respect we think of the anti-Pelagian canons, as stated by Ch. J. Hefele, *A History of the Councils of the Church from the Original Documents*, Vol. II, 1896 (ET), pp. 458f. The first two canons reject Adam's death as natural, and that new-born children would have no original sin. Can. 3 states: "If any man says that the grace of God, by which man is justified through Jesus Christ, is only effectual for the forgiveness of sins already committed, but is of no avail for avoiding sin [non etiam ad adiutorium] in the future, let him be anathema". Can. 4: "If any man says that this grace only helps not to sin, in so far that by it we obtain a better insight into the Divine commands, and learn what we should desire and avoid, but does not also give the power gladly to do and to fulfil what we have seen to be good, let him be anathema". Can. 5: "If any man says that the grace of justification was given us in order that we might the more easily fulfil the Divine commands, let him be anathema".

In the next three canons the Council rejects the claim of sinless perfection here and now, when it states that those who pray the Lord's prayer for the forgiveness of our trespasses in order to acknowledge themselves as sinners "only out of humility", deny the literal meaning of the Lord's prayer and of 1 John 1,8.

258 Cf. J. Daniélou, *Historical Theology*, "The Pelican Guide to Mod. Theol.", II, ed. R. P. C. Hanson, 1969, p. 48. According to Harnack, *H.D.* II, 319, they transformed the heathen empire into a Christian one, and Greek philosophy into ecclesiastical philosophy.

people of the world to lead them to the highest stage of Christian character and mystical experience, spiritual perfection, i.e., the beatific vision of God.[259] For our purpose the sixth and especially the seventh book of Clement's *Stromateis* are of special importance, since they deal explicitly with the steps to perfection.

It has been generally observed that Clement and Origen construe basically the same synthesis of the Christian tradition and Hellenistic philosophy as Philo had done in Judaism.[260]

### Clement's ideal of Christian perfection.

Addressing the many new Christian believers who still had an elementary faith and stained morals, Clement,[261] in his *Paidagogus*, says that all reborn Christians have "received the perfection for which we strive", i.e., the knowledge of God and perfect forgiveness.[262]

Writing his *Stromateis* for the inner circle of spiritually hungry souls, he appeals to them to progress from faith to knowledge (*gnosis*) of perfect virtue or moral perfection, i.e., right actions according to reason.[263] Clement distinguishes two kinds of believers: the class of medium believers (*tōn mesōn*) who only do medium or intermediate actions, procuring a lower grade of glory; and the perfect Gnostics who perform perfect actions (*katorthōmata*), which raise them to the height of glory.[264] Gnosis for Clement, therefore, does not merely indicate intellectual insight but ethical perfection.[265] Only the Gnostic Christian continually testifies to the truth in deed and work and thought. His piety

---

259    Clement's two other great extant writings are the *Paidagogos*, on Christian ethics, and the *Stromateis*, a summary of Christian *Gnosis*. In this last work Clement describes philosophy as a divinely ordered preparation of the Greeks for faith in Christ, just as the Law was for the Hebrews. On Origen, see below.

260    Seeberg, *H.D.* I, § 15. Harnack, *H.D.* II, 325f. Loofs, *Leitfaden*, § 23, 1. Daniélou, *o.c.*, p. 49, indicates: "The task before the Christians was to give an interpretation of Christianity as a successor to Platonism". See especially W. Völker, "Die Vollkommenheitslehre des Clemens Alexandrinus in ihren geschichtlichen Zusammenhängen", *ThZ* 3 (1947), 15-40; esp. 22ff. He states, for instances: "In der Lehre vom Ebenbilde Gottes im Menschen steht Clemens auf Philos Schultern und ist der Mittler zwischen Philo und Origenes" (29f.). On the differences between the three Alexandrians, see 30ff.

261    He died in Asia Minor c. A.D. 214.

262    *Paid.*, I, 6, 25-26.

263    *Strom.*, VII, 11 (Description of the Gnostic's life).

264    *Strom.*, VI, 14 (Degrees of glory in heaven).

265    R. N. Flew, *The Idea of Perfection in Chr. Theology*, pp. 142f., even concludes: "No one in the century after the apostolic age has fathomed the moral grandeur of the Gospel so deeply as Clement" (p. 143). Heussi, *K.K.*, § 17h, however, evaluates this *gnosis* that follows *pistis*: "Diese Gnosis aber ist hellenistische Metaphysik und Ethik mit christlichem Einschlag".

of truthfulness always secures sinlessness.[266] Through incessant ascetic exercise, virtue becomes a habit in the pneumatic soul.

This sinless moral perfection implies for Clement, as well as for Origen, the disposition of complete disinterestedness in all the distractions of matter, i.e., a continuous passionless state, undisturbed by pleasure or profit, in the contemplation of heaven.[267]

His philosophical concept of divine perfection as *apatheia*, emotionlessness, crystallizes itself in his docetic Christology. Christ, having come in a phantasmal body, "was entirely impassible (*apathès*); inaccessible to any movement of feeling – either pleasure or pain".[268]

When Flew[269] states, "Clement knows that the Christian life was meant to be a close and unbroken converse, a wondrous familiarity with God", this means to Clement the unification of the soul with a God who is habitually free from passion. Clement incidentally even calls this perfect union with God in the beatific vision of God, "deification", although he refrains from the Stoic ultimate identification of the perfect man and God.[270]

Nevertheless, S. P. Wood, C.P., apparently is correct when he concludes:[271] "There are three virtues which Clement could have learned only from the Stoa: self-sufficiency, frugality, and apathy".

Clement distinguishes basically between two "saving changes" or steps to perfection:

> The first saving change is that from heathenism to faith...; and the second, that from faith to knowledge. And the latter terminating in love, thereafter gives the loving to the loved, that which knows to that which is known. And, perchance, such an one has already attained the condition of "being equal to the angels".[272]

---

266 *Strom.*, VII, 9 (*to anamartèton pantote katorthōn, MPG* 9, 477); cf. VI, 7: "in his case perfection abides in the fixed habit of well-doing after the likeness of God" (*ANF* II, 494). In III, 8 Clement goes beyond Paul by stating that the new creation of the man in Christ is "no more sinful", *ouketi hamartètikè*; cf. Flew, *o.c.*, p. 148. Sinlessness is postulated in *Strom.*, IV, 9, 75; 20, 127. Clement seems to have contradictory statements, however, in this respect.

267 *Strom.*, VII, 13. In VII, 11, he states, in the ET of *ANF*, II, 542: "But self-control, desirable for its own sake, perfected through knowledge, abiding ever, makes the man lord and master of himself; so that the Gnostic is temperate and passionless, incapable of being dissolved by pleasures and pains, as they say adamant is by fire".

268 *Strom.*, VI, 9 (*ANF* II, 496). Cf. Loofs, *Leitfaden*, p. 131.

269 *O.c.*, p. 145.

270 *Strom.*, IV, 23, 149-155; VII, 10, 56; 13, 82; 16, 95. Cf. Flew, *o.c.*, p. 146, n. 1; Harnack, *H.D.* II, 338, n. 1.

271 *Clement of Alexandria. Christ the Educator*, "The Fathers of the Church," 23, p. xvi.

272 *Strom.*, VII, 10 (*ANF* II, 539).

The Gnostic Christian is already now deified[273] by knowledge, is already now perfect when he lives in the habit of passionlessness or impassibility and cultivates the virtue of magnanimity.[274]

Clement's Platonic-Christian ideal of perfection, which anticipates[275] even the apocalyptic-eschatological perfection of the New Testament (the "angelic" perfection of Lk. 20,36), is determined by an intellectualistic concept of sin as act rather than power. In other words, his doctrine of sinlessness or Neoplatonic perfectionism is based upon a basic denial of original sin.[276] "Salvation is effected through both well-doing and knowledge, of both of which the Lord is the teacher".[277]

*Origen's ideal of Christian perfection.*

Called the first systematic theologian,[278] Origen (A.D. 186-255) was first and foremost an exegete whose speculative genius utilized for the Bible the hermeneutical methods which the pagan philosophers used in their interpretation of Homer.[279] But, as Walther Völker has shown in his magnificent study *Das Vollkommenheitsideal des Origines* (1931), Origen was primarily a great master of the spiritual life, possessed by the idea of experiencing the ideal of Christian perfection. The basic structure of his dogmatic theology – the structure of gradations – also underlies his spirituality[280] and exegesis. As Daniélou observes:[281]

> Just as there is a movement onward from the literal meaning to the allegorical meaning, so there is a transition from the common faith to gnosis and there is a progress from the ordinary Christian life to perfection. Spirituality forms the inward dimension of this ladder.

273  *Protr.* XI, 114 (deifying man by heavenly knowledge, *ouraniōi didaskaliai theopoion ton anthrōpon, MPG* 8, 233). Also *Strom.*, VI, 15, 125 *MPG* 9, 349). VII, 16, 101 (*en sarki peripolōn theos, MPG* 9, 540). See *MPG* 8, 233, n. 39, for more references. H. E. W. Turner, *The Patristic Doctrine of Redemption,* 1952, p. 79, says that Clement is the first Father who explicitly states that the Logos deifies man by His teaching. Here mysticism begins to rule over Greek metaphysics.

274  *Strom.,* VII, 14; explained from an exposition of 1 Cor. 6.

275  Cf. *Strom.,* VI, 12 (*ANF* II, 503): "He will therefore [sc. in order to live perfectly] prefer neither children, nor marriage, nor parents, to love for God, and righteousness in life. To such an one, his wife, after conception, is as a sister, and is judged as if of the same father".

276  Cf. Ferguson, *Pelagius,* pp. 161, 163.

277  *Strom.,* VI, 15 (*ANF* II, 508).

278  His *Peri Archōn* (*De Principiis*) is the first comprehensive synthesis of Neoplatonic philosophy and Christian religion.

279  Daniélou, *Hist. Theol.,* p. 56.

280  On Origen's five gradations in his hamartiology, see Völker, *Das Vollkommenheitsideal des Origenes,* pp. 30ff.

281  Daniélou, *o.c.,* p. 60.

The threefold aspect which Origen develops in his Biblical exegesis – the typical (literal), the spiritual (moral), and the mystical (pneumatic)[282] – corresponds to the three types of believers, the common people, the spiritually growing, and those who are truly perfect.[283]

How fundamental *gnosis* as the principle of perfection is to Origen, appears from his advice to start with the Socratic "Know Thyself",[284] and *after that* to try to know God by way of a rigid, world-despising asceticism.[285] This ascetic despising of the body and the sensuous, closing the door to all things perceived by the senses in order not to be led astray, is rooted in Origen's peculiar Platonic doctrine of the pre-existence of all rational spirits. These spirits, all created equal and immaterial, had cooled off in different degrees from their attachment to God, and therefore were incorporated in soul-animated bodies.[286]

Daniélou[287] indicates the implications of Origen's concept well:

> The structure of the universe is therefore a secondary datum, created by God, but for the purpose of dealing with sin. The problem is to know how these spirits will be restored to their original condition.

Men in their present state thus have been devils before, and may now, with the help of the Logos-Christ, raise themselves up to become angels again. Ultimately God will completely conquer evil in that all spirits, including devils, will be restored in their original perfection. This is the *apokatastasis pantōn* of Acts 3,19.[288]

Within this context, it becomes clear what Origen means when he says to Celsus that – with the exception of Christ Jesus – "it is impossible for a man thus to be without sin" [sc. as having never at any time sinned].[289] On the other hand, he distinguishes sharply between sinners and "those who are already pure and who sin no more".[290] Christ was sent as a

---

282  See Daniélou, *Origen*, 1955, pp. 139-174.

283  *De Princ.* IV, 2, 4 (11): simpliciores – qui vero proficere coeperunt – qui vero perfecti sunt. Cf. Loofs, *Leitfaden*, p. 150. G. Heinrici, *RE* VII, 730f. (s.v. *Hermeneutik*).

284  Flew, *o.c.*, p. 152. Harnack, *H.D.* II, 336f.

285  Flew, *o.c.*, p. 153, concludes: "Origen has gone beyond Clement in thus introducing to his Sancta Scala an asceticism that despises the world."

286  Loofs, *Leitfaden*, p. 155. In *De Princ.*, III, 4, 4. Or. applies Rom. 7,23 to the human body as such. The body is the enemy of the soul.

287  *Hist. Theol.*, p. 57.

288  See Daniélou, *Origen*, pp. 209-220, 271-310. Harnack, *H.D.* II, 377-378. Loofs, *Leitfaden*, pp. 157f.

289  *Contra Celsum*, III, 62. Cf. Loofs, *Leitfaden*, p. 155: "So zweifellos auch die Freiheit des Menschen ist..., so tritt doch jede Seele bereits als befleckt in die Welt ein, und der materielle Leib verunreinigt sie noch mehr; dazu kommen die Versuchungen durch die Dämonen."

290  *C. Cels.*, III, 62. In III, 69, he finds these "to be few in number."

physician to the sinners, but as a "teacher of divine mysteries" to the perfect ones.[291]

The souls of the "sinners" still have to fight against flesh and blood, i.e., the body; the perfect ones, having passed beyond this stage through a radical mortification of the flesh, merely have to fight against the demonic powers.[292] Thus Origen recognizes basically two different kinds of Christians in the Church, in which the perfect Gnostics, as priests and Levites, constitute the Church proper.[293]

He applies the Stoic theory of progress to the Christian way of sanctification. Instead of a sudden break with sin through rebirth, Origen places a system of gradual ascent to perfect virtue, a long process which passes many stations.[294] To those few who strive for moral perfection in the appointed ascetic way, he indeed holds out sinlessness.[295] This doubtless may be related directly to Origen's concept of Adam as prototype of each sinner's personal guilt, not as the source of sin.[296] Origen's ideal of perfection is the deification[297] of the soul into pure spirit, i.e., the complete union with the Deity in love.[298] Since in his view conversion means only conversion of the will, and regeneration cannot mean a fundamental renewal of the ego,[299] Origen's ideal of perfection, however, is rather Neoplatonic.[300]

---

291 *Ibid.* Harnack, *H.D.* II, 369f., exposes Origen's defective Christology.

292 *De Princ.*, III, 2, 4. The first struggle was that of the Corinthians, the last struggle that of Paul and the Ephesians. The prophets and the apostles attained to perfection in this life, *Comm. in Rom., Praef.* Cf. Flew, *o.c.*, p. 155.

293 See G. Teichtweier, *Die Sündenlehre des Origines*, 1958, pp. 58-62, 65f., 160ff. He states: "Bei allen Erörterungen der Sündenfolgen für die Kirche hat Or. immer ihr doppeltes Bild vor Augen, die ideale Kirche der Vollendeten und Sündelosen muss in der real-gegenwärtigen Kirche der Unvollkommenen und Sünder sich durchsetzen" (p. 160).

294 Cf. Völker, *o.c.*, pp. 43f., who specifically refers to Origen's Numbers-homilies, esp. XXVII.

295 See Teichtweier, *o.c.*, pp. 94f., with further references in n. 18. Origen, however, in this respect is more restrained than Clement, since Origen stresses that progression in holiness is accompanied by a deepened sin-consciousness.

296 See Teichtweier, *o.c.*, pp. 96-99, for the arguments that Origen knew no original sin. Adam is conceived as man in general, *C. Cels.*, IV, 40.

297 Cf. *Comm. in Joan* XXXII, 17 (*theopoieitai*, *MPG* 14, 817). See Harnack, *H.D.* III, 164f., on the idea of deification in the ancient Church.

298 See his *Hom. in Cant. cant.* Cf. Harnack, *H.D.* II, 375f.: "Thus a union of grace and freedom takes place within the sphere of the latter, till the 'contemplative life' is reached, that joyous ascetic contemplativeness, in which the Logos is the friend, associate, and bridegroom of the soul, which now, having become a pure spirit, and being herself deified, clings in love to Deity." On Origen's synergism see Völker, *o.c.*, pp. 27f., 37ff.

299 The soul – as the *imago Dei* – has a natural knowledge of God; cf. Völker, *o.c.*, p. 23.

300 Cf. Heussi, *K.K.*, § 171: "Origenes war im Grunde christlicher Neuplatoniker." Flew, *o.c.*, p. 154.

Hampered by the Greek dichotomy of body and soul, Origen seeks perfection exclusively in the ascetic mortification of the body (passionlessness)[301] and the contemplative life of intensified, ecstatic prayer.[302]

Flew rightly calls Origen the precursor of Monasticism.[303] The pneumatic soul ought not to marry, must separate from his familiy, cannot have a wordly trade, should sell all his possessions, and live in poverty.[304] This asceticism, however, functions only as the substructure for the mystical experience of Gnostic deification or *henōsis* of the soul, the beatific vision of God.[305]

The Alexandrian focus on ascetic-contemplative perfection – more intensified in Origen than in Clement –[306] can therefore be characterized as Christian Gnostic or Neoplatonic perfectionism in the early Church.[307]

## 7. The Monastic way of perfection.

According to R. Newton Flew "Monasticism is the boldest organized attempt to attain to Christian perfection in all the long history of the Church."[308]

The origin[309] of the movement of men towards the contemplative life cannot be traced back historically to one famous example, but "before the end of the fourth century some people looked back upon Antony

301  The perfect one cannot marry, since Origen makes 1 Cor. 7 normative; cf. Völker, *o.c.*, pp. 52f.

302  By combining asceticism with mysticism Or. became the forerunner of Dionysius the Areopagite and Augustine; cf. Völker, *o.c.*, pp. 44, 199ff.

303  *O.c.*, p. 156. Already Völker, *o.c.*, pp. iv, 38, 55; especially with respect to the ascetic *imitatio Christi*, pp. 215ff.

304  See Völker, *o.c.*, pp. 52-59. In *Comm. in Mat.* XV, 25, he distinguishes several grades of perfection according to the measure of giving away goods.

305  On this Gnostic *visio Dei* as *unio mystica*, which ultimately dispenses with Christ, see Völker, *o.c.*, pp. 116-144, 190f. He concludes: "In der ekstatischen Schau Gottes ist der Höhepunkt des inneren Aufsteiges erreicht" (p. 144). On Origen's concept of deification, see Turner, *o.c.*, pp. 80f. See his whole chapter IV: "Christ the Giver of incorruption and deification", which shows that throughout the whole patristic tradition the incarnation of Christ is conceived in order that man might be deified. Cf. also J. Gross, *La Divinisation du chrétien d'après des Pères grecs*, 1938.

306  Cf. Völker, in *ThZ* 3 (1947), 35ff., who compares Clement's and Origen's mystical experience. He shows that Clement and Origen were regarded by the later mystics "als die grossen Lehrmeister des geistlichen Lebens, die Formgeber und Gestalter der aszetisch-mystischen Frömmigkeit" (40).

307  Harnack, in *RE*[3] I, 358, remarks that the Alexandrian Christian apologists have conquered Hellenistic Neoplatonism by robbing its arsenal and then overcoming it by its own weapons.

308  *The Idea of Perfection in Christian Theology*, p. 158. See pp. 158-188.

309  See Heussi, *K.K.*, § 28f. and his *Der Ursprung des Mönchtums*, 1936, O. Chadwick, *John Cassian*, 1968[2], ch. I: "The earliest Christian monks."

as the great founder of this manner of life."[310] When he heard the Gospel story read in a church about Christ's appeal to the rich young ruler in Mt. 19,21, he immediately sold all his possessions and became a hermit for the rest of his long life in order "to win fellowship with God by ceaseless prayer".[311]

It was Pachomius who c. A.D. 320 started the organized cloistral life with the rules of unconditional obedience to the abbot, sharp discipline, no private possessions, and the duty of manual labor.

Basil the Great, however, the leader of the orthodox church in Asia Minor and archbishop of Caesarea, became the most influential founder of monasticism in the East because of his standard rules of the monastic life.[312]

Whereas Basil gave the settlements in the Pontus on the banks of the river Iris their constitution and discipline, it was his younger brother Gregory of Nyssa who actually gave monastic life its spiritual form. He gave philosophical depth and theological substance to Basil's ideal of monastic perfection[313] by writing a number of ascetical works. In his trilogy *On Virginity*, *On What It Means to Call Oneself a Christian*, and *On Perfection*, written between A.D. 371 and 391,[314] Gregory, like Plato, stresses the unity of the virtues and defines virtue as the perfection of our nature.[315] In his last *De instituto Christiano* (*On the Christian Mode of Life*), Gregory explains to a group of monks, a short time before the Pelagian controversy in the West, that the grace of God and the moral

310   Chadwick, *o.c.*, p. 5.
311   Flew, *o.c.*, p. 158. The main source is Athanasius' *Vita Antonii*, MPG XXVI, 835-975. See St. Athanasius, *The Life of Saint Antony*, in "Anc. Chr. Writers," 10, ET by R. T. Meyer, 1950. K. Holl gives a fine survey of the five sections of *Vita Antonii* in his *Gesammelte Aufsätze zur Kirchengeschichte*, B II, 1964 (repr. of 1928), pp. 250ff. Heussi, *K.K.*, § 28b, presumes that Antony died in A.D. 356 at the age of 105 years. Also Basil (d. A.D. 379) was incited to the monastic way of perfection by the Gospel story of Mt. 19. He sold all his goods, gave them to the poor and refused "to let the soul have any sympathetic concern with things on earth" (quoted in Flew, *o.c.*, p. 159).
312   The *Rules* are preserved in two redactions, the *Regulae fusius tractatae*, and the *Regulae brevius tractatae*, see *MPG* XXXI, 889-1052; 1052-1305.
313   Flew, *o.c.*, p. 160, points to this general motivation: "The motive that drove all the chief founders of monasticism to forsake the world was the desire of perfection."
314   See the Text edition by W. Jaeger, *Gregorii Nysseni Opera*, Vol. VIII, 1. We do not hesitate to speak of a renaissance of Gregory-of-Nyssa studies, in view of the many works and articles on his mystical theology. See the bibliography in D. L. Balás, S. O. Cist., *Metousia Theou. Man's Participation in God's Perfections according to Saint Gregory of Nyssa*, Studia Anselmiana 55, 1966, pp. xi-xxii.
315   V. W. Callahan, ed. *Saint Gregory of Nyssa, Ascetical Works*, "The Fathers of the Church," 58, 1967, p. xiv.

302

effort of man must cooperate in a balanced co-ordination (the "synergia theory") in order to attain perfection.[316] In fact, to Gregory it is not man who cooperates with God but the grace of God that cooperates with the moral effort of man.[317]

From a dogmatic point of view Gregory defends what anachronistically can be classified as Semipelagianism.[318] Gregory, like later Semipelagianism, defends the priority of free will over divine grace, while recognizing that the perfection of man's nature can be achieved only with the help of God. It is his basic assumption, however, that man's God-given nature consists in his freedom to choose either the good or the evil.

The great Hellenistic scholar Werner Jaeger admits that Gregory's attempt to hellenize the apostolic concept of perfection by turning it into Plato's ideal of imitating the divine, or assimilating to God through ascetic virtue, definitely goes beyond the New Testament.[319]

Harnack[320] also sees a basic difference here:

> But the super-terrestrial God which Neo-Platonism proclaimed, was not the God of the Gospels, and the deliverance from the sensuous which it promised was quite different from the original Christian hope of salvation.

Following in the footsteps of the Alexandrian theologians, especially Origen, Gregory makes the *gnosis* of being (*tōn ontōn*) the supreme end of religion. The starting point of his comtemplative life is man's inborn desire for the good, or the contemplation of the soul in and of itself, i.e., self-perfection.[321]

"Perfection" designates therefore one of the basic concepts of the great master of Christian mystic theology in the Eastern Church. Using the New Testament word *teleios*, Gregory fills it, however, with the Platonic philosophical content, i.e., a life according to virtue in order to attain to self-perfection.[322]

---

316   See W. Jaeger, *Two rediscovered Works of Ancient Christian Literature: Gregory of Nyssa and Macarius*, 1954, pp. 87ff., 92ff.

317   *Ibid.*, p. 92. See the collection of relevant texts from Gregory's *De Inst. Chr.* on pp. 93-96, which clearly state that grace *follows* closely upon the efforts of virtue. On the different connotation of synergy with Clem. Al., see pp. 103-106.

318   Cf. *ibid.*, p. 89. On the Semipelagian controversies, see Seeberg, *H.D.* I, 368-382. Chadwick, *o.c.*, pp. 127ff.

319   Jaeger, *o.c.*, p. 33.

320   *Monasticism. Its Ideals and its History*, ET 1895, p. 20.

321   *Ibid.*, pp. 75f., 90. Jaeger states: "Pelagius was only an extreme representative of this perfectionist trend in the Church" (p. 90). On pp. 106ff. Jaeger traces Gregory's whole ascetic perfection idea back to Origen.

322   *Ibid.*, pp. 31f. Since also the Western Church was greatly influenced

David Balás has shown that self-perfection according to Gregory means man's *participation* in God's perfections or virtues, i.e., the presence of God in the participant, with the new emphasis that participation is essentially a continuous and everlasting progress.[323]

John Cassian (d.c. A.D. 433), the abbot of Massilia, defined perfection as the state of passionlessness, the freedom from crude temptation and disturbance, with the mind concentrated upon God.[324]

Yet Cassian denied the possibility of a state of sinlessness because of the working of original sin.[325] He therefore applied Rom. 7,14ff. to the "perfect".[326] Unceasing prayer with ecstasy became the norm in Cassian's ideal of the Christian life.[327] The monastic life is the way of salvation, to Cassian.[328]

In monastic perfection the *imitatio Christi* came to mean perfect renunciation and "complete impassivity as regards actual living".[329] It implied a renunciation even in the very thoughts, which only the very well trained, the spiritual athlete, could obtain by long *ascesis*.[330] It was taken for granted that man's ascetic endeavors, with the Spirit's help, could attain to the perfect fulfillment of God's commandments, e.g., to love God and the neighbor perfectly, and thus live sinless.[331]

Unfortunately, the monastic attitude to human affection was more influenced by the Stoic ideal of *apatheia* and by the exclusive community-

by Basil's and Gregory's monastic perfectionism, Jaeger seems not to exaggerate when he states: "One cannot easily overrate the importance of the ascetic ideal of perfection, not only for Christian life but also for the history of faith and dogma" (p. 91).

323 *Ibid.*, pp. 162-167. He shows that Gregory took the fundamental Platonic notion of "participation" and inserted it into a Christian synthesis. He criticizes Gregory because he "failed to distinguish between natural and supernatural participation and also tended to minimize the distinction between present anticipation and the future eternal fulfilment" (p. 165).

324 *Collationes* III, 10; IX, 10. Cf. Chadwick, *o.c.*, pp. 102f., who concludes on p. 103: "Cassian will allow that a monk may strip himself of his passions, destroy his faults – provided passions and faults are understood crudely. He will allow the possessions of the virtues – modesty, continence, humility and the rest, but not the possibility of keeping the mind fixed upon God. There is thus a perfection of the 'active life' here, but of the contemplative life only in heaven."

325 *Coll.* XXIII.

326 *Coll.* XXIII, 13.

327 See Flew, *o.c.*, p. 167. Also Flew's critique. Chadwick, *o.c.*, p. 104: "Prayer is the apprehension of God by the mind."

328 Flew, *o.c.*, pp. 167f.

329 Basil's *Regulae fusius tractatae* 8, 348e; 349a; quoted in Flew, *o.c.*, p. 169.

330 See the story of Macarius of Alexandria, the "record-breaker", in Flew, *o.c.*, p. 170.

331 Cf. Flew, *o.c.*, p. 172, concerning Basil.

love than by Christ's appeal to perfect love in Mt. 5,48.[332]

In Greek monasticism the perfect monk always remains the hermit, the anchorite who lives the life of Antony, and who renounces not only the world but also the Church and all communal life.[333]

Thomas Aquinas in his systematic theology has, on the one hand, acknowledged that "perfection consists essentially in the observance of the commandments [sc. of love, in Dt. 6,5; Lev. 19,18]," [334] but, on the other hand, has legalized the monastic way of chastity (continence) and poverty as the objectively best and surest way to Christian perfection by stating that the "evangelical counsels" are "directed to the removal of things that hinder the act of charity, and yet are not contrary to charity, such as marriage, the occupation of wordly business, and so forth." [335]

He recognizes that monasticism or the following of the "counsels" is not perfection as such even when it is called officially the "state of perfection", but "the means of attaining to perfection." [336] For both the Roman Catholic and the Greek Catholic Church the genuine and perfect Christian is the monk.[337]

The monastic way of life – the sinking of one's being in God, and strict asceticism – is the Christian life proper. But with this recognition a high price had to be paid: the ecclesiastical legitimization of a double moral standard within or alongside the Christian Church.[338]

---

332 Cf. the terrible example in Flew, *o.c.*, pp. 175f. Cassian tells approvingly how a monk, after having lived in seclusion for fifteen years, received a huge packet of letters from his parents and friends, but threw the packet unopened into the fire because those letters would only draw off his attention from his contemplation of heavenly things.
Also Basil's concept of the monastic community as one not dependent on the life of the Church, but as a *self-sufficing* whole, reveals how he considered brotherly love as pertaining only to the fellowmonks. See Flew, *o.c.*, p. 177.

333 See K. Holl, "Ueber das griechische Mönchtum", in *Ges. Aufs.* II, 270-282. He states: "Das Ideal der vita Antonii ist als das Ideal des wahren Mönchs in der griechischen Kirche unverändert durch alle Jahrhunderte hindurch festgehalten worden. Es ist das Ideal des Einsiedlers, des Anachoreten" (p. 272). He shows in his sympathetic evaluation of Greek monkhood why the Church sought and honored its monks so much, especially in offering them the bishopric.

334 *STh* II-II, q. 184, a. 3.

335 *Ibid.*; also I-II, q. 108, a. 4, on the difference between a counsel and a commandment. Both lead to the same end; only, the counsels do so "more assured and expeditious, more speedily." Cf. K. Adam, *The Spirit of Catholicism*, 1963[12] (Image Books ed.), pp. 218f.

336 *Ibid.*; also q. 184, a. 5, *ad* 2. For a radical rejection and refutation of monasticism as Christian perfection by the Reformation, see the *Augsburg Confession*, art. XXVII (stated positively what Chr. Perfection is, art. XXVII, 49); and the *Apology*, art. XXVII. Further Calvin's *Institutes*, IV, 13, 11-14.

337 Harnack, *Monasticism*, p. 2.

338 Harnack, *H.D.* II, 94, 123. On the great difference between Eastern and Western monasticism, see Harnack, *Mon.*, pp. 44ff.

Thomas Aquinas created a theology of merit in which he developed a system of two kinds of merits – a *meritum de congruo* and a *meritum de condigno* – on the basis of the presupposition that God had pre-ordained this to be so according to His justice.[339]

It is the decree of God's justice that the human act as such has an objective and intrinsic value, whether such an act be envisaged in the order of nature or of grace. In other words, Thomas' teaching on merit presupposes, as J. Rivière puts it, "une proportion entre l'oeuvre humaine et la récompense divine."[340] The merits of human acts correspond to the proportion of the works as such. But this proportion or congruity itself is established by divine grace.[341] Although it is true that according to Thomas man could not merit for himself the *first* grace,[342] yet he maintains that man's free will is a secondary, subordinate and providential cause of merit. He considered grace and free will basically as two separate entities besides each other.[343] And since grace does not work in the will, does not recreate the will – only the abstract soul-essence – he construes a system of co-ordination of grace and free will as if both are autonomous parties working on a contract basis.[344] This leads Thomas to the following conclusion:[345]

By every meritorious act a man merits the increase of grace, equally with the consummation of grace which is eternal life.

339 See *STh* I-II, qq. 109-114; esp. p. 114. Cf. M. McDonough, O.P., *The Law and the Gospel in Luther*, 1963, pp. 156-162.

340 In *DTC* X, 700 (s.v. *Mérite*).

341 Cf. *STh* I-II, q. 114, a. 1, *ad* 3: "Since our action has the character of merit only on the presupposition of the Divine ordination, it does not follow that God is made our debtor simply, but His own, inasmuch as it is right that His will should be carried out."

342 *STh* I-II, q. 114, a. 5, referring to Rom. 11,6. After Thomas the scholastic issue became, however, whether fallen man can earn the first bestowal of grace. See H. Oberman, *Forerunners of the Reformation*, 1966, p. 132.

343 Thomas' solution to this created dilemma was to harmonize grace and free will with the aid of the Aristotelian metaphysics, i.e., the sharp distinction between the soul and its faculties, of which the will is one. When grace is infused in the essence of the soul, creating in it a new quality or habitus, this molding of the soul takes place apart from any act of the will.

344 Significant are the remarks of W. von Loewenich, *Von Augustin zu Luther*, 1959, p. 87, in this respect concerning Luther's reaction: "Man kann allerdings fragen, ob das Problem theoretisch damals völlig durchgearbeitet wurde. Gnade und Wille sind ja nicht einfach Gegensätze. Die Gnade Gottes wirkt im Willen des Menschen. Ihr Zusammensein im Heilsvorgang lässt sich praktisch gar nicht auseinanderlegen. Es handelt sich ja nicht um ein Nebeneinander von Gnade und Wille, sondern um ein Ineinander. Von diesem Ineinander ist jedes Addition- und Subtraktionsschema fernzuhalten."

345 *STh* I-II, q. 114, a. 8, *ad* 3.

Not only Christ's life, therefore, but also that of the spiritual monks did earn merits greater than necessary because of their obedience to the counsels of perfection.[346] Monastic perfection thus produces the so-called works of supererogation (*supererogationes*), which are gathered in the spiritual treasury (*thesaurus*) of the Church and can be used by the Pope, through the granting of indulgences, to those who come short.[347]

Noteworthy is the rise of the revolutionary new theology of history and apocalyptic interpretation of perfection of Joachim of Floris, or Fiore (c. 1130-1202), the abbot of the Cistercian monastery in Corace, Italy.[348] Opposing the traditional Tichonius-Augustine view of prophetic interpretation,[349] which had given the Roman Catholic Church finality and sovereignty in human perfection, Joachim conceived the Trinity as the guiding principle for developing a new theology of human history.[350]

He conceived basically three eras – an age of the Father, to be followed by an age of the Son, which would be followed around his own time by an age of the Holy Spirit. If the era of the Father was still a carnal period, and the era of the Son partly carnal and partly spiritual in Joachim's concept, the new impending era would be the age of the triumph of the Holy Spirit.

As Froom[351] points out:

> In this era the full revelation of spiritual things would become a reality, and each individual would have a part in it, sharing in it directly and freely, without need of intercessors.
> The Spirit of God would be the guiding principle in the affairs of men.

Joachim then characterizes the three successive *status* of mankind by three orders of men, who reflect the three Persons of the Trinity. The era of the Spirit which would lead to the final end and the Last Judgment, he calls the period of monasticism, of which the Benedictines were the precursors.[352]

346  *Ibid.*, q. 107, a. 2, referring to Mt. 19,21.
347  *Suppl.*, q. 25, a. 2. Q. 26 deals with those who can grant indulgences; Q. 27 with those whom indulgences avail.
348  For an excellent treatment of Joachim of Floris' prophetic interpretations, see Le Roy E. Froom, *The Prophetic Faith of our Fathers*, I, 1950, pp. 683-716.
349  See W. Kamlah, *Apokalypse und Geschichtstheologie. Die mittelalterliche Auslegung der Apokalypse vor Joachim von Fiore.* "Hist. Stud." 285, 1935 (repr. 1965), pp. 115-129.
350  See the scholarly study of Marjorie Reeves, *The Influence of Prophecy in the Later Middle Ages. A Study in Joachimism*, 1969, pp. 16-27.
351  *O.c.* I, p. 693.
352  The first order of men were the married; the second order the clerics. See esp. M. Reeves, *o.c.*, pp. 135-144.

Then the Spirit would guide all men through a spiritual understanding, which proceeds from both the Old and the New Testament. The new order of contemplation would reveal the eternal Gospel, as predicted in Rev. 14,6.[353]

> This new era would set in, supported by a new, monastic, purely evangelical society, which would raise life to a new spiritual basis. Not clerical society, not bishops and cardinals who fight for worldly gains, but a new monastic order would dominate life in this period, which would have as its sole aim the *imitatio Christi*.[354]

Thus Joachim's revolutionary doctrine of the impending[355] Third Age as monastic perfection gave a new self-understanding and sense of mission to his followers, the Joachimites, with respect to the *ordo spiritualis*.

Containing the seeds of a radical criticism of the papal Church,[356] Joachim's idea of the coming perfect Church, the *ecclesia contemplantium*, did not conceive a new faith or a new church. The new order would be only the perfect expression of the same religion.[357] He still saw married men and clergy living in the "suburbs" of the Holy City.[358] In his concern for the general body of Christian people Joachim was continually considering the problem of relating the *ordo monachorum*, the *viri spirituales*, who lived the life of contemplation on the one hand, with the laity and the clergy on the other hand.

He assigned, therefore, to the spiritual men the responsibility of mediation, of interceding for souls, as the patriarchs did; in short, to be preachers of the truth. Like Moses and Joshua they must lead the Church through the desert and across the Jordan into the Promised Land.

Marjorie Reeves therefore concludes:[359]

> Here is no esoteric mystic who locks up the spiritual future within a select group while the masses perish. Sometimes he even visualizes the conversion of *all* peoples including the Jews to a new spiritual intelligence.

---

353 According to Joachim the order of monastic perfection had remained in sterility until his own time: *contemplativa interim perfectione usque scilicet ad hec tempora nostra in sterilitate manente, Concordia*, bk. IV, ch. 33, 57ra., quoted in G. Leff, *Heresy in the Later Middle Ages*, I, 1967, p. 75, n. 2.

354 Froom, *o.c.* I, p. 697.

355 According to Joachim's calculation the years from 1200 to 1260 were to be the culmination of the change from the second to the third age.

356 For a survey of Joachim's exposition of Daniel and the Apocalypse, see Froom, *o.c.* I, pp. 701-716. It was Joachim's revolutionary idea that the order of clergy would pass away before that of contemplatives.

357 Cf. G. Leff, *o.c.* I, 1967, p. 75.

358 See Reeves, *o.c.*, p. 140.

359 *O.c.*, p. 140.

Joachim's expectation of an imminent era of perfect humanity, led by spiritual monks, received significant influence only because of the powerful preaching of Francis of Assisi and the Spiritual Franciscans who saw themselves as the fulfillment of Joachim's prophecies.[360] After Joachim's death the year 1260 was considered as the specific date when the new age would begin.[361]

History now seems to justify the conclusion that monasticism and monastic apocalypticism both must be defined as forms of ascetic perfectionism.

## 8. *John Wesley.*

As with German Pietism in the seventeenth century, so likewise Methodism in England in the eigtheenth century arose as a direct *reaction* against the prevailing rationalism and moralism.[362] Only, England had already experienced the influence of an English Pietism, Puritanism, in the seventeenth century. But the spiritual fire had died out and the English nation had fallen a prey to a lifeless deism and shameful inhumanity at the time when Methodism started out in 1739.[363]

The unselfish consecration manifested in the Christian lives of John Wesley and John William Fletcher, who unabatedly attended to the spiritual and physical needs of their fellowmen, can only fill us with deepest respect and gratitude.[364]

Our inquiry is directed toward Wesley's concept of Christian perfection and its relation to Biblical perfection.

In 1790, near the end of Wesley's long life (1703-1791), after having preached for sixty years, he stated that the doctrine of "entire sanctification" or "Christian perfection" was "the grand depositum which God has lodged with the people called Methodists; and for the sake of pro-

360  See Froom, *o.c.* I, pp. 731ff.
361  *Ibid.*,pp. 740f. In A.D. 1260 the *flagellants* arose who believed that they could prepare the way for the new era by self-inflicted pain and suffering, thus doing penance for their sins.
362  See the religious-historical picture in C. N. Impeta, *De Leer der Heiliging en Volmaking bij Wesley en Fletcher*, 1913, pp. 6-11, 394f. E. Troeltsch, in *RE*[3] IV, 532ff. (s.v. *Deismus*). F. Loofs, in *RE*[3] XII, 750ff. (s.v. *Methodismus*).
363  See Wesley's evaluation of the English irreligiosity and immorality in his *The Works of the Rev. John Wesley*, 1829-31[3], XI, 159; VIII, 148f., 201 (further designated by *WW*).
364  Cf. Ph. Schaff, *The Creeds of Christendom*, I, 1931[6], p. 885: "The Methodist revival checked the progress of skepticism and infidelity which had begun to set in with deism. It brought the life and light of the gospel to the most neglected classes of society." Cf. Impeta, *o.c.*, p. 396: "Wesley en Fletcher hebben ons het voorbeeld achtergelaten van een Christendom in de praktijk, waarvan we verbaasd staan. Bewondering vervult ons wanneer we opzien tot zulke mannen. Zij waren 'daders des Woords'."

pagating this chiefly He appeared to have raised us up." [365]

This shows that the doctrine of perfection – and with that the perfected man, i.e., the Christian who is entirely sanctified – for Wesley was the very heart and core of the Gospel. As Philip Schaff [366] aptly brings into perspective:

> Calvin's ideal Christian is a servant of God, Luther's, a child of God, Wesley's, a perfect man in the full stature of Christ.

Many [367] are the influences that led Wesley to his concept and conviction of perfection, which appears to have a double focus or two centers basically: the Christ *for* us and the Christ *in* us. [368]

Wesley distinguished sharply between justification and sanctification. In fact, he separated them as two distinct and totally different gifts of God. Justification – and here he accepted the *sola fide* of the Reformers [369] – saves from the *guilt* of sin; sanctification from the *power* of sin. Justification, however, meant to him only the initial step toward full salvation, not yet perfect sanctification. According to Wesley the man who denies the *sola fide* could still be saved if he worked righteousness, appealing to Acts 10,35. [370]

From the time of the Holy Club at Oxford (1730), John Wesley, together with his brother Charles, became possessed with the conviction that holiness is required for full salvation, according to Heb. 12,14. [371]

---

365  *The Letters of the Rev. John Wesley, A.M.*, Standard ed., VIII, p. 238.
366  *O.c.* I, p. 892. He takes the typification from Warren.
367  Cf. E. J. Rattenbury, *The Conversion of the Wesleys*, 1938, p. 173: "Catholic and Lutheran, Anglican and Moravian influences were all blended in Wesley." Flew, *o.c.*, p. 314, esp. refers to Clement of Alexandria, Augustine and Thomas Aquinas.
368  Cf. Impeta, *o.c.*, p. 397.
369  See W. R. Cannon, *The Theology of John Wesley. With Special Reference to the Doctrine of Justification*, 1946, Ch. IV: "Within a hair's breadth of Calvinism" (pp. 81-102). He concludes: "No one ever asserted man's absolute dependence on grace any more than John Wesley did, or preached justification by faith with more zeal or steadfastness" (p. 102). "He cannot, however, agree with them [sc. Whitefield and Calvin] in their conception of the nature of the operation of God's grace. To make grace particular, restricted, special, is in the end to affirm that God himself is unjust" (p. 100). Wesley was particularly opposed to Calvin's doctrine of a double predestination, because he saw its outworking in the moral indifference of his time. See Cannon, pp. 95-100.
370  *Journal*, V, 243.
371  *WW* VIII, 300: "In 1729, two young men, reading the Bible, saw that they could not be saved without holiness, followed after it, and incited others so to do. In 1737 they saw holiness comes by faith. They saw likewise that men are justified before they are sanctified; but still holiness was their point. God then thrust them out, utterly against their will, to raise a holy people.

Holiness or Christian perfection[372] he understood as perfect love.[373] Consequently, love – to God and to the neighbor – became Wesley's central kerygmatic focus and appeal. When Wesley in 1764 reviewed the essentials of his teaching he summed them up in eleven short propositions:[374]

1) There is such a thing as perfection; for it is again and again mentioned in Scripture.
2) It is not so early as justification; for justified persons are to "go on unto perfection" (Heb. vi. 1).
3) It is not so late as death; for St. Paul speaks of loving men that were perfect (Phil. iii. 15).
4) It is not absolute. Absolute perfection belongs not to man, nor to angels, but to God alone.
5) It does not make a man infallible; none is infallible while he remains in the body.
6) Is it sinless? It is not worth while to contend for a term. It is "salvation from sin."
7) It is "perfect love" (1 John iv. 18). This is the essence of it: its properties, or inseparable fruits, are, rejoicing evermore, praying without ceasing, and in everything giving thanks (1 Thess. v. 16, etc.).
8) It is improvable. It is so far from lying in an indivisible point, from being incapable of increase, that one perfected in love may grow in grace far swifter than he did before.
9) It is amissible, capable of being lost; of which we have numerous instances. But we were not thoroughly convinced of this till five or six years ago.
10) It is constantly both preceded and followed by a gradual work.
11) But is it in itself instantaneous or not? In examining this, let us go on step by step.
   An instantaneous change has been wrought in some believers; none can deny this.

When Satan could not otherwise hinder this, he threw Calvinism in the way; and then Antinomianism, which strikes directly at the root of all holiness."

372  In Sermon XXXV on "Christian Perfection" in *Forty-Four Sermons*, ed. 1944 (repr. 1964), p. 461, Wesley calls Christian perfection "only another term for holiness." Wesley's specific writings on Christian perfection are collected in Vol. XI of *The Works*: "A Plain Account of Christian Perfection," pp. 366-445; "Brief Thoughts on Christian Perfection," p. 446; "On Christian Perfection," pp. 448-449.

373  See the superb article of F. Platt, in *ERE* IX, 728-737 (s.v. *Perfection*); esp. 730-731 on Methodist perfection.

374  *WW* XI, 441f. E. H. Sugden clarifies, however: "In spite of his assertion that his views had not changed in any material point from 1725 to 1765, he certainly modified them as time went on" (*Wesley's Standard Sermons*, II, 1956⁴, p. 148). Wesley developed the thought of the "second change", recognizing more fully (original) sin in the believers.

Since that change they enjoy perfect love; they feel this, and this alone; they "rejoice evermore, pray without ceasing, and in everything give thanks." Now, this is all that I mean by perfection; therefore, these are witnesses of the perfection which I preach.

In this respect Heick[375] observes: "His religious experience was nearer to that of Augustine than to that of Luther." But what are the constitutive elements of Wesley's doctrine of perfection in distinction from that of historic Protestantism? The difference basically arises from a different concept of grace and sin,[376] the indissoluble corollary of the concept of holiness. This is acknowledged by Leo G. Cox, in his thought-provoking study *John Wesley's Concept of Perfection*, 1968[2], in chapter II.
Cox states:

Wesley's definition of sin was different, as will be seen, from that of the reformers as well as his concept of grace ... Wesley's doctrine of perfection will stand or fall within the framework of his teachings on sin and grace (p. 28).

With regard to sin and grace Wesley considered both the Reformed and the Pelagian position as extremes.[377] While Cox denies that Wesley defends the doctrine of Semipelagianism,[378] Cannon rather identifies Wesley's concept with it.[379]
It is well known that Wesley avowedly chose Arminianism – a modified form of Calvinism – as the thought-pattern for his theology.[380]
In the ethical theology of Wesley everything hinges on the restoration and function of the human free will in order to co-operate with God.[381] According to Wesley every natural man has already the prevenient grace

375  *A Hist. of Chr. Thought* II, 40.
376  The difference is not so much in the nature of sin as selfishness, pride and the transgression of God's commandments but in the concept of the transmission and eradication of sin.
377  See Cox, *o.c.*, p. 41.
378  *Ibid.* Also Schaff, *o.c.* I, 895.
379  *O.c.*, p. 200, n. 113.
380  See *WW* X, 358-361. Cf. Schaff, *o.c.* I, 894: "The five points in which Arminius differed from the Calvinistic system are clearly and prominently brought out in Wesley's writings." He summarizes them as: freedom of the will (or power of contrary choice) as necessary to responsibility; self-limitation of divine sovereignty in its exercise and dealing with free agents; foreknowledge as preceding and conditioning foreordination; universality of redemption; resistibility of divine grace; possibility of total and final apostasy from the state of regeneration and sanctification. On the Methodist modifications of Arminianism and its own contributions, see pp. 896ff.
381  See *WW* X, 457-480, where he discusses the necessity of human freedom. Cf. Cox, *o.c.*, p. 42.

which consists of the "very first motion of good", the infusion of every good desire, the first wish to please God.[382] It is the "spark of divinity", God's antidote to original sin in each natural man.[383] With this gracious ability, the liberty of self-determination, man is capable of choosing good or evil.[384] If this grace is used and not resisted when salvation in Christ is offered, man need not sin any more.[385]

It was Wesley's specific burden to awaken the conscience of his Anglican fellowmen who excused their moral apathy by a fatalistic and antinomian use of Calvin's *decretum horribile*.[386]

He proclaimed that man is personally responsible for his own damnation.[387] Man has the power to *resist* grace and mercy. For Wesley the decisive element in a person's salvation is his own moral freedom.

In the divine act of justification the sinner is regenerated, cleansed of sin and empowered with new moral strength to obey the will of God and to overcome sin in the realm of social relationship.[388]

Wesley[389] writes:

> A Christian is so far perfect, as not to commit sin. This is the glorious privilege of every Christian, yea, though he be but a babe in Christ. But it is only of grown Christians it can be affirmed, they are in such a sense perfect, as, Secondly, to be freed from evil thoughts and evil tempers.

Cannon even states about Wesley: "There is no other theologian in the entire range of Christian history who was any more concerned with the direct relationship between Christianity and morality than was John Wesley. To him the immoral man was *ipso facto* the un-Christian man. Christianity, at least in the personal sense, without morality could not exist."[390]

382  *Ibid.*, pp. 33ff.
383  Cannon, *o.c.*, p. 100. Schaff, *o.c.* I, 897.
384  *WW* X, 234; VI, 512.
385  *WW*, XIII, 96; X, 360.
386  See Cannon, *o.c.*, p. 95.
387  Cox, *o.c.*, p. 44.
388  Cf. Cannon, *o.c.*, p. 222. Most of Wesley's thirteen sermons on the Sermon on the Mount are intended to show how Christ has revealed the true meaning of the Law, and calls us to keep it. Obedience to the Law in all its particulars through the power of the Holy Spirit is the appointed way of sanctification. See *Sermons*, Standard ed., I, 398-403. On the controversy with Antinomianism, see R. Davies, "The People called Methodists", Appendix, in *A History of the Methodist Church in Great Britain*, I, ed. R. Davies and G. Rupp, 1965, esp. pp. 176-179.
389  *WW* XI, 376. He means that the justified man does not commit outward, voluntary sin.
390  In "John Wesley's doctrine of sanctification and perfection", *MQR* XXXV (1961), 91-95. Quotation on p. 94.

Wesley, in distinction from the Reformers, stressed a sharp difference in "sinning" before and after justification.[391] If God justifies a sinner, He reckons him righteous only for the purpose of making him righteous in the process of sanctification.[392] In other words, Wesley could find no agreement with the central doctrine of the Reformation, that the Christian before God is *simul iustus et peccator* according to Romans 7. Although he agreed that sin remains in the believers – the impulses of a sinful nature, i.e., original sin – Wesley denied that Christians were still sinful in act.[393]

The *imitatio Christi* must be manifested in a new way of life, since the Christian can do all things through Christ strengthening him:

> You can love him and keep his commandments; and to you his 'commandments are not grievous'.... Glorify Christ by imitating Christ in all things, by walking as he walked.[394] By perfection I mean the humble, gentle, patient love of God, and our neighbour, ruling our tempers, words, and actions.[395]
> We mean one in whom is 'the mind which was in Christ'; a man 'that hath clean hands and a pure heart', or that is 'cleansed from all filthiness of flesh and spirit'; one in whom is 'no occasion of stumbling', and who, accordingly, 'does not commit sin'.[396]

Wesley's concept of sin, however, was different from that of the Reformers in so far as he not only distinguished between outward and inward sin but postulated the complete annihilation and eradication of both kinds of sin in the empirical reality of the perfect Christian now.

391  Where Wesley defined a Christian as one who does not commit sin (as act), Luther defined him as one to whom God imputes no sin (original sin). Cf. Luther on Rom. 4,7: "The text says: 'Blessed are they whose iniquities are forgiven'; that is to say: Blessed are they who by grace are freed from the burden of iniquity, namely, of the actual sins which they have committed. That, however, is not sufficient, unless also their 'sins are covered', that is, unless the radical evil which is in them, (*original sin*), is not charged to them as sin. That is covered when, though still existing, it is not regarded, considered and imputed by God, as we read: 'Blessed is the man to whom the Lord will not impute sin'" (*Comm. on the Ep. to the Romans*, ET J. Th. Mueller, Ed., Zondervan, 1965⁴, p. 67). See also Seeberg, *H.D.* II, 260ff.

392  *WW* V, 56f: "What is *justification?*... it is not the being made actually just and righteous. This is *sanctification*; which is, indeed, in some degree, the immediate fruit of justification, but, nevertheless, is a distinct gift of God, and of a totally different nature. The one implies what God does for us through His Son, the other, what he works in us by his Spirit" (56).

393  Cf. Cox, *o.c.*, p. 47. On Wesley's superficial knowledge of Luther's *Commentary on the Epistle to the Galatians*, see H. Carter, *The Methodist Heritage*, 1951², pp. 221-231 ("John Wesley on Martin Luther").

394  *WW* X, 369.

395  *WW* XI, 446.

396  *WW* XI, 384.

The renowned Methodist historian William B. Pope [397] even concludes:

> The Methodist doctrine is the only one that has consistently and boldy maintained the possibility of the destruction of the carnal mind, or the inbred sin of our fallen nature.

Wesley postulated that the experience of Christian perfection sprang forth from a specific divine act in the soul *after* justification,[398] as "the second change" or "blessing", by which sin would actually "cease to be" in the Christian.[399]

This particular moment, however, would only be the culmination and consummation of the gradual dying to sin and growing in grace which had started in justification. Yet it still was a specific act of God to be received and experienced instantaneously by faith only. Wesley stressed the experiential uniqueness of this distinctive gift of perfection apart from justification with the aid of the following analogy:

> And as the change undergone, when the body dies, is of a different kind, and infinitely greater than any we had known before, yea, such as till then it is impossible to conceive; so *the change wrought when the soul dies to sin, is of a different kind, and infinitely greater than any before, and than any can conceive till he experiences it.*[400]

In that moment the Christian would receive the added testimony of the Spirit that he now has "total death to sin" and "entire sanctification", i.e., perfect love.[401] This to Wesley meant the perfect uprooting of indwelling (or original) sin, of sinful nature *per se:*

---

397   *A Compendium of Christian Theology*, III, 1880, p. 97.

398   *WW* XI, 446: "I believe it is usually many years after justification; but that it may be within five years or five months after it, I know no conclusive argument to the contrary." In 1767 he conceived that this divine act generally happened at the instant of death, "the moment before the soul leaves the body" (446).

399   *WW* VI, 53. *Sermons*, Standard ed., II, 459 (in "The Scripture Way of Salvation"). In II, 390f. (in "The Repentance of Believers") Wesley explicitly states, after having said that we may conquer both outward and inward sin: "although we may *weaken* our enemies day by day; yet we cannot *drive them out*. By all the grace which is given at justification we cannot extirpate them. Though we watch and pray ever so much we cannot wholly cleanse either our hearts or hands. Most sure we cannot, till it shall please our Lord to speak to our hearts again, to speak the second time, 'Be clean'; and then only the leprosy is cleansed. Then only, the evil root, the carnal mind, is destroyed; and inbred sin subsists no more."

400   *WW* XI, 402 (italics supplied). Wesley adds that this perfection still makes room for an endless growing in grace and the knowledge of Christ, even "to all eternity."

401   *WW* XI, 401f. Cf. Pope, *o.c.*, III, 97: "Hence the fervour with which

a full salvation from all our sins, from pride, self-will, anger, unbelief .... Then the soul is pure from every spot of sin; it is clean from all unrighteousness. The believer then experiences the deep meaning of those solemn words, 'If we walk in the light as He is in the light, we have fellowship one with another, and the blood of Jesus Christ his Son cleanseth us from all sins'.[402]

Rupert Davies psychologizes too much Wesley's theological point of the *essential* annihilation of original sin, when he states that it is not just purged away but "superseded, overwhelmed, by the positive qualities of humility, tenderness, compassion, love. There is no inadequacy about an ideal such as this."[403]

In this respect Wesley even went beyond Pietism and mysticism.[404] Wesley not only considered perfection "the highest state of grace", a present reality, but also regarded it a holy duty of the perfected ones to witness of their unique blessing to the fellow believers, thus urging them to seek "a still higher salvation" than justification.[405] But how could anybody be sure of the reality of such a testimony? Although there is no infallible surety, there is "reasonable proof" on candid examination: 1) clear evidence of examplary behavior, 2) an account of the time and manner of the change, 3) blamelessness in words and actions.[406]

Wesley placed the burden of disproof on his opponents for the reliability of his message.[407] He conceded:[408]

the Hymns appeal to the Holy Ghost for the destruction of inbred sin, and the almost equal earnestness with which the Sermons urge on believers the prayer for faith in the omnipotent power of God, not only to shed abroad His perfect love, but to finish the death of the body of sin. The combination of the two elements, the negative annihilation of the principle of sin and the positive effusion of perfect love, is, it may be said, peculiar to Methodist theology as such."

402  WW VI, 46, 53. Wesley recognized this perfection in quite a number of his followers who had "the direct witness of it", WW XI, 424; VI, 420. He also believed that the apostle John and the first Christians had this perfection of soul, appealing to 1 Jn. 4,17, WW VIII, 296. Remarkably enough, Wesley himself never claimed to have had the experience of "that sudden and instantaneous change" (WW VIII, 66). Yet, he preached: "Look for it then every day, every hour, every moment! Why not this hour, this moment?" (VI, 53).

403  In *Hist. of the Meth. Church*, I, 173.

404  See Pope, *o.c.* III, 97: "But the utmost contemplated by them [sc. Mystics and Pietists] was the gradual suppression of the evil nature through the ascendency of love."

405  WW XI, 397f. ("undoubtedly he ought to speak").

406  WW XI, 398.

407  WW XI, 405: "Convince me of this [sc. deception], and I will preach it no more.... But, if there are none made perfect yet, God has not sent me to preach perfection."

408  WW XI, 406.

I want living witnesses. I cannot indeed be infallibly certain that this or that person is a witness; but if I were certain there are none such, I must have done with this doctrine.

Thus the perfect Christian has not only "the great salvation" but also the *consciousness* of this renewal.[409] It is the fulfillment of the promises in Dt. 30,6; Ps. 130,8; Ez. 36,25.29; Mt. 5,48; 22,37; 2 Cor. 7,1; Rom. 8,3-4; and 1 Jn. 3,8; 4,17.[410]

Wesley recognized many such perfected Christians among his followers:

> I know many that love God with all their heart. He is their one desire, their one delight, and they are continually happy in him. They love their neighbor as themselves . . . . They rejoice evermore, pray without ceasing, and in everything give thanks. Their souls are continually streaming up to God, in holy joy, prayer, and praise. This is a point of fact.[411]

Wesley's idea of moral perfection thus is essentially the ontological concept of *sinless* perfection of the soul. Wesley did not want to *stress* the qualification "sinless", since it suggested to him a perfection of the whole psycho-somatic man, including his physical and mental constitution.

On the basis of his presupposed substantial dichotomy of body and soul[412] Wesley distinguished sharply (sinless) perfection of the soul and (sinless) perfection of the body. With regard to the soul and character of man Wesley basically accepted[413] the attainability of sinless perfection now, in an instant. But because of the impossibility of having the perfection of the body and its faculties before the day of the resurrection of the body (the "Adamic perfection"), Wesley preferred to refrain from using the term "sinless" at all, "lest I should seem to contradict myself."[414]

409   See E. W. H. Vick, "John Wesley's Teaching Concerning Perfection", *AUSS* IV (1966), 201-217, esp. 209ff. He also summarizes Fletcher's doctrine of perfection. Fletcher, who admittedly lived a holy life, claimed to have attained to perfection. R. Davies, in *A Hist. of the Meth. Church,* I, 172, frankly concedes: "We may rightly object, however, to the doctrine that a perfect Christian has within himself the witness of the Spirit that he is perfect."

410   *WW* XI, 389ff.

411   *WW* XI, 418. Cf. *ERE* IX, 371, where it is shown that Wesley's mature judgment was more guarded.

412   On the basis of 1 Thes. 5,23 Wesley believed in the essential trichotomy of man, see *WW* XI, 447f.

413   Cf. *WW* XI, 446: "And I do not contend for the term *sinless*, though I do not object against it." This was in 1767. In 1763 he seems to have recognized that the N.T. never qualifies perfection by "sinless", *WW* XII, 257; cf. Flew, *o.c.,* p. 325, n. 4.

414   *WW* XI, 396.

This essential separation of moral soul-perfection and physical perfection which is based on his unscriptural anthropological dichotomy (even trichotomy), forced Wesley, however, also to postulate a fateful dualism in his hamartiology.

Not satisfied with the deep sin consciousness of the Reformers who only theoretically distinguished between *sins* as acts, and original *Sin* or sinful nature as the wellspring of sinful promptings, Wesley went on to create his dualistic and problematic doctrine of "proper" and "improper" sins.[415] A sin "properly so called" he defined as "a voluntary transgression of a known law".[416] From such sins, Wesley maintained, we could be perfectly freed. Sins "improperly so called" he defined as ignorance, error, infirmities which are not of a moral nature, such as "slowness of speech, impropriety of language, ungracefulness of pronunciation; to which one might add a thousand nameless defects, either in conversation or behaviour."[417] All these shortcomings, including the liability to temptation, are "necessarily connected with flesh and blood."[418] As long as the soul is not freed from the body, Christian perfection cannot be exempted from these bodily imperfections.[419]

> I believe there is no such perfection in this life as excludes these involuntary transgressions [sc. W. defines these as "deviations from the perfect law", i.e., from Adamic perfection] which I apprehend to be naturally consequent on the ignorance and mistakes inseparable from mortality. Therefore *sinless perfection* is a phrase I never use, lest I should seem to contradict myself.[420]

Wesley recognized the difficulty of discriminating accurately between sinful and sinless faults,[421] between conscious and unconscious sins.[422]

---

415   *WW* XI, 396. Cf. Flew, *o.c.*, p. 326: "Evidently Wesley is using the word sin in two distinct senses."

416   *Ibid.* Cf. also *Sermons*, Standard ed., I, 304 ("The Great Privilege of those that are Born of God").

417   Sermon XXXV, in *Forty-Four Sermons*, p. 461 ("Christian Perfection").

418   *WW* XI, 383.

419   See note 417.

420   *WW* XI, 396.

421   Cf. *WW* XI, 396f.; and *ERE* IX, 731. Flew acknowledges, *o.c.*, p. 327: "It is difficult to carry through such a distinction without contradictions." He gives as an example the fact that Wesley could classify a "wrong temper" as a sinless fault as well as a sinful fault. The ultimate criterion was love.

422   Wesley never used the term "unconscious sin", since he basically recognized only a voluntary transgression, i.e., a wilful sin, as a sin. W. E. Sangster, *The Path to Perfection*, 1943 (repr. 1945), pp. 72ff., 146, 155, severely criticizes Wesley's hamartiology, since the "serious sins of omission have slipped through the net" which constitute "the most terrible leprosy of the soul" (p. 155).

To him nothing was sin properly speaking save a conscious sin, "a voluntary transgression of a known law". In other words, in the state of sanctification there is no consciousness of sin.[423] Even the Methodist scholar Flew acknowledges that Wesley's analysis of the nature of sin was inadequate. He explains:

> Our worst sins are often those of which we are unconscious. The stress on the consciousness and deliberate intention of the agent is the most formidable defect in Wesley's doctrine of the ideal.[424]

This specific hamartiological distinction of Wesley's doctrine of perfection is exposed as a schematic construction, however, when placed in the light of Christ's atoning mediation and Priestly cleansing of sins. Wesley inevitably had to face the crucial question whether those Methodists who had received the second change, i.e., sinless perfection of the soul, still needed Christ as a Mediator.

Did they not live without sin? Were they not essentially, inherently[425] holy? On this vital point Wesley's anthropological thinking clashed with the Lutheran Reformation as represented in Zinzendorf. Wesley had a historic conversation with Zinzendorf on September 3, 1741, in Gray's Inn Gardens, London, which Wesley afterwards recorded in Latin in his Journal.[426]

The essential passage[427] on Perfection is:

> Z.  I acknowledge no inherent perfection in this life. This is the error of errors. I pursue it through the world with fire and

---

423  Cf. His Letter to Mrs. Maitland, of May 12, 1763: "But is there no sin in those who are perfect in love? I believe not; but be that as it may, they feel none; no temper contrary to pure love.... And whether sin is suspended, or extinguished, I will not dispute; it is enough that they feel nothing but love" (*WW* XII, 257f.). On the *destruction* or utter abolishing of sin, see Impeta, *o.c.*, p. 224. Also above, n. 399.

424  *O.c.*, p. 332. He admits, p. 227, that the conclusion of O. A. Curtis, *The Christian Faith*, 1905, p. 378, cannot be contradicted: "I have found no way of harmonizing all of Wesley's statements at this point; and I am inclined to think that he never entirely cleared up his own thinking concerning the nature and scope of sin." Cf. also Vick, *o.c.*, 212ff. R. D. Davies, in *A Hist. of the Meth. Church*, I, 169, 173.

425  Cf. Cannon, *o.c.*, p. 225: "What might appear as a superficial distinction, manifesting itself in the Reformers' refusal to say that man is inherently righteous in this world, as against Wesley's insistence that he *is* righteous, is really of ultimate significance."

426  *Journal*, II, pp. 487-495. H. Moore has translated the Dialogue in his *Life of Wesley*, I, 1825, pp. 481-488. The chief passage also in Flew, *o.c.*, pp. 278f.

427  *Ibid.* II, 489.

sword .... Christ is our sole perfection. Whoever follows inherent perfection, denies Christ.

W.  But I believe that the Spirit of Christ works this perfection in true Christians.

Z.  By no means. All our perfection is in Christ. All Christian perfection is Faith in the blood of Christ. Our whole Christian Perfection is imputed, not inherent. We are perfect in Christ, in ourselves we are never perfect.

W.  I think we strive about words.

Wesley obviously did not recognize the basic difference between his own anthropological-empirical perfection and Zinzendorf's Reformation doctrine of Christian perfection. When Zinzendorf continued the dialogue by stating that the Christian is holy in Christ, not in himself (*in se*), Wesley replied, But doesn't he live holy? Doesn's he have a holy heart? Zinzendorf answered. Certainly! Wesley then asked the significant question, Isn't he then, consequently, holy *in himself*? [428] To which Zinzendorf replied with the equally significant: "No, no. Only in Christ. He is not holy *in himself*. He never has any sanctity *in himself*." [429] It can hardly be doubted that Wesley in his position on *inherent* holiness or righteousness goes fundamentally beyond Luther and Calvin. In this respect he shows a definite affinity to Augustine and the medieval Scholastic tradition in which the sinful nature of man decreases essentially to the proportion that *it* becomes essentially a holy nature. [430]

428  *Ibid.*: "*Nonne, ex consequenti, sanctus est* in se?"
429  *Ibid.*: "*Non, non. In Christo tantum. Non sanctus* in se. *Nullam omnino habet sanctitatem* in se."
430  Cf. R. Prenter, *Spiritus Creator*, ET 1953, p. 39: "The Augustinian and scholastic teaching of justification which Luther opposes in the writing against Latomus permits grace to be a new nature in man, so that man is gradually changed to a new man or lifted up from the natural level to the supernatural. Righteousness in this manner becomes a 'formal justice'. Perhaps it can be stated crudely that in the scholastic teaching grace results in a gradual improvement of the old man until he insensibly has become a new man.... Man thus gradually becomes more and more righteous. Grace gradually substitutes the new nature more and more for the old sinful self." Luther fundamentally rejected this ontological-anthropological concept of Scholastic justification by his religious-theological statement of *simul iustus et peccator* which over against the traditional *partly* righteous-*partly* sinful idea placed the concept of the Christian as being simultaneously *fully* righteous and *fully* sinful. This implied the radical idea of *semper iustificandus*: the Christian needs to be justified daily anew. This means a continual *total* justification. Sinful nature itself, to Luther, never enters on a process of healing or improvement. The old man remains sinful. Luther's teaching is characterized by a deepening sin-consciousness and a radical self-condemnation which destroys all thoughts about a gradual transition to holiness or a slow process of becoming perfect. To Luther, as well as Calvin, man does not gradually become more and more righteous inherently. Progress in sanctification rather

He accepts the hymn of his brother Charles who stated: [431]

> Partner of thy perfect nature,
> Let me be Now in thee
> A new, sinless creature.

Wesley also accepted inherent holiness and progress in holiness, although he only recognized this as the fruit and consequence of justification.[432]

The perfect Christian is holy in himself, however, only when he remains in Christ.[433]

Also in Vick's analysis the fundamental theological failure of Wesley's perfectionism appears to be his mystification of "the relationship between original sin and sanctification."[434]

When Wesley created his doctrine of sinless perfection of the soul as the gift of inherent holiness or essential perfection, he and his followers had to give account of their key doctrine in 1758, when the searching question had to be answered:

> But still, if they live without sin, does not this exclude the necessity of a Mediator? At least, is it not plain that they stand no longer in need of Christ in his priestly office?[435]

The answer of Wesley is, "Far from it", supported by five points, only the fifth of which relates the perfect man to the sin problem, the actual matter at issue:

> The best of men still need Christ in his priestly office, to atone

meant progress in true repentance and deeper trust in Christ's righteousness. In this light Heick's evaluation becomes understandable: "Wesleyanism may be called a Protestant version of Franciscan-Jesuit theology" (*o.c.* II, 44).

431  In *WW* XI, 392.

432  See also *WW* V, 241, 244; VII, 314. The righteousness of Christ is our *title* to heaven; our personal righteousness is our *fitness* for heaven. Cf. Impeta, *o.c.*, p. 238. Vick, *o.c.*, 213.

433  See *WW* XI, 417. Cf. Impeta, *o.c.*, p. 238: "Derhalve: *niet* slechts *in Christus aangemerkt* is de ware Christen heilig, terwijl hij in zichzelf onheilig is; neen: *in Christus zijnde* is de Christen heilig, terwijl hij buiten Christus onheilig zou zijn."

434  *O.c.*, 213. He concludes: "[Wesley] appears to be creating an abstract ideal which does not take into full consideration the presence and the intermittent manifestation of original sin. That he virtually but vaguely recognizes this is evident in his saying that the faults of the sanctified man, while not sins, still require the blood of the Saviour to atone for them. What can these faults be but the coming to expression of the original sin which Wesley has desired to take so seriously?" (217).

435  *WW* XI, 395.

for their omissions, their short-comings, (as some not improperly speak,) their mistakes in judgments and practice, and their defects of various kinds. For these are all deviations from the perfect law,[436] and consequently need an atonement. Yet *that they are not properly sins*, we apprehend may appear from the words of St. Paul, 'He that loveth, hath fulfilled the law; for love is the fulfilling of the law' (Rom. xiii. 10). Now, mistakes, and whatever infirmities necessarily flow from the corruptible state of the body, are noway contrary to love; *nor therefore, in the Scripture sense, sin.*[437]

In other words, Wesley's perfect Christian has perfect love and therefore does not need Christ as Priest for any sinful act, word, or thought any more, since he is *essentially* holy, each sinful prompting (original sin) being annihilated.[438] The only reason why Wesley still maintains Christ as a Mediator for the Christian is for the sake of his physical infirmities and shortcomings, which are, however, *no sins* "in the Scripture sense".[439]

Wesley radically rejects the Reformation position that original sin or sinful nature is indissolubly connected with the human body, and that, consequently, the "sinful flesh" or "sinful body" – indicating the sinful relation of the whole man to God – does not exclude but include the body as the concrete sinful human existence *coram Deo*.

Wesley's anthropological separation of body and soul leads him to the statement:

> A sinful body? .... But there is no authority for it in Scripture: The word *sinful body* is never found there. And as it is totally unscriptural, so it is palpably absurd. For no *body*, or matter of any kind can be *sinful*: Spirits alone are capable of sin.
> Pray in what part of the body should sin lodge? ...
> Only the soul can be the seat of sin.[440]

---

436  By the "perfect law" Wesley means *here* the Adamic law, the law of perfect humanity. Wesley distinguishes three kinds of law: a) the Adamic law or the law of innocence, b) the Mosaic law, c) the law of faith, love and liberty, or the law of Christ. See *WW* XI, 415. Cf. also Impeta, *o.c.*, pp. 232f.

437  *WW* XI, 396 (italics supplied).

438  Wesley had to confess that some of his followers had drawn the conclusion of no longer needing Christ's atonement: "Indeed, exceeding few; I do not remember to have found five of them in England" (*WW* XI, 418; cf. *ERE* IX, 731).

439  Cf. also *WW* XI, 395: "And a thousand such instances there may be, even in those who are in the highest state of grace. Yet, where every word and action springs from love, *such a mistake is not properly a sin*. However, it cannot bear the rigour of God's justice, but needs the atoning blood" (italics supplied).

440  *WW* VI, 418 (Sermon LXXVI: "On Perfection").

The artificial manner by which Wesley is forced to maintain the necessity of forgiving grace, for the perfect ones, e.g., in the Lord's prayer, becomes strikingly apparent when he argues that "they fulfill the law of love", but, because of the "shattered body" (not original sin!), "even in this case, there is not a full conformity to the perfect law".[441]

This is certainly a curious solution for those who have received essential divine perfection of the soul.[442]

From a Biblical theological point of view Wesley's problematic hamartiology does not reach the profundity of the religious sin concept of the Reformers.

The dynamic correlation of the Christian believer, with all his "good works" through a deepening *sola fide* also in sanctification, with God, is replaced by the dilemma of proper and improper sins in the sanctified Christian, of fulfillment of the divine law of love, but yet not full conformity to the perfect law of humanity. On the Scriptural basis of the psycho-somatic unity of the human nature[443] the judgment of Edward Vick is unavoidable, that Wesley in principle repudiates his doctrine of perfection – as the annihilation of human sinfulness – by his qualification of improper "*sins*" in the perfect Christian.

For Wesley himself, however, his doctrine of sin was no contradiction or repudiation of his postulated sinless perfection, since his hamartiology and soteriology were rooted in the substantial dichotomy of his anthropology. Flew points out that Wesley, influenced by Augustine, even conceived of original sin as a substance, a thing, which might be expelled or rooted out like a rotten tooth.[444]

Original sin, as the corrupt nature of the soul before God, is completely *separated* from the body and its members. Wesley's perfectionism is based on this anthropological dualism. His corresponding schematic hamartiological dualism qualifies this doctrine of perfection as an *ethico-philosophical perfectionism*.

Its inadequate sin concept ends with the philosophical contrast of grace (perfection) with nature, the corruptible body "as such". Wesley's

---

441  *WW* XI, 419.

442  Cf. *WW* XI, 444: "It is the circumcision of the heart from all filthiness, all inward as well as outward pollution. It is a renewal of the heart in the whole image of God, the full likeness of Him that created it." Cf. also Impeta, *o.c.*, p. 234.

443  See J. R. Zurcher, *The Nature and Destiny of Man*, "Philosophical Library," ET 1969, ch. XI. Cf. also his three art. "Christian View of Man", in *AUSS* II (1964), 156-168; III (1965), 66-83; IV (1966), 89-103.

444  *O.c.*, p. 335. He asks the searching question, "How can he be delivered in an instant from that which he himself is? The man himself must be changed; and we are changed by the companionship of the Indwelling Spirit of God" (p. 335). Cf. Sangster, *o.c.*, p. 167. Also Sugden, in *Wesley's Standard Sermons*, II, 148f.

postulation leaves us with some unanswered religious-theological questions. How can Wesley's perfectly sanctified and holy Christian still stand and progress in true repentance *coram Deo*, still confess his own sinfulness before Christ as High Priest? *Could* he really do this, when he believes, and through a specific testimony of the Spirit feels, that he no longer has a sinful nature, no longer has sin, in the Scripture sense? And how can there be postulated a relapse into sin when the roots of sinful nature are supernaturally, radically erased?

It is significant that the Methodist Episcopal Church[445] later decided to disavow Wesley's perfection. This change is expressed in the revision of Charles Wesley's famous hymn "Love Divine, All Loves Excelling", in the Methodist hymnal.[446] Instead of "Let us find that second rest" the second stanza now reads "Let us find the promised rest". Many regarded this doctrinal decision as a decline of the genius and mission of Methodism and as apostasy from Scriptural truth, leading to the rise of many schisms and new sects in America.[447] Since 1867 a number of Methodist ministers started the yearly interdenominational holiness camp meetings, organized in the National Holiness Association, now embracing thirteen holiness denominations with more than one and a half million members in the United States.[448]

It is only appropriate to close with the remark that Methodism, with its Biblical concern for holiness and character perfection, restored to Protestantism the moral aspiration which it had lost in the eighteenth century. Our analysis of Wesley's theology of perfection, however, has confirmed the conclusion of George C. Cell, that Wesley's perfection is a unique "synthesis of the Protestant ethic of grace and the Catholic ethic of holiness."[449]

---

445   After Wesley, for practical reasons, had ordained preachers for America in 1784, Methodism became an autonomous Church. See Carter, *o.c.*, pp. 145-157.

446   Heick, *o.c.*, II, 45.

447   See E. T. Clark, *The Small Sects in America*, 1965, rev. ed., p. 59. He reports: "Thus Methodism is directly or indirectly responsible for over fifty of the existing American sects. These have a combined membership of over ten million persons. All may be called perfectionists so far as their official doctrines are concerned, and at least thirty of them still make sanctification one of their central principles."

448   See W. M. Arnett, "Current theological emphases in the American Holiness Tradition", *MQR* XXXV (1961), 120-129.

449   *John Wesley's Theology*, 1950, pp. 361f. Cf. also J. Orcibal, "The Theological Originality of John Wesley and Continental Spirituality", in *A History of the Methodist Church in Great Britain*, I, ed. R. Davies and G. Rupp, 1965, pp. 83-111; esp. pp. 102ff.

# SUMMARY

Manifold have been the ways in which man, before and after Christ, has tried to attain to perfection and to live the perfect life before God. With regard to the perfectionist communities and movements at least three general characteristics can be discerned.

Firstly, all types of perfectionism arose as a *reaction* against the contemporary religious-moral lethargy or apostasy. This is an indication that, in spite of all theological falsification and religious deviation in perfectionism, the motivation and intention may be acknowledged as a legitimate dissatisfaction with the present situation and a sincere will to obey the Biblical summons to walk perfectly before God, or to follow Jesus Christ in concrete reality according to His Word.

Secondly, we find that all perfectionist movements ultimately, if not in the beginning, led to the establishment of a more or less separate religious community apart from the main body of believers, even if not intended by the perfectionists themselves. In the case of monastic perfectionism the unique phenomenon can be observed that monasticism became incorporated within the Roman Catholic Church as a *legitimate* way of perfection.

The price to be paid for this solution, however, was high indeed the legitimization of a double standard or morality within the Church.[450] Still it may be maintained that perfectionism – as a misconception of Biblical and Christo-centric perfection – contains in itself the seed of separatism, mainly because its basic concern is and remains *individualistic* perfection, taking the individual too much by himself alone.

Thirdly, closely related to the previous characteristic of individualistic perfectionism, is the creation and recognition of *a new standard or authority* above the one accepted by the covenant people of God at large. This "higher" standard may have the character of a new "revelation" besides or beyond the accepted Holy Scriptures, or more subtly, of a new "interpretation" of the Scriptures. The new reformer then claims to have received special esoteric knowledge or enlightenment which functions as the *superior* norm to determine whether the Scriptures are understood and interpreted aright. Especially with respect to the Qumran sect the three mentioned characteristics become clearly evident.

In reaction against the cultic apostasy of the Jerusalem priesthood, the Righteous Teacher, a persecuted priest, organized an independent priestly community in the desert for the sake of creating an army of spiritually and physically perfect ones for the apocalyptic battle of Yahweh. The Teacher's esoteric-allegorical interpretations of apocalyptic Scripture, especially of Habakkuk, were implicitly accepted by the

---

450  See Harnack, *H.D.* II, 94, 123.

covenanters as the superior norm for Scriptural interpretation.

In the New Testament era we observed how each form of perfectionism was promoted by a reformer who, motivated by holy passion, aroused the consciences by appealing to a higher morality, a more intensified religious vision of God, a sharper separation from the world and its way of life. Whether it was Tatian or Montanus, Novatian or Pelagius, the great mystics, or Wesley, separate communities or movements to practice the proclaimed perfection inside and, ultimately, outside the established Church were the result.

We endeavored to classify theologically the different types of the perfectionist ethos. Typifying the discussed and analyzed perfectionist concepts as *apocalyptic* perfectionism (the Qumran community; Montanism; Joachim of Floris); *moralistic-ascetic* perfectionism (the Encratites; Pelagianism); *ecclesiological* perfectionism (Novatianism); *Neoplatonic-ascetic* perfectionism (the Alexandrian theologians); *monastic-contemplative* perfectionism; *ethico-philosophical* perfectionism (Wesleyan Methodism); this cannot suggest that each movement represents a clearly distinguished and different theological concept. The complex reality of life usually shows an interaction of several of the mentioned distinctive concepts in each perfectionist community.

The given classification, therefore, intends only to indicate one or two major determining motifs in a certain historical phenomenon of perfectionism. Although inadequate as descriptions by themselves, since one characterization can cover even widely diverging manifestations, e.g., in apocalyptic perfectionism, the designations serve the significant purpose of realizing that religious-theological perfectionism in the Hebrew-Christian faith is not one uniform stereotyped concept or phenomenon. In fact, each perfectionist movement has its own unique color and structure of conceptual and religious perfectionism.

The abiding phenomenon of perfectionism in the history of ancient Israel and the Christian Church, however, confronts us dramatically with the unexplainable but empirical reality of imperfection among the elected people of God. The perfectionists have not acquiesced in this religious-moral imperfection as being a matter of fact or a matter of course. They confront us with a subtle problem, as Berkouwer points out significantly: "Perfectionism presents a problem we may never lightly dismiss: the problem of the sin of those who *are* justified and those whose sanctification is Christ himself".[451]

The religious perfectionist is not satisfied with his present situation before God and man. Perfect sanctification means to him the striving for the personal feeling of holiness, i.e., the consciousness of perfection, or the essential participation in the divine nature, i.e., *inherent* holiness.

451  *Faith and Sanctification*, 1952, p. 48.

The *sola fide* he regards, at best, only as the beginning, the introduction, not the abiding essential. Is this an overzealous *anticipation* of God's apocalyptic act of redemption, of the glorious change of the *psychikon* body into a *pneumatikon* body (1 Cor. 15,51ff.; Phil. 3,21; Rom. 8,23)?

Then the worshippers of God and the Lamb will "see" God's face (Rev. 22,4), "see Him as He is" and "be like Him" (1 Jn. 3,2). But even in the great apocalyptic song of victory we hear the conquerors sing: "Who shall not fear and glorify Thy name, O Lord? For Thou alone art holy" (Rev. 15,4).

The most impressive truth of Biblical perfection is that it does not concentrate on man's nature in the abstract but on man's perfect relationship with God and his fellowman here, now as well as in the future.

In the Old Testament revelation of cultic covenant perfection Israel's love to Yahweh is conditioned and motivated by God's redeeming election *sola gratia*. The scope of Israel's cultic ethos is manifestly its social ethos, i.e., perfection in action, intending to bless ultimately all the nations of the world.

The New Testament proclaims that the promised blessing has come in the concrete, historical reality of Jesus Christ, "whom God has made our wisdom, our righteousness and sanctification and redemption" (1 Cor. 1,30).

It is the emphatic apostolic kerygma that both justification and sanctification begin and end with the communal praising of God in Christ. Christ saves the believing sinner from the beginning till the end *sola fide*, i.e., through a faith which is created by and fixed upon the divine promise, a faith which embraces Christ.

The apostle prays for such believers:

> ... that Christ may dwell in your hearts through faith; that you, being rooted and grounded in love, may have power to comprehend with all the saints what is the breadth and length and height and depth, and to know the love of Christ which surpasses knowledge, that you may be filled with all the fullness of God. (Eph. 3,17-19).

Perfectionism, therefore, seems to be inadequate not primarily because of its *concept* of holiness but its too limited *experience* of the manifold dimensions of holy love. Not the effort to attain to perfection in this life, but the *nature* of perfection itself is the crucial point.

All the manifestations of religious perfectionism have ultimately failed to solve the sin problem in the Church or the Christian community.

According to Biblical revelation, perfection participates in the same modus of being as the kingdom of God; it is present and future. There can be no ultimate solution to the sin problem until Christ has subjected all His enemies under His feet and when He as "the Son Himself will also be subjected to Him who put all things under him, that God may be everything to every one" (1 Cor. 15,28).

*Primary sources*

On Ancient Near East:

*Ancient Near Eastern Texts relating to the Old Testament.* Ed. J. B.
    Pritchard, 2d ed. 1955, Princeton (N.J.).
*The Ancient Near East. Supplementary Texts and Pictures relating to
    the Old Testament.* Ed. J. B. Pritchard, Princeton (N.J.), 1969.
*Sumerische und Akkadische Hymnen und Gebete.* Eingeleitet und über-
    tragen von A. Falkenstein und W. von Soden. Die Bibliothek der
    alten Welt. Der alte Orient. Ed. K. Hoenn, Zürich, 1953.
*The Egyptian Book of the Dead.* Documents in the Oriental Institute
    Museum at the University of Chicago. Ed. Th. G. Allen, Chicago, 1960.
*Le Livre des Morts des Ancient Egyptiens.* Introd., trad., com., de P.
    Barguet, Paris, 1967.
*The Secret Books of the Egyptian Gnostics.* An introduction to the Gnostic
    Coptic manuscripts discovered at Chenoboskion. J. Doresse. New
    York, ET 1960.
*Corpus Hermeticum.* Tomes I-II (Greek and French). Texte établi par
    A. D. Nock, et traduit par A. J. Festugière. Deuxième ed. Collection
    des Universités de France. Paris, 1960.
*The Manual of Discipline.* Translated and Annotated. With an introduction
    by P. Wernberg-Møller. "Studies on the Texts of the Desert of Judah",
    Ed. J. van der Ploeg. Leiden, 1957.
*Hodayot. Psalms from Qumran.* "Acta Theologica", Vol. II. S. Holm-
    Nielsen. Aarhus, 1960.
*The Thanksgiving Hymns.* Translated and Annotated. With an intro-
    duction by M. Mansoor. "Studies on the Texts of the Desert of
    Judah", III. Ed. J. van der Ploeg. Leiden, 1961.
*The Scroll of the War of the Sons of Light against the Sons of Darkness.*
    Edited with commentary and introd. by Y. Yadin. London, ET 1962.
Josephus, Flavius. *Complete Works.* Kregel Publ. Grand Rapids, 1966[4].

On Greek philosophy:

*The Loeb Classical Library.* Founded by James Loeb. London-Cambridge
    (Mass.) Aristotle and Plato in Greek and ET.

328

*The Work of Aristotle.* Vol. IX. Ed. W. D. Ross. Oxford. 1949 (Repr. of 1915).
*Greek Philosophy. A Collection of Texts. Selected and supplied with some notes and explanations* by C. J. de Vogel, Vols. I (1963) ; II (1967³) ; III (1964²), Leiden.


On the Early Church:


J. P. Migne, *Patriologiae cursus completus, series Graeca.* Paris, 1857ff.
—, *Patriologiae cursus completus, series Latina.* Paris, 1844ff.
*Corpus Scriptorum Ecclessiasticorum Latinorum.* Vindobonae, 1866ff.
*The Ante-Nicene Fathers.* American Reprint of the Edinburgh Edition. Wm. B. Eerdmans, Publ. Co., Grand Rapids (Michigan).
*Nicene and Post-Nicene Fathers of the Christian Church.* Ed. Ph. Schaff, Buffalo. The Christian Literature Co., 1886ff.
*Corpus Apologetarum Christianorum saeculi secundi.* Ed. J. C. Th. Otto, Vol. VI: "Tatianus". Wiesbaden, 1969 (Repr. of 1851).
A. Hilgenfeld, *Die Ketzergeschichte des Urchristentums. Urkundlich dargestellt.* Hildesheim, 1966 (Repr. of 1884).
*Tatian: Perfection according to the Saviour.* Ed. J. Rendel Harris. Reprinted from "The Bulletin of the John Rylands Iibrary", Vol. VIII, no. 1. Jan. 1924, Manchester.
*The Acts of the Martyrdom of Perpetua and Felicitas.* Ed. J. R. Harris and S. K. Gifford. London, 1890.
*Gegorii Nysseni Opera.* Ed. W. Jaeger, Vol. VIII, 1. Leiden, 1963.
*Pelagius, Expositions of Thirteen Epistles of St. Paul.* "Texts and Studies", IX (3 vols.) Ed. J. A. Robinson. Publ. by A. Souter, 1922-1931 (Repr. 1967).


On the Reformation:


*D. Martin Luthers Werke. Kritische Gesammtausgabe.* Weimar 1833ff.
*Corpus Reformatorum Ioannis Calvini. Opera quae supersint omnia.* Editors G. Baum, E. Cunitz and E. Reuss. Brunsvigae, 1863ff.
*The Book of Concord. The Confessions of the Evangelical Lutheran Church.* ET Th. G. Tappert, Philadelphia, 1959.
*De Belijdenisgeschriften van de Nederlandse Hervormde Kerk.* 's-Gravenhage, 1957.


On Roman Catholicism:


*Enchiridion Symbolorum. Definitionum et Declarationum de rebus fidei et morum.* H. Denzinger-A. Schönmetzer. Ed. 33. Freiburg i.Br., 1965.
ET *The Sources of Catholic Dogma.* (From 30th ed.) St. Louis, 1957.
*The Documents of Vatican II. All Sixteen Official Texts promulgated by*

*Ecumenical Council 1963-1965.* Ed. W. M. Abbott, S.J. An Angelus Book, New York, ET 1966.

On John Wesley:

*Wesley's Standard Sermons,* Vols. I-II. Ed. E. H. Sugden, London, 1955-56.
*The Works of the Rev. John Wesley,* Vols. I-XIV, London 1831³.
*The Letters of the Rev. John Wesley,* Vol. VIII, Ed. J. Telford, London, 1931.
*The Journal of the Rev. John Wesley,* Vols. I-VIII, Ed. N. Curnock, London, 1938.
*Forty-Four Sermons. Sermons on several Occasions,* London, 1964 (Repr. of 1944).

*Secondary sources: selective bibliography*
(Excluded are Bible Commentaries, Dictionaries, Enclyclopedias)

Aalders, G. Ch., *De Goddelijke Openbaring in de eerste drie Hoofdstukken van Genesis.* Kampen, 1932.
Abrahams, I., *Studies in Pharisaism and the Gospels.* First and second Series. Library of Biblical Studies. Ed. by Harry M. Orlinsky. New York, 1967. (Repr. 1917 and 1924).
Adam, K., *The Spirit of Catholicism.* Image Book (rev. ed.) New York, ET 1963¹².
Aland, K., "Bemerkungen zum Montanismus und zur frühchristlichen Eschatologie," *Kirchengeschichtliche Entwürfe.* Gütersloh, 1960.
Albert, E., "Ein neuer Erklärungsversuch von Gen. 2 and 3. *ZAW* 33 (1913), 161-191.
Albright, W. F., *From stone Age to Christianity: Monotheism and the Historical Process.* Baltimore, 1957².
—, *Jahweh and the Gods of Canaan.* London-New York, 1968.
Anderson, B. W., *Creation versus Chaos: The Reinterpretation of mythical symbolism in the Bible.* New York, 1967.
Andreasen, M. L., *The Sabbath.* Washington, 1942.
Arnett, W. M., "Current theological emphases in the American Holiness Tradition," *MQR* XXXV (1961), 120-129.
Balás, D. L., *Metousia Theou. Man's Participation in God's Perfections According to St. Gregory of Nyssa.* Studia Anselmiana. Bd. 55. Romae, 1966.
Bandstra, A. J., *The Law and the Elements of the World.* Kampen, 1964.
Barr, J., *Old and New in Interpretation.* New York, 1966.
—, *The Semantics of Biblical Language.* London, 1961.
Barrett, C. K., "The Eschatology of the Ep. to the Hebrews," *The Background of the New Testament and its Eschatology. FS* C. H. Dodd. Ed. W. D. Davies and D. Daube. Cambridge, 1964, pp. 363-393.
Barth, K., *Christ and Adam. Man and Humanity in Romans 5.* New York, 1962² (German, 1952).

—, *Church Dogmatics*, Vols. III, 1 (ET 1958); III, 4 (ET 1961); IV, 1 (ET 1956).
—, "Philosophie und Theologie," *Philosophie und Christliche Existenz. FS* H. Barth, Ed. G. Huber. Basel, Stuttgart, 1960.
Baumgarten, J. M., "Sacrifice and Worship Among the Jewish Sectarians of the Dead Sea (Qumran) Scrolls," *HThR* 46 (1953), 141-159.
Baumgartner, W., "The Wisdom Literature," *The Old Testament and Modern Study.* Ed. H. H. Rowley. Oxford, 1951, pp. 210-235.
Bavinck., H., "De navolging van Christus en het moderne Leven," *Kennis en Leven.* Kampen, 1922.
—, *Gereformeerde Dogmatiek.* Dl. I-IV. Kampen, 1928-30[4].
Beckmann, K. M., *Der Begriff der Häresie bei Schleiermacher.* München, 1959.
Beek, M. A., *Profiel van het Oude Testament.* 's-Gravenhage, 1960.
Begemann, A. W., *De relatie tussen wijsbegeerte en theologie en haar belangrijkste gestalten in de Hellenistische periode van het oud-Griekse denken.* Kampen, 1965.
Berkouwer, G. C., *Conflict met Rome.* Kampen, 1949[2].
—, *The Triumph of Grace in the Theology of Karl Barth.* Grand Rapids, 1956.
In the Series "Studies in Dogmatics," Ed. Wm. B. Eerdmans. Grand Rapids:
—, *Faith and Justification.* ET 1954.
—, *Faith and Sanctification.* ET 1952.
—, *Faith and Perseverance.* ET 1958.
—, *The Providence of God.* ET 1952.
—, *Man: The Image of God.* ET 1968[2].
In the Series "Dogmatische Studiën," Ed. J. H. Kok. N.V. Kampen:
—, *De Algemene Openbaring.* 1951.
—, *De Zonde II.* 1969.
Bernfeld, S., *The Foundations of Jewish Ethics. The teachings of Judaism.* Vol. I. New York, ET 1968. (Repr. of 1929).
Betz, H. D., *Nachfolge und Nachahmung Jesu Christi im Neuen Testament.* BHT 37, 1967.
Betz, O., *Offenbarung und Schriftforschung in der Qumransekte,* WUNT 6, 1960.
Beyerlin, W., *Die Rettung der Bedrängten in den Feindpsalmen der Einzelnen auf institutionelle Zusammenhänge untersucht.* FRLANT 99, 1970.
Bigg, Ch., *The Christian Platonists of Alexandria.* Oxford, 1968 (repr. of 1913).
Birkeland, H., *Die Feinde des Individuums in der Iraelitischen Psalmenliteratur.* Oslo, 1933.
Black, M., *The Dead Sea Scrolls and Christian Doctrine.* London, 1966.
—, *The Scrolls and Christian Origins.* New York, 1961.
Blass, F., and Debrunner A., *A Greek Grammar of the New Testament.* Cambridge-Chicago, ET 1961 (from 9th–10th German ed.).
Boecker, H. J., *Die Beurteilung der Anfänge des Königtums in den deuteronomistischen Abschnitten des I. Samuelbuches,* WMANT 31, 1969.

Bohlin, T., *Die Theologie des Pelagius und ihre Genesis*. Uppsala, 1957.

Bonhöffer, A., *Epiktet und das Neue Testament*, 1964 (Repr. of 1911).

Bonhoeffer, D., *The Cost of Discipleship*. New York, ET 1960².

—, *Ethik*. München, 1963⁶.

Borchert, R., *Stil und Aufbau der priesterlichen Erzählung*. Unpub. dissertation of the University of Heidelberg, 1957.

Bornkamm, G., "Enderwartung und Kirche im Matthäusevangelium," *FS* Dodd. Cambridge, 1964², pp. 222-260.

Bout, H., *Het zondebesef in het boek der Psalmen*. Leiden, 1952.

Braun, H., *Qumran und das Neue Testament*, Vols. I and II. Tübingen, 1966.

—, "Römer 7, 7-25 und des Selbstverständnis des Qumran-Frommen," *ZThK* 56 (1959), 1-18.

—, *Spätjüdisch-häretischer und frühchristlicher Radikalismus. Jesus von Nazareth und die essenische Qumransekte*, Vols. I: Das Spätjudentum; II: Die Synoptiker. Tübingen, 1957.

Breasted, J. H., *Ancient Records of Egypt*. Hist. Doc. I. Chicago, 1927³.

—, *The Dawn of Conscience*. New York-London, 1944.

—, *Development of Religion and Thought in Ancient Egypt*. London, 1959 (Repr. of 1912).

Brongers, H. A., "La Crainte du Seigneur," *OTS* V (1948), 151-173.

—, "Merismus, Synekdoche und Hendiadys in der Bibel-Hebräischen Sprache," *OTS* XIV (1965), 100-114.

—, "Schuldbelijdenis en Genadeverkondiging in het O.T.", *Kerk en Eredienst* IX (1954), 135-144.

Bronner, L., *Sects and Spearatism During the Second Jewish Commonwealth*. New York, 1967.

Brown, R. E., "The Qumran Scrolls and the Johannine Gospel and Epistles," *The Scrolls and the New Testament*. Ed. K. Stendahl. New York, 1957.

Brownlee, W. H., *The Meaning of the Qumran Scrolls for the Bible*. New York, 1964.

Bruce, E. F., *The Spreading Flame: The Rise and Progress of Christianity from its First Beginnings to the Conversion of the English*. Grand Rapids, 1964.³

Brunner, E., *The Divine-Human Encounter* (German: *Wahrheit als Begegnung*), Philadelphia, 1964².

—, *The Mediator*. Philadalphia, 1947.

—, *Revelation and Reason*. Philadelphia, 1946.

Buber, M., "Nachahmung Gottes," *Werke* II. München, 1964, pp. 1054-65.

Bultmann, R., *Jesus*, Tübingen, 1951.

—, *The Old and New Man in the Letters of Paul*. Richmond, ET 1967.

—, "Römer 7 und die Anthropologie des Paulus," in *Imago Dei. FS* G. Krüger. Giessen, 1932, pp. 53-62.

Burrows, M., *More Light on the Dead Sea Scrolls*. New York, 1958.

Cannon, W. R., "John Wesley's doctrine of sanctification and perfection," *MQR* XXXV (1961), 91-95.

—, *The Theology of John Wesley: A systematic guide to understanding Wesley's teachings as the natural development of one burning truth*.

*With Special Reference to the Doctrine of Justification.* New York-Nashville, 1946.

Chadwick, O., *John Cassian.* Cambridge, 1968.

Childs, B. J., *Myth and Reality in the Old Testament.* SBT 27, 1962².

Clark, E. T., *The Small Sects in America: an authentic study of almost 300 little-known religious groups.* Nashville, 1965.

Clavier, H., "Brèves remarques sur la notion de *sōma pneumatikon,*" *The Background of the N.T. and its Eschatology. FS* Dodd, Cambridge, 1964², pp. 342-362.

Cohn, N. R. C., *The Pursuit of the Millennium.* New York, 1962.

Colpe, C., *Die religionsgeschichtliche Schule: Darstellung und Kritik ihres Bildes vom gnostischen Erlösermythus.* FRLANT 78. Göttingen, 1961.

Cross, F. M., Jr., *The Ancient Library of Qumran and Modern Biblical Studies.* New York, 1958.

Cruvellier, J. M. E., *L'Exégèse de Romains 7 et le Mouvement de Keswick.* 's-Gravenhage, 1961.

Cullmann, O., *Christ and Time.* Philadelphia, 1964 (rev. ed.).

Curtis, O. A., *The Christian Faith.* New York, 1905.

Dahl, N. A., "Christ, Creation and the Church," *The Background of the New Testament and its Eschatology. FS* Dodd. Cambridge 1964², pp. 422-443.

—, *Das Volk Gottes. Eine Untersuchung zum kirchenbewusstsein des Urchristentums.* Darmstadt, 1963.

Daniélou, J., *The Dead Sea Scrolls and Primitive Christianity in the New Testament.* Baltimore, ET 1966.

—, *Origen.* New York, 1955.

—, A. H. Couratin, John Kent. "The Pelican Guide to Modern Theology," *Historical Theology,* Vol. 2. Baltimore, 1969.

Davies, R., "The People called Methodists," *A History of the Methodist Church in Great Britain,* Ed. R. Davies and G. Rupp. Vol. I. London, 1965, pp. 257-273.

Davies, W. D., *Introduction to Pharisaism,* Biblical Series 16. Philadelphia, 1967.

—, *Paul and Rabbinic Judaism.* London, 1965².

—, "Paul and the Dead Sea Scrolls: Flesh and Spirit," *The Scrolls and the N.T.,* pp. 157-182. Ed. Stendahl. New York, 1957.

—, *The Sermon on the Mount.* Cambridge, 1966.

—, *The Setting of the Sermon on the Mount.* Cambridge, 1964.

de Boer, P. A. H., "De Voorbede in het O.T.," *OTS* III (1943), 144ff.

de Boer, W. P., *The Imitation of Paul. An Exegetical Study.* Kampen, 1962.

de Jonge, M., "Geliefden, laten wij elkander liefhebben, want de liefde is uit God," *NTT* 22 (1967/68), 352-367.

Delekat, L., *Asylie und Schutzorakel am Zionheiligtum. Eine Untersuchung zu den privaten Feindpsalmen.* Leiden, 1967.

de Vogel, C. J., *Het Humanisme en zijn historische achtergrond.* Assen, 1968.

—, *Theoria. Studies over de Griekse Wijsbegeerte.* Assen, 1967.

de Vuyst, J., *"Oud en Nieuw Verbond" in de Brief aan de Hebreeën.* Kampen, 1964.

Dietzel, A., "Beten im Geist. Eine rel. gesch. Parallele aus den Hodajot zum paulinischen Gebet im Geist," *ThZ* 13 (1957), 12-32.

Dodd, C. H., *According to the Scriptures: The sub-structure of new Testament Theology.* London, 1952.

—, *Gospel and Law.* Cambridge, 1957⁴.

Dormer, J. A., *History of Protestant Theology, particularly in Germany,* Vol. II. Edinburgh, ET 1871.

Driver, G. R., *The Judaean Scrolls. The Problem and a Solution.* Oxford, 1965.

Du Plessis, P. J., *Teleios. The Idea of Perfection in the New Testament.* Kampen, 1959.

Dupont, J., *Gnosis: La Connaissance religieuse dans les Épîtres de Saint Paul.* Louvain, 1960².

—, *Les Béatitudes.* Bruges, 1958.

Dürr, L., "Heilige Vaterschaft im antiken Orient. Ein Beitrag zur Geschichte der Idee des 'Abbas,'" *Heilige Überlieferung. FS* I. Herwegen, 1938.

Edelkoort, A. H., *De Christusverwachting in het Oude Testament,* Wageningen, 1941.

—, *Het zondebesef in de Babylonische Boetepsalmen.* Utrecht, 1918.

Edelstein, L., *The Idea of Progress in Classical Antiquity.* Baltimore, 1967.

—, *The Meaning of Stoicism.* Cambridge (Mass.), 1966.

Eichrodt, W., *Man in the Old Testament.* SBT 4. London, ET 1966⁶.

—, *Theology of the Old Testament,* I, Philadelphia, 1961 (German, 1956⁶); II/III London, 1967 (German, 1964⁷).

Eissfeldt, O., *Einleitung in das Alte Testament.* Tübingen, 1964³ (ET 1965).

Elliger, K., *Studien zum Habakuk-Kommentar vom Toten Meer,* BHT 15, 1953.

Ellwein, E., "Das Rätsel von Römer VII," *KuD* I (1955), 247-268.

Elze, M., *Tatian und seine Theologie.* Forsch. z. Kirch. u. Dogm. gesch. 9. Göttingen, 1960.

Esser, H. H., "Thesen und Anmerkungen zum Exegetischen Paulus-verständnis des Pelagius," *Studia Patristica,* Vol. III, "Texte und Unters." Bd. 92, 443-461. Oxford, 1966.

Evans, R. F., *Pelagius. Inquiries and Reappraisals.* New York, 1968.

—, *Four Letters of Pelagius.* New York, 1968.

Fascher, E., "Jesus der Lehrer," *ThLZ* 79 (1954), 325-342.

—, *Sokrates und Christus.* Leipzig, 1959.

Ferguson, J., *Pelagius.* Cambridge (Eng.), 1956.

Finley, J. H., Jr., *Four Stages of Greek Thought.* Stanford, 1966.

Flew, R. N., *The Idea of Perfection in Christian Theology. An Historical Study of the Christian Ideal for the Present Life.* Oxford, 1968 (Repr. of 1934).

Flückiger, F., *Geschichte des Naturrechtes* I. Zürich, 1954.

Flusser, D., "The Dead Sea Sect and Pre-Pauline Christianity," *Scripta Hierosolymitana,* Pub. Hebrew Univ., Vol. IV (1965), 215-266.

Fohrer, G., *Geschichte der israelitischen Religion.* Berlin, 1969.

Frankfort, H., et al. *Before Philisophy. The Intellectual Adventure of*

*Ancient Man.* Penguin Books. Harmondsworth, 1954.

—, *Ancient Egyptian Religion.* New York, 1949[2].

—, *Kingship and the Gods.* Chicago, 1958[3].

Friedlander, G., *The Jewish sources of the Sermon on the Mount.* The Library of Bibl. Studies. New York, 1969 (Repr. of 1911).

Froom, L. E., *The Prophetic Faith of our Fathers,* I. Washington, 1950.

Frör, K., "Das Gebet des Königs Hiskia," *Humanitas Christianitas.* FS W. v. Loewennich. Ed. K. Beyschlag *et al.,* Witten, 1968.

Fuchs, E., "Jesu Selbstzeugnis nach Matthäus 5," *ZThK* 51 (1954), 14-34.

—, "Zur Frage nach dem historischen Jesus." *Gesammelte Aufsätze* II. Tübingen, 1960.

Füglister, N., *Die Heilsbedeutung des Pascha.* StANT VIII, München, 1963.

Gaddis, M. E., *Christian Perfectionism in America.* Unpubl. Diss. of Univ. of Chicago, 1929.

Gärtner, B., *The Temple and the Community in Qumran and the New Testament. A Comparative Study in the Temple Symbolism of the Qumran Texts and the New Testament,* "Soc. for N.T. Studies. Monographs I." Cambridge (Eng.) 1965.

Gispen, W. H., *De Christus in het Oude Testament,* "Exegetica". Kampen, 1952.

—, *Schepping en Paradijs.* Kampen, 1966.

Glueck, N., *Ḥesed in the Bible.* Cincinnati, ET 1967.

Goppelt, L., *Christologie und Ethik. Aufsätze zum Neuen Testament.* Göttingen, 1968.

Grant, R. M., "The Heresy of Tatian," *JThS* NS 5 (1954), 62-68.

Gray, G. B., *Sacrifice in the Old Testament.* Oxford, 1925.

Grundmann, W., "Die *nèpioi* in der Urchristlichen Paränese," *NTS* V (1959), 188-205.

Guardini, R., *Der Anfang aller Dinge. Meditationen über Genesis.* Kap. I-III. Würzburg, 1961.

Gunkel, H., *The Psalms. A Form-Critical Introduction.* Facet books, Philadelphia, 1967.

—, *Schöpfung und Chaos in Urzeit und Endzeit. Eine rel. gesch. Unters. über Gen. 1 und Ap. John. 12,* Göttingen, 1924[2].

—, and J. Berich, *Einleitung in die Psalmen.* Göttingen, 1966[2].

Guthrie, G. P., *Kant and Ritschl: A Study in the Relation between Philosphy and Theology.* Unpubl. Diss. of Univ. of Chicago, 1962.

Hadas, M., *The Stoic Philosophy of Seneca.* New York, 1968.

Haenchen, E., "Matthäus 23", *ZThK* 48 (1951), 38-63.

Harnack, A., *History of Dogma.* Vols. I-VII. Dover Publ. Inc., New York, ET (from 3d German ed.) 1961.

—, *Monasticism: Its Ideals and its History,* New York, ET 1895.

Hasler, V., "Das Herzstück der Bergpredigt. Zum Verständnis der Antithesen in Matth. 5,21-48", *ThZ* 15 (1959), 90-106.

Hefele, J., *A History of the Councils of the Church from the Original Documents,* Vols I-II. Edinburgh, ET 1896.

Heick, O. W., *A History of Christian Thought.* Vol. II. Philadelphia, 1966.

Heise, J., *Bleiben. Menein in den Johanneischen Schriften. Hermeneu-*

*tische Untersuchungen zur Theologie*. Tübingen, 1967.

Helfmeyer, F. J., *Die Nachfolge Gottes im Alten Testament*. BBB 29, 1968.

Hengel, M., *Judentum und Hellenismus*, WUNT 10, 1969.

—, *Nachfolge und Charisma. Eine exegetisch-religionsgeschichtliche Studie zu Mt. 8,21f. und Jesu Ruf in die Nachfolge*. BZNW 34, Berlin, 1968.

Hengstenberg, E. W., *Christology of the O.T.* I. Grand Rapids, 1956 (Repr. of 1872).

Herbert, A. S., *Worship in Ancient Israel*, "Ecum. Stud. in Worship" no. 5, Richmond, 1963[3].

Hermisson, H. J., *Sprache und Ritus im altisr. Kult. Zur "Spiritualisierung" der Kultbegriffe im A.T.* WMANT 19, 1965.

Heschel, A. J., *The Sabbath: Its Meaning for Modern Man*, New York, 1951.

Hessen, J., *Religionsphilosophie*, I-II. München-Basel, 1955[2].

—, *Thomas van Aquin und wir*. München-Basel, 1955.

Heussi, K., *Kompendium des Kirchengeschichte*. Tübingen, 1957[11].

—, *Der Ursprung des Mönchtums*. Tübingen, 1936.

Hicks, F. C. N., *The Fullness of Sacrifice. An essay in Reconciliation*. London, 1946[3].

Hicks, R. D., *Stoic and Epicurean*. New York, 1962.

Hoekema, A. A., *K. Barth's Doctrine of Sanctification*. Grand Rapids, 1965.

—, *The Four Major Cults*. Grand Rapids, 1965[2].

Holl, K., *Gesammelte Aufsätze zur Kirchengeschichte*. Bd. II: "Der Osten". Tübingen, 1964 (Repr. of 1928).

Hooke, S. H., *Babylonian and Assyrian Religion*. London-New York, 1953.

Horst, Fr., „Der Mensch als Ebenbild Gottes". *Gottes Recht. Ges. Stud. z. Recht im A.T.* Th.B. 12. München, 1961, pp. 222-234.

Hoskyns, E. C., "Jesus der Messias", in *Mysterium Christi. Christologische Studien britischer und deutscher Theologen*. Ed. G. K. Bell; A. Deismann. Berlin, 1931, pp. 89-115.

Hulst, A. R., "Bemerkungen zum Sabbatgebot", in *Studia Biblica et Semitica FS* Th. Chr. Vriezen. Wageningen, 1966, pp. 152-164.

Huppenbauer, H. W., *Der Mensch zwischen zwei Welten*. ATANT 34. Zürich, 1959.

Hutten, K., *Seher, Grübler, Enthusiasten. Sekten und religiöse Sondergemeinschaften der Gegenwart*. Stuttgart, 1968[11].

Hyatt, J. Ph., "On the meaning and origin of Micah 6:8", *AThR* 34 (1952), 232-239.

—, "The View of Man in the Qumran 'Hodayot' ", *NTS* II (1955/56), 276-284.

Impeta, C. N., *De leer der Heiliging en Volmaking bij Wesley en Fletcher*. Leiden, 1913.

Jacob, E., *Theology of the Old Testament*. New York, ET 1958.

Jacobsen, Th., "Ancient Mesopotamian Religion: The Central Concerns", *Proceedings to the Am. Phil. Society*. Vol. 107 no. 6 (1963), 473-484. Philadelphia.

Jaeger, W., *Two rediscovered works of ancient Christian Literature: Gregory of Nyssa and Macarius.* Harvard Institute for Classical Studies, Leiden, 1954.

Jänicke, Th., "Gott bleibt der Erde treu." *Reden über die ersten Kapitel der Bibel.* Ed. H. Gollwitzer, *et al.* Gelnhausen-Berlin, 1963.

Jenni, E., *Die theologische Begründung des Sabbatgebotes im Alten Testament.* Theologische Studien. Heft 46. Zürich, 1956.

Jeremias, G., *Der Lehrer der Gerechtigkeit.* SUNT 2. Göttingen, 1963.

Jeremias, J., *The Sermon on the Mount.* Univ. of London, ET 1961.

—, "Der Gedanke des 'Heiligen Restes' im Spätjudentum und in der Verkündung Jesu", *ZNW* 42 (1949), 184-194.

Jervell, J., *Imago Dei.* Göttingen, 1960.

Joest, W., "Paulus und das Luthersche simul iustus et peccator", *KuD* I (1955), 269-320.

Johansson, N., *Parakletoi. Vorstellungen von Fürsprechen für die Menschen vor Gott in der alt. lichen Religion, im Spätjudentum u. Urchristentum.* Lund, 1940.

Johnson, A. R., "The Psalms". *The Old Testament and Modern Study.* Ed. H. H. Rowley. Oxford, 1951, pp. 162-209.

Jonas, H., *Gnosis und spätantiker Geist,* II/1. Göttingen, 1954.

Kadushin, M., *The Rabbinic Mind.* New York, 1952.

Käsemann, E., "Zum Thema der urchristlichen Apokalyptik", *Exegetische Versuche und Besinnungen* II. Göttingen, 1965[2].

Kamlah, W., *Apokalypse und Geschichtstheologie. Die mittelalterliche Auslegung der Apokalypse vor Joachim von Fiore.* "Hist. Stud." Heft 285, Berlin, 1935 (Repr. 1965).

Kimbrough, S. T., Jr., "The Concept of Sabbath at Qumran", *RQ5* (1966), 483-502.

Klausner, J., *Jesus of Nazareth. His Life, Times and Teaching.* New York, ET 1943.

Knierim, R., *Die Hauptbegriffe für Sünde im Alten Testament.* Gütersloh, 1967[2].

Koch, K., "Tempeleinlassliturgien und Dekaloge". *Studien zur Theologie der at.lichen Überlieferungen. FS* G. von Rad. Neukirchen, 1961, pp. 45-60.

Koole, J. L., "Psalm XV – Eine königliche Einzugliturgie?" *OTS* XIII (1963), 98-111.

Kosmala, H., "Nachfolge und Nachahmung Gottes", *ASTI* II (1963), 38-85; III (1964), 65-110.

Kraemer, H., *Kerk en Humanisme.* 's-Gravenhage, 1957[2].

—, *Religion and the Christian Faith.* London, 1956. (Dutch: *Godsdienst, godsdiensten en het Christelijk geloof.* Nijkerk, 1958).

Kraft, H., "Die altkirchliche Prophetie und die Enstehung des Montanismus", *ThZ* XI (1955), 249-271.

Krahn, C., *Dutch Anabaptism. Origin, Spread, Life and Thought.* (1450-1600). The Hague, 1968.

Kraus, H. J., *Worship in Israel.* Richmond ET 1966 (German: *Gottesdienst in Israel.* "Beiträge z. evang. Theol." Bd. 19. München 1954).

Kraus, J., "Imitation and being in the ethics of the N.T.,", *Theology*

*Digest* XVII (1969), 139-143.

Kubo, S., "1 John 3:9: Absolute or Habitual?" *AUSS* VII (1969), 47-56.

Kümmel, W. G., *Promise and Fulfillment. The eschatological Message of Jesus.* London, 1961².

—, *Römer 7 und die Bekehrung des Paulus.* Untersuchungen zum Neuen Testament. Heft 17. Leipzig, 1929.

Kuhn, H. W., *Enderwartung und gegenwärtiges Heil. Untersuchungen zu den Gemeindeliedern von Qumran.* SUNT4. Göttingen, 1966.

Kuhn, K. G., "New Light on Temptation, Sin, and Flesh in the New Testament", *The Scrolls and the New Testament.* Ed. K. Stendahl. New York, 1957, pp. 94-113.

—, "Zum Essenischen Kalendar", *ZNW* 52 (1961) 165-73.

Kuyper, A., *Tractaat van den Sabbath. Hist. Dogm. studie.* 1890.

Larsson, E., *Christus als Vorbild. Eine Untersuchung zu den paulinischen Tauf- und Eikontexten.* ASNU XXIII. Uppsala, 1962.

Leaney, A. R. C., *The Rule of Qumran and its Meaning. Intr., transl. and comm.* N.T. Library. Philadelphia, 1966.

Lescow, Th., *Micha 6,6-8. Studien zur Sprache, Form und Auslegung.* Stuttgart, 1966.

Lindström, H., *Wesley and Sanctification. A study in the doctrine of salvation.* London, 1961 (Repr. of 1950).

Lisowsky, G., *Konkordanz zum hebräischen Alten Testament.* Stuttgart, 1958².

Lofthouse, W. F., "Fatherhood and Sonship in the Fourth Gospel," *ExpT* 43 (1931/32), 442-448.

—, "Imitatio Christi", *ExpT* 65 (1953/54), 338-342.

Lohfink, N., *De Actualiteit van het Oude Testament.* Hilversum-Antwerpen, 1966.

Loofs, F., *Leitfaden zum Studium der Dogmengeschichte.* 1. und 2. Teil. Herausgegeben von Kurt Aland: Alte Kirche, Mittelalter und Katholizismus bis zur Gegenwart, Tübingen, 1959⁶.

Loretz, O., *Die Gottebenbildlichkeit des Menschen.* München, 1967.

—, *Schöpfung und Mythos.* Stuttgart, 1968.

Luck, U., *Die Vollkommenheitsforderung der Bergpredigt.* ThEx 150. München, 1968.

Lüthi, W., und Brunner, R., *The Sermon on the Mount.* Edinburgh, ET 1963.

Luthardt, Chr. E., *Geschichte der christlichen Ethik.* Leipzig: I (1888), II (1893).

McDonough, M., *The Law and the Gospel in Luther. A study of M. Luthers' confessional writings.* London, 1963.

Maritain, J., *Moral Philosophy.* (French, 1960) New York, ET 1964.

Marmorstein, A., *The Doctrine of Merits in Old Rabbinical Literature and the Old Rabbinic Doctrine of God.* New York, 1968 (Repr. of 1920).

Mendenhall, G. E., *Law and Covenant in Israel and the Ancient Near East.* (Repr. from the *Biblical Archaeologist* Vol. XVIII No. 2 May 1954 and No. 3 Sept. 1954). Pittsburg, 1955.

Merki, H., *Homoiōsis Theōi. Von der Platonischen Angleichung an Gott zur Gottähnlichkeit bei Gregor von Nyssa*. Freiburg (Schweiz) 1952.

Metz, J. B., *Christelijke mensbetrokkenheid*. (German 1962) Hilversum-Antwerpen, 1964.

Metzger, M., *Die Paradieseserzählung. Die Geschichte ihrer Auslegung von J. Clericus bis W. M. L. de Wette*, Abhandl. z. Phil. Psych. u. Päd., Bd. 16. Bonn, 1959.

Michel, O., "Die Lehre von der christlichen Vollkommenheit nach der Anschauung des Hebräerbriefes," *ThStKr* 106 (1935), 333-335.

Moderau, H., "Die Moral der alten Ägypter nach Kap. 125 des Totenbuches," *Archiv für Orientforschung*, XII (1938), 258-268.

Molin, G., *Die Söhne des Lichtes*. Wien, 1954.

Moltmann, J., *Theologie der Hoffnung*. München, 1965[4].

Montefiore, H., "Thou shalt love the neighbour as thyself." *Donum gratulatorium. FS* E. Stauffer. Leiden, 1962, pp. 157-170.

Moore, G. F., *Judaism in the first centuries of the Christian Era. The age of the Tannaim*. Vols. I-II. Cambridge, 1946.

Motyer, J. A., *The Revelation of the Divine Name*. Tyndale Monograph. London, 1959.

Moule, C. F. D., "The Judgment Theme in the Sacraments," *FS* C. H. Dodd. Cambridge, 1964[2], pp. 464-481.

Mowinckel, S., *Psalmenstudien*. Six vols, in two. Amsterdam, 1966 (Repr. of 1921-24).

—, "Psalms and Wisdom," *Wisdom in Israel and in the Ancient N. East. FS H. H. Rowley*, Leiden, 1955.

—, *The Psalms in Israel's Worship*. Oxford, ET 1962.

Muilenburg, J., "A Liturgy on the Triumphs of Yahweh," *Studia Biblica et Semitica. FS* Th. Chr. Vriezen. Wageningen, 1966, pp. 233-251.

—, *The way of Israel. Biblical Faith and Ethics*. Harper Torchbook, TB 133. New York, 1961.

Murdoch, W. G., *A Study of Early Montanism and its relation to the Church*. Unpubl. Diss. of Univ. of Birmingham (Engl.), 1946.

Nielen, J. M., "Die Kultsprache der Nachfolge und Nachahmung Gottes und verwandter Bezeichnungen im neutestamentlichen Schrifttum," *Heilige Überlieferung. FS* I. Herwegen, 1938.

Niesel, W., *The Theology of Calvin*. Philadelphia, ET 1956 (German 1938).

Nigg, W., *Das Ewige Reich. Geschichte einer Hoffnung*. Zürich, 1954[2].

Nötscher, F., *Gotteswege und Menschenwege in der Bibel und in Qumran*. BBB 15. Bonn, 1958.

Noth, M., *History of Israel*. New York, ET 1958.

—, *Überlieferungsgeschichte des Pentateuch*. Stuttgart, 1948.

Nygren, A., *Agape and Eros*. Philadelphia, ET 1953.

Obbink, H. Th., *Het Bijbelse Paradijsverhaal en de Babylonische Bronnen*. Utrecht, 1917.

Oberman, H., *Forerunners of the Reformation. The Shape of Late Medieval Thought*. New York, ET 1966.

—, *The Harvest of Medieval Theology. Gabriel Biel and Late Medieval Nominalism*. Cambridge (Mass.), 1963.

Odeberg, H., *The Fourth Gospel*. Amsterdam, 1968 (Repr. of 1929).

Orcibal, J., "The Theological Originality of John Wesley and Continental

Spirituality," *A History of the Methodist Church in Great Britain.*
Ed. R. Davies and G. Rupp. Vol. I. London, 1965, pp. 81-111.
Osswald, E., "Zur Hermeneutik des Habakuk-Kommentars," *ZAW* 68
(1956), 243-256.
Ostborn, G., *Tōrā in the Old Testament.* Lund, 1945.
Otzen, B., "Die neugefundenen Hebräischen Sektenschriften und die
Testamente der zwölf Patriarchen," *StTh* 7 (1953), 125-157.
Owen, H. P., "The 'Stages of Ascent' in Hebrew V. 11 – Vi 3," *NTS* III
(1956/57), 243-253.
Pedersen, J., *Israel. Its Life and Culture.* London: I-II (1946); III-IV
(1947).
Peterson, E., "Theologie der Kleidung," in *Universitas.* Zeitschrift f. Wiss.
K. u. Lit. Stuttgart III (1948), 1409-1414.
Pope, W. B., *A Compendium of Christian Theology. Analytical Outlines
of a course of Theological Study, Biblical. Dogmatic, Historical.* Vol.
III. London, 1880².
Porteous, N. W., "Prophet and Priest in Israel," *ExpT* 62 (1950/51), 4-9.
Porúbčan, S., *Sin in the Old Testament. A Soteriological Study.* Rome,
1963.
Preisker, H., *Das Ethos des Urchristentums.* Gütersloh, 1949.
Prenter, R., "Die Einheit von Schöpfung und Erlösung. Zur Schöpfungs-
lehre Karl Barths," in *ThZ* 2 (1946), 161-182.
—, *Spiritus Creator. Luther's Concept of the Holy Spirit.* Philadelphia,
ET 1953.
Pretorius, H. S., *Bijdrage tot de Exegese en de Geschiedenis der exegese
van Romeinen VII.* Amsterdam, 1915.
Preuss, H. D., *Jahweglaube und Zukunftserwartung.* BWANT 87. Stutt-
gart, 1968.
Prümm, K., "Das neutestamentliche Sprach- und Begriffsproblem der
Vollkommenheit," *Bib.* 44 (1963), 76-92.
Quistorp, H., *Calvin's Doctrine of the Last Things.* London, ET 1955.
Rahner, K., "Philosophy and Theology," Theological Investigations, VI
(German: *Schriften zur Theol.,* VI 1965/1966) Baltimore, ET 1969.
Reeves, M., *The Influence of Prophecy in the Later Middle Ages. A Study
in Joachimism.* Oxford, 1969.
Reisel, M., *Observations on ʾehyeh ašer ʾehyeh.* Assen, 1957.
Rendtorff, R., *Die Gesetze in der Priesterschrift.* Göttingen, 1954.
Rengstorff, K. H., "Old and New Testament traces of a formula of the
Judean Royal Ritual," *Nov. Test.* V (1962), 229-244.
Richardson, H. W., *Toward an American Theology.* New York, Evanston,
London, 1967.
Ridderbos, H. N., *De Komst van het Koninkrijk.* Kampen, 1950.
—, *Paulus. Ontwerp van zijn theologie.* Kampen, 1966.
Ridderbos, N. H., "De betuigingen van 'onschuld, rechtvaardigheid' in de
Psalmen," *GTT* 50 (1950), 86-104.
—, *Is there a conflict between Gen. I and natural science?* (Dutch: *Be-
schouwingen over Gen. I*) Grand Rapids, 1957.
—, *Psalmen en Cultus.* Kampen, 1950.
Rigeaux, B., "Révélation des Mystères et Perfection à Qumrân et dans le

Nouveau Testament," *NTS* IV (1957/58), 237-262.

Ringgren, H., *The Faith of Qumran. Theology of the Dead Sea Scrolls.* Philadelphia, ET 1963.

—, *The Prophetical Conception of Holiness.* Uppsala, Leipzig, 1948.

Robinson, H. W., *Inspiration and Revelation in the Old Testament.* Oxford, 1946.

Rössler, D., *Gesetz und Geschichte. Untersuchungen zur Theologie der jüdischen Apokalyptik und der Pharisäischen Orthodoxie,* WMANT 3. Neukirchen, 1962².

Roth, C., *The Dead Sea Scrolls. A New Historical Approach.* New York, 1965.

Rothuizen, G. Th., *Primus Usus Legis. Studie over het Burgerlijk Gebruik van de Wet.* Kampen, 1962.

Rowley, H. H., *The Meaning of Sacrifice in the Old Testament.* Manchester, 1950.

—, *The Unity of the Bible.* London, 1955².

Runia, K., *Karl Barth's Doctrine of Holy Scripture.* Grand Rapids, 1962.

Rutenberg, C. G., *The Doctrine of the Imitation of God in Plato.* Philadelphia, 1946.

Sangster, W. E., *The Path to Perfection.* London, 1945.

Sarna, N. M., *Understanding Genesis.* New York, 1966.

Schaff, P., *The Creeds of Christendom.* Vol. I: "The History of Creeds." New York-London, 1931⁶.

Schechter, S., *Aspects of Rabbinic Theology. Major Concepts of the Talmud.* New York, 1961.

Schippers, R., "Cultus en ethos in het Nieuwe Testament," *Arcana Revelata. FS* W. Grosheide. Kampen, 1951, pp. 105-117.

Schleiermacher, F., *Der christliche Glaube.* Bd I⁷. Berlin, 1960.

Schlette, H. R., *Christen als Humanisten.* München, 1967.

Schmidt, H., *Die Erzählung von Paradies und Sündenfall,* Tübingen, 1931.

—, *Das Gebet der Angeklagten im Alten Testament.* BZAW 49, Giessen, 1928.

Schmidt, W. H., *Alttestamentlicher Glaube und Seine Umwelt. Zur Geschichte des alt.lichen Gottesverständnisses.* Neukircher Studienbücher, Bd. 6, 1968.

—, *Die Schöpfungsgeschichte der Priesterschrift.* WMANT 17. Neukirchen-Vluyn, 1964.

Schmithals, W., *Paulus und die Gnostiker.* Hamburg-Bergstedt, 1965.

Scnackenburg, R., *Christliche Existenz nach dem Neuen Testament.* München: Bd I (1967); Bd II (1968).

—, *Gottes Herrschaft und Reich.* Freiburg, 1959.

—, *Die sittliche Botschaft des Neuen Testaments.* München, 1954.

Schoeps, H. J., "Von der Imitatio Dei zur Nachfolge Christi," *Aus frühchristlicher Zeit. Religionsgeschichtliche Untersuchungen.* Tübingen, 1950, pp. 286-301.

Schoonenberg, P., *Het Geloof van ons Doopsel.* Dl. I-II. 's-Hertogenbosch, 1955. ET (revised) *Covenant and Creation.* London, 1968.

Schrage, W., *Die Kronkreten Einzelgebote in der paulinischen Paränese. Ein Beitrag zur neutestamentlichen Ethik.* Gütersloh, 1961.

Schubert, K., *The Dead Sea Community. Its Origin and Teachings*. New York, ET 1959.

Schulz, A., *Unter dem Anspruch Gottes. Das neutestamentliche Zeugnis*. München, 1967.

—, *Nachfolgen und Nachahmen*. StANT VI. München, 1962.

Schulz, S., "Zur Rechtfertigung aus Gnaden in Qumran und bei Paulus," *ZThK* 56 (1959), 155-185.

Schweizer, E., *Erniedrigung und Erhöhung bei Jesus und seinen Nachfolgern*. ATANT 28. Zürich, 1962² (ET *Lordship and Discipleship*. SBT 28. London, Rev. ed. 1960).

—, "Observance of the Law and Charismatic Activity in Matthew," *NTS* XVI (1969/70), 213-229.

Schwital, J., *Grosskirche und Sekte. Eine Studie zum Selbstverständnis der Sekte*. Hamburg, 1962.

Seeberg, R., *Textbook of the History of Doctrines*. Two vols. in one. Grand Rapids, 1966⁷.

Sevenster, J. N., *Paul and Seneca*. Suppl. N.T. IV. Leiden, 1961.

Snaith, N. H., *The Distinctive Ideas of the Old Testament*. London, 1950⁴.

Snijders, L. A., "Psaume XXVI et L' Innocence," *OTS* XIII (1963), 112-130.

Søe, N. H., *Christiche Ethik. Ein Lehrbuch*. München, 1957².

Spiegel, J., "Die Idee vom Totengericht in der ägyptischen Religion," in *Leipziger Ägyptologische Studien*, Heft 2 (1935), 44-71.

Stamm, J. J., *Der Dekalog im Lichte der neueren Forschung*. Bern, 1962².

—, *Erlösen und Vergeben im Alten Testament*. Bern, 1940.

Stanley, D. M., " 'Become Imitators of Me.' The Paulinic Conception of Apostolic Tradition," *Bib.* 40 (1959), 859-877.

Stauffer, E., *Die Botschaft Jesu. Damals und heute*. Bern, 1959.

Stendahl, K., "Hate, Non-Retaliation and Love," *HThR* 55 (1962), 343-355.

Süss, T., "Nachfolge Jesu", *ThLZ* 78 (1953), 129-140.

Sutcliffe, E. F., "Hatred at Qumran", *RQ* 2 (1960), 345-355.

Teichtweier, G., *Die Sündenlehre des Origenes. Studien zur Geschichte der Kath. Moraltheologie*. Bd 7. Regensburg, 1958.

Thielicke, H., *Theological Ethics*. Vol. I: "Foundations". Ed. H. Lazareth, Philadelphia, 1966.

Thompson, R. J., *Penitence and Sacrifice in early Israel outside the Levitical Law*. Leiden, 1963.

Thurneysen, E., *Die Bergpredigt*. ThEx 46. München, 1936.

Tinsley, E. J., *The Imitation of God in Christ. An Essay on the Biblical Basis of Christian Spirituality*. Philadelphia, 1960.

Turner, H. E. W., *The Patristic Doctrine of Redemption*. London, 1952.

van As, T. T., *Skuldbelydenis en Genadeverkondiging in die O.T.* Utrecht, 1961.

van der Leeuw, G., *Religion in Essence and Manifestation* II. Harper Torchbook. New York, ET 1963.

van der Ploeg, J., *The Excavations at Qumran. A Survey of the Judaean Brotherhood and its ideas*. London-New York, ET 1958.

van Groningen, G., *First Century Gnosticsm. Its Origin and Motifs*.

Leiden, 1967.

van Oyen, H., *Ethik des Alten Testaments. Geschichte der Ethik.* Bd 2, Gütersloh, 1967.

van Praag, *Humanistisch Credo.* Driebergen, 1964.

van Ruler, A. A., *Overheid en Humanisme.* Den Haag, n.d.

—, "De Waarde van het O.T.," in *Religie en Politiek*, Nijkerk, 1945.

van Unnik, W. C., *Newly Discovered Gnostic Writings.* SBT 30 (Dutch: *Openb. uit Eg. Zand*). London, 1960.

Velema, W. H., *De Geestelijke Groei van de Gemeente.* Kampen, 1966.

—, *Wet en Evangelie.* Assen, 1959.

Vermes, G., *The Dead Sea Scrolls in English.* Penguin Books. Baltimore, 1962.

Vick, E. W. H., "John Wesley's Teaching Concerning Perfection," *AUSS* IV (1966), 201-217.

Völker, W., *Das Vollkommenheitsideal des Origenes.* Tübingen, 1931.

—, "Die Vollkommenheitslehre des Clemens Alexandrinus in ihren geschichtlichen Zusammenhängen," *ThZ* 3 (1947), 15-40.

von der Osten-Sacken, P., *Gott und Belial. Traditionsgeschichtliche Untersuchungen zum Dualismus in den Texten aus Qumran.* SUNT 6. Göttingen, 1969.

von Loewenich, W., *Von Augustin zu Luther. Beiträge zur Kirchengeschichte.* Witten, 1959.

von Rad, G., *Gesammelte Studien zum Alten Testament.* Th. B. 8. München, 1965³.

—, *Old Testament Theology.* New York: I (1962); II (1965).

—, *Studies in Deuteronomy.* SBT9. London, 1953.

Vos, G., *Biblical Theology. Old and New Testaments.* Grand Rapids, 1963, (Repr. of 1948).

Vriezen, Th. C., " ᵓEhje ᵓašer ᵓehje," *FS* A. Bertholet. Tübingen, 1950, pp. 498-512.

—, *Die Erwählung Israels nach dem Alten Testament.* Zürich, 1953.

—, *De Godsdienst van Israel.* Zeist, 1963.

—, *Hoofdlijnen der Theologie van het Oude Testament.* Wageningen, 1966³.

—, *Onderzoek naar de Paradijsvoorstelling bij de Semietische volken.* Wageningen, 1937.

—, *An Outline of Old Testament Theology* (Dutch 1954²). Oxford, 1966.

Waetjen, H. C., "Is the 'Imitation of Christ' Biblical?" *Dialog* 2 (1963), 118-125.

Warfield, B. B., *Perfectionism.* Ed. S. G. Graig. Philadelphia, 1958.

Weber, O., *Grundlagen der Dogmatik.* Bd. I Neukirchen-Vluyn, 1964³.

Wendt, H. H., *Die Christliche Lehre von der menschlichen Vollkommenheit.* Göttingen, 1882.

Wernberg-Møller, P., "Some reflections on the Biblical Material in the Manual of Discipline", *StTh* 9 (1955), 40-66.

Westermann, C., *Forschung am Alten Testament. Gesammelte Studien.* Th. B. 24. München, 1964.

—, *The Genesis Accounts of Creation.* Facet Books. Philadelphia, ET 1966².

—, *Isaiah 40-66. A Commentary*. Philadelphia, ET 1969.
—, *The Praise of God in the Psalms*. Richmond, ET 1965.
Wiersma, W., *PERI TELOUS. Studie over de leer van het volmaakte leven in de ethiek van de oude Stoa*. Groningen, 1937.
Williams, G. H., *The Radical Reformation*. Philadelphia, 1962.
Williams, R. R., *A Guide to the Teachings of the Early Church Fathers*. Grand Rapids, 1960.
Wilson, J. A., *The Culture of Ancient Egypt*. Phoenix Books. Chicago, 1957[4].
—, and Frankfort, H. A., *et al. Before Philosophy. The Intellectual Adventure of Ancient Man*. Penguin Book. Harmondworth, 1954.
Wilson, R. McL., *Gnosis and the New Testament*. Philadelphia, 1968.
—, *The Gnostic Problem*. London, 1958.
Windisch, H., "Die Sprüche vom Eingehen in das Reich Gottes," *ZNW* 27 (1928), 163-189.
—, *The Meaning of the Sermon on the Mount*. Philadelphia, ET 1951.
Wingren, G., "Was bedeutet die Forderung der Nachfolge Christi in evangelischer Ethik?" *ThLZ* 75 (1950), 385-392.
Wolff, H. W., "The Kerygma of the Yahwist," *Interpr.* 20 (1966), 131-158 (= *Ev. Th.* 24 (1964), 73-94).
Wright, G. E., *Biblical Archaeology*. Philadelphia, 1962.
—, *God who Acts. Biblical Theology as Recital*. SBT 8. London, 1964[7].
—, *The Old Testament Against its Environment*. SBT 2. Chicago, 1962.
—, *The Old Testament and Theology*, New York, 1969.
Wundt, M., *Geschichte der griechischen Ethik*. Leipzig: I (1908); II (1911).
—, *Der Intellektualismus in der griechischen Ethik*. Leipzig, 1907.
Wurth, G. B., *Het Christelijk Leven*. Kampen, 1957[2].
Ziener, G., *Die Theologische Begriffssprache im Buche der Weisheit*. BBB 11. Bonn, 1956.
Zimmerli, W., *Gottes Offenbarung. Gesammelte Aufsätze zum Alten Testament*. Th. B. 19. München, 1969[2].
Zirker, H., *Die Kultische Vergegenwärtigung der Vergangenheit in den Psalmen*. BBB 20. Bonn, 1964.
Zurcher, J. R., "Christian View of Man." *AUSS* II (1964), 156-168; III (1965), 66-83; IV (1966), 89-103.
—, *The Nature and Destiny of Man*. "Philosophical Library." New York, ET 1969.

| | |
|---|---|
| ANET | Ancient Near Eastern Texts relating to the Old Testament, ed. J. B. Pritchard, 2d ed. 1955, Princeton (N.J.). |
| ANF | The Ante-Nicene Fathers. American Reprint of the Edinburgh Edition. Wm B. Eerdmans, Publ. Co., Grand Rapids (Michigan). |
| ASNU | Acta Seminarii Neotestamentici Upsaliensis. |
| ASTI | Annual of the Swedish Theological Institute in Jerusalem, Leiden. |
| ATANT | Abhandlungen zur Theologie des Alten und Neuen Testaments, Zürich. |
| AThR | Anglican Theological Review, Evanston (Illinois). |
| AUSS | Andrews University Seminary Studies, Berrien Springs (Michigan). |
| ATD | Das Alte Testament Deutsch, ed. A. Weiser, Göttingen. |
| BA | The Biblical Archaeologist, Publ. by The American Schools of Oriental Research, Jerusalem and Bagdad; Cambridge (Mass.). |
| BBB | Bonner Biblische Beiträge, Bonn. |
| BHT | Beiträge zur Historischen Theologie, Tübingen. |
| Bib | Biblica, Quarterly issued by the Pontifical Biblical Institute, Rome. |
| BK | Biblischer Kommentar, Altes Testament, ed. M. Noth, Neukirchen. |
| BWANT | Beiträge zur Wissenschaft vom Alten und Neuen Testament, (Leipzig) Stuttgart. |
| BZ | Biblische Zeitschrift (NF – Neue Folge), Paderborn. |
| BZAW | Beihefte zur Zeitschrift für die alttestamentliche Wissenschaft, (Giessen) Berlin. |
| BZNW | Beihefte zur Zeitschrift für die neutestamentliche Wissenschaft und die Kunde der älteren Kirche, Berlin. |
| C.D. (Barth) | Church Dogmatics by Karl Barth. Editors G. W. Bromiley and T. F. Torrance, Edinburgh. |
| CNT | Commentaire du Nouveau Testament, Neuchatel, Paris. |
| CR | Corpus Reformatorum Ioannis Calvini. Opera quae supersint omnia. Editors G. Baum, E. Cunitz and E. Reuss. Brunsvigae, 1863ff. |
| CSEL | Corpus Scriptorum Ecclesiasticorum Latinorum, Vindobonae, 1866ff. |

345

| | |
|---|---|
| DThC | Dictionnaire de Théologie Catholique, Paris, 1930-51. |
| ERE | Encyclopaedia of Religion and Ethics, ed. J. Hastings, Edinburgh, 1908ff. |
| EvTh | Evangelische Theologie, München. |
| ExpT | The Expository Times, Edinburgh. |
| FRLANT | Forschungen zur Religion und Literatur des Alten und Neuen Testaments, Göttingen, 1903ff. |
| G.D. (Bavinck) | Gereformeerde Dogmatiek, H. Bavinck, Dl. I-IV⁴, 1928-30, Kampen. |
| GTT | Gereformeerd Theologisch Tijdschrift, Kampen. |
| GW | Gereformeerd Weekblad, Kampen. |
| HAT | Handbuch zum Alten Testament, ed. O. Eissfeldt, Tübingen. |
| HK | Handkommentar zum Alten Testament, ed. W. Nowack, Göttingen. |
| HNT | Handbuch zum Neuen Testament, founded by H. Lietzmann, ed. G. Bornkamm, Tübingen, 1923ff. |
| HThR | Harvard Theological Review, Cambridge (Massachusetts). |
| HUCA | Hebrew Union College Annual, Cincinnati (Ohio). |
| ICC | The International Critical Commentary, Edinburgh. |
| Inst. (Calvin) | Institutes of the Christian Religion, 2 vols., in The Library of Christian Classicis, Vols. XX-XXI, ed. J. T. McNeill, ET by F. L. Battles, Philadelphia, The Westminster Press. |
| Interpr. | Interpretation, Richmond (Virginia). |
| JThS | The Journal of Theological Studies, London. |
| KAT | Kommentar zum Alten Testament, (Leipzig) Gütersloh. |
| KuD | Kerygma und Dogma, Göttingen. |
| LCC | The Library of Christian Classics, Philadelphia. |
| LThK | Lexikon für Theologie und Kirche, 2d ed., Freiburg, 1957ff. |
| MPG | J. P. Migne, Patrologiae cursus completus, series Graeca, Paris, 1857ff. |
| MPL | J. P. Migne, Patrologiae cursus completus, series Latina, Paris, 1844ff. |
| MQR | The Mennonite Quarterly Review, Goshen (Indiana). |
| NICNT | The New International Commentary on the New Testament, Grand Rapids (Michigan). |
| Nov.Test. | Novum Testamentum, Leiden. |
| NPNF | Nicene and Post-Nicene Fathers of the Christian Church. Ed. Ph. Schaff, Buffalo: The Christian Literature Co., 1886ff. |
| NTC | New Testament Commentary, Grand Rapids (Michigan). |
| NTD | Das Neue Testament Deutsch, ed. P. Althaus and J. Behm, Göttingen, 1952ff. |
| NTS | New Testament Studies, Cambridge. |
| NTT | Nederlands Theologisch Tijdschrift, Wageningen. |

| | |
|---|---|
| OTS | Oudtestamentische Studien, ed. P. A. H. de Boer, Leiden. |
| RE³ | Realencyklopädie für protestantische Theologie und Kirche, 3rd ed., Leipzig, 1896ff. |
| RGG³ | Die Religion in Geschichte und Gegenwart, 3rd ed., Tübingen, 1957ff. |
| RNT | Regensburger Neues Testament, Regensburg. |
| RQ | Revue de Qumran, Paris. |
| SBT | Studies in Biblical Theology, London, 1950ff. |
| STh (Aquinas) | Summa Theologica, Thomas Aquinas. ET by Fathers of the English Dominican Province, Vols. I-III, Benzinger Brothers Inc. 1947-48. |
| StANT | Studien zum Alten und Neuen Testament, ed. V. Hamp and J. Schmidt, München. |
| Str-B | Kommentar zum Neuen Testament aus Talmud und Midrash, Bd. I-IV, München 1922-28, by H. L. Strack and P. Billerbeck. |
| StTh | Studia Theologica, Lund, Aarhus. |
| SUNT | Studien zur Umwelt des Neuen Testament, Göttingen. |
| Suppl.VT | Supplements to Vetus Testamentum, Leiden. |
| SVF | Stoicorum Veterum fragmenta (ed. H. von Arnim), Vol. I-IV, Stuttgart 1968². |
| Th.Arb. | Theologische Arbeiten, Berlin. |
| Th.B. | Theologische Bücherei, München. |
| ThEx | Theologische Existenz heute, ed. K. G. Steck and G. Eichholz, München. |
| ThHNT | Theologischer Handkommentar zum Neuen Testament, Leipzig. |
| ThLZ | Theologische Literaturzeitung, Leipzig, Berlin. |
| ThR | Theologische Rundschau, Tübingen. |
| ThSt | Theologische Studien, Zollikon, Zürich, 1938ff. |
| ThStKr | Theologische Studien und Kritiken, Hamburg, Gotha. |
| ThWNT | Theologisches Wörterbuch zum Neuen Testament, begun by G. Kittel, ed. G. Friedrich, Stuttgart, 1933ff. |
| ThZ | Theologische Zeitschrift, Basel. |
| VT | Vetus Testamentum, Leiden. |
| WA (Luther) | D. Martin Luthers Werke. Kritische Gesammtausgabe, Weimar 1883ff. |
| WMANT | Wissenschaftliche Monographien zum Alten und Neuen Testament, ed. G. Bornkamm and G. von Rad, Neukirchen. |
| WUNT | Wissenschaftliche Untersuchingen zum Neuen Testament, Tübingen. |
| ZAW | Zeitschrift für die alttestamentliche Wissenschaft, (Giessen) Berlin. |
| ZNW | Zeitschrift für die neutestamentliche Wissenschaft, (Giessen) Berlin. |
| ZThK | Zeitschrift für Theologie und Kirche, Tübingen. |

Other abbreviations:

| | |
|---|---|
| c. | circa |
| conc. | concerning |
| cf. | confer |
| d. | died |
| esp. | especially |
| ET | English translation |
| FS | Festschrift |
| i.e. | id est |
| l.c. | locus citatum |
| LXX | Septuagint |
| MT | Masoretic text |
| n. | note |
| n.d. | no date given |
| N.T. | The New Testament |
| o.c. | opus citatum |
| O.T. | The Old Testament |
| par. | parallel |
| Repr. | Reprint |
| RSV | Revised Standard Version of the Holy Bible |
| s.v. | sub voce |

Unless stated otherwise, quotations of the Bible are from the Revised Standard Version.